OPENING SCRIPTURE

"Did not our heart burn within us
while He talked with us on the road,
and while He opened the Scriptures to us?"
Luke 24:32

OPENING SCRIPTURE

A Hermeneutical Manual
Introducing the Exegetical Study of the New Testament

PATRICK FAIRBAIRN

Solid Ground Christian Books
Birmingham, Alabama

Solid Ground Christian Books
2090 Columbiana Road
Suite 2000
Birmingham, AL 35216
(205) 443-0311
sgcb@charter.net
http://solid-ground-books.com

Opening Scripture: A Hermeneutical Manual
Introducing the Exegetical Study of the New Testament
by Patrick Fairbairn (1805-1874)

Solid Ground Classic Reprints hardcover edition September 2004
Solid Ground Classic Reprints paperback edition April 2005

Taken from the 1858 edition by T & T Clark, Edinburgh

ISBN 1-932474-51-X (hardcover)
ISBN 1-932474-72-2 (paperback)

Special thanks to Sinclair Ferguson of Westminster Theological Seminary
In Dallas, TX for his enthusiastic support of this significant project.

PREFACE.

THE alternative title prefixed to this volume has been assumed, rather than the simple designation of " Hermeneutics of the New Testament," chiefly for the purpose of indicating, that a certain latitude may be expected in it, both in regard to the range of subjects discussed, and in regard to the measure and method of treatment respectively applied to them. Works, indeed, could readily be named, bearing the title of *Hermeneutics*, which have taken nearly as much license in both respects, as I need to vindicate for myself in connection with the present publication. But the term is strictly applicable only to such works as unfold the *principles* of Interpretation, and give to these a regular, consecutive, and scientific treatment. Of this sort is the comparatively recent work of Cellerier (*Manuel d'Hermeneutique*, 1852), which, however objectionable in respect to the principles it occasionally enunciates, is one of the most systematic and complete in form,—treating, after a pretty long introduction, successively of the Psychological elements and aspects of the subject—the Grammatical, the Historical, the Scriptuary (or more peculiarly Biblical), the Doctrinal. In this province, however, it is possible to sacrifice to completeness or perfection of form greatly more than there is any reasonable prospect of gaining by it. Higher ends have here to be aimed at than can always be reached by a rigid adherence to scientific method, or a close regard to artistic proportions. For, in a field so various as that of New Testament Scripture, so complicated, touching on so many relations, and embracing topics so diverse alike in nature and in importance, it often depends, not more, perhaps even less, upon the hermeneutical principles adopted, than upon the mode of applying these principles to particular cases, and passages of more peculiar difficulty, that solid footing is to be obtained, and satisfactory results accomplished. Accordingly, in those hermeneutical works, which take the more precise and scientific form, there is always what appears to me much needless waste in one direction, and ill-judged parsimony in another. Not a little space is occupied in announcing, or illustrating principles, which every one knows and admits, and which often have no special bearing on the interpretation of Scripture; while many of the points more peculiarly calling for elucidation are summarily disposed of, and left much as they were found. Even when the simpler elements of the subject are correctly enough stated, little often in connection with them is properly wrought out; and unless the student of Scripture is content to take all on the authority of his Master, he will often feel as much at a loss as ever in respect to the things for which he more especially seeks the help of a qualified instructor.

A work that is really fitted in the present day to serve the purpose of a proper guide-book, must undoubtedly so far possess a scientific character, that it shall exhibit an acquaintance with the several branches of learning and knowledge, which illustrate the language and structure, the incidental allusions, and the main theme of the sacred books, and apply what it may thence appropriate in an orderly and judicious manner. If deficient in this, it fails in the fundamentals of the subject. But it should be allowed to move with some freedom in the selection of its topics, and in the relative care and consideration that it expends upon some of them, as compared with others. It cannot otherwise occupy, in a serviceable manner, the intermediate ground, that properly belongs to it, between Lexicons, Grammars, Books of Antiquities, etc., on the one hand, and formal commentaries on the other—turning, as it should do, to such account the materials furnished by the former class of productions, as may aid and qualify the student for an independent and discriminating use of the latter. This is the peculiar province and object of a Hermeneutical work on Scripture, and *that* will always come practically the nearest to the mark, which is the best fitted to place the student of Scripture in the position now indicated.

In works composed with such an aim, there must ever be room for some diversity of judgment as to the subjects that should be brought into notice, and the degree of consideration respectively given to them. Different persons will naturally form their opinions from somewhat different points of view; and what will appear to some the fittest arrangement to be adopted, and the points most in need of investigation, may not always be regarded in exactly the same light by others. In this respect I have simply to say, that I have endeavoured to exercise an impartial judgment, influenced, no doubt, to some extent, by what my own experience, coupled with the general tendencies of the age, may have suggested to me as of importance. Throughout the volume prominence has been given to the connection that subsists between the Old and the New in the book of God's revelation, as well in respect to words as ideas; there being nothing more essential than correct views here to an intelligent reading of New Testament Scripture, or better fitted to serve as a safeguard against superficial and fanciful interpretations. This, also, has partly operated as a reason for introducing some of the dissertations which occupy the Second Part of the volume. The whole of these, however, have reference to terms and subjects, which must always engage the special attention of those, who give themselves to the exegetical study of the writings of the New Testament. And they may further serve the purpose of exemplifying, as by a few testing cases, the principles and modes of inquiry, which it is the great object of the work to explain and recommend.

In another respect, also, I am prepared for finding occasional differences between what has approved itself as right to my own mind, and what may appear such to some of my readers :—I refer to the explanations given of several of the more difficult passages of Scripture, and the exhibitions of Divine truth therewith connected. Here, again, there is room for a certain diversity of judgment, even among those who are agreed upon the plenary inspiration of Scripture, and the great doctrines of evangelical religion. And I am not so extravagant as to imagine, that on every point I shall carry the convictions of all, who may be at one with me in fundamental principles. It is possible I may find critics, who are disposed to look with so censorious a spirit and so unkindly an eye on what I have written, that they shall even try to represent me as at fault in regard to some of those evangelical principles themselves. This, I perceive, has been attempted in a certain quarter with respect to my last publication — *Prophecy viewed in respect to its Distinctive Nature, etc.*—and, as the work is occasionally referred to in the present volume, I may be permitted here to make a brief allusion to the subject. In Chapter IV. of that work, I treated of the bearing of prophecy on human freedom and responsibility, with a consideration of the question, how far it should be regarded as conditional in its announcements. I was aware, of course, that people would think differently respecting the mode of explanation I adopted: that to some it might appear more or less satisfactory, to others not. But a writer in the *Journal of Prophecy* (for July 1857) has chosen to represent me as giving expression to views essentially at variance with the Calvinistic doctrine of predestination, or the unconditionality of the Divine decrees. Nothing certainly was further from my own mind; neither there, nor in any other part of my writings, have I consciously given expression to a thought which was intended, in the slightest degree, to impugn the statement of doctrine on that subject, contained in the Westminster Confession, or the Articles of the Church of England, and not a few things that plainly enough point in the contrary direction. But the reviewer, of course, must have some way of making out his point; and, with the adroitness of a critic, who sets himself to damage the credit of a book, and its author along with it, he does so by imposing a sense upon my words which they were not intended to bear, and so bringing them into connection with a subject that was not properly in my view. Prophecy, as he there views it, is identical with the Divine decree; so that a conditional element in the one comes to be virtually the same with a conditional ground for the other. The subject of discourse with me, however, was prophecy, simply as it appears in the written Word, as an objective communication to men. In handling this, I, no doubt, occasionally spoke of the Divine purposes; but of these, as is evident from the whole tenor and connection of the discourse, not as formed in the mind of God, and determining with infinite and unerring wisdom the entire system of the Divine administration. I purposely abstained from entering upon this higher region, and confined my attention to the intimations of the

Divine will as disclosed in the prophetic word—to these as coming into contact with men's obligations and responsibilities—and therefore, in a greater or less degree (for they differ widely in the extent to which they admit it), tinged with that anthropomorphic colouring, which is required to adapt the communications of heaven to the thoughts and feelings, the ever varying states and conditions of men. The subject, as presented by me, might be assigned to that species of accommodation treated of in Part I. sect. 5 of this volume, according to which, while the *form* given to spiritual things bears the variable type of what is human, there are not the less realities lying behind, fixed and immutable. And in the very brief and general allusion, which was made to the Calvinistic writers of a former age, nothing more was designed than to intimate, in the shortest manner possible—it was implied, indeed, rather than intimated—that the distinction (however expressed) between the secret and the revealed, or between the absolute decrees and the conditional announcements of God, did not, to my view, satisfactorily explicate the matter at issue. I thought so then, and I think so still, notwithstanding the advantage I have derived from the instructions of so learned a reviewer. To divide, as he and his authorities do, between prophecy, considered as equivalent to Divine decrees, and prophecy, as involving matter of commination or promise—the former absolute, the latter conditional—does not satisfy my " exegetical conscience," and I am afraid never can. It seems to me to introduce an artificial distinction into the prophetic word, which is not indicated in that word itself, nor admits of being properly drawn ; and has the appearance, at least, of attempting, by the mere adoption of a particular phraseology, or by arbitrarily singling out portions of the same prophetic message, to tide over difficulties in interpretation, which attach to the subject as a concrete whole, as an objective communication addressed to the fears or the hopes of mankind.

But this is not the place for minute or lengthened explanations on the subject. I wished merely, in a few sentences, to deliver my protest against a style of criticism which I hold to be essentially unfair, and which, if similarly applied to the sacred writers, might readily be made to turn one-half of them against another. It is not likely that I shall refer to anything of the same sort in future. No one, who reads with a candid and unbiassed spirit what is written in this, or in previous productions of my pen, can have any doubt that the great principles of the Reformed churches are therein maintained and vindicated. And the palpable mis-representations, and, I must add, uncourteous treatment, which have sometimes already, and may possibly be again, employed respecting me, by parties belonging to the same prophetical school with the reviewer above referred to, together with the clouds of dust that usually accompany their hostile attempts, it is my in-tention to leave to the obscurity, to which they cannot fail of themselves to descend.

The Third Part of the volume, which is devoted to the quota-tions from the Old Testament in the New, occupies a larger space than I could have wished. But it relates to a branch of the subject which, in the present day, is of special importance ; and I did not see how my main object could be served without taking it up in detail, and examining somewhat carefully the parts which are more peculiarly attended with difficulty. For those who would study the subject in its relation to Typology, and would trace the gradual evolution of the meaning of Old Testament Scripture, through the application of particular passages to the realities of the Gospel, I take leave to refer to the first volume of my Typology, and especially to the Appendix in that volume on this particular subject.

P. F.

GLASGOW, May 1858.

CONTENTS.

PART FIRST.

DISCUSSION OF FACTS AND PRINCIPLES BEARING ON THE LANGUAGE AND INTERPRETATION OF NEW TESTAMENT SCRIPTURE.

PART SECOND.

DISSERTATIONS ON PARTICULAR SUBJECTS CONNECTED WITH THE EXEGESIS OF NEW TESTAMENT SCRIPTURE.

PART THIRD.

THE USE MADE OF OLD TESTAMENT SCRIPTURE IN THE WRITINGS OF THE NEW TESTAMENT.

ERRATA.

Page 17, last line, *for* Hebraism *read* Hellenism.

37, second line, *for* Φίλλιπος *read* Φίλιππος.

101, eighth line from bottom, *for* the victory, *read* victory.

134, fifth line from bottom, *for* showing *read* shunning.

202, line eighth, after vow *insert* than that thou shouldst vow.

228, line twenty-fifth, *for* hope and despair, *read* fear and despair.

237, line twelfth, *for* ψευδιδάσκαλοι *read* ψευδοδιδάσκαλοι.

311, line twenty-first, *for* διαθήκαι *read* διαθῆκαι.

... line twenty-sixth, *for* διαθῆκη *read* διαθήκη.

319, third line from bottom, *insert* or *before* from.

PART FIRST.

SECTION FIRST.

THE ORIGINAL LANGUAGE OF THE NEW TESTAMENT.

IN the more exact and scientific study of the Sacred Scriptures, the first object, in the order of nature, that calls for examination, has respect to the state of the original records. The possession of a pure text is an indispensable preliminary to a thoroughly correct and trustworthy exposition. And, as well from its importance as from the peculiar character of the investigations belonging to it, this is now fitly assigned to a distinct branch of Biblical study. Next to it in order, and certainly not inferior in importance, is a correct and discriminating acquaintance with the original language of Scripture, and the principles that should guide our inquiries into its meaning and purport. All theology that is really sound, and that will stand the test of time, must have its foundation here. The Reformers, to their credit, clearly perceived this, and were hence led to doctrinal results, which, in the main, never have been, and never can be displaced. They proceeded on the sound maxim of Melancthon, that Scripture cannot be understood theologically, unless it has been already understood grammatically (Scriptura non potest intelligi theologice, nisi antea sit intellecta grammatice). In such statements, of course, the term grammatical must be taken in its wider sense,

A

as comprehending all that is necessary to a just discernment of the import and spirit of the original. And if such a critical acquaintance with the mere language of Sacred Scripture be but one element of success, it still is an element of very peculiar moment to the well-furnished theologian ; since it has respect to the ultimate source of all that is sound and valuable in theological attainment.

As regards the Scriptures of the New Testament, with which alone we have properly to do at present, it is only the Greek language that comes directly into notice ; since the whole of the writings that compose the New Testament are found, as to their original form, in no other language than that of the Greek. If any of them ever existed in a *prior* original, it no longer does so. Nor, with the exception of St Matthew's Gospel, and the Epistle to the Hebrews, has it ever been imagined, but by a few dreaming and speculative minds, that the books of the New Testament appeared originally in any other language. The Epistle to the Hebrews is now also held by all men of competent learning to have been originally composed in Greek. And there only remains the Gospel of St Matthew about which there may still be some room for difference of opinion—though, even in regard to it, the conviction has of late been growing in favour of the proper originality of its present form, which was certainly in current use before the close of the apostolic age.

Whence, then, did this predilection for the Greek arise ? Were our Lord's discourses, and the writings of the Evangelists, as well as of the apostles, transmitted to us in Greek, because that was the current language of the place and time ? Was this really the language in which our Lord and his apostles usually spoke ? So, some have been disposed to maintain ; and though it is a question rather of antiquarian interest, than of any vital moment for the interpretation of Scripture, it is entitled to some consideration at our hands. It has also a certain bearing on the dispute respecting the original language of St Matthew's Gospel. Indeed, it was chiefly in connection with this more special question, that the other pressed itself on the attention of Biblical students. Thus Hug, in his Introduction to the New Testament, went at considerable length into the investigation of the subject, for the purpose of vindicating the proper originality of the Greek Gospel of Matthew ; and endeavoured to prove, that the Greek language was in current use throughout Palestine at the commencement of the Christian era—so much so, that the people generally understood it, that our Lord himself often employed it, nor had His evangelists and apostles any proper reason for resorting to another in those writings, which were intended for circulation in Palestine and the neighbouring regions. But the fullest and, we believe, also the ablest defence of this view, is to be found in the treatise of an Italian Ecclesiastic, Dominici Diodati, entitled De Christo Græce loquente exercitatio, originally published at Naples in 1767, and re-published in this country not many years since. In this treatise the subject is discussed, partly on general grounds, as on its own account interesting and important to the Biblical student, and partly also with reference to its bearing on the question of the original language of Matthew's Gospel. The position which the author labours to establish, is, that "neither Hebrew, Syriac, nor Latin, was the vernacular language of the Saviour, but Greek." It will be readily understood, on the other side, that those who held the contrary opinion respecting Matthew's Gospel—viz. that it was originally written in Hebrew for the use of the Jewish believers in Syria—were naturally led to controvert the position, that Greek was generally spoken and understood in Palestine : they held, that not Greek, but Aramaic, a sort of broken Hebrew, was the only language in general use, and that also commonly employed by our Lord and his apostles in their public discourses.

Now, on a question of this kind, it is not difficult for an ingenious theorist, or an eager disputant, to sort and apply some scattered notices of ancient writers, either directly or indirectly bearing on the subject, in such a way as to give them a plausible appearance, and compel them to pay tribute to the side of the controversy he has espoused. But there are certain great principles applicable to the case which, with all sober and impartial minds, must go far to settle it, and which cannot be overthrown, or materially modified by any occasional statements or fragmentary notices culled out of ancient records. It is found, not in the history of one people, but in the history of nations generally, that there is nothing which is more tenacious of its grasp, and which more slowly yields to the force of foreign influences, than the vernacular language of a people. "Language is after all the most durable of human monuments. Conquerors may overthrow empires and states ; earthquakes may swallow up cities ; time may confound all things besides :—But the winged words, in which man gives utterance to his feelings and thoughts, often outlast all these ravages, and preserve the memory of nations long after they have ceased to exist. That which seems the most fragile, the most variable, the most evanescent of human attributes or possessions, becomes in reality the most permanent, the most indestructible. If no longer able to support an independent existence, it clings to and coalesces with some more recent and robust dialect :—if lost in one form, it is almost certain to re-appear in another—exhibiting amidst all changes and disfigurations incontestable traces of its origin. This law of decay and reproduction, of fluctuation yet permanence, is so general, that it is principally from analytical inquiries into the origin, composition, and affinities of language, that we derive what knowledge we possess of the early history and fortunes of nations." [1]

In confirmation of this, it is only necessary to point to a few well-known examples. One of the most striking is furnished by the ancient country of the Pharaohs, after the time that their dynasty came to an end, and a succession of conquests, followed by the ascendency of a foreign power, swept over the land. Persian, Macedonian, Roman, and Arabian conquerors in turn held possession of the throne of Egypt, each endeavouring to establish as firmly as possible their dominion over the vanquished, and to render their sway enduring and complete. Yet after this subduing and fusing process had been proceeding for twelve or fourteen centuries, we have the best grounds for believing that the language of the Pharaohs still survived, and continued, though not, we may well conceive, without the introduction of many foreign admixtures, to form the staple of the vernacular tongue of the people. What is called the Coptic language is but a corrupt form of the old Egyptic (as the name also, perhaps, is).[2] Into this language the Scriptures were translated in the earlier ages of Christianity ; a liturgy in common use probably about the fifth or sixth century, is still employed by the few remaining

[1] Encyclopedia Brittanica, 7th ed., Art. 'Hieroglyphics,' c. 2d.
[2] Aἰγυπτος—Gyptos, Coptos, Coptic.

Copts of the present day—though the Coptic tongue in which it is written is no longer understood by them. They adhere to it merely as a venerable relic of the better past of their history ; of which it forms an abiding, though a mournful and mummy-like witness. But its introduction into the churches of Egypt a few centuries after the Christian era testifies to the fact, that the sub stance of the ancient language had withstood the influences of foreign conquest and dominion for more than a thousand years.

We may, however, take an example nearer home. The Norman conquest took place in the year 1066 ; and it is well known to have been the policy of the first Norman kings—a policy, too, that was continued with steady aim by their successors—to get rid of the old Saxon entirely, and have it supplanted by their own Norman French. In this French the statutes of the realm were written ; so also were commentaries upon the laws, and the decisions of the courts of justice. In many places it was at length introduced into the common schools ; so that an old chronicler (Ralph Higden) complains of it as a thing "against the usage and manner of all other nations," that " children in schools are compelled for to leave their own language, and to construe their lessons and their things in French." A change in this respect only began to be introduced about the year 1385—more than three centuries after the conquest—when the English again resumed its place in the schools ;—and though it was English materially altered, betraying in many respects the influence of Norman domination, yet it still retained its old Saxon root and trunk. The power and policy of the conquerors, though in active operation for more than three centuries, could prevail no further than to superinduce some partial changes upon the mother tongue of the people, and introduce some additional terms ; and that, too, while this tongue itself was in a comparatively crude state, and very far from having reached its matured form.

Other examples might be referred to—such as the Welsh, the Gaelic, and the Irish-speaking portions of the British Isles, from which still more powerful and long-continued influences have not been sufficient to dislodge the ancient dialects from their place, as the customary vehicles of intercourse among the people. But it is needless to enlarge. The cases adduced are by no means singular ; they are but specimens of a multitude—exemplifications

of principles and habits that are inherent in human nature, operating equally among all races and in all climes.   And is it, then,
to be conceived, with such facts presenting themselves in the
linguistic history of tribes and nations, that the effect of a foreign
rule in Palestine—a rule that had not for more than two or three
centuries possessed the form of a stringent and pervasive domination—the rule, too, of masters, who themselves spoke different
languages, first Persian, then Greek, then Roman, and who never
were so closely identified with the subjects of their sway as in the
cases already noticed—is it yet to be conceived, that the effect
here was to be such, as to bring about an entire revolution in the
vernacular language of the people?   The supposition is in the
highest degree improbable—we may even say, morally impossible;
the rather so, as the Jews had reasons connected with their
religion, their history, and their prospects, for cleaving to their
language, which no other people, either in ancient or in modern
times, equally possessed.   Everything in the past and the future
contributed to throw an air of sacredness and grandeur around
the Hebrew language, which must have doubly endeared it to
their minds, and, on the part of their conquerors, have greatly
aggravated the difficulty of supplanting it by another altogether
different.

It is, therefore, against all analogy, and in opposition to the
strongest tendencies of human nature, to suppose that in such
circumstances the Greek tongue should, in the age of our Lord
and His apostles, have come into general use in Palestine, and
to any considerable extent taken the place of Aramaic.   With
far more probability might it be maintained that Norman and
not Anglo-Saxon was the language of common life among the
English in the thirteenth and fourteenth centuries, or that in the
present day English is understood and spoken by the mass of
the population in the Principality of Wales, or in the Highlands
of Scotland.   It is true, however, that the ancient language of
Palestine had undergone a certain change; it had in some degree suffered by the misfortunes of the people, and had lost its
original purity.   The long sojourn in Chaldea, in the first instance, then the intercourse kept up with the neighbouring Syrian
tribes through commerce, war, and marriage relationships, naturally brought into it foreign elements, and imparted to it a Syro-

Chaldaic form. Of this we have undoubted indications, both in the later books of the Old Testament, and in occasional notices and expressions that occur in the New. But these successive changes only affected the accidents of the language; they introduced new dialects, antiquated particular words and phrases, and obtained currency for others in their stead; but—as in all similar cases—they left the bones and sinews of the language, its structure and essence, substantially what they were. The historical proofs of this are perfectly sufficient. Josephus, for example, constantly distinguishes between his native tongue and the Greek. While he speaks of having applied diligently to domestic and foreign literature, so as even to be acknowledged by all his countrymen as a person of superior learning, he yet confesses himself to have been so long accustomed to his own tongue (πάτριος συνήθεια) that he could not attain to an accurate pronunciation of the Greek (Antiq. xx. 11, 2). In the introduction, as well to the Antiquities as to the Wars, he speaks of writing in the Greek language and in his native tongue, as two distinct things, and says, that what he originally wrote in the one he afterwards translated into the other, ('Ελλάδι γλώσση μετα-βαλὼν ἃ τοῖς βαρβάροις τῇ πατρίῳ συντάξας, Bell. Jud. Pro. 1, Antiq. Pro. 2). And once and again he represents the communications sent from Titus during the siege of Jerusalem as being interpreted by himself to the Jews, or by some other person who *Hebraised* (ἑβραΐζων), as he terms it, or spake to them in their own tongue (πατρίῳ γλώσσῃ, Bell., v. 9, 2, vi. 2, 11). At the same time he shows, by occasional allusions to Syriac or Babylonian terms, that the Hebrew current in his day was not altogether identical with that of earlier times—as when, speaking of the high priest's upper robe or girdle, he tells us the old designation for it had been drop (אַבְנֵט, *abaneth*), and it was now called by the Babylonian name *Emia* (Antiq. iii. 7, 2)— a proof that the foreign influence had reached even to the terms for sacred things, and if to these, then assuredly to many others.

When we turn to the New Testament, the evidence is not less clear on both points—both, that the language in common use in Palestine was of the Hebrew, not of the Greek character, yet Hebrew of the Aramaic, not of the older and purer Hebrew

stamp. Thus, when our Lord appears in the attitude of addressing any one very familiarly, of giving or adopting designations for common use, He is represented as speaking in Aramaic :
—as when He said to the daughter of Jairus, Talitha cumi
(טְלִיתָא קוּמִי, Mark v. 41), and to the blind man, Ephphatha (אִתְפַּתַּח,
Mark vii. 34) ; or when He referred to the terms currently employed among the people, such as *raka, rabbi, corban;* when he
applied to His disciples such epithets as *Cephas, Bar-jona, Boanerges* (בְּנֵי רְגֵישׁ) ; or when on the cross He exclaimed, *Eli, Eli,
lama Sabacthani.* Similar indications are also to be found in the
Acts of the Apostles—in the name, for example, reported to have
been given by the Jews to the field purchased by the reward of
Judas' treachery, *Aceldama* (properly Ἀκελδαμα, חֲקַל דְּמָא, i. 19) ;
or of *tabitha* as the familiar term, the native word for the Greek
δορκάς (ix. 36) ; or, finally, in the fact of St Paul addressing the
Jewish multitude on the occasion of his being apprehended in
the temple, in the Hebrew tongue, and their giving, on that
account, the more attentive heed to him, as addressing them
through a medium which was at once intelligible and congenial
to their minds (ch. xxii. 1). The composition also of Targums
among the Eastern Jews, sometime about the apostolic age
(certainly little if at all later), can only be explained on the supposition that the Aramaic language in which they were written,
was that currently employed at the time by the Jews in Palestine and the adjoining regions. Nor is there any clear or even
probable evidence of the Greek translation of the Old Testament Scriptures ever having been used in the synagogues of
Palestine and Syria. The efforts that have been made to establish this point, have utterly failed ; indeed, it can scarcely be
said, that so much as one of the proofs advanced by Diodati in
support of it, has any proper bearing on the subject.[1]

On all these grounds it appears to us a matter of historical
certainty, that the Aramaic, or later Syro-Chaldaic form of the
Hebrew, was in the age of our Lord the vernacular language
of the Jewish people, and consequently the medium of intercourse on all ordinary occasions. At the same time, it cannot

[1] The arguments by Diodati are well met by Dr Pfannkuche, in vol. II., of
Bib. Cabinet. A fair summary of the arguments on both sides is given by
Dr Davidson, in his Introduction to the New Testament, I. pp. 38–40.

be reasonably doubted, on the other side, that from a long and varied concatenation of circumstances, the Greek language must have been very commonly understood by the higher and more educated classes throughout Syria. It was the policy both of Alexander and of his successors in that part of the world, to extend the language and culture, as well as ascendency of Greece. With this view cities were planted at convenient distances, which might be considered Grecian rather than Asiatic in their population and manners. The Syrian kings, by whom the Macedonian line of rulers was continued, kept up Greek as the court language, and were doubtless followed by their official representatives, and the influential classes generally throughout the country. The army, too, though not entirely, nor perhaps even in the major part, yet certainly in very considerable proportions, was composed of persons of Grecian origin, who could not fail to make the Greek language in some sense familiar at the various military stations in the regions of Syria. Even after the Macedonian rule had terminated, and all became subject to the sway of the Romans, it was still usually through the medium of the Greek tongue that official intercourse was maintained, and the decrees of government were made known. It is in the nature of things impossible that so many Hellenizing influences should have continued in operation for two or three centuries, without leading somewhat generally to a partial knowledge of Greek among the better classes in all parts of Syria. There were also circumstances more strictly peculiar to the Jewish people, which require to be taken into account, and which could not be without their effect in bringing them to some extent acquainted with the Greek language. Partly from special encouragements held out to them at the founding of Alexandria, a Grecian city, and partly, perhaps, from the mercantile spirit which began to take possession of them from the time of the Babylonish exile, Alexandria became one of their great centres, where, as we are told by Philo, they formed about two-fifths of the entire population. They abounded also, as is clear alone from the Acts of the Apostles, in the Greek-speaking cities of Asia Minor, and in those of Greece itself. From whatever causes, the dispersion seems, for some generations previous to the Christian era, to have taken very much a Western, and

specially a Grecian direction; in every place of importance in-
habited by Greeks, members of the stock of Israel, had their
homes and their synagogues. It is only, too, what might have
been expected in the circumstances, that the culture and enterprise which distinguished the communities in those Grecian
cities, would act with stimulating effect upon the Jewish mind,
and bring its powers into more energetic play and freedom of
action, than was likely to be found among the Palestinian Jews,
who were sealed up in their national bigotry and stagnant Pha-
risaism. Hence, the only moral and religious productions which
are known to have appeared among the Jews between the
closing of the Old Testament canon and the birth of Christ—
those contained in the Apocryphal writings—came chiefly if not
entirely from the pen of the Hellenistic Jews, and exist only—
most probably never did exist but—in the Greek language.
Hence also the Greek translation of the Old Testament, which
was completed several generations before the Christian era, and
which, there is good reason to believe, was in extensive use about
that era among the Jewish people. So that, looking to the numbers, the higher intelligence, and varied resources of the Hellenistic
Jews, and taking into account their frequent personal visits to
Palestine at the ever-recurring festivals, we cannot doubt that
they materially contributed to a partial knowledge and use of
the Greek tongue among their brethren in Palestine.

As regards the question, then, whether our Lord and his immediate disciples ever spoke in Greek to their countrymen in
Judea, it may be admitted as perfectly possible, perhaps even
probable, that they *sometimes* did so—but the reverse of probable,
that such should have been their usual practice, or that their
public addresses should have been originally delivered in that
tongue;—the more so, as their intercourse for the most part lay,
not with the more refined and educated, but with the humbler
classes of society. But in respect to the further question, why
in such a case the books of the New Testament, including those
which contain our Lord's personal discourses, should, with at most
one exception—if the Gospel of Matthew *be* indeed an exception
—have been originally composed in the Greek, rather than the
Aramaic language? the answer is obvious—that at the time
those books were written, and for the individuals and communi-

ties whose spiritual good they more immediately contemplated, the Greek language was on every account the fittest medium. It was comparatively but a small portion of the people resident in Jerusalem and Judea, who embraced the Christian faith ; and those who did, having in the first instance enjoyed many opportunities of becoming personally acquainted with the facts of Gospel history, and enjoying afterwards the ministry of Apostles and Evangelists, who were perfectly cognisant of the whole, were in a manner independent of any written records. Besides, the troubles which shortly after befel their native land, and which were distinctly foreseen by the founders of the Christian faith, destined, as they were, to scatter the power of the Jewish nation, and to render its land and people monuments of judgment, presented an anticipative reason against committing the sacred and permanent records of the Christian faith to the Hebrew language. That language, itself already corrupted and broken, was presently to become to all but the merest fragment of the Jews themselves, antiquated and obsolete. The real centres of Christianity—the places where it took firmest root, and from which it sent forth its regenerating power among the nations—from the time that authoritative records of its facts and expositions of its doctrines became necessary—were to be found in Greek-speaking communities—the communities scattered throughout the cities of Asia Minor, of Greece, at Rome and the West—where also the first converts to the faith consisted chiefly of those whose native tongue was Greek. Whether, therefore, respect were had to the immediate wants of the first Christian communities, or to the quarters in which the Gospel was to find its most active agents and representatives, and the direction it was appointed to take in the world, the Greek was obviously the language in which its original and authoritative documents behoved to be written. Whatever reasons there were for the adherents of Judaism getting the Scriptures of the Old Testament rendered into Greek ; whatever reasons also Josephus could have for translating into Greek his Jewish histories, and the authors of the Apocryphal writings for adopting that language in preference to Aramaic, the same reasons existed, and in far greater force, for the inspired writings, which were to form in earlier and later times the fundamental records of the Christian faith, being composed in the Greek language, and in that language committed to the faithful keeping of the Church. Had they not been originally composed in Greek, the course of Providence would presently have required that they should be translated into Greek; and considering how much depended on the correct knowledge of them, and how many sources we have for illustrating Greek, as compared with Aramaic productions, it was unspeakably better that, from the first, they should have appeared in a Greek form.

SECTION SECOND.

THE CHARACTERISTICS OF NEW TESTAMENT GREEK.

I. Being satisfied that the books of the New Testament were written in Greek, our next inquiry naturally turns on the precise character of this Greek. Is it fashioned after the model of classical Greek, or has it laws and properties of its own? If the latter, wherein consist its distinctive peculiarities? This is evidently a subject of no small moment for the correct interpretation of the New Testament writings, and demands a careful examination. In the present day, it can scarcely be said, that there is any material difference of opinion upon the subject. This common agreement, however, is the result partly of a long controversy, and partly of the more exact and impartial treatment of Scripture, which is the general characteristic of present, as compared with earlier, times. Indeed, the question, in so far as it has been agitated, has usually turned, not so much upon the *fact* of a difference between New Testament and classical Greek (which no competent scholar could fail to perceive), as upon the *extent* of the difference, and the precise *light* in which it was to be regarded. So early as the period of the Reformation, we find distinct notice taken of the difference. Erasmus, for example, says on Acts x. 38, " The apostles had not learned their Greek from the speeches of Demosthenes, but from the language of common discourse; and I should think it best suited to the Gospel of Christ, that it was communicated in a simple

and unpolished style, and that the discourse of the apostles re-
sembled their clothing, their manners, and their whole life.
Pious persons should as little take offence at the language of
the apostles, as at their unwashed bodies, and their plebeian garments." Beza, in a long note on the same chapter, only so far
controverts the sentiments of Erasmus, as the latter had affirmed
the language of the apostles to be relatively imperfect and obscure, as well as unpolished; but he admits the existence of
Hebraistic peculiarities, and of occasional solecisms. Practically,
however, the theological writers of that period treated the language of the New Testament much as they would have done any
other production in Greek, and as if it had no very marked peculiarities of its own. The doctrinal discussions, too, in which
they, and their immediate successors in sacred learning, were so
much engaged, tended not a little to impede the exact philological study of the Greek Scriptures, and their relation in point of
dialect to other Greek writings, from a too prominent regard to
polemical discussions.

Often, indeed, Greek studies were prosecuted for the purpose
mainly of impugning or defending out of Scripture a particular
class of doctrines; and, as a natural consequence, the New
Testament came to be regarded as an ordinary specimen of
Greek, and to be commonly used as a class-book for the acquire-
ment of the language. Nor, by and by, were there wanting
persons to contend for the absolute purity of its style—including
among others the well-known printer Robert Stephens—persons
who sought to prove, that the seeming peculiarities of the New
Testament dialect were also to be met with in the contempo-
raneous and earlier writings of Greece. It was the more common opinion, however, among learned men during the seventeenth
and eighteenth centuries, that there are certain terms and modes
of expression frequently employed in the New Testament, and
derived from the Hebrew, which characteristically distinguish it
from the writings belonging to Greece proper; but yet that the introduction of these—to use the language of Pfeiffer, who speaks
the general sentiment of his age[1]—"is to be sought, not in any
degeneracy of the Greek language into a distinct Hellenistic dialect, but in an assimilation of the style of the New Testament to

[1] Klausen's Hermeneutik, p. 260.

that of the Old, through an especial direction of the Holy Spirit. Such Hebraisms are not to be reckoned solecisms, or barbarisms, but modes of speech, which are peculiar to the Holy Spirit. If the style of the New Testament (he adds) may be designated by any name, it should rather be called after the authors, the sacred Greek style, than either Hellenistic, or half Hebraistic, or Hebrew Greek, or Hebraising, to say nothing of disfigured Greek."

We have here, no doubt, in substance, the right view of the matter—though with an error in the formal representation of it, the offspring of a not unnatural, though mistaken dread, lest, in conceding the strict purity of New Testament Greek, a kind of slight should be thrown upon the medium of the Spirit's communication. The strongest representative of this feeling, perhaps, may be found in Blackwall, who, in his Sacred Classics, both denied that many of the alleged peculiarities of New Testament Greek *are* Hebraistic or Oriental idioms, and claimed for such, as he admitted to be of this description, the character of true and proper ornaments. "He did not consider," as justly remarked by Dr Campbell, in the first preliminary dissertation to the Gospels, "that when he admitted *any* Hebraisms in the New Testament, he in effect gave up the cause. That only can be called a Hebraism in a Greek book, which though agreeable to the Hebrew idiom, is not so to the Greek. Nobody would ever call that a Scotticism, which is equally in the manner of both Scotch and English. Now, such foreign idioms as Hebraisms in Greek, Grecisms in Hebrew, or Latinisms in either, come all within the definition of barbarism, and sometimes even of solecism—words which have always something relative in their signification; that term of expression being a barbarism or a solecism in one language, which is strictly proper in another, and, I may add, to one set of hearers, which is not so to another. It is in vain, then, for any one to debate about the application of the names *barbarism* and *solecism*. To do so, is at best but to wrangle about words, after admitting all that is meant by them."

So obvious is this view of the matter, and so readily does it commend itself to one's practical judgment, that it seems strange there should ever have been any unwillingness to admit it. The unwillingness, as we have mentioned, simply arose from a mistaken idea of some necessary connection subsisting between purity of diction and inspiration of sentiment ;—certainly a *mistaken* idea, for the imagined purity is expressly disclaimed by the most learned of all the apostles, who represents himself as naturally appearing to a Greek audience " rude in speech ;" and of his method of discourse generally, including doubtless the language in which it was expressed, he declares that it did not aim at excellency of words. A strictly classical diction would not have been natural to him and the other apostles. And as it was the rule of the Spirit in all His supernatural gifts and operations to proceed on the basis of what is natural, it would, in the first instance, have been contrary to the usual method of the Spirit's working, if they had given utterance to their thoughts in language of fine polish and unexceptionable purity. It would, in fact, have required a kind of *second* inspiration to secure this, and one so little in accordance with the principle usually acted on in like cases, that it might well have suggested a doubt as to the reality of the first. If the apostles had written with the classical taste, which is sometimes claimed for them, thoughtful minds would have found some difficulty in believing them to be the authors of their own productions. And we, in this remoter age, should have wanted one of the most important evidences of the authenticity and genuineness of New Testament Scripture— its being written in the style natural to the persons by whom, and the age in which, it was produced. The language is precisely what might have been expected from Jews at that particular time expressing themselves in Greek. And this, beyond doubt, is the fundamental reason for the style being precisely what it is. But the Apostle Paul connects with it in his own case—connects with its very deficencies in respect to classical refinement and rhetorical finish—the further and higher reason, that it but served the more strikingly to exhibit the direct agency of God's Spirit in the success of the Gospel. He spake, in delivering the Divine message, and of course also wrote, " not with the wisdom of words, lest the cross of Christ should be made of none effect ;" and " his preaching was not with enticing words of man's wisdom, but in demonstration of the Spirit and of power, that your faith (the faith of those who listened to his preaching) might not stand in the wisdom of men, but in the power of God" (1 Cor. ii. 4, 5). His meaning evidently is, that in himself and the other heralds of the Gospel, in their personal attributes and in their whole manner of address, there were obvious defects and imperfections, as judged by the standard of worldly taste and re-fined culture; and *that*, not as a matter of accident, but of Divine choice—for the purpose of rendering more palpable and conspicuous the operation of God's hand in the results that were accomplished through their instrumentality.

Even this is not the whole. Another reason still may be added for the same thing, and one too commonly overlooked by those who contended against the purists. There was a necessity in the case for securing the proper ends of a divine revelation—a necessity for a certain departure from the pure classical style, and calling in the aid of Jewish idioms and forms of speech, in order to exhibit in the most distinct and appropriate manner the peculiar truths of the Gospel. As these truths required the pre-paration of much time and special providences for their proper growth and development, so also did the language, in which they were to be finally presented to the world, require something of a peculiar conformation. The native language of Greece, though in some respects the most perfect medium for the communication of thought which has ever been employed by the tongue of man, yet from being always conversant with worldly things, adapted to express every shade of thought and every variety of relationship within the human and earthly sphere—but still *only* these—it was not fully adequate to the requirements and pur-poses of Christian authorship. For this higher end it needed to borrow something from the sanctuary of God, and be, as it were, baptized in the modes of thought and utterance which were familiar to those who had enjoyed the training of the Spirit. So that the writings of the Old Testament formed a necessary preparation for the language of the New, as did also the history and institutions of the one for the religious ideas of the other. Nor is it too much to say, as indeed *has* been said, "that a pure Greek Gospel, a pure Greek apostolic epistle is in-conceivable. The canonical and the Hebrew are most intimately connected."[1]

[1] Hengstenberg on the Revelation of St John, ii., p. 442.

It is perfectly consistent with all this, and no less true, that the writers of the New Testament often show a correct acquaintance with the idioms of the Greek language, and knew how to distinguish between the nicer shades of meaning in many of its expressions. There are numberless passages in their writings which are scarcely less remarkable for the lofty elevation of thought they convey, than for the graceful and felicitous form in which it is embodied. And if we must say, on the one hand, that their language, as a whole, exhibits frequent deviations from the purity of Attic Greek, we must say also, on the other, that it often makes near approaches to this—differing, if not *only*, yet most distinctly and chiefly, when the higher purposes for which they wrote required them so to do. Their language may thus be said to be of a somewhat irregular and oscillatory character. "In many cases it rises superior to the common dialect of the time, and approaches marvellously near to the vigour and precision of Attic Greek, while in other usages it seems to sink below the average standard, and to present to us the peculiarities of the later Greek, distorted and exaggerated by Aramaic forms of expression. This mixed character of the language is very interesting and suggestive. It shows us how at one time the august nature of the narrative, from the vital force of the truths it revealed, wove round itself a garb of clear and vigorous diction of Attic power, and more than Attic simplicity: and yet how, at other times, in the enunciation of more peculiarly scriptural sentiments and doctrines, the nationality of the writer comes into view, and with it his inaptitude—his providential inaptitude (we may thankfully say)—at presenting definite Christian truths in the smooth, fluent, yet possibly unimpressive [and spiritually defective] turns of language, which the native Greek—the Greek of the first century—would have instinctively adopted. Where, however, in a merely literary point of view, the sacred volume may thus seem weakest, it is, considered from a higher point of view, incomparably strongest. It is this investiture of its doctrines with the majesty of Hebraistic imagery [and the peculiar richness and force of Hebraistic modes of expression], rather than with the diffluent garb of a corrupted and decaded Hebraism, that does truly reveal to us the overruling providence and manifold wisdom of God."[1]

Whether, therefore, we look to what was in itself natural and proper at the time, to what was in fittest accordance with the purposes for which the Gospel revelation was given, or, finally, to what was required by the demands of the revelation itself, on each account there appears ground for concluding, that not the earlier and purer Greek of the classics, but the later Greek of the apostolic age, intermingled with and modified by the Hebraisms, which were natural and familiar to those whose style of thought and expression had been moulded by Old Testament Scripture, was the appropriate diction for the writers of the New Testament. Admitting, however, that such *is* and *ought* to have been its general character, we have still to inquire into the special characteristics of this dialect—to notice the more marked peculiarities that belong to it, and which require to be kept in view by those who would succeed in the work of interpretation.[2]

II. Undoubtedly the basis of the New Testament dialect is the κοινή διάλεκτος, the common, or Hellenic dialect, as it has been called, of the later Greek. This is the name given to the form of the Greek language, which came into general use after the Macedonian conquests. It was called *common*, and some-

---

[1] Fraser's Magazine for December 1855. Substantially, indeed, the correct view was given by Beza, in the note already referred to on Acts x. 46. After noticing the fine specimens of powerful and affecting writing to be found, especially in the epistles of Paul, he adds, " As to the intermixture of Hebraisms, it arose, not only from their being Hebrews, but because, in discoursing of those things which had been transmitted through the Hebrew tongue, it was necessary to retain much peculiar to it, lest they should seem to introduce some new doctrine. And certainly I cannot in the least wonder that so many Hebraisms have been retained by them, since most of these are of such a description, that by no other idiom could matters have been so happily expressed, nay, sometimes not expressed at all ; so that, had those formulas not been used, new words and novel modes of expression would have needed to be sometimes employed, which no one could properly have understood."

[2] For a short account of the earlier part of the controversy on the style of the New Testament, and a notice of some of the leading authors and works it called forth, see Planck's Sacred Philology, Bib. Cab. vii., pp. 67–76.

times also *Macedonian,* because it originated in a sort of fusion of the particular dialects which had prevailed in earlier times; and this again arose, in great measure, from the fusion of the several states of Greece into one great empire under kings of the Macedonian dynasty. Indeed, what are known as the four classical dialects of earlier times—the Ionic, Æolic, Doric, and Attic—were not so properly the dialects in common use among the people, circulating in their separate localities, as the forms appropriated to so many departments of literature, which severally took their rise among the tribes that bore the distinctive names referred to. There may have been, and most probably were, other varieties in current use throughout Greece, but none, except one or other of the four specified, were allowed to appear in written productions. The Attic, however, surpassed the others so much, both by its inherent grace, and by the number of distinguished men who employed it in their writings, that it came to be generally regarded as the model form of the Greek language, and was cultivated by nearly all who were ambitious of writing in the purest style. Certain changes began to pass upon this dialect after the period of the Macedonian conquests, arising chiefly from the Doric peculiarities which predominated in Macedonia, and which now obtained a more general currency; while, along with these, occasional peculiarities from the other dialects were also introduced, probably, in the first instance, from colloquial usage;—the whole combining to form the common speech of Greece in later times. Salmasius was among the first to draw the attention of the learned to this subject, and since his day many others have contributed to the same line of investigation. Of these Henry Planck may be named as one of the most careful and accurate, whose treatise on the subject has been translated into English, and forms part of Vol. II. of Clark's Biblical Cabinet. The characteristics of this common dialect were not quite uniform; but there are some general features which distinguish it pretty broadly from the Greek of the strictly classical times. They fall into two leading classes—Lexical and Grammatical peculiarities—the one relating to the form and usage of words, the other to their flexion and government. We shall notice under each head the more marked and important distinctions, and in each shall select only such examples as have a place in New Testament Scripture.

1. Under Lexical peculiarities, or such as relate to the form and usage of words, there are, (1.) Words that received a new termination :—such as μετοικεσία, Matt. i. 11, for which μετοίκησις or μετοικία was employed in earlier times; καύχησις often in St Paul's writings for the act or object of glorying, as previously in the Septuagint, but in Attic writers καύχη or καύχημα; γενέσια, which in the earlier Greek writers was wont to signify the solemnities offered to the dead, on the periodical return of their birth-day, was latterly used for the birth-day itself, as in Matt. xiv. 6, instead of γενέθλια; ἔκπαλαι for πάλαι; various words with terminations in μα, as αἴτημα for αἴτησις, ἀνταπόδημα for ἀνταπόδοσις, ἀσθένημα for ἀσθένεια, ψεῦσμα for ψεῦδος (though it is found also in Plato). We have also βασίλισσα, queen, for βασίλεια or βασιλίς, ἀποστασία for ἀπόστασις, and various other alterations of a like nature. (2.) Words, and forms of words, which were but rarely used in classical Greek, or found only with the poets, passed into common use in the later common dialect :—such as αὐθεντεῖν, to govern; ἀλέκτωρ, a cock; ἀλεκτροφωνία, cock-crowing; ἀλάλητος, that is not, or cannot be spoken, etc. (3.) Certain words formerly in use came latterly to acquire new meanings :—such as παρακαλεῖν, in the sense of admonishing or beseeching; παιδεύειν, of chastising; εὐχαριστεῖν, of giving thanks (originally to be thankful); εὐσχήμων, of respectable or noble standing (originally, graceful, decent, or becoming); ὀψάριον, diminutive, from ὄψον (from ἕψω), strictly, boiled meat, then anything eaten with bread to give it a relish, seasoning, sauce—in particular, at Athens, fish, which were there reckoned among the chief dainties—whence also the diminutive ὀψάριον acquired the sense of fish, as in John vi. 9, in Plutarch too, and Athenæus. Under the same class may be ranked verbs with an active meaning, which, in classical Greek, are used only intransitively; for example, μαθητεύειν, to disciple, instead of being or taking the place of a disciple; θριαμβεύειν, to cause to triumph, instead of leading in triumph. Such transitions, however, from the received intransitive to a transitive sense, should rather perhaps be ascribed to the Hebraistic impress of the New Testament diction, than regarded as a peculiarity of the common dialect of the later Greek--the

sacred writers very naturally giving, in certain cases, the force of the Hiphil to the simple meaning of the verb. But, undoubtedly, traces of such alterations are also to be found in other writers. (4.) Words and phrases entirely new entered, especially compound words; for example, ἀλλοτριοεπίσκοπος, ἀνθρωπάρεσκος, μονόφθαλμος, εἰδωλολατρεία, σπλαγχνίζεσθαι, with many others — some peculiar to the Septuagint and the writings of the New Testament, others common to these and the productions in later Greek generally. Peculiarities of this class are distributed by Planck, not inaptly, into three kinds :—the first comprehending those which were expressly asserted by the ancient grammarians to have belonged to the common language of later times ; the second, such as were not explicitly noted in this way, but are only found in the productions which appeared subsequently to the Macedonian era ; and finally, those which nowhere occur but in the Septuagint, the Apocrypha, the writings of the New Testament, and the Greek Fathers. It is quite possible that, in regard to many of the words comprised in each of these divisions, the use made of them in the later Greek writings is not absolutely novel ; they may have existed before, most likely did exist, but only as provincialisms, which had not received the sanction of any pure writer, or as expressions so seldom employed, that the earlier writings in which they occurred have not been preserved among the remains of antiquity. (5.) A fifth class consists of words imported into the Greek tongue from the Latin—a natural result of the subjugation of the Greek-speaking countries by the Romans ; of these it is enough to notice such expressions as ἀσσάριον, δηνάριον, κῆνσος, λεγεών, σικάριος, etc., λαμβάνειν συμβούλιον (consilium capere), ἐργασίαν δοῦναι (operam dare), etc.[1]

2. In regard to the other great class of peculiarities belonging to the common dialect—those relating to flexion and syntax —*Grammatical* peculiarities—they also fall into several divisions. (1.) We have peculiarities in the flexion of verbs, such as δύνῃ as 2d pers. sing. of indic. pass. for the regular δύνασαι, κάθῃ for κάθησαι ; second aorists with the terminations proper to the first, as εἶπα for εἶπον, ἔπεσα for ἔπεσον, even ἡμάρτησα for ἥμαρτον ; various endings also in αν instead of ασι, such as ἔγνωκαν for ἐγνώκασι,

---

[1] For a more complete list, see Klausen, Hermeneutik, pp. 338–343 ; also Winer's Idioms, § 2.

εἴρηκαν for εἰρήκασι. Verbs occur, too, with double augments, as ἤμελλε, ἠβούληθην, ἠδυνηθήσαν, as sometimes also with Attic writers; and again occasionally without the augment, according to the best readings, for example, in Luke xiii. 13; 2 Tim. i. 16. Besides, certain Doric forms came into general use—such as πεινᾷν for πεινῆν, διψᾷν for διψῆν, σημᾶναι for σημῆναι. (2.) Peculiarities also appear in regard to the gender and flexion of nouns: thus ἔλεος, which, with all good Greek authors, is masculine, is neuter in the New Testament and ecclesiastical writers—but occasionally also masculine; πλοῦτος in like manner used as a neuter; λιμός, which was used by the Greeks generally as a masculine, but was feminine in the Doric dialect, occurs in this gender also in the New Testament twice (Luke xv. 14, λιμὸς ἰσχυρά; Acts xi. 28, λιμὸν μεγάλην), according to the best copies. On the other hand, the sacred writers and the later Greek writers make βάτος, a bramble, feminine, as the Greeks generally were wont to do, while the Attics treated it as a masculine. The peculiarities in flexion are fewer; but χάριτα, the later and rarer form, occurs occasionally for χάριν; and ἕας of the accus. plural is always dropt for εἷς. (3.) As further distinctions, there may be added the nearly entire disuse of the dual, and a few peculiarities in respect to syntax. These latter consist chiefly (to take the summary of Winer) "in a negligent use of the moods and particles. In the New Testament the following may be noticed as examples: ὅταν used with the indicative preterite, εἰ with the subjunctive, ἵνα with the indicative present;[1] the dispensing with ἵνα in forms like θέλω ἵνα, ἄξιος ἵνα, etc.; the coupling of verbs like γεύεσθαι with the genitive, and προσκυνεῖν with the dative; the use of the genitive infinitive, such as τοῦ ποιεῖν, beyond the original and natural limit, and of the subjunctive for the optative in the historical style after preterites; and, above all, the rare use of the optative, which became entirely obsolete in the late Greek. Also a neglect of the declensions begins to be exhibited, as εἷς καθεῖς (after ἕν καθέν), and even καθεῖς; then also ἀνὰ εἷς, εἷς παρ' εἷς; so also μετὰ τοῦ ἕν, and similar instances."

These constitute the leading peculiarities of the later Greek,

[1] He might have added, what is still more peculiar, the occasional use of ἵνα with the future, as at 1 Cor. xiii. 3, Rev. vi. 11, if these are, as they appear to be, the correct readings.

appearing in the writings of the New Testament. But no doubt, as Winer also remarks, this later and more popular dialect had in some districts peculiarities which were unknown elsewhere. And in this category some have been disposed to place the expressions, which Jerome called Cilicisms of the Apostle Paul. But of such peculiarities we know too little to enable us to form any correct judgment; and examples have been found in good Greek authors of, at least, some of Jerome's alleged Cilicisms. Winer, however, is disposed to reckon of the class in question, the occasional use of ἵνα in expressions where the pure Greek writers would have used the infinitive, and would explain it as a sort of free and colloquial usage (§ 45, 9). It is, certainly, difficult to maintain the strictly *telic* use of ἵνα throughout the New Testament, as Meyer, for example, endeavours to do; nor can it be done without at times leading to strained and somewhat unnatural explanations. That the telic force should be retained in the great mass of cases, and, in particular, in the formula ἵνα πληρωθῇ, we have no doubt; for when so employed there always is the indication of design. So also is there in various passages, in which it does not at first sight appear, but discovers itself on a closer inspection; as in 1 John v. 3, "This is the love of God, ἵνα τὰς ἐντολὰς αὐτοῦ τηρῶμεν"—not that we *do* keep, as a fact—but *in order that we may* keep the commandments of God, as a scope or aim; the tendency and striving of Divine love in the heart is ever in the direction of God's commandments; or again, in Matt. v. 29, συμφέρει γάρ σοι ἵνα, κ.τ.λ., it is for thy advantage, viz., to cut off the right hand, in order that one (one merely) of thy members may perish, and not thy whole body be cast into hell-fire; this, at least, is a perfectly admissible explanation. But there are others—such as Rev. vi. 11; Matt. xviii. 6; Mark vi. 25, ix. 30 —in which it is, no doubt, possible, by copious supplementings, to bring out a design, yet scarcely to do it in a way that appears consistent with the simplicity of the sacred writers.

But of the peculiarities generally, which have been noted as characterizing the dialect of the New Testament, in common with that of the later Greek writers, there is no room for difference of opinion. They distinguish the Greek of the apostolic age from the Greek of classical times. They must, therefore, be understood, and have due allowance made for them by all, who would exhibit the precise import of Scripture, and would even avoid mistakes in interpretation, which have sometimes been committed by persons of high attainments in classical learning, from their too exclusive regard to simply classical authorities.

III. But another, and scarcely less important class of peculiarities, must be taken into account for the correct knowledge and appreciation of the original language of the New Testament—those, namely, arising from its Hebraistic impress. The common dialect of later times was, in the case of the sacred writings, intermingled with the free and frequent use of forms derived from the Hebrew, which, as already stated, was to some extent unavoidable in the case of the sacred penmen. Very commonly the Greek of the apostolic age, with the addition of this Hebraistic element, is called Hellenistic Greek, from the name Hellenists, which was usually applied to the Greek-speaking Jews, and who naturally spoke Greek with an admixture of Hebrew idioms.

It is to be borne in mind, however, that while all the writers of the New Testament partook to some extent of the Hebraistic influence, some did so considerably more than others; and they are by no means uniform in the admission of Hebraisms into their style. The Hebraistic element was a very variable one among them. It differed with the same writers in different parts of their writings—as in the Apocalypse of St John, which is considerably more Hebraistic than either his gospel or epistles—while these again have more of that element than many other parts of the New Testament. The Gospel of St Luke is decidedly less marked with Hebraisms than those of St Matthew and St Mark; and in St Paul's epistles also there are diversities in this respect. The epistle to the Hebrews approaches more nearly to the classical diction than any other book of the New Testament. Viewing the subject generally, however, and without reference to the peculiarities of individual writers, there are three several respects in which the Hebraistic influence appears in the style of the New Testament.

1. The first is of a somewhat general kind, and consists of a sensible approximation to the Hebrew in the usual cast and complexion of the style, namely, in those things in which the Hebrew

characteristically differed from the Greek. As (1.) in the more
frequent use of the prepositions for marking relations, which
were wont to be indicated in classical Greek by means of cases.
This characteristic pervades so much the style of the New Testament, that particular examples are almost unnecessary. But take
one or two :—In Heb. i. 2, ὅν ἔθηκε κληρονόμον πάντων, " whom he
appointed heir of all," is classical Greek; but Acts xiii. 22,
ἤγειρεν τὸν Δαυὶδ εἰς βασιλέα, literally " raised up David for king,"
is Hebraistic. Again, τίνι γὰρ εἶπεν ποτε τῶν ἀγγέλων, " for to
which of the angels said He at any time," is pure Greek,—but
the use of the preposition in the following expressions is Hebraistic, τίς ἐγκαλέσει κατὰ ἐκλεκτῶν Θεοῦ, Rom. viii. 33; ἀγανακ-
τοῦντες πρὸς ἑαυτούς, Mark xiv. 4; ἀθῶος ἀπὸ τοῦ αἵματος, Matt.
xxvii. 24 (so Sept. transl. נָקִי מִ in 2 Sam. iii. 28); ὁμολογεῖν ἐν αὐτῷ,
Matt. x. 32, etc. (2.) It formed another marked difference between the two languages—the paucity of conjunctions which
existed in the Hebrew, and their great abundance, one might
almost say, their superfluity, in the Greek. But the New Testament writers constantly show an inclination to adhere to the
simplicity of the Hebrew in this respect, rather than to avail
themselves of the greater wealth of the Greek. How often in
their productions do we meet with a καί, where we would rather
have expected an ἀλλά, a καίπερ, or a καίτοι? and a γὰρ or an
οὖν where we would have looked for an ἐπεί, a ὥστε, or a ὅτι, if
judging from the usage of classical writers? In the narrative
portions, more especially, of the New Testament, it is the remarkable nakedness and simplicity of the Hebrew language, as
to conjunctions and other particles, which presents itself to our
notice, rather than the copiousness of the Greek. (3.) A further
Hebraistic turn appears in the frequent use of the genitive pronouns, instead of the possessives—σοῦ, μοῦ, αὐτοῦ, ἡμῶν, ὑμῶν,
αὐτῶν. This naturally arose from the inspired writers being
used to the Hebrew suffixes, and was also encouraged by a
growing tendency in the Greek language itself to substitute the
genitives of the personal pronouns for the possessives. The
practice, however, is greatly more frequent in the New Testament and the Septuagint, than in other productions of the same
period. Indeed, we often meet with the personal pronouns
generally in the Greek Scriptures, where simply Greek writers

would have altogether omitted them; as in Gen. xxx. 1, δός μοι
τέκνα, εἰ δὲ μή, τελευτήσω ἐγώ; Ex. ii. 14, μὴ ἀνελεῖν με σὺ θέλεις,
ὃν τρόπον ἀνεῖλες χθὲς τὸν Αἰγύπτον (in both cases imitating the
Hebrew); so in John iii. 2, ταῦτα τὰ σημεῖα ποιεῖν ἃ σὺ ποιεῖς;
Rev. v. 4, καὶ ἐγὼ ἔκλαιον πολύ; 2 John 1, οὓς ἐγὼ ἀγαπῶ ἐν ἀλη-
θείᾳ, etc. (4.) Another pronominal peculiarity, arising from
assimilation to the Hebrew, is occasionally found in the New
Testament, and abounds in the Septuagint. In Hebrew there
is only one relative pronoun, אֲשֶׁר (sometimes abbreviated into
שׁ); and this without any distinction as to number, gender, or
case:—on which account the suffixes of the personal pronouns,
or these pronouns themselves with a preposition, required to be
added, in order to give the necessary point and explicitness to
the reference. Hence such expressions as the following: "the
land in which ye dwell upon it," " the place in which ye sojourn
in it," and so on. As the Greek language possessed a declinable
relative ὅς, and adverbs derived from it, οὗ, ὅθεν, ὅπου, there was
no need, when employing it, to resort to this kind of awkward
circumlocution. But those who had been accustomed to the
force and emphasis of the Hebrew usage, appear still occasionally
to have felt as if they could not give adequate expression to
their mind without availing themselves of the Hebrew form.
Hence such passages in the Septuagint as the following: ἡ γῆ
ἐφ᾽ ἧς σὺ κατοικεῖς ἐπ᾽ αὐτῆς, Gen. xxviii. 13; πᾶς σοφὸς τῇ διανοίᾳ,
ᾧ ἐδόθη σοφία καὶ ἐπιστήμα ἐν αὐτοῖς, Ex. xxxvi. 1; also Deut. ix.
28; Ex. xxx. 6; Deut. iv. 5, 14, etc. In the New Testament
the peculiarity occurs more rarely; but still it is found, as in Mark
vi. 55, "They carried about the sick on couches," ὅπου ἤκουον ὅτι
ἐκεῖ ἐστίν; vii. 25, ἧς εἶχεν τὸ θυγάτριον αὐτῆς πνεῦμα ἀκάθαρτον;
Rev. vii. 2, οἷς ἐδόθη αὐτοῖς; xii. 6, ὅπου ἔχει ἐκεῖ τόπον ἡτοιμασμένον;
ver. 14, ὅπου τρέφεται ἐκεῖ καιρόν. The usage is found also in some
quotations from the Old Testament (Acts xv. 17; 1 Pet. ii. 24),
but it is certainly of rare occurrence in the New Testament writings themselves. (5.) A further distinctive impress arose from a
marked difference between the Hebrew and the Greek in respect to the tenses of the verb, giving rise to a peculiarity in the
general character of the New Testament style, and imparting to
it something of a Hebraistic air. Here again the Hebrew was
as remarkable for the fewness, as the Greek for the multiplicity

of its forms—the one having its simple past and future tenses, while the other had its present, imperfect, perfect, pluperfect, first and second aorists, first and second futures, and paulo-post future—certainly a plentiful variety, if not, in some respects, a needless redundancy ; and all these, again, subject to variations of mood—indicatives, subjunctives, optatives—which are unknown in Hebrew. There can be no doubt that the New Testament writers were well acquainted with the principal tenses of the Greek verb, and some of its more peculiar modes of construction, such as those with neuter plurals, with ἵνα and ἄν; at the same time, there are occasional anomalies, with a manifest preference for the simple past and future of the Hebrew, and, as in the latter, a tendency to use the future, as expressive of necessity and continued action (*must* and *is wont*), somewhat more frequently than is usual in ordinary Greek. (6.) Once more, there are some peculiar case-usages, though rare in the New Testament, as compared with the Septuagint. The most noticeable of these is the employment, though in the New Testament occurring only in the Apocalypse, of a kind of nominative absolute—not such as is to be found in Acts vii. 40, ὁ γὰρ Μωϋσῆς οὗτος ὁ ἄνθρωπος, in which, merely for the purpose of giving prominence to the leading noun, the sentence begins with it in the nominative, and of which examples are to be met with in ordinary Greek—but one in which the nominative comes after, and stands in apposition with, other nouns in the oblique cases. This arose from a close imitation of the Hebrew, prefixing the indication of case, or the preposition, to the first noun in a sentence, and dropping it in those that followed. Thus at Num. xx. 5, εἰς τὸν τόπον τὸν πονηρὸν τοῦτον· τόπος οὗ οὐ σπείρεται ; Deut. iv. 11, καὶ τὸ ὄρος ἐκαίετο πυρὶ ἕως τοῦ οὐρανοῦ· σκότος, γνόφος, θύελλα ; also ver. 22 ; Deut. viii. 8, x. 7. Though an anomalous construction, it had the effect, as Tiersch justly remarks (*Pent. Versione Alexandrina*, p. 133), of giving force and emphasis to the terms placed thus absolutely in the nominative—which were thereby isolated. This also is very decidedly the effect of the employment of the nominative in Rev. i. 4, where grace and peace are sent ἀπὸ ὁ ὢν καὶ ὁ ἦν καὶ ὁ ἐρχόμενος ; retaining in the nominative the words, which express the Lord's eternal Being, and so taking them, as it were, out of the common category of declinable nouns, and placing them in

an independent position.   Other examples occur in Rev. ii. 20,
iii. 12.   In the same connection may be mentioned a kind of
Hebraistic extension of the accusative of place, this accusative
being sometimes coupled with a following genitive, in a way not
usual with the Greeks ; of which we have such examples in the
Old Testament as Deut. xi. 30, οὐκ ἰδοὺ ταῦτα πέραν τοῦ Ἰορδάνου,
ὀπίσω, ὁδὸν δυσμῶν ἡλίου ; i. 19 ; Exod. xiii. 17.   And in the New
Testament, the peculiar expression in Matt. iv. 14, γῆ Ναφθαλεῖμ,
ὁδὸν θαλάσσης, which has its parallel in the passages of the Old
Testament referred to, and should not have been regarded in so
exceptional a light as it is by Winer (Gr. § 32, 6).   But such
peculiarities exercise comparatively little influence on the Greek
of the New Testament.

2. Secondly, The Hebraistic cast of the New Testament style
appears in the use of words and phrases, which have their correspondence only in the Hebrew, but are not found in profane
Greek writers, whether of the earlier or of the later periods.
Among these, certain words might be included, which are transferred from the Hebrew and other Oriental languages into the
text of the New Testament :—such as ἄββα, ἀβαδδών, ἀμὴν, παρά-
δεισος, γέεννα, σατᾶν, etc.   Terms of this sort are merely Oriental
words in Greek letters, or with a Greek termination ; and it is
by a reference to their Oriental usage that their meaning is to
be determined.   It is not these, however, so much that we have
in view under the present division, as words and phrases which
are strictly Greek expressions, but expressions thrown into a
Hebraistic form, and conveying a sense somewhat different from
what would naturally be put upon them by a simply Greek
reader.   There is a considerable number of this description,—
among which are εἷς in the sense of τις or πρῶτος, according to the
Septuagint rendering of אֶחָד (εἷς γραμματεύς, Matt. viii. 19, εἰς
μίαν (ἡμέραν) τῶν σαββάτων—μίαν for πρώτην), ζητεῖν τὴν ψυχήν τινός,
θανάτου γεύεσθαι, θάνατον ἴδειν, περιπατεῖν ἐνώπιον τίνος, ποιεῖν ἔλεος,
πρόσωπον πρὸς πρόσωπον, λαμβάνειν πρόσωπον τινός, σάρξ καὶ αἷμα, etc.

To refer more particularly to one or two examples, the
phrase πᾶσα σάρξ, for all men, mankind at large, is quite a Hebraism, being a literal translation of the Hebrew כָּל־בָּשָׂר by two
terms, which in the one language, as well as the other, signify
all flesh—while still native Greek writers never used σάρξ in the

sense of *men*, and such an expression, if employed by them, would have meant, not all mankind, but the whole flesh (of a man or an animal, as it might happen). Sometimes the Hebraism is further strengthened by the addition of a negative, in a manner different from the practice of good Greek writers. In Hebrew, בָּל־בָּשָׂר לֹא *not all flesh*, is equivalent to *no flesh*, and in this same meaning οὐ πᾶσα σάρξ is used in New Testament Scripture; as when our Lord says, Matt. xxiv. 22, " If the days should not be shortened οὐκ ἂν ἐσώθη πᾶσα σάρξ," no flesh should be saved; or St Paul, 1 Cor. i. 29, ὅπως μὴ καυχήσηται πᾶσα σάρξ, so that no flesh might glory. Such phrases are to be explained by coupling the negative with the verb, and regarding the two together as predicating the negation or want of something—the *all* comprehending the entire circle or genus to which such predicate extends. Thus, in the sentence last quoted, the not being in a condition to glory is the thing predicated, and the πᾶσα σάρξ, the all flesh, which follows, denotes the sphere of being to which the predicate applies—the entire compass of humanity. So that, when rightly viewed, the expression presents no material difficulty, though it is a form of speech not native to the Greek, but imported into it from the Hebrew.

The Vulgate has not been sufficiently observant of this peculiar idiom; hence it renders the passage in Matt. non salva fieret omnis caro, and that in 1 Cor. ut non glorietur omnis caro. Our translators, however, in the authorised version have commonly attended to it, and given the correct rendering— though still in one case they appear to have missed it. The passage we refer to is 1 John ii. 19, where the apostle is speaking of those who had once belonged to the true Church, but had since fallen into Gnostic errors, and assumed an antichristian position :—" They went out from among us, but they were not of us ; for if they had been of us, they would have continued with us ; but that (the sentence here is plainly elliptical, and we must again supply ' they went out' that) they might be made manifest, ὅτι οὐκ εἰσὶ πάντες ἐξ ἡμῶν"—that they were not all of us, our version has it—but the apostle had already said of them, wholly and absolutely, that they were not of us ; and it would be strange, if now, at the close, he should have introduced a limitation, and, when speaking of the evidence of their having assumed an antichristian position, or being in deadly heresy, should have used terms that were applicable only to a portion of them. The terms, however, become quite plain, if understood in conformity with the idiom now under consideration ; *i.e.*, if the negative and the verb (οὐκ εἰσι) are taken together, as constituting the predicate, and the πάντες following as indicating the extent of its application—embracing the totality of the parties spoken of. Their going out from the company of the faithful, the apostle then affirms, shows, that they are not—all of them—of us ; *i.e.*, that none of them are of us ; the whole went out, that they might be seen—one and all—not to be of the true Church of Christ. Such, substantially, is the view adopted, not only by several foreign commentators, but also in the English Annotations of 1645, by Hammond, Guyse, Whitby, Peile, and others.

This, however, is rather a digression, and we return to our proper subject—simply remarking further, in respect to the second class of Hebraisms, that a considerable portion of the words and phrases comprised in it, are still to be taken in their ordinary sense, but, at the same time, with such reference to the Hebrew use and application of them, that in the sense necessary to be put upon them they must be regarded as Hebraisms. For example, in the common expression αἷμα ἐκχεῖν, to pour out, or shed blood, what is really meant, is not the simple shedding of blood, but the pouring out of this unto death—the words being those used in rendering the Hebrew דָּם שָׁפַךְ—the usual sacrificial formula for taking the life of an animal victim, when presenting it to God. It hence passed into a common phrase for taking the life of any one ; and in the lips of a Jew, the phrase naturally became more peculiarly and distinctly indicative of death, than it should have done when uttered by a Greek. In like manner, in the use of the word ὄνομα, in a great variety of expressions, such as "calling upon the name," or doing anything in the name of another, "hallowing God's name," "believing on the name of Christ," "trusting in the name of the Lord," and such like—while the ὄνομα precisely corresponds to the שֵׁם in Hebrew, and *name* in English to both, it is still only through the Hebrew usage that we can get at the proper import of the expressions. The Hebrews were wont to regard the name of an individual, as, what it doubtless originally was, the index to the nature ; and when the primary name failed properly to do this, they very commonly superseded it by another, which yielded a more significant or fitting expression of the individual properties. Hence, with them, the *name* was very much identified with the *person*, as, on the other side, the person was very often contemplated in the light of the name. Among the Greeks the significance of names never assumed the same place that it did among the Hebrews; they were regarded more as arbitrary signs, having their chief use in distinguishing one person or one object from another; and consequently the same identification did not prevail in the ordinary Greek usage, as in the Hebrew, between the name, and the person or properties of the individual. In dealing with such expressions, therefore, as those specified above, we must have recourse to the Hebrew, in order to arrive at the proper import.

3. There is still a third respect, in which the Hebraistic cast of the New Testament dialect appears; viz., in the formation of derivatives from words belonging, in the sense employed, to the Hebrew, and not to the Greek. For example, the word σκάνδαλον, the rendering of the Septuagint for מִכְשׁוֹל, a stumbling-block, or offence, is the root of a verb found only in the New Testament, σκανδαλίζω, to stumble, or cause to stumble (corresponding to (נִכְשַׁל הִכְשִׁיל); σπλαγχνίζεσθαι from σπλάγχνα (as in Hebrew רֶחֶם and רַחֲמִים)—ἀναθεματίζεσθαι from ἀνάθεμα, and so on. In such cases one is thrown entirely upon Hebrew ideas and usages; and from these it is necessary to ascertain and determine the precise meaning to be attached, if not to the original noun, at least to the verb derived from it.

IV. It is plain, therefore, from the occurrence of such Hebrew or Aramaic peculiarities as we have referred to, that the Greek of the New Testament adds to the later Greek—the common Hellenic dialect—elements derived from the vernacular language of the sacred writers, on account of which it may justly be denominated a peculiar idiom. It exhibits single Greek words, which are nowhere found in Greek writers out of Palestine; it exhibits also Hebrew and Chaldaic phrases, expressed in Greek terms, but conveying a sense different from what a simply Greek reader would naturally have put upon them; and, finally, it exhibits in the grammatical construction various features of a Hebraistic kind :—all necessarily requiring, in order to attain to a correct interpretation of New Testament Scripture, an acquaintance with the Hebrew as well as with the Greek languages, and, in particular, with the usages established by the Septuagint Version of Old Testament Scripture. But there are two important considerations, which ought to be borne in mind in connection with those Hebraisms—the one having respect to their number, and the other to the proper mode of dealing with them.

(1.) In the first place, they are not nearly so numerous as they were at one time represented to be; nor much more numerous than was rendered necessary by the circumstances of the writers. By far the greater part of them are so essentially connected with the position of the writers, as not only trained under the economy of the Jewish dispensation, but called also to unfold truths and principles, which were but the proper growth and development of such as belonged to it, that they could not justly have been dispensed with. They entered, by a kind of moral necessity, into the cast of thought and expression adopted by the apostles of the New Testament. And hence also they occur less frequently in grammatical constructions than in other respects, and only so as to impart to the style, in that particular respect, an occasional Aramaic colouring. The Greek syntax differs in many things from the Hebrew; the one has its own marked and peculiar characteristics, as well as the other; yet in most of these we find the New Testament writers regularly accommodating themselves to the foreign idiom—as in the distinctive use of imperfects and aorists, in the coupling of neuter plurals with a verb in the singular, in the construction of verbs with ἄν, in the attraction of the relative, etc. It may not be improper to point to an example or two, in a single line, of this conformity to the foreign idiom :—in the discriminating use of the aorist and perfect tenses—the aorist as denoting the historic past, and the perfect as denoting the past in its relation to the present, the past continuing with its effects and consequences to the present. Even St John, who has often been treated as ignorant of the commonest Greek idioms, we find, at the very beginning of his Gospel, carefully observing this distinction, when he says of the work of the Logos, ἐγένετο οὐδὲ ἕν ὃ γέγονεν, nothing whatever that has come to be, and still is in being, was made without Him. So also in Col. i. 16, pointing to the act of creation by Christ in the indefinite past, ἐν αὐτῷ ἐκτίσθη τὰ πάντα ; but when Christ's continued relation to, and interest in, what was created, is in view, then the apostle changes from the aorist to the perfect, τὰ πάντα δι᾽ αὐτοῦ καὶ εἰς αὐτὸν ἔκτισται. Another striking example of a similar change may be seen in ch. iii. 3 of the same epistle, in the ἀπεθάνετε used of the old life once and for ever put away, and the κέκρυπται of the new begun at conversion, but continuing still on. In connection with such discriminating employments of the aorist and perfect tenses, it is justly remarked by the late Professor Scholefield, that the English translation is often obscured by failing to mark the distinction as observed in the original, and consequently inserting or omitting at the wrong place the auxiliary *have.*—(*Hints for Improvements in the Authorised Version,* Preface X.)

In respect, however, to the excessive multiplication of Hebraisms, Titmann very justly says, in his Synonyms, ii. p. 163, " Many expressions in the New Testament have been stamped with the name of Hebraisms, for no other reason whatever than because it was taken for granted that the writers of the New Testament have imitated the Hebrew mode of speaking ; just as if they could not have derived those forms from the like usage of the Greek language, which they were writing. Many Hebraisms have thus been pointed out by Vorstius, Leusden, and others, which might with equal justice be called *Hellenisms.* Because, forsooth, they appear in the New Testament, in writers Ἐβραΐζοντες, they are Hebraisms ; while the same things, when found in Demosthenes, Thucydides, Xenophon, or Polybius, are pronounced to be good and elegant Greek. Thus, in the New Testament, the use of the demonstrative pronoun without apparent necessity after a noun or relative pronoun, has been regarded as a Hebraism, inasmuch as the Hebrews do indeed use this construction, as also the Arabs, Syrians, Greeks, and Romans (we might add the Germans and English). Still that cannot surely be reckoned as a *Hebrew* idiom, which is also employed by the best writers of other nations." He proceeds to give various examples of the usage,—among which are, from Cicero, Illud *quod* supra scripsi, *id* tibi confirmo; from Sallust, Sed urbana plebes, *ea* vero præceps ierat; from Thucydides, " the most Attic of all Greek writers," τῷ δὲ Ἱπποχράτει ὄντι περὶ το Δήλιον, ὡς αὐτῷ ἠγγέλθη; and concludes by saying, " The construction in all these usages is evidently the same as in Matt. iv. 16, viii. 5; John xv. 2, xviii. 11."

Michaelis remarked sharply, but not without cause, on this tendency to discover Hebraisms in New Testament Scripture, " It is extraordinary, that those very persons who are least acquainted with the Hebrew are the most inclined to discover Hebraisms; and it has been as fashionable, as it is convenient, to ascribe the difficulty of every passage to an Oriental idiom."— (Introd. iv. 6.) Yet he has not himself altogether escaped the contagion; for we find him, in the same chapter, ranking some things as Hebraisms, and giving them on that ground a false rendering, which ought to be taken in their strictly Greek meaning; for example, εἰς νῖκος, in 1 Cor. xv. 54, which he designates " a harsh Hebraism" signifying " for ever," while really the proper import is best given by the literal rendering, " into victory," *i.e.*, towards this as the end aimed at—death being viewed as the great enemy, with whose swallowing up the final victory comes. Gerard (Bib. Criticism, p. 54), as usual, follows Michaelis in this; and, along with many others then and since, he also gives ῥῆμα, in the sense of thing, as a Hebraism, in such passages as Luke i. 37, ii. 15; Acts v. 32. But it always bears the sense of *word* or *saying*, or of things only in so far as they have become matters of discourse. Thus, at Luke i. 37, the exact rendering undoubtedly is, " No word shall be impossible with God;" and hence the verb is in the future, ἀδυνατήσει, pointing to the futurity of the accomplishment, as compared with the period when the word was spoken.

(2.) Then, while we should thus beware of multiplying Hebraisms in the New Testament beyond what really exist, we should, in the second place, also beware, in handling what really are such, and the peculiarities generally of the New Testament dialect, of setting them down as mere extravagancies, or barbarous departures from a proper diction. On the contrary, we should endeavour to ascertain the idea in which they originated, and get at the precise shade of meaning, or aspect of a subject, which they set before us. This *is* the course, as Winer remarks, which has latterly been taken by grammarians in their investigations concerning the Greek language : " The idea which gave rise to each particular form has been accurately apprehended, and its various uses reduced to the primary signification. The *language* thus becomes a directly reflected image of the Greek *thought*, as a *living idiom*. One does not stop at the mere externals, but there is a reference of each form and inflexion of the language to the thinking soul, and an effort to apprehend it in its existence in the mind itself. For a long time Biblical philologists took no notice of these elucidations of Greek grammar and lexicography. They followed Viger and Storr, and separated themselves entirely from the profane philologists, under the impression that the New Testament Greek, being Hebraistic, could not be an object of such philological investigations. No one believed that the Hebrew, like every other language, admitted and required a rational mode of treatment. The rational view is now gaining ground. It is believed that the ultimate reasons of the phenomena of the Hebrew must be sought out in the nation's modes of thought ; and, above all, that a plain, simple people could not contravene the laws of all human language. It is no longer, therefore, considered proper to give a preposition diverse meanings, according to one's own pleasure, in a context superficially examined. Nor must it be supposed that a Hebrew, instead of ' this is my brother,' could say *pleonastically*, ' this is of my brother,' or ' this is in the wise man,' instead of ' this is a wise man ;' but the origin of changes so contrary to rule must be sought for in the speaker's mode of thought, as with every rational being each deviation has its reason."—(Idioms, pp. 19, 20.)

This, it will be understood, is said simply of the manner in which deviations of the kind here referred to should be considered and explained ; and determines nothing as to what may be called the comparative pureness and elegance of the diction, or the reverse. In some of them, possibly, the thought expressed may be cast into a form, which is not justified by the usage of the most correct writers, nor accordant with the native idioms of the language ; but possibly also there may be no real departure from these ;—and the apparent deviation, or peculiarity, may lie in the thought expressed being somewhat different from what a superficial consideration, or a common point of view, might be apt to suggest. Such, no doubt, will be found sometimes to be the case. But the question at present has respect, not simply, nor indeed so much to the purity of the diction, as to the proper and rational mode of explaining its real or apparent peculiarities. These should, in every case, be considered with reference to the specific circumstances and mental habits of the writer. And had they been so—had due regard been paid to the considerations which have just been advanced—not only would many senseless and improper laxities have been spared from our grammars, lexicons, and commentaries, but the received text also of the New Testament and our authorised version would have been in a better state than they at present are. Schleusner's Lexicon of the New Testament, and Macknight's Commentary on the Epistles, may be referred to as specimens, out of the more learned class, which egregiously err in the respect now mentioned, more especially in the laxity with which they render the prepositions and the particles of the New Testament Greek. For example, in Schleusner, the prepositions εἰς and ἐν have ascribed to them, the one 24, the other no fewer than 30, distinct uses and meanings; and, though Macknight does not carry it quite so far, yet, from the diverse and disconnected senses he puts upon them in his Preliminary Essays, it seems as if, when handled by a Hellenistic Jew, these prepositions might express almost any relation whatever. Εἰς, as it happens, may be *into* or *in*, *concerning* or *with*, *against*, *before*, *by*, *in order to, among, at, towards*, or it may stand without *any* definite meaning—as a mere expletive—and had better been wanted. So also with ἐν.[1]

Of course, in the writings of the New Testament, as in all popular productions, there is a considerable freedom in the use of such parts of speech—especially in what are called pregnant constructions and current phrases—yet never without a respect to the fundamental meaning of the word—never with a total abnegation and disregard of this. Thus, in the New Testament, as with Greek writers generally, the preposition εἰς is not unfrequently coupled with verbs of rest, and hence comes to be

---

[1] This looseness has also been countenanced to some extent by Ernesti, and still more by his foreign and English annotators.—See Bib. Cabinet, vol. iv. 153, 154.

rendered as if it were ἐν:—as Matt. ii. 23, κατῴκησεν εἰς πόλιν λεγομένην Ναζαρέθ ; Acts viii. 40, Φίλιππος εὑρέθη εἰς Ἄζωτον ; John i. 18, ὁ ὢν εἰς τὸν κόλπον τοῦ Πατρός. But in all such cases there is an implied reference to the preceding motion towards the place indicated, or some sort of terminal relation to it. Thus, in the examples noticed, we must explain, in the first, having gone so far as to the city called Nazareth, having entered into it, he dwelt there; in the second, Philip was found as far as Azotus, carried thither, and so at it ; in the third, He that is (viz. set, who has His proper place of being) into the bosom of the Father, so close, so deep into the personal indwelling, and union with, the Father. In none of the cases is there properly an interchange of one preposition for another ; but a complex thought is uttered in an abbreviated and elliptical form.

In many cases of this description, however, it is only by a comment that the full and proper meaning can be brought out, and in a simple translation it is scarcely possible to keep up the peculiarity of the original. But there are others, in which that was perfectly possible, and in which our authorised version has suffered from the too prevalent notion of Hebraistic laxity—nor has even the received text of the original escaped occasional corruptions. Under those of the latter description we may point to Rev. ii. 14, where the undoubtedly correct reading of what is said of Balaam is, ὃς ἐδίδασκεν τῷ Βαλὰκ βαλεῖν σκάνδαλον ἐνώπιον τῶν υἱῶν Ἰσραήλ; but which, from the apparent anomaly of the verb διδάσκω being coupled with a noun in the dative, for its direct object (as was supposed), the resort was made by grammarians and commentators to Hebrew usage, according to which it was alleged the dative was put for the accusative ; and certain copyists went a step further, and, taking the dative for an error, substituted the accusative in its place, which is the reading of the received text—τὸν Βαλὰκ. It is not a Hebraism, however, to couple such a verb with the dative ; the Greek and Hebrew usage here entirely correspond; and that John was perfectly cognisant of the Greek usage is manifest from his coupling the same verb with an accusative in ver. 20, as in every other instance, in which he has placed a noun in regimen with it, except the one before us (John vii. 35, viii. 2, 28, ix. 34, xiv. 26 ; 1 John ii. 27, thrice). This sufficiently shows, that the dative in

Rev. ii. 14 is put, not by oversight or from the usage of a foreign idiom merely, but on purpose ; that it is what grammarians call the *dativus commodi*, indicating that what was done, was done, not *upon* the individual concerned, but *in his interest*—not that Balaam taught Balak (as in the English version), but that he taught *for* Balak, on his account and in his behalf, to cast a stumbling-block before the children of Israel. We are not, in short, told *whom* he taught, though we know from the history it was the people of Balak, but *for whose advantage* he did so ; he taught in the service of the king of Moab, not of the God of Israel.

We must refer to a few other passages, in which, though the received text remains correct, the authorised version has missed the precise shade of meaning by giving way to the idea of laxity on the part of the original writers. Thus, in the prayer of the converted malefactor, Luke xxiii. 42, Remember me when Thou comest ἐν τῇ βασιλείᾳ σου—not *into* Thy kingdom, which might seem to point to the glory into which the Lord was presently going to enter—but *in* Thy kingdom, viz., when the time comes for Thee to take to Thyself Thy great power and to reign among men ; for this future manifestation of glory was undoubtedly what the faith of the penitent man anticipated and sought to share in, not the glory which lay within the vail, which only the answer of Christ brought within the ken of his spiritual vision. The same preposition has also been unhappily translated in another important passage—Phil. ii. 10, ἵνα ἐν τῷ ὀνόματι 'Ιησοῦ— not *at*, but *in* the name of Jesus, every knee should bow; in it as the ground and principle of the act, not at its mere enunciation. Again, in Eph. iii. 19, " That ye may be filled εἰς πᾶν τὸ πλή- ρωμα τοῦ Θεοῦ," not strictly *with*, which would imply an infinite recipiency, but *into* all the fulness of God—lifted, like empty vessels, into the boundless pleroma of Godhead, that ye may take to the full satisfaction of your desires, and the measure of your capacity. So, again, in 2 Pet. i. 3, where God is said to have given to us all things pertaining to life and godliness, through the knowledge of Him καλέσαντος ἡμᾶς διὰ δόξης καὶ ἀρετῆς, who called us—not, as in our version, *to* glory and vir- tue, which puts a most arbitrary and unauthorised sense upon the διὰ, and converts, besides, the means into the end—but *by* or *through* glory and virtue—namely, the glory and virtue, the divine energy exhibited in the way and manner, in which we *are* called of God, in consequence of which, as is presently added, there have also been given to us exceeding great and precious promises; the promises are so great and precious, because the call conducting to them was so distinguished by divine power and glory. The very next verse but one of the same epistle, ver. 5, furnishes another example of unfortunate laxity in the translation, which in consequence misses the precise shade of thought expressed in the original : the words, καὶ αὐτὸ τοῦτο δὲ, rendered, " And besides this "—altogether sinking the adversative particle δὲ, and mistaking also the force of the adverbial accusative αὐτὸ τοῦτο. The object of the clause, is partly to suggest a difference, and partly to mention an agreement, between what precedes and what follows : " And on this very account indeed," or " but for this same reason, give all diligence," etc.

These are only a few specimens out of many, that might be adduced, of the evil that too long and generally prevailed, of supposing that the sacred writers of the New Testament were so Hebraistic, or otherwise so peculiar in their use of words and phrases, that any sort of license might at times be taken with their language. It is but rarely that the evil discovers itself in the authorised version, and within narrow limits, compared with what has appeared often in later versions and commentaries. But it is still occasionally found there ; and special notice has been taken of it, not for the purpose of disparaging that version, which, as a whole, is so admirable, but in order to show, how even there, when the proper line has been deviated from, and with the best intentions, the effect has only been to substitute one shade of meaning for another—a meaning that could only at first view have seemed the natural and proper one, for another more accordant both with the idioms of the language and with the truth of things.

V. To pass now, however, from the real or alleged Hebraisms of the New Testament, we may mention as another characteristic feature of its diction, that which it occasionally derives from the new ideas and relations introduced by the Gospel. These of necessity called into existence a class of expressions, not in themselves absolutely new, but still fraught with an import which could not attach to them as used by any heathen writer, nor even in the production of any Greek-speaking Jew prior to the birth of Christ. With the marvellous events of the Gospel age, a fresh spring-time opened for the world; old things passed away, all things became new; and the change which took place in the affairs of the Divine kingdom could not fail to impress itself on those words and forms of expression, which bore respect to what had then for the first time come properly into being. In so far as the terms employed might embody the distinctive facts or principles of Christianity, their former and common usage could only in part exhibit the sense now acquired by them; for the full depth and compass of meaning belonging to them in their new application, we must look to the New Testament itself, comparing one passage with another, and viewing the language used in the light of the great things which it brings to our apprehension.

When handling such terms as those now referred to, it is peculiarly necessary to understand and apply aright the fundamental principles of language, as to the relation in which the spoken word stands to the internal thought, of which it serves as the expression. "Language," it has been justly said,[1] "is the outward appearance of the intellect of nations: their language is their intellect, and their intellect their language; we cannot sufficiently identify the two. . . . Understanding and speaking are only two different effects of the same power of speech." In confirmation of this statement, we may point to the twofold meaning of the Greek word λόγος, which denotes alike the internal and the external reason—either reason as exercising itself and forming conceptions in the mind itself (λόγος ἐνδιάθετος), or reason coming forth into formal proposition, and embodying itself in the utterances of human speech (λόγος προφορίκος)—comprising, therefore, in one term, what the Latins, with their more objective and realistic tendencies, took two words to express—ratio and oratio. Now, as the external reason, or reason embodied in the form of spoken or written words, ought to be the exact image of the internal, a correct represen-

[1] William Von Humboldt, quoted in Donaldson's Cratylus, p. 56.

tation of the thoughts and conceptions of the mind, so, in proportion as these thoughts and conceptions vary, the language employed to express them must present a corresponding variation; and if the same terms are retained, which may have been previously in use, there must be infused into them a somewhat new and more specific import. To some extent this is done, even in comparatively common circumstances, and as the result of individual thought and feeling; for speech, as has also been well said by the writer just referred to, " acquires its last definiteness only from the individual. No one assigns precisely the same meaning to a word that another does, and a shade of meaning, be it ever so slight, ripples on, like a circle in the water, through the entirety of language." That is—for the sentiment must be understood with such a limitation—it will so perpetuate and diffuse itself, if circumstances favour it, and the particular shade of meaning introduced is one not confined to too narrow a sphere of thought, not merely local or temporary, but requiring, by the exigencies of human thought, to have an abiding place in its medium of communication. Whenever that is the case, it *will* certainly ripple on like a wave, widening and enlarging its range, till it has embraced the whole field.

Such peculiarly has been the case in respect to those terms, which the great events of Gospel history served to bring into general use, and through which expression is given to some of the more distinctive ideas and relations of Gospel times. Among the foremost of these is the phrase, βασιλεία τοῦ Θεοῦ, or τῶν οὐρανῶν—a phrase composed of words perfectly familiar to all accustomed to the Greek tongue, but, as applied to the state of things introduced by Christ, and growing out of the events of His earthly career, expressive of ideas essentially novel to heathen minds, and but partially possessed even by Jewish. We can have no doubt about its origin, and the reason of its employment in this connection. It points back to those prophecies of the Old Testament, in which promise was made of a King and kingdom, that should unite heaven and earth, God and man, in another way than could be done by a merely human administration; and especially to the prophecies of Daniel, in ch. ii. and vii., where, after a succession of kingdoms, all earthly in their origin, and ungodly in their spirit and aims, the Divine

purpose was announced, of a kingdom that should be set up by
the God of heaven, and that should never be destroyed—a
kingdom imaged by one like a Son of man coming in the clouds
of heaven, and destined to be possessed by the saints of the
Most High.   *Some* notion might, therefore, be obtained of the
import of the expression, by those who were acquainted with
Old Testament Scripture; yet only a vague and imperfect one,
as the precise nature of the kingdom, and its distinctive characteristics could only be correctly understood, when they were
brought clearly to light by the facts and revelations of the
Gospel.   The general unbelief and apostacy of the Jewish people,
after Christ came, showed how little previous intimations had
served to bring them properly acquainted with the nature of
the kingdom; and both that, and the palpable errors and mistakes regarding it, which frequently discovered themselves even
among the followers of Christ, but too clearly proved how difficult it was for the minds of men to rise to a just apprehension
of the subject.   The difficulty, no doubt, chiefly arose from the
imperfect earthly forms under which the prophetic Spirit had
presented it to their view, and from the not unnatural tendency
in their minds to shape their idea of it too much after the monarchies and governments of this world, which kept them from
realising the change in spirit, aim, and administration, involved
in the divine character of its Head.   But as soon as the true
idea came to be realised, and the kingdom in its real properties
began to take root in the world, as a natural result, the phrase
βασιλεία τοῦ Θεοῦ, which gave expression to the idea, became
informed, we might say, with a new meaning, and bore a sense
which it were vain to look for anywhere but in the writings of
the New Testament.   Even there the sense which it bears is
not quite uniform; for in a subject so complex, and branching
out into so many interests and relations, the expression could
not fail to be used sometimes with more immediate reference
to one aspect of the matter, and sometimes to another.   This is
clearly the case in the parables, where a manifold variety is
found in the images employed to represent the kingdom of God,
with the view of presenting under diverse, though perfectly consistent and harmonious representations, a comprehensive exhibition of the truth respecting it:—some (as in the parable of the

mustard-seed) pointing more to its growth from small beginnings : others (as in the parables of the ten virgins and the husband-man), to its final issues in evil and good, according to the part taken on earth by its members ; others, again, to its internal principles of administration (as the parable of the talents, or of the labourers in the vineyard); to its external means and agencies, with the diversified results springing from them (as the parables of the sower, the tares and wheat, the fishing-net) ; or to the relation of the members of the kingdom to its Divine Head, and to each other (as the parable of the unforgiving servant). But with all this variety in the use of the expression, two ideas are never lost sight of, which in truth form the two most prominent things connected with it, viz., those of a Divine king on the one hand, and of human subjects on the other—the one order-ing, providing, directing, and controlling all ; the other, accord-ing to the line of conduct they pursue, receiving at His hand blessing or cursing, life or death.

If these remarks are kept in view, there will appear no need for dividing (as Dr Campbell, for example, does, in his Preli-minary Dissertations and Translation of the Gospels) and ren-dering βασιλεία τῶν οὐρανῶν sometimes the *reign* of heaven, and sometimes the *kingdom* of heaven. This is not only unnecessary, but fitted also to mislead ; since it gives, whenever the word *reign* is used instead of *kingdom*, only a partial and imperfect represen-tation of the proper idea. It was one of the prevailing tendencies of Campbell's mind—a mind certainly of great penetration, of remarkable clearness of perception, of much philosophical acumen, and singular perspicacity in thought and diction—partly in con-sequence of these very excellencies, it was a tendency in his mind to make precision, rather than fulness of meaning his aim ; and for the sake of that precision, both in his Preliminary Dis-sertations and his Notes, he often seizes only a part of the mean-ing, couched under a particular phrase or expression, and exhi-bits that as the whole. This is, indeed, the most characteristic and general defect of his work on the Gospels, which, notwith-standing that defect, however, and a few others that might be named, is well entitled to a perusal. It was the tendency now referred to which led Dr Campbell to substitute so often the word *reign* for that of the *kingdom* of heaven, on the ground, that the expression most commonly relates to that " sort of dominion," as he terms it, which is understood by the dispensation of grace, brought in by the Gospel ; while the phrase, " kingdom of heaven," he thinks, properly indicates " the state of perfect felicity to be enjoyed in the world to come." Now, this is to divide what Scripture seeks to preserve entire, and fixes the mind too exclusively on a *part* merely of the idea, which it ought to associate with the expression. It was never intended that we should think of the Messiah's kingdom as having to do merely with the inner man, and, for the present, laying claim only to a sway over the thoughts and affections of the mind. His kingdom, according to its scriptural idea, is no more a divided empire, than He is Himself a divided person. It comprehends the external as well as the internal—although, from having its seat in the latter, it is most frequently depicted with special relation to this ; but still it comprehends both, and embraces eternity as well as time— though its condition, now on this side, now on that, may at times be brought most prominently into view. But even in those passages, in which it points to the present mixed state, and imperfect administration of the affairs of the kingdom, we should take nothing from the full import of the expression, but retain it in its completeness ; as it serves to keep before the Church the idea of a kingdom in the proper sense, and to prompt her to long for, and aim at, its realisation.

We have dwelt at the greater length on this particular example, as it is one of considerable moment, and it affords an intelligible and ready explanation of the peculiarity with which it has been here associated. But it is only one of a class belonging to the same category : such as αἰων μέλλων, δικαιοῦσθαι, δικαιοσύνη, εὐαγγελίζω, ζωή and θάνατος (understood spiritually), κλῆσις, μυστήριον, νόμος, παράκλητος, πίστις, πλήρωμα, χάρις, χάρισμα, πνευματικός, ψυχικός. All these, and, perhaps, several others that might be named, are used in New Testament Scripture with the same radical meaning, indeed, as elsewhere ; but, at the same time, with so much of a specific character derived from the great truths and principles of the Gospel, that their New Testament import must be designated as peculiar.

VI. Once more, it may be given as a still further note of distinction characteristic of the New Testament Greek, that, while there are peculiarities of the several kinds already described, distinguishing the language as a whole, there are also peculiarities distinguishing the Greek of one writer from that of another— words and phrases used by one and not used by the others, or used in a manner peculiar to himself. There is an *individual,* as well as a *general,* impress on the language. And if, as in the class last mentioned, a special regard must be had to the revelations and writings of the New Testament as a whole, there should, in the class now under consideration, be a like regard had to the writings of the particular person by whom the expressions are more peculiarly employed.

The terms belonging to this class are not of so extensive a range as some of the preceding ones ; and they are to be found chiefly in two writers of the New Testament—the Apostles Paul and John. In the writings of John we meet with various expressions, which, as used by him, are almost peculiar to himself : such as ἀλήθεια, in the specific sense of denoting what is emphatically *the truth*—the truth of the Gospel ; ποιεῖν τὴν ἀλήθειαν, in the sense of giving practical exhibition of that truth ; γεννηθῆναι ἄνωθεν, or ἐκ τοῦ Θεοῦ ; ὁ λόγος, as a personal designation of the Saviour in respect to His Divine nature and relationship ; ὁ λόγος τῆς ζωῆς, ὁ μονογενὴς υἱός, ὁ παράκλητος, ἄρχων τοῦ κόσμου, ἔρχεσθαι εἰς τὸν κόσμον, etc. In like manner, there is a set of phrases nearly as peculiar to the Apostle Paul : such as γράμμα put in contrast to πνεῦμα, ἀποθνήσκειν τινί, δικαιοῦσθαι, ἔργα σαρκός, καινὴ κτίσις, πλήρωμα τοῦ Θεοῦ, νόμος ἐν τοῖς μέλεσι, σταυροῦσθαι τινί, στοιχεῖα (taken in a figurative sense of rudimental principles), τύπος, etc.

We refrain at present from entering on the examination of any of these peculiar forms of expression—the greater part of which, viewed simply in themselves, properly belong to some of the preceding classes, and are now mentioned only as connected with a further peculiarity—their exclusive or prevailing use by particular writers. And, as they undoubtedly acquired this further peculiarity from some mental idiosyncrasy on the part of the person using them, or from some determinative influences connected with the circumstances of his position, these ought, as far as possible, to be ascertained, that the several expressions may be considered from that point of view, which was held by the writer, and may be interpreted in accordance with the laws of thought under which he wrote.

SECTION THIRD.

COLLATERAL SOURCES FOR DETERMINING THE SENSE AND EX-
PLAINING THE PECULIARITIES OF NEW TESTAMENT SCRIP-
TURE.

OUR attention has hitherto been confined to the original language itself of the New Testament, and to the things which concern both its general character and its more distinctive peculiarities. In considering these, it has been implied, rather than formally stated, that for the correct and critical study of the writings of the New Testament, there must have been acquired a competent acquaintance, not only with the common dialect of the later Greek, but also with the idioms of the Hebrew tongue, and with that combination of Greek and Hebrew idioms, which appears in the Septuagint version of the Old Testament. In this version all the leading peculiarities, as well of the later Greek as of the Hebraistic style, which have been noticed in connection with the language of the New Testament, are to be found; and some of them, those especially of the Hebraistic class, in greater abundance, and in bolder relief, than in the writings of the New Testament. In regard to the earlier portions of the Septuagint, this has been exhibited with scholarly acumen and precision in a late publication by the younger Thiersch (De Pentateuchi Versione Alexandrina, Libri Tres, 1851), to which reference has already been made. Considerable use has for long been made of the materials supplied by the Hebrew Bibles and the Septuagint for illustrating the diction of the New Testament in some of the more learned commentaries; particularly those of Grotius, Wetstein, Koppe, Kuinoel, and the more recent commentaries both of this country and the Continent. Some additional service has been rendered in the same line by the Editio Hellenistica of the New Testament of Mr Grinfield, which is devoted to the single purpose of collecting under each verse examples of the same or of similar words and phrases occurring in the Septuagint, and other writings of the period. The Lexicons also of Biel and Schleusner, and, above all, the Grammar of Winer, have contributed to establish and elucidate the connection between the Greek of the New Testament and of the Septuagint, and the characteristics of the dialect in which they are written. All this, however, has respect to the elements of the subject under consideration; it bears directly upon the form and structure of the language itself of the New Testament; so that, without a certain knowledge of the one, there can be no accurate and discriminating knowledge of the other. But there are also certain collateral sources of information, from which incidental and supplementary aid may be derived, to illustrate both the phraseology and some of the more characteristic notices and allusions of New Testament Scripture. These we must now briefly describe, with the view of indicating the nature and amount of the aid to be derived from them, before entering on the examination of specific rules and principles of interpretation.[1]

I. The sources that may be said to lie nearest to the inspired writings, and which should first be named, are the contemporary Jewish writers, who used the Greek language. These are simply two—Philo and Josephus; the former, there is reason to believe, born about a quarter of a century before Christ, though he appears to have outlived the Saviour; and the other fully as much later. The birth of Josephus is assigned to A.D. 37. In a strictly exegetical respect, little help, comparatively, is to be obtained from the first of these writers. Philo was much more of a philosopher than a religionist; and living in Alexandria, and ambitious mainly of ranking with its men of higher culture, both his sentiments and his style stood at a wide distance from those peculiar to the writers of the New Testament. Even in respect to the points, in which his writings bear a kind of formal resemblance to those of the Apostle John, in the use of a few terms

---

[1] It should be borne in mind by those who are entering on the prosecution of such studies, that the Septuagint is far from being a close translation, and that those commentators and grammarians, who have proceeded on the principle of always finding in it the key to the exact meaning of particular words and phrases, are by no means to be trusted.

relating to the Being and operations of Godhead, no real advance
has been made by the efforts that have been put forth to interpret the one by the other.   It has turned out rather—the
more carefully the subject has been examined—that as their
conceptions of divine things were essentially different, so their
language, even when it seems most nearly coincident, is by no
means agreed; and little more has resulted from such comparative investigations than learned disputations about the meanings
of words and phrases, which sometimes look as if they yielded
what was sought, but again deny it.   As for the principles of
interpretation adopted by Philo, they have, indeed, a close enough
affinity with what is found in many of the Fathers of the third
and fourth centuries, but are by no means to be identified with
those sanctioned by the writers of the New Testament.   Such
deliverances, therefore, as the following of Ernesti, which has
often in substance been repeated since—" Philo is particularly
useful in illustrating the allegorical and mystical reasonings, so
much used by St Paul"[1]—must be rejected as groundless, and
fitted to lead in a wrong direction.   The statement is made by
Ernesti with apparent moderation, as it is again in recent times
by Klausen,[2] with the view simply of pointing attention to Philo
as a master in that kind of allegorizing, which was pursued especially by the Apostle Paul—not that Paul was actually conversant with the writings of the Alexandrian, and followed in his
wake.   This latter is noted by Ernesti as a fanciful extreme,
advanced by Wetstein and some others, and is declared to be
destitute of historical support; unnecessary also, since both Paul
and Philo but imbibed the spirit of their age, and adopted a style
of exposition which was already common.   In opposition to this
view, we maintain, that the allegorizings of Philo and those, as
well of the Jewish cabbalists who preceded, as of the Christian
theosophists who followed, belonged to another class than the
so-called allegorical interpretations of the New Testament.   The
latter are not allegorical, in the distinctive sense of the term;
they are not, as allegorical meanings properly are, adaptations of
matters in one sphere of things to those of another essentially
different, and consequently arbitrary and uncertain.   On the
contrary, they are applications of the truths and principles em-

---

[1] Institutes, P. III., ch. 8.   [2] Hermeneutik, pp. 96, 97.

bodied in the institutions or events of preparatory dispensations to the corresponding events or institutions of an ultimate dispensation, to which, from the first, they stood intimately related. In short, they are typical explanations, as contradistinguished from allegorical, and have nothing about them of the caprice and extravagance to which the others are liable. But as we have investigated this elsewhere,[1] it is needless to do more here than mark the confusion of ideas, on which this assimilation of Paul and Philo is grounded, and reclaim against the dishonour which is thereby done to the character of the apostolic teaching.

So far, therefore, as Philo is concerned, there is little to be reaped from his writings for the exposition of New Testament Scripture; his language, his style of thought, and his manner of dealing with Old Testament Scripture, all move in different channels from those followed by the apostles; and his references also to existing manners and circumstances are extremely few and unimportant. In this last respect, however, his contemporary Josephus may justly be said to compensate for the defect of Philo. A man of affairs, and bent on transmitting to posterity an account of what he knew and understood of the events of his times, as well as of former generations, his writings abound with details, which are calculated to throw light on, at least, the historical parts of the New Testament. In the words of Lardner, who has done more than any other person to turn to valuable account the notices of Josephus, " He has recorded the history of the Jewish people in Judea and elsewhere, and particularly the state of things in Judea during the ministry of our Saviour and His apostles; whereby he has wonderfully confirmed, though without intending it, the veracity and the ability of the evangelical writers, and the truth of their history."[2] It was for the richness of materials in this respect, contained in the writings of Josephus, that Michaelis strongly recommended a diligent study of his works, from the beginning of Herod's reign to the end of the Jewish Antiquities, and spake of him as furnishing the very best commentary on the Gospels and the Acts.[3] Of course, a commentary so furnished could only have been of the external and historical kind, which too much accorded with

---

[1] Typology of Scripture, vol. i., c. 1, and App. B, § 1.
[2] Works, vi. p. 502.   [3] Introduction, vol. iii. P. 1, c. 9.

the taste of Michaelis; but, in a revelation pre-eminently historical, the incidental light and attestations derived from such a source
are not to be undervalued; and though, doubtless, the imperfections in Josephus' accounts, and what probably we may call his
occasional errors and studied omissions (in respect to the subject
of Christianity), have given rise to some perplexities, yet his
writings, on the whole, have contributed greatly to elucidate and
confirm the narratives of the New Testament. His style, however, which he aimed at having as pure as possible, is of little
service in illustrating the more peculiar idioms of Scripture;
though, in regard to some of those common to it and the later
Greek dialect, and the meaning also of particular words and
phrases, considerable benefit has accrued from the study of his
productions. Two works, of about the middle of last century
(the *Observationes* of Krebs, and the *Specilegium* of Ottius), were
specially directed to the elucidation of the New Testament from
this source; and many of the examples adduced by them, with
others gathered by subsequent inquirers, have found their way
into recent grammars and commentaries.

It is proper to add, that there are questions on which even the
silence of Josephus is instructive, and fairly warrants certain conclusions respecting the existing state of things in the apostolic
age—for example, on the subject of Jewish proselyte-baptism;
since, treating, as he does, of matters bearing upon the reception
of proselytes, and remaining silent regarding any such practice,
this, coupled with the like silence of Scripture, is well-nigh conclusive on the subject. (But see Dissertation on βαπτίζω in Part
II.) Again, there are other points, chiefly of a formal or legal
description, on which the testimony of Philo and Josephus runs
counter to that delivered in the later Jewish writings; and in
such cases, we need scarcely say, the testimony of those who
lived when the Jewish institutions were actually in force is entitled to the greater weight. Nothing of this sort, however, has
to be noted in connection with New Testament affairs.

II. The next source of illustrative materials that falls to be
noticed, is that supplied by the Jewish Rabbinical writings—
writings composed near to the apostolic age, though subsequent
to it, and composed, not in Greek, but in modern Hebrew.

These writings consist of two main parts, the Mischna and the Gemara,—the Mischna being the text, viz., of the traditions about the law, and the Gemara the comments of learned men upon it. Two sets of comments grew up around it,—the one earlier, produced by the Palestinian Jews, and called, along with the Mischna, the Jerusalem Talmud ; the other, originating with the Chaldean Jews, and forming, with the Mischna, the Babylonian Talmud. It is important to bear in mind the ascertained or probable dates of these productions, in order to determine their relation to the writings of the New Testament. The Mischna being a compilation of traditional lore, may, of course, in many of its parts, be really more ancient than the Gospels ; but as it was not committed to writing till the latter half of the second century after Christ, and probably even later than that,[1] there can be no certainty as to the actual existence of particular portions of it before that period ; and still more does this hold with the Talmudical comments, which were not produced, the one till 300, and the other till 600 years after Christ. Besides, undoubted traces exist in these writings of references to the events of Gospel history, showing the posteriority of some of the things contained in them to that period ; and if some, who can tell how many ! They were, it must be remembered, the productions of men who wrote in the profoundest secrecy, and who, though not formally assuming a hostile attitude toward the Christian cause, could not but be conscious of a certain influence from the great events of the Gospel and the writings of apostolic men.

There are few ancient writings extant, perhaps, that contain a larger proportion of what may be called rubbish than these Talmudical productions. Lightfoot speaks of the *stupenda inanitas et vafrities* of the subjects discussed in them, and says of them generally, *nugis ubique scatent.* There is the more reason that we should cherish feelings of gratitude and admiration toward him, and such men (in particular the Buxtorfs, Bochart, Vitringa, Surenhusius, Schoettgen), who, with the simple desire of finding fresh illustrations of the meaning of sacred Scripture, have encountered the enormous labour, and the painful discipline, of mastering such a literature, and culling from it the comparatively

---

[1] See Prideaux, Connection, at B.C. 446 ; Lightfoot's Opera, i., p. 369.

few passages which bear on the elucidation of the Word of God. They have undoubtedly, by so doing, rendered important service to the cause of Biblical learning ; although it must also be confessed, that a very considerable proportion of the passages adduced might as well have been left in their original quarries, and that some have been turned to uses which have been prejudicial, rather than advantageous, to the right understanding of Scripture. The special benefit derived from them has been in respect to ancient rites and usages, the meaning of Aramaic expressions occasionally occurring in New Testament Scripture, the synagogal institution and worship, and the state of things generally in the closing period of the Jewish commonwealth, to which so many allusions are made. But in respect to the points in which the Scriptures of the New Testament may be said to differ from those of the Old—the doctrines, for example, relating to the person of Messiah, His peculiar office and work, the characteristics of the Christian community, etc.—nothing definite can be learned from the Rabbinical sources under consideration. Endless quotations have been made from them, apparently favouring the Christian views ; but it were quite easy to match them with others of an opposite description ; so that all belonging to this department was evidently but idle talk or free speculation. In regard also to the treatment of Scripture—especially the method of expounding and applying it to things, with which it might seem to have ·no very direct connection—this, which Surenhusius (in his Βιβλος Καταλλαγης) and Eisenmenger (in his Entwecktes Judentum) have shown to be so much the practice with the Rabbinical Jews, and which rationalistic interpreters have so often sought to connect also with the writers of the New Testament, must be held to be altogether foreign to the territory of inspiration. It was quite natural to the Talmudists and their followers ; for *they* could find separate meanings, not only in every sentence, but in every word, and even letter of Scripture, and in the numerical relations of these to each other. With them, therefore, Scripture admitted of manifold senses and applications, of which some might be ever so remote from the natural import and bearing. But apostles and evangelists belonged to another school ; and when they apply Old Testament Scripture to a circumstance or event in Gospel times, it must be in the fair and legitimate sense of the terms; otherwise, their use of it could not be justified as a handling of the Word of God in simplicity and godly sincerity.

We may add, that on points of natural history the Talmuds seem just about as capricious guides as on texts of Scripture. The writers would appear to have wantoned sometimes with the field of nature around them, much as they did with the volume of God's revelation in their hands; and to have found in it what no one has been able to find but themselves. A fitting specimen of this peculiarity may be seen in the quotations produced by Lightfoot in connection with the cursing of the fruitless fig-tree. Among other wonderful things about fig-trees there noticed, mention is made of a kind which bore fruit, indeed, every year, though it only came to maturity on the third; so that three crops, in different stages of progress, might be seen on it at once; and on this notable piece of natural history an explanation of the evangelical narrative is presented. In such matters it is greatly safer to trust the accounts of scientific naturalists and travellers than Jewish Rabbis; and when *they* report the existence of such figs in Palestine, it will be time enough to consider what aid may be derived from the information, to illustrate the narrative referred to. Meanwhile, no great loss is sustained; for the narrative admits, without it, of a perfectly satisfactory explanation.

There are points, however, of another kind, in respect to which this species of learning is not unfrequently applied, not so properly for purposes of elucidation, as with the view of showing how the teaching of the Gospel appropriated to itself elements and forms of instruction already existing in the Jewish schools. Here the question of priority is of some moment; and though the things themselves remain the same, their relative character is materially affected, according as the priority may appear to have belonged to the authors of the Gemara, or to the originators of Christianity. The teaching of our Lord, for example, by parables, is certainly one of the most distinctive features of His public ministry; and, accordingly, when He began more formally to employ it, the Evangelist Matthew saw in it the realisation of a prophetic utterance (Matt. xiii. 35); nor can any one attentively read the Gospels, without discerning in the parables the most impressive image of the mind of Jesus. But this impression is apt to be considerably weakened by the array of quotations sometimes produced from those Rabbinical sources, to show how the Jewish teachers delighted in the use of parables, and even exhibiting some of our Lord's choicest parables as in the main copies of what is found in the Talmud.[1] The same thing has also been done in regard to the Lord's Prayer; so that not only its commencing address, " Our Father which art in heaven," but nearly all that follows, is given as a series of extracts from Jewish forms of devotion. Now, this style of exposition proceeds on a gratuitous assumption; it takes for granted that the existing forms in the Talmud were there before they were in the Gospels,—and, of course, that the Rabbinical gave the tone to the Christian, rather than the Christian to the Rabbinical. The reverse is what the palpable facts of the case tend to establish. The prayers of the synagogue before the Christian era were doubtless moulded after the devotional parts of the Old Testament, and to a large extent composed of these. But in none of them does the suppliant, even in his most elevated moments, rise to the filial cry of " My Father in heaven;" it was the distinctive glory of the Gospel to bring in this spirit of adoption; and the theological, as well as the historical probability, is in favour of the supposition, that Rabbis here followed in the wake of Jesus, not Jesus in the wake of Rabbis. The same probability holds equally in regard to the parables. The parabolical *form*, possibly, to some extent appeared among the earlier traditional lore of the Jews; for it is not unknown in Old Testament Scripture; but the parable, such as it is found in the teaching of our Lord, bears on it the impress of originality; and the few straggling specimens that have been produced from Rabbinical sources, nearly identical with those of Christ, may confidently be pronounced to be the echoes of the latter—the productions of men, who were greatly too feeble and puerile to invent, but who had enough of sagacity to imitate. The slaves of the letter and of tradition were not the persons to originate anything new or fresh, not even in form.[2]

---

[1] Lightfoot, Horæ Heb. on Matt. vi. xiii. ; and Schoettgen, Horæ Heb. on Matt. xx. xxi., Luke xv.

[2] Owen, in his Theologoumena, Lib. v., c. 15, Dig. 4, discusses the ques-

III. The more ancient versions may be mentioned as the next collateral source, from which aid should be sought in endeavouring to ascertain the meaning, and expound the text of New Testament Scripture. Those versions have their primary use, as among the helps for determining the text itself that should be preferred; since they exhibit the one that *was* preferred at an early period by some, and possibly should still be retained, where there is a variation in the readings. In this respect, however, they can never amount to more than subordinate authorities; since it must ever remain doubtful whether due pains were taken by the translator to obtain a pure text, and doubtful, still further, whether the translation may not to some extent have been tampered with in the course of its transmission to present times. There is necessarily the same kind of relative inferiority adhering to the use of versions in connection with the import of the original. While, in the simpler class of passages, they could scarcely fail to give the natural meaning of the original, it must still be a matter more or less problematical, how far they did so in those cases where there is some dubiety or difficulty in the passage, and consequently some possibility of the precise import having been misunderstood. Still, considerable weight must always be attached, especially in respect to the meaning of particular words and phrases, to those versions, which were made by competent persons at a time when the original language of the New Testament continued to exist as a living tongue. And of such versions ˙so made, the Vulgate seems entitled to hold the first place. The Vulgate, that is, as it came from the hands of Jerome, and as it appears with probably substantial correctness in the Codex Amiatinus, the oldest MS. of the Vulgate extant, not the common Vulgate of the Romish Church, which in many parts has undergone alteration to the worse. In point of learning and critical tact, Jerome, we have reason to believe, was the most competent man in the ancient Church for executing a translation of the Scriptures; and the version he produced would have been probably as near perfection as the translation of a single individual, and in so early an age, could well be ex-

tion of our Lord's relation to the Talmudical doctors, but chiefly with respect to religious usages and services. He indignantly rejects, however, the idea of a borrowing on the part of Christ.

pected to be, if he had been left altogether free to exercise
his judgment in the performance of the work.   His version of
the Old Testament, with the exception of the Psalms, *was* the
unfettered production of his hand; it was made directly from
the Hebrew, as he himself testifies once and again, although, as
it now exists, it contains not a few accommodations to the Septuagint, and departs from the Hebrew.[1]   But in regard to the
New Testament, he professed to do nothing more than fulfil the
request of Pope Damasus,—revise the current versions, and select out of them the best; so that, as he said, "he restrained his
pen, merely correcting those things which appeared to affect the
sense, and permitting other things to remain as they had been."
What was called the Old Italic, or Latin version, therefore, was
simply the current version, in one or other of the forms in which
it existed before it had been the subject of Jerome's collating
and emendatory labours.   It now exists only in part, but most
fully in the Codex Claromontanus, which is of great antiquity.
In some things the **rendering** contained in it is even preferable to
that adopted by Jerome, and, consequently, where access can be
had to it, it is worthy of being consulted.   But it is not so properly a distinct version from that of Jerome, as a variation of
what became his.   And, as a whole, Jerome's form of the Latin
version must be held to be the best.   Restrained and limited as
his object was, he undoubtedly accomplished much good.   And
with all the defect of polish that appears in the version that goes
by his name, its occasional Hebraisms, the imperfect renderings,
and even erroneous representations of the original, sometimes to
be met with in it, there can be no doubt that it is in general a
faithful translation, and has rendered essential service toward
the elucidation of the sacred text.

Some of the blemishes in the Vulgate, especially in the New
Testament portion, are obvious, and have often been exposed;
such as the pœnitentiam agite, in Matt. iii. 2, and other parallel
places; Ave gratia plena, Luke i. 28; mortuus est autem et
dives, et sepultus est in inferno, Luke xvi. 22; et (Jacob)
adoravit fastigium virgæ ejus, Heb. xi. 21; panem nostrum
supersubstantialem da nobis, Matt. vi. 11; etc.   And, unfortu-
nately, they are mistranslations which too often afford a sort of

[1] See Walton's Prolegomena, x. c. 9.

handle to the advocates of corruption in the Church of Rome. Yet it is proper also to add, that some of the examples occasionally referred to in that connection yield no real countenance to those corruptions; and some again, that are more correct than the English translation, which has been exalted to the prejudice of the other. Thus at 1 Pet. iii. 19, the rendering, in quo et his, qui in carcere erant, spiritibus veniens prædicavit, is substantially correct (though the meaning expressed, of course, may be, and often is, perverted by Romanists to a wrong use), and the *in quo*, in which, is more exact than the *by which* of the authorised version. In not a few cases, indeed, the Vulgate is decidedly more correct than our version in the rendering of prepositions and connecting particles :—as, to refer to one or two examples partly mentioned already in another connection, ut *in* nomine Jesu omne genu flectatur, Phil. ii. 10; gratia vobis et pax adimpleatur *in* cognitione Dei, 2 Pet. i. 2; qui vocavit nos propria gloria et virtute, ver. 3; ut impleamini in omnem plenitudinem Dei, Eph. iii. 19. In these, and many other cases, the Vulgate contrasts favourably with our English version in respect to grammatical precision; and, if judiciously used, it may often be of service in suggesting some of the nicer shades of meaning. It is due also to the memory of Jerome to notice (though it does not belong to the criticism of the New Testament), that the well-known mistranslation in the authorised Vulgate of Rome, of Gen. iii. 15, ipsa conteret caput tuum, which ascribes to the woman the victory over the tempter, and which the Romanists usually apply direct to the Virgin, is a later corruption. The correct reading, as given by Vallarsius, runs, ipse conteret caput tuum, and, in a note, he declares this to be beyond doubt the reading established by the authority of MSS.

The version next in importance to the Vulgate of Jerome, and undoubtedly prior to it in origin, is the Old Syriac, or Peschito—a production, in all likelihood, of the latter part of the second century. We know nothing of the author of this version (which, however, wants the second Epistle of Peter, the two last of John, Jude, and the Apocalypse); but without going into the extravagance of Michaelis, who pronounced it " the very best translation of the Greek Testament he had ever read," we may safely regard it as, in general, a faithful and

spirited translation. The chief use, to which it has hitherto
been turned, is as a witness in behalf of the genuine text. This
may have partly arisen from the Syrian language being so little
understood, even by Biblical scholars. They may, however, to
some extent, avail themselves of its aid by means of the transla-
tions which have been made of it. It has for long existed in
Latin ; and a few years ago the portion containing the Gospels
was rendered into English by Mr Etheridge, accompanied with
preliminary dissertations.

The remaining versions which, from their age or their fidelity
to the original, are entitled to consideration, and calculated to be
of occasional service in the work of exposition, are the Ethiopic,
the Memphitic, and the Gothic of Ulphilas. The aid, however,
to be derived from any of them is extremely limited. Mr Ellicott,
in the preface to his last volume (his Commentary on the Epistles
to the Philippians, Colossians, and Philemon) speaks in strong
terms of the excellence of the Ethiopic version, and of the satisfaction he has derived from consulting it, since he has been enabled
to find his way with some certainty to its meaning. But, in truth,
we have so many more helps for getting at the precise import of
the Greek New Testament, than for arriving at an intelligent acquaintance with the old Ethiopic version of that Greek, that most
people will feel greatly more assured of coming at the object of
their search by repairing directly to the original source ; nor, with
the defective literature of Ethiopia in the early centuries, can such
a version—even if it were thoroughly understood—attain to a
place of much authority. Its renderings can, at the most, confirm
meanings obtained by other and surer lines of investigation. And
the same may be said of the Memphitic and Gothic versions.
So that, whatever incidental benefits or personal satisfaction the
study of such versions may yield, little comparatively can now be
expected from them as to the correct understanding of New Testament Scripture.

IV. Among the collateral sources of information, that may be
turned to account · in the interpretation of New Testament
Scripture, we must unquestionably reckon the writings of the
earlier Fathers. It is, certainly, but a mixed service they
render ; since, from the strong tendency among them to al-

legorical and arbitrary modes of interpretation, if they are not used discriminatingly, they will often prove false guides. They were as a class defective in critical discernment, and that well-poised balance of mind, which in such matters is rarely possessed, excepting as the result of an efficient training in linguistic and critical studies, such as they did not enjoy. Had the earlier Fathers but possessed a little more of the critical faculty, and employed in connection with it the advantages of their position for the good of the Church in future times, they would have directed their minds particularly to the investigation of the facts and circumstances of the Gospel age, examined with minute care the information that lay within their reach respecting the local and historical allusions in the New Testament, searched into the meaning of all words that in any way bore upon them the peculiar impress of the time, and by philological or antiquarian researches endeavoured to make plain the obscurer passages in the Gospels and Epistles. These, however, are the provinces which they have most thoroughly neglected to cultivate, and in respect to which, apparently, they felt least conscious of any need of special application. We have scarcely left the inspired territory, till we find ourselves involved in the strangest misconceptions even as to matters of fact, and, instead of careful discriminations between fable and history, are presented with a confused jumbling of both together. In what is probably the earliest of sub-apostolic writings extant, one also of the best—the epistle of Clement to the Corinthians—we have the fables about the Danaids and the Phœnix classed with the biographical notices of sacred history, and treated as equally deserving of credit (c. 6, 24). Justin, in like manner, swallows without a suspicion the story of Aristeas about the translation of the Septuagint, and even speaks of Herod as having sent to Ptolemy the seventy elders who executed the work; as if the two had been contemporaries! (Apol. c. 31, Exhor. ad Græcos, § 11). Even in the face of plain statements in the Gospel history to the contrary, he once and again, in his Trypho, represents Jesus as having been born in a cave or grotto. Irenæus falls into mistakes and inanities still more extraordinary; not only accrediting the senseless tradition of Papias respecting the fruitfulness of the millennial age (B. V. c. 33), but also affirming it to have been the teaching of St John, that our Lord's personal ministry lasted from His thirtieth till His fiftieth year (ii. c. 4, 5). Even when we come down to the more regular and elaborate expositors of New Testament Scripture, Augustine, Jerome, Chrysostom, while they contain much that deserves, and will repay a careful perusal, they are marvellously deficient on those points in which their comparative proximity to apostolic times, had they known how to avail themselves of its opportunities, should have given them an acknowledged superiority over more distant generations. In respect to dates and places, customs and manners, they knew nothing of the accuracy of our age. Their references to Old Testament affairs contain often the most egregious blunders (of which a striking example will be found in the Dissertation on the Genealogies) ; and of the spirit and design of the Old Testament economy, both as a whole, and in its several parts, they are ever evincing the most defective understanding. Not unfrequently, also, in matters connected with the New, we meet with explanations utterly puerile and fantastic ; as in the instance produced by Archdeacon Hare from Augustine respecting the gift of the Spirit to the disciples on two distinct occasions—an explanation that turns on the mystical value of numbers—and of which Hare justly remarks :— " The striking thing is, not that the explanation is a bad one, but that it implies an ignorance of what an explanation is, and of the method in which we are to attain it ; and the same thing we find perpetually, as well in the Fathers, as in the contemporary grammarians and rhetoricians."[1]

Another thing, that may equally be characterised as striking in the mode of exposition adopted by the Fathers, is the perpetual interchange between the most spiritualistic meanings and the grossest literalism ; so that one is puzzled to understand how the same minds that took pleasure in the one could possibly rest satisfied with the other. For example, we have not one merely, but a whole series of the Fathers (Barnabas, Tertullian, Clement Alex., Ambrose, Augustine, etc.), finding in the letter T, when occurring as a numeral in the old Testament, an indication of the cross, numbers of all kinds spiritualised, the spring in Eden with its four streams made to signify Christ and the four

---

[1] Mission of the Comforter, p. 312.

cardinal virtues (Ambrose de parad. 3); and, in short, the principle of Augustine carried out in all directions, "that whatever in Scripture cannot be referred to purity of manners or the realities of faith, is to be understood spiritually" (De Doc. Chris. iii. 14). But, on the other hand, there ever and anon meets us the most literal and fleshly application of the prophecies; if these speak of New Testament things under the images supplied by the Old, of priesthood and sacrifice, they are interpreted to mean things equally outward and earthly still. Some of the Fathers (such as Irenæus, Tertullian, Ambrose, Lactantius) even carried this species of carnalism into the future world, and held, that flesh and blood, only in the sense of unregenerate nature, shall not inherit the kingdom of God; but that the bodies of believers —limb for limb, member for member, precisely the same bodies as now—shall be raised up from the dead, and shall regale themselves with corporeal delights (Tert. de resur. c. 35, Irenæus, v. 9, etc). This exegetical caprice, which oscillated between two extremes, and inclined to the one or the other as the fancy or exigence of the moment might prompt, unfits the patristic writings for being employed as exegetical guides; and, along with the other defects mentioned, obliges the student at every step to exercise his discretion.

Still, considerable benefit is to be reaped for Scriptural interpretation from the perusal of the more eminent Fathers—although one that we must be content to seek in fragments. To say nothing of the bearing they have on the text of Scripture, the development of Christian doctrine, and the varied evolution of evil and good in the history of the Church, which constitute their chief historical interest, they are valuable for the manifestation they give of mind in the ancient world, when brought into contact with the revelation of God in Christ, and of the effect produced by this in turning the tide of thought and feeling, and directing it into a channel somewhat accordant with the realities of the Gospel. Even when the explanations given of Scripture are one-sided and imperfect, they are far from being uninstructive; for, when not absolutely erroneous, they still present one aspect of the truth, which the events and relations of the ancient world served more particularly to call forth. In this respect they contribute an element—often a very important element—

to the full understanding of the Divine record. And in writers
of the higher class—writers like Augustine and Chrysostom—
one is continually rewarded with passages, which discover the
profoundest insight into the truth of Scripture, and present it to
our view in the sharpest outline. The Greek expositors, too,
among the Fathers, have a value of their own in regard to
occasional words and phrases, the precise import of which they
not unfrequently enable us to apprehend, or at least to determine, in a way that might otherwise have been impracticable.
With all the exceptions, therefore, and serious abatements that
require to be made, in regard to the exegetical value of the
Fathers, there are advantages to be derived from their judicious
perusal, which no well-furnished interpreter can dispense with;
and however, in certain quarters, their employment may have
been pushed to excess, the full and correct knowledge of New
Testament Scripture has certainly gained by the revived study
of their writings.

V. In the way of collateral sources, nothing further requires
to be mentioned, excepting the occasional employment of the
various materials, furnished partly by ancient, partly by modern
research, which serve to throw light on the historical, social, or
geographical allusions of the New Testament. If the earlier
Christian writers have done little to supply us with such
materials, the deficiency is in a great degree made up by con-
tributions from other quarters. From the nearly stationary
character of society in the lands of the East, the manners and
usages of the present time, which have been amply illustrated by
modern travellers, have brought us almost equally acquainted with
those of the Gospel age. All the scenes, too, of Gospel history,
not only the places trodden by the footsteps of Jesus, but those
hallowed by the labours, the journeyings, and voyages of the
apostles, have been with laborious accuracy explored. The
chronology of the New Testament has been so frequently and so
fully investigated, that the probable period of every event of any
moment has been ascertained. And even the local details,
and casual occurrences of single chapters—such as the 27th
of the Acts—have been verified and explained with a minute-
ness and fidelity, which leaves nothing further to be desired

(Smith on the Voyage and Shipwreck of St Paul). With sources of such a kind the intelligent interpreter of Scripture must make himself familiar; and be prepared at fitting times to use the information, which past care and industry have accumulated. In its own place this is valuable, and, in a sense, indispensable; yet still only as a subsidiary aid; and the work of exposition turns into a wrong channel, when it finds its chief employment in matters of so incidental and circumstantial a kind.

SECTION FOURTH.

GENERAL RULES AND PRINCIPLES TO BE FOLLOWED IN THE INTERPRETATION OF PARTICULAR WORDS AND PASSAGES.

WE must now make the supposition, that the points adverted to in the preceding sections have been duly attended to; that an acquaintance has been formed with the peculiar dialect of the New Testament, and with the collateral sources of information fitted to throw light on its terms and allusions. It by no means follows, however, that when we *have* become thus furnished with knowledge in such elementary matters, we have all the qualifications necessary to render us safe or skilful interpreters of New Testament Scripture, capable of unfolding with clearness and accuracy the meaning of its several parts. For this various other things are requisite, the want or neglect of which may as certainly ensure our failure in the work of interpretation, at least as regards the more select portions of Scripture, as if we had yet to learn the peculiar structure and characteristics of the language. We proceed, therefore, to lay down some general rules and principles, which it is of essential moment that we be in a condition to embrace and act upon, in order to exhibit aright the meaning of Scripture.

1. The first we shall notice is one, that bears on the state of mind of the interpreter—*he must endeavour to attain to a sympathy in thought and feeling with the sacred writers, whose meaning he seeks to unfold.* Such a sympathy is not required for the inter-

pretation alone of the inspired writings ; it is equally necessary
in respect to *any* ancient author ; and the possession of it, to
some extent, must be held to be altogether indispensable.   Language is but the utterance of thought and feeling on the part of
one person to another, and the more we can identify ourselves
with the state of mind out of which that thought and feeling
arose, the more manifestly shall we be qualified for appreciating
the language in which they are embodied, and reproducing true
and living impressions of it.   An utter discordance or marked
deficiency in the one respect, cannot fail to discover itself in the
other by corresponding blunders and defects.

It is the virtual abnegation of this principle, and the palpable want of the qualification which it presupposes, that has
rendered the really available results so inadequate, which have
been accomplished by the rationalistic school of interpreters.
Not a few of them have given proof of superior talents, and have
brought to the task also the acquirements of a profound and
varied scholarship.   The lexicography and grammar, the philology and archæology of Scripture, have been largely indebted to
their inquiries and researches ; but, from the grievous mental
discrepancy existing between the commentator and his author,
and the different points of view from which they respectively
looked at Divine things, writers of this class necessarily failed to
penetrate the depths of the subjects they had to handle, fell often
into jejune and superficial representations on particular parts,
and on entire books of Scripture never once succeeded in producing a really satisfactory exposition.   What proper insight,
for example, into the utterances of the Apostle John—utterances that are remarkable for the combination they present of
simplicity in form, with depth and comprehensiveness of meaning—could be expected from one, who calls, indeed, upon the
reader to sympathise with the sacred writer, but how to do so ?
To sympathise " with the apostle, as being, at the time of his
writing the Epistle, a weak old man, who had no longer the
power of thinking in any connected manner." Such is the
manner in which even Langé speaks, though in many respects
greatly in advance of the proper Rationalists.   Dr Paulus of
Heidelberg was for long one of the leading champions of this
school—a man of no ordinary gifts, both natural and acquired,

and a man, too, who possessed what many learned and useful commentators have wanted—the power of so far sympathising with the sacred penmen, as to realize, in a vivid and attractive manner, the scenes of their history, and the circumstances in which they were placed. But all being brought to the test of a so-called rational—namely, an anti-supernatural—standard, the spirit evaporates in his hands, and everything in a sense becomes common and unclean. The most miraculous occurrences shrink into merely clever transactions or happy coincidences; and even when he comes to such a passage as this, " Blessed art thou, for flesh and blood have not revealed it to thee, but My Father that is in heaven," he can see nothing but a reference to the force of circumstances in awakening the mind to reflection, and giving it a practical direction and impulse toward what is good; or to such another passage as this, " I must work the works of Him that sent Me while it is day : the night cometh, when no man can work," the whole he can extract from it is, " I must heal the diseased eyes before the evening twilight comes on, because when it is dark we can no longer see to work." [1]

This school of interpretation, however, at least in the extreme shape represented by Dr Paulus, has become virtually extinct. In Germany itself the tide has long since turned, and been steadily setting in a better direction; nor would it be easy to find anywhere better specimens of a truly sympathetic and congenial spirit in the work of interpretation, than are furnished by some of the later expository productions from that country. There still is, no doubt, and probably will ever be, both there and here, a class of interpreters, who in a certain modified form exhibit a defect in the respect under consideration; but a conviction, as to the real nature of the things which constituted the great aim and substance of the Gospel, and to the necessity of a correspondence in belief and spirit between the inspired penmen

[1] The entire note on the first of the two passages is: " All circumstances leading to insight and pursuit after the good are, in the New Testament, considered as grounded in the Godhead, educating men in a spontaneous and moral, not juridical manner. When they awaken the mind to reflection, furnish to its activity matters of practical insight, keep these before it, and thereby quicken the energetic working toward what is good, then the paternally inclined Godhead reveals to man something which the grovelling and earthly disposition in man could not have discovered to him."

E

and those who would engage in the work of interpretation, such a conviction being now more generally diffused and constantly growing, renders it probable, that that specific work will in the future be left more in the hands of persons, whose productions shall manifest a becoming unison of sentiment between the original author and the modern disciple.   Hence it is laid down as a fundamental point by a distinguished German theologian— by Hagenbach in his Encyclopedia, that " an inward interest in the doctrine of theology is needful for a Biblical interpreter.   As we say, that a philosophical spirit is demanded for the study of Plato, a poetical taste for the reading of Homer or Pindar, a sensibility to wit and satire for the perusal of Lucian, a patriotic sentiment for the enjoyment of Sallust and Tacitus, equally certain is it, that the fitness to understand the profound truths of Scripture, of the New Testament especially, presupposes, as an indispensable requisite, a sentiment of piety, an inward religious experience.   Thus is it ever true, that the Scriptures will not be rightly and spiritually comprehended, unless the Spirit of God become Himself the true interpreter of His words, the *angelus interpres*, who will open to us the real meaning of the Bible."

The more we take into consideration the distinctive character of Scripture, as a revelation from God, the more shall we be convinced of the necessity and the importance of the principle now stated.   That character constitutes a special reason for a harmony of spirit between the interpreter and the original writer, beyond what belongs to Scripture in common with other ancient writings.   For, as an authoritative revelation of the mind of God, it unfolds things above the reach of our natural desire and apprehension, and unfolds them, not as things that may be coolly surveyed and thoroughly understood from a position of indifference, but as things affecting our highest interests, and demanding our implicit and cordial acceptance.   In such a case something more is evidently required than mere intellectual discernment, or competent scholarship.   The heart as well as the head must be right ; there *must* be the delicacy of a spiritual taste, and the humility of a childlike disposition.   So true is the sentiment, which Neander took for his motto, Pectus est quod theologum facit.   Our Lord, indeed, declared as much at the outset, when He said, in His address to the Father, " Thou hast hid these things from the wise and prudent, and hast revealed them unto babes." It is only with the attainment of such a spiritual condition, that the eye opens to a clear perception of the truth, or that the mind is able to discern the full import of the words which embody it, and catch the nicer shades of meaning they convey. So that what has been said of religion generally, may be specially applied to the interpretation of its sacred records: "As in all subjects we can understand language only as far as we have some *experience* of the things it reports, so in religion (by the very same principle) the spiritual heart alone can understand the language of the Spirit. In every book whatever, it is the mind of the reader that puts meaning in the words; but the language of the New Covenant is a celestial language, and they who would give their fulness to *its* blessed words, must have caught their secret from heaven." [1]

2. Necessary, however, and important as this sympathetic spirit, this *spiritus interpres*, is, on the part of the interpreter of Scripture, when possessed in fullest measure, it can never entitle any one to use arbitrariness in the explanation of its words, or warrant him to put a sense on these different from that which properly belongs to them. Its value lies simply in guiding to the real import, not in modifying it, or in superinducing something of its own upon it. And we, therefore, lay it down as another principle to be sacredly maintained in Scriptural interpretations, that *nothing should be elicited from the text but what is yielded by the fair and grammatical explanation of the language.* The import of each word, and phrase, and passage, must be investigated in a manner perfectly accordant with the laws of language, and with the actual circumstances of the writers. Not what we may think they *should* have said, or might possibly wish they *had* said, but simply what, as far as we are able to ascertain, they *did say*—this must be the sole object of our pursuit; and the more there is of perfect honesty and discriminating tact in our efforts to arrive at this, the more certain is our success. For in the words of Bengel:[2] "It is better to run all lengths with Scripture truth in a natural and open manner, than to shift, and twist, and accommodate. Straightforward conduct

[1] Sermons by Mr A. Butler, First Series, p. 94.
[2] Life by Burck, p. 259.

may draw against us bitterness and rancour for a time, but sweetness will come out of it. Every single truth is a light of itself, and every error, however minute, is darkness as far as it goes."

Nothing is more directly at variance with this principle of interpretation, and more surely fatal to success, than a party or polemical bias, which brings the mind to the examination of Scripture with a particular bent, and disposes it to work for an inferior end. No doubt, it may be alleged, the possession of a spirit in harmony with that of the sacred penmen implies something of this description—as such a spirit cannot exist without the recognition of vital truths and principles common to us with the inspired writers, and in conformity with which our interpretation must proceed. To some extent it must be so. But there is a great, and, for the most part, easily marked distinction, between holding thus with the writers of New Testament Scripture in a natural and appropriate manner, and doing it in a controversial and party spirit—between holding with them so as to give a fair and consistent interpretation of their language, and doing it, or professing to do it, while we are ever and anon putting a constrained or inadequate meaning on their words. If the latter be our mode of procedure, it will not fail to betray itself in the manifest violence occasionally done to the words of the original, and the various shifts resorted to for the purpose, either of evading their proper force, or foisting upon them a sense they cannot fairly be made to bear.

Previous to the Reformation, divines of the Romish Church were wont to carry this style of interpretation to the worst extreme. Individual writers, here and there, gave evidence of a certain degree of candour and impartiality; but, for the most part, the sacred text was treated in abject deference to the authority of Rome, and the most arbitrary expositions were fallen upon to establish her doctrinal positions. It was only such a vigorous and general movement as the Reformation,—a movement basing itself upon the true sense of Scripture, and perpetually appealing to that for its justification,—which could break the trammels that had so long lain upon men's minds in this respect, and recall sincere students of Scripture to the simple, grammatical sense of its words. To a great extent, it actually did this. Luther, Melancthon, Calvin, and the other leading Reformers, were of one mind here, though they sometimes failed, and differed from each other, in the results to which the principle actually led them. Their fundamental rule was, that "the sense of Scripture is one, certain, and simple, and is everywhere to be ascertained in accordance with the principles of grammar and human discourse." (Elem. Rhet. II. of Melancthon.) "We must not," says Luther, "make God's word mean what we wish; we must not bend *it*, but allow it to bend *us;* and give it the honour of being better than we could make it; so that we must let it stand." Of this fair, straightforward, grammatical mode of handling Scripture, as characteristic of the spirit of the Reformation, the commentaries of Calvin are the noblest monument of the period, scarcely surpassed in that respect, as in certain others not equalled, to the present day. It was more, indeed, by what the Reformers did in their exegetical productions, and their comments on Scripture, than by any formal announcement or explanation of their hermeneutical principles, that both they themselves and their immediate followers gave it to be understood what those principles really were. A hermeneutical work by Flacius Illyricus did appear in 1567—entitled, Clavis Scripturæ Sacræ—somewhat cumbrous, indeed (comprising, along with his explanation of Scripture figures and expressions, two large volumes), and in certain parts not a little prolix; but strong and earnest in its advocacy of the great principle now under consideration, and for the period altogether a respectable and useful production. It stood alone, however, in the 16th century, and was not followed up, as it should have been, by Biblical students of a more strictly exegetical and less controversial spirit. The author himself in this, as in his other works, was too much influenced by doctrinal prepossession and interest,—although he justly condemns Papists and sophists on this account, who (he says) "pick out select passages from the sacred books at their own pleasure, and combine them together again in the most arbitrary manner; so that they speak, indeed, in the plain words of Scripture, but at the same time utter their own thoughts, not those of Scripture."

It is proper to note, however, that on this very point—the point in respect to which the Reformation wrought so beneficial a change—Dr Campbell pronounces a most severe and caustic judgment against Beza, one of the most learned and able expositors of the Reformation ; he charges him with allowing his doctrinal tendencies to impart an improper bias to his translation and notes. It cannot be questioned, we think, that Beza did lay himself open to objection on this ground, and his adversary Castalio proved himself quite ready to take advantage of it· *Some* of the examples produced by Castalio, and reproduced by Campbell, are certainly instances of wrong translation and false exposition, such as but too clearly originated in undue doctrinal bias. But neither is it quite fair, with Campbell, to ascribe them all to this source, nor are they such as to merit that bitter acrimony which pervades the critique, and which looks more like the expression of personal antipathy to Beza for the *kind* of doctrines he espoused, than for occasional indiscretion in the way of introducing them. That something of this sort did mingle in Campbell's animadversions, one can scarcely doubt, not only from the pungency of their general tone, but also from the evident desire betrayed in some of the examples to aggravate as much as possible the charge of bad faith :—As when, in regard to Beza's rendering ψυχή, in Acts ii. 27, by *cadaver* in his first edition, he is represented as quite singular and arbitrary, while for that sense (though in itself, we believe, a wrong one) Beza produces the authority of Jerome ; and Suicer, in his Thesaurus, says of it, *Quæ Beza in prima editione sua* RECTE *interpretatus erat,* —referring, as Beza had done before him, to Virgil Æn. iii., Animamque sepulchro condimus. So, again, in regard to the word χειροτονήσαντες, in Acts xiv. 23, which Beza renders *per suffragia creassent,* Dr Campbell can see nothing in the *per suffragia* but Beza's desire to thrust in his own views respecting the popular election of ministers. Beza, however, only professes to give what he held to be the full and proper import of the word, and what was undoubtedly its *original* meaning ; as Suicer also admits, when he says, it designates, according to its primary signification, " *an election, quæ fit per suffragia manuum extensione data*"—*eligere per suffragia ad Episcopatum*—a practice, he truly remarks, which long survived in the Church. It may be questioned, whether the word should have this definite meaning ascribed to it in the passage under consideration, as the word was often used in the more general sense of designating or appointing. Suicer himself thinks it does not; but Erasmus had already translated *cum suffragiis creassent*, and the same sense is vindicated by Raphelius, who supports it by examples from profane writers; to say nothing of Doddridge and others in later times. There is, therefore, no just reason for charging Beza with bad faith, as if, in ascribing such a sense to the word, he deliberately tampered with the integrity of Scripture. These remarks have been introduced merely for the purpose of guarding against what appears an exaggerated representation of Beza's partiality, and of correcting the too depreciatory estimate formed by Dr Campbell of his merits as an interpreter of Scripture.

It may be confidently affirmed, that the parties, who, next to the Papists, have erred most through doctrinal bias in perverting and narrowing the proper import of Sacred Scripture, have been the elder Socinians and the modern Rationalists. These, if not the only, are at least the chief parties, who from the ranks of Protestantism, and under a show of learning, have systematically tampered with the sense (sometimes even with the text) of Scripture; and have sought to obtain from it something else or something less than that which the words by a natural interpretation yield. But the arts plied for this purpose have signally failed. The forced interpretations and arbitrary methods of the Socinian party have been obliged to give way. By the establishment of a more accurate criticism, by sounder principles of interpretation, and a more intimate acquaintance with the original languages, it has been found that Scripture will not surrender up any of its peculiar doctrines; so that, as has been remarked by Winer,[1] "the controversies among interpreters have usually led back to the admission, that the old Protestant views of the meaning of the sacred text, are the correct ones." These views *are* there, the Rationalists of a past generation confessed, though only by way of accommodation to the antiquated notions and doctrinal beliefs of the Jews, not as being in themselves absolutely true or strictly Divine:—they *are* there, the Rationalists of the present day still admit, but only as the temporary and imperfect forms of the truth, suited to an immature age, now to be supplanted by higher and worthier conceptions. We thank

[1] *Litteratur Zeitung*, No. 44.

them both for the admission ; in *that* we have the confession of
those, whom nothing but the force of truth could have constrained
to own, that the doctrines of the orthodox faith are those which
are elicited from Scripture by the grammatical rendering and
fair interpretation of its words.   And by this faith it behoves us
to abide—till, at least, He who gave it may be pleased to give
us another and better.

The principle, however, of abiding in interpretations of Scripture by the grammatical sense, not only requires a spirit of
fairness, as opposed to a doctrinal bias or polemical interest, but
also a spirit of discrimination in regard to the various elements,
the Lexical and Syntactical peculiarities, by the observance of
which the real grammatical sense is to be ascertained.   It is
obvious, that if no proper discrimination is made between the later
and the more classical Greek—if due respect is not had to the
Hebraistic element, which appears in some of the phrases and
constructions of New Testament Scripture—if either the more
distinctive meanings of particular words, or the characteristic
peculiarities of individual writers are overlooked, failures and
mistakes in a corresponding degree will inevitably be made in
the exhibition of the correct meaning.   From deficiencies in one
or more of these respects it is possible to give an unfair and
erroneous view of a passage, not only without any improper bias
prompting one to do so, but even with the most honest purpose
of attaining to correctness, and many qualifications to aid in accomplishing it.   When the Apostle Paul, for example, in Gal. ii.
2, speaks of going up to Jerusalem κατὰ ἀποκάλυψιν—if, from undue regard to classical analogy, we should interpret with the
learned Hermann, *explicationis causa*—for the purpose, that is,
of rendering certain explanations to parties residing there, we
should certainly not give what is either the grammatical sense
of the expression, or what accords with the Apostle Paul's use
of the term ἀποκάλυψις ; by whom it is always employed in the
higher sense of a Divine communication.   And in such an expression it is not so much classical analogy, as *scriptural*, and
we may even say *Pauline*, usage, that must determine the exact
import.   It is in fact, as formerly stated, very much from the
more careful and discriminating attention, that has latterly been
paid to the various peculiarities both of the Greek language

generally, and of the New Testament style and diction in particular, that advances have been made in precision and accuracy of interpretation. Nor should it be forgotten, in strictly critical expositions, what has been justly remarked by Mr Ellicot in his preface to the Epistle to the Galatians, that "in the Holy Scriptures every peculiar expression, even at the risk of losing an idiomatic turn, *must* be retained. Many words, especially the prepositions, have a positive dogmatical and theological significance, and to qualify them by a popular turn, or dilute them by a paraphrase, is dangerous in the extreme."

3. Assuming, however, what has been stated—assuming that our primary object in interpreting Scripture, should be to ascertain what sense the words of every passage *may*, by a fair and grammatical interpretation, and in reality *do* yield:—assuming, moreover, that we both know and are disposed to keep in view the more distinctive peculiarities belonging in whole or in part to the language of the New Testament, there are still guiding principles of great importance to be remembered and followed, especially in those parts that have some degree of difficulty about them. One of these, which we therefore specify as the *third* point to be noticed in this connection, is *the regard that should be had to the simplicity which characterises the writings of the New Testament.* "The excellence of an interpreter," says Ernesti justly, "consists much in simplicity; and the more any interpretation bears the mark of facility, and it appears as if it ought to have struck the reader before, the more likely is it to be true. Ῥᾴδιον τὸ ἀληθὲς, says Lycurgus; and Schultens, in his Preface to Job, well remarks, that the seal of truth is simple and eternal."

It is necessary, however, to explain here. The simplicity that should characterise our interpretations of Scripture is very different from shallowness, or from what lies entirely on the surface and is found without difficulty. On the contrary, great skill and study may often be required to come at it. The simplicity we speak of is the proper counterpart of the simplicity of Scripture itself—a simplicity that is compatible with the most profound thought and the most copious meaning—and which had its ground partly in the *circumstances*, and partly in the *design* of the sacred penmen. In respect to their circumstances, the position they occupied was that of the comparatively humbler ranks of life ; they lived and thought in a simple, as contradistinguished from an artificial state of society. Their manners and habits, their modes of conception, and forms of speech, are such as usually belong to persons similarly circumstanced ; that is, they partake, not of the polish and refinement, the art and subtlety, which too commonly mark the footsteps of high cultivation and luxurious living, but of the free, the open, the natural—as of persons accustomed frankly to express, not to conceal their emotions, or to wrap their sentiments in disguise. On this account—because written by persons of such a type, and depicting characters and events connected with such a state of society, the narratives of Scripture are pre-eminent above all other writings for their simplicity ; they are nature itself, in its unvarnished plainness and clear transparency ; and from this they derive a charm, which is more or less felt in every bosom. But what so strikingly characterises the narrative portions of Scripture, has also given its impress to the others ; the whole are pervaded by the direct, the guileless simplicity of men, who had to do with the realities of life, and were wont to speak as from heart to heart.

But if the circumstances of the sacred writers tended to produce, the *design* with which they wrote expressly called for, this simplicity in writing ; and, indeed, secured it. It was to inform, to instruct, to save, that they wrote—this was their one grand aim. They had no personal, no literary ends in view ; they were simply witnesses, recording the wonderful things they had seen and heard, or ambassadors conveying messages from another, not on their own behalf, but for the interests of their fellow-men. Hence, they naturally lost themselves in their subject. Having it as their one object to unfold and press this upon the minds of others, they used, as the apostle says, great plainness of speech—language the most natural, the most direct, the most fitted to convey in appropriate and impressive terms the thoughts of their heart. The simplicity which thus characterises their writings is that of men, who had a single aim in view, and so went straight to the mark.

Such is the kind of simplicity which the writings of the New Testament possess ; and corresponding to this is the simplicity which should appear in our manner of interpretation. How, then, *should* it appear? Primarily, no doubt, and mainly, in putting a natural construction on their words, and ascribing to them, precise indeed and accurate, yet not recondite and far-fetched meanings. As in writing what they were moved to in-dite by the Holy Ghost, the sacred penmen were guided by the simplicity of an earnest purpose and a lofty aim, so we should prescribe to ourselves (as Titmann has said) this quality of sim-plicity as a rule, and not recede, except for grave reasons, from that sense, which seems to be the nearest and most direct. It may be quite possible, in certain cases, by the help of lexicons and other appliances, to bring out interpretations of an in-genious nature, and display a good deal of skill in supporting them; but no satisfactory results shall thus be obtained, unless the meanings put upon the different words, and the sense extracted from them, are such as might seem appropriate to men using the language of ordinary life, and using it with the view, not of establishing subtle distinctions, but of unfolding in the most effective manner the great principles of truth and duty.

This, however, has respect only to our treatment of the *language;* the kind of thoughts and feelings of which that language might be expressive is another thing. Here there was room for infinite depth and fulness. It is of the nature of grace, in all its operations, to give a subjective elevation to the soul— to increase, not only its appetency, but its power of discernment also, for the inward and spiritual; and by the help even of com-mon things, through the instrumentality of the simplest language, to open veins of thought, and awaken chords of feeling, which lie beyond the reach of those who are living after the course of nature. In the spiritually enlightened mind there is, what may be called, a *divine* simplicity, which, by drawing it into closer connection and sympathy with the mind of God, discovers to it views and meanings, which would otherwise never have sug-gested themselves. So, we see with the inspired writers of the New Testament themselves, that not unfrequently they discern an import in the earlier dispensations of God, or indicate thoughts in connection with the facts of later times, such as would not have occurred to persons, even of superior and cultivated minds, looking from a merely natural point of view. Yet not the less in what they thus discern and indicate—in the inferences they deduce, and the conclusions they build, as well as in the more substantive part of their announcements, are there to be found the proper characteristics of simplicity—a style of thought and expression, direct, plain, natural.

We simply add further, that in endeavouring to preserve and copy this simplicity, we are in no respect precluded from the necessity of applying careful thought and the resources of solid learning to the work of interpretation. It is only through these, indeed, that we can hope to surmount the difficulties which lie across the path of a thoroughly successful exegesis of Scripture. In aiming at this we have to throw ourselves back upon the times and circumstances of the sacred penmen—to realize their position—make ourselves familiar with their modes of thought and forms of expression, so as to be able to judge what would have been for them a natural and fitting mode of representation —what forced and unnatural. And this we can only expect to do by close study, and the judicious employment of the resources of learning. Not the learning merely which is confined to the use of grammars and lexicons, but all that can serve to throw light on the language, the manners, the opinions and habits of those, among whom Christ and His apostles lived and spoke. Whatever is calculated to aid us in arriving at such intimate knowledge, must also be serviceable in enabling us to attain to a proper simplicity in our interpretations of Scripture.

4. It is only following out the same line of thought, and rendering the principle it involves specific in a particular direction, when we mention as another, a *fourth* rule to be attended to in scriptural interpretations, that in settling the meaning of words we must have respect chiefly to the *usus loquendi, the current sense, or established usage at the time—to this more than to their etymology.* The reason for such a rule is no further peculiar to the writings of the New Testament, than that they are of a popular and practical nature ; which rendered it expedient, and, in a sense, necessary, that words and phrases should be taken in their prevailing signification. But this signification often differs greatly from what might be conjectured by looking simply to their etymology. For the spoken language of

a people is ever passing through certain processes of change and fluctuation. Many of its terms depart considerably, in the course of time, from their original import, acquire *new shades* of meaning, and sometimes even become so entirely transformed in their progress, that the *ultimate use* scarcely exhibits a trace of the *primal signification*. A familiar example of this from our own language is to be found in the word *villain*—the English form of the Latin *villanus*—originally, the poor serf attached to the villa or farm of a proprietor—then, from the usual condition and manners of such, the low, selfish, dishonest peasant—and, finally, when villenage in the original sense became extinct, those capable of the most base and dishonourable actions—the *morally* vile and mean. Another instance is furnished by a word, which by a strange coincidence has had the like fortune in its English, that it seems formerly to have had in its Greek form. *Sycophant* in the earlier stages of our literature meant simply an *accuser*—by-and-by a *false accuser*—but in process of time it lost this sense, and came to signify a *fawning flatterer*, one who speaks, not ill of a person behind his back, but good of him before his face, though only for a sinister and selfish purpose—the only sense now retained by the word. In like manner, the Greek συκοφάντης, according to the ancient grammarians, and according also to its apparent composition, originally a *fig-shower*—an *informer* (as is said, though there is no certain proof of such a use) *against persons exporting figs from Attica*—then a *common informer*—and ultimately a *false accuser*, or a *false adviser*, its only signification in classical writings—while in the New Testament it bears the still further, but collateral sense, of extorting money under false pretences (Luke iii. 14).

Not only do words thus in current use sometimes escape altogether from their original meaning, but there are also words, which, etymologically considered, *ought* to be identical in their import, and should admit of being interchanged as synonymous, which yet come to differ materially as to their actual use. To refer only to one example : our two terms *foresight* and *provision* are each made up of two words precisely similar in meaning—only the one pair of Saxon, the other of Latin origin. Undoubtedly *fore* by itself answers to *pro*, and *sight* to *vision ;* yet usage has appropriated the two words to different ideas—the one to indicate what is anticipated in the future, the other to what is laid up or done with a view to the future. A foreigner not acquainted with the usage, and guided merely by the etymology, might readily substitute the one for the other. And it is but lately that I noticed in a letter written from abroad the expression used respecting some one, that his "provisions were disappointed," evidently meaning by provisions what should have been expressed by foresight—the anticipations that had been formed in respect to the future.

A similar sense of incongruity, as in this case, is occasionally produced in one's mind, when a word occurs in some of our older writers, which since their day has undergone a considerable change of meaning—especially if, as sometimes happens, it is employed by them, not only in its original acceptation, but also in conjunction with an epithet, which seems to indicate what is incompatible with the other. Thus in one of Caxton's prefaces, his preface to a translation of a Life of Charles the Great, printed by him in 1485, beseeching the reader's indulgence toward his translation, he says, " Though there be no gay terms in it, nor subtle, nor new eloquence, yet I hope, that it shall be understood, and to that intent I have especially reduced (translated) it after the simple cunning that God hath lent me,"—the *simple cunning*, two words that now bear antagonistic meanings, and seem incongruously united together. Certainly, as now understood, a man of cunning is anything but a simple person; simplicity and cunning cannot exist together. But *cunning* originally implied nothing of a sinister kind. It has its root in the German *kennen*, to know, from which our *ken* comes, and merely denoted the kenning, or knowing, which one might have of anything in art or science. Applied to works of art, it became nearly synonymous with *skill* or *power*—approaching to another cognate German word, *kœnnen, canning*, having the power or ability to accomplish anything—in which sense it occurs in our English Bible, " Let my right hand forget her cunning," namely, her acquired skill to play upon the harp. It is only in comparatively late times, that the word lost this meaning, and came to denote that sort of deceit, which is united with a low kind of skill or cleverness.

Such examples show how cautiously etymology should be applied in determining the sense of words, as these come to be used in a living tongue. As our examples have been chiefly taken from our own language, it may be added in passing, that the person, who did most to turn the attention of English scholars in this direction, and who originated inquiries which have led to many interesting and profitable results—Horne Tooke—has also exhibited in some of his deductions one of the most striking examples of the danger of pushing such inquiries to excess, and of being guided simply by the etymological element in ascertaining the import of words. In the spirit of a thorough-going Nominalist, he maintains, in his "Diversions of Purley," that as words are merely the signs of ideas, and as all our words, not excepting the most abstract, are ultimately traceable to a meaning derived from sensible impressions, so words must be understood not in their acquired or metaphorical, but always substantially in their primitive and sensational meaning :—consequently, as we have no words, neither have we any ideas, of a properly absolute description—both alike cleave inseparably to the dust. So in regard even to truth : " Truth is nothing (he says) but what every man troweth ; whence there is no such thing as eternal, immutable, everlasting truth ; unless mankind, such as they are at present, be also eternal, immutable, and everlasting ; and two persons may contradict each other, and yet both speak truth, for the truth of one person may be opposite to the truth of another." This is carrying the subjective principle in our natures to an extravagant height, and making words govern ideas in a manner, which few, we should think, will be disposed to accredit. We refer to it merely as a proof of the folly of pushing such a line of investigation to the utmost, and making what is the primary ground of our words and ideas also their ultimate standard and measure. Even with soberer inquirers and safer guides we sometimes perceive an excess in the same direction. It may be noticed occasionally in a work, which as a whole is marked by just thought and fine discrimination, and will well repay a careful perusal—Dr Trench on "the Study of Words." Thus, when treating of *kind*, he says, " a *kind* person is a *kinned* person, one of *kin*, one who acknowledges and acts upon his kinship with other men. And so man*kind* s

man*kinned.* In the word is contained a declaration of the relationship which exists between all the members of the human
family ; and seeing that this relation in a race now scattered so
widely and divided so far asunder can only be through a common head, we do in fact, every time that we use the word *mankind*, declare our faith in the common descent of the whole
human race " (p. 42). We *would*, indeed, declare it, if, as often
as we used the word, we had respect to that derivation, and as-
sented to the principle implied in it ; but how few in reality do
so ! In the language of every-day life, we employ the word
simply as current coin—we take it as expressive of the multitude of beings who possess with ourselves a common nature,
but at the same time, perhaps, thinking as little of their common
origin, as, when speaking of truth, we have respect to what every
individual troweth.

But in all this we point only to the excess. There can be no
doubt, in regard to the thing itself, that it is of great importance
to attend to the derivation of words, and that without knowing
this we cannot get at those nicer shades of meaning which they
often express, or make a thoroughly intelligent and proper use of
them. In the great majority of cases, the *etymological* is also the
actual sense of the word ; and even when the acquired or metaphorical use comes materially to differ from the primary one, the
knowledge of the primary is still of service, as most commonly a
certain tinge or impress of it survives even in the ultimate. How
often does a reference to the original import of some leading
word in a phrase or sentence, enable us to bring out its meaning
with a point and emphasis that we must otherwise have failed to
exhibit ! How often, again, when terms nearly synonymous are
employed—so nearly, perhaps, that in rendering from Greek to
English we can only employ the same word for both,—does a
glance at the fundamental import disclose the difference between
them ! Thus, in Gal. vi. 2, we have the exhortation, " Bear ye
one another's burdens, and so fulfil the law of Christ ;" and presently afterwards, in ver. 5, we have the announcement, " For
every one shall bear his own burden." Even an English reader
may see, by looking at the connection, that the burden in the one
case cannot be the same with what is meant by it in the other ; that
the one, as Augustine long ago remarked, is the burden of one's

own trials or infirmities, which may be shared in by others, while the other is something altogether proper to the individual —the burden of his personal responsibility, or rather, perhaps, the burden of his personal state and destiny—which he must bear himself alone. But the difference at once presents itself when we turn to the original, where we find two distinct words employed, each having their respective shades of meaning. The burdens we are to bear one for another are τὰ βάρη, the *weights*, the things which press like loads upon those who come into contact with them, and in a manner call for friendly help : but the burden each one has to bear for himself is τὸ ἴδιον φορτίον, that charge of what is more properly his own, which is indissolubly linked to his personal consciousness and rationality, and of which no one can relieve another.

Again, in Rom. ix. 15, Ἐλεήσω ὃν ἂν ἐλεῶ, καὶ οἰκτειρήσω ὃν ἂν οἰκτείρω, we have two verbs, which are of such cognate meaning, that they are often loosely interchanged, and sometimes the one, sometimes the other, is held to be the stronger expression. Even Titmann (Synon. I. p 122), and after him Robinson, in Lex., designates ἔλεος and ἐλεεῖν as stronger than οἰκτιρμός, and οἰκτείρειν, because the former carry along with them the additional notion of beneficence, a desire to relieve the miserable. But if the greater strength had been there, we should rather have expected the clauses in this passage of the Epistle to the Romans to be in the inverse order—the weaker to be first, and the stronger last. A more exact analysis justifies the existing order; for, as Fritzsche has justly remarked on the passage, the words, ὁ οἰκτιρμός and οἰκτειρεῖν signify more than ὁ ἔλεος and ἐλεεῖν. The latter stand related to ἵλαος, ἰλάομαι, ἰλάσκομαι (the being propitious, kind, or gentle) ; the other to οἴ (the Oh ! the cry of distress or sympathy), and οἶκτος (the tender pity or compassion, of which that cry is one of the first and most natural expressions). Hence ὁ ἔλεος denotes that sorrow which a kindly disposition feels at the misery of another, and is the proper word to be used when the general notion of mercy is to be expressed ; ὁ οἰκτιρμός, however, denotes the sorrow awakened by the sense of another's misery, which calls forth tears and lamentations—not pity merely, but pity in its keener sensibilities and most melting moods. So that the passage referred to has in it a real progression : " I will

F

have mercy on whom I will have mercy, and will have pity on whom I will have pity."

An expression in 2 Cor. xii. 9 may be referred to as an example of a somewhat different kind. The apostle there says that he would most willingly rather glory in infirmities, ἵνα ἐπισκηνώσῃ ἐπʼ ἐμὲ ἡ δύναμις τοῦ Χριστοῦ, the full import of which is but imperfectly conveyed by the common rendering, " that the power of Christ may rest upon me." The verb employed belongs to the later Greek, and is found in Polybius in the sense of dwelling in a tent, or inhabiting. This, however, is not sufficient to explicate the meaning of the word here; nor is any aid to be obtained from the Septuagint, since it does not occur there. It can only be explained by a reference to what is said in Old Testament Scripture of the relation of the Lord's tabernacle or tent to His people; by such a passage, for example, as Isa. iv. 6, where it is written, " And there shall be a tabernacle for a shadow in the day time from the heat;" that is, the Lord's gracious presence and protection spread over them as a shelter. So in Rev. vii. 15, the Lord is represented as " tabernacling upon" the redeemed in glory. In like manner, the apostle here states it as the reason why he would rejoice in infirmities, that thereby Christ's power might tabernacle upon him—might serve, so to speak, as the abiding refuge and confidence in which he should hide himself.

We need not multiply examples further of this description. But we may add, that for those who would know generally how much may be gained in drawing out the more precise and delicate shades of meaning, by a reference to the radical and primary sense of words, one of the best helps will be found to be Bengel's Gnomon, which, notwithstanding occasional failures, is in a short compass the happiest specimen extant of this kind of interpretatation. This should be taken as an habitual companion. But occasionally, also, in writers of a more popular cast, good examples are to be met with of the same tact—in none, perhaps, more than in Leighton, who, if he sometimes strains rather unduly the original meaning, more commonly turns it to good account, and that in a natural and happy manner. As in the following example : " *God resisteth the proud*—ἀντιτάσσεται—singles it out as His grand enemy, and sets Himself in battle array against

it ; so the word is. It breaks the ranks of men, in which He hath
set them, when they are not subject—ὑποτασσόμενοι,—as the word
is before ; yea, pride not only breaks rank, but rises up in rebel-
lion against God, and doth what it can to dethrone Him, and
usurp His place; therefore He orders his forces against it ;" and
so on.

On the other hand, in passages presenting some difficulty, or
affording scope for the display of fancy on the part of the interpreter, it is quite possible, and, indeed, very common, to err by
pressing unduly the etymological import of words. Horsley,
for example, gives a marked and somewhat ludicrous exhibition
of this, when rendering, as he occasionally does, the Greek word
ἰδιῶται by the English word derived from it, *idiots*,[1]—a word, no
doubt, bearing much the same signification with its Greek original—denoting, first, the merely private man, as contradistinguished from one conversant with affairs and offices of state ;
then a person of rude and unskilled condition—in manners and
intellect unpolished ; and, finally, one altogether destitute of the
ordinary powers of human intelligence—bereft of reason, to
which last sense it has long been confined in the common intercourse of life. So that, with Horsley, to turn the expression
used of the apostles in Acts iv. 13, " unlearned men and idiots,"
is only, by a misplaced literalism, to give a false representation
of the meaning. Not much better is his rendering and interpretation of Luke i. 4, " That thou mightest know the exact truth
of those doctrines wherein thou hast been catechized"—περὶ ὧν
κατηχήθης :—on which he remarks, " St Luke's own Gospel, therefore, if the writer's own word may be taken about his own work,
is an historical exposition of the *Catechism*, which Theophilus
had learned when he was first made a Christian. The two first
articles in this historical exposition are, the history of the Baptist's birth, and that of Mary's miraculous impregnation. We
have much more, therefore, than the testimony of St Luke, in
addition to that of St Matthew, to the truth of the fact of the
miraculous conception ; we have the testimony of St Luke, that
this fact was a part of the earliest catechetical instruction ; a
part of the catechism, no doubt, which St Paul's converts learned

---

[1] Tracts against Priestley, p. 46.

of the apostle."[1] We see here, too plainly, the polemical interest, endeavouring to make the utmost of an argument, but overreaching its purpose by putting an undue strain on the principal word in the passage. That our word *catechize* might originally correspond to the Greek word κατηχέω, from which it obviously comes, may be certain enough ; but it does not follow, that what κατη-χέω imports, as used by St Luke, is fairly given by *catechize*, in its current acceptation. The Greek verb did not originally bear the technical import of *catechize*; it meant, to *sound out towards*, to *resound*, or *sound in one's ears ;* then more specially to do this by *word of mouth*, to *instruct*, and ultimately to instruct by way of question and answer. As used in the New Testament, and Greek writers generally, except the Fathers, it indicates nothing as to the specific mode of instruction ; and to represent it by the word *catechize*, would only render our translation in most cases unintelligible or ridiculous. Thus, at Gal. vi. 6, it would run, " Let him that is catechized in the word communicate to him that catechizeth in all good things ;" and at Acts xxi. 22, " But they have been catechized concerning thee, that thou teachest all the Jews to forsake Moses." To sound forth, or communicate instruction, in the active voice, and in the passive, to hear by way of rumour, or be instructed anyhow,—these are the only senses which the word bears in the New Testament. In later times the κατηχούμενοι were those who were under special instruction for admission to the Church, and, as we might say, the *catechized* portion in Christian communities.

In Dr Campbell's Fourth Preliminary Dissertation will be found some good remarks and apposite illustrations on the subject before us. Not, however, without some grounds for exception. His jealousy in respect to etymological considerations is carried to excess, and in some of the instances he produces, leads him, more or less, into error. We formerly alluded to his remarks on χειροτονέω, as used in Acts xiv. 23, and his severe denunciation of Beza for so far giving heed to its etymological formation, as to express in his translation a reference to the mode of appointment to church offices by popular election, signified by holding up the hand. He would exclude everything from its import but the simple idea of appointment, although in the only other passage

[1] Sermon on the Incarnation.

in the New Testament, where it is similarly used of appointment to church offices (2 Cor. viii. 19), it plainly does include the element of popular suffrage. We shall rather point, however, under the present division, to another example, in which Dr Campbell is still less successful, though he labours hard to make good his point. It turns on the word προγινώσκω, whether this should be rendered, as its component elements would lead us to expect, by *foreknow*, or by some more general mode of expression. Dr Campbell holds, it should be less strictly taken in Rom. xi. 2, where we read in our common version, "God hath not cast away His people, whom He foreknew" (ὃν προέγνω); he would separate the preposition, πρό, from the verb, and also impose on the verb itself a somewhat different meaning,—that, namely, of acknowledging or approving; and thus he obtains a, no doubt, very plain and intelligible sense: "God hath not cast off His people, whom heretofore He acknowledged." But is this really the sense intended by the apostle? We find him using the same compound verb a little before at ch. viii. 29, "Whom He did foreknow (οὓς προέγνω), them He also did predestinate;"—and *there* it is scarcely possible to understand it otherwise than in the sense of *foreknowing* given to it by our translators, being plainly used of an act of the Divine mind toward His people, prior to that of their predestination to blessing: He foreknew, then He fore-appointed. Is there any necessity for departing from the same literal sense in the passage before us? None that appears worthy of notice. Dr Campbell has, indeed, said, that to speak there of God's people as those whom He foreknew, "conveyed to his mind no meaning whatever;" and, by a strange oversight in so acute a mind, he founds his statement on the assertion, that to foreknow "always signifies to know some event before it happens"—as if it might not equally import, when used in reference to an act of God, to know a *person* before he exists. Presently, however, he resorts to another consideration, which implies a virtual abandonment of the other, and objects, that "God knew Israel before, in the ordinary meaning of the word *knowing*, could never have been suggested as a reason to hinder us from thinking, that He would never cast them off; for, from the beginning, all nations and all things are alike known to God." True, indeed, in one sense, but not in another. They were not all alike

known to God as destined to occupy toward Himself the same
relation, and to receive the same treatment; and *that* is precisely
the point in the eye of the apostle. God *could* not cast away
His own people, whom He foreknew *as* His own. Their friendly
relation to Him being descried as among the certainties of the
coming future, nothing in that future could arise to hinder its
accomplishment. In another passage (2 Tim. ii. 19) of quite
similar import, the apostle finds the ground of the believer's
security from perdition in the simple fact, which he calls a seal,
that " the Lord knoweth them that are His"—a thought which
had consoled the Psalmist ages before, as appears from the words
in the first Psalm, " The Lord *knoweth* the way of the righteous."
For such knowledge necessarily implies a corresponding treatment. " If the way of the righteous is known by God as the
omniscient, it cannot but be blessed by Him as the righteous.
Hence, there is no necessity to ascribe to *know* the sense of *having
care and affection for, loving,* which it never properly possesses.
It is enough, if only God with His foreknowledge is not shut up
in the heavens; the rest flows spontaneously from His nature,
and does not need to be particularly mentioned."[1]

We have referred under this division to so many illustrative
examples, on the one side and the other, because it is chiefly
through these, that the danger of running into an extreme is
made apparent; and along therewith the necessity of care and
skill in avoiding it. It is, no doubt, one thing to know, in what
direction a tendency to excess in such a matter lies, and another
thing to keep clear of it. Yet it *will* be of importance to remember, that while one should always seek to be acquainted
with the etymological import of words, this cannot in every case
be taken for the actual meaning; this is determined by the current usage, which must be ascertained and adhered to.

So far as concerns the language of the New Testament, or the
precise meaning and interpretation of its words, the general rules
and principles now given appear to comprise all that is necessary.
They will serve to mark out the course of inquiry that must be
pursued, if any measure of success is to be attained. For the
actual result, much will necessarily depend upon the greater or
less degree of exegetical tact possessed by the student, and the

[1] Hengstenberg on Ps. i.

extent to which it has been cultivated by personal application and proper exercise. Hermeneutical skill, like skill of other kinds, must not only have something in nature to rest upon, but have that also matured by diligent and well-directed practice, without which no proficiency can be expected.

For those cases, in which some more peculiar difficulty is felt in getting at the precise sense of a passage, there must, first of all, be brought into play the requisite qualifications connected with the application of the rules and principles already laid down. There must be an acquaintance with the original language, in its proper idioms, the etymology and usage of its words—a knowledge of the distinctive peculiarities of the writer, in whose productions the passage occurs—of the circumstances of the time in which he wrote, its manners and customs, modes of thought, and principles of action—in a word, an insight into the nature of the language employed, and the various things, of a circumstantial description, fitted to tell upon the views of the writer and his more immediate circle. It is clear, that without knowledge of such compass and variety, no one can reasonably expect to succeed in dealing with a passage, which involves any difficulty in respect to the proper construction of its words, or the real meaning which they bear. But it is possible, that where so much is possessed and used, the difficulty may still fail to be overcome. In that case, the next, and more special thing that should be done, is to look very carefully and closely to the connection in which the passage stands—which will often do much to remove the darkness or uncertainty that rests upon its import. Then, let the peculiar phrase or construction, which occasions the difficulty, be examined in connection with others of the same, or nearly the same description, in what remains besides of the individual writer;—or if none such may occur, then in other parts of Scripture; and, still again, in other writings of the apostolic age, and periods not remote from it. The nearer to the passage itself, then the nearer to him who indited it, that any light can be found, the more likely to prove satisfactory. So that the examination should usually be made in the order of his own writings first, next of the other inspired productions, and, finally, of writings as near as possible to the age and circumstances in which he wrote. In such investigations, we need scarcely say,

all available helps, whether ancient or modern, should be brought
into requisition. Access to these in any considerable degree
must always be a special advantage to those who enjoy it. But
even where it is very imperfectly possessed, no inconsiderable
progress may be made in the exact knowledge and interpretation
of Scripture, if this Scripture itself is but carefully studied, with
a few good grammars and lexicons; as, when so used, it will be
found to supply many materials for interpreting itself. Let no
one, therefore, wait till he has all requisite means within his
reach; but let each rather endeavour to make the most profitable use of what he can command—in the persuasion, that though
he may be far from accomplishing all he could wish, he will still
find his labour by no means in vain. And, however he may
stand as to inferior resources, let him never forget to seek the
enlightening and directing grace of the Holy Spirit, who to the
humble and prayerful mind will often unlock secrets, which remain hid to the most learned and studious.

SECTION FIFTH.

OF FALSE AND TRUE ACCOMMODATION; OR, THE INFLUENCE THAT SHOULD BE ALLOWED TO PREVAILING MODES OF THOUGHT IN FASHIONING THE VIEWS AND UTTERANCES OF THE SACRED WRITERS.

THE previous discussions have had respect mainly to the language
of the New Testament, and the principles or rules necessary to
be followed, in order to our arriving at the precise and proper
import of its words. There are, however, elements of various
kinds, not properly of a linguistic nature, which must yet, according to the influence allowed them, exercise an important bearing on
the sense actually obtained from the words and phrases of Scripture—elements, which will affect the interpretation of some parts
of Scripture more than others, or tend to modify the meaning
put on certain of its passages. The points referred to less properly concern the explanation of particular terms, than the nature

of the ideas contained in them. They respect the question, what
is there precisely of truth to be received, or of practical instruction to be obeyed, in the portions which have been analysed and
explained ? It is quite possible, that one may know with perfect
correctness every word in a passage, and yet, from some false
conceptions or misleading bias, may have a very imperfect apprehension of its real purport, or, perhaps, give a wrong turn to the
thoughts it expresses. It is necessary, therefore, on the basis of
the principles already unfolded, to proceed to this higher line of
hermeneutical inquiry, and endeavour, if possible, to set up some
proper landmarks upon it.

I. Now, the first point that here calls for investigation is, the
general one, in what relations the sentiments of the sacred writers
stand to the spirit of their age—to its prevailing modes of thought
and popular beliefs. Were they in any material respect modified
by these ? Or did they pursue an altogether independent course
—never bending in aught under the prevailing current, if this at
all deviated from the exact and natural line of things ? Or, if
they did to some extent accommodate themselves to this, how far
might we expect the accommodation to go ? At a comparatively
early period a certain doctrine of accommodation was introduced
with reference to representations in Scripture—which Origen,
and others of the Fathers, were wont to regard as spoken or done
κατ᾽ οἰκονομίαν, by way of dispensation, or through συγκατάβασις, a
condescension, or an accommodation to the position and infirmities of the persons addressed. Advantage, it was believed, was
taken of these, in order the more readily to gain the confidence
or reach the understanding of those who were in an unfit state
for receiving the naked truth. It is difficult to say precisely,
how far the Fathers, who introduced this principle, meant to carry
it, in respect to the teaching of Christ and the apostles; for they
are neither very explicit nor altogether consistent in their statements upon the subject. For the most part they appear simply
to have understood by it an adaptation in the *form* of Divine
communications to the modes of human thought and speech,
while the *matter* not the less remained true and divine; as in
conduct the Apostle Paul became as a Jew to the Jews (1 Cor.
ix. 20), or externally conformed himself to their manners and

customs, without in the least detracting thereby from the claims
and principles of the Gospel. In this way, Scripture was explained as accommodating itself to men's infirmities or habits,
when it speaks of God as possessing human parts and passions,
or uses parables, proverbs, and familiar images, to set forth to
our view things spiritual and divine. But occasionally they seem
to indicate an application of the principle beyond this limit, and
to include the *matter* of what was taught or done, as well as the
form : as when Origen (in his Principia, L. iv.) speaks of mystic
dispensations employed by God, which, in their literal sense or
obvious meaning, were opposed to enlightened faith and reason—
or when Jerome, in his Epistle to Augustine, teaches that Paul,
as well as Peter, feigned himself to be a Jew, and yet reproved
Peter at Antioch by what he calls *honesta dispensatio,* which the
one administered, and the other submitted to feignedly, that they
might show the prudence of apostles. It requires no arguments
to prove, that honest dispensations of this sort but ill accord
with that godly simplicity, which we are wont to ascribe to the
apostles, and would, if generally believed in, somewhat shake
their credit as inspired writers. Fortunately, however, the
Fathers erred comparatively little in this direction; and it was
rather from inadvertence, or from perplexity in dealing with particular passages, than from any general laxity of principle, that
they have been occasionally betrayed into rash and unguarded
statements upon the subject.

It was reserved for modern times to apply the principle of accommodation to the teachings of Scripture in the full and proper
sense, and to represent Christ Himself and the apostles as pan-
dering to the mistaken views and narrow prejudices of their
time. Wetstein was among the first to lay down a formal principle of this sort, although Grotius in some of his comments had
before virtually acted on it. But Wetstein, in a little work on
the criticism and interpretation of the New Testament (A.D.
1724), gave it out as a canon of interpretation, in respect to
those passages, which seem to be at variance with truth, or with
each other, that the sacred writers should be viewed " as not
always expressing their own opinion, nor representing matters as
to their real state, but occasionally also expressing themselves
according to the sentiments of others, or the sometimes am-

biguous, sometimes erroneous, opinions of the multitude." And he indicates, that this mode of explanation should be especially adopted in regard to what is often said in the New Testament of sacrifices, of Satan, of angels and demons. Shortly after, Semler (both in a new edition of Wetstein's treatise, and in works of his own) took up the principle of interpretation thus announced, and with characteristic ardour and industry applied it to the explanation of the New Testament writings. His fundamental position was, that the exposition of the New Testament should be pre-eminently historical; that is, that one should have respect to the spiritual conditions of the time—the prevailing thoughts and opinions, as well as external circumstances, of those among whom Christ and His apostles lived; and these he represented to be such, that the truth could not always be spoken as it should have been, and required a use to be made of Old Testament Scripture in reference to Gospel events, such as cannot be justified on principles of grammar or grounds of abstract reason. Our Lord and His apostles, therefore, spoke at times *ex vulgari opinione*, not precisely according to the truth of things; yet so as that, by instituting a comparison of the different parts of their writings, and making the more general and comprehensive rule the more special and peculiar, we may arrive at the ultimate and permanent ideas of the Gospel. The door was thus fairly opened for exegetical license,—and from Semler's day to this, there have never been wanting men fully disposed to avail themselves of the liberty which it invited them to take. Loose as Semler's views were, and great as was the havoc which he carried into the received views of Scripture, he lived to see (with grief, it is said) others far outstripping him in the same line of accommodations. By degrees everything was reduced to a subjective standard; and if in anything an interpreter found statements recorded, or doctrines taught, which did not accord with *his* notions of the truth of things, the explanation was at hand, that such things had found a place in Scripture merely on a principle of accommodation; the people at the time were capable of appreciating nothing higher, or the writers themselves as yet understood no better. And so, in the hands of many on the Continent, and of some also in this country, of some here still, the proper teaching of the Gospel came to be

reduced to the scanty form of a Sadducean creed. The doctrines of the Trinity, of the Divine Sonship of Messiah, of the
atonement, of the personality of the Spirit, of a corporeal resurrection and a final judgment, have all been swept away by the
abettors of the principle under consideration ; and even the idea
of Christianity's being in any peculiar sense a revelation from
Heaven, has been sometimes represented as merely a mode of
speech suited to the time of its appearance.

Such has been the practical result of the accommodation theory,
or the historical principle of interpretation (as it has been sometimes called)—a result, which carries along with it the virtual doom
of the principle itself. For, obviously enough, to deal in such
an arbitrary and magisterial manner with sacred Scripture, is
not to interpret, but to sit in judgment upon it, as we might do
upon any human composition, and receive or reject what it
contains, according to our preconceived notions. The proper
revelation—the real standard of truth and error, is in that case
within ; we stand upon essentially infidel ground ; and seeing
that Scripture as much contradicts, as coincides with our views
of things, it were better to discard it as an authority altogether—
treat it merely as a help.

Most commonly, however, the accommodation principle is
confined within a comparatively narrow range, and applied to
what are called innocuous errors. So Seiler, for example, in his
Hermeneutics, who says, that in such a matter we must be careful to distinguish between innocuous and nocuous errors. Among
the innocuous he includes chiefly errors of an historical and
chronological kind—such as he conceives occur in the speech of
Stephen, Acts vii.—and exegetical errors, or false interpretations
of several passages of the Old Testament, which were erroneously
supposed to contain what the words did not really indicate. So,
too, Rosenmuller, in his Historia Interpretationis, I. p. 27, who
thinks, that as the Jews had a fondness for something out of the
direct and simple style of writing, loved to exhibit their sentiments in an allegorical dress, and to seek for them strained and
fanciful supports in Scripture, so the apostles acted wisely in
adapting themselves in these respects to the genius and habits of
their countrymen. Whence with him, and many others in this
country and America (including such names as Moses Stuart,

Horne, Adam Clarke, Albert Barnes), the formula, "that it might be fulfilled," or "then was fulfilled what was spoken," is held to have been used often as a kind of Rabbinical flourish, an embellishing of the narrative or discourse with quotations, which, though they had properly another sense, yet were so expressed as to admit of being happily applied to the circumstances and events of Gospel history.

But would this really have been a wise, or even a justifiable procedure, on the part of our Lord and the apostles? Would such a fanciful application of Scripture have been an *innocuous* error? Is it so light a thing for inspired men to misquote the writings of each other? It is precisely to their use of Old Testament Scripture—to the elucidations they give of its meaning, and the specific applications they make of its several parts, that we are indebted for our more certain knowledge of its design, and especially for our insight into the connection that subsists between the Old and the New in God's dispensations. To bring looseness and ambiguity into such a region, were in reality to destroy all certainty of interpretation, and open the door on every hand for fanciful conceits or groundless conjecture. Surely the same majestic authority which said of the Old Testament writings, "And the Scripture cannot be broken," virtually said, at the same time, It must not be arbitrarily dealt with; it is too sacred a thing to be coupled with mock fulfilments, or brought into connection with events, to which it bore no proper reference. And the rather may we thus conclude, when we think of the slender nature of the reasons for which, it is supposed, an accommodation should have been made. To give fancied ornateness to a discourse, or show a sort of Rabbinical adroitness in the mere handling of texts—and thereby to win for the moment a readier attention to what they said or wrote—were *these* sufficient motives for our Lord and His disciples travestying the great laws of sound exegesis, and bringing confusion into the sense of ancient Scripture? No—we may rest assured, they knew their calling better; and as in other things they were not afraid to meet the strongest prejudices of their countrymen, and lay the axe to the most rooted corruptions, it were folly to think, that in this, and for such trivial considerations, they should have entered into compromises about the truth. Least of all

could *they* be guilty of such improper trifling with the oracles of
God, who brought it as one of their heaviest charges against the
men of that generation, that they erred in not knowing the
Scriptures, or in making them void with their own traditions.

We hold it, therefore, to be contrary to any right views of the
mission of Christ and His apostles, to suppose, that they in such a
sense accommodated themselves to the modes of thought and contemplation around them, as to admit error into their instructions
—whether in respect to the interpretation of Scripture, or in
respect to forms of opinion and articles of belief. " This," as
Heringa has justly said in his notes to Seiler, " were consistent
neither with wisdom, nor with honesty ; it had not been suited
to the case of extraordinary ambassadors of God, furnished with
such full powers, and assisted by such Divine interposition as
they were. There is a vast difference between leaving errors
untouched, which would in time expire either of themselves, or
by deeper views of the very doctrine preached, and the confirmation of the same errors, by admitting them into their own
instructions." It is, plainly, one thing to desist from unfolding
a doctrine, because men are for the time incapable of apprehending or bearing it, and another and very different thing to
countenance them in the mistakes and delusions, in which that
incapacity has its ground. The one course, in either respect,
was compatible with inspired wisdom, the other was *not;* and
whenever explanations are given, which would involve our Lord
and His apostles in the formal admission or inculcation of what
is in itself erroneous, out of deference to existing circumstances,
we must hold it to be a *false* accommodation : since, if *knowingly*
done by them, it must have been, in the sphere of religious instruction, doing evil that good might come ; but if *without* conscience of the evil, on their part, then it must have bespoken their
participation in the errors of the time, and their consequent un-
fitness for being the infallible guides and instructors of the
world.

II. In rejecting, however, this false accommodation, because
it trenches on the *matter* of the teaching contained in the New
Testament, we say nothing against such an accommodation as
has respect to the *form* merely of the doctrines or lessons taught,

which might be perfectly admissible, and, in a sense, even necessary. In this direction there was abundant room, in *New* as well as *Old* Testament times, for a true accommodation, of which the inspired writers wisely availed themselves, and which must be duly taken into account by those who would fairly interpret their writings. The limits within which such accommodation might be practised, cannot always, perhaps, be very precisely defined ; but, in the general, it may be stated to consist in the *falling in with prevalent modes of thought or forms of conception, so as, not to lend countenance to error, but to serve for the better apprehension of the truth.* An accommodation of this sort might be employed under two kinds—one more general, the other more specific; the former grounded in characteristics of thought common to mankind at large, the latter in such as were peculiar to the age and country in which the sacred penmen lived.

(1.) To the first or more general class of accommodations are to be referred the representations given of Divine and spiritual things—things which lie beyond the region of sense, and are not directly cognisable by any faculties we possess. Such things can only be made known to us by an accommodation from the visible to the invisible, from the known to the unknown ; and though, in such cases, the form is necessarily imperfect, and conveys an inadequate idea of the reality, it still is the fittest representation of the idea, the nearest to the truth of things, which it is possible for us in present circumstances to attain to. What is said, for example, of God's anger towards sinners—or of His being revealed (through Christ) in flaming fire for the execution of judgment upon the wicked—or of the possibility of moving Heaven by prayer to depart from some purpose already formed, as if there could be passion or mutability with God—everything of this sort manifestly proceeds upon that necessity, which is inherent in our natures, of thinking and speaking of God in a human manner. It is impossible, otherwise, to gain definite ideas of His perfections and government; and the only way of guarding against the abuse of such representations, is by the employment of counter-representations, which declare God to be in Himself essentially spiritual, unchangeable, and incapable of being carried away by the feelings and impulses of finite beings.

We must, nevertheless, think of Him, and conduct ourselves towards Him, as if the human form of conceptions respecting Him conveyed the exact truth;—He *will* act toward impenitent sinners precisely as if He were moved to anger by their sins— His appearance for judgment against them *will* be as if He were encompassed with devouring fire—He *will* give effect to earnest and believing prayer, as if He could be changed by the entreaties of His people.

Essentially similar, and belonging to the same class, are the representations given of Satan and his agents. Being in themselves simply spirits, without bodily parts, the language used concerning them could not have been intelligible, unless it had taken its hue and colour from human forms and earthly relationships. So that when Satan is spoken of as falling from heaven, as being chained or set loose, as overcoming the saints or being bruised under their feet—or when the demons generally are spoken of as going into men, as driven out of them, as wandering in dry and desert places, and such like, it is open for consideration, how far in such things there is an accommodation in the form of the truth exhibited to what is cognizable by the senses. To a certain extent there *must* be an accommodation—as several of the things mentioned are, if literally understood, incompatible with the nature of incorporeal creatures, and some, if closely pressed in the literal sense, would be found inconsistent with others. Due allowance, therefore, must be made in our interpretations for the sensuous and external form of such statements —not to the extent, certainly, of explaining away the existence of those evil spirits (which were to tamper with the very substance of the representations);—but yet so as to render what is contained in them a description of the relative, rather than of the absolute state of things—of what Satan and his agents are or do in reference to human interests, and as contemplated through a human medium. Viewed thus, the whole, probably, that can be understood, for example, by Satan being cast down from heaven, is losing the place of godlike power and influence he had reached —and by the demons wandering in dry and desert places, their being bereft for a season of that malignant satisfaction, which they find in inflicting evil upon the unhappy subjects of their sway—being left, like persons in a desert, without refreshment and without a home. It is needless, at present, to pursue the subject into further details, as from what has been said the principle of interpretation may be distinctly understood.

It may be added, however, that the same kind of accommodation, which appears in the language used of essentially Divine and spiritual things, is also required in many descriptions of the still undeveloped future. For, although that future may lie within the region of sensible and earthly things, yet, if the world's affairs are then to assume an aspect essentially different from what has hitherto belonged to them, they can only be distinctly imaged to our view under the form of the present or the past. Partial, of course, and imperfect such prophetical representations of the higher things to come must always be, but they are the only ones adapted to our existing condition; and the nearest approach to the truth, the best practical conception we can form, of what is hereafter to be realised, is by the help of representations so drawn from the theatre of actual and known relations. But this opens too wide a field of thought for investigation in a general course of hermeneutical instruction; it is enough to have indicated the fundamental principle, on which the structure of prophecy is framed, and on which its interpretation should proceed.[1]

(2.) But there is another and more specific class of accommodations, which cannot thus be said to have their explanation in the necessary limitations of the human mind, in its relation to the objects and beings of a higher sphere, but which arose out of the modes of thought and expression peculiar to the age and country in which the sacred writers lived. Every age and country has certain peculiarities of this description; and as the inspired penmen were not prevented by the Spirit, but rather led thereby, to think and write in a manner agreeable to the usage of the times, such peculiarities must be taken into account, if we would fully understand the passages, where they occur, or even sometimes avoid serious misconceptions of their meaning. The peculiarities referred to are often no further remarkable, than that they are connected with what seems a singular turn of expression—some peculiarity in the mode of conception embodying

[1] For the particular investigation, see "Prophecy viewed in respect to its Distinctive Nature," etc.

itself in a corresponding peculiarity in the form of representation.
For example, both Hebrews and Greeks were in the habit of
conceiving certain states of mind or body, indicated by some verb
or adjective, as limited or particularised by a related noun in a
way not natural to *us*—they simply placed the limiting noun in
the accusative, without anything to mark the nature of the connection, while *we* invariably attach it to the verb or adjective by
a preposition. The expressions in Greek, ποδὰς ὠκὺς, κάμνειν τοὺς
ὀφθαλμοὺς, τὰς φρένας ὑγιαίνειν, θαυμαστὸς τὸ μέγεθος, and such like,
are familiar to every one acquainted with the Greek language;
and precisely similar are many phrases in Hebrew—such as
חָלָה אֶת־רַגְלָיו, he was diseased the feet of him; יְשׁוּפְךָ רֹאשׁ, he will
crush thee the head; הִכָּהוּ נֶפֶשׁ, he smites him the soul or life;
קוֹלִי אֶקְרָא, my voice I will cry. In all such cases, *we* find it
necessary to use some preposition before the noun—*with, in respect to, upon,* or such like—in order to bring out the idea we
wish to express. This arises from our conceiving the state expressed by the verb or adjective as something by itself, as having
no necessary connection with any particular object; and so,
when there is such an object to be specified, we must connect
the two by terms that will fitly indicate the connection. The
Hebrews and Greeks seem to have viewed matters more concretely;
they conceived of the state indicated as inseparably connected with
some individual person or thing, and thought it enough to name
in the loosest way the particular part or property affected. They
were satisfied with the *accusative*, as it is called, *of nearer definition*—or that which expresses the relation of the particular to the
general.

It arose partly, perhaps, from the same tendency in ancient
times to a more concrete mode of contemplation than prevails
now, that the Hebrews, and to some extent also the Greeks, express relations in a more inward manner than we do—*they* look
to the sphere or element in which a thing is, or is done; while
we, viewing the matter more *ab extra*, speak of the way or instrument by which it comes to be so. Thus they said, to drink
in a cup, while we say, to drink *from* it, or *out of* it; to walk *in*
the counsel of any one; " in murder in my bones," Ps. xlii. 10,
as if my bones were actually undergoing murder; Eccl. vii. 14,
in the day of joy be thou in joy (joyful)—הֱיֵה בְטוֹב—live in it

as thy proper element. Quite similar in the New Testament are such passages as Apoc. xiii. 10, " If any one ἐν μαχαίρᾳ ἀποκτενεῖ," literally, kills in sword—identifies himself, in a manner, with the sword, so as to make its proper action, killing, his own—" he must be killed ἐν μαχαίρᾳ :"—Rom. ii. 12, " As many as have sinned ἐν νόμῳ, shall be judged ἐν νόμῳ," the ἐν denoting the *status* of the persons spoken of, in respect to law—*in it*, as possessing the knowledge of its requirements and its penalties :—1 Cor. iv. 21, " What will ye? Shall I come to you ἐν ῥάβδῳ ἢ ἐν ἀγάπη "— *in a rod*, as if a rod led and impelled me, or love :—And to mention no more, 2 Pet. i. 5–7, we have a whole series of graces coupled with ἐν, Englished in the authorised version by *to*, " add to your faith virtue," and so on ; but more properly the ἐν points to the spiritual state of the persons addressed, as standing in the several graces mentioned ; and the exhortation given them is, that in the spirit and power of these they should go on and have themselves established in others of a like kind. For *us*, however, it is more natural to regard faith and the other graces as principles or dispositions to be possessed and exercised ; and in such a manner, that the cultivation of one should lead on to the possession and exercise of others.

These may seem somewhat minute distinctions ; and it is only in a limited sense, that we can regard the expressions noticed as accommodations : they are such, only in so far as they show a falling in, on the part of the inspired writers, with a somewhat peculiar mode of conception, belonging to their age and country —and one, with which we must acquaint ourselves, if we would catch the precise shades of thought they meant to express. But we have only to follow out the same line of reflection a little further, to find it supplying us with some very natural and important explanations. The same tendency to the concrete, as contradistinguished from the isolating and analytic spirit of modern times, discovers itself occasionally in statements and forms of expression, which, if considered from a modern point of view, must appear loose and incorrect. For example, in the genealogy of Matthew, ch. i., Joram is said to have begotten Ozias, or Uzziah, although in reality there were three intervening generations between the two. And in the Dissertation on the Genealogies of Matthew and Luke, there will both be found

many other instances noticed of the same description in Old
Testament Scripture, and the mistakes also pointed out, into
which many have been led by overlooking the practice adverted
to. Mr Layard, in his work on *Nineveh and Babylon*, p. 613,
when noticing an inscription, which seems to designate a certain
king as the son of another, though he was only a successor, not
the offspring of that other, remarks, that " the term, *son of*, appears to have been used throughout the East in those days, as it
still is, to denote connection generally, either by descent, or by
succession." It is well, that an existing practice in the East can
thus be appealed to in confirmation of a usage, that seems so
manifestly sanctioned in the genealogies ;—but it is strange, that
any students of Scripture should have been so regardless of the
terms employed in other and similar portions of its records, as to
have required any extraneous or modern proof of the usage.

It was only to advance a step farther in the same line, and
view another class of related objects in a like concrete manner,
if successive exemplifications of one great principle, or substantial
repetitions of one line of procedure, instead of being precisely
discriminated, were treated as in a manner one. The prominence
given in the mind to the common principle or homogeneous
action, appearing in the several cases, had the effect of practically
obliterating the individual differences, which separated one part
of the transactions from another, and made the differences seem
not worth noticing. In this way, Abraham and his posterity are
often identified, in regard to the principle of faith, on account of
which he was justified,—it is alike Abraham's faith, whether appearing in him personally, or in them ;—and so in regard to the
blessing connected with it—Abraham's blessing comes upon
them, and the inheritance of Canaan is indifferently spoken of as
given to him or to them. Many similar examples occur in those
Scriptures, which afford scope for the play of lively feeling or a
warm imagination—those, therefore, more particularly, in which
the facts and personages of history are worked up into the delineations of prophecy, or are considered as exponents of great
and vital principles. It is thus we would explain a statement
in the speech of Stephen before the Jewish council, which has
often been treated as a demonstrable historical error, but which
has only to be viewed as an accommodation to the mode of con-

templation now referred to, in order to its being satisfactorily explained. The statement is that in which Stephen says, " So Jacob went down into Egypt, and died, he, and our fathers, and were carried over into Sychem, and laid in the sepulchre that Abraham bought for a sum of money of the sons of Emmor, the father of Sychem" (Acts vii. 15, 16). Now, there can be no doubt, that viewing the matter critically and historically, there *are* inaccuracies in this statement; for we know from the records of Old Testament history, that Jacob's body was not laid in a sepulchre at Sychem, but in the cave of Machpelah at Hebron;— we know also that the field, which was bought of the sons of Emmor, or the children of Hamor (as they are called in Gen. xxxiii. 19), the father of Sichem, was bought, not by Abraham, but by Jacob. It would appear, therefore, that to a critical eye there are no less than two distinct blunders here—and blunders so palpable, that a mere school-boy, who had read Old Testament Scripture, might without difficulty detect them. But this very circumstance, that the incongruities are so palpable and easy of detection, must surely render it very improbable, that they could have been fallen into by a man of Stephen's penetration and discernment—to say nothing of his supernatural endowments by the Spirit. There must be some other explanation of the matter, than that which would resolve it into mere ignorance or forgetfulness of the facts of the case—the rather so, as it occurs in a speech remarkable for the insight it displays into the connection and bearing of Old Testament history. And that explanation is to be found in the principle of accommodation, considered merely as determining the form and manner of the representation. Stephen here, as in his speech generally, is not acting the part of a simple narrator of facts; he has in view throughout important principles, substantially the very same principles, which were then struggling for the victory in the cause with which he was identified; and it is only as connected with these, and serving to throw light on them, that he notices and groups together the occurrences of the past. In this part of his statement, where he is speaking of the godly fathers of the nation, he is silently contrasting *their* faith in God with the unbelief and hardness of subsequent generations, his own in particular; and the special proof of it, to which he points, is the purchase of ground from the Canaanites, at a time when it seemed little likely to the eye of sense that the land should ever be theirs, and destining their bodies to be deposited in the ground so purchased, as a pledge of the ultimate realisation of their hopes. As the faith in this respect was one, and the way in which it showed itself the same, Stephen (after the manner of his countrymen) throws all together;—he does not distinguish between what was done by Abraham, and what was done by Jacob, as if they were separate and independent acts; he looks at the matter concretely, and as Abraham originated the procedure of buying ground for a sepulchre, and Jacob merely trod in his footsteps, so the whole is identified with Abraham,—the ground at Sychem is also contemplated as his purchase, in which, according to Jewish tradition, the patriarchal heads of the nation were brought from Egypt and buried; and the distinction is in a manner lost sight of between the transactions connected with Mamre, and those with Sychem,—because one character and one bearing belonged to them in the light contemplated by Stephen.[1]

It appears, therefore, that there is a perfectly legitimate application of the principle of accommodation; and one that it may be of considerable importance rightly to understand and employ, for the proper elucidation and defence of New Testament Scripture. It is carefully to be borne in mind, however, that the accommodation has respect merely to the form and manner in which the statements are made, not to the substance of the truth therein communicated;—its whole object is to render the truth more distinctly comprehensible, or to give it greater force and prominence to the mind. And as it proceeds upon forms of thought and conception prevalent, it may be, only in the times and places where the inspired writers lived, or, at least, more markedly prevalent there than elsewhere, it must always be our first concern, to get ourselves well acquainted with the peculiarities themselves, and the state of mind out of which they originated. For thus alone can we come to perceive in what respects there was an accommodation, and know how to give due allow-

---

[1] It is much in the same way, and on substantially the same principle, that two prophecies—the utterances of quite different men—are sometimes thrown together, and treated as one. See the remarks on Matt. xxvii. 9, 10.

ance to it, without, at the same time, impairing the substance of the truth that might be couched under it.

SECTION SIXTH.

THE RESPECT DUE IN THE INTERPRETATION OF THE NEW TES-
TAMENT TO THE ANALOGY OF THE FAITH, OR FROM ONE
PART OF SCRIPTURE TO ANOTHER; AND THE FURTHER
RESPECT TO BE HAD TO THE RELIGIONS OF THE ANCIENT
WORLD, THE TRUE AND THE FALSE.

FROM what concerns the *form*, we proceed now to what rather relates to the *substance* of the sacred writings; with the view of considering whether this may not itself be subject to modifying influences—whether it is to be always taken in an absolute, and not also sometimes in a merely relative point of view.

I. Here our first line of inquiry shall be, into the relation of one part of New Testament Scripture to another—whether any respect, or, if any, what respect, should be had in our inter-pretations to what is called *the analogy* or *rule of faith.* The expression, *the analogy of faith,* is derived from Rom. xii. 6, where the subject of discourse is the exercise of spiritual minis-trations or gifts, and where, in regard to the gift of prophecy, it is said, that they who possess the gift, should employ it κατὰ τὴν ἀναλογίαν τῆς πίστεως, *according to the analogy of the faith,* as some would render it;—and when so rendered, it becomes very nearly synonymous with *according to the rule of faith.* For *analogy* in such a connection can only be understood as denoting the com-mon agreement, the standard κανών, or rule, which results from a comparison of one part of Scripture with another. And there can be no doubt, that the word ἀναλογία is sometimes so used; for it is defined, by the old lexicographer Hesychius, *measure, canon, rule.* Yet the sense, which is thus obtained, is not suitable to the connection in the passage before us, and is now generally abandoned by commentators, although it is still retained by

Hodge. When treating of persons, who do not merely pretend
to possess, but who are actually endowed with, the gift of prophecy, an exhortation to use it in accordance with the great
principles of the Christian faith seems out of place ; for it were
really no gift at all, unless it took of itself this divinely prescribed
course. The faith here meant is to be understood, not *objectively*
as a comprehensive term for the truths and doctrines of the
Christian religion, but *subjectively*, for the internal principle of
spiritual discernment and apprehension, on which the soul's recipiency in respect to prophetical gifts, and fitness for exercising
them, depends. According to the measure or proportion—such
is undoubtedly the *usual* import of ἀναλογία—of this faith, says
the apostle, let each one prophesy, who is spiritually endowed
for that work ; let him ply his function, or give forth the instructions he has to communicate, agreeably to the light and strength
enjoyed by him—not seeking to go beyond it, on the one
hand, and not falling short of it, on the other. Understood thus,
the exhortation comes to be much of the same import as that of
Paul to Timothy, to "stir up the gift that was in him"—meaning, that he should not allow the spiritual endowments conferred
on him to slumber, nor divert them to a wrong use, but should
endeavour to bring them into full and proper exercise.

Some of the early Fathers make mention of a rule of faith
(regula fidei), to which all teaching in the Church was to be
conformed, or, if contrary to it, condemned. By this was
originally meant, no specific creed or set form of words, but
merely the general principles of the faith, of which various sum-
maries are given by Irenæus, Tertullian, Origen, agreeing in
the main, but by no means altogether the same. Augustine, in
his Treatise de Doc. Christiana III. 2, expressly defines it to be
the sense or doctrine, which is gathered from the plainer parts
of Scripture. Speaking there of the difficulties which the student
of Scripture sometimes meets with in his efforts to ascertain the
meaning, he says, Consulat regulam fidei, quam de Scripturarum
planioribus locis et Ecclesiæ auctoritate percepit ; *i.e.* Let him
rule the sense of the more obscure and difficult parts of Scripture by such as are of plainer import, and the common faith held
by the orthodox Church. And should this prove insufficient,
then, he adds, let him carefully examine the connection, and en-

deavour to get light to the particular text from what goes before or follows. The expression, however, of the rule of faith came by-and-by to be understood of the creeds publicly authorised and sanctioned by the Church; and in the hands of Vincentius Lirinensis it came to assume the form of an all-embracing principle of conformity—in the famous maxim, Quod ubique, quod semper, quod ab omnibus creditum est. By thus establishing universality, antiquity, and general consent as the great criterion of truth and duty, tradition was virtually exalted above Scripture—and the maxim has hence passed as a watchword among Roman Catholic theologians, and their High Church imitators. In this sense the rule is, of course, rejected by all sound Protestant writers. Yet there is also a sense in which it has been accepted by them, and has commonly had a place assigned it in the Hermeneutics of the New Testament. Ernesti, for example, thus writes of it in his Institutes: " Analogy of doctrine or of faith, which is rarely defined with sufficient accuracy, depends not upon the system received by any sect of Christians, as unfair and ignorant men falsely assert; for in that case the rule would be variable;—nor on the mutual relation of its parts—just as legal analogy does not consist in the body of laws, nor in the mutual connection and dependence of single laws; nor grammatical analogy in the words themselves. But as grammatical analogy is the law and form of language established by usage, to which is opposed *anomaly*, that is, departure from the established usage and forms of speech; so the analogy of doctrine or faith rests upon the main points of Christian doctrine evidently declared in Scripture, and thence denominated by the Latin doctors, the Regula Fidei. To these everything is to be referred, so that no interpretation can be received, which is not consistent with them. Nor, as far as relates to matters of faith and practice, is the analogy of Scripture anything different from the analogy of doctrine."

This is a very plain and reasonable account of the matter; although one may justly say, with Dr Terrot, the translator of Ernesti, that the expression has not been happily chosen, and that it were better to say, Scripture, like all other books, ought to be interpreted consistently. When the analogy or rule of faith is mentioned as a standard or rule of interpretation, it naturally suggests something apart from Scripture—some sort of compend or exhibition of its leading principles; whereas all that is really meant, is, that one part of Scripture should not be isolated and explained without a proper regard being had to the relation in which it stands to other parts. This is a consideration, which must be taken into account generally, without respect to any peculiarity in the nature of the writings we have to deal with; but it should have place more especially in the interpretation of Scripture; for the Word of God *must* be consistent with itself, while the word of man may not. "The books of Scripture were not handed down to us by chance or accident; neither are we to regard them only as a manual of sayings and examples, or as isolated relics of antiquity, from which no perfect whole, no comprehensive and finished plan, can be educed; but as a matchless, regular account of God's dealings with man through every age of the world, from the commencement to the end of time, even to the consummation of all things. They indicate together one beautiful, harmonious, and gloriously connected system. For, though each scriptural book is in itself something entire, and though each of the inspired penmen has his own manner and style of writing, one and the self-same spirit breathes through all; one grand idea pervades all."[1]

Thus understood, the principle of which we speak is not fairly open to the objection urged against it by Dr Campbell in his 4th Prelim. Dissertation. He represents it as implying, that we have first somehow learned the scheme of truth revealed in Scripture, and that, with this previously arranged scheme in our heads, we then go to Scripture, not in order to learn the truths it contains, but in order to find something that may be made to ratify our opinions. This is, no doubt, what has too often been done; and, whenever done, ought to be strongly repudiated by all who have a proper reverence for the authority of Scripture. But in its fair and legitimate application the principle has respect only to the more doubtful or abrupt parts of the Word of God, and simply requires, that these should be brought into comparison with the other and clearer statements contained in it; so that no erroneous or partial meaning may be imposed on them, and amid various possible interpretations such an one may

[1] Life and Remains of Bengel, p. 254.

not be adopted as would place them at variance with the fundamental truths and pervading spirit of Scripture. The selection
of one or two examples will serve to exhibit more distinctly its
true nature and proper application.

In Matt. iv. 1 it is stated, respecting our Lord, that " He was
led up of the Spirit into the wilderness, to be tempted of the
devil;" while in James i. 13, the general principle is laid down,
that God tempteth no man ; and it is the plain import of what
is taught in Scripture concerning God, that being Himself infinitely wise and good, He cannot take a course with His children
which has for its object the enticing of them to sin. This general
doctrine, therefore, so frequently announced, and so necessarily
flowing from the character of God, must so far be allowed to
qualify the statement respecting the design of our Lord's being
led into the wilderness, that we dissociate from it the idea, which
we usually couple with tempting—that of an intention to draw
into evil. The leading, on the Spirit's part, into the field
of temptation, was for the purpose of victory over sin, not
of subjection to its power. In the course of that temptation,
Satan brought into remembrance a promise, contained in Ps.
xci., expressing in the strongest and most comprehensive terms
the charge, which the Lord gives to the angels over His own
people, and the certainty with which, in consequence, they shall
be kept in all their ways. But, in reply to the use made of this
promise by the tempter, for the purpose of inducing our Lord to
cast Himself down from the pinnacle of the temple, He placed,
not as an antagonistic, but as a restrictive consideration, the precept, " Thou shalt not tempt the Lord thy God "—showing that
here, as in respect generally to the promises of Scripture, the
whole is to be understood as bounded and qualified by the plain
rules of duty—nothing promised is ever meant to supersede
or disannul what has been commanded. The special promise
given to the Apostle Peter, in Matt. xvi. 18, as to his being the
Rock on which Christ should build His Church, is to be dealt
with in a similar manner ;—instead of being isolated, as is done
by Romanists, and the meaning of its terms pressed to the utter-
most, as if the subject of promise stood in no sort of connection
with any other passages of Scripture, it ought to be viewed in
connection with similar promises and statements made concern-

ing the other apostles, according to which they were all to be, in an instrumental sense, foundation-stones and pillars (Matt. xix. 29 ; Gal. ii. 9 ; Eph. ii. 20; Rev. xxi. 14) ; and also with what Peter himself wrote in the latter period of his earthly labours, in which, for himself, and for all others, he denounces that spiritual lordship, which, on the ground of the original promise, has been attributed to him (1 Pet. v. 1–4), and gives to Christ the whole and undivided glory of procuring and distributing the blessings of salvation (ch. i. 2, 3, ii. 3–6, etc.)   Take one example more : In Prov. xxv. 21, 22, and again in Rom. xii. 20, kindness instead of revenge is enjoined toward an enemy—giving him food when he is hungry, when thirsty giving him water to drink—by the consideration, "for in so doing thou shalt heap coals of fire upon his head."   Now this, if taken simply by itself, is capable of a twofold meaning : it may mean, either thou shalt by these acts of kindness sorely aggravate the guilt and the doom of thine adversary,—or, thou wilt altogether destroy in him that which makes him an adversary—thy kindness, in recompense for his malice, will consume the spirit of evil that works in him, and win him to the position of a friend.   If the clause were entirely isolated, either of these explanations might be adopted.   But, surely, when we consider the whole tenor of the Gospel of Christ—when we think even of what goes immediately before, of the benignant spirit and the active charities, which it is the object of the apostle to enforce, it is scarcely possible to doubt which of the two should be preferred.   Could the apostle, as a sequel to such exhortations, and when seeking to have the disciples penetrated by a full sense of the mercies of God, have meant to ply them with the diabolical motive of deepening the guilt of an adversary, and rendering his doom more intolerable ? No—we instinctively feel this could not possibly be ; what he intended, must have been the practising upon him of that noble and generous revenge, which should convert him from being an enemy into a friend.

These illustrations may suffice to show, in what manner, and within what limits, the principle of analogy, or, as it had better be called, the principle of consistency, in the interpretation of Scripture may be applied.   It undoubtedly requires to be used with caution, and in a spirit of fairness and candour—if it is to be turned to any valuable account, or even not abused to the support of dangerous error. The faith, according to which the sense of particular passages is determined, must be that which rests upon the broad import of some of the most explicit announce- ments of Scripture, about the meaning of which there can be, with unbiassed minds, no reasonable doubt. And in so far as we must decide between one passage and another, those passages should always be allowed greatest weight in fixing the general principles of the faith, in which the subjects belonging to it are not incidentally noticed merely, but formally treated of and dis- cussed; for, in such cases, we can have no doubt that the point on which we seek for an authoritative deliverance was distinctly in the eye of the writer.

2. The principle of interpretation now considered has respect to the relation that one part of New Testament Scripture bears to another—the more difficult and obscure to the plainer and more explicit. But there is another relation also that must be taken into account—the relation in which the writings of the New Testament stand to those of the Old. It is scarcely pos- sible to throw this into a specific principle of interpretation; at least not further than that it must be remembered, we have in the New Testament a higher, but very closely related, exhibition of truth and duty; and consequently must have respect alike to the agreements and the differences subsisting between them. This relation, of necessity, exercised a very marked and import- ant influence upon the writings of the New Testament—upon its writings, both in respect to ideas, and the forms of expression in which the ideas are clothed. It is, of course, necessary, in the first instance, that a correct apprehension be formed of the rela- tion as regards the ideas involved in it, the ideas common to both dispensations; for the knowledge of the ideas bears on the foundation, and touches the ground and nature of every particu- lar view that may be exhibited. This, however, is too wide a field to be entered on particularly here. If considered fully, it would require a discussion of the nature and principles of the typical connection between the law and the Gospel, and lead to investigations fully as much connected with the dogmatical as with the exegetical departments of theology. So far, however, the relation must be understood, that it has to do as well with

the *agreements* as with the *differences* between the affairs of the Old and those of the New Covenants. Indeed, if any distinction were to be made between the two, we should say, that the *agreements* ought more especially to be regarded, because they lie deeper, and concern the more essential elements in the two dispensations ; while the *differences* are of a more circumstantial and formal nature. From the position of matters at the commencement of the New dispensation, more particularly from the determination on the part of many to exalt to an undue place the temporary and shadowy things, in which the Old dispensation differed from the new, it became necessary for the inspired writers of the New Testament to bring out with peculiar prominence the *differences ;* with the view of manifesting the superior and more perfect nature of the work and economy of Christ. But they scarcely ever do this, without, at the same time, pointing to the essential agreements pervading both economies.

Now, it is in accordance with this twofold nature of the relation which subsists between the Old and the New in God's dispensations, that the language of New Testament Scripture, in so far as it bears respect to the Old, is constructed, and ought to be interpreted. In the great majority of cases, the precise nature of the reference is manifest ; we can see at a glance whether it is the agreements or the differences that are in view. For example, when our Lord is described by the Baptist as " the Lamb of God, who takes away the sins of the world ;" or when the Apostle Paul says, " Christ our Passover is sacrificed for us," the simplest reader will perceive, that there is an agreement or correspondence indicated between the sacrifices of the Old Testament and the one great sacrifice of the New—that what the lamb of atonement, especially the paschal lamb, was to the Israelite, as regards his interest in the blessings of the Old Covenant, *that* Christ now is to believers, in respect to the greater things of His redemption. No one can doubt, that like is compared to like ; although, from the nature of the objects brought into comparison, differences of an important kind were necessarily implied. But, in explaining the passages, we would naturally lay stress upon the resemblances between Christ and the Old Testament things referred to, and would only notice subordinately the points which distinguished the one from the other. In like manner, when, in Col. ii. 11, the apostle calls baptism "the circumcision of Christ," and, in Phil. iii. 3, describes believers as "the circumcision which worship God in spirit," the meaning obviously is, that the essential design of circumcision, its real spirit and object, are attained in those who, as baptized believers, have entered into fellowship with Christ. So that it is the *correspondences*, which must again, in such passages, be brought out; it is these which must be rendered prominent; however, also, occasion may be taken to indicate the points, in which the new surpasses the old circumcision.

Again, there is another class of passages in which, with equal plainness, our attention is drawn to the *differences* subsisting between the New and the Old :—as when, in Heb. viii. 2, Christ is called "a minister of the true tabernacle, which the Lord pitched, and not man;" and, in ch. x. 20, where believers are said to enter the holiest of this higher tabernacle "by a new and living way"—in such passages, while the language bears distinct allusion to the things of the Old Covenant—expresses the New, indeed, under the form and aspect of the Old, yet it is for the purpose of showing the vast superiority of the New. So that, in such cases, it is the *differences* we are naturally led to think of—these now become the prominent things, and the resemblances fall into the background.

But there are other passages, in which it is less easy to decide —passages, in which Old Testament language is employed, without any clear indication being given, whether the resemblances or the differences are more particularly referred to. For example, in Heb. x. 22, the apostle exhorts us to make a fiducial approach to the throne of grace, as persons "having their hearts sprinkled from an evil conscience, and their bodies washed with pure water." Now, what is here meant by our bodies being washed? Corporeal ablutions held an important place under the Old economy; and continually, as the priests entered the sanctuary, they had to wash their hands and their feet at the brazen laver, which stood in the outer court. But what corresponds to this in Christian times? We have no external sanctuary, like that which existed in the Jewish commonwealth, and consequently no corporeal ablution to perform, when drawing near to engage in the worship of God. When, therefore, the

apostle speaks of having the body washed with pure water, he
must mean, not formally the same thing as of old, but something
corresponding to it in nature—bearing the same relation to a
Christian, that the other did to a ceremonial worship.   And this
is not far to seek; it is simply a freedom from all manifest stains
and blemishes in the conduct.   It was precisely these stains and
blemishes, which were imaged by outward defilements on the
body of one entering into the material sanctuary :—his washing
of these off was a symbol of the separation, which then also had
to be maintained by sincere and accepted worshippers, from all
overt acts of iniquity.   And now that the symbol has dropt, as
no longer needed—now that the reality alone remains, it is of
this reality that the language should be understood ;—we are to
regard the apostle as intimating, that along with a purged conscience, we must also have a blameless and untarnished life —
and then, with the two together, we may draw near with confidence to God.

It is, therefore, to the *resemblances* that this expression also
points.   In explaining its import, we should endeavour chiefly to
bring out the correspondence, that subsisted between the ritual
service of the Old, and the spiritual worship of the New economy.
This, obviously, cannot be done by exhibiting merely the ritual,
on the one side, and the spiritual, on the other ; for that would be
to present a contrast rather than a resemblance.   We must
penetrate into the symbolical import of the ritual, and show, that
in the outward action, in which it consisted, there lay concealed
a spiritual element, for the sake of which it was required and
done.   So that it is not properly a contrast, to be put after this
manner : Such an *outward* thing then, and such another inward
now, or fleshly then, and spiritual now ; but a similarity with a
difference :—A *similarity*, since under both covenants alike freedom from open impurities is required of God's acceptable worshippers—there must be clean hands, or a blameless life, as well
as a pure heart; and yet a *difference*, since from the clearer
revelation now made of all things spiritual and divine, and
the abolition of the worldly sanctuary, the symbolical action has
gone into desuetude, and the naked reality is alone brought into
view.

Let us still look at another example, and we shall thus more readily perceive the justness of the rule, which we are seeking to deduce for guiding our interpretations in respect to such portions of New Testament Scripture. In Rom. xii. 1, we have this exhortation given by the apostle, "I beseech you, by the mercies of God, that ye present your bodies a living sacrifice—more exactly, a sacrifice, living,—holy, acceptable to God, which is your reasonable service." There is evidently a reference in the language to the ancient sacrificial worship ; and, in particular, to the service of the whole burnt-offering, in which at certain times an entire animal was presented upon the altar to God. The only question is, what is the nature of the reference? Is it by way of resemblance, or by way of contrast? If the apostle had stopt at θυσίαν—if he had said merely, " present your bodies a sacrifice," the matter would have been quite plain; it would have been manifest, that the resemblance only was indicated. But he adds a series of epithets, characterizing the nature of the service, which Christians are called to render ; and these are usually regarded by commentators as expressing the kind of service, not *positively* merely, as to what it is in itself, but *negatively* also, as to what it is not, viewed in reference to the ancient ritual of Judaism. The λογικὴν λατρείαν, the reasonable service, at the close, is in particular held to indicate this idea,—as in the following comment of Haldane : " This evidently refers to the distinction between the service of the Jews by sacrifices and ceremonial worship, and the service of Christians. Sacrificial worship, and in general the whole ceremonial ritual of the Jews, were not worship according to reason. It is, indeed, reasonable to worship God in whatever way He prescribes ; but had not man fallen, he would not have been required to worship by such ceremonies as the Jewish law enjoined. Sacrificial worship is not in itself rational ; and was appointed by God, not for its own excellence, but from its adaptation to prefigure the good things to come." He adds, and certainly not without reason, that many commentators hesitated about adopting this explanation of the λογικὴν, under the impression, that it was disrespectful to the Divine appointments to have them represented as not rational. But might we not, on the same ground that is assigned here for the non-rational character of the Old Testament worship, also deny rationality to the New? For it, too, proceeds on a basis

H

different from the natural and proper one; it is offered on the foundation of what has been done by another in our stead, while the original and strictly proper idea of sacrifice is that of a *personal* surrender and dedication to God.

We may feel the rather inclined to doubt the correctness of this mode of explanation, at least in the strongly antithetic form expressed above, when we look to the other epithets applied by the apostle to the sacrifice of Christians—living, holy, acceptable. *Living*, we are told, stands opposed to the dead sacrifices presented under the law, slain victims; but what, then, shall be put in contradistinction to the *holy* and *acceptable*? Were these epithets not applicable to the burnt-offerings of the Old Testament? On the contrary, they are precisely the epithets that are most commonly applied to them. The flesh of the sacrifices generally, as of everything laid upon the altar, was declared to be holy—in token of which the victims were required to be without any external blemish; while of every sacrifice offered according to the law the set phrase is, that it was an offering of sweet savour—in other words, acceptable to God. These two expressions, then, beyond a doubt, indicate a *resemblance;* and it would surely be somewhat strange—a confusion in the use of language we should not have expected in the apostle—if the one going immediately before them, and the other coming immediately after them, should have pointed to a *formal contrast.* Such a throwing together of agreements and differences in one continuous description, is in the highest degree improbable.

A good deal of this confusion imputed to the statement of the apostle, arises from the inadequate notions that prevail respecting the Old Testament sacrificial worship—as if the outward actions had formed the one and all of this, and there were no outgoings of spiritual desire and affection on the part of the worshipper accompanying them. According to the true idea, the outward service was merely the symbolical expression of what was thought and felt, done or purposed to be done, by the person who performed it. The sacrifice was in the closest manner identified with the sacrificer. Thus, in the case of the burnt-offering, which is here more particularly referred to, the occasion of presenting it usually was, when an individual had experienced some great mercy, or felt upon his soul a special call to devoted gratitude and love; and his feelings in this respect were embodied in the offering—he expressed thereby his personal surrender to God, and the dedication of all he had to the Divine service and glory. Without this grateful feeling and purpose of devotedness on the part of the offerer, the offering would have been simply a piece of hypocrisy—a sign without anything signified thereby. The proper connection between the external and the internal was beautifully brought out by David in the fifty-first Psalm, when, after having expressed his deep contrition for past sin, and renewed the dedication of himself to God, he prays for fresh tokens of the Lord's favour, that, as the natural result of what was to be imparted on the one hand, and felt on the other, the Lord might receive and be pleased with sacrifices of righteousness, with the whole burnt-offerings that should be laid upon His altar. In offerings so drawn forth, and so presented, would there be no life? Could the service with any propriety be designated as a dead one? Assuredly not; the soul of the offerer was itself on fire with love and gratitude to God, and a spirit of life animated its movements, not the less that it had to express itself by means of slain victims laid and consumed upon the altar.

We entertain no doubt, therefore, that here also the direct and prominent thing in the apostle's description is a *resemblance,* and not a *contrast.* His object is, to show how those, who are partakers of the rich grace and mercy of God under the Gospel, may and should exhibit a substantial agreement with the service of the burnt-offering, which was wont to be rendered by such as had received peculiar tokens of the Lord's goodness. They should present to God their bodies—*i. e.* the active powers and energies of their nature (for it is through the body that these come into operation)—present these as a sacrifice, living, holy, acceptable—a real dedication, instinct with life and purity, and on that account well-pleasing to God. On the same account also a λογίκη λατρεία, a reasonable service—not, however, in the sense of *rational,* as opposed to a former *ir*-rational service; but in the sense of *spiritual*—a reasonable or spiritual service, in which the soul and conscience are exercised, and hence opposed to what is simply σωματική, corporeal or outward. In no part of the description is there properly a contrast marked between the Christian and the Jewish service; for, in the Jewish also, when rightly performed, there were the same spiritual elements, as in the Christian : there, too, the soul and conscience were engaged; the service was one of life and holiness, on the part of the worshipper, and on the part of God crowned with acceptance. Still, no doubt, a difference is implied, though not distinctly and formally expressed; —it is implied in the very prominence which is given to the spiritual elements of the service required, presented apart from any external accompaniments or outward rites. For there being so much of what was outward in the Old Testament service, it naturally tended to take off the mind to some extent from the more inward and vital part; the mind *could*, and doubtless too often *did*, view the sacrifice as something apart from itself—a thing done *for* one, rather than *by* him and *with* him :—While now, the temptation to a lifeless externality is in great measure removed, the service is of a strictly personal and spiritual nature, springing from the soul's proper consciousness of grace and bless- ing, and appearing in the willing obedience of the members of the body, as instruments of righteousness unto God.

Now, from these examples and illustrations there is plainly deducible a twofold rule of interpretation in regard to those por- tions of the New Testament, which represent spiritual things in language derived from the relations and ritual of the Old. The rule is, that in those passages, which distinctly and formally ex- hibit the *difference between New and Old Testament things, it is this difference, which ought to be rendered prominent in our ex- planation*, yet not without also pointing attention to the funda- mental agreement, which lies underneath the superficial diversity; —while, on the other hand, in those passages, which simply pre- sent Christian things *under the form and aspect of those, that be- longed to the Old Covenant, it is the correspondence or agreement that should be mainly dwelt upon*. The Old should, in that case, be ex- hibited as a lively image or palpable representation of the New— though a representation in an inferior line of things, and with com- paratively inadequate results. In the former case, our object should be to unfold a marked and obvious difference with an under- lying substantial agreement ; in the other, to unfold a substantial agreement, though accompanied with formal and ostensible differ- ences—such as necessarily pervaded the relations of an inferior and preparatory, to an ultimate and permanent state of things.

3. If now we pass, for a moment, from the one true, to the many false religions of the ancient world, from Judaism to the endless forms of heathenism, we have to mark in Christianity toward them a relation of an essentially different kind—one simply of an antagonistic nature. The heathen religions of antiquity, therefore, had no direct or positive influence in moulding the language of the New Testament, and imparting peculiar shades of meaning to its expressions. Yet the subject is not to be passed altogether unnoticed. For, though the respect had to heathen modes of thought and forms of expression is chiefly of a negative kind, yet even that is instructive; since it shows in what a different region the Christian religion moved, and what different elements it embraced from those, out of which heathenism was constructed. Amid the freedom, with which Christianity proceeded to diffuse itself in the world, and its adaptation to the modes of thought and forms of expression in current use, it still manifested a careful reserve in respect to all that savoured of heathenism; it abstained from the use of such terms as had become associated with the false worship, or impregnated with the false notions, of the pagan world.

For example, in so far as the language of the New Testament bears respect to sacrificial usages, it borrows the terms it employs from the Old Testament, or makes use only of such as are common to the Septuagint and the writings of Hellenic authors. It refrains from employing such expressions as, though of similar import, had been linked to usages, which rendered them suggestive of the pollutions of idolatry. Of this description are περικάθαρμα and περίψημα, which both bear, in the old lexicographers, the signification of ransom or sacrifice—the equivalents given are ἀντίλυτρον, ἀντίψυχον. The Septuagint also, at Prov. xxi. 18, has περικάθαρμα δικαίου ἄνομος, the wicked is a ransom for the righteous. But as the words acquired this sense from the horrid custom of sacrificing criminals and worthless persons to make expiation for the state in times of public calamity, they are never used in the New Testament with reference to religious worship. That custom prevailed especially at Athens, where persons of a worthless caste were regularly kept against the occurrence of any plague or public calamity, and then thrown into the sea, in the belief that they should wipe off the guilt of the nation. Such persons were called καθάρματα, περιψήματα, and other epithets of a like import. The terms are used only once in the New Testament: it is by the Apostle Paul, when speaking, in 1 Cor. iv. 13, of the indignities he had received; but it is in the original sense of sweepings, offscourings, or filth, the vilest portions of society.

The common term for the altars on which the heathens offered their victims, might have been thought less objectionable for Christian uses. This term is βωμός; yet it occurs only once in the whole of the New Testament; and on that solitary occasion it is employed, not of a Jewish altar, or anything corresponding to it in Christian times, but of the heathen altar, with its inscription to the Unknown God, which Paul found at Athens. The term uniformly employed in the New Testament, whether in a literal or a figurative sense, is θυσιαστήριον:—an evidence of the care with which the sacred writers sought to keep the true religion at a distance from all contact, even in name, with idolatry.

In the use also of δαίμων, and its compounds, we see a similar instance of the wisdom and the propriety with which the speech of the sacred writers was guided. The word had become thoroughly inwoven with the ideas and the worship of heathendom; and as the evil, as well as the good—bad, and malignant, not less than gracious and benign divinities, were embraced in the religions of Polytheism, so the word δαίμων extended equally to both. It was in that respect a word of indifferent meaning. The whole religion of the Greeks and the Romans might be called, and, indeed, was familiarly called, demon-worship, δεισιδαιμονία. It could not, therefore, be counted a reproach, it might rather be esteemed an honour for any one to be spoken of as δεισιδαιμονέστερος; it simply marked him out as peculiarly given to the worship of the gods. And when Paul, in the Areopagus, applied that epithet, at the commencement of his speech, to the men of Athens, inferring their title to it from what he had observed of their altars, there can be no doubt that he meant to indicate nothing that should prove offensive to them. He merely intended to express the fact, that they were, in their own sense of the matter, a very religious people. And it is certainly a somewhat unhappy turn that is given to this, the opening part of the apostle's address, in the authorised version, when he is made to say, that he perceived " they were in all things too superstitious." Had such been the native import of his language, the apostle would have been guilty of the misdemeanour of creating a prejudice against himself at the outset—a fault, we may be sure, he did not commit at *any* time, and least of all in that which is, artistically considered, the most perfect of all his recorded discourses. There is another instance of a like use of the word—though in this case *really* misapplied—in Acts xxv. 19, where Festus says of the case of Paul to Agrippa, that it touched upon questions περὶ τῆς ἰδίας δεισιδαιμονίας; it should have been rendered, " concerning their own *religion*," to give the fair impression of what Festus actually meant; since, speaking as Festus did to Agrippa, a professed Jew, he never could have intended to stigmatise the worship which was paid by the king and his countrymen as a superstition, in *our* sense of the term. It was, however, a wrong term to apply to the religion of a Jew, and in making use of it Festus spoke from a merely heathen point of view. The Jewish religion was a θεοσεβεία, a reverential fear and worship of God, but not a δεισιδαιμονία, a religious homage to the divinities. In the Jewish sense, demon-worship was devil-worship—abominable idolatry. And hence δαιμονία was the common term employed to designate the malignant powers, that so often held possession of the souls and bodies of men at the Gospel era. Hence also the term εὐδαιμονία, which so frequently occurs in heathen authors to express human happiness and prosperity, is never—because it indicates prosperity as the gift of the divinities—similarly employed in the New Testament. Not even once is it used there to express, in any way, the blessedness enjoyed by God's people.

These examples may suffice, as the subject they are brought forward to illustrate is rather negative in its bearing on the interpretation of Scripture, than of a positive description. They are signs, impressed upon the language of the New Testament, that the religion of the Gospel has no proper affinity to that of heathenism, and convey a silent protest against all pollutions of idolatry.

SECTION SEVENTH.

THE RELATION OF THE OLD TO THE NEW IN GOD'S DISPENSA-
TIONS MORE EXACTLY DEFINED, WITH THE VIEW OF PRE-
VENTING MISTAKEN OR PARTIAL INTERPRETATIONS OF SUCH
PORTIONS OF NEW TESTAMENT SCRIPTURE AS BEAR ON IT.

To lay more securely the ground of some of the directions given
in the preceding section, and to provide, so far as can be done
within a small compass, a clue to the right path in the treatment
of those passages, which bear upon the mutual relations between
Christianity and Judaism, it seems advisable, before entering on
a fresh topic, to devote a little space to the further consideration
of these relations.   We do this more especially for the purpose
of guarding against a twofold error, which is constantly reap-
pearing, in the one or the other of its aspects, with those who have
not attained to accurate views of the connection between the
Old and the New in God's dispensations :—the error of either
ascribing too much of the carnal element to Judaism, or of imposing too much of the Judaistic on Christianity.   These are
the two opposite extremes, into which certain diverse tendencies
in Christianity are ever apt to run.   They both began at an early
period to develop themselves.   The Judaizing tendency naturally
appeared first, as it was out of Judaism that Christianity sprung;
and in making the transition from the one to the other, many
found it difficult to realise the extent of the change which the
work of Christ had introduced—they clung to what was temporary in the Old, even after it had been supplanted by something
higher and better; like persons, according to the similitude of
our Lord, who have been accustomed to old wine, and cannot
straightway relish new—although in this case the new *was* the
better.   It was providential, that this Judaizing tendency did appear so early—at Jerusalem, at Antioch, in the churches of
Galatia, and elsewhere—as it obliged the apostles at the very
first to meet it.   In various parts of the New Testament, we
have their formal deliverance on the subject, and their condemnation of the error which it involved.   The Epistles to the

Galatians, to the Colossians, and to the Hebrews are, in this point of view, especially important; as they show conclusively, that the external forms of the ancient worship, its visible temple, Aaronic priesthood, fleshly sacrifices, stated festivals, and corporeal ablutions, were no longer binding on the conscience, and naturally led, if perpetuated, to carnalize the Gospel. It might have been thought, that these apostolic efforts and explicit deliverances would have been sufficient to check the evil, and prevent its recurrence in the Christian Church. But this was far from being the case. With some non-essential modifications, the old error reappeared, bringing in a train of forms and ceremonies, purgations and sacrifices, feasts and solemnities, which differed only in name from those of the Old Economy; and a Christian priesthood established itself as an essential part of the Church's constitution, of which the most characteristic feature was, that it should be able to trace up by successive links to Christ its hereditary power and authority, precisely as the ancient priesthood had to show their genealogical descent from the loins of Aaron. And the result has been, that, notwithstanding the strong and repeated protest lodged in New Testament Scripture against such institutions and practices, as at variance with the genius of the Gospel, in what once formed nearly the whole, and what still forms the largest part of Christendom, sacred times and seasons, altars and sacrifices, external purifications and an official priesthood, have their recognised place now, much as in ancient Israel. To such a mournful extent has Christianity been Judaized.

Exactly the opposite tendency, however, began also in early times to discover itself, and still continues to do so, though it has not proved nearly so powerful or so general as the other. The Gnostic spirit, which was just beginning to make its appearance in the Christian Church at the close of the apostolic period, was the first representative of this extreme. In its self-elated and ethereal flights, Gnosticism sought to soar above Christianity— to become spiritual above *its* spirituality; and to raise at least the loftier and more contemplative believers of the Gospel into a kind of Divine-like superiority to everything outward and material. In this vain attempt, however, it only corrupted Christianity, by disparaging or denying the great historical facts on which it is based, and entering into profitless speculations respecting heavenly things. Along with this tendency, and as a kind of natural corollary to it, it sought to break the chain between Christianity and Judaism—holding the former to be indeed of God, but not so the latter, on account of the fleshly ordinances and material accompaniments with which it was connected; it was, therefore, assigned to the agency of an evil, or, at least, inferior spirit. In this anti-scriptural form, Gnosticism was, of course, repelled by the Church; its special views and conclusions were universally reprobated by believers. But the *spirit* of Gnosticism crept in through many avenues into the Church; and in the case of some of the fathers—more especially Clement of Alexandria and Origen—it led them to draw too broadly the distinction between Christianity and Judaism, and to seek the instruction couched in the ordinances of the Old Testament, not in their immediate design or symbolical import, but in an allegorical interpretation of an entirely fanciful and arbitrary nature. The natural inference from their mode of treating the Old Testament ritual and worship was, that, considered by itself, in its obvious and historical reality, it was too carnal to have much in common with Christianity. *Now*, of course, the relations of those times no longer exist; the leaven, which then wrought with insidious and corrupting influence, can scarcely be said to work after the same fashion that it did then. And yet there have been, and there still are, certain sections of the Christian Church, and particular individuals in almost every section, in whom the tendency to over-spiritualize (if we may so express it) in Christianity, and, as a natural consequence, to carnalize in Judaism, does not fail in some way to manifest itself.

Writers belonging to the Baptist communion are under some temptation to give way to this tendency, and not unfrequently do so. Take as an example the following passage, in a commentary, by a late respectable member of that body: " Israel was a stiff-necked and rebellious people; their law was written on tables of stone, and enforced by temporal sanctions; he that despised Moses' law died without mercy. But all Christ's disciples are taught of God; they are the circumcision of Christ; they worship God in the Spirit; His law is written on the fleshly tables of the heart."[1] If there is any propriety in this contrast, it must be, that Israel, as such, were a carnal and ungodly people, yet were not the less entitled to God's ordinances, nay, these ordinances were just for such a people; whereas the Church of the New Testament, as well in respect to its people as its ordinances, is strictly spiritual and holy. The conclusion, therefore, in regard to the Israelites, as the author distinctly states (p. 193), is, that their privileges were all carnal, that the relation in which they stood to God was carnal, and all properly growing out of it fleshly and temporal; and that the covenant, under which they were placed, had attained its object, if only it preserved a worshipping people visibly separated from the idolatrous Gentiles. In like manner, another writer, belonging to the same communion,[2] says of circumcision (and, of course, he might equally have said it of any other Jewish ordinance), that it was " quite irrespective of personal character, conduct, or faith," that the covenant of which it was the sign " included solely temporal blessings ;" and that " the rite was instituted to distinguish the Jews from the other nations, and to show their title to the land of Canaan :"—all simply outward and carnal. Another writer still—and one belonging to an entirely different school, a minister of the Church of England—in a late work, gives forth substantially the same views respecting the people and ordinances of Israel; does so, too, in the most assured tone, as if there could be no reasonable doubt upon the subject—as if, in announcing it, he was entitled to demand the assent of the whole Christian world: " The Old Covenant (he says) had nothing whatever to do with eternal life, except by way of type or suggestion; it had nothing whatever to do with any, except with the nation of Israel; and nothing whatever with any mere individual in that nation. It was made with the nation collectively (as if the collective nation did not consist of an aggregate of individuals !), and was entirely temporal. God promised to give the land of Canaan to the nation of Israel; but only so long as the nation collectively acknowledged Jehovah as the one God."[3] And, further, as regards the nature of the holiness aimed at by the

[1] Haldane on the Epistle to the Galatians, pp. 113, 193.
[2] Dr Cox, as quoted by Dr Wardlaw on Baptism, pp. 55, 60.
[3] Johnstone's Israel after the Flesh, p. 7.

covenant, he says, that " it was quite irrespective of individual
righteousness. Notwithstanding any sins, short of the national
infraction of the covenant, Israel was still the holy nation."
And he adds, " This very manifest sense of the Old Covenant
holiness is constantly lost sight of, and errors of the most dis-
tructive kind are caused."[1]

Quotations of a similar kind might be furnished in great profusion,
but those given may suffice. They abundantly show what crude
and ill-digested notions prevail still among persons, otherwise well-
informed, and holding evangelical views, respecting the nature
of the Old Economy, and the real position of God's people under
it. On the hypothesis of such views, there are some queries that
naturally suggest themselves to one's mind, and to which it seems
impossible to produce a satisfactory answer. Circumcision, and
the other ordinances of the Old Testament, were (it is alleged)
altogether carnal, and irrespective of personal holiness—how,
then, could Israel in the wilderness, when simply standing under
a covenant with such ordinances, have been reproved and
punished for murmuring against God, and want of faith in God's
promises—spiritual acts—acts committed by the people, while
they still collectively acknowledged God—and both acts and
punishments so personal, that the two individuals (Joshua and
Caleb) who stood aloof from the rest in sin, were also excepted
from them in judgment? How could it be reconciled with the
notion of a God essentially holy and spiritual, to have imposed
such merely carnal services upon His people, with promises of
blessing if performed, and threatenings of evil if neglected and
despised? How could He have represented it as the end He
had in view in establishing such a covenant, that He might have
a godly seed? (Isa. vi. 13; Mal. ii. 15.) How could there
come to exist in the midst of Israel such a seed at all—a seed
possessing the elements of real holiness? Whence could its members have their being? How were they born? Was it altogether apart from the ordinances? In that case, must not their
existence have been an anomaly, a miracle accomplished by
Divine power without the intervention of appropriate means?
And the more pious individuals of that seed, such as David, and
those who acted with him, how could they possibly long for, and

[1] Johnstone's Israel after the Flesh, p. 87.

rejoice in waiting upon, ordinances which were wholly carnal, and without any adaptation to a spiritual taste? To such questions no satisfactory answer can be returned, on the supposition of the Old Testament ordinances being what those persons would represent. We know of no way by which a spiritual seed can be expected, in *any* age, to come into existence, and find life to their souls, otherwise than through the ordinances which God is pleased to appoint ; and how God could either appoint ordinances altogether carnal, or how, if appointed, spiritual life and nourishment could be derived from them, is a mystery that seems inexplicable on any grounds of reason or of Scripture.

Without going very minutely into the subject, there are a few leading principles that may be laid down upon it, sufficient, if clearly understood, and kept properly in view, to guard us against any material error on either side.

1. It must be held, in the first place, as a fundamental principle, that whatever difference may exist between Judaism and Christianity, as to their respective services and forms of administration, there still must have been an essential agreement between them at bottom—an essential oneness in their pervading character and spirit. We say, *must* have been so ; there was a Divine necessity in the case, grounded in the nature of Him who is the Author of both covenants, and who makes Himself known as "Jehovah that changes not." Unchangeable in His own nature, He must be such also in the principles of His government among men, not less than in the personal attributes of His being. The adversaries of the faith in every age have well understood this ; and hence, from the Manicheans of early times to the infidels and rationalistic writers of the present day, they have ever sought to overthrow the foundations of Divine truth by playing off one part of Scripture against another— exposing what they deemed the contrarieties between things established in the Old, and things taught in the New Testament ; or, through alleged defects and immoralities in the one, aiming a blow at the authority of the other. Had they succeeded in such attempts, their object had been gained ; since Scripture could no longer be vindicated as the actual product and authoritative revelation of an unchangeable God.

It is true, as indeed appears on a moment's inspection, that

the religion of the Old Testament addressed itself more immediately to the outward man, while that of the New addresses itself
more to the inward.   In ancient times, the business of religion
—if we may so speak—was transacted under the form and aspect
of what pertained to visible and earthly relations : its rites and
services had respect primarily to a worldly sanctuary, an earthly
inheritance and a present life—in these exhibiting the shadow
or sensible image of what relates to the concerns of an unseen
world, and an eternal existence.   They *did*, however, present
such a shadow of higher realities ; and did it, not as an incidental and subsidiary, but as an essential part of their design ; and
not for some merely, but for all the worshippers.   Through the
external and corporeal, God continually spake to them of the
internal and spiritual.   Under the outward shell, and along with
it, He conveyed to as many as would receive it, the kernel of
Divine truth and holiness ;—so that the same description, as to
its substance, will serve at once for the true Israelite and for the
genuine Christian.   As in that given by the Apostle Paul, " He
is a Jew who is one inwardly, and circumcision is that of the
heart, in the spirit and not in the letter ; whose praise is not of
men (the mere outside observer), but of God (who looks directly
upon the heart)."
     We find the truth in this respect distinctly apprehended by
Augustine, and correctly expressed in the writings he composed
against the Manicheans and other errorists of his day.   Referring,
in his work against Faustus (Lib. xii. 3), to what the apostle
says, in Rom. iii. and ix., of the advantage possessed by the Jews
in having had God's oracles and covenants, he asks, " Why did
he say that the covenants belonged to them, had it not been that
the Old Covenant was given to them, and that the New was
imaged in the Old ?   These men, in their senseless folly, are in
the habit of denouncing the legal institution, which was given to
the Israelites, not understanding its dispensation, and because
God has thought good now to place us, not under law but under
grace.   Let them, therefore, give way to the authority of the
apostle, who, in lauding the condition of the Israelites, mentions
it among their advantages, that to them had belonged the giving
of the law, which could not have been matter of praise, if it had
been in itself bad."   And again, in another work, written against

one who had published a treatise containing many things of an
offensive nature against the law and the prophets, he shows
the pervading and essential agreement of these with the Gospel,
even in those things, in which this adversary had sought to represent them as utterly opposed to each other.   In regard, for
example, to the punishment of sin, he both mentions what precepts
and examples there were under the Old Testament of a forgiving
spirit, and places alongside the temporal inflictions of the one the
eternal retributions of the other, thereby making it manifest that
" in each Testament alike (as he says) there was at once a goodness to be loved, and a severity to be dreaded."   Then, referring
to the inferior nature of the Old Testament dispensation, on
account of its having had so much to do with outward and
temporal things, he says, " Nevertheless, in those times also there
were spiritual and righteous persons, whom the letter of command did not kill, but the aid-giving Spirit quickened.   Whence
both the faith of a coming Saviour dwelt in the prophets, who
announced beforehand that He should come ; and now, there are
many carnal persons who either give rise to heresies by not
understanding the Scriptures, or in the Catholic Church itself
are like babes that can only be fed with milk, or, still worse, are
preparing like chaff to be burned in the fire.   But as God is the
sole and true Creator of both temporal and eternal goods, so is
He also the Author of both Testaments; because the New is as
well figured in the Old, as the Old is revealed in the New (quia
et Novum in Vetere est figuratum, et Vetus in Novo est revela-
tum)."[1]

2. Very nearly allied to the fundamental principle just stated
is another, viz., that the ordinances of Judaism were all of a
symbolical nature, not simply outward or typical.   If they had
been *simply* outward as regards the service they required, and
typical as regards their religious value, they would have been
nothing more than bodily exercises for those who engaged in them
—exercises that had respect to their purification from a merely
ceremonial uncleanness, and the preservation of a present life ;
while, in addition to this, a few persons of superior discernment
might have descried through them the higher and better things,
which they prefigured for a coming age.   This is the whole that

[1] Contra Adversarium Legis et Proph., i. 35.

many persons would find in the ordinances of the Old Covenant; and thence arises much of the confusion and misconception in which the subject has been enveloped. An important element is omitted—the symbolical—lying mid-way between the other two, and forming in reality the link that unites them together. By calling them symbolical, we mean, that they expressed, by means of the outward rite or action, certain religious views and principles, which the worshipper was expected in the perform- ance of the service to recognise, and heartily concur in. It was the conscious recognition of these views and principles, and the exercise of the feelings growing out of them, for which more immediately the outward service was appointed, and in which its acceptability with God properly consisted. Without these the whole would have been a false parade—an empty and mean- ingless form. Take as an example the corporeal washings, which on so many occasions were required under the law—these were not appointed for the purpose merely of removing bodily defilement. Often, as in the case of the restored leper, purifica- tion from the touch of a dead body, or from sprinkling the water of cleansing on others, there was not even the semblance of anything of that sort to be removed. The washing, in *every* case, was appointed as a natural and appropriate symbol of per- sonal purity on the part of the worshippers, and was perfectly understood by all serious and thoughtful worshippers to carry such an import. Even Pilate, though a heathen, showed his un- derstanding of this symbol, by taking water and washing his hands before the people, to express more emphatically than he could do by words his refusal to participate in the condemnation of Jesus. And the Psalmist, when he spake of " washing his hands in innocency," and the prophet, when he called on the crimson-stained sinners of his day to " wash themselves, and make themselves clean," gave plain indication of the symbolical import of the transaction. In like manner—to refer to the initiatory ordinance of the whole series—the rite of circumcision, when brought into connection with the Divine covenant as its sign and seal, was by no means a merely external badge. Its proper aim and object were not the affixing of a corporeal mark upon the Jew, and thereby distinguishing him from the people of other countries. If that had been all, it should have been very imperfectly fitted to serve the end in view ; as it is certain, that at least the Egyptian priesthood, if not also some of the higher grades of the people, and not a few of the Syro-Arabian races, practised the rite from the very earliest times. It is, in fact, one of those customs, the origin of which is lost in a remote antiquity. But when adopted by God in connection with His covenant as its appropriate token and seal, it thenceforth became a symbol of purification from the guilt and pollution of the flesh —the symbol of a transition from nature's depravity into a spiritual and holy life. This transition *should* have been effected in all who stood within the bonds of the covenant ; and in those whose state accorded with their profession, it must in reality have been effected. It was, therefore, the distinctive badge of Israel, not simply as a separate people, but as God's *covenant*-people, called and bound to cast off nature's impurity, and walk in righteousness before God. This, too, was perfectly understood by all the more serious and thoughtful portion of the Israelites ; and they did not need the higher revelations of the Gospel to disclose its import. Moses himself pointed to it as a thing which even then was familiarly known and understood, when he repre-sented the people, in their state of impenitence and guilt, as being of uncircumcised hearts (Lev. xxvi. 41) ; and on this very account,—because circumcision had a strictly moral import, it was suspended during the thirty-eight years' sojourn in the wilderness ; since the people being then under the judgment of heaven for their sins, they were held to be in an unfit state for having the ordinance administered to them. Such, at least, ap-pears the main reason for the disuse of the ordinance during that long period. Circumcision, therefore, if viewed according to the design of God, and its own emblematic import, was no more a merely outward and corporeal thing, than baptism now is ; the one had respect to the believer's spiritual position and call to righteousness, not less than the other. In both cases alike the opus operatum might stand alone ; the sign might be without the thing signified ; since no ordinance of God ever has salvation indissolubly linked to it ; while yet the two would always in point of fact be connected together, if the ordinances were used in a spirit of sincerity and truth.

2. This second principle, which ascribes a symbolical or spiritual

I

import to all the rites and ordinances of the Old Covenant, like the first, has its ultimate ground in the nature of God—in the essential holiness of His character. Precisely as God's unchangeableness rendered it necessary, that there should be in everything of vital moment a fundamental agreement between Judaism and Christianity; so the pure and unspotted holiness of God, which comes out in the very first revelations of the Bible, and holds in all of them the most prominent place, rendered it necessary, that the Covenant, with every rite and institution belonging to it, should have respect to moral purity. What is essential and preeminent in God Himself must appear also essential and preeminent in His public administration. And hence in the very centre of the Mosaic polity—as the standard by which everything was to be judged, and the end to which it pointed—lay the two tables of the moral law—the comprehensive summary of love to God and man. Hence also, in some of those parts of the laws of Moses, which prescribe the more peculiar ceremonial institutions, the *reason* of their appointment is placed in immediate connection with the holiness of God ; as in Lev. xx. 25, 26, where the command is reinforced as to the distinction to be put between clean and unclean in food, it is added as the ground of the requirement, " And ye shall be holy unto Me, for I the Lord am holy, and I have severed you from other people, that ye should be Mine." So again in ch. xxii., after a multitude of prescriptions regarding sacrifice, and the eating of the flesh of peace-offerings, the whole is wound up by pointing to the fundamental reason, " I am Jehovah ; therefore shall ye keep My commandments and do them ; I am Jehovah. Neither shall ye profane My holy name ; but I will be hallowed among the children of Israel ; I am Jehovah, that hallow you." The entire ritual had its foundation in God, in the principles of *His* character and government, whither the people were directed to look for the ultimate ground of the laws and institutions they were commanded to observe. As the one was pre-eminently moral, so, of necessity, was the other ; and no enlightened Israelite could regard the services of his symbolical worship, any more than the statutes and judgments of his theocratic polity, in any other light than as a system of means and appliances for securing purity of heart and conduct.

3. It is clear then—and we state it, as equally a deduction

from what has preceded, and a *third point* to be kept in view, in all the representations that may be made in such matters—that the true Israelites, those who were such in the reckoning of God, were a spiritual, not a fleshly seed; and that the rearing of such a seed, not any outward and formal separation from the world, was the direct aim of the laws and institutions of Moses. That the dwelling of the people alone, in a state of isolation from the other nations of the earth, or antagonism to them, could never of itself have been designed to form the principal reason of the ancient economy, is evident—not only from the considerations already advanced—but also from the very end of their peculiar calling in Abraham, which was to be first blessed in themselves, and then to be a blessing to others—a blessing even to all the families of the earth. It can never be by an isolating and frowning exclusiveness, that they could fulfil this ulterior part of their destination; it could only be by operating in a kindly and beneficent manner upon the nations around them, diffusing among them the knowledge of God, and extending the boundaries of His kingdom. That this was from the first contemplated by God may certainly be inferred from the admission of proselyte strangers, even in Abraham's time, into the bosom of the covenant (Gen. xvii. 12), and from the law afterwards prescribed regarding it (Ex. xii. 48). It is still further evident from the prayer of Solomon at the dedication of the temple, which made express mention of the case of strangers coming to intermingle their devotions with those of the house of Israel; and from the fact, that whenever the covenant-people were in a lively and prosperous state, there was a disposition, on the part of others, to share with them in their privileges and blessings, as in the times of David and Solomon (1 Chron. xxii. 2; 2 Chron. ii. 17). So far, indeed, were David and the prophets from thinking it the glory of Israel to be alone, that they anticipated with joy the time when kings would bring presents to Jerusalem, and the Lord's house should become a house of prayer for all nations. So long, certainly, as the people of other countries abode in heathenism, it was inevitable that Israel should dwell apart—if they remained faithful to their calling. But the separation in that case was only the necessary result of Israel's holiness, on the one hand, and the corruptions of the Gentiles, on the other;—

nor was it for any other end, than as the fittest means, in the existing state of the world, for producing and maintaining that holiness in the families of Israel, that the laws and ordinances of the Old Covenant were established. So, indeed, the Apostle Paul distinctly declared, when in Gal. iii. 19, he said, " Wherefore, then, serveth the law ?   It was added because of transgressions,"—added, that is, to the prior covenant made with Abraham, on account of the people's proneness to transgress.   That covenant was not of itself sufficient to restrain them ; and the law with its explicit requirements of duty, and its terrible sanctions was given to supplement the deficiency.   The law, therefore, when rightly understood and properly used was in perfect harmony with the covenant ; it occupied an inferior and subsidiary place, but in that place was alike designed and fitted for qualifying the people to carry into effect the objects of the covenant.   And as it was not the aim of the covenant to make Israel merely a separate people, walled-off by certain distinctive peculiarities from others, as little could it be the proper aim of the law.   The scope and tendency of both, indeed, was for righteousness, and their common end was accomplished only in so far as there was produced a spiritual and holy seed to God.

4. It follows from what has been said, in the fourth place, that the difference, as to privilege and character between the genuine members of the Old and of the New Covenants, must be relative only, and not absolute.   It should be exhibited, not as a contrast between two opposites, but as an ascending gradation, a rising from a lower to a higher stage of development.   A contrast, no doubt, is sometimes presented in the New Testament between law and grace, between the darkness and servile condition before Christ's coming, and the light and liberty that followed.   But the darkness was not that of total ignorance, nor was the bondage properly that of slaves, but of children rather, who from their imperfect discernment and feeble powers required to be hemmed in by outward restraints, and stimulated by artificial expedients. When the Prophet Jeremiah represents (ch. xxxi.), the distinction between the Old Covenant then existing, and the New and better one sometime to be introduced, as consisting in the putting of the Divine laws into the hearts of the people, and engraving them in their inward parts, the representation can

only have been meant to indicate a more effectual and general accomplishment of this spiritual result, than had hitherto appeared, not its absolute commencement. For, beyond all question, the internal revelation of the law was to a certain extent possessed also in former times—possessed by every true Israelite, of whom it was written, "The law of God is in his heart," and "he meditates therein day and night." And in what chiefly did the reforming agency of David and many of the prophets appear? Was it not in their earnest striving to awaken the people to the insufficiency of a dead formalism, and have them brought to the cultivation of such holiness as the law required?

There was something more, then, in the relation between Judaism and Christianity, than that of type and antitype—in the sense commonly understood by these terms; there was the relation also of germ and development, beginning and end. The Christian Church, if in one respect a new thing in the earth, is, in another, a continuation and expansion of the Jewish. As was long ago well stated by Crucius, "Israel is the basis and the body itself of the Church, which must continue to grow and diffuse itself more and more; and this it does, not by virtue of its corporeal descent, but on account of its faith and obedience towards God's covenant of grace with it, in virtue of which it obtains the heritage of the heathen. When Paul in Gal. vi. 16, speaks of the true Israel of God, he means thereby believing Israelites, whom he opposes to the enemies of Christ. And these Israelites did not pass over to the heathen, but the heathen to them (Eph. ii. 19, iii. 6; Phil. iii. 3; Col. ii. 11; Acts xiii. 32, xxvi. 6, 7). In this sense true Christians are reckoned to Israel; and as the ancient Israel of God could, before Christ's appearance, receive proselytes among themselves, who thereafter became part of the covenant people; so now, since the appearance of Christ, they have by reason of the covenant and the promise, already become greatly enlarged through the incorporation of multitudes of the heathen, and shall at length receive the whole earth for a possession. And this entire body of the Church, of which the believing portion of Israel formed the foundation, shall one day also receive the remnant of the other portion, the apostasy, into its bosom."[1]

[1] In Delitzsch's Biblisch. proph., p. 132.

5. From all these premises, there arises still another conclusion, a fifth point to be kept steadily in view, viz., that the ordinances of the two covenants, like the conditions of their respective members, can admit only of relative differences. Differences certainly exist, corresponding in nature to the change in the Divine economy, and the spiritual condition of those placed under it ; and these must be carefully marked and explained in accordance with the truth of things—otherwise, countenance may be given to grievous mistakes. It was here that Augustine, in common with so many of the fathers, chiefly erred, though holding correct views in the general as to the connection between Judaism and Christianity. The one was clearly enough seen to be the preparation and shadow of the other ; but in drawing out the connection to particular points, too little account was made of the rise that had taken place from a lower to a higher sphere ; a tendency rather was shown to regard the antitype as equally outward and formal with the type. Hence, in the first instance, the typology of the Old Testament was caricatured, by having the most fortuitous and superficial resemblances turned into adumbrations of Gospel mysteries ; and then the theology of the New was carnalised, by being cast into the form and pattern of the Old ; the observance of days and seasons in the one inferring, it was thought, a like observance in the other—and, as of old, so also now, it was held, that there should be an altar, with its consecrated priesthood and material oblations—a visible unity in the Church, from which it was heresy, even in matters of ceremony, to deviate—and, at last, a supreme earthly head, on whose will were conceived to hang the issues of life and death for entire Christendom. A mournful result in any circumstances ; but rendered greatly more so by the consideration, that among the forces tending to produce it must be placed the venerable name of Augustine, who, in his interpretations, often falls into the mistaken carnalism, out of which the evil might be said to have originated.

But while showing this form of error, care must be taken to avoid falling into another. And the principle must be held fast, that in the ordinances of the two covenants there can be room only for differences of a relative kind. The sacrifices and ablutions of the Old Testament were not simply carnal institutions, no more than baptism and the Lord's Supper now are. They also pertained to the conscience, and, to be acceptably engaged in, required faith on the part of the worshipper. It is true, that " as pertaining to the conscience, they could not make the comers to them perfect;" they could not present to the worshippers a full, complete, and permanent ground of peace ; whence a perpetual renewal of the sacrifices was needed to reassure the conscience after fresh acts of transgression. Yet, this by no means proves, that they had to do merely with the purification of the flesh. There *were* certain fleshly or ceremonial defilements, such as the touching of a dead body, for which purification was obtained by means of water, mixed with the ashes of a red heifer; —and to that the apostle refers in Heb. ix. 13. But it is an utter misapprehension of his meaning, to understand him there to assert, that *all the offerings* of the law were of force merely to purify the flesh. What could purifications of such a kind have availed one, who had been guilty of fraud, or oppression, or deceit, or false swearing? Yet for such sins, forgiveness was attainable through the appointed offerings, Lev. vi. 1–7.

We hold it, therefore, as most certain, that there was also a spiritual element in all the services of the Old Covenant, and that their unsuitableness to Gospel times does not arise from their having been exclusively carnal and outward. It arises, partly from their being too predominantly symbolical for a religion, which contains a full revelation of the truth ; and partly also from their having been peculiarly adapted for bringing into view the demands of law, and the liabilities of debt, while they provided only a temporary expedient as to the way of relief—no more than a shadow of the real satisfaction. So that for men to cleave to the Old Testament services after Christ had come, as a matter essential to salvation, was in effect to say, that they did not regard the death of Christ as in itself a perfect satisfaction for the guilt of sin, but that it needed the purifications of the law to render it complete—thereby at once dishonouring Christ, and taking the legal ceremonies for something more than they really were. But still, these ceremonies, when rightly understood, differed from the ordinances of the Gospel only in degree, not in kind; and it is perfectly competent for us to draw conclusions from the nature and administration of the one, to the

nature and administration of the other.   Here, as in so many
other things, there is a middle path, which is the right one ; and
*it is just as easy to err from it by carnalizing too much in Judaism,
as by Judaizing too much in Christianity.*

SECTION EIGHTH.

ON THE PROPER INTERPRETATION OF THE TROPICAL PARTS OF THE NEW TESTAMENT.

AMONG the portions of New Testament Scripture which require
a separate hermeneutical consideration, are those in which tropes
or figures are employed.   Some of the examples given under the
two last divisions might in part be referred to this head, for there
is also a figurative element in them.   But other portions belong
more properly to it ; and the class is of sufficient compass and
moment to entitle it to special inquiry.   The subject, however,
does not hold so large a place in the hermeneutics of the New
Testament as it does in those of the Old; for the poetical enters
more into the composition of the Old, and poetry, from its very
nature, delights in the use of figure.   In both the prophetical,
and the more distinctively poetical books of Old Testament
Scripture, the boldest images are introduced, and the language
has throughout a figurative colouring.   But of these we are not
called to treat at present.   We have to do merely with that
more sparing and restricted use of tropical language, which appears in the New Testament, and was not incompatible with its
clearer revelations and its more didactic aim.   Reference, however, may also be occasionally made, by way of illustration, to
passages in the Old Testament.

It is, perhaps, scarcely necessary to state, yet, in case of any misapprehension, it may as well be stated, that the terms *figurative* and
tropical, on the one side, and those of *literal* and *grammatical*, on
the other, may be employed indiscriminately, as being substantially of the same import.   The one pair happen to be derived
from the Greek, and the other from the Latin, but, in each case,

from words that precisely correspond. *Literal,* from the Latin *litera,* denotes the meaning of a word, which is according to the letter, the meaning it bears in its original or primary use ; and nothing else is indicated by the term *grammatical,* in this connection, the word of Greek derivation for what is according to the γράμμα or letter. But when a word, originally appropriated to one thing, comes to be applied to another, which bears some real or fancied resemblance to it, as there is then a τρόπος or turning of it to a new use, so the meaning is called *tropical,* or, if we prefer the Latin form of expression, *figurative*—there being always some sort of figure or image suggested to the mind in this new use of the term, founded either on resemblance or some other link of connection, and forming a natural transition from the original to the derived sense. Very commonly also the word *proper* is used to denote the original import of words, and *improper* the figurative. But as these epithets are fitted to suggest wrong ideas, it is better not to employ them in such a connection.

All languages are more or less figurative ; for the mind of man is essentially analogical, and delights to trace resemblances between one object and another, and embody them in forms of speech. In strictly mental operations, and in regard to things lying beyond the reach of sense or time, it is *obliged* to resort to figurative terms ;—for only through the form and aspect of sensible objects can it picture to itself and express what lies in those hidden chambers of imagery. And the more vivid its own feelings and conceptions are respecting spiritual and Divine things, or the more it seeks to give a present and abiding impression of these to the mind of others, the more also will it naturally call to its aid the realistic language of tropes and metaphors. Hence the predominant use of such language in sacred poetry ; and hence also its occasional employment by Christ and His apostles, in order to invest their representations of Divine things with the greater force and emphasis.

I. In applying our minds to this subject, the first point that naturally calls for inquiry, has respect to the proper mode of ascertaining when words are employed, not literally, but tropically. *How* may we assure ourselves, or *can* we assure ourselves, against any mistake in the matter ?

This branch of hermeneutical inquiry began to receive some consideration in comparatively early times ; and in Augustine's treatise De doctrina Christiana, we find certain rules laid down for determining what in Scripture should be taken literally, and what figuratively. These are, certainly, somewhat imperfect, as might have been expected, considering the period when they were written : yet they are not without their value, and if they had been followed up by others, with any measure of Augustine's discernment, they might have kept the early Church from many false interpretations, on which the most unscriptural and superstitious views leant for support.

1. In the first place, it may be noted, that in a large number of cases, by much the larger number of cases, where the language is tropical, the fact that it is so, appears from the very nature of the language, or from the connection in which it stands. This holds especially of that kind of tropical language, which consists in the employment of *metaphor—i.e.* when one object is set forth under the image of another ; and in the employment of parable, which is only an extended metaphor. Thus, when Jacob says of Judah, " Judah is a lion's whelp, from the prey, my son, thou art gone up ;" or when our Lord designated two of His disciples by the name of Boanerges, " Sons of thunder ;" or, again, when He spake of the difficulties connected with an admission into His kingdom, under the necessity of " being born again," and of " entering a strait gate and treading a narrow way :"—in all these and many examples of a like nature, the tropical element is palpable ; a child, indeed, might perceive it ; and the only room for consideration is, how the lines of resemblance should be drawn between the literal and the figurative sense of the terms. The same also may be said, and with still stronger emphasis, of formal similitudes and parables, in which the literal interpretation is expressly, or by plain implication, taken as the mere cover of something higher and greater.

2. Another class of passages, in which the figure is also, for the most part, quite easy of detection, are those in which what is called *synechdoche* prevails—*i. e.* in which a part is put for the whole ; as a cup for its contents, " Take this cup and drink it," or, " Ye cannot drink the cup of the Lord and the cup of devils."

It is manifest, that in such cases the cup does not stand alone; it is viewed merely as the symbol of the draught presented in it. So in other passages, where there is a kind of metonymy, such as putting a cause for an effect, or an effect for a cause :—for example, when our Lord says of Himself, " I am not come to send peace upon earth, but a sword;" or when, inversely, the Apostle Paul, in another connection, says of Him, " He is our peace." In examples of this description also there is no difficulty; it is obvious, that a particular result is in the eye of the writer, and that, for the sake of point and brevity, the object or person is identified with that result, or with the natural cause and instrument of effecting it,. as if they were one and the same.

But still, when all such examples as those now referred to have been taken into account, there remains a considerable number,—especially of the class called *metonymies*, in regard to which it is not so easy to determine, whether the language should be understood literally or tropically. It may, for instance, be questioned, whether our Lord, in Matt. v. 23, where He speaks of bringing a gift to the altar, means an actual altar for the presentation of sacrificial offerings, or something in the spiritual sphere that might be held equivalent to it :—whether, again, when speaking of His followers eating His body and drinking His blood, He meant a corporeal or a spiritual participation :—or Paul, when he makes mention of a fire that is to try every man's work (1 Cor. iii. 13), whether he has respect to the material element of fire, or to a process of judgment, which in spiritual things will have the same effect as a searching fire in earthly. It is well known, that these questions are answered very differently, and that great points of doctrine hang on the specific interpretations adopted. Nor is it possible, by any sharply defined rules to settle conclusively the view that should be taken; for the settling of the rules would necessarily involve a discussion of the particular cases, to which we wish to apply them. It is more, therefore, to the general principles of interpretation—to the proper mode and habit of dealing with the Word of God, the accurate analysis of its terms, the close and discriminating examination of the scope and connection :—it is to this more, than to any specific directions, that we are to look for obtaining the skill to determine between the literal and the tropical in the less obvious cases. At the same time, there are two or three leading principles, which if fairly and consistently applied, might in the majority of cases, be sufficient to guide to a right decision.

(1.) The first of these is, that when anything is said, which, if taken according to the letter, would be at variance with the essential nature of the subject spoken of, the language must be regarded as tropical. This principle requires to be little more than enunciated; it carries its own evidence along with it. No single act, no particular attribute can be ascribed by an intelligent writer to a person or an object, which is inconsistent with their proper nature. So that, on the supposition of that nature being known to us, we can be at no loss to understand in what sense the language should be taken. Thus, it is essential to the nature of God, that He is spirit and not flesh—a Spirit infinite, eternal, and unchangeable; consequently without bodily parts, which are necessarily bounded by space and time; without liability to passionate excitation or erring purposes, which arise from creaturely limitations. Hence all those passages, which represent God as possessed of human powers and organs, as seeing, or hearing, or having experience of such affections as are the result of human weakness and infirmity, must be understood in a figurative sense. Nor can it be otherwise with those things, which are spoken of the soul and its spiritual life in terms borrowed from what pertains to the body :—As when our Lord calls on His followers to cut off their right hand and pluck out their right eye, or when St Paul speaks of crucifying the flesh, and putting off the old man of corruption. In such cases the path is clear; we must keep strictly in view the *essential nature* of the subject discoursed of; and since that is not such as to admit of an application of the language in the literal sense, we can have no hesitation about understanding it tropically.

(2.) A second principle applicable to such cases, is, that if the language taken literally would involve something incongruous or morally improper, the figurative, and not the literal sense, must be the right one. If the literal implies nothing contrary to sense and reason—if the instruction it conveys is in accordance with the great moral distinctions impressed upon the conscience, and written in the Word of God, then it may safely be adhered to as the sense actually intended. But if otherwise, we must abandon the literal for the figurative. The passage formerly referred to in another connection—Rom. xii. 20—may be taken as an example; it is the exhortation to heap coals of fire on an enemy's head, by showing kindness to him in the time of want and necessity. The action itself here specified (whatever may be understood of the motive involved in it) must in any case be understood figuratively; since the heaping of coals of fire on the head of another must plainly have respect to the moral influence of the things done to him upon his state or character. But further, in regard to the kind of operation intended, or the nature of the effect to be wrought, held out as the motive for exertion in the manner specified, it must be, as Augustine long ago remarked, of a beneficial, not of an injurious description, since it is brought in to enforce a precept of benevolence, and must, therefore, have contemplated the good of the parties interested.[1] There are many similar examples in the Proverbs, where the one just noticed originally occurs; as—to mention only another—when a person sitting at meat with a ruler is exhorted to put "a knife to his throat," meaning that he must set bounds to his appetite—slay, in a manner, his voracity. In like manner, our Lord says, "If any man will come after Me, let him take up his cross and follow Me,"—"whosoever loveth his life, shall lose it,"—"make to yourselves friends of the mammon of unrighteousness:"—in each of which passages there must be a certain amount of figure; since, to bear a cross, and to love life, in the natural sense of the expression, cannot be regarded as things fitted to carry with them the consequences of good and evil with which they are associated, nor can it be deemed proper, otherwise than by a figure, to make for one's self a friend of what is unrighteous. In such cases, we can only gét at the true meaning by penetrating beneath the surface, and apprehending a moral act or line of behaviour as the object presented to our notice.

(3.) A third direction may be added, viz. that where we have

[1] Aug. De Doc. Christiana, iii. 16, Ne igitur dubitaveris figurate dictum; et cum possit dupliciter interpretari, uno modo ad nocendum, altero ad præstandum; ad beneficentiam te potius charitas revocat, ut intellegas carbones ignis esse urentes pœnitentiæ gemitus, quibus superbia sanatur ejus qui dolet se inimicum fuisse hominis, a quo ejus miseriæ subvenitur.

still reason to doubt whether the language is literal or figurative, we should endeavour to have the doubt resolved, by referring to parallel passages (if there be any such) which treat of the same subject in more explicit terms, or at greater length. The really doubtful cases, in which we can avail ourselves of this help, may not, perhaps, be very numerous; but they are still to be found. Thus, in the first beatitude of the Sermon on the Mount, in which the simple designation *poor* occurs, in the Gospel of Luke, "Blessed are ye poor:" this has its fuller explanation in St Matthew's Gospel, where we read, "Blessed are the poor in spirit:"—plainly indicating that, if literal poverty is not excluded, respect is mainly had to the spiritual frame. In like manner the passage in the same sermon, respecting bringing a gift to the altar, in so far as regards its bearing on the Christian Church, has its meaning clearly determined by the Epistle to the Hebrews, and other parts of the New Testament, which declare earthly altars, and the offerings proper to them, to have no longer any place in the Church of God. And the word of Jesus, "Destroy this temple, and in three days I will raise it up again," though spoken with apparent literality, was afterwards found, when the progress of events and the illumination of the Spirit laid open its meaning, to have had a figurative import. It referred, not to the building usually designated the temple, but to the Lord's body, although this also was in reality a temple, which is but another name for the dwelling-place of Deity; nay, was such in a sense more strictly appropriate than could be affirmed of the other.

Now, if we apply these simple and just principles of interpretation to the passage in Corinthians (1 Cor. iii. 13), we can have no difficulty in ascertaining the result that ought to be arrived at. The declaration there made is, that "the day," viz. of coming trial, "shall be revealed by fire, and the fire shall try every man's work, of what sort it is." What is the *nature* of the work to be tried? That is naturally our first question. Is it of a moral, or simply of an external and earthly kind? The only work spoken of in the context is that which concerns the foundation and progress of Christ's Church, and man's relation to it— work, therefore, in a strictly moral sense; and so, by our first principle, the fire that is to try it must be moral too. For how incongruous were it to couple a corporeal fire with a spiritual service, as the means of determining its real character ?   And if, in accordance with our last principle, we have recourse to other passages, which speak of the day of future trial and final decision, we find statements, indeed, to the effect that the Lord will be revealed in flaming fire, or, as it again is, in the clouds of heaven ; but as to what shall really fix the character and the award of each man's work in the Lord, we are left in no room to doubt that it shall be His own searching judgment :—this it is that shall bring all clearly to light, and give to every one according to his desert. The result, therefore, is obvious ; the fire spoken of, and spoken of simply in respect to its property as an instrument of trial, must be understood tropically of what, in spiritual things, has the like property.

Let us also try, in the same way, what our Lord says about eating His flesh and drinking His blood.   The Romanists contend that the expressions must be taken literally, even as recorded in John vi. 53, long before the sacrament of the Supper was instituted.   Ernesti, who was a Lutheran, admits it must be understood tropically there ; but he maintains that the words at the institution of the Supper must be taken literally.   When treating of the interpretation of tropical language, in his Institutes of Biblical Interpretation, he states that, as at Matt. xxviii. 19, in the formula of baptism, the word baptize is to be taken literally, so the words at the institution of the Supper, about eating and drinking, must be taken literally.   And he refers to what he regards as a kind of parallel passage, Heb. ix. 20, where the words of Moses are quoted, " This is the blood of the covenant which God hath enjoined unto you," and draws the conclusion that, as in this case the blood of the covenant must be literally understood, so our Lord must have meant His blood to be understood in the same manner.   Nor could this expression, he adds, convey any other than its proper sense to the minds of the disciples, who were accustomed to take up our Lord's declarations in their proper or literal sense.   No doubt they *were* accustomed to do this ; greatly too much accustomed : it was their failing and their error to be so.   Hence our Lord had once and again to complain of their inaptitude to perceive the real import of His words ; and specially in regard to this very form of expression, when, on one occasion, He spoke of having Himself bread to eat that others knew not of, and on another, cautioned His disciples to beware of the leaven of the Pharisees ; so far was He from justifying them for understanding His words literally (as He discovered they did), that He reproved them on that very account for their dulness of apprehension.   If Ernesti's reasoning were sound, and the use he makes of the words of Moses in Hebrews were valid, the natural conclusion would be, not only that the corporeal presence of Christ in the Supper should be maintained, but also that the whole legal economy should remain in force—the altar of sacrifice, with the blood of slain victims, the distinction of Jew and Gentile, the continued teaching of the scribes in Moses' seat, etc.; for these are all distinctly mentioned by Christ, and, in all probability, were at first understood in the most literal sense by the disciples.

We must plainly have other rules for our direction in such a case.   It is surely one thing to say, that Christ literally ratified the covenant with His own blood, and a very different thing, that bread and wine became His blood, and as such were to be eaten and drunk, at a feast instituted in commemoration of His act in ratifying the covenant.   Indeed, it is only by a sort of figure that we can speak even of the covenant being ratified by His blood—a figure derived from the ancient sacrifices ; for, in reality, it was the simple death of Christ, the free surrender of His soul through the pains of dissolution to the Father, which, in His case, established the covenant; and would equally have done so, though not a drop of blood had been outwardly shed. There is a failure, therefore, as to *formal resemblance* at the very outset, in the actions that are brought into comparison.   And when we come to the participation spoken of, there is no resemblance whatever.   Even Augustine, with all his leanings toward ritualism, and his mystic notions on the virtue of the Sacraments, saw that the literal in its strict sense could not stand. On the passage in St John's Gospel, about eating the flesh and drinking the blood of Christ, he says, " It appears to order a wicked and abominable action ; it is, therefore, a figure, teaching that we must communicate with our Lord's passion, and have it sweetly and profitably laid up in our memory, that His flesh was crucified and wounded for us (præcipiens passioni dominicæ communicandum, et suaviter atque utiliter recondendum in memoria quod pro nobis caro ejus crucifixa et vulnerata sit).[1] Whether we look to this passage, or to the words, " This is My body broken for you," and " This cup is the New Covenant in My blood, shed for the remission of sins, drink ye of it," the literal interpretation violates every one of the three leading principles, which we have laid down as applicable to such cases.   It is against the *first* principle ; for what our Lord was speaking of in the one passage, and the privilege He was establishing in the other, was a joint-participation with Himself as the Redeemer of men.   But this is a thing in its very nature spiritual ; and a carnal amalgamation with His bodily parts—were such a thing possible—could be of no benefit ; in that respect, as our Lord Himself testified, " The flesh profiteth nothing."   Not oneness of outward standing or corporeal substance, but unity of soul, identity of spiritual life—this is what alone avails in such a matter.   Then, the literal interpretation is against our *second* principle of interpretation, inasmuch as it ascribes an action to Christians, nay imposes as the highest and most sacred duty an action, which is abhorrent to the common instincts of humanity—an action which has no parallel in real life, except among the lowest types of human nature—the most untutored savages.   These alone among mankind are known, and even these only in extreme cases, to eat human flesh and drink human blood ; and it is utterly inconceivable, that the most solemn rite of Christianity should have been designed to be formally the same with the most unnatural and savage practice which exists in the world.   And, finally, the parallel passages may also be said to be against it ; for though, from the singularity of the case, as to the Sacrament of the Supper, we cannot appeal to any passages absolutely parallel, yet passages substantially parallel are not wanting—passages, in which Christ is represented as identifying Himself with an external object, much as He does with the bread and wine in the Sacrament :—Such as, " I am the door," " I am the vine," " The Church which is His body," " And that Rock was Christ."   We have also passages, in which the bread of this ordinance, after consecration, the bread as actually partaken by the communicants, is still designated bread, and not flesh ;—as when the apostle says, in 1 Cor.

[1] De Doc. Christiana, iii. 16.

K

x. 16, 17, " The bread which we break is it not the communion of the body of Christ ?   For, we being many are one bread, and one body ; for we are all partakers of that one bread"—from which one might as well argue, that believers are turned into bread, as from the words in Matthew, that the bread is turned into flesh.   And in Acts, ch. ii. 42, xx. 7, 11, we have the expression, " breaking of bread," used as a common phrase to denote the celebration of the Supper, manifestly implying, that the participation of bread, and not what could be termed flesh, constituted the formal act in this part of the Communion.

We say nothing of the doctrinal positions based upon the literal sense, but contemplate the matter in a simply exegetical point of view.   Apart altogether from the doctrinal consequences and results, the close and comparative examination of the words leads to the adoption of the tropical, in contradistinction to the literal import.

II. We turn now to what forms naturally the second subject of consideration in this branch of inquiry, viz., the proper mode of treating the tropical or figurative portions of Scripture.   This necessarily varies to a considerable extent, as does also the use of figure in Scripture :—so that uniform rules, applicable to all cases of figurative language, cannot possibly be given.   The field must be surveyed in successive portions.

1. In the first place, there are in Scripture, as in other compositions, words and phrases, which are really used in a figurative manner, but in which the figurative has become so common, that it has ceased to be regarded as figurative.   Examples of this in ordinary language are not far to seek.   *Expression*, for example, which in its original sense means a *squeezing out*, but is now almost invariably appropriated to the specific act of pressure outwards, which takes place in speech, when the thought conceived in the mind is put forth into intelligible words—*ardour*, which is primarily burning or heat, but by usage has come to be confined to states of mind—*reflect, ruminate*, and many others, of which what was once the tropical, has now come to be the ordinary usage.   Examples of the same description are found in Scripture, in such words as *edify* (" edify one another in love"), *train-up* (originally *draw-up*, but now usually *educate*, instruct,

rear), *synagogue, church*: in all which the secondary or tropical meaning is the current one; and if occasionally a reference may with advantage be made to the primary sense, generally it is best to treat them as no longer tropical, but to regard the common acceptation as the only one, that has any particular claim for notice.

2. A second point to be noted is, that there is often a complex tropical meaning in the words and phrases of Scripture (as of language generally)—one tropical meaning, by some addition or subtraction in respect to the principal idea, giving rise to another, and that, perhaps, still to another. So that there is sometimes trope upon trope; and it is of importance, not only to have a general acquaintance with the whole, so as to be able the more readily to choose the proper one for the occasion, but also to understand something of their successive growth—to be able to trace, in a manner, their genealogy, so as fitly and intelligently to connect one with another. This can now, for the most part, be done with comparative ease, and usually requires nothing more than the careful use of the grammar and the dictionary; for of late years the progress of philological study has been such as to determine pretty accurately almost all the primary and derived meanings of the words in New Testament Scripture, with their relative order and gradation. As an example of the accumulation of tropes in the meaning of some words, we may refer to Rev. iii. 12, " Him that overcometh will I make a pillar in the temple of my God," in which not the nearer, but a more remote tropical meaning is given to *pillar*. The literal is that of a strong support to a material building; whence comes the more immediate tropical meaning, of some kind of like support in the sphere of moral and spiritual things; but a further tropical meaning also arises, suggested by the thought of pillars being usually the strongest and most securely fixed parts of the building—the meaning of a stable and abiding position. This is the idea intended to be conveyed in the passage referred to; and hence it is added, as what naturally arises from the subject of the promise having the position of a pillar assigned him, that " he shall go no more out "—his place in the region of bliss and glory shall be one of eternal continuance.—We may point for another example to Matt. xxiii. 14, where our Lord says to the Scribes and Pharisees,

" Ye devour widows' houses "—τὰς οἰκίας τῶν χηρῶν, evidently
meaning the goods or substance of those widows. The first
transition from the natural to the figurative import consists in
taking *house*, by metonymy, for family—what contains for the
principal objects contained in it—and then by a further limitation, putting the means of support, belonging to the house or
family, for this itself—on the implied ground, that the one as to
substantial existence is identified with the other, and that he who
lays his hand on the means of sustenance to a house virtually
lays his hand on the house itself. This second trope, therefore,
growing out of the first, is quite natural; and we can easily see,
how much, by the throwing together of the several things which
make up this last idea, the language of our Lord gains in strength
and vivacity. It leads us to think, not merely of the avaricious
and fraudulent appropriation of some earthly goods, but of the
result also flowing from such conduct—the actual absorption of
a whole house, in order to gratify a base and selfish appetite.

3. As a third direction for the proper explanation and manage-
ment of the tropical language of Scripture—and, indeed, the
principal one—we mention this, that care should be taken to
give a fair and natural, as opposed to a far-fetched or fanciful,
turn to the figure employed. We do so, on the ground, that
figurative language is essentially of a popular caste, and is founded
on those broader and more obvious resemblances, which do not
need to be searched for, but are easily recognised and generally
perceived. When the apostle, for example, says, " Let not the
sun go down upon your wrath," the reference plainly is, to the
time that should be set to the continued indulgence of angry
feelings; if these *should* arise in your bosom, let them not be
harboured, let them at least expire ere the day closes, on which
they have arisen. But see how oddly, and we may say phantasti-
cally, Thomas Fuller draws out the figure, " St Paul saith, ' Let
not the sun go down on your wrath,' to carry news to the anti-
podes in another world of thy revengeful nature. Yet"—he
adds, as if intending to give a more simple view of the matter,
" let us take the apostle's meaning rather than his words, with
all possible speed to depose our passion; not understanding him
so literally, that we may take leave to be angry till sunset; then
might our wrath lengthen with the days, and men in Greenland,

where day lasts above a quarter of a year, have plentiful scope of revenge." It is evident on a moment's consideration, that such turns given to the image are quite fanciful; they could not have been in the apostle's mind, nor would they readily suggest themselves to an ordinary reader of the epistle: and they serve rather to amuse, or to divert attention from the right point, than guide it into the proper channel. Even writers much less fanciful than Fuller, and who have their imaginations more under control, often err in this direction. Thus Leighton, in his first sermon on Isa. lx. 1—as a whole an admirable discourse—when referring to Canticles vi. 10, where it is said of the spouse, " She is fair as the moon and clear as the sun," thus explains, " The lesser light is that of sanctification, *fair as the moon;* that of justification the greater, by which she is *clear as the sun.* The sun is perfectly luminous, but the moon is only half enlightened; so the believer is perfectly justified, but sanctified only in part; his one-half his flesh, is dark; and as the partial illumination is the reason of so many changes in the moon, to which changes the sun is not subject at all, so the imperfection of a Christian's holiness, is the cause of so many waxings and wanings, and of the great inequality of his performances, whereas in the meanwhile his justification remains constantly like itself." Doctrinally, indeed, this is perfectly correct; but it is certainly not in the passage, on which it is founded. The reference there to the two objects in nature, sun and moon, is merely to these as they strike the eye of a spectator—therefore, to the intense brightness of the one, and to the milder radiance of the other. And the Church is compared to the two luminaries of nature, only for the purpose of exhibiting under two similar, though slightly diversified aspects, the imposing and attractive appearance, which would belong to her, if she were in her normal condition of light and purity.

Take still another example. In Matt. x. 16, our Lord exhorts His disciples, since they were to go forth like sheep in the midst of wolves, to be " wise as serpents "—on which Augustine remarks, by way of explanation, " It is known respecting the serpent, that it presents to those striking it, instead of the head, the whole body; and this shows, in connection with our Lord's word, that we should offer to those persecuting us our body, rather than our head, which is Christ, lest the Christian faith should be, as it were, slain in us, if by sparing our body we should disown God." " Or, again "—taking another view of the matter—" since it is known, that the serpent, when compressed by the straitness of its den, casts off its old skin, and thereby, it is said, receives new strength, it admonishes us to imitate that same cunning of the serpent, and put off the old man, as the apostle says, that we may put on the new, and put it off through straits, entering (as the Lord says) through the strait gate."[1] I need scarcely say, that these points in the natural history of the serpent (if they were real) would serve little to illustrate our Lord's maxim, in the connection, in which it is introduced ; since, plainly, the wisdom He recommends, and finds imaged in the serpent, is wisdom, not to enter into a Christian state, nor to brave persecution and death, when entered, rather than betray the cause of Christ, but to guide one's self discreetly and pru- dently in the midst of danger, so as, if possible, to escape the evil threatened by it.   Indeed, there is scarcely anything known in the natural history of the serpent-brood, which can be of ser- vice in illustrating the comparison ; for in their existing condi- tion serpents are not remarkable for wisdom, in the respect now mentioned, and possess lower instincts and sagacity than many other irrational creatures.   Yet there can be no doubt, that in ancient times the serpent was very commonly taken as a symbol of wisdom, was even extensively worshipped as having something Divine about it.   But this most probably sprung out of the tradi- tion respecting its primeval state, as the wisest among the beasts of the field, and the part it was in consequence employed by the arch-deceiver to play in the fall of man.   Scripturally, and tra- ditionally, the serpent was peculiarly associated with the attri- bute of wisdom—and it is best to regard our Lord as simply founding on this historical belief, and the deeply significant facts connected with it.

The danger of erring in the manner now referred to is not, perhaps, so great in our day, as it was in former times, when general literature abounded with laboured ingenuities and fanci- ful conceits.   We live in an age, which gives more play to the unsophisticated feelings and instincts of nature, and which is less disposed to seek for remote and curious analogies.   But when in

[1] De Doc. Christiana, ii. 16.

public discourses a passage is selected, which contains a similitude, there always is some danger of pressing this, in some respects, too far, so as to make it the cover of a more varied or lengthened instruction than it naturally suggests. The best way to avoid this, is to cultivate simplicity of thought and style, and to rest in the conviction, which experience will amply justify, that two or three points, well chosen and vigorously handled, will make both a happier and a more lasting impression, than double the number, if not properly grounded in the text, or really germane to the subject.

SECTION NINTH.

THE PARABLES OF CHRIST, THEIR PROPER INTERPRETATION AND TREATMENT.

WE have considered as yet only the commoner and briefer forms of figurative language in the New Testament writings—those which consist of single expressions, or admit of being compressed into one sentence. But a very considerable and important part of our Lord's discourses exhibits the use of figurative representations of a much more extended and diversified kind. We refer to the parables, which, both on account of their intrinsic importance, and the peculiarities connected with such a mode of instruction, demand a separate treatment.

It is marked by the Evangelists as a sort of era in our Lord's ministry, when He began to teach in parables. Each of the Synoptic Evangelists takes notice of it, and connects it with specific reasons. The period itself is not very definitely indicated; but it must have fallen, if not actually within the last year of His ministry, at least not far from its commencement; and if not absolutely the whole, certainly by much the greater number of His parables must be ascribed to the last year. At the same time, the formal employment of parabolic teaching was not the introduction of something entirely new. Christ's manner of teaching from the outset partook largely of figure; and some even of His earlier recorded utterances were parables of a shorter kind; for, while conveying a spiritual lesson, they bore a distinct and intelligible meaning also in the natural sense. Of this description are some parts of the Sermon on the Mount; for example, ch. v. 25, " Agree with thine adversary quickly, whiles thou art in the way with him; lest at any time the adversary deliver thee to the judge, and the judge deliver thee to the officer, and thou be cast into prison." Here human and earthly relations alone are directly mentioned, though it is plain, from the connection in which they stand, and the whole tenor of the discourse, that they are employed merely as the cover of a higher instruction. Not materially different are other things in the same discourse, and especially the concluding verses, in which the two classes of hearers—the fruitful and fruitless—are represented under the similitude of two builders, the one of whom erected his house on the sand, and the other on the solid rock. And in the interval between the delivery of the Sermon on the Mount, and the commencement of the more regular system of parabolic instruction, we find on record a few instances of similitude, which are always ranked with the parables—those, namely, of the old garment and the new patch, of the new wine and the old bottles (Matt. ix. 16, 17), and of the creditor and the two debtors in the house of Simon (Luke vii. 41, 42). So that the parabolic mode of instruction, to a certain extent, pervaded the ministry of Jesus; it was not altogether limited to any one period; only, at a particular stage, somewhere between the middle and the close, He commenced a more regular, frequent, and systematic use of the parabolic style. And to this later period it is, that the parables distinctively so called, belong.

I. In regard, first of all, to the reasons which may have led our Lord to adopt this mode of instruction, and to resort to it more especially in the concluding stages of His ministerial career, a variety of considerations may be named as having each had a certain share in the result.

1. In the first place, a foundation is laid for it in the nature of things, " in the harmony that exists, and that is unconsciously felt by all men between the natural and spiritual worlds, so that analogies from the first are felt to be something more than illus-

trations, happily, but not arbitrarily chosen."[1] Something more
—because they are the signs and witnesses of that happy adjust-
ment, which God has established between the external and internal worlds, between matter and mind, time and eternity ;
according to which the things that are seen are in many respects
the image of those which are not seen, and nature-processes are
at once designed and fitted to be emblems of the operations of
grace. In saying this, we do not need with some, among others
with Dr Trench, to go to the extreme of holding, that everything in nature has been pre-ordained expressly to shadow forth
and represent Divine mysteries ;—to hold, for example, that " all
the circumstances of our natural birth had been pre-ordained to
bear the burden of the great mystery of our spiritual birth," or
that the title of King, as applied to Christ, is not taken from
the kings of the earth, but " rather that He has lent His title to
them." We designate this an extreme, because it is an invert-
ing of the natural order of things as they present themselves to
our minds, and is also at variance with the whole current of
Scriptural representation on the subject. *There* the natural ever
precedes the spiritual, and the supernatural bases itself on the
natural; so that creation does not anticipate redemption, but redemption pre-supposes creation—pre-supposes it as in itself good
and right; and, in like manner, regeneration pre-supposes generation, and elevates it to a higher sphere. All we have to affirm
and hold is, that the author of the spiritual kingdom (as Tholuck,
on John xv., has very correctly and fitly expressed it) " is also
the author of the natural kingdom, and both kingdoms develop
themselves after the same laws. For this reason, the similitudes
which the Redeemer drew from the kingdom of nature, are not
mere similitudes, which serve the purpose of illustration, but are
internal analogies ; and nature is a witness for the kingdom of
God. Hence was it long since announced as a principle, that
'whatever exists in the earthly, is found also in the heavenly
kingdom.' Were it not so, those similitudes would not possess
that power of conviction, which they carry to every unsophisticated mind."

On this ground alone, then, we have a valid ground for the
employment by our Lord of the parabolic method of instruction.

[1] Trench on the Parables, p. 13.

He thereby drew the attention of His followers in every age to the profound and intimate connection that subsists between the realms of nature and of grace, and taught them to look through the one to the other. It was the more important that *He* should do this, as the kingdom He came to introduce stood in so many respects opposed to the world as it existed in His time, through the false views, grovelling superstitions, and horrid crimes under which it groaned. It had become, so to speak, a worn-out world,—corrupt nature had spent apparently its last efforts on it in vain ; and it seemed as if there was little more to be learned from it, or to be done for it. But our Lord, while mainly intent upon unfolding new views of the mind and purposes of Heaven, at the same time directed a new look into the secrets and principles of nature. By means especially of His inimitable parables, He showed, that when nature was consulted aright, it spoke one language with the Spirit of God ; and that the more thoroughly it is understood, the more complete and varied will be found the harmony which subsists between the principles of its constitution and those of Christ's spiritual kingdom.

2. A second reason very naturally suggests itself for this method of instruction, in the near assimilation, into which it brings a large portion of the teaching of Jesus with the acted lessons of His life, and with sacred history in general. That so much of the revelation of God to men consists of the facts of history, especially of biographical facts connected with the lives of God's saints, has ever been regarded by wise and thoughtful men as a striking proof of its adaptation to our natures, which so much more readily imbibe clear and lasting impressions in this way, than by set and formal instructions. And not only so, but by this means they can be taught much more in a brief compass than it is possible otherwise to impart to them. For, in a life, especially in such lives as are recorded in the Word of God, there is a great variety and fulness of instruction, admitting of a manifold applicability to the diversified fortunes and conditions of men. There is this, pre-eminently, in the life of Jesus, with its wondrous details of doing and suffering, and the unfathomable depths of wisdom and love, which it was ever exhibiting— alike incomparable in itself, and in the artless, engaging manner, in which it is presented to our view by the Evangelists. The

parables of Jesus, from the historical element in them, and the attractive form in which it appears, possess much of the same excellence. They are based, if not on what has actually occurred in the world of realities, at least on what *may* have occurred there, and often in effect *has* done so. Ideal histories they are, yet derived as to all their leading features from the actual, and these grouped together, and portrayed with the simplicity of nature itself. They are hence, in a brief compass, copious treasures of Divine wisdom, from which lessons, new and old, may be continually drawn. And however much we may strive to exhibit the several aspects of the Divine kingdom, we shall still find, that we can present nothing under any of them so complete, as is contained in some one of the parables, which is devoted to its illustration.

3. A third reason for our Lord's teaching in parables may be found in the opportunity it afforded of presenting more truth to the minds of His disciples than, from their continued dulness and carnality of spirit, could otherwise have been communicated to them. Steeped in prejudice, and, even when holding the truth in substance, mingling with it such partial, or mistaken apprehensions, they could with difficulty be got to receive with intelligence some of Christ's plainest revelations; and, at last, He was obliged to stay His hand in respect to the more direct and open communications of His mind, as He found the disciples were not able to bear, or to profit by it. But, by teaching in parables, and presenting the concerns of His kingdom under the image of familiar objects and earthly relations, He laid the ground-work of a most comprehensive and varied instruction. Many aspects of the kingdom were thus unfolded to them in a form they could easily grasp and distinctly comprehend—though, for the time, all remained, like the symbols of the Old Testament worship, very much as a dark and unintelligible cypher to their view. That cypher, however, became lighted up with meaning when the personal work of Christ was finished, and the Spirit descended with power to make application of its blessings, and the minds of the disciples were enabled to grasp the higher as well as the lower scheme of doctrine exhibited in the representation. Through the earthly form they could now descry the spiritual reality; and the advantage they derived from the types, when rightly

understood, they also derived, and in a still higher degree, from the parables.

4. Once more, another reason, and, indeed, the one that is most distinctly announced in the Gospels, for our Lord teaching so much in the latter part of His ministry in parable, was the judicial treatment involved in it—the practical rebuke it administered to the people generally, on account of their failure to receive the truth when presented in its simple and more direct form. After the parable of the sower and some others had been delivered, the disciples asked Jesus, " Why speakest Thou to them in parables?" And the answer pointed chiefly to the measure of darkness connected with them : " Unto you it is given (said He) to know the mysteries of the kingdom : but to them it is not given ; for whosoever hath, to him shall be given, and he shall have more abundance ; but whosoever hath not, from him shall be taken away even that which he hath. Therefore"—He added, with reference to the people, who belonged to the latter class, the persons who *had not*, as the disciples did to the former—" Therefore speak I to them in parables ; because they seeing, see not ; hearing, they hear not, neither understand." The import of the statement is, that the disciples, having to a certain extent used the privilege they possessed—having improved the talents committed to them —were to be intrusted with more ; while the body of the people, having failed to make a similar use of *their* opportunities—remaining destitute of Divine knowledge, notwithstanding all that had been taught them—were to have their means of knowing abridged, were to be placed under a more indirect and veiled method of instruction. This mode of dealing was in perfect accordance with the whole nature and tendency of the work of Christ in its relation to the hearts of men—which always carried along with it two ends, the one displaying the severity, and the other the goodness of God. From the first He was " set for the fall," as well as " the rising again," of many in Israel—for the enlightenment and salvation first, but, if that failed, then for the growing hardness and aggravated guilt of the people.

In the parable, viewed as a mode of instruction, there was necessarily a veiling of the truth for such as neither sought, nor obtained through private explanations, the key to its spiritual bearing. And in that *veiling* there was an act of judgment for previous indifference and contrariety to the manifestation of the truth. Because the people had not received it in love, when more openly presented to them, it now became wrapt in an obscurer guise, and was placed at a greater distance from their view. Even this, had it been rightly viewed, would have wrought beneficially upon their minds. For, had they not wilfully blinded their eyes and hardened their hearts, they would have seen in such a darkening of the Divine counsel something fitted to rouse and startle them; it would have fallen on their ear as the warning-note of coming retribution; and, perceiving that the Lord was showing Himself froward to the froward, they would have fled to the arms of mercy before severer judgment overtook them. This, undoubtedly, was what our Lord designed as the effect that *should* have been produced upon them by the change He adopted in His manner of teaching. And in certain cases it may have done so; but, with the greater part, the evil only proceeded from one stage to another, and, before leaving for the last time the cities in which most of His mighty works had been done, and His discourses delivered, He uttered against them those memorable woes which announced their approaching doom.

Such appear to have been the chief considerations which induced our Lord in the later period of His ministry, to use so commonly the parabolic mode of instruction. It is not so properly an additional reason, as a particular mode of representing those that have been specified, when the Evangelist Matthew says of Christ's speaking to the people in parables, " that it might be fulfilled which was spoken by the prophet, saying, I will open my mouth in parables, I will utter things which have been kept secret from the foundation of the world." What is here regarded as a prophecy, is a somewhat general declaration respecting the form of utterances common to the more special messengers of heaven. With certain characteristic differences, there still was something proper to them all in this respect, more particularly in those communications which had a prospective reference to the kingdom of God; there was a certain amount of figurative and analogical discourse required to their fulfilling aright their prophetic office. And it was unavoidable, that the greatest messenger and prophet of all should also exhibit this mark of the prophetic calling. It behoved to appear in *some* form; but the specific form it actually assumed in his hands was determined by the several considerations already mentioned. So that the allusion of the Evangelist to the passage in the forty-ninth Psalm, does not indicate anything new or different upon the subject, but is comprehensive of all the considerations, which actually weighed with our Lord, and induced Him to adopt the parabolic style.

II. We proceed now to the second leading point of inquiry respecting the parables of Jesus, viz., the proper mode of interpreting and handling them. We are not left here entirely to our own resources; for, on two occasions, very near each other, the disciples asked our Lord for an explanation of the parables He had delivered, and we have, in consequence, His interpretation of two of them. We are, doubtless, entitled to regard these examples of Divine exposition as specimens of the kind of exposition generally, that should be employed upon the parables, and the main features in them should be steadily kept in view by all interpreters.

1. The first thing, however, that requires to be attended to is one not noticed in our Lord's explanations, but taken for granted there as perfectly understood, viz. the correct reading of the parabolical representation itself, which forms the ground and cover of the spiritual instruction. We must obtain a clear understanding, and be able to give an accurate exposition of the meaning of the words, and the natural or historical allusions which they may contain. And the image or delineation, as a whole, in its merely natural aspect and relations, should be set forth in its proper fulness and simplicity, preparatory to our drawing from it the instruction it is fitted to convey. For the most part, this is not difficult—if only a moderate amount of scholarship is possessed, and such a cast of mind as is capable of taking up a fair impression, and giving forth a distinct representation of what is narrated:—not difficult, because usually the language in these portions of Scripture is remarkable for simplicity, and the parabolical narratives relate to the more familiar objects in nature and history. In a few cases only is some difficulty experienced. As an example of one in the language, we may point to the parable of the wheat and the tares—as it is commonly termed.

The difficulty lies here in determining exactly what is meant by ζιζάνια, the seed which the enemy scattered among the wheat, and which, it appears, did not attract any notice or excite any uneasiness, till the full blade had been put forth, and the ear had been formed. The tares, the ancient vicia, by which our translators have rendered the word, plainly do not altogether accord with the description; both because they are so different in form and appearance from wheat, that they should be detected the moment they rose above ground, and also because they are not of a noxious nature, but are grown for purposes of nourishment. Our Lord, there can be little doubt, referred to some weed with which His hearers were familiarly acquainted, and which was wont to be found in the corn-fields of Syria. The term *zizania* is, therefore, in all probability a Syrian word; and, accordingly, it never occurs in any Greek or Latin author, except in the writings of the Fathers, where they refer to this parable. They explained it differently, and if we except Jerome, none of them quite correctly. But there is a plant, which the Rabbins call *zunim*, and the Arabs of the present day *zulzan* (neither of them very far from the *zizania* of Scripture), which abounds in the corn-fields of Syria—a plant, which is at first very like wheat in appearance, which belongs to the same family, and which, when analysed, contains nearly the same ingredients, yet so different in its effects upon the human frame, that when the seeds remain mixed with the wheat, the flour thus produced always occasions dizziness and other injurious effects. There can be little doubt, that this is really the plant referred to. The only question (but one that can scarcely be said to affect the exposition of the parable) is, whether it is a distinct plant, or a sort of degenerate wheat—*afterwheat* as it is sometimes called. The Rabbinical doctors held it to be the latter: they said, as quoted by Lightfoot, "Wheat and zunim are not seeds of different kinds," but "zunim is a kind of wheat, which is changed in the earth, both as to its form and as to its nature." The ancient scholiast, too, writes on Virgil's infelix lolium, "Triticum et hordeum in lolium mutantur." This, certainly, may be reckoned doubtful; for the Rabbis and scholiasts were no great naturalists; and it is more common now to regard the zizanion as a separate plant, the *bearded darnel*, lolium temulentum, of naturalists. At all events, this plant, and not our tares, is what must be understood by the term in the parable—although it would be unwise now to substitute the one term for the other in our Bibles.

In the figurative representation of the parable, apart from the language in which it is expressed, there is seldom any difficulty. Only, it is necessary to exercise caution, so as not to extend the representation too far—carry it beyond the bounds within which it was intended to move. Thus, in the parable of the unjust steward, who is set up as a representative in the worldly sphere, of a selfish and carnal wisdom, choosing skilfully its means for the accomplishment of a desired end, we must take care to confine it to that one point, and abstain from giving it a more general direction. There is a higher wisdom even in the world than what is there exhibited, a wisdom that extends to the choice of a proper end, as well as to the employment of proper means:— but this is not brought into view in the representation of the parable.

2. The next thing to be attended to in the interpretation of the parables, is the main theme or leading idea, which they are severally intended to illustrate. For, there always is what may be so characterised—some special aspect of the Divine kingdom, or some particular line of duty to be followed, or of danger to be shunned, which the parable aims at exhibiting, and to which all its imagery is subservient. This, as Lisco has justly observed, " is the centre and kernel of the parable, and till it has been discovered and accurately determined, we need not occupy ourselves with the individual parts; since these can only be seen in their true light, when contemplated from the proper centre. We may compare," he adds, " the whole parabolical representation to a circle, the centre of which is the Divine truth or doctrine, and the radii are the several figurative traits in the narrative. So long as we do not stand in the centre, neither does the circle appear in an entirely round form, nor do the radii seem in their proper order, as all tending to the centre, and in beautiful uniformity:—this *is* done, when the eye surveys everything from the centre. So is it precisely in the parable. If we have brought clearly and distinctly out its central point, its principal idea, then also the relative position and right meaning of its several parts

become manifest, and we shall only dwell upon these in so far as the main theme can thereby be rendered more distinct."

In order to arrive correctly at this main theme, beside an exact and careful examination of the parable itself, the chief help is to be sought in the connection; and if this is closely considered, and the light it furnishes applied to the illustration of the subject, we shall rarely, if ever, be left in doubt as to the principal idea or doctrine, which it was designed to unfold. A few of the earlier parables, all those recorded in the 13th ch. of Matthew, and which were delivered about the same time, having been uttered one after another, without anything intervening between them in speech or action, can consequently derive no benefit from the immediate context. But with that exception, all the parables in the Synoptic evangelists are connected with occasions of an historical kind, very often also are preceded by a direct address; and then the principle couched in the address, or which the historical occasion served to bring out, is resumed, and for all times thrown into the form of an attractive and striking parable. Possibly, the parable may carry the instruction somewhat farther than was done by what immediately preceded, but it will be found to be only in the same line. Thus the beautiful and impressive parable of the rich fool, recorded in the 12th ch. of Luke, was occasioned by a person rudely interrupting Jesus, and requesting his interference with that person's brother, in order to obtain a division of the inheritance. Our Lord first repelled the intrusion by asking, "Man, who made Me a judge or a divider over you?" and then delivered to His followers the appropriate counsel, "Take heed, and beware of covetousness: for a man's life consisteth not in the abundance of the things which he possesseth." Now, the parable that follows is simply an embodiment of this great lesson, which is thrown into the parabolic form, to clothe it with life-like freshness, and give it a more impressive and touching influence on the heart. In like manner, the three parables in the 15th ch. of Luke—those of the lost sheep, the lost piece of money, and the prodigal son—all took their rise in the taunt thrown out by the Pharisees against Christ, that He received sinners and ate with them; and they each unfold, under so many different, yet closely related aspects, the grounds of the procedure, out of which the taunt originated; they explain and justify, on the common

L

principles and feelings of humanity, the merciful and considerate treatment, which the adversaries vilified.

These examples are comparatively simple; but there are others, in which the proper result is not so easily arrived at. It is, how- ever, to be sought in the same way; the connection, when closely surveyed, will generally be found the best help to ascertain the principal idea in the parable. In the case which, probably, pre- sents the greatest difficulty in this respect—that of the parable of the labourers in the vineyard, Matt. xxi.—we shall not search in vain if we look in the direction now indicated. By referring to the close of ch. xx., we find the parable was delivered for the purpose of embodying and illustrating a great principle, which Peter's self-complacent exhibition of the sacrifices he and the other apostles had made for Christ's sake, had elicited from the Saviour, " that many who were first should be last, and the last first." The main theme of the parable, which is summed up with the reiteration, in a somewhat stronger form, of this prac- tical saying, is comprised in the twofold truth therein contained. It teaches that the one class, the outwardly first, represented by the early called labourers, were unfit for the kingdom, because of the sense of merit, grounded on their early and long-continued services, rendering them indisposed to the simple reception of the gifts of grace, on which the Divine kingdom is founded. The other class, the outwardly last, represented by those who went into the vineyard at the eleventh hour, and who had nothing almost of their own on which to ground *any* claim to blessing—these, the parable teaches, *are* the proper subjects of the kingdom, having that deep spirit of humility, which disposes them to receive without a murmur whatever the Divine house- holder might give.

It is needless to multiply examples further. But it will be perceived, from what has been already stated, that the parable should be viewed in each case as one whole. If it is pervaded by some great idea, or specific lesson, it should be viewed and treated with a reference to this; and it cannot but suffer if it is broken up into a variety of separate parts, and each handled in- dependently of the others. At the same time, individual traits may, on certain occasions, be selected as the basis of a discourse, if only care is taken to exhibit the connection in which it stands with the unity of the entire representation, and a view is given of it properly consistent with the place belonging to it in that connection.

3. There is still another point, which requires consideration in the treatment of parables, but on which it is scarcely possible to lay down a very explicit direction. We refer to the regard that should be paid to the individual traits—how far they should, or should not, be looked upon as having a separate significance. It is here more especially that our Lord's interpretation of the two parables formerly noticed is fitted to yield an important service. From this we see, that every specific feature in the earthly type has its correspondence in the higher line of things it represents. Nothing, on the one hand, appears merely for ornament; while, on the other, nothing is wiredrawn, or made to bear a meaning that seems too much for it. It may, doubtless, be regarded as one of the indications of comparative perfection belonging to the parables of our Lord, that they admit of such a close and particular application; for the more numerous the points of agreement in such a case, the more perfect must be deemed the form of the discourse.

In connection with this, however, the distinctive nature of the parable should be borne in mind, which is not fitted for unfolding the particular facts or the more specific doctrines of the kingdom of Christ, as its more fundamental laws and broader features. In their nature, parables are a species of allegory, or symbol; and whatever variety or depth of meaning this is capable of embodying, it still must relate more to the great lines of truth and duty, than to the minuter details of either. If we should, therefore, go to the interpretation of them in a spirit of partizanship, eager to find support for some particular dogma we may be anxious to uphold, the result is sure to be an unnatural wresting of certain portions of the parable. And in all ages such has too frequently been the case in the treatment that has been given to this species of discourse.

In early times we find many indications of it. For example, the Manicheans sought support for their independent principle of evil, the essentially divine and creative power of the wicked one, in the representation given in the parable of the tares, respecting the sowing of the bad seed in the field—as if the existence of the bad were something altogether new, and not rather the depravation of what existed before. It is not, as Augustine contended, and many others of later times, that something is brought into being apart from the creation of God, or accomplishing what God alone could effect. The zizania were of God, as well as the wheat, only in the wrong place, and in that place a depravation—a travestying of the proper order and harmony of God's productions—an evil, as every work of Satan is. Nor can we regard it as anything but another, and, in principle, similar misinterpretation of the same parable, when many in modern times find in the sowing of the zizania, and the refusal of the householder to have them plucked up, an argument for the utter relaxation of discipline in the Christian Church. They thus place it in antagonism to the instruction contained in other portions of the New Testament; for example, the Epistles to the Seven Churches of Asia, and the First Epistle to the Corinthians, in which the strictest charges are given to maintain a watchful discipline, and the severest rebukes and threatenings are uttered on account of its neglect. The proper application of that part of the parable has respect only to such admixtures as spring up unperceived—those which the most vigilant oversight cannot prevent, or which, when they appear, are not so flagrantly offensive to Christian sense and purity, that they may at once be proceeded against as utterly opposed to the character of a Christian Church. It is only of such things that the representation can justly be understood, as of them only could it be said, that the judicial treatment of them by human instrumentality might involve the exclusion also of some of the true children from the state and privileges of grace. Comparing this parable with that of the sower, what is said in the one of the tares, nearly corresponds to what is said in the other of the third class of hearers—those in whom the cares of this life, and the deceitfulness of riches, spring up and choke the word. Both alike seem to include such as might be within the pale of the Christian Church, though becoming by degrees alien to it in spirit and character, yet still preserving so much of the form of godliness, that no merely human eye has sufficient discernment to draw the line of demarcation between them and others, nor could any human hand administer the proper discipline, without sometimes, at least, confounding together the children of God and the children of Satan.

A misuse, similar to those already noticed, has also frequently been made of the representation given in the parable of the prodigal son, of the reception which that son met with on his return to the father. No mention is there made of anything being necessary to secure the father's reconciliation, or provide for the son access to the bosom of his love, excepting the son's own penitent frame of mind, and actual return; and hence, it is argued, in the higher sphere of things represented by these, there can also be no need for more—an atonement in the ordinary sense cannot be required. But here the cases are not parallel— the representation, by this use of it, is stretched beyond the proper line; since it is not as a *father*, but as a *righteous governor*, that God requires an atonement for the guilty; and to press a feature of this kind in an exclusive sense, is simply to place it in antagonism to other parts of Scripture. This parable, like all the others, was intended to represent Divine things under the image of the human, only in *so far* as the one *could* present a parallel to the other. In the case of the earthly parent and child, there was *no room* for the introduction of an atonement as the basis of reconciliation; the whole that could, with any propriety, be exhibited, was the play of feeling from the one side to the other, with the results to which it led—every- thing of a more fundamental kind, or connected with other aspects and relations of the subject, being left, for the present, out of view.

Reference may still further be made in this connection to the treatment often given to the parables in a prophetical respect. Undoubtedly, they do generally contain a prophetical element, referring as well to the future progress and results of Messiah's kingdom, as to its existing character and condition. But they commonly do so under some particular aspect, one parabolical representation being chosen to give prominence to one feature, that was going to be developed, and another to another. Care, therefore, should be taken to keep in view the partial nature of each representation; otherwise particular traits will have undue significance attached to them, and the instruction conveyed by one parable will be brought into conflict with that of another.

Thus, the parable of the tares and wheat presents the future aspect of the kingdom as to the intermingling of the evil with the good—presents this as a state of things that should, more or less, continue to the end of time;—while the parable of the leaven hid in meal represents the Divine element in the kingdom working on till the whole was pervaded by it.   They are two different aspects, but perfectly consistent, if the parts in which they differ are not unduly pressed; but if otherwise, then the apparent continuance of evil in the one case, and its gradual extinction in the other, must become, not the complements, but the antitheses of each other.   The Divine leaven cannot spread onwards till all is leavened, without, at the same time, causing the tares of error and corruption to disappear.   But that there shall still, till the time of the end, be a certain admixture of the evil with the good, can readily be supposed; while, on the whole, the good continues to grow and spread, and becomes ultimately triumphant.

These hints, perhaps, may suffice.   It is impossible, on such a subject, to lay down precise and definite rules; and the exact line in each case can only be ascertained by careful consideration, a well-exercised judgment, and a spiritual sense, derived from a living acquaintance with the truths of the Gospel, and close attention to the manner in which they are revealed in Scripture.

SECTION TENTH.

ON THE SUBJECT OF PARALLELISM AS BEARING ON THE STRUCTURE AND INTERPRETATION OF NEW TESTAMENT SCRIPTURE.

IT seems to be the invariable tendency of the human mind— the consequence of its partial and imperfect working—that when it gets hold of a right principle, it cannot rest till this has been pushed in some direction to excess; and the subject of Scripture parallelism forms no exception to the rule.   It was to the fine discernment and poetical taste of Bishop Lowth that we owe the first correct appreciation of the distinctive characteristics of Hebrew poetry, and the establishment of what he denominated *parallelism*, as the peculiar feature of its rhythmical structure. He showed, first in his Prelections on Hebrew Poetry, and afterwards in his Preliminary Dissertation to his work on Isaiah, that while the poetry of the Hebrews did not admit of rhyme, nor of the regular metrical measures we meet with in the classical poets in Greece and Rome, yet it possessed a clearly marked rhythmical structure, consisting in a certain correspondence of the lines—not, however, in respect to the *sound*, but in respect to the *sense;* " a certain equality (as he defined it), resemblance, or relationship between the members of each period, so that in one or more lines or members of the same period things shall answer to things, and words to words, as if fitted to each other by a kind of rule or measure" (Prelec. xix.). Lowth gave to this rhythmical structure, as we have said, the name of Parallelism, or the parallism of members—a name which is sufficiently indicative of the reality, and is not likely, in this country at least, to be displaced by the " verse-rhythm," or " thought-rhythm" of Ewald. It is, however, in the thought or the sense that the rhythm properly lies. It is not simply, as Ewald justly states, a harmony of the members of the verse, but along with this, and as the foundation of this, " the rhythmical outpouring of the subject and life of the thoughts which fill the verse; and the beauty of the verse, as a whole, rises in proportion to the equilibrium and symmetry with which the sense is poured forth."

We are not called here to enter into any formal investigation of the subject of parallelism, as connected with the poetical portions of Old Testament Scripture. But it may be proper to state, that under the general principle of parallelism Bishop Lowth comprehended the different forms, which he called severally *synonymous, antithetic,* and *synthetic* or *constructive* parallels. The synonymous parallel lines are those which correspond one to another, by expressing the same sense in different but equivalent terms—when a proposition is delivered, and is immediately repeated in whole or in part, the expression being varied, but the sense entirely or nearly the same. As when it is said—

> " O-Jehovah, in-Thy-strength the-king shall-rejoice,
> And-in-Thy-salvation how greatly shall-he-exult!
> The-desire of-his-heart Thou-hast-granted unto-him,
> And-the-request of-his-lips Thou-hast-not-denied."

The correspondence here is confined to two lines, the second of the two having a formal resemblance both in thought and in membership to the first. But the correspondence may also extend to three, to four, or even to five lines.—The antithetic parallels are those " in which two lines correspond with one another by an opposition of terms and sentiments; in which the second is contrasted with the first, sometimes in expressions, sometimes in sense only." One of the simplest examples is Prov. x. 7, " The memory of the just is blessed, But the name of the wicked shall rot." Or this, Prov. xxvii. 6, " Faithful are the wounds of a friend, But deceitful are the kisses of an enemy." The antithesis expressed may differ both in kind and degree; and is found, indeed, to exist in very considerable variety, both in the Proverbs, where this species of parallelism particularly abounds, and in other parts of Scripture.—The synthetic or constructive parallel lines are those, " in which the parallelism consists only in the similar form of construction; in which word does not answer to word, and sentence to sentence, as equivalent or opposite; but there is a correspondence and equality between the different propositions in respect of the shape or turn of the whole sentence, and of the constructive parts: such as noun answering to noun, verb to verb, number to number, negative to negative, interrogative to interrogative."—From its very nature, this species of parallelism is of a somewhat looser, and more discursive sort than the others; but, as one of the best, and most familiar examples of it, we may point to Ps. xix., " The law of the Lord is perfect—converting the soul; The testimony of the Lord is sure —making wise the simple," etc.

Now, looking to this parallelism, as first explained by Bishop Lowth, and applied by him to the more strictly poetical portions of Scripture, one can easily see the propriety and fitness of having the rhythmical structure of those portions confined to such a characteristic. It is the simplest of all rhythmical forms, and the freest, and, as such, peculiarly adapted to inspired strains, in which, whatever scope may be allowed to the fancy, the form must still be subordinated to the sense. The artificial and complicated measures of classical poetry would have been unsuited to such a purpose; for it would have been difficult, next to impossible, for us to regard what was written, if thrown into such forms, as the unconstrained and fresh utterances of men, who spake as they were moved by the Holy Ghost. It is the chaste and natural simplicity of parallelism which peculiarly adapts it for sacred purposes, and renders the discourse so true, hearty, and confidential.[1] For, when the heart pours itself forth, there naturally flows stream upon stream—which is parallelism ; or it turns over the image, and shows the reverse side, in order to impress the matter more deeply upon the heart—and this again is parallelism. Only a measure which possessed such freedom and simplicity could have been worthy of being employed as the poetry of revelation. And this alone, too, properly consisted with the design of the Bible, as destined for the use of men, in every nation and of every language. It is the excellence of the simple rhythmical structure of Hebrew poetry, that it is " transfusible (to use the words of Bishop Jebb) into all languages—an excellence, not only unattainable in classical poetry, but prevented by classical metre. Classical poetry is the poetry of one language, and of one people. The words are, I shall not say *chosen* (though this be sometimes the case), but *arranged*, with a view, not primarily to the sense, but to the sound. In literal translation, therefore, especially if the order of the original words be preserved, not only the melody is lost, but the sense is irreparably injured. Hebrew poetry, on the contrary, is universal poetry, the poetry of all languages and of all peoples : the collocation of the words is primarily directed to secure the best possible announcement and discrimination of the sense ; and so, if a translator be only literal—if he only preserve, so far as the genius of his language will admit, the original order of the words, he will infallibly put the reader in possession of all, or nearly all, that the Hebrew text can give to the best Hebrew scholar of the present day."[2]

Bishop Lowth has himself—in the Introduction to his work on Isaiah—given examples of this : he has shown how, by adhering closely to the order of the original, not only may the parallelism be preserved, but a more lively and spirited exhibition also of the sense be given, than is done by neglecting it. And he has further shown, that by means of the parallelism the interpretation is sometimes aided, in those cases especially, in which rare words are employed, or words of doubtful import ; the plainer meaning of

[1] Herder, Hebr. Poesie, i. 21.   [2] Sacred Literature, p 20.

one member throwing light upon the corresponding one. At the same time, the help to be derived from this source is of a somewhat ambiguous character, and is very apt to lead astray. In the hands of Lowth himself, and of some of his followers, it led to not a few arbitrary interpretations, and unwarranted tamperings with the sacred text ; as a change in the received import of a word, or in the existing text, when it seemed favoured by the parallelism, presented itself as an easy mode of getting over a difficulty, while, perhaps, it only led to a departure from the true meaning of the original. As a help to interpretation, therefore, the parallelism of Hebrew poetry always requires to be used with much caution. It does so more especially on this account, that there is both a considerable diversity, and a great freedom manifested in the use of the parallel arrangement. So that what is called the *synonymous* parallel is not always, and indeed very rarely, altogether synonymous ; with a general similarity, it usually exhibits some distinct shade of meaning ; and, again, when there is something of antithesis, the sentiment expressed is often but partially antithetic.

Bishop Lowth was not insensible of such freedoms and shades of diversity ; for, when speaking of the second member of synonymous parallels, he represents it as containing either *entirely*, or *nearly*, the same sense as the first. And in his 4th Prelection, when treating generally of the subject of parallelism, he says not merely that they repeat, but also that they vary and strengthen the sense (idem iterant, variant, augent). Practically, however, this was too much overlooked both by him, and by his followers ; and the custom sprung up and grew, among lexicographers and commentators, of ascribing many unwarranted meanings to words, on the simple ground, that the sense as determined by the parallelism seemed to require them. On this practice, which extended to the Greek Scriptures also, Bishop Jebb very properly cautioned biblical students : he said, " The *assumed* synonyme of periods, members, or lines, has, in many instances, occasioned the consequent *assumption,* that in the Alexandrine translators of the Old Testament words are synonymous, which in all other writers have totally diverse meanings ; and the same principle has been applied to several words and passages in the New Testament." He adds, " Let the cited passages be carefully examined, and I venture to affirm, that instead of a synonyme, there will almost universally be found an important variation of meaning, between the related members; commonly a progress in the sense; but always such a variation as will quite supersede the necessity of resorting to an unusual, much less an unprecedented, acceptation of the terms employed" (p. 51).

Jebb, however, fell into something like an opposite extreme; and, instead of being satisfied with showing a general variation in the meaning of one parallel line as compared with another, he sought to establish a uniform and regular progression of thought in the sentences. Hence, the parallels of the first class, instead of being called *synonymous*, have come to be usually designated *gradational*—though Jebb himself preferred the term *cognate*. We call this an *extreme* in the opposite direction; for though there can be no doubt, that in a very large proportion of the parallelisms of Scripture, there is a gradational advance, an intensifying of the sense in the second parallelistic line as compared with that given in the first, yet in a considerable number of cases there is a substantial agreement, or a diversity without anything that can fitly be called a progression of thought. And the attempt to make out a uniform gradational sense in the parallelism has led, not unfrequently, to forced interpretations. Take, for example, one of Jebb's illustrative passages:—

> " Who shall ascend the mountain of Jehovah?
> And who shall stand within His holy Place?
> The clean of hands, and the pure in heart."—Ps. xxiv. 3, 4.

" To ascend," says Jebb, "marks progress; to *stand*, stability and confirmation; the *mountain of Jehovah*, the site of the Divine sanctuary; His *holy place*, the sanctuary itself; and in correspondence with the advance of the two lines which form the first couplet, there is an advance in the members of the third line: the clean of hands, and the pure in heart:—the clean of hands shall ascend the mountain of Jehovah, the pure in heart shall stand within His holy place" (p. 40). Augustine, as Jebb acknowledges, had in substance made the same distinction; but whenever, or by whomsoever made, I hold it to be quite fanciful—at least in the form in which it has now been presented.

The Psalmist is plainly describing, in this part of the Psalm, the sincere worshipper of God, and doing so in respect to his going to appear before God at the appointed place of worship under the Old economy. But nothing seems farther from his mind, than the thought of delineating different degrees of purity, and of privilege connected with it—one to occupy a certain position of nearness, and another to occupy a higher and a holier. To ascend God's mountain, in the sense here contemplated, was all one, in substance, with standing in His holy place ; for, it was for the purpose and with the view of standing in such a place, that the worshipper comes into consideration as ascending the mountain ;—and the law of Moses recognised no distinction of the kind here indicated—between cleanness of hands fitting for one act of worship, or one stage of approach, and purity of heart fitting for another. Cleanness of hands has no other significance than as a symbol of moral purity ; if it differs at all from the other expression—purity of heart—it can only be in pointing more to the life as embodying the purity, which has its seat in the heart ;—but the two expressions at most denote, not different *degrees* of goodness, but different *aspects* of the same goodness. Besides, in a continuous description of this sort, how can you stop simply at the second term of the description ? If there is a progression in the two first, why should it not extend also to what follows ? It is added, " Who hath not lifted up his soul to vanity, nor sworn deceitfully." Do these denote a gradation of excellence beyond purity of heart ? Or is the one clause here also to be connected with ascending the mountain, and the other with standing in the holy place ? Neither of these assertions can with any propriety be made. And on this ground also we hold, that the distinction is an entirely fanciful one ; and that the description ought to be viewed in its entireness, as the description, under a variety of aspects, of one who might appear with acceptance among God's sincere worshippers. The several epithets are not absolutely synonymous, but neither are they gradational ; they are merely diverse representations of the righteous man's state and character.

It is, therefore, my conviction, that the principle of parallelism has been carried to excess by Dr Jebb and his followers, in the way of discovering correspondences or relations of a somewhat more complicated and artificial kind, than really exist. But the chief excess has been in connection with what is called the *introverted* parallelism—a *fourth* form introduced by Jebb—and its application to portions of the New Testament writings. On this sort of parallel, Jebb says, "There are stanzas so constructed, that whatever be the number of lines, the first line shall be parallel with the last; the second with the penultimate; and so throughout, in an order that looks inward, or, to borrow a military phrase, from flanks to centre." One of the longest examples given of this by Jebb is also, perhaps, the best for his purpose that could have been selected : it is in Psalm cxxxv. 15–18, and consists of eight lines, of which the first and eighth are held to be parallel—then the second and seventh—the third and sixth—and finally, the two beside each other, the fourth and fifth, in the centre. The passage is the following :—

" The idols of the heathen are silver and gold,	" They have ears, but they hear not;
The work of men's hands:	Neither is there any breath in their mouths.
They have mouths, but they speak not;	They who make them are like unto them;
They have eyes, but they see not;	So are all they who put their trust in them."

" In the *first* line," says Dr Jebb, " we have the idolatrous heathen ; in the *eighth*, those who put their trust in idols; in the *second* line the fabrication, in the *seventh* the fabricators ; in the *third* line mouths without articulation, in the *sixth* mouths without breath ; in the *fourth* line eyes without vision, and in the *fifth* ears without the sense of hearing." No doubt, a sort of correspondence throughout, but, at the same time, no organic connection, or peculiar relationship between the lines thus artificially brought together—nothing that materially contributes to help the meaning. Thus, in the first and last, " the idols of the heathen are silver and gold—so are all they who put their trust in them." What is gained, we ask, by bringing these far-distant lines into juxtaposition ? So far from the sense thereby gaining in force and clearness, it is not even preserved ; and though, it is true, idolatrous persons are the subjects in both of them, yet this is no more than what may be said of the seventh line—" they who make them are like to them,"—and one might as well join together the first and seventh as the first and eighth. Indeed, rather do so, as this collocation would make sense, while the other does not. The parallelism, therefore, viewed in respect to the sense, which is the main point, fails in the manner it is here attempted to be carried out; and we gain nothing by throwing ourselves back from the later to the earlier line, with which it is supposed to have some special affinity. On the contrary, we are in danger of losing the real progression of thought, which appears in the passage, when viewed consecutively, for a somewhat fanciful arrangement of its several parts. So also in multitudes of passages, that might be produced from human compositions, it might be perfectly possible to throw the successive lines of thought into similar combinations, although these were quite remote from the mind of their respective authors; but by doing so we should gain nothing, we should rather lose by making the attempt.

It may be well to give proof of this by pointing to some examples; but let me first present some idea of the extent to which the parallelistic principle has been carried. A great portion of Bishop Jebb's work on Sacred Literature was devoted to the purpose of applying that principle, and more especially this latter form of it, to New Testament Scripture. Of course, there *are* parallelisms there. The language of the New Testament, as well as its doctrines, spring out of the Old; and where the poetical element enters, it naturally assumes much of the ancient form; the parallelistic structure is more or less preserved. It is not, therefore, the fact of the existence of parallelisms in New Testament Scripture, but the limits within which they should be confined, or the form they may be made to assume, that can be regarded as just matter of controversy. It is not the presence, but the excess of the principle, as exhibited by the class of writers referred to, to which we object. But this principle, first of all, is often sought for in cases where there is nothing peculiar— where there is merely such a structure of the sentences as the mind naturally adopts when tersely expressing its thoughts, without thinking of any regular measures or parallel lines. Thus, in Luke xii. 48, " Unto whomsoever much is given, of him shall much be required; and to whom they have committed much, of him shall they demand the more;"—or Gal. vi. 8, " He who soweth to the flesh, shall of the flesh reap corruption; and he who soweth to the Spirit, shall of the Spirit reap life eternal." In Matt. viii. 20, we have an example of what is called the triplet, there being three lines in parallelism,—" The foxes have dens, And the birds of the air have nests, But the Son of Man hath not where to lay His head;" and again, in Rev. xiv. 18, " Put forth thy sharp sickle, And gather in the clusters of the vine of the earth, For its grapes have become fully ripe." Then, there is the quatrain, consisting of two parallel couplets, the pairs of which are termed sometimes directly, sometimes inversely parallel—of which the passages just cited from Luke and Galatians may be taken as specimens;—or this in John xv. 10, " If ye keep My commandments, Ye shall abide in my love, Even as I have kept My Father's commandments, And abide in His love:"—And even this in Mark xii. 12, " And they sought to seize Him, And they feared the people; For they knew that against them he spake the parable; And having left Him, they departed." But examples of longer stanzas, having five, six, and even more lines, are produced—such as John xi. 9, 10, " Are there not twelve hours in the day? If a man walk in the day he stumbleth not; Because he seeth the light of this world: But if a man walk in the night he stumbleth; Because the light is not in him" (*five*);—also Matt. xxiv. 7, 8; 1 Thess. v. 7, 8; Rom. ii. 28, 29. For those of six, see Matt. xvi. 2, 3 (" When it is evening, ye say, ' a calm!' For the sky is red: And in the morning, 'to-day a tempest;' For the sky is red and lowering: Hypocrites! the face of the sky ye know how to discern, But ye cannot [discern] the signs of the times"). Also Luke xii. 4, 5, 47, 48; 1 Cor. xv. 47–49; and many parts of the Sermon on the Mount.

Now, that there is nothing of the proper parallel arrangement in such passages as these, is evident from the difficulty often of knowing where precisely the division of the lines should be made, or which part is to be held as corresponding with another. One has to cast about for a time, to see how the sentences can be brought into shape; and were it not for the stanza-form, into which they are thrown by the advocates of parallelism, very few persons would ever have imagined, that they really admitted of such an arrangement. They belong to that species of composition, which consists of apophthegm, or short sententious utterances, usually embodying some sort of comparison or contrast; and in which the mind naturally—in modern as well as ancient times, in its ordinary as well as in its loftier moods—throws its words

into set forms and relative proportions—but without ever thinking of anything like remote and complicated parallels. Open,
for example, Lord Bacon's Collection of Apophthegms, and take
one of the very first that occurs. As presented by him, it forms
two short sentences; but in the hands of the Parallelists it would
make a choice specimen of the introverted quatrain—thus:

> Good fame is like fire:
> When you have kindled it, you may easily preserve it;
> But if once you have extinguished it, you will not easily kindle it again,
> At least not make it burn as bright as it did.

Here, it might be stated, the first and the last lines correspond;
they both speak of fire in its capacity of burning, or shining
brightly. Then, the two intermediate clauses refer to two different conditions, with their respective effects—the fire, when
once kindled, easily preserved; when extinguished after having
been kindled, not easily lit up anew. But what is gained by this
sort of introversion? Does it throw additional light on the
thoughts expressed, or present them in a more striking aspect?
Not in the least; it only suggests an artificial arrangement, where
none whatever was intended, and the mind of the writer was
merely following the natural course of its thoughts and feelings.
—We might say substantially the same of another example in
Bacon: " In great place, ask counsel of both times—Of the
ancient time, what is best; and of the latter time, what is
fittest :"—quite natural and orderly as it stands, but incapable of
being improved by being drawn out into parallels. Or, look at
this longer specimen from the same quarter :—

> " The empirical philosophers are like pismires,
>   They only lay up and use their store ;
> The rationalists are like the spiders,
>   They spin all out of their own bowels.
> But give me a philosopher who is like the bee,
>   Who hath a middle faculty,
>   Gathering from abroad,
> But digesting that which is gathered,
>   By his own virtue."

Thrown into so many lines, this passage, doubtless, presents a
great variety of parallels—parallels, too, much more distinctly
marked, and more easily detected, than many of those found in
New Testament Scripture. But what advantage is gained by

presenting the passage in such a form ? Was this form present to the mind of the writer ? Or, when exhibited, does it serve to bring out the thoughts in a more lucid and impressive manner? The writer himself has simply put them down as so many consecutive sentences—each growing naturally out of what preceded; and, so far from making any improvement upon the manner of exhibiting the truths stated, the introduction of parallelisms would tend rather to lead our minds in the wrong direction—make us conceive of him as busying himself about artificial forms of expression, while in reality he was intent only upon giving distinct utterance, or logical sequence, to the ideas which had formed themselves in his mind. The proper parallelism—that which by way of distinction should be so called—is a particular form of that measured diction, which the mind in an elevated state of feeling instinctively adopts, as necessary to give adequate expression to the fiery glow, or swelling fulness of sentiment, of which it is conscious : it cannot be satisfied with itself, till it has thrown its conceptions and feelings into such a compressed and regulated form. But in the examples that have been adduced both from Bacon and the New Testament, it is the reflective or logical faculties that are at work. The mind is in its ordinary mood, and merely seeks in a pointed and consecutive manner to present its thoughts on some particular topic. So that introverted parallelisms, or complicated structures of any kind, are out of place ; nor can they serve any purpose but that of suggesting the idea of constraint or art, where in reality nothing of the kind existed.

Not only, however, does this extreme fondness for parallelisms, and the attempt to discover them in the simply didactic or historical portions of New Testament Scripture, tend to give too artistic and constrained an appearance to such portions, but it leads occasionally to fanciful conceits, and false interpretations. The most part, as we have said, of the Sermon on the Mount has been turned into examples of parallelisms—some of them of the most involved and intricate description, but never with the effect of throwing any fresh light upon its different parts—sometimes, however, with the effect of arbitrarily changing the connection, and obscuring the natural import. In proof of this we may take one of Jebb's examples, which is re-produced by Dr Forbes, in

M

his work on Scripture Parallelism—viz., Matt. vii. 6 : " Give not, that which is holy to the dogs, Neither cast your pearls before swine ; Lest they trample them under their feet, And turn about and rend you." This is considered as a specimen of the introverted parallelism ; so that the first and the fourth go together, then the second and the third. It is, therefore, according to Dr Jebb, to be read thus : " Give not that which is holy to the dogs, Lest they turn about and rend you ; Neither cast your pearls before swine, Lest they trample them under their feet." And this interpretation is justified on the ground, that our Lord wished to place the more dangerous act of imprudence first and last, so as to make it, and its fatal result, produce the deepest impression on the mind ;—while the other, and less senseless form, that represented by the image of casting pearls before swine, is placed in the middle. But, in that case, by the ordinary laws of construction, something would have been required to carry back our thoughts from the last to the first member : and Dr Jebb, sensible of this, shoves in a *those* before the verbs in the last line—" Lest *those* turn about and rend you." And, indeed, to make the matter quite right, the *they* in the preceding clause should have been *these :* it should have stood thus : " Give not that which is holy to the dogs, Neither cast your pearls before swine : Lest *these* (the swine) trample them under their feet, And *those* (the dogs) turn about and rend you." In this way, no doubt, the references become tolerably plain ; but it is a plainness, for which we are indebted to the invention or arbitrariness of an interpreter who has a theory to support, and adjusts the words to the theory, rather than the theory to the words. Plainness of this kind is too easily found to be of much value, and in the present case it is not needed. For, while both dogs and swine might be included in the latter part of our Lord's statement, it is the swine more especially, not the dogs, that must be meant. The one, as well as the other, might turn about and rend those, who threw something in their way ;—but from the very nature of the case, it is the swine we are here naturally led to think of as acting such a part :—both, because they are the more voracious and savage in disposition, and because the thing cast to them, pearls, being fitted to mock, rather than to satiate their appetite, it was quite natural for them to turn about and

rend the person, who had thus provoked, without satisfying their
greed.   The dogs, on the other hand, had no temptation to act
so ferocious a part; for in having what was holy given to them,
they doubtless had what they wished—they got flesh to eat;
only, being *holy* flesh, they were incapable of appreciating its
distinctive character, and treated it as a common thing.   Understood spiritually, the dogs represent those, who are in such a
grovelling and debased condition, that they have no aptitude for
the things of God—no relish or capacity for spiritual exercises
and enjoyments; so that to admit *them* to sacred privileges, or
to spread before them the joys of the Divine life, were only to
give them an opportunity of treating as common, *profaning*, what
should be handled with holy reverence and spiritual relish.   The
characters represented by the swine, however, are such as have
reached a more advanced stage in the course of depravity—not
grovelling, merely, and sensual, but also devilish—ready to re-
sent as evil what has been *meant* for good, but does not suit their
unhallowed appetite; hence disposed, not only to treat with
despite or scorn the pearls of Gospel truth and promise, but also
to vilify, abuse, or persecute those, who would press these on
their regard.   It is such, therefore—the characters represented
by the swine—the sour, ungenial, repulsive, or furious, as well
as worldly spirits, who are chiefly referred to, and warned against
as likely to turn again, and rend those who might offer the
precious things of the Gospel to them.—Thus, it appears, that
the natural order and connection is also the best; and the search
after a more artificial arrangement only leads to a mistaken application of the images employed.

The same line of remark in substance might be extended to
many other passages in New Testament Scripture, to which the
principle of parallelism has been applied.   And the objections
already urged are *a fortiori* valid in regard to a still further extension of the principle, which has occasionally been made—in
particular by Mr Boys, in what he designates a *Key to the
Book of Psalms*, and more recently adopted by Dr Forbes.   By
this more extended application of the principle, whole chapters,
and passages long enough to form a chapter, are treated as specimens of the introverted parallelism.   The entire Epistle of
Philemon is held to be constructed on this principle—the two

verses at the centre (ver. 15, 16) having something in common,
viz. one and the same subject, Onesimus; and then the respective
verses on each side, as they recede from this centre, possessing what
is thought to render them parallel one to another. The merest
glance over the arrangement is sufficient to convince any unbiassed
mind, that it is altogether fanciful; since what are called parallel
verses have often so little in common, that no one, who was not
in search of resemblances, would ever have thought of them. But
even if there had been more to countenance the idea in appearance, we should still have rejected it. The very conception of
such complicated and artificial structures has something palpably
and painfully unnatural about it, and is utterly opposed to the
simplicity, which we cannot but associate with the epistolary and
didactic parts of Scripture. It is as if one should compress the
free and spontaneous movements of Spirit-stirred minds within
bones of steel, and make art, rather than nature, the ground-form
of the utterances of God's Spirit. Such applications of parallelism,
therefore, must be ranked as a vicious excess—unsound in principle, and sure, in practice, to lead to frivolous conceits. Parallelism, as already remarked, properly belongs to the poetical
province, being the simplest of the measured and regular forms,
into which a poetical elevation throws the conceptions and feelings, which it strives to give forth. If judiciously applied to those
portions of Scripture which partake of this elevation, the beauty
of the composition, and the fulness and force of the thoughts
expressed in it, will be more distinctly perceived, and may be
more impressively set forth. But when brought into the province
of history, of epistolary writing or familiar discourse, if admitted
to a place at all, it must be within very narrow bounds, and in
connection only with the simpler modes of construction.

PART SECOND.

DISSERTATIONS ON PARTICULAR SUBJECTS CONNECTED WITH THE EXEGESIS OF NEW TESTAMENT SCRIPTURE.

I.

THE TWO GENEALOGIES OF CHRIST, GIVEN RESPECTIVELY BY THE EVANGELISTS MATTHEW AND LUKE.

THERE are several marked and characteristic differences between the two genealogical tables presented by the Evangelists of the human ancestry of our Lord—differences that from a very early period have occasioned embarrassment to interpreters, and have often been pronounced inexplicable discrepancies. Nor is it only in the things in which they differ that they have given rise to trouble and dispute; but a still more perplexing circumstance, if possible, has been found, in a matter on which they are, at least, *apparently* agreed; namely, that it is with Joseph, not with Mary, that the genealogical descent of Jesus is formally connected. What renders this the more remarkable is, that the two Evangelists, who thus agree in dropping the name of Mary from any *ostensible* or *direct* connection with the descent from David and Abraham, are precisely those, who expressly record the miraculous conception of Jesus, and so provide an explicit testimony to the fact, that He was strictly the Son only of Mary, and not of Joseph. There can be no doubt that this is, in some respects, the greater difficulty adhering to these tables, since it touches the point of our Lord's title to the name and office of Messiah. It is, therefore, the point to which our attention shall be primarily directed, yet so as not to neglect the others, which are also of considerable interest and importance.

I. Here we observe at the outset, that there are certain preliminary considerations, which ought, in all fairness, to be borne
in mind, and which, apart from all minutiæ belonging to the
construction of the genealogies, go far to determine the chief
historical question.   It is certain, for example, that up till the
period of our Lord's birth, and even after His death, genealogical
registers were kept in Judea, both publicly and privately; so
that ample materials must have existed for investigating all that
concerned the lineage of Jesus.   This fact, like most others in
Gospel history, has been questioned, chiefly on the ground of a
statement of Julius Africanus, who wrote, in the earlier part of
the third century, a chronicon, of which a fragment on this subject has been preserved by Eusebius (Hist. Eccl. i. 7).   Africanus
there reports, that Herod, conscious of the infelicity of his birth,
and anxious to prevent the possibility of detecting it, burned the
public family registers, "imagining that he should then appear
noble, when no one could derive from the public monuments the
evidence of a descent from the patriarchs, or the proselytes, and
the mixed multitude that was called *georæ*."   On what grounds
this statement was made, nothing is known; nor does it appear,
that Africanus himself had any great confidence in its historical
correctness; for he introduces the narrative as delivered by the
descendants of those who were the kinsmen of Jesus, "either
for the purpose of display [in respect to their own pedigree], or for
simply declaring the truth;" and at the close introduces the
qualifying clause, "Whether the matter actually stood thus or not"
(εἴτ᾽ οὖν οὕτως, εἴτ᾽ ἄλλως ἔχει).   The story must be held to be, if
not entirely fabulous, at least a great exaggeration of some law-
less proceedings on the part of Herod or his abettors.   Josephus
is altogether silent respecting any such destructive measures,
which, if they had actually occurred to the extent described,
could scarcely have been practicable: more than that, he expressly testifies, that he took the materials of the abstract he gave
of his own family descent from those same public registers
(δέλτοις δημοσίοις ἀναγεγραμμένην εὗρον, Vit. i. 1), and at a period
considerably later than that of the birth of Christ.   The reference, too, of the Apostle Paul once and again to genealogies,
as matters with which certain Jewish teachers were wont need-
lessly to entangle themselves and others (1 Tim. i. 4; Titus iii.

14), is a sufficient proof of the plentiful existence of such documents. And so also is the reference made to them in the Protevangelium of James, which, though a spurious production, is yet of very great antiquity. There can, therefore, be no reasonable doubt of the late existence of registers, or genealogical tables, public as well as private; and the means must have been accessible to all, who had a mind to examine the point, for determining whether Jesus was really of the house and lineage of David. Nor can we doubt, from the nature and intensity of the opposition made to Him, that, if the evidence on this point had not been known to be of the most conclusive kind, the defect would certainly have been discovered, and pressed to the prejudice of His claims. If His title to a Davidic origin was not impugned, the reason could only be, that it was incapable of being gainsayed.

It is further to be borne in mind, that both Christ's title to be regarded as the Son of David, and the evangelical testimony in favour of that title, by no means rests exclusively, or even principally, upon the preservation in the Gospels of the two Genealogies. There is much evidence besides upon the subject, and evidence of a more patent and obtrusive kind. In the annunciation of His birth to the Virgin, it was declared, that the *throne of His father David* should be given to Him—implying, that simply as born of her, He stood connected with the throne and family of David. During the course of His public ministry, He allowed Himself to be openly addressed as the Son of David (Matt. ix. 27, xv. 22)—again implying both what He Himself claimed, and what was commonly believed respecting Him. On the day of Pentecost, St Peter proclaimed to the assembled thousands, that God had raised Him up of the fruit of David's loins, to sit upon his throne (Acts ii. 30); and in several passages St Paul represents Him as having been of the seed of David, according to the flesh (Rom. i. 3; 2 Tim. ii. 8; Acts xiii. 23). Finally, in the Apocalypse He is designated "the root and offspring of David" (ch. xxii. 16). Most plain, therefore, it is, that neither our Lord Himself, nor His immediate followers, made any secret of His strict and proper relationship to the house of David—itself a conclusive proof, that it had a solid ground to rest upon, and could challenge the fullest scrutiny. The very objections urged against Him may be cited as evidence; for, while they occasionally grazed the border of this important point, they never actually struck upon it, and so yielded a virtual testimony in its support.   It was perfectly understood, that if He was the Son of David, and the heir to his throne, He behoved to be born at Bethlehem (Matt. ii. 5; John vii. 42); and on this account the objection *was* raised against Jesus, that He was a Galilean, and came forth from Nazareth, whence nothing good in the spiritual sphere might be looked for (John i. 46, vii. 52); but it never took the form of an allegation laid, or even a suspicion uttered, against His connection by birth with the house of David.   This is the more remarkable, as His residence from childhood in Galilee gave His adversaries a *prima facie* ground to question it; doubts could scarcely fail to be stirred in many minds on the subject; and that these doubts did not find any audible utterance or assume a tangible form, can only be accounted for by the conclusive evidence which existed of His royal parentage.

Still further, the report of Hegesippus concerning the relatives of Jesus in a subsequent generation, furnishes a collateral proof, as it clearly indicates the general and settled belief of the time. He states, as quoted by Eusebius (Hist. Eccl. iii. 20), that the grandchildren of Judas, the brother of Jesus, were accused to the Emperor Domitian, and brought before him for examination, because of their reputed connection with the royal line of David; but that when Domitian ascertained their humble circumstances, and the spiritual nature of the kingdom they ascribed to Jesus Christ, he despised them and sent them away.   It thus appears, that amid all the circumstances that had become known concerning Christ down to the close of the first century—the claims put forth on the part of His followers, and the objections or surmises raised on the part of His adversaries—the belief of His personal relationship to the house of David remained unshaken.

The fact, therefore, of our Lord's real descent from David must be held as certain, whatever difficulties concerning it may hang around the two genealogical tables.   The subject of inquiry in respect to them narrows itself to the point, how they can be made to appear consistent with the truth of things, and not in antagonism with each other.   There are certain palpable differences between them, which are fitted to suggest the idea of their having been drawn up on somewhat different principles; and the thought very naturally suggests itself, that if these could only be ascertained, a satisfactory explanation would be found of the diversities subsisting between them.

II. Is this diversity of principle in the construction of the two genealogies to be sought—as regards the main point at issue— in the one evangelist presenting the genealogy of Jesus through Joseph the reputed and legal father, and the other through Mary the only real parent, according to the flesh? If this were a practicable mode—exegetically considered—of understanding what is written, it would, no doubt, present a comparatively natural and easy solution of the greater differences. But so far is it from appearing on the face of the language, that it seems never so much as to have occurred to the earlier writers, who had their minds specially directed to the subject. With one consent they referred both genealogies to Joseph, and appear to have been little troubled by the absence of any specific mention of the lineage of Mary. Africanus, who made the subject a matter of very careful investigation, makes no allusion to this point, as tending to create in his mind any embarrassment. Jerome, indeed, refers to it; but thinks it enough to say, that Joseph's relation to the tribe of Judah and the house of David determined also Mary's, since by the law people were obliged to marry from among their own tribe :[1]—although he could scarcely be ignorant, that however customary this might be, there is no express enactment upon the subject; and, indeed, in the case of the daughters of Zelophehad, the legislation actually made proceeded upon the usual liberty of the females to marry into any tribe, and prescribed a limit in *their* case, and cases of a similar kind, only for the sake of perpetuating the inheritance. When there was nothing peculiar in this respect, it was perfectly allowable, and not uncommon, for the husband to belong to one tribe

[1] Quærat diligens lector et dicat : Quum Joseph non sit pater Domini Salvatoris, quid pertinet ad Dominum generationis ordo deductus usque ad Joseph? Cui respondebimus primum, non esse consuetudinem Scripturarum, ut mulierum in generationibus ordo texatur. Deinde, ex una tribu fuisse Joseph et Mariam; unde ex Lege eam accipere cogebatur ut propinquam. —In Matt. i. 18.

and the wife to another. In the Gospel age, also, when remnants of all the tribes were thrown together, such intermarriages would naturally be more frequent. Augustine, the contemporary of Jerome, goes, somewhat singularly, into the opposite extreme; and while of opinion that Mary must have had some connection (he does not state what) with the house of David, he is rather disposed to lay stress upon her relationship to Elizabeth, and her connection with the house of Aaron; for, he says, " it must be held most firmly, that the flesh of Christ was propagated from both stems, that alike of the kings and of the priests, the personages in whom among the Hebrews was figured that mystic unction (namely, chrism), whence the name of Christ beams forth, so long before also pre-intimated by that most evident sign."[1] Chrysostom, in his second homily on St Matthew, reverts to Jerome's mode of explanation, and puts it in a still stronger form. He says, " not only was it not lawful to marry from another tribe, but not even from another family (οὐδὲ ἀπὸ πατριᾶς ἑτέρας) ; that is," he adds, " kindred (συγγενείας)." This is the chief explanation he gives, although he also points to the words used by the angel Gabriel, of whom it is said, that he was sent to " a virgin espoused to a man whose name was Joseph, of the house of David "—understanding the latter expression, " of the house of David," to refer, not to Joseph the immediate, but to Mary the remote, antecedent; in which he is not followed by the better class of interpreters. He indicates no doubt, however, any more than the other writers of early times, that both genealogies bore respect to the ancestry of Joseph.

This general agreement, for so long a time, as to the fact of Joseph's lineage being exhibited in both tables—the absence of any idea, that either of them did, or by possibility might be understood, to trace the descent of Mary, undoubtedly affords a strong presumption against the idea itself, as proceeding on a too subtle or somewhat forced interpretation of the text. It was only about the period of the Reformation that the opinion seems to

---

[1] Firmissime tenendum est carnem Christi ex utroque genere propagatam, et regum scilicet et sacerdotum, in quibus personis apud illum populum Hebræorum etiam mystica unctio figurabatur, id est, chrisma, unde Christi nomen elucet, tanto ante etiam illa evidentissima significatione prænuntiatum. —De Consensu Evang. ii. 2.

have been distinctly brought out and advocated, of Mary's genealogy being given in Luke, and Joseph's in Matthew—the one for the satisfaction of the Jews, who, in matters of this description, made account only of males; and the other for the satisfaction of mankind in general, who might seek to know the lineage of Jesus, not through his reputed or legal father, but through his one real earthly parent. Calvin refers to it as a view which had its known advocates in his day, but rejects it as untenable; and, though it has since numbered many learned names on its side—those, among others, of Osiander, Calov, Spanheim, Lightfoot, Rosenmüller, Paulus, Kuinoel—yet it must be held to be without any just foundation in the text, and even to do violence to its plain import. The view is based on the words of the Evangelist Luke, when introducing the subject of the genealogy, "And Jesus Himself was about thirty years of age when beginning (viz. His ministry), being, as was supposed, the Son of Joseph, who was the son of Eli," etc. ($ὤν, ὡς ἐνομίζετο, υἱὸς Ἰωσὴφ, τοῦ Ἡλί$). But the words, taken in their natural and obvious sense, connect Jesus with Joseph as his reputed father, and then this Joseph with Heli, as *his* father. The native import and bearing of the $ὡς$ $ἐνομίζετο$, was precisely given by Euthymius, $ὡς ἐδόκει τοῖς Ἰουδαίοις·$ $ὡς γὰρ ἡ ἀλήθεια εἶχεν, οὐκ ἦν υἱὸς αὐτοῦ$—in the common reckoning of the Jews He was Joseph's Son, but He was not so in reality. The latter idea, however, was only implied, not distinctly stated, in the Evangelist's expression. If the meaning had been: the Son, as was supposed, of Joseph, but in reality of Eli, that is Eli's grandson (through Mary the daughter of Eli),—the passage would have required to run (as justly stated by Meyer), $ὤν, ὡς μὲν ἐνομίζετο$ $υἱὸς Ἰωσὴφ, ὄντως δὲ Μαρίας, τοῦ Ἡλί$, or something similar. It is possible enough, and may even be deemed probable, that the genealogies of Mary and Joseph coincided at a comparatively near point, but this can only be matter of probable conjecture, or, at most, natural inference; for, as regards the genealogy itself of St Luke, we have no direct notice of Mary's pedigree, but only of Joseph's.

To our view, this silence regarding Mary in the genealogical tables, and the stress that is laid in the Gospels upon Joseph's connection with the house of David, certainly seems strange. It appears to imply, that the Davidic descent of Joseph somehow

carried that of Christ along with it; for the genealogies are produced as evidence of that very point. In much the same way,
Joseph, when meditating the repudiation of the Virgin, is addressed by the angel in terms that make special reference to his
royal descent,—" Joseph, thou son of David" (Matt. i. 20); and,
again, when the reason is assigned for the journey to Bethlehem,
which led to the birth of Jesus there, it was because, not Mary,
but Joseph, was of the house and lineage of David (Luke ii. 4).
How is this to be explained? Does the determination of Joseph's
genealogy really involve and carry along with it that of Mary's
and Christ's? So Augustine conceived, and in a profound remark expressed, when commenting on the designation of Joseph
and Mary by St Luke as the parents of Jesus. " Since, therefore," says he, " the Evangelist himself relates that Christ was
born, not from intercourse with Joseph, but of Mary, as a virgin,
whence should he call him (Joseph) His father—unless we rightly
understand, both that he was the husband of Mary, without carnal intercourse, by the bond simply of the marriage-tie; and that
he was on this account also Christ's father, Christ being born of
his wife, in a manner far more intimate than if He had been
adopted from another family? And on this ground," he adds,
" even if any one should be able to prove that Mary had no
blood-relationship to David, it was competent to hold Christ to
be the Son of David, for the very same reason that Joseph was
entitled to be called His father."[1] This view, though not formally referred to Augustine, has been taken up and ably ex-
pounded by Delitzsch, in an article on the genealogies in Rudel-
bach's Zeitschrift for 1850, p. 581, sq. He holds that, in consequence of the Divine revelation made to Joseph, and his entire
acquiescence in the arrangements announced to him, Jesus was
really the fruit of his marriage, and, as such, his Son. Joseph
acknowledged and owned the child, not, indeed, as begotten of

[1] Cum igitur ipse narret, non ex concubitu Joseph, sed ex Maria virgine
natum Christum; unde eum patrem ejus appellat, nisi quia et virum Mariæ
recte intelligimus sine commixtione carnis, ipsa copulatione conjugii; et ob
hoc etiam Christi patrem multo conjunctius, qui ex ejus conjuge natus sit,
quam si esset aliunde adoptatus? Ac per hoc, etiam si demonstrare aliquis
posset, Mariam ex David nullam consanguinitatis originem ducere, sat erat
secundum istam rationem accipere Christum filium David, qua ratione etiam
Joseph pater ejus recte appellatus est.—*De Consensu Evang.* ii. 1.

his body, but as a sacred gift, which God had most wonderfully granted to him through his wife. In all cases children are God's gifts; but this child was so in the most peculiar sense, there being an exclusion of human agency, and the direct intervention of the Divine. Now, if Jesus was the Son of Joseph, in his married relation, for the same reason also He was the Son of David; for He was born to a descendant of the house of David—was conceived and born of a virgin, who, simply from her espousals to Joseph, was already introduced into the house of David, and, within that house, as Joseph's spouse, brought forth her child. So the Evangelist Matthew contemplated the matter; for, according to the law and the established convictions of Israel, all depended upon Joseph's descent from David, not upon Mary's; and, by virtue simply of his relation to Joseph, Jesus was born in the house of David, was therefore the child of a Davidic person, and so was justly held to have sprung out of the house of David.

Such is the view of Delitzsch, which is undoubtedly in accordance with Jewish notions on the subject, and rests upon a solid basis of truth; since Mary, before the birth of the child, had actually, and by Divine ordination, become the spouse of Joseph, so that what was hers, through her became also her husband's. Yet, as God's work is ever perfect—not in design and nature merely, but in the way and manner also of its accomplishment— so doubtless it was here. We have the best reasons for supposing that the relationship of Mary, immediately to Joseph, and remotely to the house of David, was such, and so well known, that the genealogy of the one, at a point comparatively near, was understood to be the genealogy also of the other. This relationship on Mary's part seems plainly taken for granted by the angel, who announced the conception and birth of the child, when he said, "And the Lord God shall give unto Him the throne of His father David,"—an announcement that was made to her before her marriage to Joseph, before she could be sure of such a marriage ever being consummated, and so implying that, simply as born of her, through the power of the Holy Ghost, the child should stand in a filial relation to David. The statements in other parts of Scripture, designating Christ as, beyond dispute, of the seed of David, are also to be taken into account; so that,

if the genealogies do not of themselves establish the personal relation of Mary to the house of David, they may be said to involve
it ; since, when viewed in connection with the entire representation of the sacred writers, they seem to proceed on the ground of
a common interest in this respect belonging to Joseph and Mary,
and to Jesus through them.   Certain other probabilities will also
present themselves as we proceed.

III. But, meanwhile, difficulties start up from the ground we
have already won.   For, if the two genealogical tables are both
those of Joseph's proper pedigree, how should they differ at so
many points from each other—differ, even in respect to the
immediate father of Joseph—and differ so regularly in the latter
divisions, that between David and Christ they present only two
names in common?   This is a difficulty, which has long exercised the ingenuity of interpreters, and has given rise to a variety
of schemes.   It would occupy a considerable time to recount all
these, and could serve no valuable purpose.   We shall simply
state what we deem to be the correct explanation of the matter
—prefacing it, however, by a few considerations, which ought to
be kept in view by those who would arrive at right conclusions
on the subject.   The first is, that in these, as in genealogical
tables generally, there may be several diversities without any
actual incorrectness.   This holds of such tables generally, and
arises from the diversity of names sometimes borne by individuals
mentioned in them, and from various circumstances and relations occurring to alter in some respect the natural course of
descent, and thereby leaving room for one genealogist departing
from the exact route or nomenclature of another.   It is perfectly
well known by those, who are at all acquainted with Jewish
genealogies, how much this is the case ; and the reference of the
apostle to disputes in his day about endless genealogies (1 Tim.
i. 4 ; Tit. iii. 9), clearly implies, that the circumstances just
noticed were wont to involve considerable diversity in details,
not readily settled or explained.   It may well be expected,
therefore, especially at this distance of time, that there should
be points of divergence in the two tables before us, either altogether inexplicable now, or admitting of explanation only by the
help of suppositions which can at most be considered only as

probable. A more full and intimate knowledge of the particulars might have made all perfectly plain.

Another consideration to be kept in mind is, that whatever precise form the genealogical tables might assume—whether they traced the lineage in an ascending or a descending order—whether each successive generation is presented to our view as begotten by the preceding, or as standing to this in the relation of a son to a father—in either case alike the table is to be regarded as possessing the same character; and the same allowances or qualifications that may have to be made in the one case, are also quite allowable in the other. Mistakes and false theories have arisen from the neglect of this consideration. It was thus, indeed, that Julius Africanus was misled, and became the instrument of misleading many others, regarding the principles on which the two tables were constructed, by supposing that the phrase in Matthew, 'such an one begat such another,' is of a stricter kind than the phrase in Luke, ' such an one was the son of another;' he was of opinion that the former always denoted a natural connection as of parent and child, while the latter might include other connections—sons by adoption, or by marriage, or by legal standing, as the case might be. In reality, however, the Hebrews observed no distinction of the kind; they were accustomed to use both forms of expression in the same way; and the one as well as the other was sometimes applied to denote, not descendants by actual procreation, but the next of kin, or descendants in the wider sense. The table itself in Matthew's Gospel affords conclusive evidence of this; for it has " Joram begat Ozias," or Uzziah, although we know for certain that three links of the chain are there dropt out, and that Joram begat Ahaziah, then Ahaziah Jehoash, and Jehoash Uzziah. As a proof of the freedom sometimes used in such cases, we may point to the statements in Gen. xlvi. 26 ; Ex. i. 5, where Jacob is himself included among those that came out of his loins ;[1] and to Gen.

---

[1] See, for example, the Jewish commentator Raphall, on Gen. xlvi. 26, who, after referring to the opinions of other Jewish authorities, and showing how the 66 persons said to have come out of Jacob's loins were made up (32 by Leah, 16 by Zilpah, 11 by Rachel, 7 by Bilhah), thus sums up : " Now, as the family of Leah is said to consist of 33, though only 32 are enumerated, and as the former number would give us 67 persons (which the Septuagint

x. 13, 14, " Canaan begat Sidon his first-born, and Heth, and
the Jebusite, and the Amorite," etc.,—where evidently whole
races are said to have been begotten by the person who was no
further related to them than that he was their common progeni-
tor. We even occasionally find cities or districts associated in
the same way with an individual as their parent; thus in 1
Chron. ii. 50, " Shobal the father of Kirjath-jearim, Salma the
father of Bethlehem, Hareph the father of Beth-Gader." And
not only did the Levirate law afford occasions of pretty frequent
occurrence, when a person must have had children reckoned to
him that were not strictly his own, but women also—for example,
Sarah and Rachel—are represented as speaking of the possibility
of obtaining children born to them through their handmaids
(Gen. xvi. 2, xxx. 3).

Such being the case, there is plainly nothing in the way of our
holding, that the table of Matthew may, equally with that of
Luke, admit of relationships being introduced not of the nearest
degree; nor, further, anything, so far as form is concerned, to
render the position untenable, that in the one we may have the
succession in the strictly royal line, the legal heirs to the throne
of David (Matthew's), and in the other (Luke's) the succession
of our Lord's real parentage up to David. So that, were this
view to be accepted, we should have Christ's legal right to the
kingdom established, by the list in the one table; and by that of
the other, the direct chain which connected Him with the person of David. This is substantially the view that was adopted
by Calvin, though not originated; for he refers to some as pre-

actually has), whereas the text expressly declares, that the number of those
who proceeded from Jacob's loins were 66, and no more : And as, moreover,
the only members of Jacob's family whom the text mentions as being in
Egypt were three, namely, Joseph and his two sons; and as these three, with
the 66 above named, are only 69, whereas the text declares, that all the
persons of the house of Jacob who came into Egypt were 70; and as Jacob
must, of course, be considered as a member of his own house, it follows, that
the 70th person who came, can have been no other than Jacob himself.
And if this be so, then the 33d person numbered with, but not among, the
descendants of Leah, can also have been no other than Jacob; for if it had
been any other person, the total number of Jacob's house would have been
71—contrary to the text, since Jacob can in no wise be excluded from his
own house."

ceding him in the same view. It was first, however, fully brought out, and vindicated against the errors involved in the current belief, by Grotius. In opposition to that belief, which owed its general prevalence to the authority of Africanus—the belief that in St Matthew we have the natural, and in Luke the legal, descent—Grotius remarks, " For myself, guided, if I mistake not, by very clear, and not fanciful grounds, I am fully convinced, that Matthew has respect to the legal succession. For he recounts those who obtained the kingdom without the intermixture of a private name. Then Jechonias, he says, begot Salathiel. But it was not doubtfully intimated by Jeremiah, under the command of God, that Jechoniah, on account of his sins, should die without children (ch. xxii. 30). Wherefore, since Luke assigns Neri as the father of the same Salathiel, a private man, while Matthew gives Jechoniah, the most obvious inference is, that Luke has respect to the right of consanguinity, Matthew to the right of succession, and especially the right to the throne—which right, since Jechoniah died without issue, devolved, by legitimate order, upon Salathiel, the head of the family of Nathan. For among the sons of David Nathan came next to Solomon."

This view has lately been taken up, and at great length, as well as in a most judicious and scholarly manner wrought out by Lord Arthur Hervey, in a separate volume. The work as a whole is deserving of careful perusal. On this particular part of the subject he reasons somewhat as follows:—First of all, since St Matthew's table gives the royal successions, as far as they go, one can scarcely conceive why another table should have been given, unless it were that the actual parentage of Joseph did not properly coincide with that. If Joseph's direct ancestors, and Solomon's direct successors, had run in one line, there had been no need for another line ; since having already the most honourable line of descent, there could have been no inducement to make out an inferior one. But, on the supposition that a failure took place in Solomon's line, and that the offspring of Nathan (the next son of David) then came to be the legal heirs to the throne, another table was required to show, along with the succession to the inheritance, the real parentage throughout. A second consideration is derived from the pro-

N

phecy of Jeremiah already noticed, in which it was declared
concerning Jehoiakim, "He shall have none to sit upon the
throne of David" (ch. xxxvi. 30); and again, of Jehoiachin or
Jechoniah, the son, who was dethroned after being for a few
months acknowledged king, "Write ye this man childless, for
no man of his seed shall prosper, sitting upon the throne of
David, and ruling any more in Judah." After such explicit
declarations, it is not conceivable that these men should yet
have been the parents of a seed, out of which was at last to
spring the ultimate possessor of David's throne. A third consideration is supplied by the names found in both tables immediately after Jehoiachin. It was precisely there, that the
lineal descent from Solomon was broken; and there, accordingly,
the two tables again coincide; for the next two generations the
names Salathiel and Zerubabel occur alike in both tables—
brought in, we may reasonably suppose, from Nathan's line, to
supply the place of Solomon's, when it became defunct, and so
are connected with Solomon's line by Matthew, but with
Nathan's by Luke. So that, the line being traced by one
Evangelist through Solomon, by the other through Nathan, the
double object is served, of showing Christ to be at once David's
son and Solomon's heir, the latter being the type of Christ as
David's immediate son and heir. And thus also the genealogy
of the one Evangelist supplements that of the other, by showing
the validity of the right of succession as traced by Matthew,
since Joseph was Solomon's heir only by being Nathan's descendant.

A collateral confirmation is obtained for this view in certain
double genealogies which occur in the Old Testament Scriptures;
the one having respect to the parentage, the other to the inheritance. One of the most remarkable of these is that of Jair, who,
in 1 Chron. ii., has his genealogy ranked with the house of Judah,
being the son of Segub, the son of Hezron, the son of Pharez,
the son of Judah. By Moses, however, he is always called the
son of Manasseh (Num. xxxii. 41; Deut. iii. 14, 15), and is represented as having come to the possession of a number of small
towns in Gilead, which he called Havoth-Jair, i.e., the towns of
Jair. A notice in the genealogy of 1 Chron. ii. 22–23 explains
the discrepancy. We there learn that Hezron, his grandfather,

in his old age married the daughter of Machir, the son of Manasseh, who bare him Segub, and that Segub begat Jair—while Ashur, another son by the same marriage, had his inheritance in Judah. So that Jair, by his real parentage, was a descendant of Judah; though, in respect to his inheritance, and, no doubt, in the reckoning of the public registers, he was of the tribe of Manasseh. Another example is found in the case of Caleb, who, in the earlier records, is always called the son of Jephunneh (Num. xiii. 6, xiv. 6, etc.), and is reckoned of the tribe of Judah; while yet, it would seem, he did not originally and properly belong to that tribe: for, in Josh. xiv. 14 he is called "Caleb the son of Jephunneh *the Kenezite*," and, in ch. xv. 13, it is said that Joshua "gave him a part among the children of Judah, according to the commandment of the Lord to Joshua." If he had by birth belonged to that tribe, there should have been no need for a special commandment appointing his inheritance to be given out of what fell to that tribe; this would have happened to him as a matter of course; and both, therefore, on this account, and from his being called a Kenezite, we are led to infer that, not by birth, but by adoption, he had his place and portion fixed in the tribe of Judah. But, in order to this, he must be reckoned to some particular family of that tribe; and, accordingly, in the public genealogy given in 1 Chron. ii. 18–20, the paternity of Jephunneh is dropt, and that of Hezron, the son of Pharez, the son of Judah, put in its stead: "And Caleb, the son of Hezron, begat children of Azubah, his wife, and of Jerioth," etc. It is probable that one or other of these wives belonged to the family of Hezron, and that Caleb became, by marriage, connected with it; while afterwards, on account of his steady faith and resolute behaviour, he had the honour conferred on him of a special allotment in the tribe of Judah. We have thus the interesting fact brought out, through these comparatively dry details, that Caleb was originally a stranger, probably a native of Egypt, or an Arab of the Desert, but that he joined himself to the Lord's people, and was not only counted of the seed of Jacob, but became one of the most distinguished heads of its chief tribe.

A still further proof in support of the principles supposed to be involved in the construction of the two tables, as to the points now under consideration, is found in the recurrence of certain names in both of them during the period subsequent to the captivity. In St Luke's list the name of Nathan's son is Matthata (ver. 31) ; another son, in the eleventh generation, was called Matthat (ver. 29); and, between Salathiel and Joseph, the name of Mattathias occurs twice (ver. 25, 26), and that of Matthat once (ver. 24) :—all but different modifications of the original name Nathan (from נָתַן, he gave), and so affording internal evidence of the genealogy being really that of Nathan's line. In the other table, we find Matthan (the same person, in all probability, as Luke's Matthat), in the third generation before Joseph; and, at the same time, several names taken with little alteration from the royal household of former times—Eliakim, Zadok (Zedekiah), Achim (an abbreviation of Jehoiachim) ; as if, while the lineage in this part was really that of Nathan, there was an effort to keep up the connection with the latter days of the elder branch, the line of royal succession down to the period of the exile. The descendants of Nathan, who afterwards stept into their place in the genealogy, though not in the kingdom, seemed, by the very names they assumed, to be conscious of their peculiar relationship to Solomon's house, and desirous of indicating their claim to the throne.

This is all quite natural ; and it affords a very probable explanation at once of the agreements and the differences between the two genealogical tables. Now it only requires one or two very natural suppositions to bring the closing parts of the tables into correspondence ; for, on the supposition that the Matthan of St Matthew is the same with the Matthat of St Luke (of which there can be little doubt), then Jacob the son of Matthan, in Matthew, and Heli, the son of Matthat, in Luke, must, in fact, have been brothers—sons of the same father. And if Jacob had no sons, but only daughters, and Joseph, Heli's son married one of these—perfectly natural suppositions—then he became (on the principle of Matthew's table) also Jacob's son, and the lineal heir of the throne, as Jacob had been. It only requires that we make the further supposition—no ways extraordinary or unreasonable—of that daughter being the Virgin Mary, in order to meet all the demands of the case ; for thereby the principle of each table would be preserved : and Mary and Joseph being, in that case, first cousins, and cousins in that line which had the right of succession to the throne, the birth of our Lord was in every respect com-

plete, whether viewed in respect to consanguinity or to relationship
to the throne. The whole ordering of the matter exhibits a conjunction of circumstances which it was worthy of the Divine
oversight to accomplish, and which yet might, in the common
course of events, have readily come about.

It may be added, that the last circumstance in the series of
suppositions now mentioned—the marriage of Joseph and Mary,
as of two cousins, the one the son of Heli, the other the daughter
of Jacob, dying without sons—perfectly accords with Jewish
practice; as appears alone from the case of Jair marrying into the
tribe of Manasseh, and thenceforth taking rank in that tribe; and
still more, from the case of Zelophehad's five daughters, who
married their five cousins, and retained their inheritance. It was
the constant aim of the Jews to make inheritance and blood-
relationship, as far as possible, go together. And it could not
seem otherwise than natural and proper, that the daughter of the
nearest heir to the throne of David, should be espoused to the
next heir. Nor is it undeserving of notice—as, at least, negatively favouring the supposition respecting Mary—that, while we
read of a sister, we never hear of a brother belonging to her;
excepting Joseph, female relatives alone are mentioned. So that,
in the supposed circumstances of the case, there is nothing that
even appears to conflict with the facts of Gospel history; everything seems rather to be in natural and fitting agreement with
them.

IV. The few remaining peculiarities in the two tables are of
comparatively little importance, and need not detain us long.

(1.) The existence of a second Cainan in only one of the
tables—in that of Luke (v. 36)—between Sala and Arphaxad—
is one of these minor difficulties. In the corresponding genealogy
of our Hebrew Bibles, the name is not found. The only Cainan
that appears in the early Hebrew records belongs to the antediluvian period; and it is still a matter of dispute how the second
Cainan has originated—whether it had somehow been dropt from
the Hebrew text, or had been unwarrantably inserted into the
Greek. It is found in all the copies extant of the Septuagint,
except the Vatican; but the Septuagint itself omits it in the
genealogies of 1 Chron. i.; and it is wanting in the Samaritan,

Pentateuch, and seems not to have been known to Josephus, Berosus, Eupolemus, Polyhistor; nor does it even appear to have been in the copies of the Septuagint used by Theophilus of Antioch in the second century, by Africanus in the third, or by Eusebius in the fourth. Jerome, too, in his comments on that part of Genesis, omits all mention of Cainan, though he has annotations on the precise verse, where the name of Cainan is now found. Augustine, however, had the name in his copy both of the Septuagint and of St Luke. The probability seems to lie decidedly against the original existence of the name of Cainan in the genealogy, either in the Old or the New Testament tables. But the precise time or occasion of its introduction can be matter only of conjecture. Possibly, it may have originated in some mystical notions about numbers, which often had a considerable influence in the form given to genealogies. Bochart was of opinion, it probably arose from some clerical oversight in the transcription of the table in Luke, and was thence transferred to the Septuagint; but the common opinion rather leans to the view of its having first appeared in the Septuagint; certainty, however, is unattainable. Bochart's statements on the subject are worth consulting—Phaleg, L. ii. c. 13.

(2.) A peculiarity of a minor kind also belongs to the other table, and one, in respect to which we can have no difficulty in perceiving the influence of numbers. It is the division into three tesseradecades. For the purpose of securing the three fourteens certain names are omitted in the second division—Ahaziah, Joash, Amaziah—which would have unduly swelled the number, if they had been inserted. And closely connected with the same point is a peculiarity in respect to Josiah, who is said to have " begot Jeconias and his brethren, about the time they were carried away to Babylon" (v. 11). It is scarcely possible to doubt, that some corruption must have crept into the text here; for, in reality, Josiah begot Jehoiakim, not Jeconias; and the birth of Jehoiakim took place a considerable time before the exile. But Jehoiakim begat Jeconias much about that period; and the natural supposition is, that the original text here must have had Jehoiakim as the son of Josiah, and then Jeconias as the son of Jehoiakim. The two might very readily have been run together by a copyist, as, in one form of them, the names differed only in a single letter—Jehoiakim being written Ἰωακείμ, and Jeconias Ἰωαχείμ. A scribe might quite naturally take these for but one name, and so leave out Jehoiakim. This view is strengthened by the consideration, that unless we take in Jehoiakim, as well as Jeconias, we want one to complete the fourteen of this middle division; at least, it can only be made out by the somewhat awkward expedient of including the name of David at the beginning of this division, as well as at the close of the preceding one. If this really had required to be done, one does not see why the evangelist should have omitted three names together in order to shorten the list; it had been a much simpler expedient to leave out only two. And on each account the probability is very great, that Jehoiakim has been dropt from the text in the manner just stated.

In regard, however, to the general characteristic of the division of the entire table into so many fourteens; and the adoption of certain abbreviations to effect this, it has the support of a very common practice among the Jews. Schöttgen has produced from the Synopsis of Sohar a genealogy constructed in a quite similar manner to the one before us: " From Abraham to Solomon there are 15 generations, and at that time the moon was full; from Solomon to Zedekiah there are again 15 generations, and at that time the moon was down, and Zedekiah's eyes were put out." Lightfoot also produces on Matt. i. several artificially framed genealogies. The number 14 was here, doubtless, fixed on as the basis of the arrangement, and made to rule each period; because, in the first period, that from Abraham to David, it comprehends the entire number of links, when both Abraham and David are included. No higher number, therefore, could have been assumed; and in this fact we discover the most natural reason for the ground of the arrangement.

In the preceding remarks we have touched on everything that is likely to create difficulty in connection with the two genealogies. For various other points of a collateral kind, or of antiquarian interest, and occasionally bearing on peculiarities in the Old Testament chronology, we refer again to the volume of Lord A. Hervey, which will be found well deserving of a careful perusal from those, who are desirous of prosecuting the subject into its minuter details.

SECTION SECOND.

THE DESIGNATIONS AND DOCTRINE OF ANGELS, WITH REFER-
ENCE MORE ESPECIALLY TO THE INTERPRETATION OF PAS-
SAGES IN NEW TESTAMENT SCRIPTURE.

ANGELIC agency meets us at the very threshold of the Gospel.
The first communications made respecting the new order of
things, then on the eve of emerging, came through the mediation
of angels : it was they who at length broke the silence of ages.
Nor may this be matter of surprise, if, together with the long
cessation of prophetical gifts among men, respect be had to the
part, that in earlier times was wont to be taken by angels in
supernatural revelations.   The only thing that may seem somewhat strange is the assumption of a name (Gabriel) by one of
those angelic messengers, for the purpose more immediately of
confirming the certainty of those things which he came to announce, and magnifying the guilt incurred by Zecharias in enter-
taining doubt concerning the possibility of their accomplishment
(Luke i. 19).   This, however, admits of a satisfactory explanation ; but as there are various other points and passages of
Scripture connected with angelic agency, which also call for explanation, we shall take the whole subject into consideration,
and discuss the several topics relating to it, in the order that
seems most natural and appropriate.

I. And, first, in regard to the *general designation and its use*
in Scripture.   The Greek ἄγγελοι, like the Hebrew מַלְכִים, has a
general as well as a more specific sense : it may denote any individuals sent forth with a message to carry, or a commission to
execute—*messengers*, as well in the natural as in the supernatural
sphere of things.   When the reference is plainly to the former,
then the rendering ought commonly to be *messenger*, as it usually
is in the English version—for example, Job i. 14 ; 1 Sam. xi. 3 ;
Luke ix. 52 ; James ii. 25.   There are passages, however, in
which, while the reference still is to persons or things belonging

to the earthly sphere, the name is applied to them in a sense quite peculiar, and so as sometimes to leave it doubtful whether *angel* or *messenger* might be the more fitting translation. In this I do not include such passages as Acts xii. 7, or 1 Cor. xi. 10, where, by " the angel of the Lord," in the one case, and by " the angels," in the other, some would understand merely human delegates; entirely, as I conceive, against the proper import and interpretation of the passages. Of this, however, afterwards. But, in Ps. civ. 4, we have the words, which are quoted in Heb. i. 7, " who maketh His angels spirits, His ministers a flaming fire;" and as the discourse there is of natural things, in their relation to the beneficent disposal and ever present agency of God, it seems fittest to understand by the *spirits* winds, and by the *flaming fire* lightning; so that the sense comes to be, that God makes the winds of heaven, as angels or messengers, do His bidding, and the lightning of the clouds minister to His will: not certainly (as Kingsley interprets it, *Village Sermons*, p. 7), " showing us that in those breezes there are living spirits, and that God's angels guide those thunder clouds :" no, but showing that these very breezes and thunder-clouds *are* His angelic or ministering agents. Of course, they are poetically so designated; and the language is of the same kind, as when it is said of God, that " He makes the clouds His chariot, and flies upon the wings of the wind." In like manner, but with closer approximation to the ordinary meaning of the word, prophets are sometimes called God's *melakim*, or angels, though the rendering of *messengers* is adopted in the authorised version (Hag. i. 13; Mal. iii. 1); and the epithet is even applied to Israel generally, with special reference to the prophetical nature of his calling, appointed by God to be the light and instructor of the world (Isa. xlii. 19).

It formed but a comparatively slight transition from this use of the word, and indeed, was but connecting it with another aspect of the delegated trust committed to the covenant-people, when the priesthood were styled God's angels; as in Mal. ii. 7, " The priest's lips should keep knowledge, and they should seek the law at his mouth; for he is the angel (Engl. version, messenger) of the Lord of Hosts." This obviously is said, not so much of any individual member of the priestly class, as of the class itself collectively; the priesthood was God's delegated ministry for making known the things pertaining to His will and worship—in that respect, His angel-interpreter. And thus we obtain a ready explanation of another passage, which has often been much misunderstood : " When thou vowest a vow unto God, defer not to pay it ; for He hath no pleasure in fools ; pay that which thou hast vowed. Better is it that thou shouldst not vow and not pay. Suffer not thy mouth to cause thy flesh to sin ; neither say thou *before the angel*, that it was an error" (Eccl. v. 4–6) ; that is, neither rashly utter with thy lips what thou hast not moral strength and fixedness of purpose to perform ; nor, if thou shouldst have uttered it, go before the priesthood, the Lord's deputed agents to wait on such things, and say it was an error, as if by making an easy confession of having done wrong in uttering the vow, the evil could be remedied. On the ground, especially of this last application of the word *angel* in Old Testament Scripture, we find the most natural explanation of the address under which, in the Apocalypse, the epistles were sent to the seven churches of Asia :—" to the angels of the churches." The term is adopted, like so many others in the Apocalypse, from the prophetical usage, and from that usage more especially as employed in later times with respect to the priesthood. It can determine nothing, therefore, as to the question, whether the party designated *angel*, might at the time consist of one individual, or of a collection of individuals ; without in any way defining this, it indicates the high position of the party, whether single or collective, as having had committed to it the authoritative instruction and oversight of the Christian community in the several churches. That party stood, as it were, between heaven and earth, and was charged with God's interest in that particular locality.[1]

Usually, however, when angels are mentioned in Scripture, it is with reference to another kind of existences than such as pro-

---

[1] This very charge and the responsibility implied in it, is itself quite fatal to the notion of Dean Stanley, " that the churches are there described as personified in their guardian or representative angels " (*Apostolic Age*, p. 71). Angels are nowhere else spoken of as having to do in such a manner with the life and purity of the churches ; and the notion is altogether opposed to the general doctrine of angels.

perly belong to this present world—to *spirits*, as contradistinguished from men in flesh and blood, and the occupants of regions suited to their ethereal natures. Yet even when thus limited, there is considerable latitude in the expression, and the name may be said to comprise several orders of being. (1.) First, there are those more commonly understood by the expression—the angels of God, as they are sometimes called, or of heaven (Matt. xxiv. 36; Mark xiii. 32; John i. 51; Matt. xxii. 30). They are named in connection with heaven, because they have their more peculiar abode there, in the region of God's manifested presence and glory. God's angels also they are emphatically called, not merely because they derived their being from His hand, and are constantly sustained by His power—for this belongs to them in common with all creation—but more especially because they are in a state of peculiar nearness to God, and are His immediate agents in executing the purposes of His will. It is as possessing the ministry of such glorious agents, and possessing them in vast numbers, as well as invincible strength, that He takes to Himself the name of "The Lord of Hosts." (2.) Then there are the angels of darkness, who are never, however, like the others, designated simply *the angels*, but always with some qualifying epithet indicative of their real character and position; such as "the Devil's angels," as contrasted with the angels of God, or "the angels that sinned," "that kept not their first estate," in contradistinction as well to what they themselves once were, as to the party that remained stedfast (Matt. xxv. 41; 2 Pet. ii. 4; Jude ver. 6). (3.) Finally, there is one who is called *the* angel, by way of eminence, or "the Angel of the Covenant," and who, as regards angelic ministrations, occupies a place altogether peculiar to himself. As we shall have occasion to refer at some length to this angel-prince under the next division, it is needless to be more particular here.

II. We turn now to the *individual or proper names sometimes applied to angels* in Scripture, one of which occurs so near the commencement of the Gospel history. It is at a comparatively late period of the elder dispensation, and only in the book of Daniel, that we find any specific names given to particular angels, or beings acting in the capacity of angels. *There*, for the first time, occur the names of Gabriel and Michael; nor do any other names beside these occur. The late appearance of such designations, together with the local position of him who employed them, was sufficient ground for the Rationalists to rush to the conclusion, that such names were of heathen origin, and that Daniel and his captive brethren learned them from the Chaldeans. It were impossible to admit such a view, without bringing into doubt the prophetical gifts of Daniel, and involving in just suspicion the supernatural character of his communications. For the angelic names he uses were not applied by himself, but were heard by him in vision, as applied one to another, by the heavenly messengers themselves. So that whatever may have been the reason for their introduction, it can with no fitness be ascribed—if Daniel's own representations are to be accepted— to an adoption of the heathen notions prevalent around him. Nor was such a tendency in the direction of heathenism to have been expected here. Nowhere more strongly than in the book of Daniel does the theocratic spirit keep the ascendant—the resolute determination to abide at all hazards by the old foundations, and, in things spiritual and divine, to make the heathen the learner merely, not the instructor or the guide. The aim and design of the whole book is to show the real superiority and ultimate triumph of Judaism over heathenism. And it was not, to say the least, by any means likely that in this one point Daniel should have been disposed to renounce his claims as a messenger and prophet of the true God, and become a disciple of the magicians over whom his better wisdom carried him so far aloft.

It is true, no doubt, that the Jews, after the Babylonish captivity, in the interval that elapsed between that period and the Christian era, showed a disposition to deal somewhat lavishly with angelic names and orders. The book of Tobit, which was composed during this interval, not only finds one of the principal characters of the story in an angel called Raphael, but makes this personage say of himself, " I am Raphael, one of the seven holy angels, which present the prayers of the saints, and which go in and out before the glory of the Holy One :"—evidently showing that something like a system of angelology, branching out into offices as well as names, had sprung up among the Jews of the dispersion. As commonly happens, when the elements of super-stition begin to work, the false tendency developed itself more fully as time proceeded. In the book of Enoch, a spurious production that appeared some time about the Christian era, and undoubtedly embodying the notions of many of the more specu-lative Jews of that period, we are told of the " four great arch-angels, Michael, Raphael, Gabriel, and Uriel," who perpetually bring reports to the Creator, of the corrupt state of the world, and receive from Him their respective commissions. Rabbinical writers descend into still further details, specify the exact posi-tions of those superior angels in the presence of God (setting Michael on the right, Gabriel on the left, Raphael behind, Uriel in front), tell us how Gabriel attended at the nuptials of Adam and Eve, how he taught Joseph the 70 languages of the world, and many similar things both of him and of the other archangels (Eisenmenger Ent. Judenthum, vol. i., p. 374, sq.). Such were the fanciful and ridiculous vagaries into which the Jewish angelology ran ; but it by no means follows, from such a system having de-veloped itself among the later Jews, that it had its origin in the Chaldean influence, to which they were exposed in Babylon—least of all, that Daniel and his godly companions led the way in surrendering themselves to the direction of such an influence. Considering the jealousy with which not only they, but the stricter Jews generally, felt toward the corruptions of heathenism, after the Babylonish exile, the more natural supposition is, that they spun their theories of angelical existences out of the few actual notices that occur of the world of spirits in their own Scriptures—in this, as in other things, pushing some scattered elements of truth into many groundless and frivolous extremes. It is in perfect accordance with what is known of Jewish or Rab-binical speculations in general, to affirm, that the real basis of what they imagined respecting the names and offices of angels, was to be found in the writings of the Old Testament, though the opinions of those among whom they lived might come in at one quarter or another, to give a particular turn to the current of their speculations.

Now, it is to be remembered that, while we meet with specific names of those heavenly messengers only in Daniel, yet in earlier revelations there is a certain approximation to the same thing ;

and the change cannot be characterized as very abrupt, or the feature in Daniel marked as absolutely singular. Even in one of the earliest notices of angelic visitation, that which occurred to Abraham on the plains of Mamre (Gen. xviii.), it is evident from the sacred narrative that, of the three personages who then appeared, one was manifestly superior in dignity, if not also in nature, to the other two. He remains behind, and, in the name of the Lord, speaks to Abraham respecting the destruction of Sodom, while they go in the humbler character of messengers to take personal cognizance of its state. Then, in later times, we have the designations of "the Angel of the Covenant," "the angel of the Lord's presence," "the angel in whom the Lord's name is" (Mal. iii. 1 ; Isa. lxiii. 9 ; Ex. xxiii. 21) ; constantly represented as different from, and superior to, a mere angel—for, in the first of the passages just referred to, he is identified with the Lord Himself, whom the people professed to be seeking after ; in the second he is described as the Saviour of the covenant-people ; and, in the third—the earliest of the three, and the foundation of the others—He is in a pointed manner distinguished from an angel, in the ordinary sense (comp. the passage with ch. xxxiii. 2, 12, 14), and is characterized as the same that afterwards appeared to Joshua, at once as the Lord and as the Captain of the Lord's host (Josh. v. 14, 15, vi. 2). Still further, we find this highest angel, the Angel or messenger of the covenant, identified with the Messiah, and designated by a variety of names, such as Immanuel, Jehovah Zidekinu, the prince, or the prince of the host, etc. And not only is this leader of the Lord's hosts thus individualized and indicated by name, but a specific designation is also frequently applied to the great adversary of God and man—Satan. So that it was not to strike into a path altogether new, but merely to take an additional step in a direction already formed, when Daniel introduced the names of Michael and Gabriel into our heavenly vocabulary.

But why should even such a step have been taken ? Was this done in a way which admits of being intelligently explained and justified ? Or does there appear in it something arbitrary and fanciful ? In answer to such questions, it may be replied generally, that, if such designations were proper to be introduced anywhere, it is precisely in the book of Daniel that they might be most fitly looked for. His writings possess considerably more of a dramatic character than those of the other prophets, and in his own book those are the most dramatic visions in which the names occur. It was, therefore, in them that the actors in the spiritual drama might be expected to be most distinctly portrayed. And then the individual names, which are used for this end, are found on examination to be, not proper names in the ordinary sense, but appellatives designating the nature and office of those who bore them, and most naturally growing out of the special communications which they were engaged in making. To see this, we have only to glance at the names themselves.

1. Beyond doubt the highest in rank and importance is MICHAEL. This name occurs twice in Daniel, and is also found in the Epistle of Jude and the Revelation. It is compounded of three words, which together express the meaning, *Who is like God?* (מִיכָאֵל). The *El*, which denotes God, has respect to God as the God of might; so that the idea indicated by the appellation is, the possession, either of absolutely Divine, or of Divine-like majesty and power—the former, if the name is applied to one in whom the nature of God resides; the latter, if applied to a created intelligence. Here, however, there is considerable diversity of opinion. The Jewish and Rabbinical authorities, as already noticed, understand by Michael one of the four highest angels, or archangels, as they are sometimes termed—though with a certain superiority possessed by him above the rest; for they call Michael the Princeps Maximus, the tutelary angel of Judea, God's peculiar angel, the Prince of the World. He was, therefore, in their account, decidedly the highest of created intelligences, but still himself a part of the creation. We find the same view exhibited in one of the earliest Patristic productions, the Shepherd of Hermas; and it became the prevailing opinion among the fathers. But the divines of the Reformation very commonly adopted another view, and understood Michael to be a name of Christ. So, for example, Luther (on Dan. x. 21 and xii. 1), and Calvin, who, at least, expresses his preference for the same opinion, though without absolutely rejecting the other; in the next age, also Cocceius, Witsius, Turretine, Lampe, Calov, the last of whom even affirms the opinion which represents the Michael in Dan. xii. 1 as a created angel, to be impious. This certainly appears

to be the correct view, and we shall present in as brief a compass
as possible the grounds on which it is based.

(1) The name itself—*who is like God?* This seems to point to
the Supreme Lord, and in a way very common with the earlier
writers of the Old Testament ; as in Ex. xv. 11, " Who is like
Thee among the gods, O Lord ?" or, in Ps. lxxxix. 8, " Who is
like the Lord among the sons of the mighty ?"   Such an ascrip-
tion of peerless might and glory, when turned into a personal
appellation, seems most naturally to imply, that the qualities expressed in it belonged to the individual ; it fixes our regard upon
Him as the representative and bearer of what the appellation
imports ; and the turn given to it by Bengel (on Rev. xii. 7), as
if it were a mark of humility rather than of weakness—as if the
possessor of the title pointed away from himself to God—is quite
unnatural, and contrary to the Scriptural usage in such appella-
tions.   Nor, in that case, would it have formed a suitable designation for the highest of the angels, since it could have indicated
nothing as to any peculiar honour or dignity belonging to him.
As a distinguishing epithet, it is appropriate only to Christ, who
actually possesses the unrivalled properties of God ; and who,
expressly on the ground of his possessing these, and being able
to say, " All that the Father hath is Mine," has charged Himself
with the interests of the covenant-people, and is found adequate
to the establishment of its provisions (John v. 18, xvi. 15 ; Isa.
ix. 6, 7 ; Phil. ii. 6–11).   (2) Another argument is found in the
collateral, and, to some extent, epexegetical, or explanatory designations, which are applied to the same personage.   Thus in
Dan. xii. 1, He is called emphatically *the Great Prince* (הַשַּׂר
הַגָּדוֹל) apparently referring to, and closely agreeing with, the
name assumed by the angel of the Lord in Josh. v. 14, captain,
or rather, *prince of Jehovah's host* (שַׂר־צְבָא־יְהוָֹה), that is, the
leader of the heavenly forces of the Great King.   So again,
in ch. x. 21, Michael is styled the prince of the covenant-people,
" *Your* prince," the one who presides over their state and
destinies ; or, as it is at ch. xii. 1, " Who standeth up for the
children of thy people," namely, to protect and deliver them.
These descriptions seem plainly to identify Michael with the
Angel of the Covenant, who sometimes appears as God, and
sometimes as his peculiar representative.   Even the Rabbinical

Jews could not altogether escape the conviction of the identity
of Michael and this personage; for the saying occurs more than
once in their writings, that " wherever Michael appeared, there
was seen the glory of the Shekinah itself." The passage, which
tended chiefly to lead them in the wrong direction, was Dan. x.
13, where he is called " *one* (אֶחָד) of the chief princes," or, as it
might equally be rendered, " first of the chief princes," head of
the angel-chiefs. The Jewish writers understood it to indicate
merely precedence or superiority in respect to others essentially
of the same class. But, taken in connection with the other
passages and expressions in Daniel, it seems intended simply to
exhibit the relation of Michael to the angels, to present him to
our view as their directing and governing head. It is substantially, indeed, of the same import as *archangel*, which is
never used in the plural, and never receives a personal application but to Michael (Jude ver. 9; 1 Thess. iv. 16); so that
there is no Scriptural warrant for understanding it as an indication of an angelic hierarchy, or otherwise than as a designation
of the head of angelic hosts. (3) Lastly, the descriptions given
of Michael, both of his person and his acts, seem to confirm the
same view : they are such as properly belong to the Messiah, the
essentially Divine Head and King of His Church, but are
scarcely compatible with the position of a created intelligence.
Take, for example, the delineation of his person as given in Dan.
x. 5, 6, " And I looked, and behold a certain man in linen,
whose loins were girded with fine gold of Uphaz : his body also
was like the beryl, and his face as the appearance of lightning,
and his eyes as lamps of fire, and his arms and his feet like in
colour to polished brass, and the voice of his words like the voice
of a multitude"—the description has been almost literally transferred to the vision of the glorified Redeemer by St John in the
Apocalypse (ch. i. 13–17, ii. 18). With representations so
nearly identical, we naturally conceive the same personages to
have been intended by them. Some, indeed, have taken the description in Daniel as referring to Gabriel, and not to Michael ;
but this is plainly against the natural import of the narrative ;
which represents Gabriel as coming and talking familiarly with
the prophet, while the vision of the glorious One was so over-
powering, that he was unable to bear the sight. It is necessary,

therefore, to understand it of Michael, who appeared in glory at some distance, and on the opposite bank of the river. What is afterwards said of Michael, at ch. xii. 1, as standing up to deliver the Lord's people in a time of unparalleled tribulation, and the co-relative action ascribed to him in the Apocalypse (ch. xii. 7–9), of overcoming and casting down from the heaven of his power and glory the great adversary of God and man, serve also to confirm the identification of Michael with Christ. For, the actions referred to are manifestly proper to Christ, as the Head of His Church, not to any inferior agent. Scripture constantly represents it as the sole and peculiar glory of Christ to put down all power and authority that exalts itself against God, or to execute the judgment written upon the adversary. On these grounds we conclude, that Michael is but another name for the Angel of the Covenant, or for Christ. It is the *name* alone that is peculiar to Daniel; and the reason, apparently, why such a name was chosen in the revelations given through Him, was to render prominent the Divine power and majesty in the angel-mediator, which assured the covenant-people of a triumphant issue out of those gigantic conflicts and troubles that were before them, if only they proved stedfast to the truth. (Compare Ode de Angelis, pp. 1054–58, Hengstenberg on Daniel and on Rev. xii. 7–9).

(2) In regard to the other specific name, GABRIEL, it is clear, both from the name itself, and from the historical notices given of the bearer of it, that a created angel is to be understood. The word may have a slightly different explanation put upon it, according as the *iod* is held to be paragogic merely, or the pronominal affix: in the former case, it means *hero*, or *mighty one of God*; in the other, *my hero*, or *mighty one, is God—God is my strength*. Either way the leading thought conveyed by it is much the same; it embodies a twofold idea—that the bearer of the name is distinguished by heroic might, and that he has this might, not of himself, but of God. Such an appellation could only be given to a created intelligence, to one whose part it was to recognise his dependence upon God, and in the exercise of his might to show forth something of the almightiness of the Creator. Appearing under this designation, it indicated that the business, which led to his appearance, was one that would

call for the manifestation of heroic energy, such as could be found only in close connection with the all-sufficient Jehovah. The times and circumstances referred to in the vision of Daniel, in which Gabriel acted a prominent part (ch. viii., ix. 21), were precisely of such a description; they bore respect to the great struggles and conflicts, through which ultimate security and blessing were to be attained for the covenant-people; and the revelation of the progress and issue of the contest by one, whose very name carried up the soul to the omnipotence of Jehovah, was itself a pledge and assurance of a prosperous result. Nor was it materially different at the commencement of the Gospel, where the name of Gabriel again meets us in Divine communications. These communications bore upon matters encompassed with peculiar difficulty, and capable of being brought about only by the supernatural agency of Godhead. The very first stage in the process lay across a natural impossibility, since to furnish the herald of the new dispensation an aged and barren woman (Elizabeth) must become the mother of a child. The next, which was presently afterwards announced to Mary, involved not only a natural impossibility, but the most astounding and wonderful of all mysteries—the incarnation of Godhead. In such circumstances, what could be more fitting and appropriate, than that the Divine messenger, sent from the Upper Sanctuary to disclose the immediate approach of such events, should come as the personal representative of the heroic might and energy of Heaven?—should even make himself known as the Gabriel, the God-empowered hero, who in former times had disclosed to Daniel the purpose of God to hold in check the powers of evil, and in spite of them to confirm for ever the eternal covenant? The remembrance of the past, in which the purpose of God had been so fearlessly proclaimed and so successfully vindicated, now came in aid of the testimony, which the same Divine messenger was sent to deliver; so that the tidings, all strange and startling as they might appear, should have met from the children of the covenant with a ready and believing response.

Even the miraculous, temporary suspension of the power of speech, with which the appearance of Gabriel to Zacharias came to be attended, was full of meaning and in perfect keeping with the whole circumstances of the time. Viewed in connection with these, the aspect of harshness, which at first sight it may seem to carry, will be found to disappear. That the measure of unbelief, which arose in his mind on seeing the angelic vision, and on first hearing the announcement made to him, was deserving of rebuke, must be regarded as certain from the rebuke actually administered; no such, even slight and temporary, punishment would have been inflicted, had it not been amply justified by the existing state of mind in Zacharias. But Zacharias is chiefly to be contemplated here as a representative of the people, whose prayers he was at the time symbolically offering; and in him, as such, were embodied, along with the better elements that continued to work among them, a portion also of the worse. The unbelief, therefore, that discovered itself in connection with the angelic announcement, was but too sure an indication of the evil, that slumbered even among the better part of the covenant-people. And the instant, and visible, though still comparatively gentle rebuke it met with in the case of Zacharias, was meant to be a salutary and timely warning to the people at large; and, taken in connection with the name, Gabriel, made known along with it, it was also a palpable proof that this name was no empty title, but gave assurance of the immediate operation of the infinite power of Godhead. Thus the miracle of dumbness wrought upon Zacharias became a sign to all around—a sign of the certainty with which the things should be accomplished that were announced by Gabriel (whatever might be required of miraculous power for their performance), and a sign also of the withering and disastrous result, which should infallibly emerge, if the manifestations of Divine power and goodness that were at hand should be met by a spirit of distrust and unbelief.

It thus appears, when the history and relations of the subject are duly considered, that there is nothing greatly peculiar in the use of the names Michael and Gabriel, whether in the Book of Daniel, or in New Testament Scripture. The names here also, as in those of Immanuel, Branch of the Lord, Angel of the covenant, Satan, were really descriptive of nature and position. And their appearance only in the later revelations of the Old covenant finds a ready explanation in the circumstance, that the progressive nature of the Divine communications necessarily led to a progressive individualizing, both in regard to the Messiah Himself, and to the various persons and objects connected with His undertaking. Hence, it naturally happens, that in the later books of the Old Testament, and in those of the New, the individual features and characteristics of all kinds are brought most distinctly out. In this respect, therefore, the appearance is precisely as the reality might have led us to expect.

III. Having so far cleared our way to a right understanding of the subject of angels, by examining the language employed, both in its more general and its more specific forms, we naturally turn to inquire next, what, according to the revelations of Scripture, is *their personal state?*—the state, namely, of those, who are always understood, when angels generally are spoken of— the angels in heaven. In Scripture they are uniformly represented as in the most elevated condition of intelligence, purity, and bliss. Endowed with faculties which fit them for the highest sphere of existence, they excel in strength, and can endure, unharmed, the intuition of God (Ps. ciii. 20; Matt. xviii. 10). Nor in moral excellence are they less exalted; for they are called emphatically " the holy angels," " elect angels," " angels of light " (Mark viii. 38; 2 Tim. v. 21; 2 Cor. xi. 14); and are represented as ever doing the will of God, doing it so uniformly and perfectly, that men on earth can aim at nothing higher or better than doing it like the angels in heaven. In the sphere, too, of their being and enjoyment, all is in fitting harmony with their natural and moral perfections; not only no elements of pain or disorder, but every essential provision for the wants and capacities of their immortal natures; so that to have our destiny associated with theirs, to have our condition made equal to theirs, is presented to our view as the very glory of that resurrection-state to which Christ has called His people (Luke xx. 36; Heb. xii. 22). The two, indeed, may not be in all respects identical, can hardly, indeed, be so; but that which is made to stand as the pattern cannot in anything of moment be inferior to what is represented as bearing its likeness.

That the angelic state was from the first substantially what it still is, can scarcely be doubted from the general tenor of the Scriptural representations. Yet in these a certain change also

is indicated—not, indeed, from evil to good, or from feebleness
to strength, but from a state, in which there was, at least, the
possibility of falling, to another in which this has ceased to be
possible—a state of ever-abiding holiness and endless felicity.
The actual fall and perdition of a portion of their number, implies that somehow the possibility now mentioned did at one
period exist; and the angels, that kept their first estate, and have
received the designation of *elect* angels, nay, are assigned an
everlasting place among the ministers and members of Christ's
kingdom, must have made some advance in the security of their
condition.   And this, we inevitably conclude, must infer some
advance also in relative perfection; for absolute security to
rational beings in the enjoyment of life and blessing, we can only
conceive of as the result of absolute holiness; *they* have it—they
alone *can* have it—we imagine, in whom holiness has become so
deeply rooted, so thoroughly pervasive of all the powers and susceptibilities of their being, that these can no longer feel and act
but in subservience to holy aims and obedience to principles of
righteousness.   So far, therefore, the angels appear to have *become* what they now are, that a measure of security, and, by
consequence, a degree of perfection (whether as regards spiritual
knowledge, or moral energy) is now theirs, which sometime was
not.

From the representations of Scripture, there is room also for
another distinction in regard to the state of angels, though, like
the one just noticed, it cannot be more than generally indicated
or vaguely apprehended.   The distinction referred to is a certain
diversity in rank and power, which there seems ground for believing to exist among the heavenly hosts.   There are indications
in Scripture of something like angelic orders.   For, though the
term *archangel* cannot be applied in this connection, being used
(as we have seen) only as the designation of a single personage,
and that, apparently, the Messiah, yet the name Gabriel, when
assumed as a distinctive epithet, appears to imply that he stood
in a nearer relationship to God than certain others, or partook to
a larger extent than they of the might of Godhead.   So also in
Rev. xviii. 21, we read of " a mighty angel," as if not every
angel could be called such.   And in various places there is an
accumulation of epithets, as of different orders, when referring to

the heavenly intelligences ; as in Eph. i. 20, 21, where Christ is said to be exalted " above all principality and power, and might, and dominion, and every name that is named, not only in this world, but also in that which is to come ;" and in 1 Pet. iii. 22, where He is again said, in His heavenly exaltation, to have " angels, principalities, and powers made subject to Him." But if such expressions appear to render probable or certain the existence of some kind of personal distinctions among the angels of glory, it leaves all minuter details respecting it under a veil of impenetrable secrecy. And to presume, like the ancient Jews, to single out four or seven primary angels ; or, like the Rabbins, to distribute the angelic hosts into ten separate classes ; or, still again, with many of the Scholastics, to range them in nine orders, each consisting of three classes, regularly graduated in knowledge and authority, the class below ever standing in dependence upon the one above :—to deal with the matter thus, is to do precisely what the apostle has discharged any one from attempting on such a subject, " intrude into those things which he has not seen, vainly puffed up by his fleshly mind " (Col. ii. 18). Of persons who discourse familiarly upon such points, and discuss the most subtle questions regarding angelic being and agency, Gerhard very justly, as well as wittily said, " They naturally dispose one to ask, how recently must they have fallen from heaven !" (quam nuper sint de cœlo delapsi.) And Calvin with his accustomed sense and gravity remarks, " If we would be truly wise, we shall give no heed to those foolish notions, which have been delivered by idle men concerning angelic orders without warrant from the Word of God " (Inst. i. c. 14, 4).

We are assuredly entitled to affirm, that in whatever the distinctions among angels may consist, or to whatever extent it may reach, it cannot in the least interfere with the happiness they individually enjoy. For this happiness arises, in the first instance, from each standing in a proper relation to the great centre of life and blessing ; and then from their being appointed to occupy such a sphere, and take part in such services and employments, as are altogether adapted to their state and faculties. These fundamental conditions being preserved, it is easy to conceive, how certain diversities, both in natural capacity, and in relative position, may be perfectly compatible with their mutual satisfaction and general well-being, and may even contribute to secure it.

IV. *The proper function and employment of angels relatively to us*, is what next calls for consideration ; and on this point we are furnished in Scripture with information of a more varied and specific nature, as it is that which more nearly concerns ourselves. In not a few passages we find their knowledge of what pertains to affairs on earth distinctly intimated, and also their interest in it, as proving to them an occasion of joy, or yielding a deeper insight into the purposes of God. Thus, they appear taking part in communications made from heaven to earth, desiring to look into the things which concern the scheme of salvation, learning from the successive evolution of the Divine plan more than they otherwise knew of God's manifold wisdom, rejoicing together at the birth of Jesus, and even over the return of individual wanderers to His fold (1 Pet. i. 12 ; Eph. iii. 10 ; Luke ii. 13, xv. 10). But there are other passages, in which a still closer connection is indicated—passages which represent them as engaged in directly and actively ministering to the good of believers, and shielding or delivering them from the evils incident to their lot. The office of angels in this respect was distinctly understood even in Old Testament times ; as appears alone from the designation, "Lord of Hosts," so commonly applied to God in respect to the forces He has at command for the execution of His purposes ; and still more from the frequent interposition of angels to disclose tidings or accomplish deliverances for the covenant-people, as well as from express assurances, such as these : " The angel of the Lord encampeth round about them that fear Him, and delivereth them " (Ps. xxxiv. 7). " He shall give His angels charge concerning thee, to keep thee in all thy ways ; they shall bear thee up in their hands, lest thou dash thy foot against a stone" (Ps. xci. 11, 12). Similar representations of angelic agency are found in New Testament Scripture, and come out, indeed, with greater prominence there, conformably to the general character and design of the Gospel, in rendering more patent the connection between this lower region and the world of spirits. So that it is only what we might have expected beforehand, to learn that our Lord in the days of His flesh was from time to time ministered to by angels; that on ascending to the regions of glory, He had the angels made subject to Him for carrying forward the operations of ·His kingdom; that commissions of importance were executed through their instrumentality during the life-time of the apostles; and that, generally, they are declared to be " all ministering spirits, sent forth to minister to those who are heirs of salvation" (Mark i. 13; Luke xxii. 43; Phil. ii. 10; 1 Pet. iii. 22; Acts xii.; Heb. i. 14).

In regard, however, to the kind of services which are actually rendered to believers by the ministry of angels, or the benefits which may justly be expected from it, we know too little of the nexus, which binds together in any particular case the world of sense with the world of spirits, to be able with much accuracy to determine. Negatively, there are definite boundaries that may be set down; we must hold· as excluded from their agency the actual communication of life and grace to the souls of men. Nowhere is this ascribed to them in Scripture; on the contrary, it is uniformly represented as an essentially Divine work, and, as such, lying beyond the agency of created beings. Father, Son, and Spirit are here the only effective agents, working, in so far as subordinate means are employed, through a human, not through an angelic instrumentality. The things which come within the sphere of angelic ministrations, bear incidentally upon the work of salvation, rather than directly touch it; and as regards the ordinary history of the Church and the common experience of believers, they have to do with the averting of evils, which might too seriously affect the interests of righteousness, or the bringing about of results and operations in the world, which are fitted to promote them. When it is reflected how much even the children of God are dependent upon the circumstances in which they are placed, and how much for the cause of God, whether in the world at large or in the case of single individuals, often turns upon a particular event in Providence, one can easily see what ample room there may be in the world for such timely and subtle influences as the quick messengers of light are capable of imparting. It might be too much to say, as has occasionally been said by divines, and seems to be held by Mr Kingsley, that all the active powers of nature are under angelic direction, and every event—at least every auspicious event—is owing to their interference; there are certainly no testimonies in Scripture sufficient to warrant so sweeping an inference. But, on the other hand, it is equally possible to err in the opposite direction; and as we have explicit information in Scripture of the fact, that there are myriads of angelic beings in heavenly places, who are continually ascending and descending on errands of mercy for men on earth, it may not be doubted, that in many a change which takes place around us, there are important operations performed by them, as well as by the ostensible actors, and by the material agencies of nature.

But whatever individuals, or the collective body of believers, may owe to this source, there are certain laws and limitations, under which it must always be understood to be conveyed. The fundamental ground of these is, that the efficiency of angels is essentially different from that of the several persons of the Godhead; it is such merely as one finite being is capable of exercising toward another. Consequently, it never can involve any violent interference with the natural powers of reason in those who are the subjects of it : it must adapt itself to the laws of reciprocal action established between finite beings, and so, can only work to the hand, or set bounds to the actings of nature, but cannot bring into operation elements absolutely new. Hence, as a further necessary deduction, all that is done by angels must be done in connection with, and by means of natural causes; and only by intensifying, or in some particular way directing these, can they exert any decisive influence on the events in progress. Thus, at the pool of Bethesda, the angel's power wrought through the waters, not independently of them; at Herod Agrippa's death, through the worms that consumed him; at the jail of Philippi, through the earthquake that shook the foundations of the building :—and if thus in these more peculiar, certainly not less in the more regular and ordinary interpositions of their power. But this takes nothing from the comfort or efficacy of their ministrations; it only implies, that these ministrations are incapable of being viewed apart from the channels through which they come, and that the beings who render them are not to be taken as the objects of personal regard or adoring reverence. Hence, while the hearts of believers are cheered by the thought of the ministry of angels, the worshipping of angels has from the first been expressly interdicted (Col. ii. 18; Rev. xxii. 9).

Various fanciful and groundless notions have been entertained on the subject of angelic ministrations, and have sought for countenance in isolated statements of Scripture. It has been held, for example, that a part of their number are separated for the special work of praise in the heavenly places, and observe hours of devotion; that angels act at times as subordinate intercessors, mediating between believers and Christ; that individual angels are appointed to the guardianship of particular kingdoms, and even of single persons; and that they have also, whether individually or collectively, a sort of charge to be present in the assemblies of the saints. As this latter class of notions still extensively prevails, and has an apparent foundation in certain passages of Scripture, it will be necessary to subject it to a particular examination.

(1) In regard to the guardianship or protection of particular kingdoms by individual angels, the notion can scarcely, perhaps, be said to exist, as a substantive belief in the present day, in Protestant Christendom; but it is held by not a few interpreters of Scripture as a doctrine of the book of Daniel, though not a doctrine they are themselves disposed to accredit. Rabbinical writers have certainly from an early period found it there. On the supposition, that Michael was a created angel, and the guardian angel of the Jews (designated as such, "their prince"), coupled with the further supposition, that what is said in the same book of the prince of the kingdom of Persia, who is represented as withstanding Gabriel for twenty-one days (x. 13), has respect to another angel, exercising a like guardianship over the Persian empire:—on these suppositions, the notion became prevalent, not only among the doctors of the synagogue, but also among the Christian fathers, from whom it went down, like other crudities, as a heritage to the Catholic theologians, that the several states or kingdoms of the earth have each their protecting genius, or tutelary angel—a created, but high and powerful intelligence. The idea—as the divines of the Reformation justly contended—is at variance with all right views of the general teaching of Scripture respecting those kingdoms, which are represented as in a condition that must have placed them be-

yond the pale of any such guardianship, even if it had existed; nor do the particular passages leant upon, when fairly interpreted, countenance the idea of its existence. We have already seen, how the proof fails in respect to Michael, he not being an angel, in the ordinary sense, but the Lord Himself as the Angel of the Covenant. He, the Jehovah-Mediator, the King and Head of the Old, as well as of the New Dispensation, was fitly denominated the שׂר, or Prince of the covenant-people. But the prince of the kingdom of Persia, who stands, by way of contrast, over against this Divine Head of the Theocracy, is the mere earthly potentate, the only real head of that kingdom. Such also is the prince of Grecia, afterwards mentioned. The Lord in the heavens, by His angelic agencies, and providential arrangements, contends with these earthly powers and dominions : in the exercise of the freedom granted them, and the resolute application of the re-sources they possessed, they might succeed in gaining certain advantages, or creating a certain delay, but in such an unequal contest the result could not be long doubtful; and the victory is soon announced to be on the Lord's side. This is the substance of the representation in Daniel, which contains nothing at vari-ance with the other representations in Scripture, nor anything, indeed, peculiar—unless it be the designation of the heads alike of the Divine and of the human kingdoms by the name of *prince*, instead of using the more common appellation, *king*. A peculiarity scarcely deserving of notice.[1]

(2) The idea of guardian-angels for each particular believer, or, as it is often put, for each individual child—the natural child in the first instance, then the spiritual—has met with much more general acceptance than the one already noticed, and still has the support of distinguished commentators. It is chiefly based on our Lord's statement in Matt. xviii. 10, " Take heed that ye despise not one of these little ones; for I say unto you, that in heaven their angels do always behold the face of my Father, which is in heaven." Alford, as well as Meyer, holds the plain teaching of the passage to be, that individuals have certain angels appointed to them as their special guardians; and on Acts xii.

---

[1] For a similar contrast between the Divine Head of the Jewish state, and the merely earthly heads of the surrounding states, see the explanation given in Part Third of Isa. vii. 14, as quoted in Matt. i. 23.

15, where he again refers to the passage, he affirms, not only that the doctrine of guardian-angels had been distinctly asserted by our Lord, but that the disciples, on the ground of His teaching, naturally spoke of Peter's angel, and believed that the guardian-angel sometimes appeared in the likeness of the person himself. So also Stier (on Matt. xviii. 10), while he admits, that the language points only by way of allusion to special guardian-angels of persons, holds the doctrine on this ground, and the unanimous sense of the Fathers, to be beyond any reasonable doubt. " Every child," he affirms, " has his angel until sin drives him away, as we may still be able to trace in the reflection of the angelic appearance in the countenance and aspect of children. Every believer, again, who may have come into a saved condition through the grace of redemption, gets, as a new spiritual child, his angel again, whom now he especially needs in the weakness of his spiritual commencement, for deeper-reaching experiences of guardianship and admonition, than weak and foolish children in times of bodily danger." I am no way moved by these high authorities and confident assertions; for they seem to me to impose a sense upon the words of our Lord, which they neither necessarily bear, nor naturally convey. The readiness and unanimity with which the Fathers found in them the doctrine of guardian-angels, is easily understood from the universal belief in the heathen world— a belief accredited and often largely expatiated upon in its highest philosophy—of attending genii or demons attached to single persons; and which naturally begat in the Fathers, whose early training was to a greater or less degree received in the school of heathenism, a predisposition to discover the same doctrine in a Christian form. On such a point they were peculiarly disqualified for being careful and discriminating guides; of which the following comment of Jerome on the passage may serve as a sufficient proof: " *Because their angels in heaven always see the face of the Father*: the great dignity of souls, that each should have from his natural birth (ab ortu nativitatis) an angel appointed for his guardianship. Whence we read in the Apocalypse of John, *Write these things to the angel of Ephesus, Thyatira, and to the angels of the other churches.* The apostle also commands the heads of women to be veiled in the churches, on account of the angels." How much sounder and more discriminating, not only than this confused and puerile annotation, but also than the interpretations of the modern expositors referred to above, is the note of Calvin? " The view taken by some of this passage, as if it ascribed to each believer his own peculiar angel, is without support. For the words of Christ do not import, that one angel is in perpetuity attached to this person or that, and the notion is at variance with the whole teaching of Scripture, which testifies, that angels encamp round about the righteous, and not to one angel alone, but to many has it been commanded, to protect every one of the faithful. Let us have done, therefore," he justly adds, " with that comment concerning a good and evil genius, and be content with holding, that to angels are committed the care of the whole Church, so that they can bring succour to individual members as necessity or profit may require." This plainly appears to be the correct view of the passage. It does not speak of little children simply as such, but of believers under this character (to which in humility and lowliness of spirit they had immediately before been assimilated); nor does it speak of individual relationships subsisting between these and the angels, but of the common interest they have in angelic ministrations, which extend to the apparently least and lowest of their number. But of a separate guardianship for each individual there is not a word dropt here, nor in any other part of Scripture. Even in Acts xii. 7, where a very special work had to be accomplished for Peter by the ministry of an angel, there is nothing of the historian's own that implies any individual or personal relationship of the one to the other : the angel is not called Peter's angel, nor is the angel represented as waiting upon him like a tutelary guardian; on the contrary, he is designated " the angel of the Lord," and is spoken of as coming to Peter, to do the particular office required, and again departing from him when it was done. It is true, the inmates of Mary's house, when they could not credit the report of the damsel, that Peter himself was at the door, said, as if finding in the thought the only conceivable explanation of the matter, " It is his angel." But as Ode has justly stated (De Angelis, Sec. viii. c. 4), " It is not everything recorded by the Evangelists as spoken by the Jews, or even by the disciples of Christ, which is sound and worthy of credit. Nor can what in this particular case was true of Peter be affirmed of all believers, or ought it to be so. And, indeed, that Peter himself did not believe, that a particular angel was assigned to him for guardianship, clearly enough appears from this, that when Peter got out of the prison, and followed the angel as his guide, he did not as yet know it to be true, that an angel was the actor, but thought he saw a vision; and at length, after the departure of the angel, having come to himself, he said, ' Now I know of a surety, that the Lord hath sent *His* angel, and delivered me from the hand of Herod.' "

(3) The last notion we were to consider respecting the ministry of angels, is the special charge they are supposed to take of Christian assemblies. This notion rests entirely upon two passages—the one, Eccl. v. 4–6, which has already been examined, and shown to have no proper bearing on this, or any other point, connected with angelic agency; the other, 1 Cor. xi. 10, in which the apostle says, " For this cause ought the woman to have power on her head, because of the angels." It is said in the course of the discussion, which the apostle introduces on the subject of female attire in the public assemblies. At the same time, it is proper to bear in mind, what expositors too commonly overlook, that the immediate object of the statement is of a general kind, and has respect to the relation of the woman to the man, as determined by the order of their creation: " For the man is not of the woman, but the woman of the man; neither was the man created for the woman, but the woman for the man: for this cause (namely, on account of that relative position and destiny) ought the woman to have power on her head, because of the angels." It is plainly the attire and aspect of the woman, as indicative of her proper place, that the apostle has here more immediately in view, and not merely nor directly her appearance and bearing in the church; this last and more specific point he would derive simply as a practical conclusion from the other. Now, as to the import of what he says on that other and more general subject, there can be little doubt, that what is meant by having power or authority ($\dot{\epsilon}\xi o \upsilon \sigma \dot{\iota} \alpha$) on the head, is having what visibly exhibited that; viz. a veiled, or covered appearance, which is the natural symbol of a dependent or subordinate position. There is no force in the objection to this, that it is rather the want of authority, than the possession of it, which is ascribed to the

woman; for it proceeds on a mistaken view of the expression, as
if the apostle meant she had the power to use it as her own. The
reverse, rather, is what is indicated. The expression is entirely
similar to that used by the centurion in Matt. viii. 9, when he
said of himself, " For I also am a man under authority " (ὑπὸ
ἐξουσίαν)—he stood, as it were, under its law and ordination—
having a right and a call to do whatever it authorised him to do
—*that*, but no more. So the woman here, as standing under the
man in a relation of subservience, *ought* (ὀφείλει) to have authority or power upon her head; in other words, something in the
very attire and aspect of her head to denote, that authority lay
upon her. Her veiled appearance—naturally, by her long hair,
and artificially, by an appropriate head-dress—is such a thing;
it is a token of respect and submission toward the higher authority lodged in the man, and betokens that it is hers to do with
ministrations of service, rather than with the right of government
and control.

Hence the feminine aspect which, in the ancient ordinance of
the Nazarite vow, the person bound by it had to assume, in regard
to his head. The Nazarite was one who, by a special vow,
placed himself in strict subservience to God; the authority of God
rested upon him in a manner quite peculiar; and, to mark this,
he had to let his hair grow like a woman's; so that, as the woman
in relation to man, so he in relation to God, might be said to have
power or authority on his head; and the parting with the symbol
of his position (as in the case of Samson) was in effect abandoning the covenant-engagement under which he stood—breaking
loose from God.

We see, then, the fitness and propriety of the veiled appearance
of the woman's head—it is the becoming sign of her place and
calling, as made *of* man, and, in a sense also, *for* man. But why
should this be said to be *because*, or, *for the sake of the angels?*
Whatever may be meant by the expression, one thing should be
distinctly understood regarding it—that, from the brief and
abrupt manner in which the allusion is made—not a word of
explanation going before or coming after—it can have reference
to no recondite or mysterious point—nothing in itself of doubtful
speculation, or capable of being ascertained only by minute and
laborious search. Points of such a nature, together with the

Rabbinical or heathen lore, on which they are grounded, must be out of place here, as the allusion (had it referred to such) could only have tended to perplex or mislead. Proceeding, therefore, on the ground now laid down, we have to dismiss from our minds all the peculiar and unusual applications of the term angels sometimes adduced by commentators ; and also all fanciful notions regarding the acts of real angels—such as their supposed habit of veiling their faces before God (which is never mentioned of angels, strictly so called), or having a sort of superintendence and oversight of Christian assemblies (a matter also nowhere else intimated in any earlier Scripture) :—and we have simply to consider, whether there be any broad and palpable facts respecting the angelic world, which, without violence or constraint, may be fitly brought into juxtaposition with the proper place and bearing of women. We know nothing of this description, unless it be what their very name imports—their position and calling as ministering spirits before God, from which one section of them, indeed, fell, but which the rest kept, to their honour and blessing. This, however, is enough ; it furnishes precisely the link of connection between them and woman. Her place, in relation to man, is like that of the angels of God ; it is to do the part of a ministering agent and loving help—not independently to rule and scheme for herself. It is by abiding under law to man, that she becomes either a subject or an instrument of blessing. Hence, when she fell, it was by departing from this order, by attempting to act an independent part, as if no yoke of authority lay upon her, and she might be an authority and a law to herself—quitting her appointed place of ministering, for the coveted place of independent action. So, too, was it, in the higher regions of existence, with the angels that lost their first estate ; they strove, in like manner, against the prime law of their being, which was to minister and serve, and aspired to be and act as from themselves. By this vain and wicked attempt they fell ; and the fall of Eve, through their instrumentality, was but the image and echo of their own. Now, is it unnatural to suppose that the apostle, while tracing up the matter concerning woman's place and bearing in society to the origin and fountain of things, should also have reminded them of these instructive facts ?˅ should have pointed their thoughts to the higher region of spirits ? The order

P

here—he virtually said to them—the order of things in this lower world, serves as an image of the heavenly. Relations of superiority and subservience exist there as well as here; and the harmony and blessedness of both worlds alike depend upon these relations being duly kept; to disregard them, is the sure road to confusion and every evil work. Let the woman, therefore, recognising this, and remembering how the evil that originated in ambitious striving in the heavenly places, renewed itself on earth by the like spirit taking possession of her bosom—feel that it is good for her to wear perpetually the badge of subjection to authority. It is at once safe and proper for her to retain it; and so, instead of constantly repeating the catastrophe of the fallen angels, she will show her readiness to fulfil that angel-relationship, with its ministrations of service, for which she was brought into being, and exhibit before the blessed ministers of light a reflection of their own happy order and loving obedience.

It may be added, in respect to the false views of angelic ministration which we have combated, and as an additional proof of their contrariety to the truth of Scripture, that the countenance they too commonly received from the Fathers produced its natural fruit throughout the early Church in a prevailing tendency to angel-worship. The Fathers, however, opposed this tendency, and sometimes by formal synodal acts denounced the practice, in which it showed itself, of dedicating particular churches to certain angels, and calling them by their names. In the rightness of this opposition, the inconsistence with which it was connected may be overlooked; but it were hard to see how, if the guardianship of distinct regions, of particular persons, and of Christian assemblies, were assigned to individual angels, these should not have received a share in the semi-divine honour that was paid to the saints. Angelic adoration and saint-worship are but different forms of the same idolatrous tendency.

V. The doctrine of the fallen angels, and their agency among men, though it should not be totally omitted here, yet does not call for lengthened consideration; since, while it gives rise to many metaphysical questions and baffling difficulties, these have comparatively little to do with the interpretation of Scripture. For the most part, the passages in which the fallen angels are referred to, are plain enough in their meaning; and it is the subjects themselves discoursed of, not the language used in discoursing of them, which more peculiarly exercise the powers of the mind. At present, it will be enough to indicate a few points nearly connected with, or naturally growing out of, the principles that have been unfolded regarding the angels of God. (1) It is, first of all, to be held fast respecting them, that, in common with those who still retain their place in light and glory, they were originally created good. The teaching of Scripture throughout is altogether opposed to the idea, which, from the earliest times, was so extensively prevalent in the East, of an independent, uncreated principle of evil, whether as embodied in one, or in a multiplicity of concrete existences. Every being in the universe, that is not God, is a part of the creation of God; and, as His works were all, like Himself, very good, the evil that now appears in any of them must have been a perversion of the good, not an original and inherent malignity. And, in the case of the evil angels, the fact of a fall from a preceding good state is distinctly asserted (John viii. 44 ; Jude 6 ; 2 Pet. ii. 4). But nothing is said as to the period of this fall, whether it came immediately after their creation, or after the lapse of ages—nor as to the circumstances that gave rise to it, and the precise form it assumed. The expression of our Lord, in John's Gospel, that Satan was a liar from the beginning (ἀπ' ἀρχῆς), does not necessarily refer to the commencement of his own existence, but seems rather, from the connection, to point to the beginning of this world's history. It is more natural for us to suppose, that the fall of the angels, like that of our first parents, was nearly coeval with their existence, as it is next to impossible for us to conceive how they should, for any length of time, have enjoyed the intuition and the blessedness of God, without having all the principles of goodness in their natures strengthened and rendered continually less capable of turning aside to evil ;—but this is a region into which Scripture does not conduct us, and it is best to avoid it as one that can only involve matters of uncertain speculation. (2) The total depravity, and consequent misery of the evil angels, is also constantly asserted in Scripture. In both respects they are represented as the antithesis of the good and blessed angels. Inveterately hostile to God Himself, whatever is of God excites their enmity and opposition : falsehood instead of truth, instead of love, selfishness, hatred and malice, have become the elements of their active being; and, themselves utterly estranged from all good, they appear incapable even of apprehending the feelings of those who love it, and actuated only by the insatiate desire of, in every possible way, resisting and overthrowing it.   Hence their policy is characterised by mingled intelligence and blindness, cunning and folly, according as it is directed to those who, like themselves, are inclined to the evil, or to such as are wedded to the good : with the one it is skilfully laid and reaches its aim, with the other it perpetually miscalculates and defeats itself.   Of all this the recorded actings of Satan and his angels, in the history of our Lord and His apostles, supply ample proof (comp. besides Matt. xiii. 39 ; 1 Pet. v. 8 ; Eph. vi. 12 ; Heb. ii. 14).   So that sinning and doing evil may be said to have become a moral necessity in their natures, as love and holiness with the elect angels.   " Hence they are necessarily miserable.   Torn loose from the universal centre of life, without being able to find it in themselves; by the feeling of inward void, ever driven to the outward world, and yet in irreconcileable hostility to it and themselves ; eternally shunning, and never escaping, the presence of God ; always endeavouring to destroy, and always compelled to promote His purposes ; instead of joy in the beatific vision of the Divine glory, having a never-satisfied longing for an end they never reach ; instead of hope, the unending oscillation between hope and despair ; instead of love, an impotent hatred of God, their fellows, and themselves :—can the fearful condemnation of the last judgment, the thrusting-down into the bottomless pit of destruction (Rev. xx. 10), add anything to the anguish of such a condition, excepting that they shall there see the kingdom of God for ever delivered from their assaults, their vain presumption that they can destroy or impede it scattered to the winds, leaving to them only the ever-gnawing despair of an inward rage, which cannot spend itself upon anything without, and is, therefore, for ever undeceived as to its own impotence !"—(Twesten's Lectures, see Bib. Sacra, i., p. 793).   (3) Lastly, in regard to the agency of the evil angels, and the mode in which it is exercised in the world, the general limitations already deduced from Scripture in respect to the good, undoubtedly hold also here.   Negatively, it cannot assume a substantive existence or separate action of its own, nor come into direct contact with the minds of men. It has no other way of operating, either upon men's souls or bodies, but by entering into the series of second causes, and giving such additional potence to these as it may consist with the Divine purpose to admit of being employed. So that the temptations of the powers of evil, and the effects of every kind wrought by them, are not (in ordinary cases) to be distinguished from the operation of the moral and physical laws which prevail in the world. No record is contained of external injuries inflicted by them, except by means of external causes, which they were allowed, in some unknown manner, to intensify—as in the case of Job's calamities, or Paul's thorn in the flesh. And the moral hardening, or intense addictedness to evil, which is sometimes ascribed to the working of Satan, or his fellows, always appears as the result of a previous course of wickedness, and as consisting simply in a more thorough abandonment to the carnal lusts and affections, which have gained dominion of the heart. The cases of Saul in the Old Testament, of Judas, Ananias and Sapphira, the followers of Antichrist, etc., in the New, fully confirm this (1 Sam. xvi. 14, xviii. 10 ; Luke xxii. 3 ; Acts v. 1–9 ; 2 Thess. ii. 11, etc.). The nearest contact with the individual that any of the notices of Scripture give reason for supposing to have ever taken place, or to be compatible with the nature of things, lies in some such operation on the bodily organism, as is fitted to inflame the existing tendencies to evil, and shut their unhappy victim more entirely up to their dominion. And hence the utter fallacy of the whole theory and practice of witchcraft, which proceeded on the assumption of direct, personal intercourse with the Wicked One. That the possibility of such a traffic should have been believed in Christian times, and especially that it should have led to the sacrifice of thousands of lives in every state of European Christendom, is one of the greatest scandals in the history of modern civilization.

SECTION THIRD.

ON THE NAMES OF CHRIST IN NEW TESTAMENT SCRIPTURE, AND, IN PARTICULAR, ON THE USE OF Χριστός, AND Υἱὸς τοῦ ἀνθρώπου.

ALL the names of the Redeemer were originally appellatives. They expressed some leading property, or exhibited some specific aspect of His person, His mission, or His kingdom. The term *Christ* is no exception, nor even *Jesus*, which simply denotes Him as emphatically the Saviour—although being the individual name borne by Him from His infancy, it was familiarly used, and might from the first be regarded, as a proper name. The Old Testament designations not only were originally, but for the most part continued still to retain an appellative character; such, for example, as *The Angel of the Lord, The Angel of the Covenant, Immanuel, The Prince, The Son of God.* But in others the appellative passed, even in Old Testament times, into a kind of proper name; and, as a consequence, the article, which was originally prefixed to them, ultimately fell away. In one of them, indeed, Michael— which has already been investigated in connection with the subject of angels—the article was not prefixed; for in the only book where it occurs (Daniel) it was employed substantially as a proper name; yet it was really an appellative, and, for the purpose of indicating more distinctly the Divine nature and exalted position of Messiah, was preferred to some of the earlier and more common designations used by the prophets. As a proper example, however, of the change from the appellative to the individual form, let us trace the manner in which the term *Zemach*, or Branch, came to be applied definitely and personally to Christ. Isaiah first speaks in ch. iv. 2, with reference probably to Messianic times, but in a somewhat general way, of the Lord's branch (צֶמַח יְהוָה), which he said was yet to be beautiful and glorious; and at ch. xi. 1, a little more specifically, at least with a more special reference to the house of David, and an individual member of that house, he gives promise of a stem of Jesse, and a branch, or sucker, from his roots. Here, however, the word

Zemach is not used, but חֹטֶר and נֵצֶר, showing that such terms were employed simply in an appellative sense, and merely because indicating a certain characteristic of the future scion of the royal house. With a still nearer approach to the personal, Jeremiah, in ch. xxiii. 5, prophesies of a time, when the Lord would raise up to David a righteous branch (*Zemach*), and a king (viz. the branch already mentioned) should reign and prosper. And, finally, when through these earlier prophecies the appellative had come, in the general apprehension, to be associated with the one object of hope and expectation, to whom it pre-eminently pointed, it is used as a sort of proper name by the prophet Zechariah—though still with an obvious reference to its appellative import: ch. iii. 8, " Behold, I bring my servant, Branch ;" and again, ch. vi. 12, " Thus saith the Lord, Behold a man, whose name is Branch."—Much in the same manner *Melek*, king, is occasionally used; for example in Ps. xlv. 1, Ps. lxxii. 1, where the theme is that King by way of eminence, to whom even then the eye of faith looked forward as the crowning-point of Israel's glory; it is applied to Him individually, and without the article, as a strictly personal designation.

This progression, however, from the appellative to the proper use of names, appears still more distinctly in the epithet, by which in ancient times the coming Redeemer was most commonly known—*the Messiah*, or, adopting the Greek form, *the Christ*. In its primary import and application there was nothing strictly personal, or even very specific, in the term. A participle or verbal adjective from מָשַׁח to anoint, it was applied to any one so anointed; for example, to the high-priest, who is called in Lev. iv. 3, " the priest the anointed" (*hamaschiach*), rendered in the Septuagint ὁ ἱερεὺς ὁ χριστός. At a later period it is similarly used of Saul by David—not of Saul as an individual, but of him as the possessor of a dignity, to which he had been set apart by a solemn act of consecration; as such, he is designated ὁ χριστὸς τοῦ Κυρίου, the christ or anointed of the Lord (1 Sam. xii. 3, 5, etc.) It was Hannah who first gave the term this kingly direction, when, at the conclusion of her song of praise, she proclaimed the Lord's intention to give " strength to His king, and exalt the horn of His anointed (*meschiho*)"—evidently using *His Messiah*, or anointed, as synonymous with *His king* in the preceding

clause; and, singularly enough, doing so, before there was an
actual king in Israel, and when as yet the act of anointing had
not been applied to any one filling the kingly function. The
prophetic spirit, in which her song was conceived, and the elevation especially of its closing sentences, seem to point above and
beyond the immediate future, and to bear respect to that universal King, of whom Jacob had already spoken as the Shiloh,
and to whom the gathering of the peoples was to be—whom
Balaam also descried as " the Star that should come out of Jacob,
and the Sceptre that should rise out of Israel, who was to smite
the corners of Moab, and destroy all the children of tumult."
This was the child of hope more especially in the eye of Hannah;
for the anointed King, of whom she speaks, was to stand pre-
eminent above the states and powers of the world, and through
Him the adversaries of the Lord were to be broken, and the ends
of the earth to be judged. Not long after we find the term
Messiah applied in the same manner by David—not to a merely
human and earthly monarch, but to the Son of the Highest,
to whom as such the heritage of the world, to its utmost bounds,
by Divine right belongs. And at length it became so appropriated to this higher use, in the diction of the Spirit and the
expectations of the people, that its other possible applications
were lost sight of; it came to be regarded as the distinctive name
of the promised Saviour—as in Dan. ix. 25, " Know, therefore,
and understand, that from the going forth of the commandment
to restore and to build Jerusalem, unto Messiah, Prince" (no
article); and again in the next verse, " And after threescore
and two weeks shall Messiah be cut off."

These remarks will explain some apparent grammatical anomalies in the New Testament use of the term Χριστός. But before quitting the Old Testament usage, it is not unimportant to
notice, that there are two or three passages, in which the term is
applied to persons not precisely included in the cases already
noticed; applications which have given rise to the idea, that the
term was loosely extended to include any person of note, and in
particular the collective people of Israel. This is a mistaken
view, and loses its apparent plausibility, when respect is had to
the symbolical import of anointing with oil, out of which the
word Messiah arose. Such anointing, as a religious ceremony,

was always symbolical of the communication of the gifts of the
Holy Spirit. Thus the anointing of the tabernacle and all its
furniture bespoke the indwelling of the Spirit for purposes of life
and blessing among the members of the Theocracy. Hence,
when David was anointed to be king in the room of Saul, it is
immediately said, that "the Spirit of the Lord came upon him
from that day forward, and that the Spirit of the Lord departed
from Saul" (1 Sam. xvi. 13, 14); and David himself, when by his
iniquity he had forfeited his title to the place he held in the kingdom, prays that God would not take His Holy Spirit from him
(Ps. li.)—would not deal with him as He had dealt with Saul,
and leave his anointing a shell without a kernel. Still more explicitly Isaiah, pointing to Gospel times, and personating the
Messiah himself, says, "The Spirit of the Lord is upon me, because He hath anointed me to preach glad tidings to the meek"
(ch. lxi. 1)—the possession of the Spirit because of the anointing; as if the one necessarily inferred the other; and, indeed, in
this case the reality alone was made account of; the symbol was
dropt as no longer needed. And, to mention no more, in the
vision presented to Zechariah, ch. iv., there is first the symbol of
two olive-trees, pouring a perpetual stream of oil into the candlestick, with its seven branches—emblems of the Church; and then
the explanation of the symbol in what is said to Zerubbabel, "Not
by might, nor by power, but by My Spirit, saith the Lord of
Hosts:"—So that the presence of the Spirit, pervading the affairs
of the covenant, and carrying these triumphantly over the difficulties and dangers around them, is the reality indicated by the
oil that flowed from the olive-trees into the candlestick.

Now, it is by a reference to this symbolical import of the practice of anointing that the passages in question are to be understood and explained. One of them is Isa. xlv. 1, where Cyrus
is designated by the name of Messiah ("Thus saith the Lord to
His anointed, to Cyrus"); so designated, however, not from his
being simply a prince or a ruler, but from the peculiar relation
in which he stood to the covenant-people, and the important
service he rendered to their interests. On these accounts he
was justly regarded as one possessed of a certain measure of the
Spirit, having the reality, though not the outward symbol of an
anointing, which qualified him for discerning in some degree the

truth of God, and for acting as God's chosen instrument at an important crisis in the affairs of His Church.   In the judicious language of Vitringa, " The anointed person here is one who was separated by the Divine counsel, and ordained to accomplish a matter that pertained to the glory of God, and was furnished for it from above with the necessary gifts ; among which were his justice, his regard for the Divine Being, his prudence, fortitude, mildness, and humanity; so that he could not seem to be unworthy of being made an illustrious means of executing the counsels of God."   Again, in Hab. iii. 13, it is said, " Thou wentest forth for the salvation (help) of Thy people, and for the salvation of Thine anointed" (Sept. τοὺς Χριστοὺς σου) ; where the *anointed*, in the last clause, is often viewed as synonymous with *people* in the first.   But this is erroneous ; the former expression points to the God-anointed king of the people, in whose behalf the Lord is often also in the Psalms represented as coming, or entreated to come, for the purpose of bringing deliverance (Ps. xxviii. 8, xx. 6).   Finally, in Ps. cv. 15, it is said respecting the patriarchs, " Touch not Mine anointed, and do My prophets no harm ;" and the reference is still of the same kind—it points to those heads of the Jewish nation as vessels and instruments of God's Spirit, to whom were communicated revelations of the Divine will, and by whom were accomplished the more peculiar purposes of Heaven : on which account also Abraham is expressly called a prophet (Gen. xx. 7).   To style thus the patriarchal heads of the covenant-people, and even Cyrus the heathen prince, by the name of God's anointed, is itself convincing evidence of the respect that was had, in Old Testament times, to the reality in the symbol, and shows how, where the external form of anointing had failed, this might still be regarded as virtually present, if the things signified by it had actually taken effect.

To return, however, to our more immediate object, we have seen that while the term Messiah was properly an appellative, yet, toward the close of the Old Testament writings, it came to be used of the expected Redeemer much as a proper name, and hence, naturally, without the article ; still, not as if it thereby lost its appellative import, but only because this import was seen concentrating all its fulness in Him, so that He alone seemed

worthy to bear the appellation. It should not, therefore, excite
any surprise; it is rather in accordance with what might have
been expected, if, sometimes at least, and especially when persons
spoke, who were peculiarly under the influence of the Spirit, or
who had no doubt as to the individual to whom the name properly belonged, it is found to be similarly used in New Testament Scripture. It is in reality so used on the very first occasion on which Χριστὸς occurs in the Gospels, viz., when the angels
announced to the shepherds on the plains of Bethlehem that there
had been born a Saviour, ὅς ἐστιν Χριστὸς Κύριος, " who is Christ,
Lord" (Luke ii. 11). In like manner, the woman of Samaria,
when speaking, not of any definite individual, but of the ideal
Messiah, or the specific, though still unknown individual, in
whom the idea was to be realized, uses the term absolutely, or as
a proper name, " I know (she said, John iv. 25) that Messias
comes, who is called Christ (ὁ λεγόμενος Χριστός) : when he shall
have come, He will tell us all things." So, yet again, Jesus
Himself, in the only passage in which He is recorded to have
applied the term directly to Himself, John xvii. 3, " And Jesus
Christ, whom Thou hast sent." Here especially commentators
have often found a difficulty, from not seeing the matter in its
proper light; and Dr Campbell even suspects, in the face of all
the MSS., that the article has somehow been lost before Χριστόν.
He might, however, as well have suspected a like omission in the
address of the angels to the shepherds, or in Dan. ix. 24, 25,
before Messiah. The same principle accounts for the omission
in all the cases, and satisfactorily explains it; viz., the distinctive
application of the term Messiah, even before the close of Old
Testament Scripture, to the promised Redeemer, which rendered
it substantially a proper name, when used by those who looked
with some degree of confidence to the individual that was entitled
to bear it.

But from the circumstances connected with our Lord's appearance in the world, which were such as to occasion doubts in
many minds respecting His Messiahship, it was quite natural that
when the term was used during the period of His earthly sojourn,
it should not commonly have been employed as a proper name,
but should rather have been taken in its appellative sense, and as
only with a greater or less degree of probability applicable to the

Saviour. The question, which at the time either consciously agitated, or silently occurred to men's minds, was, whether this Jesus of Nazareth was entitled to be owned as *the* Messiah ; whether He was in reality the person, in whom the characteristics and properties implied in that designation were to be found. Hence, being commonly used with reference to the solution of such a question, the name Messiah, or Christ, usually has the article prefixed, till after the period of the resurrection, when all doubt or uncertainty vanished from the minds of His followers, and the name began, equally with Jesus, to be appropriated to our Lord as a strictly personal designation. We can thus mark a general progress in the usage of the sacred writers, and a diversity in respect to Χριστός, quite similar to that, which was noticed in the Old Testament respecting Messiah : an earlier use, in which respect is had more to the appellative import, and a later, in which the word comes chiefly to be applied as a proper name. And, accordingly, in the Gospels it is but rarely found *without* the article, while it is almost as rarely found *with* the article in the Epistles.

This more advanced stage of matters, when Christ as well as Jesus had come to be used as a proper name, had already entered when the Gospels were written. Hence we find the Evangelists, at the beginning of their narratives, and when speaking from the point of view which had then been reached, employing the term Christ in as personal a manner as Jesus. Thus Matthew, at the beginning of his genealogy, " The book of the generation Ἰησοῦ Χριστοῦ," of Jesus Christ ; and again at the close of it, " Jacob begat Joseph the husband of Mary, of whom was born Jesus, who is called Christ" (ὁ λεγόμενος Χριστός). In like manner Mark heads his Gospel, " The beginning of the Gospel of Jesus Christ, Son of God." So also John in ch. i. 17, " The law was given by Moses ; grace and truth came by Jesus Christ." But immediately after such introductory statements, when they begin to report what persons thought and spake, while the events of Gospel history were in progress, we mark in the use of the article the regard men had to the appellative import of the word. Thus in John i. 20, the Baptist is reported as confessing, that he was " not *the* Christ ;" and at ver. 42, Andrew says to Peter, " We have found *the* Messias." In Matt. ii. 3, Herod demands of the chief priests and scribes, " Where *the* Christ is born ;" *i.e.* the person to whom that appellation should really belong. And Peter in his memorable confession says, " We believe that Thou art *the* Christ, the Son of the living God."

It would undoubtedly have been better, and would have contributed to the more easy and distinct understanding of some passages in New Testament Scripture, if our translators had been more generally observant of the difference in style now under consideration, and had more commonly rendered the article when it exists in the original. We miss it particularly in some passages of the Acts—as at ch. iv. 42, " They ceased not teaching and preaching Jesus Christ," properly, Jesus the Christ, meaning, that Jesus is the Christ; ch. xvii. 3, " This Jesus whom I preach to you is Christ," ch. xviii. 28, " Showing by the Scriptures that Jesus was Christ "—where in both passages the meaning would evidently gain in distinctness by inserting the article, as in the original, " That Jesus is the Christ." At the same time, as the name, even when it became a kind of personal designation, always bore a reference to its original import, so it never wholly loses this in the minds of thoughtful readers of the Bible ; and there are probably not very many, at least of serious and thoughtful readers, who are in the position described by Dr Campbell, when he says, that they consider Jesus Christ as no other than the name and surname of the same person, and that it would sound all one to them to say, that Paul testified that Christ was Jesus, as that Jesus was Christ.[1] No one could possibly be insensible to the difference in these statements, who reads with ordinary attention the authorised version — excepting in the sense, which would not suit Dr Campbell's purpose, of ascribing an appellative import to Jesus as well as Christ. In that case it would be much the same to say, that Jesus or Saviour is Christ, and that Christ or Messias is Jesus. All, however, that can with propriety be affirmed is, that the omission of the article in such cases renders the meaning less palpable and obvious than it would otherwise have been.

Even when the word *Christ* was passing, or had already passed into a sort of personal designation, pains were taken by the apostles to keep up in the minds of the disciples an acquaintance

[1] Preliminary Dissertations.

with its proper import. Thus Peter on the day of Pentecost
speaks of God having made the Jesus who had been so recently
crucified both Lord and Christ — καὶ Κύριον καὶ Χριστὸν; and,
somewhat later, the assembled company of apostles, after the
liberation of Peter and John, say in their joint address to God,
" Thy holy child Jesus, whom Thou didst christen," or anoint
(ὃν ἔχρισας, Acts iv. 27).   Still more explicitly was this done in
the address of Peter to the household of Cornelius, when, after
briefly adverting to the general outlines of our Lord's history,
and styling Him simply, Jesus of Nazareth, he adds, " how God
anointed him with the Holy Spirit and power" (ὡς ἔχρισεν αὐτὸν
ὁ Θεὸς Πνεύματι Ἁγίῳ καὶ δυνάμει, Acts x. 38).   Indeed, the verb
χρίω, on this very account—that is, because of its symbolical connection with the gift of the Spirit, and in particular with the
name and consecration of Jesus—itself acquired a kind of sacred
value, and in New Testament Scripture is only used of this
higher, spiritual anointing. With one exception, it is never used
but of Christ Himself, as the Spirit-replenished servant of Jehovah ; and even that exception is not without a close respect to
the same. It is in 2 Cor. i. 21, where the apostle says, " He
that establisheth us together with you into Christ, and hath
anointed us, is God" (ὁ δὲ βεβαιῶν ἡμᾶς σὺν ὑμῖν εἰς Χριστὸν, καὶ
χρίσας ἡμᾶς, Θεός)—that is, He has so knit and consolidated us into
Christ, that we have ourselves become Christ-like, replenished
with a portion of His enlightening and sanctifying Spirit. The
verb ἀλείφω is the word employed in reference to anointings of
an inferior sort, done for the sake of refreshment merely, and
without any sacred design.

In some of the later passages of the New Testament this reference to the original meaning of the term is undoubtedly lost sight
of; and Jesus is designated Christ, when, as far as we can see,
Lord, or Redeemer, might have been equally appropriate. Thus
in Eph. v. 21, according to the correct reading, we have " being
subject to one another in fear of Christ" (ἐν φόβῳ Χριστοῦ);
Christ being simply an appellation of the Divine and glorified
Redeemer, as the object of humble reverence and submissive regard. Passages of this sort, however, are not very frequent; and
where there is no distinct, there often is a concealed or implied
reference to the appellative import of the term. It is to this,

that we would ascribe the occasional employment of Christ, rather than any other name of the Redeemer, to denote the organic union between Him and His people. Thus in Gal. iv. 19, the apostle says, "My little children, of whom I travail in birth again, until Christ be formed in you;" and in Eph. iv. 20, "Ye have not so learned Christ." In these passages we are not to dilute the term *Christ*, so as to take it for a kind of concrete designation of Christian doctrine; we are rather to regard it as pointing to that intimate spiritual fellowship between the soul and Christ, which renders genuine believers so many images of Himself—smaller vessels and partial embodiments of that grace, which in infinite fulness and perfection is treasured up in Him. So again in 1 Cor. xii. 12, we read, "For as the body is one, and hath many members, and all the members of that one body, being many, are one body; so also is Christ;" *i.e.* Christ and those who are His—the whole corporate society of the faithful; they are together designated by the name of Christ, as having their spiritual being in Him, and in Him receiving the unction of the same Spirit. It is quite possible also, and even probable, that out of this import and use of the word Χριστός, may have grown that common name Χριστιανοί, Christians, by which the followers of Jesus became so early, and have so uniformly been distinguished. We are told in Acts xi. 26, that they were so called first in Antioch; and Mr Trench (in his *Study of Words*, p. 98), as well as many in former times, have thought, that the name was imposed upon them by their heathen adversaries, and consequently at first had somewhat of the aspect of a nickname. We cannot positively affirm it was otherwise; but the phraseology of St Paul approaches so very near to the use of the word as a common designation, that if it did not actually originate in the Church itself, we might almost say, it should have done so; nor, assuredly, would it have become so readily owned, and so extensively employed among the Christian communities, unless it had, either spontaneously arisen from within, or as soon as heard awakened a response among the members of the Church. Hence, as conscious of no reproach in the appellation, yea, rather as owning and accrediting its propriety, the Apostle Peter says, "But if any of you suffer as a Christian—ὡς Χριστιανός—let him not be ashamed" (1 Pet. iv. 16). And as regards the spiritual use to be made of the appellation, the most natural and appropriate turn, in our judgment, to be given to the matter, is, to direct attention—not to the supposed accident of the origin of the term —but to the real meaning involved in it, when rightly understood; in other words, to the fulness of grace and blessing, which ought to distinguish those, who have their calling and designation from Him, who is THE CHRIST—the Spirit-anointed Saviour.

Another thing to be noted, in connection with this name and its cognate terms, is the rise that took place from the outward and symbolical, to the inward and spiritual. This had begun, as we have noticed, even in Old Testament times; persons were even then designated as Christs or anointed ones, who had received no outward consecration with holy oil. The application of the term to the patriarchs in Psalm cv., and to Cyrus by Isaiah, was manifestly of this description; and in the New Testament the external symbol, so far as regards the use of χρίω in all its forms, falls entirely away; it is applied only to the inward communication and endowment with the Spirit's grace, which was symbolized by the external anointings with holy oil. The spiritual reality was so well understood, that while the old language was retained, the ancient symbol was felt to be no longer needed; so that the anointed one now is simply the vessel of grace—Jesus pre-eminently and completely, because in Him resides the plenitude of the Spirit's grace; then, subordinately to Him, the members of His spiritual body, because out of His fulness they receive grace for grace.

It is proper, still further, to note the relative order and gradation, that appears in the names usually applied to our Lord as regards their individual import and common use. The first name by which He was known and addressed was Jesus, which, though of deep and comprehensive import, and requiring the exercise of lively faith and spiritual discernment, if used with a proper knowledge and apprehension of its meaning, was yet for the most part regarded as simply a proper name. When called Jesus of Nazareth by the men of His generation, our Lord was merely distinguished from the other persons of the place and neighbourhood. The first question that came to be stirred in men's bosoms, was, whether He was entitled to have the further name of the Christ, or simply to be called Jesus Christ. As soon as inquirers attained to satisfaction on that point, they took their place among His disciples; they recognised Him as the promised Messiah, and confessed Him as such. It was a further question, however, and one not so readily decided, what personally this Christ was? Was He simply a man, distinguished from other men by superior gifts of nature and of grace? Or was He, in a sense altogether peculiar, the Son of God? A considerable time elapsed before even the immediate followers of Christ reached the proper position of knowledge and conviction upon this point; and the first distinct, or, at least, thoroughly intelligent and assured utterance of the truth, was that which came from the lips of Peter, when he said, " We believe, that Thou art the Christ, the Son of the living God." If he had stopt at " the Christ," there had been nothing very remarkable in the confession; Philip virtually confessed as much at the outset, when he said to Nathanael, " We have found Him, of whom Moses in the law and the prophets wrote, Jesus the Son of Joseph;" and by Andrew, when he informed Simon, " We have found the Messiah." But it was greatly more to be able to add, with a full understanding and conviction of what was said, " the Son of the living God." Peter appears to have had precedence of the other disciples in the clearness and strength of his convictions on the subject. Nearly the same confession in words had been uttered at an early period by Nathanael, when he exclaimed, " Rabbi, Thou art the Son of God, Thou art the King of Israel;" but we can scarcely doubt that his mind was still imperfectly enlightened regarding the person of Jesus, and that he really confessed to nothing more than some kind of indefinite superiority in Jesus over ordinary men. But the truth had been communicated to Peter by special revelation, and had taken firm possession of his soul; and the Sonship of Jesus to which he confessed was that essentially Divine one, of which Christ spake when He said, " All things are delivered to Me of M Father; and no man knoweth the Son but the Father; neither knoweth any man the Father save the Son, and he to whomsoever the Son will reveal Him" (Matt. xi. 27). And it was, beyond doubt, in this higher sense, which had been indicated in various discourses of Christ, that the Jewish high priest used it,

Q

when he solemnly put the question to Jesus, whether He were the Christ, the Son of God; and on receiving an affirmative answer, condemned Him for blasphemy. So that to confess Jesus, as at once the Christ, and the Son of God, was to own Him to be all that the prophets foretold He should be—all that His Divine mission required Him actually to be; it declared Him to be possessed of a nature essentially Divine, as well as human, and thereby rendered capable of receiving the entire fulness of the Spirit, to qualify Him for executing in every part the work of man's redemption.

It is somewhat singular, that our Lord Himself never, except on one occasion—the one already referred to in John xvii. 3—appropriated the names, Jesus and Christ; and only on a very few occasions, and even then somewhat obliquely, did He take to Himself the title of Son of God (Matt. xi. 27; John v. 25, ix. 35, xi. 4). The epithet, under which He usually spoke of Himself, was that of the " Son of Man." There are on record upwards of forty distinct occasions on which He is represented to have employed it in His discourses. Yet it was never applied to Him by the Evangelists, when relating the events of His earthly ministry; nor is He ever mentioned as having been addressed under this title either by friends or foes. Stephen, however, after the resurrection of Jesus, made use of it, when in ecstasy he exclaimed, " Behold, I see the heavens opened, and the Son of Man standing on the right hand of God" (Acts vii. 56). On no other occasion do we find it used, either of Christ or to Him, in New Testament Scripture—unless we may so regard what is written in Rev. i. 13, where the Apocalyptist speaks of seeing in vision one ὅμοιον υἱῷ ἀνθρώπου, "like to"—not, as in the authorised version, the, but—" a son of man." It is in itself a quite general expression, although it doubtless points to the glorified Redeemer. This, however, we only learn from what follows: from the connection it appears, that the individual, who in the vision bore such resemblance to a son of man, was none other than the once crucified but now exalted Saviour; but the description, " like a son of man," is not in itself more specific and personal than the corresponding phrase in Daniel, ch. vii. 13—where, after the vision of the four wild beasts rising from the sea, and representing the four successive worldly monarchies, one appeared in the night visions " like a son of man (no article in the original), coming with the clouds of heaven, and receiving dominion, and glory, and a kingdom, that all people, nations, and languages should serve Him."

There can be no doubt that this passage in Daniel is the fundamental one, on which not only that in Revelation, but also our Lord's favourite and familiar use of the phrase in question, is based; and without knowing the precise import and bearing of the representation in the prophet, it is impossible rightly to apprehend the reason and object of the language derived from it in New Testament times. There are two points of contrast brought out in the prophet between the representative of the fifth, the really universal and everlasting kingdom, and the representatives of the earthly kingdoms that preceded. These latter are all exhibited as deriving their origin from beneath; they appeared coming out of the sea, that is from the world, in its heaving, troubled, and agitated state; and not only so, but they, one and all, bore the aspect and possessed the nature of wild beasts, having only earthly properties about them, and these of the more savage and selfish description. In marked contrast to both of these broad characteristics, the representative of the fifth and ultimate kingdom was seen descending from above, borne on the clouds of heaven, the distinctive chariot of Deity, and bearing the aspect, not of a nameless monster, or savage tenant of the forest, but of " the human face Divine"—ideal humanity. Introduced in such a connection, and with the obvious design of exhibiting such a contrast, it is surely a meagre representation of its import, which is given by many commentators—for example, by Dr Campbell, when it is said, " Nothing appears to be pointed out by the circumstance, ' one like a son of man,' but that he would be a human, not an angelical, or any other kind of being; for, in the Oriental idiom, *son of man* and *man* are terms equivalent."[1] Be it so; the question still remains, Why only in respect to this last—the sole world-embracing and perpetual monarchy—was there seen the attractive form of a *human* likeness, while the others, which were certainly to be constituted and governed by men, had their representation in so many irra-

[1] Dissertation v. 13.

tional and ferocious wild beasts? And why, possessing the likeness of a man, should the former have appeared, not coming
from beneath, like the others, cast up by the heaving convulsions
of a tumultuous and troubled world, but descending from the
lofty elevation of a higher region, and a serener atmosphere?
These things assuredly were designed to have their correspondences in the realities to which they pointed; and the difference
indicated is but poorly made out in the further statement of Dr
Campbell, when he says, " This kingdom, which God Himself
was to erect, is contradistinguished from all the rest by the figure
of a man, in order to denote, that whereas violence, in some shape
or other, would be the principal means by which those merely
secular kingdoms should be established, and terror the principal
motive by which submission should be enforced, it would be
quite otherwise in that spiritual kingdom to be erected by the
Ancient of Days, wherein everything should be suited to man's
rational and moral nature; affection should be the prevailing
motive to obedience, and persuasion the means of producing it."
True, so far as it goes; but the question is, How was such a
spiritual and Divine kingdom to be set up and administered
among men? And when a prophetic representation was given
of the fundamental differences betwixt it and the merely worldly
kingdoms that were to precede, was the human element alone
thought of? Did the Spirit of prophecy mean to exhibit a simple
man as destined to realize, on the wide field of the world, the
proper ideal of humanity? That certainly is by no means
likely; and if the whole vision of the prophet is taken into
account, is plainly not the case. The simply terrene or human
kingdoms are there represented by the wild beasts; and if one
like a son of man is brought in to represent another and better
kingdom, and one both receiving His kingdom from above, and
descending thence, as on the chariot of Deity, to take possession
of His dominion, the obvious inference and conclusion is, that
here at last Divine and human were to be intermingled in blessed
harmony, and that till such intermingling took place, and the
kingdom based on it was properly erected, the ideal of humanity
should remain an ideal still, bestial properties should really have
the ascendant, and should retain their sway, till they were dis-
lodged by the manifestation and working of Him who, with Di-

vine aid, should restore humanity to its proper place and function in the world.

Such is the fair and natural interpretation of that part of Daniel's vision which relates to the fifth monarchy, and its representation under one bearing the likeness of a son of man. And it sufficiently explains our Lord's partiality for this epithet, when speaking of Himself, and some of the more peculiar connections in which He employed it. He was announced to Israel by His forerunner as coming to set up " the kingdom of God," or " of heaven." It was this kingdom which John declared was at hand—in other words, the fifth monarchy of Daniel, which was to come from above, and which was destined to supplant every other. How natural, then, for our Lord, in order to keep prominently before men this idea, and impress upon their minds correct views of the nature of His mission, to appropriate to Himself that peculiar epithet, " Son of Man," under which this kingdom had been prophetically exhibited, as contradistinguished from the kingdoms of the world? In so appropriating this epithet, He by no means claimed simple humanity to Himself; on the contrary, He emphatically pointed to that union of the Divine with the human, which was to form the peculiar characteristic of this kingdom, as that through which its higher ideal was to be realized. He was that Son of Man personified, to whom prophetically, and in vision, were committed the powers and destinies of the kingdom, which was of God—the kingdom, in which humanity was to be made to re-assume its proper type. Hence we can readily explain, and see also the full propriety of such representations as that in John i. 51—the first occasion on which the phrase in question is recorded to have been used— " Verily, verily, I say unto you, ye shall see heaven opened, and the angels of God ascending and descending on the Son of Man" —on Him, as uniting, according to Daniel's vision, heaven and earth, the Divine and the human. Or that in John iii. 13, " And no man hath ascended up to heaven but He that came down from heaven, who is in heaven"—a seeming contradiction, if taken by itself, but, when placed in connection with the passage in Daniel, embodying a most important truth. For it tells us that no one, who is simply a man, fallen and degenerate, ever has ascended to heaven, or can do so—the tendency is all in the opposite direction—not upwards to heaven, but downwards to hell. The Son of Man, however, in whom the idea of humanity was to be realized, is of a higher mould; He belongs to the heavenly—*that* is His proper region; and when He appears (as in the person of Christ He did appear) on earth, it is to exhibit in Himself what He has received from the Father, and raise others to the possession of the same. By the very title He assumed, He claimed to be the New Man, the Lord from heaven, come for the purpose of making all things new, and conforming men to the image of Himself. Hence, too, the peculiar expression, embodying another seeming incongruity, in John v. 27, where our Lord says of Himself, that the Father " has given Him authority also to execute judgment, because He is Son of Man." To execute judgment is, undoubtedly, a Divine work; and yet it is committed to Christ precisely because He is the Son of Man. How? Not, assuredly, because in Him there were simply human properties; but because there was the realization of that form in Daniel's vision, which represented the nature and aspect of the Divine kingdom among men—*the* Son of Man, in whom humanity was to attain to its proper completeness, and in whom, that it might do so, the human should be interpenetrated by the Divine, and hold its powers and commission direct from a higher sphere. He, therefore, *could* execute judgment; nay, as concentrating in Himself the properties of the kingdom, it was His peculiar province to do it; since to man, as thus allied to heaven, God has put in subjection the powers of the world to come. And there is still another peculiar passage, which derives a clear and instructive light from the same reference to the original passage in Daniel; it is Matt. xxvi. 64. The high priest had adjured our Lord to confess whether He were indeed " the Christ, the Son of God;" and His reply was, " Thou hast said [rightly]; nevertheless [rather, *moreover*, in addition to what I have declared] I say unto you, Hereafter ye shall see the Son of Man sitting on the right hand of power, and coming in the clouds of heaven." It is very striking, how our Lord here drops the title, " Son of God," to which He had confessed when put by another, and immediately reverts to His wonted appellation, " Son of Man;" while, at the same time, He affirms of this Son of Man what might have seemed to be more fitly associated with

the Son of God. The explanation is found in the passage of
Daniel, the very language and imagery of which it adopts; and
our Lord simply asserts Himself to be the Head and Founder of
that Divine kingdom, which was presented to the eye of Daniel
in vision, under the appearance of one like a Son of Man coming
in the clouds of heaven; but which a moment's reflection might
have convinced any one He could be, only by, at the same time,
being in the strict and proper sense the Son of God.

SECTION FOURTH.

ON THE IMPORT AND USE OF CERTAIN TERMS, WHICH EXPRESS AN ANTAGONISTIC RELATION TO CHRIST'S PERSON AND AUTHORITY, ψευδιδάσκαλοι, ψευδοπροφῆται, ψευδόχριστος, ἀντίχριστος.

It is more especially the two last of the terms just mentioned,
which call for particular investigation; but as the other two are
nearly related to them, and belong substantially to the same line,
we shall in the first instance direct some attention to them.

1. The two may be taken together, as they appear to be used
in senses not materially different. So early as in the Sermon on
the Mount, we find our Lord warning His disciples against false
prophets: προσέχετε ἀπὸ τῶν ψευδοπροφητῶν (Matt. vii. 15); and
the test He suggests to be applied to them is one chiefly of character; "They come," says He, "in sheep's clothing, but within
they are ravening wolves." The warning is again given in our
Lord's discourse respecting the last times, "And many false
prophets shall arise and deceive many" (Matt. xxiv. 11); and
further on, at ver. 24, He returns to the subject, coupling false
prophets with false Christs, who, He said, "should arise, and
give great signs and wonders, so as to deceive, if it were possible,
even the elect." From these intimations, we are led to understand, that the appearance of such characters in considerable
numbers was to form one of the precursors of the dissolution of
the Jewish State, and was also to be a characteristic generally of
the time of the end. As to the precise import, however, to be

attached to the terms, we must bring under review one or two of the passages, in which they are mentioned as actually appearing. Thus in Acts xiii. 6, the Jew, Barjesus, who was with Sergius Paulus, the proconsul of Cyprus, and who there withstood Paul's preaching, is called ψευδοπροφήτης; and partly in explanation of this designation he is styled Elymas the magos—Ἐλύμας ὁ μάγος —two words of different languages expressing substantially the same meaning; Elymas (from âlim) in the Arabic or Aramaic, and μάγος in the Persian, *wise*—wise, however, in the Eastern sense, that is, given to learned pursuits and the skill of hidden and sacred lore. It did not necessarily denote what is now commonly understood by the term, magician or sorcerer; but comprehended also the better wisdom of that higher learning, which was cultivated in the East, with its attendant fancies and superstitions. In the Gospel age, however, this learning had become so much connected with astrology, and kindred arts, that too often—and in the case particularly of the Barjesus mentioned above—it did not materially differ from what is denominated magic or sorcery. The persons, who bore the name of *Magi*, in the districts of Syria, were for the most part mere fortune-tellers. It was such, who swarmed about Rome, and are celebrated in the Latin classics, as " Chaldean astrologers," " Phrygian fortune-tellers," " dealers in Babylonian numbers," etc. ;[1] rushing in, amid the decay of the old faith, with their delusive arts of divination, to play upon the credulity of an age alike sceptical and superstitious. It is clear from the allusions of the ancient satyrists and historians, that those pretenders to the secrets of the gods and the knowledge of futurity drove a very lucrative trade, and had the ear of men, as well as women, high in rank, and by no means deficient in intellect. Marius is reported by Plutarch to have kept a Syrian witch or prophetess in his camp, and to have been much guided by her divinations in regulating his military and political movements. Tiberius is described by Juvenal (x. 93, sq.), sitting on the rock in Capreæ, " surrounded by a flock of Chaldeans." Even such men as Pompey, Crassus, Cæsar, appear to have had frequent dealings with them; for Cicero speaks of having heard from each of them many things, that had been said to them by the Chaldeans, and, in particular, of the as-

---

[1] Hor. Sat. I. 2, 1 ; Od. I. 11, 2.   Juv. Sat. III. 6.

surances they had received, that they should not die, excepting in a ripe age, at home, and in honour (De div. ii. 47). Certainly, most fallacious predictions! and calculated, as Cicero justly remarks, to destroy all confidence in such prognostications! Yet it failed to do so; for men must have something to repair to for support and comfort in the hour of need; if destitute of the true, they inevitably betake to the false; and infested as Rome was with the elements of religious darkness and moral evil, the soothsayers were a class that, according to the profound remark of Tacitus, were sure to be always shunned, and yet always retained (genus hominum, quod in civitate nostra et vitabitur semper et retinebitur).

It was, then, to this fraudulent and essentially profligate class of persons, that Barjesus belonged; he was a false prophet of that low and reprobate caste. But he had evidently acquired a certain sway over the mind of Sergius Paulus, much as the other leading men of the age yielded themselves to the spell of a like delusive influence. It may well seem strange, that there should have been found Jews addicting themselves to such magical arts and false divinations, considering the express and solemn condemnation of such things in the law of Moses. But there can be no doubt of the fact; not this man alone, but vast numbers of the Jews in apostolic times, plied sorcery and divination as a regular trade. It was one of the clear proofs of their sunk condition, and a presage of approaching doom. Jewish females are represented by Juvenal (Sat. vi. 542), as emerging from their lurking places in the woods, and for the smallest pittance whispering into the ear of Roman matrons some revelation of heaven's secrets. But such were only the lower practisers of the art. There were others, like Barjesus, who made loftier pretensions, who insinuated themselves by their apparent learning and divine insight into the counsels of the powerful; and their number, we can easily conceive, as well as the disposition to give heed to their fallacious arts, would acquire considerable accession from the fame of the wonderful deeds performed by Christ and His immediate followers in Judea. The manifestation of the true, in the knowledge of Divine mysteries and the exercise of supernatural power, with the mighty fermentation it produced, created, as it were, a new field for the display of the false; whence, as our

Lord foretold, many false prophets arose, deluding the ignorant, and even seeking to press into the Christian fold.[1]

The Apostle John, who lived to the close of the first century, testifies that many such prophets had already appeared. In ch. iv. 1 of his first Epistle, he says, " Beloved, believe not every spirit, but try the spirits, whether they are of God; because many false prophets are gone out into the world" (ὅτι πολλοὶ ψευδοπροφῆται ἐξεληλύθασιν εἰς τὸν κόσμον). He does not say, that they had found their way into the Church, but merely that they had made their appearance in the world, and were there making such pretensions to supernatural insight, that believers in Christ, as well as others, had need to stand on their guard against them. They might partly be the subtle and audacious diviners, of whom we have just spoken, who went about deceiving the simple and the crafty by their vaunted ability to explore the depths of futurity. That class may certainly be included in the description of the apostle; but from what follows in the Epistle, it is clear, that he more especially points to the false teaching, the anti-christian forms of error, which were springing up, if not actually within, yet on the borders of the Christian Church. For, he presently states, that the spirits are not of God, which do not confess Christ to have come in the flesh; and " this," he adds, namely, the denial of Jesus as the incarnate Son of God, " is that of the antichrist, of which ye have heard that it comes, and even now is it in the world." This apostle, therefore, virtually identifies the false prophets with false teachers, and both with the spirit of antichrist.

It may, indeed, be affirmed generally, so far as regards the manifestation of error in reference to the early Christian Church, that the ψευδοδιδάσκαλοι were scarcely to be distinguished from the ψευδοπροφῆται, or that false prophesying chiefly assumed the form of false teaching. The more arrant impostors—the astrologers and fortune-tellers—the false prophets in *that* sense, were rather to be looked for *beyond* the pale of the Church; as they could only be found in persons, who either ignored the

---

[1] It is well known, also, that the last struggles and convulsions in Judea were accompanied with prophetical delusions. Josephus speaks of " a great number of false prophets" playing their part, and notices one in particular (Wars, VI. 5, § 2, 3).

authority of Jesus, or set up their own in rivalry to His. But *within* the Church, the spirit of falsehood would more naturally show itself in assuming the name of Christ to teach what was inconsistent with the character and tendency of His Gospel. It is evidently of such—rather ψευδοδιδάσκαλοι than ψευδοπροφῆται in the ordinary sense of the term—that the Apostle Paul speaks, in Acts xx. 29, 30, as sure to arise, after his departure, among the converts at Ephesus—" grievous wolves," as he calls them, " not sparing the flock ;" some of them also from their own number, " speaking perverse things, and drawing away disciples after them." In his epistles, also, it is false teaching, chiefly, with which he had to struggle, and in regard to which his warnings were more particularly uttered. And Peter, in his second Epistle, at the commencement of the second chapter, draws thus the parallel between Old and New Testament times : " But there were false prophets also among the people (*i.e.* ancient Israel), even as there shall be false teachers among you ;" the latter now, as the former then. And in the description that follows of the kind of false teachers to be expected, he gives as their leading characteristics the introduction of heretical doctrines, tending to subvert the great truths of the Gospel, and the encouragement, by pernicious example as well as by corrupt teaching, of licentious and ungodly behaviour. To do this was, no doubt, to act the part of false prophets, since it was to give an untrue representation of the mind of God, and to beget fallacious hopes of the issue of His dealings with men on earth ; but, as it did not necessarily involve any formal predictions of the future, it was more fitly characterized as false teaching than false prophesying, while the place its apostles were to occupy in New Testament times should virtually correspond to that of the false prophets in the Old.

In general, therefore, we may say in respect to these two terms, that while the false prophets were also false teachers, and the two were sometimes viewed as nearly or altogether identical, the first term usually had more respect to the pretenders to prophetical insight outside the Church, the other to the propagators of false and pernicious doctrinal views within the Church. The same persons might, and, doubtless, occasionally did sustain both of these characters at once ; yet by no means always, and never necessarily so; since there might be the most heterodox doctrine and corrupt behaviour without any attempt at divination; and in certain cases the art of divination might be carried on as a traffic by itself.

2. We proceed now to the two other, and more peculiar terms of this class, which must also, in great measure, be taken conjointly. In regard to ψευδόχριστοι there can be little doubt; it can only indicate false pretenders to the name and character of Messiah. Precisely as false prophets are such as laid claim to gifts that did not belong to them, by false Christs must be meant those who assumed to be what Jesus of Nazareth alone is. In the strict sense, therefore, false Christs could only arise outside the Christian Church, and among those who had rejected the true. In so far as they did arise, there was in their appearance the fulfilment of another word of Jesus,—" I am come in My Father's name, and ye receive Me not; if another shall come in his own name, him ye will receive" (John v. 43). The most noted example of the kind, as well as the earliest, was that furnished by Barchochbas—Son of a star, as he chose to call himself, with reference to the prophecy of Balaam, which he would have his followers to believe was going to find its fulfilment in his victorious struggles, and his establishment of a Jewish dominion. False expectations of a similar kind have often been raised among the Jewish people, and reports of persons answering to them circulated; but they have never reached such a height as they did in the pretensions and the exploits of Barchochbas.

It would scarcely be right, however, to limit the declaration of our Lord respecting false Christs to such Jewish pretenders; the more especially as the place where He made it was in a discourse addressed to His own disciples; and for *them* the danger was comparatively little of being misled by such manifestly wandering stars. There *was* a danger in that direction, near the beginning of the New Testament Church, for persons, whose leanings might be on the side of Christianity, but who were very imperfectly enlightened in their views, and strong in their national predilections. Such persons might, amid the tumults and disorders, the false hopes and fermenting excitement, which preceded the downfall of the Jewish State, have for a time caught the infection of the evil that was at work, and even, in some instances, have precipitated themselves into the general delusions. But such cases would certainly be rare; and we cannot suppose that our Lord looked no farther than that: we are rather to conceive, in accordance with the whole structure of His discourse, that He wished them to regard what was then to take place but as the beginning of the end—a beginning that should be often in substance, though under different forms, repeating itself in the future. It matters little whether persons call themselves by the name of Christ, or avowedly set up a rival claim to men's homage and regard, if they assume to do what, as Christ, He alone has the right or the power to perform; for in that case they become in reality, if not in name, false Christs. Should any one undertake to give a revelation of Divine things, higher than and contrary to Christ's; to lay open another way to the favour and blessing of Heaven, than that which has been consecrated by His blood; or to conduct the world to its destined state of perfection and glory, otherwise than through the acknowledgment of His name and the obedience of His Gospel;—such an one would be as really acting the part of a false Christ, as if he openly challenged the Messiahship of Jesus, or explicitly claimed the title to himself. There is, therefore, a foundation of truth in the statement of Hegesippus, in which, after mentioning the Menandrians, Marcionites, Carpocratians, and other Gnostic sects, he says, that " from these spring false Christs, false prophets, false apostles, the persons who, by their corrupt doctrines against God and against His Church, broke up the unity of the Church" (Euseb. Hist. Eccl., iv. 22); although they could hardly be said to bring division into a body, to which they did not themselves strictly belong. The tendency of the doctrines, however, propounded by those advocates of heresy and corruption, undoubtedly was to supplant or supersede Christ, and the spiritual doctrines of the Gospel. While paying a certain deference and respect to the name of Jesus, their teaching in reality breathed another spirit, and drew in another direction than that of Christ. And the same, of course, may be said of many authors and systems of later times,—of all, indeed, in every age, that have maintained, or rested in the sufficiency of nature to win for itself a position of safety before God, or to acquire a place of honour in His kingdom. These, in reality, disown the name of Jesus, and set themselves up in His room as the guides and saviours of the world. And we cannot fail to perceive an indication of the varied forms such characters were to assume, and the many different quarters whence they might be expected to appear, in the warning of our Lord respecting them :—" If they shall say unto you, Behold he is in the desert, go not forth; behold he is in the secret chambers, believe it not."

But in what relation, it is proper to ask, does ψευδόχριστος stand to the ἀντίχριστος? Is this last but another name for the same idea of assumption, in some form or another, of Christ's peculiar office and work? Or, does it denote contrariety and opposition of a different kind? The word ἀντίχριστος was not used by our Lord Himself; nor does it occur in any of the writings of the New Testament, except those of the Apostle John. There are descriptions which virtually indicate what the word, as used by him, imports; but the word itself is found only in his writings; and there it occurs altogether four times—thrice in the singular, and once in the plural. Before looking at these, let us first endeavour to determine the force of the preposition ἀντί in the word. There are some who hold that it necessarily denotes *contrariety* or *opposition to*, and others who with equal tenacity contend for the sense of *substitution, in the room of*: If the former were the proper view, the antichrist would necessarily be the enemy of Christ; but if the latter, it would be His false representative or supplanter. The original meaning of the preposition is *over against*, and all its uses, whether alone or in composition, may be traced without difficulty to this primary idea, and express but different shades of the relation it involves. What is over against may be so in one of three different respects : in the way (1) of direct antithesis and opposition; or (2) of substitution, as when one takes the place which belongs to another; or (3) of correspondence, when one thing or person answers to another— an image or counterpart. This last aspect of the relation, involved in the ἀντί, cannot, of course, come into consideration here. But it is not unknown in New Testament Scripture, either as regards the simple or the compound use of the preposition. Thus, at John i. 16, " Of His fulness we all have received, and grace for grace"—χάριν ἀντὶ χάριτος—*i. e.*, grace corresponding to grace—grace in the believer becoming the counterpart of

Christ's—line for line, feature for feature. So also in composition, when occurring in such words as ἀνταπόδοσις, a giving back in return, a recompense; or ἀντίτυπος, the correspondence to the τύπος.

This, however, is the less common form of the relation denoted by the ἀντί; and of the other two, we find instances of both in Scripture. In such words as ἀντιλογία, ἀντίθεσις, ἀντικείμενος, the relation of *formal opposition* is denoted; as it is also in ἀντινομία, contrariety to law, ἀντίδικος, an adversary in a suit, ἀντίχειρ, what is over against the hand, the thumb. But there is another class of words, in which the idea of *substitution*, or contradistinction, in the form of taking the place of another, whether by deputy or as a rival, is also indicated; for example, ἀνθύπατος, the substitute of the consul, pro-consul; ἀντιβασιλεύς, pro-rex, or viceroy; ἀντίλυτρον, substitute or equivalent for a forfeit, ransom. It is plain, therefore, that the single term ἀντίχριστος cannot of itself determine the precise meaning. So far as the current use of the preposition is concerned, it may point either to contrariety or to substitution; the antichrist may be, indifferently, what sets itself in opposition to Christ, or what thrusts itself into His room—a ψευδόχριστος—and it is only by the connection in which the word is used, and the comparison of the parallel passages, that we can determine which may be the predominant or exclusive idea.

In the first passage, where the word occurs, 1 John ii. 18, the literal rendering of which is, " Little children, it is the last hour (or season); and as ye heard, that the antichrist cometh, even now many have become antichrists (ἀντίχριστοι πολλοὶ γεγόνασιν); whence we know it is the last hour." Here there is no precise definition of what forms of evil are included in the antichrist; there is merely the assumption of a fact, that the idea expressed by the term had already passed into a reality, and that in a variety of persons. This, however, is itself of considerable moment, especially as it conveys the information, that while the name is used in the singular, as of an individual, it was not intended to denote the same kind of strict and exclusive personality as the Christ. Even in the apostolic age, John finds the name of antichrist applicable to many individuals. And this, also, may so far help us to a knowledge of the idea, since, while there were numbers in that age who sought within the

Church to corrupt the doctrine of Christ, and without it to disown and resist His authority, we have yet no reason to suppose,
that there were more than a very few, who distinctly claimed the
title of Christ, and presumed to place themselves in Messiah's
room. The next passage occurs very shortly after the one just
noticed, and may be regarded as supplementary to it; it is in the
22d verse. The apostle had stated, that no lie is of the truth;
and he then continues, " Who is the liar ($ὁ$ ψεύστης, the liar by
pre-eminence), but he who denieth that Jesus is the Christ?
This is the antichrist, who denieth (or, denying) the Father and
the Son." Here it is the denial of the *truth* concerning Christ,
not the formal supplanting of Christ by an impious usurpation
of His office, to which the name of antichrist is applied. Yet it
could not be intended to denote every sort of denial of the truth;
for this would have been to identify antichristianism with Jewish
infidelity or with heathenism, which certainly was not the object
of the apostle. The denial of the truth by the antichrist was
denial after a peculiar manner, not as from a directly hostile and
antagonistic position, but under the cover of a Christian name,
and with more or less of a friendly aspect. While it was denied
that Jesus was the Christ, in the proper sense of the term, Jesus
was by no means reckoned an impostor; His name was still
assumed, and His place held to be one of distinguished honour.
That this was the case is evident, not only from the distinctive
name applied to the form of evil in question, but also from what
is said in ver. 18, 19, of the origination of the antichrists.
" Many," says the apostle, " have *become* antichrists;" they were
not so originally, but by a downward progress had ended in becoming such. And again, " They went out from us, but were
not of us;" that is, they had belonged to the Christian community, but showed, by the course of defection they now pursued,
that they had not formed a part of its living membership, nor
had really imbibed the spirit of the Gospel. When, therefore,
the apostle says, in the verse already quoted, that those whom
he designated antichrists denied Jesus to be the Christ; and
when, in another verse, he says, " Every spirit that confesseth not
Jesus Christ as having come (ἐληλυθότα) in the flesh, is not of
God; and this is that spirit of antichrist whereof ye have heard,
that it cometh, and is even now in the world" (ch. iv. 3); and,

still again, when he says, " For many deceivers have entered into the world, who confess not Jesus Christ having come in flesh (ἐρ- χόμενον ἐν σαρχί) ; this is the deceiver and the antichrist" (2 John v. 7). In all these passages, it can only be of a virtual denial of the truth, that the apostle speaks. He plainly means such a depravation of the true doctrine, or abstraction of its essential elements, as turned it into a lie. And when, further, he represents the falsehood as circling around the person of Jesus, and disowning Him as having come in the flesh, we can scarcely entertain a doubt, that he refers to certain forms of the great Gnostic heresy—to such, as held, indeed, by the name of Jesus, but conceived of Him as only some kind of shadowy emanation of the Divine virtue, not a personal incarnation of the Eternal Word. Only by taking up a position, and announcing a doctrine of this sort, could the persons referred to have proved peculiarly dangerous to the Church—so dangerous, as to deserve being called, collectively and emphatically, *the Deceiver*, the embodiment, in a manner, of the old serpent. In an avowed resistance to the claims of Jesus, or a total apostasy from the faith of His Gospel, there should necessarily have been little room for the arts of deception, and no very pressing danger to the true members of the Church.

We arrive, then, at the conclusion, that in St John's use of the term *antichrist*, there is an unmistakeable reference to the early heretics, as forming at least one exemplification of its idea. Such, also, was the impression derived from the apostle's statements by many of the Fathers ; they understood him to speak of the heretics of the time, under the antichrists who had already appeared. For example, Cyprian, when writing of heretics, Ep. lxxiii. 13, and referring to 1 John iv. 3, asks, " How can they do spiritual and divine things who are enemies to God, and whose breast the spirit of antichrist has possessed?" On the same passage Œcumenius says, " He declares antichrist to be already in the world, not corporeally, but by means of those who prepare the way for his coming; of which sort are false apostles, false prophets, and heretics." So, too, Damascenus, L. iv. orth. fid. 27, " Every one who does not confess the Son of God, and that God has come in the flesh, and is perfect God, and was made perfect man, still remaining God, is antichrist." And

R

Augustine, in the third Tractatus on 1 John, speaking to the
question, Whom did the apostle call antichrist? extends the
term, indeed, so as to make it comprehend every one who is contrary to Christ, and is not a true member of His body, but places
in the first rank, as being the characters most directly meant,
" all heretics and schismatics." It is manifest, indeed, that the
existing antichrists of John, the abettors and exponents of *the
lie*, or deniers, under a Christian name, of what was emphatically
the truth, belonged to the very same class with the grievous
wolves and false brethren of St Paul, of whom he so solemnly
forewarned the Ephesian elders, and of whom he also wrote in
his epistles to Timothy (1 Tim. iv. 1; 2 Tim. iii. 1), as persons
who should depart from the faith, teach many heretical doctrines,
and bring in perilous times upon the Church. St John, writing
at a later period, and referring to what then existed, calls attention to the development of that spirit, of which Paul perceived
the germ, and described beforehand the future growth. The
one announced the evil as coming, the other declared it had
already come; and with reference, no doubt, to the prophetic
utterances of Paul, reminded believers of their having previously
heard that it was to come. So that the *antichrists* of John are
found to coincide with one aspect of our Lord's *false Christs*;
they were those who, without renouncing the name of Christians,
or without any open disparagement of Jesus, forsook the simplicity of the faith in Him, and turned His truth into a lie. They
might, *so far*, also be said to supplant Him, as to follow *them*
was to desert Christ; yet, from the circumstances of the case,
there could be no direct antagonism to Jesus, or distinct unfurl-
ing of the banner of revolt.

We cannot, therefore, concur in the statement of Dean Trench
(New Testament Synonyms, p. 120), that " resistance to, and
defiance of, Christ, is the essential mark of antichrist." Defiance of Christ betokens avowed and uncompromising opposition, which was the part, not of deceivers, who had corrupted the
truth by some specious lie of their own, but of undisguised enemies. We concur, however, in the other part of his statement,
that, according to St John's representation of the antichrist,
there was not the false assumption of Christ's character and
offices—no further, at least, than in the modified sense already

explained, of committing one's self to a kind of teaching, which was virtually subversive of the truth and authority of Christ.

It is still, however, a question, whether we are to regard the Scriptural idea of the antichrist as exhausted in those heretical corrupters of the Gospel in the apostolic age, and their successors in apostolic times; or should rather view them as the types and forerunners of some huge system of God-opposing error, or of some grand personification of impiety and wickedness, to be exhibited before the appearing of Christ? It was thought, from comparatively early times, that the mention so emphatically of *the antichrist* bespoke something of a more concentrated and personally antagonistic character than the many antichrists which were spoken of as being already in the world. These, it was conceived, were but preliminary exemplifications of some far greater embodiment of the antichristian spirit, some monarch, probably (like Antiochus of old) of heaven-daring impiety, and unscrupulous disregard of every thing sacred and divine, who, after pursuing a course of appalling wickedness and violence, should be destroyed by the personal manifestation of Christ in glory. This view, however, was founded, not simply, nor even chiefly, upon the passages above referred to in the Epistles of John, but on the representation of St Paul, in 2 Thess. ii. 3–10 (taken in connection with certain portions of the Apocalypse). Amid many crude speculations and conflicting views on this passage, none of the Fathers appears to have doubted, as Augustine expressly states (De Civ. Dei, xx. 19), that it referred to antichrist, under the names " Man of Sin," and " Son of Perdition." And, beyond all question, the evil portrayed here is essentially of the same character as that spoken of in the passages already considered, only with the characteristic traits more darkly drawn, and the whole mystery of iniquity more fully exhibited. As in the other passages, the antichristian spirit was identified with a departing from the faith, and a corrupting of the truth, of the Gospel; so here the coming evil is designated emphatically *the apostasy—ἡ ἀποστασία—*by which we can think only of a notable falling away from the faith and purity of the Gospel; so that the evil was to have both its root and its development in connection with the Church's degeneracy. Nor was the commencement of the evil in this case, any more than the other, to be far distant.

Even at the comparatively early period when the apostle wrote, it had begun to work; and in his ordinary ministrations he had, as he reminds his disciples (v. 5, 7), forewarned them concerning it; plainly implying, that it was to have its rise in a spiritual and growing defection within the Christian Church. Then, as the term *antichrist* evidently denoted, some kind of antithesis in doctrine and practice to Christ—a certain use of Christ's name, with a spirit and design utterly opposed to Christ's cause—so, in the passage under consideration, the power personified and described is designated the opposer, ὁ ἀντικείμενος—one who sets himself against God, and arrogates the highest prerogatives and honours. Yet, with such impious self-deification in *fact*, there was to be nothing like an open defiance and contempt of all religious propriety in *form*; for this same power is represented as developing itself by a " mystery of iniquity;" *i. e.*, by such a complex and subtle operation of the worst principles and designs, as might be carried on under the fairest and most hypocritical pretences; and by " signs and lying wonders, and all deceivableness of unrighteousness," beguiling those who should fall under its influence, to become the victims of " a strong delusion," and to " believe a lie"—viz., to believe that which should, to their view, have the *semblance* of the truth, but in reality should be at complete variance with it. Not only so, but the Temple of God is represented as the chosen theatre of this impious, artful, and wicked ascendency (ver. 4); and in respect to Christian times, the Apostle Paul knows of no temple but the Church itself. Nor can any other be understood here. It is the only kind of temple-usurpation which can now be conceived of as affecting the expectations and interests of the Church generally; and that alone, also, which might justly be represented as a grand consummation of the workings of iniquity within the Christian community. So that, as a whole, the description of the apostle presents to our view some sort of mysterious and astounding combination of good and evil, formally differing from either heathenism or infidelity—a gathering up and assorting together of certain elements in Christianity, for the purpose of accomplishing, by the most subtle devices and cunning stratagems, the overthrow and subversion of Christian truth and life. It is, therefore, but the full growth and final development of St John's idea of the antichrist.

Of the descriptions generally of the coming evil in New Testament Scripture, and especially of this fuller description in the Epistle to the Thessalonians, nothing (it appears to me) can be more certain on exegetical grounds, than that they cannot be made to harmonise with the Romish opinion—which Hengstenberg and a few others in the Protestant Church have been attempting to revive—the opinion that would find the evil spoken of realised in the power and influence exerted in early times by Rome, in its heathen state, against the cause and Church of Christ. In such an application of what is written, we have only some general coincidences, while we miss all the more distinctive features of the delineation. If it might be said of the heathen power in those times, that it did attempt to press into the temple or Church of God, and usurp religious homage there, the attempt, as is well known, was successfully repelled; and it never properly assumed the appearance of an actual sitting, or enthroning one's self there (as the words import), for the purpose of displacing the true God and Saviour from their rightful supremacy. Nor, in the operations of that power, do we perceive any thing that could fitly be designated "a mystery of iniquity"—the iniquity practised being that rather of palpable opposition and overbearing violence —in its aim transparent to every one, who knew the Gospel of the grace of God, and involving, if yielded to, the conscious renunciation of Christ. As to the signs and lying wonders, and deceivableness of unrighteousness, and strong delusions, which the apostle mentions among the means and characteristic indications of the dreaded power, there is scarcely even the shadow of them to be found in the controversy which ancient heathenism waged with Christianity. On every account, therefore, this view is to be rejected as wanting in the more essential points of correspondence between the apostolic description and the supposed realisation in Providence.

Another view, however, has of late been rising into notice, which, if well founded, would equally save the Romish apostasy from any proper share in the predicted evil; and which, we cannot but fear, if not originated, has at least been somewhat encouraged and fostered by that softened apologetic hue, which the mediæval and antiquarian tendencies of the present age have served to throw around Romanism. The view we refer to would

make the full and proper development of the antichrist an essentially different thing from any such depravation of the truth, as
is to be found in the Papacy—a greatly more blasphemous
usurpation, and one that can only be reached by a Pantheistic
deification of human nature. So Olshausen, who, on the passage
in Thessalonians, thus writes, "The self-deification of the Roman
emperors appears as modesty by the side of that of antichrist; for
the Cæsars did not elevate themselves *above* the other gods, they
only wanted to have a place *beside* them, as representatives of the
genius of the Roman people. Antichrist, on the contrary, wants
to be the only true God, who suffers none beside him ; what
Christ demands for Himself in truth, he, in the excess of his presumption, claims for himself in falsehood." Then, as to the way
in which he should do this, it is said, " Antichrist will not, as
Chrysostom correctly remarks, promote idolatry, but seduce men
from the true God, as also from idols, and set himself up as the
only object of adoration. This remarkable idea, that sin in antichrist issues in a downright self-deification, discloses to us the in-
most nature of evil, which consists in selfishness. In antichrist
all love, all capability of sacrifice and self-denial, shows itself entirely submerged in the making of the I all in all, which then
also insists on being acknowledged by all men, as the centre of
all power, wisdom, and glory." The proper antichrist, therefore,
according to Olshausen, must be a person, and one who shall be
himself the mystery of iniquity, as Christ is the mystery of godliness—a kind of embodiment or incarnation of Satan. He can
regard all the past manifestations and workings of evil, only as
serving to indicate what it may possibly be, but by no means as
realizing the idea ; and he conceives, it may one day start forth in
the person of one, who shall combine in his character, the elements
of infidelity and superstition, which are so visibly striving for the
mastery over mankind. Some individual may be cast up by the
fermentation that is going forward, who shall concentrate around
himself all the Satanic tendencies in their greatest power and
energy, and come forth at last in impious rivalry of Christ, as the
incarnate son of the devil. Dean Trench seems substantially to
adopt this view, though he expresses himself more briefly, and
also less explicitly, upon the subject. With him, the antichrist is
" one who shall not pay so much homage to God's word as to

assert the fulfilment in himself, for he shall deny that word altogether ; hating even erroneous worship, because it is worship at all ; hating much more the Church's worship in spirit and in truth ; who, on the destruction of every religion, every acknowledgment that man is submitted to higher powers than his own, shall seek to establish his throne ; and for God's great truth, ' God is man,' to substitute his own lie, 'man is God'" (Synonyms, p. 120).

It may be admitted, with reference to this view, that there are tendencies in operation at the present time, fitted, in some degree, to suggest the thought of such a possible incarnation of the ungodly and atheistic principle ; but nothing has yet occurred, which can justly be said to have brought it within the bounds of the probable. At all events, it is an aspect of the matter derived greatly more from the apprehended results of those tendencies themselves, than from a simple and unbiassed interpretation of the passages of Scripture, in which the antichrist is described or named. Such an antichrist as those authors delineate, the impersonation of unblushing wickedness and atheism, has every thing against it, which has been already urged against the view, that would identify the description with the enmity and persecutions of heathen Rome. Instead of seating itself in the temple of the Christian Church as its own, and arrogating there the supreme place, an antichristian power of that sort could only rise on the ruins of the temple. And whatever audacity or foolhardiness there might be in the assumptions and proceedings of such a power, one cannot, by any stretch of imagination, conceive how, with such flagrant impiety in its front, it could present to God's people the appearance of a *mystery* of iniquity, and be accompanied with signs and wonders and deceitful workings, destined to prevail over all who had not received the truth in the love of it. Conscience and the Bible must cease to be what they now are, cease at least to possess the mutual force and respondency they have been wont to exercise, ere so godless a power could rise to the ascendant in Christendom. It may even be said, the religious susceptibilities of men, in the false direction as well as the true, would need to have sustained a paralysis alike unprecedented and incredible. And, besides, the historical connection would be broken, which the passages, bearing on the antichristian apostasy, plainly establish between the present and the future. In what already existed the apostles descried the germ, the incipient workings of what was hereafter more fully to develop itself; while the antichrist now suggested to our apprehensions, if it should ever attain to a substantive existence, would stand in no proper affinity to the false doctrine and corruptions of the apostolic age. It would be a strictly novel phenomenon.

It were out of place, however, to prosecute the subject further here, where exegetical investigations are what chiefly demand attention. For those who wish to see the subject viewed more in its doctrinal and historical aspects, I must refer them to *Prophecy, Viewed in Respect to its Distinctive Features*, etc., p. 359, sq., from which some of the last preceding pages have been mainly taken. It will be enough here to state my conviction, which may be readily inferred from the preceding remarks, that the conditions of the Scriptural problem respecting the antichrist, have met their fullest, and incomparably most systematic and general fulfilment in the corruptions of Popery. And, in as far as any other forms of evil, either now existing, or yet to arise, may be comprehended under the same designation, it can only be because they shall contain a substantially similar disfiguration of the truth, and undue exaltation of the creature into the place and prerogatives of Godhead.

SECTION FIFTH.

ON βαπτίζω AND ITS COGNATES, WITH SPECIAL REFERENCE TO
THE MODE OF ADMINISTERING BAPTISM.

It is a somewhat striking circumstance, that when our Lord's forerunner came forth to prepare the way for His Master, he is represented as not only preaching the doctrine, but also as administering the baptism of repentance; while still a profound silence is observed as to the manner in which he administered the ordinance to his disciples. St Luke, in his first notice of the subject, couples the two together—the doctrine and the

ordinance—and says, "John came into all the country about
Jordan, preaching the baptism of repentance." And St Matthew,
after briefly mentioning his call to repent, and referring to the
prophecy in Isa. xl. 3, with like simplicity relates, that "all
Jerusalem went out to him, and all Judea, and all the region
round about Jordan, and were baptised of him in Jordan, confessing their sins." Whence may we suppose such reserve upon
the matter to have arisen? Was it from the practice of religious baptism being already in familiar use among the Jews,
so that no specific information was needed respecting the mode
of its administration? Or did the word itself, βαπτίζω, so distinctly indicate the kind of action employed, that all acquainted
with the meaning of the word would understand what was
done? Or, finally, did it arise from no dependence being
placed on the precise mode, and from the virtue of the ordinance being necessarily tied to no particular form? Any of
these suppositions might possibly account for the peculiarity;
but as they cannot be all admitted, it is of some importance,
that we know which has the preferable claim on our belief.

I. To look first to the term employed—βαπτίζω has the form of
a frequentative verb from βάπτω, which is rarely used in the New
Testament, and never in this connection. Βάπτω means simply
to *dip;* the Latin synonyms are *mergo, tingo;* and βάπτος has the
sense of *tinctus.* The word was used of dipping in any way, and
very commonly of the operation of dyeing cloth by dipping; whence
it has the figurative import of *dyeing,* with a collateral reference
to the manner in which the process was accomplished. Taking
βαπτίζω for a frequentative of βάπτω, the earlier glossaries ascribed to it the meaning of *mergito,* as is stated by Vossius in his
Etymologicon: Cum autem βάπτω sit *mergo,* βαπτίζω commode
vertamus *mergito;* and he adds, respecting the Christian ordinance, præsertim, si sermo de Christianorum baptismo, qui
trinâ fit immersione. If this view were correct, it would be
necessary, to a right administration of baptism, that the subject
of it should not only be immersed in water, but should be immersed several times; so that not *immersion* only, but *repeated*
immersion, would be the constitutional form. In mentioning
definitely *three* times, as Vossius does, reference is made to a

custom that came early into use, and in certain portions of
Christendom is not altogether discontinued, according to which
a threefold action was employed in order more distinctly to
express belief in a triune God. Thus Tertullian writes, Adv.
Praxeam, c. 26 : Novissime mandavit (viz. Christus) ut tingue-
rent in Patrem, et Filium, et Spiritum Sanctum, non in unum.
Nam nec semel, sed ter, ad singula nomina in personas singulas
tinguimur. Chrysostom, in like manner, affirms, that the Lord
delivered one baptism to His disciples in three immersions of
the body, when He gave the command to baptize in the name of
the Father, Son, and Holy Ghost (Hom. de fide, 17). Jerome
and others mention the head as the part on which the threefold
immersion was performed. Thus Jerome, adv. Luciferanos :
Nam et multa alia, quæ per traditionem in ecclesiis observantur,
auctoritatem sibi scriptæ legis usurpaverunt, velut in lavacro ter
caput mergitare, deinde aggressos, lactis et mellis prægustari
concordiam ad infantiæ significationem, etc. We have no
definite information as to the time and manner in which this
three-fold immersing of the head in baptism began to be practised. Jerome admits, that there is no authority for it in Scripture, and that it was observed in his day, and was to be vindicated
merely as an ancient and becoming usage. It very probably
took its rise about the period when the doctrine of the Trinity
came to be impugned by the theories of ancient heretics, toward
the middle or latter part of the second century, with the view of
obtaining from each subject of baptism a distinct and formal
acknowledgment of the doctrine. But the head being so specially mentioned as the part immersed, seems to imply that the
entire person did not participate in the action.

   This, however, only by the way. The point we have at present
more immediately to consider, is the precise import of $\beta\alpha\pi\tau i \zeta\omega$,
and whether, as commonly used, it was taken for the frequenta-
tive of $\beta\acute{\alpha}\pi\tau\omega$. We have said, that if it really were a frequentative, it must indicate, not immersion simply, but repeated
immersion, as the proper form of administering baptism. This,
however, is not borne out by the usage. The word is applied to
denote the enveloping of objects in water, in a considerable
variety of ways, and without any distinct or special reference to
the act of dipping or plunging. Thus it is used by Polybius of

ships, i. 51, 6, καὶ πολλὰ τῶν σκαφῶν ἐβάπτισον; and in like manner by Josephus, κυβερνήτης, ὅστις χειμῶνα δεδοικὼς πρὸ τῆς θυέλλης ἐβάπτισεν ἑκὼν τὸ σκάφος (Bel. J. iii. 8, 5) : in both cases, the general meaning, *sink*, is evidently the sense to be adopted ; in the first, " many of the skiffs sunk ;" in the second, " of his own accord the pilot sunk the skiff." Speaking of Jonah's vessel, Josephus uses the expression, " the vessel being all but ready to be overwhelmed," or sunk (ὅσον οὔπω μέλλοντος βαπτίζεσθαι, Ant. ix. 10, 2) ; and again, in his own life, § 2, of the ship that he sailed in to Rome being swamped in the Adriatic (βαπτίζοντος ἡμῶν τοῦ πλοίου), so that they had to swim through the whole night. The same word is used by Diod. Sic. i. 36, of animals drowned by the overflowing of the Nile, ὑπὸ τοῦ ποταμοῦ περιληφθέντα διαφθείρεται βαπτζόμενα, and by Polybius, both of horses sinking in a marsh, v. 47, 2, and of infantry being plunged, or covered up to the waist, ἕως τῶν μαστῶν βαπτιζόμενοι ; so that, whether the objects were covered by the water flowing over them, or by themselves sinking down in it, the word βαπτίζω was equally applied. In consideration of such passages, and others of a like kind, Dr Gale, in his Reflections on Wall's *History of Infant Baptism*, feels constrained to say, that " the word, perhaps, does not so necessarily express the action of putting under water, as in general a thing being in that condition, no matter how it comes to be so, whether it is put into the water, or the water comes over it ; though, indeed, to put it into the water is the most natural way, and the most common, and is therefore usually and pretty constantly, but it may be not necessarily implied."[1] In plain terms, βαπτίζω does not always mean *dip*, but sometimes bears the more general import of being under water. And even this requires to be qualified ; for when dipping appears to be meant, not the whole, but only a part of the object seems sometimes to have gone under water. Pressed by such uses and applications of the term, Dr Gale says, " We readily grant that there may be such circumstances in some cases, which necessarily and manifestly show, that the thing spoken of is not said to be dipt all over ; but it does not therefore follow, that the word in that place does not signify *to dip*. Mr Wall will allow his pen is *dipt* in the ink, though it is not daubed all over, or totally im-

[1] Wall's History of Infant Baptism, iii., p. 122.

mersed."[1] This, as justly remarked by Wall, is, indeed, to contend for the word, but at the same time, " to grant away the
thing ;" since, " if that which he allows be dipping, the controversy is at an end." It resolves itself into a petty question, not
worth contending about, how much or how little water should be
used in baptism—whether this or that part of the body should be
in the element. Liddle and Scott, in their Lexicon, beyond all
reasonable doubt, give the fair import of the word, as used by
profane writers and Josephus, when they represent it as signifying to *dip under water*, to *sink*, to *bathe* or *soak*. It denotes
somehow, and to some extent, a going into, or being placed
under water ; but is by no means definite as to the precise mode
of this being done, or the length to which it might be carried.

When, however, we turn to the use of the word in the Apocrypha and the New Testament, we find a still greater latitude in
the sense put upon it. In the apocryphal book Judith, ch. xii. 7,
it is said of the heroine of the story, that " she went out every
night to the valley of Bethulia, and baptized herself in the camp
at the fountain of water"—$\varkappa\alpha\iota\ \dot{\varepsilon}\beta\alpha\pi\tau i\zeta\varepsilon\tau o\ \dot{\varepsilon}\nu\ \tau\tilde{\eta}\ \pi\alpha\rho\varepsilon\mu\beta o\lambda\tilde{\eta}\ \dot{\varepsilon}\pi\iota\ \tau\tilde{\eta}\varsigma$
$\pi\eta\gamma\tilde{\eta}\varsigma\ \tau o\tilde{\upsilon}\ \ddot{\upsilon}\delta\alpha\tau o\varsigma$: which can scarcely be understood of anything
but some sort of ablution or washing, since the action is reported
to have been done in the camp, and not in, but at the fountain
of water. Immersion seems to be excluded, both by the publi-
city of the scene, and by the relation indicated to the fountain.
Another, and, if possible, still more unequivocal example, occurs
in the Wisdom of Sirach, xxxiv. 25, " When one is baptized from
a dead body—$\beta\alpha\pi\tau\iota\zeta\dot{o}\mu\varepsilon\nu o\varsigma\ \dot{\alpha}\pi\dot{o}\ \nu\varepsilon\varkappa\rho o\tilde{\upsilon}$—and touches it again, ot
what avail is his washing" ($\tau\tilde{\omega}\ \lambda o\upsilon\tau\rho\tilde{\omega}$) ? The passage evidently
refers to what the law prescribed in the way of purification for
those who had come into contact with a corpse. And this we
learn from Numb. xix. 13, 19, included a threefold action—
sprinkling the person with water, mixed with the ashes of a red
heifer, bathing it, and washing the clothes. Plainly, therefore,
the $\beta\alpha\pi\tau\iota\zeta\dot{o}\mu\varepsilon\nu o\varsigma$ of the son of Sirach is a general term expressive of the whole of these ; it includes all that the law required
as to the application of water for the purposes of purification in
the case supposed. Nothing but a controversial aim could lead
any one to think of ascribing another meaning to the word in

[1] D. p. 145.

this passage. Dr Gale informs us, that " he remembered the time, when he thought it a very formidable instance ;" but bracing himself for the occasion, he again recovered his composure, and corrected, as he says, his mistake ; nay, he even came to " think it exceeding clear to any who are willing to see it, that a further washing is necessary beside the sprinklings spoken of, and that this washing was the finishing of the ceremony. The defiled person was to be sprinkled with the holy water on the third and on the seventh day, only as preparatory to the great purification, which was to be by washing the body and clothes on the seventh day, with which the uncleanness ended."[1] Such is the shift to which a controversialist can resort, in order to recover his equanimity from a formidable instance ! So far from any sort of bathing at the close being the chief thing in the ordinance, and that from which the whole might be designated, the bathing was evidently one of the least ; for it is not so much as mentioned in the Epistle to the Hebrews, where the service is referred to (ch. ix. 13). The whole stress there is laid on the sprinkling the unclean with water, mixed with the ashes of the red heifer ; nor can any one take up a different impression, who reads the passage in Numbers with an unbiassed spirit. For there, when the state of abiding uncleanness is denoted, nothing is said of the absence of bathing, but account alone is made of *the water of separation not being sprinkled on him*, which is thrice emphatically repeated, ver. 9, 13, 20. He that was to be cut off from his people, on account of this species of uncleanness, was to suffer excision simply " because the water of separation was not sprinkled upon him." So that the βαπτιζομένοι of the son of Sirach, if it should be connected with one part of the transaction rather than another, ought plainly to be viewed as having respect chiefly to the sprinkling of the unclean with the water, which had the ashes of the heifer mingled with it ; but the fairer interpretation is to view it as inclusive of all the ablutions practised on the occasion.[2]

[1] Wall iii., p. 154.
[2] An explanation has been given of the passage in Numbers, which goes to an extreme on the opposite side, and would deny that the person who underwent the process of purification from the touch of a dead body, required to be bathed at all. Thus Dr Armstrong, in a late work on the *Doctrine of*

In New Testament Scripture we find the same general use of the word, embracing, in like manner, various ceremonial ablutions. Thus in Heb. ix. 10, the ancient ritual is described as " standing in meats and drinks and divers washings—διαφόροις βαπτισμοῖς— and carnal ordinances." The *diverse* evidently points to several uses of water, such as we know to have actually existed under the law, sprinklings, washings, bathings. If it had been but one mode or action that was referred to, the *diverse* would have been entirely out of place. In Mark vii. 3, 4, 8, it is said, " The Pharisees, and all the Jews, except they wash their hands oft (ἐὰν μὴ πυγμῇ νίψωνται τὰς χεῖρας), eat not, holding the tradition of the elders ; and when they come from the market, except they are baptized (ἐὰν μὴ βαπτίσωνται), they eat not." This latter expression is undoubtedly of stronger import than the former one, and marks a difference between what was done when they came from the market, and what was done on other and commoner occasions. Dr Campbell, who, on this subject, lends his support to the views of the Baptists, concurs with them in making the distinction to be—in the one case a simple washing of the hands, or pouring water on them, and an immersion of them in the other. Dr Campbell even throws this view into his translation ; he renders the one clause, " until they wash their hands, by pouring a little water on them ;" and the other, " until they dip them." This mode of explanation, however, is grammatically untenable ; it would have required the repetition of the τὰς χεῖρας, in the second clause, after the βαπτίσωνται, if the verb had referred to the dipping of *them* alone. But on another ground this supposition must be abandoned ; for βαπτίζω is

Baptisms, holds respecting Numb. xix. 19, " And the clean person shall sprinkle upon the unclean on the third day, and on the seventh day ; and on the seventh day he shall purify himself, and wash his clothes, and bathe himself in water, and shall be clean at even," that this is meant of the person sprinkling, not of the person sprinkled upon. And he thinks this is made quite certain by ver. 21, which ordains it as a perpetual statute, that he who sprinkles the unclean shall wash his clothes, and be unclean till the evening (p. 72). But such an explanation will not stand. For the latter person was not required to bathe his body at all ; he had simply to wash his clothes. And if *he* had been meant in ver. 19, there could have been no propriety in laying stress on the *seventh* day, any more than the *third*. This points manifestly to the person defiled by the touch of the dead.

never applied to a *part* of the body, nor is even λούω; these always have respect to the body or person as a whole; while νίπτω is invariably the word used when some particular member or select portion is meant.[1] Having respect to this usage, and marking also that the verb is here in the middle voice, having a reflective sense, we must render the clause, which speaks of what the Pharisees did on coming from market, " except they baptize (or wash) themselves, they eat not ;" *i.e.* they first perform a general ablution ; for, having mingled with the crowd in the market-place, and possibly come into contact with some unclean person, not the hands alone, as in ordinary circumstances, but the whole body, was supposed to need a purification. Yet not such an one as involved a total immersion ; for the law only required this in extreme cases of actual and ascertained pollution ; in cases of a less marked or palpable description, it was done by sprinkling or washing. And we are the rather led to think of this mode of purification here, as the Evangelist, in v. 4, speaks of the Pharisees having " many other things which they received to hold, baptism of pots and cups, and brazen things, and couches ;" obviously meaning, not immersions, in the ordinary sense, but washings and sprinklings, which are the forms of purification proper to such things as brazen utensils, pots, and couches.

A still further, and very decisive use of the verb is given in Luke xi. 38, where we read of the Pharisee marvelling, that our Lord οὐ ἐβαπτίσθη πρὸ τοῦ ἀρίστου, had not washed before dinner. Even Dr Campbell finds himself obliged to render here, " had used no washing ;" judging from his views on other passages it should rather have been, " had not immersed, or bathed himself." If the Pharisees had been wont to practise immersion before dinner, we might then have supposed, that it was the disuse of such a practice, on the part of our Lord, which gave occasion to the wonder. But there is conclusive evidence to the contrary of this. The passage already cited from the Gospel of Mark alone proves it ; for the washing of the hands merely is there mentioned

---

[1] Titmann's Synonyms: " λούω νίπτω; they differ as our *bathe* and *wash*. Therefore νίπτεσθαι is used of any particular part of the body, not only of the hands or feet ; but λούσασθαι of the whole body. Acts ix. 37 ; Hom. Il. ω. v. 582." See also Trench's Synonyms under the words.

as the ordinary kind of ablution practised by the Pharisees before dinner. And Josephus notices it among the peculiarities of
the Essenes, that they bathed themselves before dinner in cold
water; plainly implying, that in this they differed from others.
There is no evidence to show, and it is against probability to believe, that private baths were common in Judea; and, indeed,
the scarcity of water for a great part of the year rendered it next
to impossible to have them in common use.

Nor was Judea singular in this respect in more ancient times,
and in states of society similar to what existed there in the apostolic age. In countries also, where water was greatly more
abundant than in Judea, bathing by immersion was comparatively
little practised till effeminate and luxurious habits had become
general, and even then it was not always so frequent as is commonly represented. It is doubtful if the Greeks in earlier times
practised it. Ulysses, indeed, is represented by Homer as going
into the bath in the palace of Circe, but the bath (ἀσαμίνθος) was
only a vessel for sitting in; and the water, after being heated,
was poured over the head and shoulders. In the Dictionary of
Greek and Roman Antiquities, edited by Dr Smith, it is stated
(Art. Balneal) that, " on ancient vases, on which persons are represented bathing, we never find any thing corresponding to
a modern bath, in which persons can stand or sit; but there is
always a round or oval basin (λουτήρ or λουτήριον) resting on a
stand, by the side of which those who are bathing are represented
standing undressed, and bathing themselves." " The daily bath,"
says Bekker (Charicles, p. 149), " was by no means so indispensable with the Greeks as it was with the Romans; nay, in some
instances the former nation looked on it as a mark of degeneracy
and increasing effeminacy, when the baths were much frequented."
Various proofs are given of this; and it is further stated, that in
the Grecian baths there appear usually to have been, beside the
λουτήρες already mentioned, some sort of tubs, in which the persons sat or stood. Some of the paintings represent women standing, and a kind of shower-bath descending on them.

To return, however, to the subject more immediately before us
—it seems unquestionable, that according to Hellenistic, and
more especially to Apocryphal and New Testament usage, the
verb βαπτίζω did not always signify immersion, or even the being

totally under water, but included the more general notion of ablution or washing. Nor is there any reason for supposing it to have borne a narrower meaning when applied to the baptism of John or of Christ. We thus quite naturally account for the different construction used in coupling the act of baptizing with the instrument employed. Very commonly the baptism is said to have been done, ἐν ὕδατι, " in water ;" but Luke has simply the dative after the verb, ἐγὼ μὲν ὕδατι βαπτίζω (ch. iii. 16), " I indeed baptise you with water"—with that as the instrument, but leaving altogether indeterminate the mode of its application.[1] We can readily conceive the practice to have varied. When administered at the Jordan, or where there was plenty of water, there might be an actual immersion, or, at least a plentiful affusion. But how could there well be such a thing at Jerusalem about the time of Pentecost, in the height of summer, when the rite had to be administered to several thousands at once? We are informed by a most credible witness, that in summer there is no running stream in the vicinity of Jerusalem, except the rill of Siloam, a few rods in length, and that the city is, and was supplied with water from its cisterns, and public reservoirs chiefly supplied by rain early in the season.[2] It is not unworthy of notice also, what we learn from the same competent authority, that the baptismal fonts still found among the ruins of the most ancient Greek churches in Palestine, and dating, it is understood, from very remote times, are not large enough to admit of the baptism of adult persons by immersion, and from their structure were obviously never intended to be so used.[3] And it may be still further noted as an additional confirmation of the view taken, that in the old Latin version the verb βαπτίζω was not rendered

---

[1] Dr Campbell most unwarrantably translates this passage in Luke's Gospel, " baptize in water," as if it were ἐν ὕδατι; and so, has rendered himself justly liable to the rebuke which, in his note on Matt. iii. 11, he has administered to those who translate ἐν ὕδατι, with water: " It is to be regretted that we have so much evidence, that even good and learned men allow their judgments to be warped by the sentiments and customs of the sect which they prefer. The true partizan always inclines to correct the diction of the Spirit by that of the party." So, sometimes, does the man who unduly presses a particular opinion.

[2] Dr Robinson's Researches, vol. i., sec. 7, § 9.

[3] Ibid., vol. ii., sec. x.

S

by *immergo* or *mergito*—as if those words were somehow too definite or partial in their import to be presented as equivalents. It preferred adhering to the Greek, and simply gave *baptizo*.

II. A second point demanding examination, is that which respects proselyte-baptism among the Jews. Did this exist prior to John's baptism? In other words, did he simply adopt an existing institution? or did he introduce what might be designated a new ordinance? Both sides of this question have been zealously maintained, and the discussion of it has given rise to long and learned investigations, both in this country and on the continent, into that department of Jewish antiquities. In favour of the prior existence of Jewish proselyte-baptism we find, among others, the names of Lightfoot, Schöttgen, Selden, Buxtorf, Wetstein, Michaelis, Hammond, Wall, etc.; and against it Owen, Carpzov, Lardner, Paulus, De Wette, Schneckenburger (in an elaborate, separate treatise), Ernesti, Moses Stuart, etc. The existence of Jewish baptism, as an ancient initiatory rite for proselytes, was more commonly believed in former generations, than it is now. Not a few of the writers mentioned in the first of the above lists, spoke of it as a matter about which it was scarcely possible to entertain a shadow of doubt. Thus Wall gives expression to their views, "It is evident that the custom of the Jews before our Saviour's time (and as they themselves affirm, from the beginning of their law), was to baptise, as well as circumcise any proselyte, that came over to them from the nations. This does fully appear from the books of the Jews themselves, and also of others, that understood the Jewish customs, and have written of them. They reckoned all mankind beside themselves to be in an unclean state, and not capable of being entered into the covenant of Israelites without a washing or baptism, to denote their purification from their uncleanness. And this was called the baptising of them into Moses."[1]

Now, there can be no doubt, that ample quotations can be produced (Dr Wall has great store of them) in support of these positions. But then what sort of quotations? Are they of a kind to bear with decisive evidence on the state of matters in the Gospel age? It is here, that when the authorities are looked

[1] History of Infant Baptism, vol. i., p. 4.

into, they prove insufficient for the end they are intended to serve ; for, so far from finding any attestations among them respecting the existence of proselyte-baptism in the apostolic age, we are rather apt to be struck with the total want of evidence on the point ; and the want of it in writings which, if it could have been had, might have been confidently expected to furnish it. In the inspired writings of the Old Testament no notice is taken of any ordinance connected with the admission, either of native Jews or converted Gentiles, into the Covenant, except that of circumcision. Nor is mention once made of any other in the Apocrypha, or in the Targums of Onkelos and Jonathan, or in Philo and Josephus, notwithstanding the references which abound in their writings, to Jewish rites and customs. There is a like silence upon the subject in the Patristic productions of the first three or four centuries, and in those of the Jewish Rabbis for the same period. So far as the direct evidence goes, the very utmost that can be said is, that indications appear of Jewish proselyte-baptism as an existing practice during the fourth century of the Christian era. And as there is no historical ground for supposing it to have been then originated, it may, with some probability, be held to have been commonly in operation for a certain time previously. But if we inquire *when*, or *how*, we can find no satisfactory answer ; all is involved in uncertainty.[1]

[1] Schneckenburger, in the treatise above referred to, besides giving a clear historical survey of the opinions and literature upon the subject, has satisfactorily established the following positions, (1) The regular admission of strangers into the Jewish religion, while the temple stood, was done through circumcision and sacrifice — a lustration, however, preceding the sacrifice, which, like all other lustrations, obtained merely as a Levitical purification, not as an initiatory rite. This appears from a variety of sources, and especially from several passages in Josephus (such as Ant. xiii. 9, xx. 2, xviii. 3, 4), in which the reception of individuals from other lands is expressly treated of, and no mention is made of baptism. (2.) The lustration performed on the occasion did not differ in outward form from the ordinary lustrations, but, like these, was practised by the proselytes merely upon themselves. (3.) This lustration by and by took the place of the discontinued sacrifice, yet not probably till the end of the third century ; and was then, for the most part, still performed as a self-lustration in connection with the circumcision that followed it : but in the case of women was done apart from the latter, and in process of time came to be applied, as a proper initiatory rite, as in the case of slaves and foundlings. (4.) Hence, a derivation

From the state of the evidence, therefore, respecting proselyte-baptism among the Jews, we are not entitled to found anything on it in respect to the subject under consideration, since it is not such as to enable us to draw any definite conclusions regarding its existence or form in the Gospel age. We are not on that account, however, to hold that there was nothing in the usages of the time tending in the direction of a baptismal service, and that the institution of such a service in connection with a new state of things in the kingdom of God, must have had an altogether strange and novel appearance. For, in the ancient religions generally, and in the Mosaic religion in particular, there was such a frequent use of water, by means of washings, sprinklings, and immersions, to indicate the removal of defilement, that the coupling of a great attempt towards reformation with an administration of baptism, could scarcely have appeared other wise than natural and proper. In the Greek and Roman clas sics we find constant references to this symbolical use of water. Thus, in Virgil, Æn. ii. 17, Tu, genitor, cape sacra manu, patriosque Penates; Me bello è tanto digressum et caede recenti, Attrectare nefas; donec flumine vivo abluero. Macrobius, Sat. iii., Constat Diis superis sacra facturum corporis ablutione purgari. Porphyry, de Abstin. iv. 7, says of the priests of Egypt, τρὶς τῆς ἡμέρας ἀπελούσαντο ψυχρῷ. Ovid speaks of the belief in the efficacy of ablutions as not only prevailing, but prevailing too extensively among the Greeks and Romans:—Omne nefas, omnemque mali purgamina causam credebant nostri tollere posse senes. Graecia principium moris fuit; illa nocentes Impia lustratos ponere facta putat. Ah! nimium faciles, qui tristia crimina caedis, Flumina tolli posse putetis aqua (Fasti, ii. 35). Many other passages might be cited to the same effect, but these are enough. The state of feeling and practice among the Jews was only so far different, that they had a better foundation to rest upon, and ordinances of service directly appointed by Heaven to observe. Among these, as already noticed, divers baptisms—

of the baptism of John or Christ from this Jewish custom, is not to be thought of; but it is to be accounted for from the general use and significance of lustrations among the Jews, taken in connection with the expectations entertained respecting the new state of things to be introduced by the Messiah.

baptisms by washing, sprinkling, and immersion—were imposed on them; and both the priests daily, when they entered the Temple, and the ordinary worshippers on ever-recurring occasions, had ablutions of various kinds to perform. Not only so, but it was matter of public notoriety, that the Essenes, who carried their notions and practices somewhat farther than others in ceremonial observance, admitted converts into their number by a solemn act of lustration, making it strictly an initiatory rite; for only after this purifying service had been undergone, and two years of probation had been passed, could the applicant be admitted into full connection with the society (Josephus' Wars, ii. 8, 6). Taking all these things into account, and remembering, besides, how frequently in the Old Testament the purification to be effected upon the soul of true penitents, and of those especially who were to live when the great period of reformation came, is represented under the symbol of a water-purification (Ps. xxvi. 6; Isa. i. 16, lii. 15; Ezek. xxxvi. 25; Zech. xiii. 1), we can scarcely conceive how it should have appeared in any way startling or peculiar that John, who so expressly called men to repentance and amendment of life, as preparatory to a new phase of the Divine administration, should have accompanied his preaching with an ordinance of baptism. The ideas, the practices, the associations, the hopes of the time, were such as to render an act of this kind both a natural expression and a fitting embodiment of his doctrine. Hence, when John gave a succession of denials to the interrogatories of the Pharisees, such as they understood to be a renunciation of any claim on his part to the character, either of Messiah or of Messiah's forerunner, they asked him, "Why baptizest thou, then, if thou be not that Christ, nor Elias, neither that prophet?" (John i. 25);—they would have been nowise surprised had any one of these come with an ordinance of baptism; they only wondered that John, disclaiming, as they thought, being identified with one or other of them, should still have made himself known as the dispenser of such an ordinance.

After what has been stated, it is scarcely necessary to add, that it is a matter of no moment in what manner Jewish proselyte-baptism was administered, when it came to be regularly established. For, as we have no certain, or even very probable evidence of its existence till some centuries after the Christian era, the mode of its administration can have no bearing on the question of baptism by John or the apostles. According to the descriptions given of it by Maimonides and other Jewish writers (as may be seen in Wall), it appears to have been done by immersion; but these descriptions belong to a period long subsequent to the apostolic age. In describing the practice of the Essenes, which, perhaps, comes the nearest to the new rite of any known existing custom, Josephus uses the words ἀπολούω (wash off), and ἁγνεία, cleansing; pointing rather to the operations of the lavacrum or λουτήριον, than to the act of immersion in a pool or bathing-tub. And it is always by words of a like nature—words indicative of washing, cleansing, and such like, that the ablutions of the Old Testament ritual are described; as in Lev. xvi. 28, where it is in the Septuagint, πλυνεῖ τα' ἱμάτια καὶ λούσεται τὸ σῶμα αὐτοῦ ὕδατι, he shall wash his clothes, and bathe (in any of the forms) his body with water. It was not, in short, by any *precise mode* of applying the water, but to the *cleansing property or effect* of the water, when applied, that respect appears to have been had in the descriptions referred to.

III. A third line of reflection will be found to conduct us substantially to the result we have already arrived at. It is derived from the incidental allusions and explanatory expressions occurring in Scripture, both in respect to the symbolical use of water generally, and to the ordinance of baptism in particular. In nearly all of these it is simply the *cleansing* property of the water, its washing virtue, which is rendered prominent. For example, in Acts xxii. 16, " Arise, and be baptised, and wash away thy sins, calling on the name of the Lord ;" or in Eph. v. 25, 26, " Christ loved the Church, and gave Himself for it, that He might sanctify and cleanse it, by the washing of water by (lit. *in*) the Word." Here the reference is not exclusively to the ordinance of baptism; for the cleansing spoken of is represented as finding its accomplishment " in the Word "—being wrought mainly in the soul through the belief of the truth. Yet, along with this more direct and inward instrumentality, the apostle couples that of baptism, and points, while he does so, to the cleansing property of the symbolical element employed in its administration. The same also is done in such expressions as "But ye are washed," "He hath washed us from our sins," "He hath saved us by the washing of regeneration and renewing of the Holy Ghost;" in each of them the language employed is founded on the baptismal use of water, and bears respect simply to its natural adaptation to purposes of cleansing. On this alone the attention is fixed.

It adds force to the argument derived from these considerations, to observe, that the word baptism is sometimes used of circumstances and events, in regard to which the mode was entirely different, and only the main, fundamental idea alike. Thus in 1 Cor. x. 2, the apostle represents the Israelites as having been all baptised into Moses in the cloud and in the sea; where nothing but the most fanciful imagination, or the most determined partizanship can think of an immersion being indicated.[1] The two actions classed together were quite different in form; and neither the one nor the other—neither the passing under the cloud, nor the going dry-shod through the Red Sea, possessed the reality, or even bore the semblance of a dipping. In 1 Peter iii. 20, 21, the preservation of Noah by the waters of the deluge, which destroyed the ungodly, is represented as a species of baptism—baptism in the type. And there also it was plainly of no moment what corporeal position Noah occupied relatively to the waters—whether above or below them. This is not brought at all into notice. The simple point of comparison between the Old and the New is, that with Noah, as with us, there was an element accomplishing a twofold process—the destruction of the evil, and the preservation of the good. He was saved in the ark through that which destroyed others; precisely as we, when our baptism becomes truly operative in our experience, are saved by that regenerative and sanctifying grace, which at once destroys the inherent evil in our natures, and brings to them a participation of a Divine life. In each of these illustrative cases no stress whatever is laid upon the particular form or mode, in which they respectively differed; in

---

[1] One would almost think it was in a *jeux d'esprit* some one had said of Moses walking through the sea on dry ground, "He got a dry dip. And could not a person, literally covered with oil-cloth, get a dry immersion in water?" But it is Dr Carson who has put his name to such solemn trifling.

regard to none of them is it so much as distinctly referred to, and the whole point of the comparison is made to turn on the separation, the cleansing process effected between the evil and the good—the corruption of nature, on the one side, and the saving grace of God, on the other.

Even the passages in Rom. vi. 3, 4, and Col. ii. 12, 13, in which the apostle speaks of baptism as a burial, and which Baptists usually contend is founded on the specific mode of immersion—even these, when viewed in connection with the representations already noticed, instead of invalidating, rather confirm the deduction we are seeking to establish. For, on the supposition of a reference being made merely to the mode of administration, it would surely be to present us with a most incongruous association, if one and the same act were held to be significant, in its simply external aspect, at once of an interment and a cleansing. What natural relation have these to each other? What proper affinity? Manifestly none whatever; and if the same ordinance *is* somehow expressive of both ideas, it cannot possibly be through its form of administration; it must be got by looking above this (whatever precisely that may be), and taking into account the spiritual things symbolised and exhibited in the ordinance. Indeed, as burial was commonly practised in the East, it did not present even a *formal* resemblance to an immersion in water; for, usually the body, and in particular our Lord's body, was not let down, as with us, into an open sepulchre, but placed horizontally in the side of a cave, and there not unfrequently lifted up as on a ledge. Such an act could not be said to look like a dip into water; and if, on the ground of an external resemblance, they had been so associated by the apostle, it would have been impossible to vindicate the connection from the charge of an unregulated play of fancy. But there is here nothing of the kind. The apostle is viewing baptism as the initiatory ordinance that exhibits and confirms the believer's union to Christ—the crucified and risen Redeemer; and to give the greater distinctness to the representation, he places the believer's fellowship with Christ successively in connection with the several stages of Christ's redemptive work—His death, burial, and resurrection, reckoning these as so many stages in the believer's personal history. And as thus, the very substance of the statement shows, how Paul was looking to the *realities*, not to the mere *forms* of things, so, as if the more to take our thoughts off from the forms, he varies the figure, passes from the idea of being buried with Christ, to that of being, like saplings, planted in the likeness of His death and resurrection. But if immersion in water has little resemblance to an Eastern burial, it has still less to the process of planting a shoot in the ground, that it may spring up into life and fruitfulness. Thus, the figures, with the truth couched under them, only become intelligible and plain, when they are viewed in relation to the spiritual design of the ordinance.

There is still another passage, to which, in this connection, reference should be made; for although it does not directly discourse of baptism, it proceeds on the ideas commonly associated in our Lord's time with the religious use of water, and on which the ordinance of baptism is certainly founded. The passage is John xiii. 1–17, which narrates the action of washing the disciples' feet by our Lord. The action had a twofold significance. It was intended, in the first instance, to exhibit an affecting and memorable proof of our Lord's lowly and loving condescension toward His disciples—one, He gave them to understand, which in spirit must be often repeated among themselves. But, besides this, it pointed to the necessity of spiritual cleansing—to its necessity, even in the case of those who have already become the disciples of Christ. They must be perpetually repairing to Him for fresh purifications. Of this symbolic import of the action Peter soon betrayed his ignorance—though really not more ignorant, but only more prompt and outspoken than the others—when he declared that Jesus should never wash *his* feet. The reply this drew forth was, " If I wash thee not, thou hast no part with Me," indicating that a deep symbolic import attached to the service, on account of which all the disciples behoved to submit to it. And now Peter, catching a glimpse of his Master's meaning, exclaimed, " Lord, not my feet only, but also my hands and my head." To this Jesus again replied, Ὁ λελουμένος οὐ χρείαν ἔχει ἢ τοὺς πόδας νίψασθαι, ἀλλ' ἔστι καθαρὸς ὅλος;—where we are to mark the change of verb in the first member—the λελουμένος, referring to a *general* washing, the cleansing of the whole body, and the νίψασθαι, the cleansing merely of the *feet*—

in accordance with the usage previously noticed (p. 271). By reason of their relation to Christ, the disciples (all except Judas, who is expressly distinguished from the rest in what immediately follows) had been, in a manner, washed; that is, they were in an accepted or justified condition, which, with reference to the action of washing, our Lord designated *clean*. But they could only abide in this condition (our Lord would have them to understand) by perpetually repairing to Him for deliverance from the partial defilements which they contracted in the world; so that the one great baptism into a forgiven and purified condition must be followed up by ever recurring lesser baptisms. But in both cases alike, it is the *cleansing* virtue alone of the outward service that is made account of; it is the washing away alone of contracted defilement; and if *that* idea is made prominent in the use of the water, we naturally and reasonably infer, the design of the symbol will in any case be accomplished.

On the whole, two things seem perfectly clear, from all that is written in Scripture respecting what is external in the ordinance of baptism. The first is, that there is nothing, either in the expressions employed concerning it, or in the circumstances of its institution, to fix the Church down to a specific form of administration, as essential to its proper being and character. This sufficiently appears from the considerations already adduced; but the view might be greatly strengthened, by comparing the indeterminateness which characterizes the language respecting baptism, with the remarkable precision and definitiveness with which the appointments were made in Old Testament ordinances. In these the form *was* essential, and hence its minutest details were prescribed—the day, the place, the materials to be employed, and the manner of employing them : all were matter of explicit legislation. But in the New Testament ordinance it is otherwise, because, while the rite itself is imperative, nothing of moment depends upon the precise form of administration. The second conclusion is, that the use of water in baptism is chiefly, if not exclusively, for the purpose of symbolising the cleansing and regenerative nature of the change, which those, who are the proper subjects, must undergo on entering the Messiah's kingdom. So that the prominent idea—the one point on which the general tenor of Scripture would lead us to lay stress—is the cleansing property of the element applied to the body, not the precise manner of its administration. And we may fairly regard it as an additional confirmation of the soundness of our views in both these respects, that when we look from the external symbol to the internal reality, we find the same disregard as to form, coupled with the same uniformity as to substantial import. It is said, we are baptised *in* the Spirit (ἐν πνεύματι ἁγίῳ, Matt. iii. 11 ; John i. 33 ; Acts i. 5) ; but this is described as taking effect by the Spirit descending into us, not by our being immersed into the Spirit—by His being poured out upon us, or coming to abide in us. The cloven tongues as of fire, which at the first imaged the fact of His descent on the apostles, appeared *sitting* on them ; it was not an element, into which they themselves were plunged, but a form of power *resting upon* them. In a word, it is the internal, vivifying, regenerative agency, which alone is important ; the mode in which it is represented as coming into operation is varied, because pointing to what in the ordinance is not absolutely fixed or strictly essential.

We have confined our attention, in the preceding line of inquiry, to what properly belongs to the exegetical province. Our immediate object has been to ascertain, by every fair and legitimate consideration, the Scriptural import of βαπτίζω and βάπτισμα, as applied to the baptism of John and our Lord. The *doctrine* of baptism—the truths it involves, the obligations it imposes, its proper subjects, and the parties by whom it should be administered—these are topics that belong to another department of theological inquiry. We shall merely advert, in conclusion, to one or two expressions, in which the word to baptise is coupled with certain adjuncts, used to indicate more definitely its nature and object. In respect to John's baptism, the common adjuncts are, εἰς μετάνοιαν, εἰς ἄφεσιν ἁμαρτιῶν, into repentance, into remission of sins—that is, into these as the aim or result of the ordinance. The same general relation is sometimes expressed in regard to Christ's baptism, only the object is different ; as when it is said to be εἰς ἓν σῶμα (1 Cor. xii. 13), εἰς Χριστὸν Ἰησοῦν, or εἰς τὸν θάνατον αὐτοῦ (Rom. vi. 3)—into these, as the end or object aimed at in the ordinance. To be baptized into a person—into Christ, for example, or into His body—means, to be through baptism formally admitted into personal fellowship with Him, and participation in the cause or work associated with His name. And not materially different is the expression of being baptized, ἐν τῷ ὀνόματι τοῦ Κυρίου (Acts x. 48), also ἐπὶ τῷ ὀνόματι Ἰησοῦ (Acts ii. 38); the import of which is—not that the original formula given by the Lord was dispensed with—that instead of it Christ's name simply was pronounced over the baptized; but that they were baptized into the faith of His person and salvation, or into the profession and hope of all that His name indicates for those who own His authority, and trust in His merits.

SECTION SIXTH.

IMPORT AND USE OF HADES, Ἅδης, IN SCRIPTURE.

THIS is one of the few words employed by the sacred writers, which played a prominent part in the mythologies of Greece and Rome ; and it is of importance, for the correct interpretation of certain portions of New Testament Scripture, to ascertain, whether the sense which it bears in the sacred, is the same with that which it bore in the profane territory ; or what, if any, may have been the modifications it underwent in being brought into contact with the spiritual revelations of the Bible.

1. To look first to the heathen use of the term,—the derivation and primary meaning cannot be pronounced absolutely certain ; yet what has been the most general, continues still to be the most approved opinion—that it is a compound of privative α and ἰδεῖν; so that, if applied to a person or power, it would designate *what makes invisible*, if to a place, the *invisible region*. We may the rather hold this to be the correct etymology, as in the more ancient writers the iota is very commonly written and pronounced as a constituent part of the word; and ᾄδης may consequently be regarded as an abbreviation of ἀΐδης. One does not see how this could have happened, if the derivation had been from ἄδω or χάδω, to receive. In the elder Greek writers, the word is generally used to designate a person or power ; it is

but another name for Pluto, Dis, or Orcus. In Homer it is always so used; but in later writers it is applied sometimes to the power, and sometimes to the abode or region, over which he was supposed to preside. And as people felt unwilling (according to Plato) to designate the Deity by the dreaded name of Hades, preferring that rather of Pluto, so the term Hades came in process of time to be generally appropriated to the region. Nor can there be any doubt that this region, in respect to locality, was understood to occupy a relatively lower position than the earth—hence the Latin designations, *inferi* and *inferna*, the people or places beneath ground; and that, in respect to its nature and design, it was the common receptacle of the departed. Πάντας ὁμῶς θνητοὺς Ἀΐδης δέχεται. This common receptacle, however, they held to be divided into two distinct spheres—one for the good, and another for the bad—Elysium and Tartarus. Delineating the two paths, which at a certain point led off to the different habitations, Virgil says, Æn. vi. 540:—

> " Hâc iter Elysium nobis: et laeva malorum
> Exercet pœnas, et ad impia Tartara mittit."

But notwithstanding this division, and the possibility, according to it, of a state of happiness being enjoyed in the nether world, the notion of Hades was still a predominantly gloomy and forbidding one to the heathen mind. Pluto and his subordinates were always imaged under a grim and stern aspect; and the whole region, over which their sway extended, looked dull and mournful. The passage of souls thither was commonly represented as a transition from the region of light and life to the mansions of darkness, and the possession, at the most, of a kind of shadowy, semi-real existence, a sort of mid-way condition between proper life and death. The poets, who partly expressed, and partly also formed the popular belief upon the subject, inclined so much in their representations to the shady side, that Plato would only admit them into his Republic, if the passages bearing on this point were erased from them; because, filling the minds of men with such uninviting representations of the state after death, they inevitably tended, he conceived, to unnerve the spirits of men, and dispose them to prefer slavery to defeat and death (Rep. iii. 1–4). This dark and gloomy portraiture of the state of the departed in heathen mythology arose, doubtless, in part from the want of any definite revelation to guide and elevate men's views regarding the future ; but still more, from a want of another kind—the want of any proper satisfaction for the guilt of sin, such as should, on solid grounds, have restored peace to the conscience. Their imperfect ablutions and sacrifices were *felt* to be insufficient for so great an end, especially when the thought of future retribution hove distinctly in view. Yet, uninviting as the prospect of an entrance into Hades was, even for the better portion of mankind, it was greatly preferred to exclusion ; and the classes that were denied admission for a time, were deemed peculiarly unhappy. These were the unburied, the unripe (such as had been carried off at an immature age, hence supposed to be not ready), and those who had met a violent death. The first class till their funeral rites were performed, the other two, till the natural period of death had arrived, were doomed to flit about the outskirts of Hades.[1] Itself a proof of the superficialism of heathen mythology, and of the undue regard that was had in it to merely natural considerations ! since all the circumstances, which were supposed to exclude from the proper receptacles of the dead, belonged to the outward and fortuitous, rather than to the moral. But whatever may be thought of such imaginations, there can be no doubt of the two leading points already noted—namely, that the Hades of ancient heathenism was believed to be the common receptacle of departed souls, and that it was understood to possess a compartment of bliss for the good, and a compartment of retributive punishment and misery for the bad.

2. Turning now to the territory of Scripture, we look in the first instance to the light that is furnished on the subject in the writings of the Old Testament. *There* the place of departed spirits is designated by the Hebrew name of *Sheol;* which is most commonly, and I believe rightly, derived from שָׁאַל, to demand or ask : So called, to use the words of Michaelis, a poscendo, quod non desinat postulare, et homines alios post alios ad se trahere. With reference to this primary import of the term, as well as to the reality indicated by it, it is said in Prov. xxvii. 20, " Sheol and the abyss are never satisfied," and in Hab. ii. 5, the Chaldean

---

[1] See Tertullian de Amina, c. 56 ; also the long note of Pearson on the subject under Art. V. of the Creed, note *l*.

monarch is likened to Sheol, "because he gathereth unto him all nations, and heapeth unto him all people." Gesenius's later derivation, as if it were for שְׁאוֹל, a hollow, then a hollow and subterranean place, seems to rest on no solid foundation. But nothing of importance depends on the etymology; other and more certain sources of information exist as to the notions involved in it. The Sheol of the Hebrews bore so much of a common resemblance to the Hades of the Greeks, that in the Septuagint ᾅδης is the word commonly employed as an equivalent; and in the latter periods of the Jewish commonwealth the two words were viewed as of substantially like import. According also to the Hebrew mode of contemplation, there was a common receptacle for the spirits of the departed; and a receptacle, which was conceived of as occupying, in relation to this world, a lower sphere —underground. Hence they spoke of *going down* to Sheol, or of being *brought up* again from it. Josephus, when describing in this respect the belief of the Pharisees, which was, undoubtedly, the common belief of his countrymen, says, "They believe that souls have an immortal vigour in them, and that under the earth (ὑπὸ χθονὸς), there will be rewards or punishments, according as they have lived virtuously or viciously in this life; that the latter are to be detained in an everlasting prison, but that the former shall have power to revive and live again" (Ant. xviii. 1, 3). The language of earlier times perfectly accords with these views, so far as it refers to the points embraced in them. Jacob, for example, speaks of being brought down to Sheol with sorrow (Gen. xlii. 38); and David, in one place, Ps. cxxxix. 8, contemplates the possibility of making his bed in Sheol, and in another, Ps. xxx., after deliverance from the sore calamity, which had enveloped him for a time as in an atmosphere of death, gives thanks to God, like one actually restored to life, for having brought his soul up again from Sheol. At the same time, that the wicked were regarded as going to Sheol, is so often expressed in Old Testament Scripture, that it is almost needless to produce any particular examples of it. The passage alone of Isa. xiv., which, though highly figurative, is certainly based on the existing beliefs of the Israelitish people, is conclusive proof. The king of Babylon is there represented as thrown from his lofty elevation by the judgment of Heaven, and sent as a humbled captive into the chambers of Sheol, the inmates of which appear moved with wonder at the thought of his downfall, and raise over him the shout of exultation. Beyond doubt, therefore, Sheol, like Hades, was regarded as the abode after death alike of the good and the bad. And the conception of its low, deep, subterranean position is not only implied in the general style of thought and expression upon the subject, but is sometimes also very forcibly exhibited;—As when in Deuteronomy, ch. xxxii. 22, the Lord declares that a fire was " kindled in His anger, which should burn to the lowest Sheol;" and in Job xi. 7–9, " Canst thou by search-ing find out God? canst thou find out the Almighty unto per-fection? It is high as heaven, what canst thou do? Deeper than Sheol, what canst thou know?" And still again in Amos ix. 2, " Though they dig into Sheol, thence shall My hand take them; though they climb up into heaven, thence will I bring them down." In these passages Sheol, like Hades, is manifestly put in opposition to what is elevated in height; it is the antithesis of heaven, and stands as a concrete designation of the lowest depths.

From what has been stated, it is clear, that the Sheol of the Hebrews much more nearly coincides with the Hades of the Greeks, than with either our hell (in its now universally received acceptation[1]) or the grave. In some of the passages referred to, indeed, the meaning would not materially suffer by one or other of these terms being employed as an equivalent. Substantially, we should give the sense of Jacob's declaration, if we rendered, " Ye shall bring down my grey hairs with sorrow to the grave;" nor should any violence be done to the general import of the pas-sage in Deuteronomy, if, as in the authorised version, the wrath of God was said to burn to the lowest hell; because here it is the wicked only that are contemplated, and these as pursued by Divine vengeance to the farthest bounds of their possible exist-ence. Yet, the terms in either case are not precisely equivalent, and hence are not convertible; we could not substitute hell for grave in Jacob's declaration, or grave for hell in the passage from Deuteronomy. With this general agreement, however, between

[1] Originally, it had much the same meaning as Hades, being derived from the Saxon *helan*, to cover, and denoting simply the covered or hidden space —the invisible regions.

Hades and Sheol, there may still be shades of difference between them, and such as involve important principles. The term Hades certainly came nearer to Sheol than either hell or the grave, especially in these two respects, that both alike were viewed as the common receptacle of departed souls, and as lying far under-ground : In two other points also there might be said to be a substantial agreement. First, in regard to the diverse conditions of the departed; for, though in what is said of Sheol we do not find by any means such a distinct separation into the two regions for their respective classes of occupants, as in the case of Hades with its Elysium and Tartarus, yet the existence of such a sepa-ration is not doubtfully indicated. It is implied in the represent-ations given of the doctrine of Divine retribution, as reaching beyond the boundaries of sense and time into the realms of the dead. It is again implied in the hope, which was possessed by the righteous in his death—the rooted conviction, that he was safe in the keeping of the all-present and omnipotent Jehovah, even when appointed to find his bed in the viewless chambers of Sheol; —a very different condition from that of those, who, like the god-less monarch of Babylon, were represented as cast down thither with the marks upon them of shame and dishonour. Such things leave no room to doubt, that while Sheol might be regarded as but one region, it was known to possess quite different receptacles for those received within its gates, and that *there* still, there, in-deed, pre-eminently, it should be well with the righteous and ill with the wicked. With all this—and here lies the other point of substantial agreement with the Hades of heathendom—a cer-tain degree of gloom and repulsiveness hung around the region even to the eye of the believing Israelite. He felt alarmed and saddened at the thought of his entrance into it—as if his nature must there suffer a kind of collapse; and not only the commoner sympathies of flesh and blood, but the holiest affections also of grace, must be denied the exercise they delighted in on earth. In the Book of Psalms Sheol is spoken of as the land of forget-fulness and of silence, where no celebration is made of God's praise, or active service is done for Him, like what is ever pro-ceeding on earth. David asks respecting those who have entered that nether world, " Who shall give Thee thanks ?" (Ps. vi. 5). And Hezekiah, in like manner, declares " Sheol cannot praise

T

Thee, nor death extol Thee. The living, the living, he shall praise Thee, as I do this day" (Isa. xxxviii. 18).

Were expressions of this nature to be taken absolutely, they would bespeak even a darker and gloomier view of Sheol, on the part of Old Testament believers, than was held by the better sort of heathens respecting the Elysium of Hades. But it is evident, from what has been stated, that they cannot be so taken. If the retributive justice of God followed men into Sheol, distinguishing there also between the righteous and the wicked, there could not possibly, with either class, be total silence and forgetfulness; the soul must have been conceived capable of happiness or misery, and consequently to have had continued recollection and consciousness, as discerning in the elements of its new state the issues of that which it had left. The ideal scene, too, in Isaiah, of the Chaldean monarch's reception among the departed, and the historical representation of Samuel's reappearance at Endor to rebuke Saul and proclaim his approaching doom, should have wanted their proper basis, if the tenants of Sheol had been supposed to be bereft of consciousness and power. The language, which *seems* to betoken such a complete cessation of thought and energy, could be nothing more than relative. It meant, that, as compared with the present life, so replete with busy, and in many respects pleasurable activities, existence in Sheol presented itself to the apprehension of the Hebrews, as an obscure, inactive, torpid repose. In truth, they had no revelation on the subject; and, wiser than the heathen, they stopt where their light forsook them ; they did not attempt to supply the lack of supernal illumination by silly fables, which were fitted only to deceive. It was the further development of God's scheme which alone could relieve the gloom ; and waiting for that, they rested meanwhile in the conviction—though not without many recoils of feeling and faintings of heart—that He, who had kept and blessed them through the troubles of life, would not leave them a prey to evil in the undiscovered regions that lay beyond.

Along, however, with those points of obvious or substantial agreement, between the Sheol of the Hebrews and the Hades of the Greeks, there were points—two in particular—of actual diversity. One was, that Sheol was not, in the estimation of the

Hebrews, a final, but only an intermediate state. It was the soul's place of rest, and, it might be, for aught they knew, of absolute quiescence, during its state of separation from the body, but from which it was again to emerge, when the time should come for the resurrection of the dead. The prospect of such a resurrection was cherished from the very first by the believing people of God, to whom the promise was given of a reversion of the evil brought in by sin, and, by consequence, of the destruction of death, in which that evil found its proper consummation. So that every true believer was a man of hope—of a hope that penetrated beyond the mansions of Sheol ; his final resting-place, he knew, was not to be there. And when the Psalmist spake concerning himself, " God will redeem my soul from the hand (or power) of Sheol, for He shall receive me" (Ps. xlix. 15) ; or the prophet Isaiah, of the righteous generally, " Thy dead men shall live, my dead body shall arise ; awake and sing, ye that dwell in dust" (xxvi. 19) ; or Hosea, " I will ransom them from the power of Sheol, I will redeem them from death : O death, I will be thy plagues ; O Sheol, I will be thy destruction"(xiii. 14) ; or Daniel, " Many of them that sleep in the dust of the earth shall awake, some to everlasting life, and some to shame and everlasting contempt" (xii. 2) :—they but gave varied expression to that hope, which lay in the breast of every pious Israelite— namely, that there should be a resurrection of the just and of the unjust—that for the just, at least, there should be a release from Sheol, with its unnatural abridgments of life and being, that they might enter on their proper heritage of blessing.

In this consisted one important element of difference between Sheol and Hades ; for the heathen idolater could see nothing beyond Hades ; its bars to him were eternal ; the thought of a resurrection was alien to all his conceptions of the possible future. And closely connected with that was this other, that Sheol was not viewed as a separate realm, like Hades, withdrawn from the primal fountain of life, and subject to another dominion than the world of sense and time. With the heathen, the lord of the lower regions was the rival of the King of earth and heaven ; the two domains were essentially antagonistic. But with the more enlightened Hebrew there was no real separation between the two ; the chambers of Sheol were as much God's as the habitations of men on earth, or the mansions of the blest in glory ; there, as well as here, the one living Jehovah was believed to be in all, through all, and over all.

Now, it is impossible but that these two leading principles, associated with the Hebrew Sheol, but not with the Grecian Hades, must have materially affected the views currently entertained upon the subject; and though the Hellenistic Jews employed Hades as the nearest equivalent in the Greek language to Sheol, it must yet have called up ideas in the mind of an enlightened Israelite, which found no place in the bosom of a heathen. The word was a different thing in the mouth of the one from what it was in the mouth of the other.

3. So much, then, for the Old Testament usage and ideas ; we come now to those of the New Testament. Here the word Hades is of comparatively rare occurrence ; it is not found in more than eight passages altogether. The first time it meets us is in our Lord's denunciation upon Capernaum, the place where He had usually resided during the time of His active ministry in Galilee ; and it is employed, as in some of the passages cited from the Old Testament, merely as one of the terms of a contrast :— " And thou, Capernaum, which art exalted unto heaven, shalt be brought down to Hades" (Matt. xi. 23)—i. e., from the most towering elevation to the deepest debasement. From a proverbial use of this description nothing very definite can be inferred as to the nature of the place ; the reference proceeds simply on the popular apprehension respecting its position in the lowest depths. The next use of the term by our Lord is also of a somewhat rhetorical character ; it is in the memorable words addressed to Simon Peter, which contained the declaration, " And on this rock I will build My Church, and the gates of Hades shall not prevail against it" (Matt. xvi. 18). This no further determines the nature of Hades, than that somehow it is conceived of as standing in opposition to the continued existence or prosperity of the Church ; so that the ascendency of the one would be the defeat or overthrow of the other. Hades is referred to as a realm or kingdom, having, like earthly kingdoms in the East, seats of council and authority at its gates, where deliberations were held, and measures taken, in regard to all that concerned its interests ; and these, the Lord affirms, should never prevail against *His*

cause on earth; this cause should ever maintain its ground. But on another occasion still—the *only* occasion besides on which the term occurs in the recorded sayings of our Lord—in the parable of the rich man and Lazarus, it is there said of the former, that " in Hades he lifted up his eyes, in torments." And it cannot but be regarded as a noticeable circumstance, that in the solitary example, wherein Hades is mentioned by our Lord explicitly as a receptacle for the departed, it is in connection with the wicked, and as a place of torment. True, no doubt, Lazarus also, the child of faith and the heir of glory, was so far associated with the lost worldling, that he appears, as it were, within sight and hail of the other; but still, it is only to the compartment, where the lost had their portion, that the name Hades is applied; and betwixt that locality and the abodes of the blest an impassable gulph is represented as being fixed. Coupling with this the circumstance, that in the other two cases also, in which the term Hades was employed by our Lord, it appears in a kind of antithesis to His cause and kingdom, one can scarcely avoid feeling as if there had been taken from Hades somewhat of that common aspect and relation to the whole of mankind, which in more ancient times was ascribed to Sheol. The rather may we thus conclude, when we call to remembrance the words of Christ on another occasion; words which exhibit a marked contrast to those spoken of the rich man in the parable, and which, from the emphatic moment when they were uttered, might be said to designate for future time the receptacle of departed saints. It was on the cross, when Jesus said to the penitent malefactor, " To-day shalt thou be with Me in paradise" (Luke xxiii. 43). Paradise! the region, not of gloom and forgetfulness, but of beautiful and blessed life—the primeval home and heritage of man; and so, proclaiming Jesus to be that Second Man, the Lord from heaven, who had prevailed to recover what was lost by the first.[1]

[1] The full significance of our Lord's language on this occasion has been sadly marred by our rabbinical commentators (Lightfoot, Wetstein, etc.), who have thought they sufficiently explained it by adducing passages from Jewish writings, in which the Garden of Eden is used as a name for the place of departed believers. As if such writings were entitled to rank even in antiquity with the Gospels! Or, as if the kind of hap-hazard employment of terms by blind Rabbis, as often wrong as right, when referring to

Notwithstanding, however, this studied avoidance, on the part
of our Lord, of the term Hades to denote the place of His temporary sojourn, and that of His people, between death and the resurrection, the next passage in which we meet with the word,
seems to make Hades such a place of sojourn for the Redeemer
Himself. It is in Acts ii. 27–31, where, after quoting a portion
of the 16th Psalm, and applying it to Christ, the Apostle Peter
says, that David spake there as a prophet—" spake of the resurrection of Christ, that His soul was not left in Hades, neither
did His flesh see corruption." By the great body of Christian
writers this passage is held conclusive as to the fact of Christ's
soul having actually been in Hades; since it could not have been
represented as not left there, had it not actually been there; and
by many of them it is deemed the only very clear and decisive
text on the point.[1] Yet it is rather pressing the language too
far, when it is alleged in proof of Hades being the proper designation of the place, whither our Lord's soul went at the moment
of death. For it is an Old Testament passage, and like other
passages of a prophetic nature, which pointed to New Testament
times, it naturally spoke of the future under the form and image
of the things then present or past. It should, therefore, be understood of the actual event in Gospel times with such a measure
of qualification, as the altered circumstances of the new dispensation might require. And if, as we have seen reason to believe,
the language of our Lord Himself gave indication of a change in
respect to Hades, as regards the souls of believers—if in His discourses he carefully distinguished between Hades and the receptacle of His own and His people's disembodied spirits, we can
scarcely be warranted in pressing the Old Testament passage
quoted by St Peter, so as to impose on it still an Old Testament
sense. But, in reality, neither the original Hebrew, nor the Septuagint Greek, which is adopted by the apostle, give any precise
indication of the place where our Lord's spirit sojourned; they
do not define so closely, as is supposed, his relation to Hades.
The words in the Greek, which represent quite exactly the sense
of the Hebrew, are, οὐκ ἐγκαταλείψεις τὴν ψυχήν μου εἰς ᾅδην, Thou

the mysteries of the kingdom, gave the key to Christ's pregnant and select
diction! But see at Part I., sec. 3, p. 51, sq.

[1] See Pearson on the Creed, Burnet or Browne on the 39 Articles.

wilt not relinquish, or abandon, my soul to Hades—wilt not surrender it as a helpless prey to that hostile power, or unwelcome abode. It might, indeed, mean, that the soul was to be allowed to enter there, though not to be shut up for a continuance; but it might also, and even more naturally intimate, that the soul should not properly fall under the dominion of Hades. The expression is general as regards the matter of relationship; Hades is simply eyed as the antagonistic power, the hostile quarter, *against* which security was to be provided, or *from* which deliverance was to be granted.

Another passage commonly referred to in the same connection, were it justly so employed, might also be treated as deriving its impress from Old Testament times. Having quoted Isa. xxv. 8, " He will swallow up death in victory," St Paul breaks out into the fervid exclamation, " O death, where is thy sting ? O Hades, where is thy victory?" (1 Cor. xv. 55). Such is the reading of the received text; but there can be no doubt, that θάνατε, O death, should be in this clause, as well as the preceding one. So that the passage does not come into consideration here ; and the English version, which merely substitutes *grave* in the second clause for *death* in the first, is really more correct than the original it professed to follow. Grave answers more nearly to θάνατε than it should have done to ᾅδη.

Passing this, then, as not applicable, the only remaining passages, in which Hades occurs, are in the Book of Revelation. There it is found four times. In ch. i. 18, the Lord re-assures John, who had fallen at His feet as dead, by saying, " Fear not: I am the first and the last ; He that liveth and was dead ; and, behold, I am alive for evermore ; Amen, and have the keys of death and of Hades." The second is in the description of the rider on the pale horse, in ch. vi. 8, whose name was Death, and who was followed by Hades, slaying on every hand with sword and pestilence. The two others occur in successive verses, at ch. xx. 13, 14, where, amid the changes that usher in the final condition of things, it is said, " And the sea gave up the dead that are in it, and death and Hades gave up the dead that are in them, and each were judged according to their works. And Death and Hades were cast into the lake of fire, which is the second death." In these representations it were too much, perhaps, to affirm with some, that Hades is necessarily restricted to the place of torment, the temporary prison-house of the lost. For, when Christ speaks of having the keys of death and of Hades, He might refer to the invisible world generally ; He might intend to comfort the Apocalyptist with the assurance, that He, who then appeared to him in glory, had supreme control over the mansions of life and death, and that excepting under His direction no one could be sent into the nether world from the scenes and habitations of the living. At the same time, when the connection of the words is taken into account—when it is remembered that John, together with the church he represented, was then threatened with destruction by a powerful adversary, and that he felt at the moment on the point of dissolution, the conviction forces itself on our minds, that there also death and Hades are chiefly contemplated as evils—objects shrunk from and dreaded, on account of their connection with sin, and from which exemption was to be sought and obtained in Christ. That such is the aspect in which death and Hades are presented in ch. vi. 8, where the one follows the other in the work of carnage and desolation, admits of no doubt ; for the work given them to do was one emphatically of judgment, to take effect on the adversaries of God. The same reference to the wicked, and to the consequences resulting from their misdeeds, if less obvious in the remaining passage of Revelation, is scarcely less certain. For, while the sea is spoken of, along with death and Hades, as giving up the dead that were in it, and of all the dead, so given up, being judged out of the books that were written in them according to their works, it is not to be forgotten, that in the Apocalypse *sea* is the usual symbol of the world, in its sin-heaving, agitated, and troubled state—the world as opposed to the peaceful and blessed kingdom of Christ ; and in such a case the books are most naturally regarded as the ideal records of human guilt and depravity. I am inclined, therefore, to the opinion, that the souls here represented as coming out of the sea, death, and Hades, and being judged according to the things written in the books, are the non-elect portion of mankind—all, whose names were not found in the book of life. And this is confirmed by what is said immediately after, that death and Hades were cast into the lake of fire ; for what reason could there have been for such an utter perdition, if Hades included in its domain the paradise to which Christ went with the penitent malefactor? Could the realms of bliss and woe, life and destruction, be so indiscriminately confounded together? Manifestly a Hades, which was to find its outgoing in the devouring fire of Heaven's wrath, was a very different region from that, in which our Lord tasted the sweets of paradise, or even the lap of Abraham's bosom, wherein a pious Lazarus is said to have reaped his reversion of comfort from the sorrows of an afflicted life.

On the whole, there seems ample ground for maintaining, that a marked difference lies between the use of Hades in the New Testament and of Sheol in the Old. Sheol is plainly and uniformly represented as the common receptacle of the good and the bad; for the one class, indeed, containing the elements of a very different portion from what awaited the other; yet even for the good wearing an aspect somewhat cheerless and uninviting. Hades, in New Testament Scripture, is not once explicitly employed as a designation for the common region of departed spirits; when speaking of the intermediate state for the good, our Lord carefully abstained from associating it with the mention of Hades; and both as referred to by Him, and as personified in the Book of Revelation, Hades is placed in a kind of antagonistic relation to the interests of His kingdom—is even viewed as standing in close affinity with death, and destined to share in its final extinction. Not, however, that we are therefore warranted to deny the existence of an intermediate state for the souls of believers, differing in place or character from their ultimate destination; or that it must on no account be identified with Hades. No; but simply that this is no longer the *fitting* epithet to apply to the temporary receptacle of departed saints; and we cannot but regard it as unhappy, and tending to convey a partially wrong impression respecting Christ, that the article in the Apostle's Creed should have taken the form of representing His disembodied soul as descending into Hades. He Himself introduced a change in the phraseology respecting the state of the departed, such as appears to have betokened a corresponding change in the reality. Assuredly, by the incarnation and work of Christ, the position of the Church on earth was mightily elevated; and it is but natural to infer, that a corresponding elevation extended to those members of the Church who had already passed, or might henceforth pass, within the veil; that a fresh lustre was shed over their state and enjoyments by the entrance of Christ, as the triumphant Redeemer, into the world of spirits; and that for them now the old Hades, with its grim and cheerless aspect, was to be accounted gone, supplanted by the happy mansions in the Father's house, which Christ opened to their view. Hence also, instead of shrinking from the immediate future, as from the grasp of an enemy, the children of faith and hope should rather look to it as a provisional paradise, and confidently anticipate in its realms of light and glory a higher satisfaction than they can ever experience in the flesh.

In this statement, however, nothing is to be understood as affirmed in respect to the locality assigned for the spirits of the departed—as if it had been removed to another sphere by the agency of Christ, and a new and higher region had taken the place of the one originally appointed. This was a very common view among the later Fathers—those who lived subsequently to the fifth century—and became at length the received opinion of the Church. It was supposed that, up till the death of Christ, and His descent into Hades, the souls of the righteous were kept in what was called *Limbus Patrum*—not absolutely hell, but a sort of porch or antechamber in its outskirts; and that Christ, after having finished the work of reconciliation, went thither to deliver them from it, and set them in the heavenly places. Bede expresses this to be the general faith of the Church in his day;[1] although many of the greatest authorities before him had opposed it, both because it seemed to bespeak the existence of too much evil in the condition of ancient believers after death, and also to ascribe too great a change to the personal descent of Christ. The notion undoubtedly rested on fanciful grounds, and had various errors, of a collateral kind, associated with it. Its propounders and advocates too much forgot that the language

---

[1] Catholica fides habet, quia descendens ad Inferna Dominus non incredulos inde, sed fideles tantummodo suos educens, ad celestia secum regna perduxerit. So also Isidore Hispalensis, *Sentent.* L. I. c. 16, Ideo Dominus in Inferno descendit, ut his, qui ab eo non pœnaliter detinebantur, viam aperiret revertendi ad cœlos. See other authorities in Pearson on the Creed, Art. V.

used of this province of the invisible world, as well as others, is to a large extent relative, and, as regards circumstantial matters, was never meant to impart precise and definite information. When represented as a lower region, as stretching away even into the profoundest depths, it was, doubtless, the world of sense that supplied the form of the representation. The body, at death, goes down into the earth; and it became natural to think and speak of the soul as following it in this downward direction, and finding its proper abode in the shades below. But this no more determined the locality, than our conception of heaven as a higher region necessitates its position over our heads; which, indeed, would require it to shift perpetually with the seasons of the year, and with the revolutions of day and night. Hence it is ridiculous to say with Horsley, as if such language aimed at philosophical precision, "The sacred writers of the Old Testament speak of a common mansion in the inner parts of the earth; and we find the same opinion so general among the heathen writers of antiquity, that it is more probable that it had its rise in the earliest patriarchal revelations, than in the imaginations of man, or in poetical fiction."[1] Did not the sacred writers as well, though less frequently, also speak of the spirit of a man going upwards, while that of a beast went downwards—of God taking the most eminent saints to Himself, of their being made to see the path of life, and dwelling in the house of the Lord for ever?[2] In speaking of what pertains to the soul after death, we necessarily speak under a veil; the discourse we make must fashion itself after the appearances, rather than the realities of things; and we wander into a wrong path whenever we attempt to turn the language so employed into a delineation of exact bounds and definite landmarks. What is written of departed believers is intended only to give us some idea of their *state*, but not of their local habitation; and the comparison of the later, with the earlier revelations, as already stated, warrants the belief, that with the progress of the scheme of God, and especially with its grand development in the person of Christ, that state did also partake of some kind of progression, or

---

[1] Sermon on 1 Pet. iii. 18–20.
[2] Gen. v. 24; Eccl. iii. 21, xii. 7; Ps. xvi. 11, xxiii. 6.

experience some rise, though we want the means for describing wherein precisely it consisted.

It is scarcely necessary to add, that the same qualifications attach to what is sometimes indicated as to the relative nearness of the two regions appropriated respectively to the saved and the lost in the separate state. An actual nearness is inconceivable, if the better portion are really to exist in a state of blissful consciousness ; for what room could there be for an Elysium of joy, with the existence of such a mass of wretchedness perpetually pressing on their view ? The scene of the rich man's cognisance of and interview with Lazarus can be nothing more than a cover to bring out the elements of remorse and agony, that torment the bosom of the lost. So far, disembodied spirits might be viewed as occupying a common territory, that they are alike tenants of a region physically suited to such spirits, and a region not yet parted into the final destinations of heaven and hell. But nearer determinations are impracticable, and the attempt to make them is to enter into profitless and haply misleading speculations.

4. The preceding remarks have touched upon everything that calls for consideration as regards the import and application of the term Hades in Scripture. The *doctrine* of our Lord's temporary withdrawal into the world of spirits, its historical reality, the relation it bears to the experience of His people, and the results to which it may be applied in respect to the constitution of His person and the completeness of His work,—all this properly belongs to another department of theological inquiry. Or, if treated exegetically, it would be more fitly discussed in connection with a few texts, in which the term Hades does not occur. One of these is the application made in Eph. iv. 9 of an Old Testament passage, in which the Lord is represented as ascending up on high, leading captivity captive ; and on which the apostle remarks, " Now that He ascended, what is it but that He also descended first into the lower parts (τὰ κατώτερα) of the earth ? " The Fathers, undoubtedly, made frequent use of this passage in establishing the descent of Christ into Hades, and they have also been followed by many in modern times. But this, as Bishop Pearson long ago remarked, and for stronger reasons than he alleged, is a very questionable interpretation ; for the contrast marked in the apostle's statement is not, betwixt one part of the

earth and another, but rather betwixt earth as the lower region, and heaven as the higher. The one is brought into view simply as expressive of His humiliation, preceding and preparing for the exaltation, announced in the other ; and to understand the words of a farther descent into the bowels of the earth, would not only be to press them to a sense which cannot fairly be regarded as before the mind of the writer at the time, but also to *make them include a portion of our Lord's history, yea specially to single out that, as the distinctive mark of His humiliation, which does not strictly belong to it.* This will appear from what follows in connection with another text—the one that chiefly bears on the point under consideration—1 Pet. iii. 18–20, in which the apostle points to the sequence and result of Christ's sufferings in the flesh. He suffered once, says Peter, for sins, " the just for the unjust, that He might bring us unto God, being put to death, indeed, in flesh, but quickened in spirit, in which also he went and preached (or, made proclamation) to the spirits in prison, that sometime were disobedient in the days of Noah," etc. (Θανατωθεὶς μὲν σαρκὶ, ζωοποιηθεὶς δὲ πνεύματι, ἐν ᾧ καὶ τοῖς ἐν φυλακῇ πνεύμασιν πορευθεὶς ἐκήρυξεν, ἀπειθήσασίν ποτε, ὅτε ἀπεξεδέχετο ἡ τοῦ Θεοῦ μακροθυμία, κ.τ.λ.)

This is, certainly, one of the most remarkable, and, if isolated from the context, one of the most obscure passages of New Testament Scripture—bringing in so abruptly, and with such rapidity passing over, some of the more remote and peculiar points in the Divine economy. The greatest theologians have not only differed from each other in their views respecting it, but also differed from themselves at one period as compared with another ; of which instances may be found in Augustin, Luther, and Calvin. It would be out of place here, however, to give a history of opinions on the subject ; they may be seen, for example, in Steiger's Commentary (Biblical Cabinet), and, in part also, in Pearson's Notes under Art. V. It will here be enough to indicate a few guiding principles and textual explanations, which it is hoped may serve to show, that when contemplated in the proper light, the passage is neither inexplicable in meaning, nor in the least at variance with the general teaching of Scripture.

First, then, it must be held as fixed and certain, that our Lord's visit to the world of departed spirits, between His death and

His resurrection, *was* an historical reality, whatever He might
have felt or done when there. His departed soul did not ascend
to the proper heaven of glory, as He expressly declared, till after
the resurrection; while yet it went, according to another declaration, to a region so blissful, that it could be called by the name
of paradise. One alternative alone remains, that His spirit went
to the company of those, who are waiting in hope of a better
resurrection.

Secondly, Christ's presence and operations in that world of
spirits must be held to have taken place in free and blessed
agency; they are to be associated, not with the *passive*, but with
the *active* part of His career. His sufferings were at an end
when He expired upon the cross; for then the curse was exhausted, and, with that, the ground of His appointment to evil finally
removed—whence the change explains itself of the difference
that forthwith appeared in the Divine procedure toward Him.
Shame and contumely now gave place to honour: not a bone
of Him was allowed to be broken; He was numbered no longer
with the vile and worthless, but with the rich and honourable, and by these, after being wrapt in spices, He was committed
to a tomb, where no man had lain :—all, so many streaks of that
dawn, which was to issue in the glory of the resurrection-morn.
Whatever, therefore, was done by the soul of Christ subsequent
to His death, must have been in free and blessed agency; and
it were abhorrent to all right notions of the truth respecting Him,
to suppose, as some have done, that His sufferings were prolonged
in the world of spirits, and that He there for a time had experience of the agonies of the lost. This were in effect to say, that
His work of reconciliation on the cross was not complete, that
the sacrifice then paid to Divine justice was not accepted of the
Father. Even the modified view of Bishop Pearson must be
rejected, that " as Christ died in the similitude of a sinner, His
soul went to the place where the souls of men are kept who die
for their sins, and so did wholly undergo the law of death ;" for,
in that case, a certain measure of penalty and satisfaction should
still have been implied in the transaction. The language of St
Peter in the passage more immediately before us gives no countenance to such an idea, nor admits it under any modification;
for he represents Christ's spirit as being vivified, or quickened—

starting into fresh life and energy of action, from the moment that in flesh He underwent the stroke of death, and, as so invigorated, going forth to preach.[1] In short, the culminating point of His humiliation and suffering was His death upon the cross (as already prefigured in the Old Testament sacrifices),[2] and from that point, both in respect to soul and body, the process of exaltation, strictly speaking, began.

Thirdly, In regard to the more specific points —why the Apostle Peter should have made such particular mention of this agency of Christ's disembodied spirit, why he should have coupled it only with the spirits of those who had perished in the flood, and what may have been the nature and intent of his preaching to them :—for all this we must look to the connection. Now, it must be carefully remembered (for chiefly by overlooking this have commentators gone so much into the wrong tract), that the apostle is not discoursing of these topics doctrinally ; they are referred to merely as matters of fact, which had a practical bearing on the great moral truths that were the more immediate subject of dis-

[1] In this explanation, it will be observed, the ζωοποιηθεὶς πνεύματι is taken to refer to the spiritual part of Christ's human nature, precisely as the θανατωθεὶς σαρκί to His corporeal part ; for it is impossible to deny, that this is the natural, and, indeed, the only grammatical mode of interpreting them. As Flacius long ago remarked, "The antithesis clearly shows, that He is said to have been put to death in one part of Him, or in one manner of life, but vivified in another." In like manner Horsley, "If the word *flesh* denote, as it most evidently does, the part in which death took effect upon Him, *spirit* must denote the part in which life was preserved in Him, *i.e.*, His own soul." Perfectly right thus far, though scarcely right when he adds, that "the word *quickened* is often applied to signify, not the resuscitation of life extinguished, but the preservation and continuance of life subsisting:" no, not preservation and continuance simply, but rather freshened energy and revived action. The interpretations, which understand by *spirit* the Holy Ghost, and regard the preaching spoken of as either the preaching of Noah through the Spirit to the antediluvians, or that of the apostles to the wicked around them, hence fall of themselves ; they are but ingenious shifts resorted to for the sake of getting over a difficulty, but twisting the passage into an unnatural sense. Giving to the words πορευθεὶς ἐκήρυξεν their legitimate import, they must mean, that Christ went away and preached—as a spirit to spirits. And the spirits being described as having been *sometime*, or formerly disobedient, also plainly implies, that the period of disobedience was a prior one to that, to which the preaching belonged.

[2] See Typology of Scripture, vol. ii. p. 347.

course. What were these? They were, that Christians should seek to avoid suffering by maintaining a good conscience; but that if they should still, and perhaps on this very account, be called to suffer, it was greatly better to do so for well-doing, than for ill-doing. Then, in confirmation of this complex truth, he points to a twofold illustration. In the first instance, he fixes attention on Christ as having suffered, indeed, the just for the unjust—suffered as the Righteous One, but only *once* suffered; and on *that* (the ἅπαξ ἔπαθεν) the special stress is here to be laid; it was, so to speak, but a momentary infliction of evil, however awful in its nature while it lasted; still, but once borne, and never to be repeated, because borne in the cause of righteousness. Not only so, but it carried along with it infinite recompenses of good—for sinful men, bringing them to God; and for Christ Himself, limiting the reign of death to a short-lived dominion over the body, while the soul, lightened and relieved, inspired with the energy of immortal life, went into the invisible regions, and, with buoyant freedom, moved among the spirits of the departed. How widely different from that mighty class of sufferers!—the most striking examples in the world's history of the reverse of what appeared in Christ—the last race of antediluvians, who suffered, not for *well*-doing, but for *ill*-doing; and suffered, not *once* merely in the flood, that swept them away from their earthly habitations, but even now, after so long a time, when the work on the cross was finished—still pent up as in a prison-house of doom, where they could be only haunted by memories of past crime, and with forebodings of eternal retribution! What a contrast! How should the thought of it persuade us to suffering for well-doing, rather than for evil-doing! And for those lost ones themselves, Christ's spirit, now released from suffering, fresh with the dew of its dawning immortality, *preached;* preached by its very entrance into the paradise of glory. For even this, seen from afar, must have been to them like the appearance of a second Noah, " the preacher of righteousness;" since it proclaimed—proclaimed more emphatically than Noah ever did—the final establishment of God's righteousness, and a sure heritage of life and blessing for those, but for those only, who were ready to hazard all for its sake. Such, doubtless, was the kind of preaching meant; it is that alone which the case admits of—whether, as to its formal character, it may have consisted in the simple presentation of the Spirit of Christ among the spirits of the blest, or may have included some more special and direct intercourse with the imprisoned hosts of antediluvian time. In either case, it was to them like the renewal, in a higher form, of the old preaching of righteousness; for what the one had provisionally announced the other finally confirmed and sealed; yea, was itself the radiant proof of an eternal distinction between those, in whom suffering triumphs because of sin, and those who through righteousness triumph over suffering.[1]

Viewed thus, the whole passage hangs consistently together; one part throws light upon another; and the agency ascribed to Christ is in perfect keeping with all that is elsewhere written, both of His own mediatorial work, and of the condition of departed spirits. On the one hand, it rescues the words from the arbitrary meanings, which doctrinal considerations have so often led pious minds to put on them; and, on the other, it removes the ground, which has too often been sought in the passage, not only by Romish, but even by some Protestant writers, to find a door of hope for certain classes of those who have lived and died in sin. The reference to the antediluvians in the age of Noah is not to some individuals among them, for whom possibly some better fate might have been reserved, but to the collective race as a well-known class in sacred history; and to them as still detained in the prison of judgment, not as having any prospect of deliverance from it. Nay, on this very circumstance the great moral of the reference properly turns; *for it is their protracted, everlasting destination to a doom of suffering, as contrasted with Christ's suffering but once, and, that over, entering on a fresh career of life and glory, which lent all its weight to the exhortation given, to prefer suffering for righteousness-sake to suffering for sin.* In what follows also the same account substantially is made of their case; they are thought of

---

[1] It is no objection to the view now given, that κηρύσσω is commonly used in the sense of a *gospel* proclamation; for it is neither necessarily, nor always so used. In Rom. ii. 21, it is coupled with abstinence from stealing as its object—a preaching of moral duty. Here the reference manifestly is to the ancient preaching of Noah; and to connect this action of Christ with his the term might justly seem the fittest.

simply as reprobate and lost. It is in Noah alone, and the little
remnant in the ark, whom the waters, that destroyed the corrupt
and pestilential mass around them, saved, to be the seed of a new
world, that the prototypes are found of the genuine subjects and
fruits of Christian baptism. And what does this imply of the
mass whom the waters engulphed? Plainly, that their counterpart in Christian times is to be sought in the corruptions of the
flesh and the world, from which it is the design of baptism,
through the power of Christ's resurrection, to save His people—
corruptions which, like their antediluvian exemplars, are irre-
concileably opposed to the life of God, and can have no end but
destruction.

SECTION SEVENTH.

ON THE IMPORT AND USE OF διαθήκη IN THE NEW TESTAMENT.

THE word now to be considered is of frequent occurrence, both
in Scripture and in the classics, but usually in a somewhat different sense. In the classics it commonly signifies *disposition,
arrangement,*—or, more specifically, that particular disposition
which is denominated a *man's will and testament*—the deed by
which he finally disposes of his effects. The latter is the more
common usage ; whence the old glossaries gave *testamentum* as
the Latin synonym. The cases are so rare in which with classical authors it is found in any other sense, that little account
needs to be made of them. They do occur, however, and in one
passage at least, the Aves of Aristophanes, l. 430, the phrase,
διαθέσθαι διαθήκην, is used to express the making of a compact or
covenant, to be carried out between two parties. But the common noun for such cases was undoubtedly συνθήκη. Yet for
what was emphatically *the* covenant in ancient times, the Septuagint has preferred διαθήκη, which, accordingly, among Greek-
speaking Jews, became the appropriate term for the covenant of
God with Israel. The first occasions on which the word was
used had respect to transactions which strikingly displayed the

goodness of God, in making sure provision for the present safety and highest well-being of man (Gen. ix. 9, xvii. 7). It is possible, we may even say probable, that on this account mainly the term διαθήκη was employed rather than συνθήκη, for the latter might justly seem an inadequate expression to characterise arrangements, in which it appeared so prominent an object to make men recipients of the Divine goodness, personally partakers, or instrumentally channels of blessing. It seemed more fitting to employ a term which, without altogether losing sight of the mutual relationship, as between two parties somehow standing in contract, should still give chief prominence to the beneficence of God in disposing of His affairs, so as to provide a suitable heritage of good for His people. In this light it appears to have been understood by some of the Fathers. Thus Clemens Alex. describes διαθήκη as that " which God, the Author of the universe, makes ;" namely, *His* arrangement or disposition of the riches of His bounty. Suidas defines it as ἡ Θεοῦ πρὸς Αβραὰμ, καὶ τοὺς λοιποὺς προπάτορας γενομένη ἐπαγγελία, the promise which God made to Abraham and the other patriarchs. Isidore of Pelusium gives it a somewhat different turn, and points to a more special characteristic, but one also that is derived from its more peculiar reference to God. He says, " συνθήκη is called in Scripture a testament, because the promise it contains is firm and permanent; pactions, indeed, are often broken up, but legal testaments never" (see Suicer).

But however we may thus be able to account for the use of διαθήκη rather than of συνθήκη, as a translation of the Heb. *berith*, we must not allow it to assume, in its ordinary use, the classical sense of *testament*, rather than of *covenant*. There can be no doubt, that *covenant* is the proper rendering of *berith;* and as διαθήκη was employed as its synonym by the Septuagint, it must be taken in the sense of the original—unless the connection should determine otherwise. Indeed, for anything that appears in the Hebrew Scriptures, the Israelites knew nothing of testaments in the ordinary sense of the term ; their rights of property were so regulated as to render these for the most part unnecessary ; if only the means were at hand for ascertaining the family descent and relationship of the parties concerned. They consequently made much account of genealogies, but none, so far as

we know, of testaments. When God, however, designated the
transactions into which He entered with their fathers by the
name of *covenant*, even though the pledged and promised goodness of God might be the most prominent feature in them, the
idea of a mutual paction or agreement was still meant to be kept
steadily in view ;—the Lord sustained one part, and the people
another. And this was done, primarily, that they might have a
clear and affecting proof of His desire to assure them of the certainty of the things guaranteed in the covenant. Not for this
only, however, but for the farther purpose of impressing upon their
minds the feeling, that they had a part to perform to God, as
well as God to them, and that faithfulness in duty, on the one
side, must keep pace with bountifulness in giving on the other.
Such was the case even in the Abrahamic covenant, which is
called, by way of eminence, the covenant of promise ; for the
assurance it contained of a numerous and blessed offspring carried along with it the condition, that parent and offspring alike
should abide in the faith of God and keep His charge.

In the English Bible the word *covenant* is the uniform rendering adopted for the Heb. *berith ;* and so is it also in New Testament Scripture for διαθήκη, whenever the word points to the covenants made with the patriarchs or at Sinai. Yet in the designation of the Scriptures, which belong to the periods embraced by those covenants, the sense of *testament* has been generally introduced. By a natural metonymy, the writings that per-
tain to a period during which a διαθήκη was in force had this applied to them as an appropriate name. Thus, in 2 Cor. iii. 14,
St Paul speaks of the veil remaining on the minds of the Jews,
ἐπὶ τῇ ἀναγνώσει τῆς παλαιᾶς διαθήκης, at the reading of the Old
Testament, as our translators have rendered it, not of the Old
Covenant. We have become so much accustomed to the use of
Testament in this application, that we rarely think whether it is
altogether appropriate or not. Yet had it been proposed for the
first time to our consideration, it could hardly have failed to
strike us as a sort of anomaly in language, that the term *Testament* should be employed as the distinctive epithet for writings
in which the term itself never occurs, while the term *covenant* is
of frequent use, and in the later Scriptures, old covenant is employed to designate a period altogether or nearly past, in contra-

distinction to a new and better era approaching (Jer. xxxi. 31).
The Old covenant, therefore, was clearly the fitting designation
for the earlier half of the Bible, rather than the Old Testament.[1]
The Vulgate, however, by its adoption of *testamentum*, instead of
fœdus, has in this respect given the law to modern times. Some
of the earlier versions presented both terms, at least in respect to
New Testament Scripture, as Beza's Testamentum Novum, Sive
Fœdus Novum, and the Genevan French, Le Nouveau Testament, c'est à dire la Nouvelle Alliance. But the alternative
phrase never came into general use; and the only prevailing designation has been, and still is, The Scriptures of the Old and
the New Testaments.

Of course, as a convenient term for simply designating the
two component parts of the Bible, it is of little moment whether
we use the one or the other. The current epithets serve well
enough to distribute the inspired writings into two sections or
parts, standing related to each other, the one as the earlier, the
other as the later revelation of Divine truth; the one springing
up in connection with that state of things which preceded the
birth of Christ, and has vanished away; the other with that
which was introduced by Christ, and abides for ever. But as
there can be no doubt that the substitution of Testament for
covenant, in the designation of Scripture, arose from a disposition
to regard the economy of Christ's salvation in the light of a *testament* rather than of a *covenant*—as on this account the writings
of evangelists and apostles came to be denominated The *New*
Testament, and in conformity with this appellation that of *Old*

[1] Kohlbrugge, in a treatise *Wozu das alte Testament* objects also to this
designation, and deems it not warranted by the language of the Apostle in
2 Cor. iii. 14. He conceives the Apostle to be there speaking of the Hebrew
Scriptures, not absolutely, but as they are to the unbelieving and blinded Jews;
to these they are merely the *old* covenant, while to the enlightened believer,
who can read them with open eye, they display the *new* covenant. Undoubtedly the books are very different things to the two classes mentioned;
but the plain and natural import of the Apostle's language points to the
books themselves, as containing what pertains to the Old Covenant. Their
further and prospective reference is not here taken into account. And if
persons now think themselves entitled to disregard those books, because
they are specially connected with the *Old* Covenant, this is an abuse charge-
able on their own ignorance and sin.

Testament was assigned to the Law and the Prophets—the question very naturally presents itself, whether such be the Scriptural view of the matter? Whether the gift of Christ, and the benefits of His redemption, are exhibited in the light of a testamentary bequest? For if they are not, then the testamentary aspect of redemption must be pronounced formally incorrect, however in substance accordant with the truth of things; but if they are, the form also is capable of vindication. In neither case is any doctrine of Scripture involved in the inquiry; it touches merely the mode of representation.

Now, as διαθήκη constantly bears in the Old Testament the sense of *covenant*, it may justly be inferred to carry the same meaning in the New, unless the connection should, in certain cases, plainly decide in favour of the other rendering. So far as regards our Lord's personal teaching, there is no room for any difference of view on the subject. Though He frequently referred to both the affairs and the writings of the old economy, He was very sparing in the use of the term διαθήκη. He does not employ it to designate the revelation of law from Sinai; nor are the transactions entered into with the patriarchs, as the heads of the Jewish people; or with David, as the founder of the royal house, called by this name. The first, and the only time that the word appears in our Lord's discourses, is at the institution of the Supper. The words of institution slightly vary in the accounts of the three evangelists, and of the Apostle Paul (1 Cor. xi.); but in each of them He is represented as using the expression ἡ καινὴ διαθήκη. And using it, as He does, without a word of explanation, we cannot doubt that He intended it to be taken by the disciples in its current acceptation; namely, in the sense of covenant; for in that sense alone had it hitherto been employed. Nor can we but regard it as unfortunate, that at that special moment in our Lord's ministry, and in connection with the most sacred and distinctive institution of His kingdom, the later rendering of *testament* should have been substituted for the earlier one of *covenant*. For it confuses the expression in words which are of perpetual recurrence, as well as solemn import, and in respect to which it was desirable that the greatest clearness and certainty should exist; and in so far as the language may be distinctly understood, it presents the great redemption in an aspect which had not at least been previously exhibited, and could not therefore have been intended at the time.

How, then, it may naturally be asked, should such a sense have been so generally put upon it? Are there other passages in subsequent portions of New Testament Scripture, in which the word, in its connection with the work of Christ, conclusively bears the meaning of *testament*? There is a remarkable one in the Epistle to the Hebrews, in which it certainly *appears* to have that meaning, and which will call for special investigation. Leaving that passage, however, for a moment (which is in ch. ix.), there are various other places where the word διαθήκη is used; and always, it is proper to note, in reference to what was strictly a covenant. In the Epistle to the Hebrews itself, we read once and again of two covenants—an old and a new; the former imperfect in its nature and provisions, and destined to last only till the time of reformation; the latter, founded on better promises, complete in all its arrangements, consequently declared to be everlasting. In like manner, in Gal. iv. 24–31, we have a discourse upon the two covenants, the covenants of law and of promise, as allegorized or typified by the facts and relations of Abraham's family; the term διαθήκαι being used as the common designation of both. Again, in the third chapter of the Second Epistle to the Corinthians, a contrast is drawn between the two covenants—the old and the new—in respect to the points, in which the one differed from, by rising superior to, the other. In this comparison, however, the word διαθήκη is only once used; and our translators, following the vulgate, and the earlier English versions, have rendered it *testament* ("who hath made us able ministers of the New Testament," ver. 6). Such was their regard to those guides, that on one occasion they have even adopted this rendering in connection with a phrase which, in all the other passages where it occurs, has been otherwise translated. The passage is Rev. xi. 19, where the temple presented itself in vision to the prophet, and he saw "the ark of the testament," as we find it rendered, but, as it should rather have been, "the ark of the covenant." In all these cases, there can be no reasonable doubt that, whether referring to the old or to the new things in God's dispensations, the word διαθήκη is to be understood in the ordinary sense of *covenant*. So that if, in the one remaining passage where it occurs, we

should see reason for adopting the sense of *testament,* this would
furnish no ground for altering the translation in the other passages that have been referred to. The less so, indeed, as the
passage in the ninth chapter of Hebrews, as far as regards what
is denoted by διαθήκη, is of a somewhat general nature; it does
not point exclusively, or even specially, to the transactions bearing that name in Scripture, but rather to the nature of διαθῆκαι
generally—what those of Scripture have in common with others.

But let us turn to the passage itself. Commencing with verse
15, for the sake of the connection, it reads thus in the authorised version, " For this cause He (viz. Christ) is the Mediator of
the New Testament, that by means of death, for the redemption
of the transgressions that were under the first testament (διαθήκη
both times), they that are called might receive the promise of
the eternal inheritance. For where a testament is, there must
also of necessity be the death of the testator (ὅπου γὰρ διαθήκη,
θάνατον ἀνάγκη φέρεσθαι τοῦ διαθεμένου). For a testament is of force
after men are dead (ἐπὶ νεκροῖς) ; otherwise, it is of no strength at
all, while the testator liveth (ὅτε ζῇ ὁ διαθεμένος). Whereupon
neither the first (viz. testament) was dedicated without blood."
The meaning obtained by this rendering may be briefly stated
thus : A will does not become valid so long as the person making it is alive; it is a disposition of his affairs proceeding on the
contemplation of his death, and can only take effect when he
has himself ceased to live ; whence also Christ, as the testator of
an inheritance of blessing for His people, must die before the
benefit provided by Him can be reaped. So understood, and
viewed with reference to the practice known to exist among
Greeks and Romans respecting wills, the sense of the passage is
plain enough. The only question is, will the sense obtained suit
the connection, and meet the real circumstances of the case ?
There are, obviously, some apparent incongruities in the way ;`
both at the commencement and at the close. The statement is
brought in to illustrate a certain correspondence between the
preparatory and the final in God's dispensations : Christ is the
Mediator of a new διαθήκη, that by His death He might purchase
redemption for those who could not obtain it by the old ; for
where a διαθήκη is there must of necessity be the death of the
διαθεμένος. But the notion of testament here involves some diffi-

culty; since a mediator, in ordinary circumstances, has nothing
to do with a testament; nor is there any essential link of connection between a mediator and a testator. Then, again, at the
close, where it is said, " Whence the first also—the first διαθήκη
—was not consecrated without blood," it is not death, as of a
testator, but consecration from defilement, that is represented as
constituting the establishment of the earlier διαθήκη. So that
the connection at both ends seems to hang somewhat loosely
with the notion of a testament; and if that notion is here the
correct one, its justification must be sought in some peculiarity
connected, either with the transactions referred to, or with the
point of view from which they are contemplated. It is possible,
that such may be found, when the subject is properly considered.

Meanwhile, it is right to state, that the difficulties are by no
means lessened by resorting to the other translation, and rendering by *covenant*. The late Professor Scholefield, who preferred
this rendering, still found himself so beset with difficulty, that the
passage appeared to him the " most perplexing in the whole of
the New Testament."[1] He would render ver. 16, 17, " For where
a covenant is, there must of necessity be brought in the death of
the mediating [sacrifice]. For, a covenant is valid over dead [viz.
sacrifices]; since it is never of any force while the mediating
[sacrifice] continues alive." Here, we are first of all struck with
the number of ellipses in so short a passage; sacrifice or sacrifices requiring to be supplied no less than three times—to διαθεμένου, in ver. 16, then to ἐπὶ νεκροῖς, in the first part of ver. 17,
and again to διαθεμένος in the second. It is plainly too much;
especially as a transition is made from the singular to the plural,
and back again from the plural to the singular. Sacrifice and
sacrifices were not wont thus to be interchanged in the reality.
Then, to speak of sacrifices as *dead,* is altogether unusual, still
more to put *dead* simply for sacrificial victims; no proper parallel can be produced to justify such a licence. And, finally, the
rendering of διαθέμενος by *mediating sacrifice* is equally unwarranted; when used in regard to covenant transactions, it is so
naturally understood of him who makes the covenant, that, as
Professor Scholefield remarks, a strong nerve should be required

[1] Hints for Some Improvements in the Authorised Version of the New
Testament, p. 142.

for any one, that would be conscious of no difficulty in giving it
a different sense here.   In short, it is an entirely arbitrary translation, and no support can be found for it in the whole range of
Greek literature.   This alone is fatal to the view under consideration ; and when taken along with the objections previously urged,
leaves the matter under this aspect utterly hopeless.

It could serve no end to examine in detail the other modifications of the view, which proceeds on the adoption of *covenant*
for the ˙sense of διαθήκη, and "over dead sacrifices" for ἐπὶ
νεκροῖς.   The same objections substantially, or others equally
valid, apply to each of them.   We revert, therefore, to the apparently natural sense of *testament*, and inquire, whether there
be not some point of view, from which, if the subject be contemplated, a natural and satisfactory vindication may be gained for
it.   This, we are persuaded, is to be found.   The statement, it
will be perceived in this aspect of the matter, proceeds upon
the apprehension of a certain agreement between a covenant
made by God for the good of men, and a will or testament
made by a man in behoof of his heirs.   There are, no doubt,
obvious points of difference between the two ; in this respect
especially, that in a covenant strictly so called, there is something of the nature of a mutual engagement or contract between
the covenanting parties.   This, however, is not the aspect in
which the Divine covenants are contemplated in this portion of
the Epistle to the Hebrews.   From ch. viii. 6, where a formal
comparison begins to be instituted between the New and the Old,
they are viewed in the light of a disposition or arrangement, on
the part of God, for the purpose of securing certain blessings to
His people—imperfectly and provisionally in the Old Covenant,
adequately and finally in the New.   On this account, the *contracting* element in them naturally falls into the back-ground,
and the *beneficiary* or *promissory* alone comes into view ; the
discussion turns upon what God has done and laid up for them
that fear Him, scarcely, if at all, upon what they are taken
bound to do for God.   Now, it is precisely here, that a point of
contact is to be found between a covenant of God and a testament of man ; the very point which led to the adoption of
διαθήκη as the fittest term for expressing the Heb. *berith ;* because
a covenant of God, in this aspect of it, is not, in the ordinary sense,

a συνθήκη or compact, but rather a διαθήκη or disposition, an unfolding of the way and manner in which men may attain to a participation or inheritance in the riches of Divine grace and goodness. It is to this common element, that the apostle points, and on it that he founds this part of his argument for the superiority of the New over the Old. The first, he in effect tells us, *did* contain a disposition from the Lord's hand as to the participation of His riches; but one only provisional and temporary, because of its presenting no proper satisfaction for the sins of the people. It left the guilt of these sins still standing unatoned, in the eye of Divine Justice, and so, if taken simply by itself, it could not provide for men the eternal inheritance which God destines for His people. Christ, who comes actually to provide, and confer on men, a title to this inheritance, must therefore come as the executor of a new διαθήκη, to make good the deficiencies of the Old, and by a valid atonement remove the sins, which continued to lie as a bar across the path to the inheritance. He must (as stated in ver. 15) through His death provide redemption for the transgressions pertaining to the first covenant, that they who had been called under it, as well as those called now, might have the promise of the inheritance made good in their behalf. Thus it comes to pass, that to do here the part of an effective mediator, in establishing a complete and valid covenant, Christ has, at the same time, to do the part of a testator; He must lose the personal possession of His goods, before He can secure for His people a right to participate in them; to enrich them He must, for a time, impoverish Himself—die the death that they (along with Him) may ultimately inherit eternal life. And so, in this fundamental respect, the two ideas of covenant and testament coalesce in the work of Christ; He is at once Mediator and Testator; at one and the same moment He establishes for ever what God pledges Himself in covenant to bestow, and by His voluntary death transmits to others the inheritance of life and blessing wherein it consists. It is, therefore, as true of this Divine διαθήκη, as of any human testament, that it could not be of force till the διαθεμένος had died. Till then the inheritance was bound up indissolubly with His own person; and through His death alone was it set free for others; as was plainly intimated, under a natural image, by our Lord Himself, when He said,

" Verily, verily, I say unto you, Except a corn of wheat fall into
the ground and die, it abideth alone ; but if it die, it bringeth
forth much fruit" (John xii. 24).

When viewed in the light now presented, the allusion of the
inspired writer is very different from what is commonly represented—a mere play upon words.   On the contrary, each word
is retained in its natural and appropriate meaning, while, at the
same time, there appears a strictly logical connection in the argument.   The train of thought proceeds, not upon a fanciful or
fictitious, but upon a real point of coincidence and agreement
between a Divine covenant and a human testament ; hence also,
between Christ the mediator of the covenant, and Christ the
testator of the eternal inheritance ; since it is the great object of
the covenant, whether in its old or its new form, to instate men
in the possession of that inheritance, and the great end of Christ's
work as mediator, to open the way to the possession by His sacrificial death.   With perfect propriety, therefore, might the apostle,
in confirmation of his principle respecting the necessity of an
intervenient death, point back to the offerings of blood at the
ratification of the old covenant, and identify death (as of a testator) with consecration by blood (as through sacrifice).   For as
the old covenant did make a provisional or temporary arrangement for men attaining to the inheritance of life and blessing, it
had in consequence to be ratified by a provisional or typical
death.   The death inflicted there was Christ's death in symbol,
as the blessing inherited was Christ's blessing by anticipation.
But in the passage before us, the typical blood is presented in
the more common aspect of a consecration (ver. 18) ; and, under
that aspect, its necessity and value are set forth, in the verses
that follow, as the one grand medium of access for sinners to the
region of eternal glory.   This simply arose from the two aspects
of death—death as necessary to the participation of the inheritance, and death as necessary to purification from sin—happen-
ing to coalesce in Christ ; so that the same act, which was needed
to secure, and did secure a title to the inheritance, was also
needed to consecrate, and did consecrate, a way to the eternal
inheritance ; and but for the one necessity, the other should
never have existed.   The two ideas, therefore, so far as Christ is
concerned, run into each other ; and as that of consecration was

both the more usual, and the most immediately connected with the great theme of the epistle, the sacred penman quite naturally resumes and prosecutes it—quitting the other, which had been but casually introduced for the sake of confirming a truth, and marking a point of connection between things sacred and common.

Such appears to us the correct interpretation of the passage, and the proper mode of explicating its meaning. The difficulty felt in arriving at this has arisen mainly from overlooking the special ground of the apostle's statement; that is, the common element or point of coincidence between a human testament and a Divine covenant in the particular aspect referred to. Both alike contain a disposition in regard to the joint participation by others of the goods of him who makes it; and a participation that requires, as its indispensable condition, his own subjection to the power of death. We thus obtain a clear and natural sense from the passage, without interfering with the received, which is certainly also the apparent, import of the words.[1] At the same time, while we here vindicate the received translation, we cannot but regard it as somewhat unfortunate, that on the ground of a thought so casually introduced, and a meaning of διαθήκη nowhere else distinctly exhibited in Scripture, many, both of the ancient, and of the more modern theological writers, should have given such prominence to the testamentary aspect of the scheme of redemption. The Cocceian school, to which several of our own older divines belonged, had a sort of predilection for this mode of exhibiting Christ's relation to his people, and thereby gave a somewhat artificial air to their explanations of things connected with the covenant of grace. They were wont to treat formally of the testament, the testator, the executor, the legatees, and the legacies. Such a style of representation, though not altogether unwarranted by Scripture, has yet no broad and comprehensive ground to rest upon there. When salvation is exhibited in connection with a covenant, it is always (with the exception just noticed in Heb. ix. 15–17) covenant in the ordinary sense that

---

[1] The considerations, on which the above explanation is made to turn had not suggested themselves to me when I wrote the article on the Epistle to the Hebrews in the *British and Foreign Evangelical Review* for Sept. 1854. I there adopted substantially Ebrard's view.

is to be understood—a sense, that involves the idea of mutual engagements—individual parts to be fulfilled, and corresponding relations to be maintained—though the place occupied by God is pre-eminently that of a bountiful and gracious benefactor. And to keep attention alive to the strictly covenant aspect of redemption, it had, doubtless, been better to have retained in the authorized version the rendering of *covenant* for διαθήκη in all but the one passage of Hebrews, and to have designated the Bible the Scriptures of the Old and New Covenants, rather than of the Old and New Testaments. In particular, it had been better, in the words connected with the celebration of the Lord's Supper, to have retained the common rendering, and read, " This is the new covenant in My blood ;" since all should thus have readily perceived, that the Lord pointed to the Divine covenant, in its new and better form, as contradistinguished from that which had been brought in by Moses, and which had now reached the end of its appointment. Due pains should be taken to instruct the unlearned, that such *is* the import of the expression, and also to inform them, that while the covenant, as established in His blood, bears the epithet *new*, it is so designated merely from respect to the order of exhibition ; while, if viewed with respect to the mind and purpose of God, this is the first as well as the last—the covenant, which was planned in the counsels of eternity to retrieve the ruin of the fall, and out of the depths of perdition to raise up a spiritual and blessed offspring for God.

SECTION EIGHTH.

ON THE IMPORT OF CERTAIN TERMS EMPLOYED IN NEW TESTA-
MENT SCRIPTURE TO INDICATE THE NATURE AND EXTENT
OF THE RENOVATION TO BE ACCOMPLISHED THROUGH THE
GOSPEL ; μετάνοια, παλιγγενεσία, ἀνακαίνωσις, ἀποκατάστασις.

THE mission of the Lord Jesus Christ, and the institution consequent on it of His spiritual kingdom, have for their object the accomplishment of a great and comprehensive renovation.

And in addition to such expressions as βασιλεία τοῦ Θεοῦ, ἡ καινὴ διαθήκη, which, in different respects, indicate the design and character of the change to be introduced, and which have already been considered, there is a class of expressions pointing also to the change in question, but with a more special respect to its renovating character. There are altogether four of these terms, which, while they form a sort of whole, must yet be considered separately, in order to obtain a correct idea, both of their distinctive meanings, and of the relation in which they stand to each other.

I. The first in order of the terms referred to is μετάνοια, which need not detain us long. The verb meets us at the very threshold of the Gospel, in the Baptist's call of preparation for the kingdom—μετανοεῖτε—which was afterwards also taken up by our Lord. The first and most immediate change, which was required of men in expectation of the Lord's appearance and kingdom, was an altered state of thought and purpose in regard to things spiritual and divine; and, to impress the necessity of this more deeply upon the minds of all, the call to enter into it was coupled with an administration of baptism—a baptism εἰς μετάνοιαν. Even after the personal ministry of Christ was finished, and He had left the work to be prosecuted among men by his apostles, the call was still the same; μετανοήσατε καὶ βαπτισθήτω was the closing and practical point of St Peter's address to the multitudes on the day of Pentecost; and in St Paul's brief summary of the Gospel he everywhere preached the first article named is τὴν εἰς Θεὸν μετάνοιαν (Acts xx. 21). In all these passages, it is μετάνοια or the cognate verb, which is employed, not μεταμέλεια and μεταμέλομαι; and this, no doubt, because the former more significantly and correctly indicated the change intended than the latter. Both, indeed, by etymology and usage μετάνοια points more to the change itself in thought and purpose, while μεταμέλεια fixes attention chiefly on the concern or regret, which the consideration of the past has awakened. Of itself, μετάνοια expresses nothing as to the nature of the change, in what particular direction taken, or how far in that direction carried; this is left to be determined by the connection, from the nature of the case. In the New Testament it is always used in a good sense, and in reference to a sincere practical reforma-

tion of mind and conduct. Not this, however, in the aspect of
a change wrought by the power of God, but rather in its relation
to human responsibilities, as an amendment that men are bound
to aim at and strive after ; hence the verb is used in the imperative ; the thing to be done is bound as an obligation upon men's
consciences. The other verb, μεταμέλομαι, is never so used—the
thought it expresses being a matter of suffering rather than of
action, the recoil of feeling or inward sorrow and dissatisfaction
which rushes upon the soul's consciousness, when a past course
of transgression is seen in its true light. Whenever the μετάνοια
is of the right description, there will always, of necessity, be
something of this sort ; since it is impossible for the mind to turn
from the love and practice of sin, to even the heartfelt desire
after righteousness, without a certain degree of sorrow and remorse. But, from the varieties that exist in human temperaments,
and the diversified effects apt to be produced by the circumstances
of life, no definite measure or uniform rule can be laid down in
this respect; there may be considerably less of such conscious
and painful regret in some cases than in others, where the
change is alike genuine; and there may also be a good deal of
it where there is no actual μετάνοια—the recoil of feeling passing
away without leading to any permanent result. Accordingly, it
is not the μεταμέλεια, but the μετάνοια, which is indispensably
required of those who would find a place in the Messiah's kingdom—a μετάνοια, as is expressed in 2 Cor. vii. 10, εἰς σωτηρίαν ἀμε-
ταμέλητος, a repentance unto salvation not to be repented of.

The word *repentance*, however, as is evident from the preceding
remarks, is but an imperfect synonym for μετάνοια ; it does not
sufficiently distinguish between this and μεταμέλεια in the respects
wherein they differ, but gives a partial indication of the import
of both. As commonly understood, it points fully as much to the
sorrow or regret which ensues upon a proper change of mind, as
to the change itself. Yet we have no other word that can fitly
take its place; for, though *reformation* or *amendment* may seem
more closely to correspond with the original, and have been formally proposed as a better rendering, they carry the thoughts too
much outward to meet with general approval as a substitute for
repentance. It is the excellence of this last, as a translation of
μετάνοια, that however otherwise defective, it points inward, and

marks the state of the soul—not merely of the outward behaviour
—as different from what it formerly was : it is expressive of a
changed action of the *heart* in respect to sin and holiness; only it
leaves the action in a state of incompleteness, as if it had respect
merely to the evil perceived to have existed in the past. It is
right, however, as far as it goes. He who repents has come to
see that to be evil which he previously loved and followed as good ;
and it is only necessary to think of this altered bent of mind, as
taking a direction toward the future equally with the past, in
order to find in the term *repentance,* which is used to express
it, a fair representation of the New Testament μετάνοια.

The call to this μετάνοια, as necessary for admission into the
Messiah's kingdom, proceeds on the existence of a state of alienation and disorder in respect to the things of God ; it implies, that
the νοήματα, the thoughts and intents of the mind, have gone in
the wrong direction, and must be turned back upon the right
objects. As a people, the Jews were in such a state when the
call was originally addressed to them ; and, notwithstanding the
call, they, for the most part, continued to abide in it. In respect
to the state itself, however, there was nothing singular in their
case ; the same alienation of heart belongs naturally to every individual, and the spiritual change, or conversion, which consists
in its abandonment, is the one door-way for all into the kingdom.
The great question—when once the heart has begun to grapple
in earnest with the Divine call—is how the change is to be
effected ? It is man's duty and interest to have it done; for, till
it *is* done, he is an enemy of God, a child of perdition ; and to
bestir himself to the task of reformation is his immediate and
paramount concern. But if in reality he does so, he will presently find that other powers than his own are needed for the end
in view; he can himself see the necessity for the change, can
think with sorrow and remorse of the errors of the past, can
anticipate with dread the dangers of the future, can wish and pray
that it were otherwise with him—but nothing comes to perfection,
unless the effort to convert bring the soul into contact with the
regenerating grace of God, and make it conscious of a vital
influence from above.

II. It is this second, but most important stage in the process,

X

that is marked in the next term—παλιγγενεσία, or regeneration. Considered doctrinally, either of these terms might be made to include the other, and the one or the other might indifferently be put first. Regeneration might be represented as necessary to conversion, and determining what belongs to it; since it is only when the Divine element implied in regeneration works upon the soul, that the conversion it undergoes is sufficiently deep and earnest to be lasting. On the other hand, conversion, if viewed in its entire compass and perfected results, must be made to comprehend, as well the regenerating grace that effects the change, as the desires and struggles of the soul, while travailing in birth for its accomplishment. But, viewed in the order of nature, and also as commonly represented in Scripture, the μετάνοια, or conversion, must be placed first; for it is with this that man's responsibilities have immediately to do : and it is in addressing himself to the things connected with it, that he is driven out of himself, and brought to surrender himself to the working of that Divine power on which he depends for the necessary result. Scripture never puts regeneration, or what is implied in regeneration, before conversion ; but it does press the work of conversion, as in some sense prior to the possession of a regenerated state :—as in the original call of the Baptist to repent, or be converted, that men might be prepared for the baptism of the Spirit ; or in St Peter's address to the inhabitants of Jerusalem, exhorting them to convert and be baptized, that they might receive the gift of the Spirit. Of course, when so represented, conversion is to be understood as spoken of only in respect to its initial stages, and as a work demanding men's earnest application ; in which respect it may be said to " precede regeneration, and to be the condition and qualification for it ;"[1]—if by condition and qualification we understand simply that without which, on the sinner's part, he has no valid reason to expect the further and higher good implied in regeneration. And there is undoubtedly this further difference implied in the terms themselves, that, while conversion is a change of mind which, so far as the mind that experiences it is concerned may possibly change again, regeneration is a change of state, *a new being*—and so, we may say, carries the idea of fixedness and perpetuity in its bosom.

[1] Mozley on Baptismal Regeneration, p. 58.

The term itself παλιγγενεσία, which exactly answers to our *re-generation*, is found only twice in the New Testament (Matt. xix. 28 ; Titus iii. 5), and in the second alone of the two cases, has it respect to spiritual renovation. There are, however, various other expressions which are employed to indicate the same thing. In point of time, the first was that used by our Lord in His conversation with Nicodemus—one also of the most explicit—in which He declared the necessity for every one who would enter His kingdom, of being born again. Ἄνωθεν γεννηθῆναι is the expression used, and is most exactly rendered, perhaps, *born afresh*—but obviously all one as to meaning with πάλιν γεννηθῆναι or γίνεσθαι; for both alike indicate a kind of starting anew into being, or re-entering upon life, in some new and higher sense. In the explanations given immediately after by our Lord, it is connected with water and the Spirit—with the Spirit alone, however, as the effective agent; for He calls it "a birth of the Spirit," as contradistinguished from a birth of the flesh (ver. 6); and, after referring for illustration to the somewhat similar operation of the wind in nature, He sums up by saying, "So is every one that is born of the Spirit" (ver. 8.) The Evangelist John himself, in ch. i. 13, says of all genuine believers, ἐκ Θεοῦ ἐγεννήθησαν, they were born of God, and that in a manner different from every form of natural generation. So again in his first Epistle, ch. v. 4, the believer, on account of his faith, is "born of God." In 1 Pet. i. 23, and Jas. i. 18, the new birth is asserted equally of all Christians, and ascribed directly to God, but connected instrumentally with the operation of the word (διὰ λόγου, or λόγῳ ἀληθείας). So, still further, St Paul, who not only designates believers once and again " new creatures" (2 Cor. v. 17 ; Gal. vi. 15); but in the passage already referred to, Titus iii. 5, characterises the change that passes on them, when they become true Christians, as a regeneration. The whole passage runs thus, " After that the kindness and love toward man (φιλανθρωπία) of our Saviour God (τοῦ σωτῆρος ἡμῶν Θεοῦ) appeared ; not by works of righteousness which we did (ἐποιήσαμεν), but according to His mercy He saved us— διὰ λουτροῦ παλιγγενεσίας καὶ ἀνακαινώσεως πνεύματος ἁγίου—through washing (or laver) of regeneration and renewing of the Holy Ghost."

The whole of these passages describe in terms substantially

alike, the spiritual change which passes over those who become
Christ's true people; differing only in connecting it, some more
immediately with the word, understood and received in faith,
others with the baptismal font or water. As this connection
can only be of a subordinate and instrumental kind, it does not
affect the nature of the thing itself, which must be determined
by the plain import of the language employed concerning it.
But the language, in its plain import, undoubtedly expresses an
actual change—a new birth; not the mere capacity for such, but
its realised possession. Were this παλιγγενεσία anything short of
a work of God, brought into actual existence in the case of the
person who is the subject of it, the term would be an entire mis-
nomer, such as we cannot conceive to have a place in the volume
of inspiration. But this becomes still more certain, and is established beyond all reasonable doubt, when along with the natural
import of the language we couple what is said of those, who have
undergone the regenerating change. " He that is born of God,"
says the Apostle John, " doth not commit sin, for his seed re-
maineth in him, and he cannot sin because he is born of God."
And, he adds, " in this the children of God are manifest, and the
children of the devil; whosoever doeth not righteousness is not
of God." (1 John iii. 9, 10.) In like manner St Paul describes
the sons of God as those, who are led by the Spirit of God, and
declares that if any have not this Spirit they are none of His
(Rom. viii. 9, 14.) Not only so, but he characterises them, on
the ground of their regeneration, as dead to sin, risen again with
Christ to walk in newness of life, and already sitting together
with Him in heavenly places (Rom. vi. 4 ; Eph. ii. 6 ; Col. ii. 12).
The apostles of our Lord can no longer be regarded as persons,
who used great plainness of speech, or even gave intelligible
utterance to their thoughts, if such expressions were employed
by them to denote anything else than an actual change from death
to life, from sin to holiness ;—if nothing more was meant, for example, than the bestowal of some mysterious gift or capacity,
which might be held by the worst in common with the best of
men—by one who continues practically a child of the devil, as
well as by him who breathes the spirit and does the works of a
child of God. " Such a monstrous perversion of language,"
it has been justly said, " would never approve itself to any one,

who did not come to this subject with his mind pre-occupied with a particular view.   But it is in vain, that Scripture is plain and express to the effect, that the Divine gift of regeneration *is* actual holiness, so long as men are pre-occupied with an idea, that actual holiness *cannot* be a Divine gift.   They will go on to the last, not seeing the plainest assertions of Scripture as to the nature of regeneration."[1]

It can serve no good purpose, therefore, to dwell longer on this aspect of the matter; since exegetical efforts must be altogether misspent in endeavouring to impart light to those, who cannot afford to see.   But in regard to the point of the instrumental relationship of regeneration to the Divine ordinances, we may remark, that while it is specially and frequently connected with baptism, it is not connected with that ordinance alone; the Word of God equally shares in the honour.   It is not to be denied, that when our Lord speaks of being born of water and spirit, and when St Paul couples the laver with regeneration, and represents believers as being buried and rising again with Christ, a close relationship is established between Christian baptism and spiritual regeneration.   But there are other passages referred to above, which equally connect it with the word of the Gospel, of which also it is said generally, that it is " the power of God to salvation to every one that believeth"—that it is " quick, powerful, and sharper than a two-edged sword"—that it is even " spirit and life." Nothing stronger than this is said of baptism in respect to regeneration ; so that the relationship of baptism to the spiritual change is by no means exclusive ; and as the change itself is inward and vital, neither baptism nor the word can have more than a subordinate and instrumental relation to it.   As to efficacious power it is " the spirit that quickeneth,"—not, however, apart from the ordinances, but in connection with their instrumentality ; nor yet by indissoluble union and invariable efficiency through these, but in such manner and ways as seem good to Him, who quickeneth whom He will.   It is enough for us to know, that in this spiritual birth, as in the natural, the internal links itself with the external, the Divine with the human ; so that if the word is honestly handled, and the sacrament of baptism believingly received and used, the spiritual effect will infallibly

[1] Mozley on Baptismal Regeneration, pp. 29, 30.

result. When so received and used baptism saves, and the baptised are regenerated, because the manifested grace of God meets with a suitable recipiency, on the part of man ; as also the word of truth brings salvation, quickens and renews, when its promises of grace and blessing are rested on in humble faith. But abstract the supposition, which is commonly made in Scripture, of this faithful and honest dealing with these ordinances of God, and there is nothing of regenerative power or saving effect in either ; the hearer of the word only treasures up for himself a heavier condemnation, and the baptised, so far from rising to newness of life, remains, even when baptised by an apostle, in " the gall of bitterness and the bond of iniquity."

There is, doubtless, so far a difference in the scriptural statements referred to, as to the relation in which baptism and the word respectively stand to regeneration, that the former, being a symbolical and sealing ordinance, it more distinctly and personally exhibits the things connected with the soul's regeneration. It has somewhat of the nature of a covenant transaction, in which the individual presents himself, or is presented by others, for a personal participation in the regenerating grace exhibited in the ordinance ; and personally, or through others for him, professes to accept what is there offered to his hand, and engages to act accordingly. Contemplating the matter, therefore, as an honest transaction—a transaction in which the human subject seems truthfully to respond to the Divine condescension and favour shown him—our Lord and His apostles represent baptism as, according to its true idea, an instrument or channel of regeneration, and speak of those as regenerate persons, who have in sincerity, complied with it. But that is a very different thing from saying, that baptism, simply as an ordinance, carries regeneration in its bosom, or that all who have passed through the outward rite are regenerate. Such language is in Scripture applied only to those who have actually been born of the Spirit, or who, in the judgment of faith and charity, may be considered to have been so born again. And precisely on account of regeneration being thus essentially a Divine work, in which man, as a spiritual being, has to be the recipient, through the grace of the Spirit operating vitally within, it is not directly laid as an obligation upon his conscience. He is entreated and bound to do the things, which, in their full compass, involve it, and which also bring him into immediate contact with the living agency that works it; but for the change itself—the actual regeneration of his soul to God—he must be a partaker and not a doer, become a subject of the Spirit's renewing grace.

III. This interconnection, however, between the human and the Divine, as directly related to men's responsibilities, comes out in the next term of the series, ἀνακαίνωσις, which is occasionally, though not very frequently, used in New Testament Scripture. In the passage cited from the Epistle to Titus, it is coupled with παλιγγενεσία, and placed after it, as denoting something consecutive—a carrying forward of the regeneration to its proper completion; which again brings us into the region of human responsibility and active working. For, while it belongs to God, through the internal agency of His Spirit, to implant the principle of divine life in the soul, it belongs to man—not independently, indeed, and as at his own hand, but in connection with the promised grace of God—to guard, and nourish to perfection the gift conferred upon him. Hence this ἀνακαίνωσις is matter of express command; for example, in Eph. iv. 23, where the apostle charges believers—who had already " been taught as the truth is in Jesus"—to " renew themselves (ἀνανεοῦσθαι) in the spirit of their mind;" and in Rom. xii. 2, they are called to be transformed, or to transform themselves, in the renewing of their mind (τῇ ἀνακαινώσει τοῦ νοός). This growing renewal of mind and spirit, which is only rendered possible by a preceding regeneration, it is the imperative duty of every believer to press forward; it should be the object of his daily watchings, strivings, and prayers, which, if rightly directed, shall have for their great end his progressive advancement in the divine life, and assimilation to the image of his Father in heaven.

We have here to note the manner in which the new life of Christianity has formed for itself a language, to give adequate expression to the thoughts and aspirations it has awakened. Of the two words just mentioned, one of them ἀνακαίνωσις, is found only in the New Testament, as is also the verb ἀνακαινόω. The classical word for expressing a somewhat similar action of mind, was ἀνακαινίζω, which occurs in Heb. vi. 6, but is found nowhere

else in the New Testament.   It was, we may conceive, felt to be
too feeble, or, from its ordinary application, indicative of too
partial and defective an improvement, to bring out the Christian
sense that was meant to be conveyed; and so a distinct word, of
the same root, but with a different termination, was brought into
requisition.   The other word, παλιγγενεσία, was, indeed, employed
by heathen writers, but in a sense so inferior, that it may be said
to have become instinct with new meaning, when turned in a
Christian direction.   As employed elsewhere, it expresses such
renovations as take place, from time to time, within the natural
sphere, and on the same line of things with itself.   Thus Cicero,
on the close of his exile, and referring to his restoration to honour
and dignity, speaks of hanc παλιγγενεσίαν nostram (Ad Attic vi.
6).   In like manner, Josephus applies the word to that political
resuscitation, which was granted to his people and country, on
the return from the Babylonish captivity (Ant. xi. 3, 9).   Mar-
cus Antoninus and the Stoics generally designated the revivals,
which, at shorter or longer intervals, occur in the constitution and
order of earthly things, and which they believed would ultimately become fixed, τὴν περιοδικὴν παλιγγενεσίαν τῶν ὅλων, the periodical regeneration of the world.   And approaching a step nearer,
though basing itself on a fanciful foundation, it was the doctrine
of the Pythagoreans, as we learn from Plutarch (De Em. Cat.
i. 7)—part of their general doctrine of the transmigration of
souls—that there was a παλιγγενεσία to each particular person
when his soul returned to the body, and again made its appearance on the theatre of an earthly existence.   From such applications of the word, one sees at a glance what an elevation was
given to it when it entered into the sphere of Christian ideas,
and came to denote that high *moral* renovation, which Christ
ever seeks to accomplish in His people—the formation in them
of a life fashioned after the life of God.   Here we find ourselves
in another region than that of nature's feebleness and corruption;
the supernatural mingles with the natural; and the earthly in
man's being is transformed, so as to receive the tone and impress
of the heavenly.

But the παλιγγενεσία of the Gospel, and its attendant ἀνακαινώ-
σις, do not stop here; while commencing with the soul of the
individual believer, they thenceforth proceed to other operations

and results. The internal renovation is but the beginning of a process, which is to extend far and wide—to spread with regenerating power through all the relations and departments of social life—to defecate and transfigure the corporeal frame itself into the fit habitation of an immortal spirit—yea, and embrace the whole domain of external nature, which it will invest with the imperishable glory of a new creation. It was this more extended and comprehensive application of the word παλιγγενεσία, which was made by our Lord in Matt. xix. 28, when He gave assurance to the disciples of the immortal honour and dignity that was to be their position in the closing issues of His kingdom, " Verily, I say unto you, that ye who have followed Me, in the regeneration (παλιγγενεσία)—when the Son of Man shall sit on the throne of His glory, ye also shall sit upon twelve thrones, judging the twelve tribes of Israel." It was a prevalent opinion among the Fathers, that by *regeneration* here, our Lord pointed explicitly to the resurrection of the body. Thus Augustine, De Civ. Dei. xx. 5, " When he says, *in the regeneration*, beyond doubt He wishes to be understood thereby the resurrection from the dead ; for thus shall our flesh be regenerated through incorruption, even as our soul has been regenerated by faith." To the like effect Jerome, who says on the passage, " *In the regeneration*, that is, when the dead shall rise incorruptible from corruption." Gregory, Theophylact, Euthymius, and others, follow in the same line. It is, however, too narrow a reference to give to our Lord's words. The resurrection of the body is, doubtless, implied in what He says ; for when the Son of Man sits upon the throne of His glory, or is manifested in His kingly state, the saints shall certainly have been raised up to sit with Him ; according to the testimony of the apostle, " When Christ, who is our life, shall appear, then shall we also appear with Him in glory." Undoubtedly, too, the resurrection may be fitly designated a regeneration ; as it shall be in the most emphatic sense a renovating of the old, casting it entirely into a fresh mould, and giving it a kind of second birth, unspeakably better than the first. So, the Apostle Paul in effect, though not in express terms, calls it, when in Rom. viii. 23, he speaks of the general body of believers groaning in themselves, and " waiting for the adoption, the redemption of the body ;" as if their proper filia-

tion only began then, and not till it took place did they fairly
enter into the state and heritage of the sons of God. Then only
indeed shall they reach it in its completeness, or in respect to
their entire personality. The regeneration is already theirs; it
is theirs from the first moment of their spiritual life, in so far as
their souls are concerned, but still only as in a mystery; since
the corporeal and visible part of their natures continues as before, in the frailty and corruption of the fall. At the resurrection, however, this anomalous state of things shall be terminated;
the old man shall in this respect also be exchanged for the new;
and the children of the regeneration shall at last look like their
state and destiny—they shall possess the visible seal of their
adoption, in the redemption of their bodies from the law of mor-
tality and corruption.

On these accounts, the resurrection of the body may fitly be
called a παλιγγενεσία; it is certainly to be included in the general
renovation, which the Lord will introduce at the proper time;
but it is this general renovation itself, not simply the resurrection
of the body, which is to be understood as pointed to in the declaration of our Lord. The παλιγγενεσία there mentioned is the
bringing in of what is elsewhere called the new heavens and the
new earth, the constitution of every thing after a new and higher
pattern; in consequence of which, that which is in part shall be
done away, evil in every form shall be abolished, and universal
peace, harmony, and perfection established. For, such is the
proper issue and consummation of Christ's work, who, as the
Lord's anointed, has received from the Father the heritage of
all things, and received it, not to retain them in their state of
corruption and disorder, but to rectify and bless them; so that,
throughout the entire domain, there shall be nothing to hurt
and offend, and all shall reflect the spotless glory of its Divine
Head.

IV. The regeneration in this large and general sense is much
of the same import as another word—the last we have to notice
in this connection—ἀποκατάστασις. The noun occurs, indeed,
only once with reference to the work of Christ (Acts iii. 21);
but the verb is found, on two occasions, with a somewhat similar
reference. In Matt. xvii. 11, our Lord replied to a question re-

specting Elias, " Elias indeed cometh and restoreth (or shall restore—ἀποκαθιστανει, Mark; ἀποκαταστήσει, Matt.) all things." It was the purpose or destination for which John came that Christ here speaks of; His mission was of a restorative nature, being appointed in respect to a people, who had gone away backward, and were practically in a state of alienation, first from the God of their fathers, and then from these fathers themselves. To turn again this tide of degeneracy, and bring the hearts of the people into a friendly relationship as well to God, as to their pious ancestors, was the special calling of this new Elias; he came to the intent, that He might restore all things to their normal state of allegiance to God, and mutual respondency between parent and child (Luke i. 16, 17).   But in respect to the event, all was marred by the perverseness and carnality of the people; they frustrated the grace of God, and did to the Elias " whatever they listed."   In this case, it was plainly but a provisional moral restoration that was meant to be accomplished; but even this was arrested in its course, and only in a very partial manner reached its end.

Still more immediately, however, in connection with Messiah's work, we find the expression used by the apostles after the resurrection, when they asked Christ, " Lord dost Thou at this time restore the kingdom to Israel (εἰ ἐν τῷ χρόνῳ τούτῳ ἀποκαθιστάνεις τὴν βασιλείαν τῷ 'Ισραήλ)? The answer returned simply conveyed a rebuke for their too prying curiosity regarding the future, and an instruction as to present duty : " It is not for you to know the times and seasons, which the Father has put in His own power; but ye shall receive power, when the Holy Ghost comes upon you," etc. In short, there was to be no ἀποκατάστασις such as they were looking for, of a present resuscitation of the temporal kingdom ; and for themselves, they had other and higher things to mind, for which the needed power was shortly to be conferred on them from above. They were not on this account, however, discharged from expecting an ἀποκατάστασις,— only it was to be one (as they themselves soon understood), which carried in its bosom the elements of a nobler renovation— fresh successions of spiritual revival in the first instance, and these culminating at last, in a complete, final restitution. So, in a comparatively brief period, the Apostle Peter gave expression to his views, and showed the vast moral elevation that had been imparted to him by the descent of the Spirit : "Repent, therefore, and be converted, that your sins may be blotted out, so that times of refreshing may come (ὅπως ἂν ἔλθωσιν καιροὶ ἀναψύξεως) from the presence of the Lord ; and He may send Jesus Christ that before was preached unto you ; whom the heaven must receive until the times of restitution of all things (ἀποκαταστάσεως πάντων), of which (of which times) God spake by the mouth of His holy prophets, since the world began (or, from the earliest times)."

The slightest inspection may convince any one, that this was spoken under the direction of a far more enlightened and elevating impulse, than that which dictated the question, " Wilt Thou at this time restore the kingdom to Israel ?"   In the one case there is a manifest savouring of the things of the flesh, in the other, of those of the Spirit ; the first thoughts were characterised by a narrow exclusiveness, and a desire for some sort of temporal ascendency, while in the latter there is a noble breathing after things heavenly and divine, a just appreciation of the spiritual in comparison of the earthly, and a lively expectation of the complete triumph over all evil yet to be effected by the presence and power of the glorified Redeemer.   The ἀποκατάστασις now looked and longed for by the apostles was nothing short of a general and thorough renovation—the same, that prophets had from the first been heralding, when they pointed to the glory which was to follow the obedience and sufferings of the Redeemer—a re-establishment of the original order and blessedness of the world, or its final deliverance from all the troubles and disorders that afflict it, and along therewith its elevation to a higher even than its primeval condition.   But the general carries no antagonism to the particular ; the restitution of all things now hoped for should also be, in the truest sense, the restitution of the kingdom to Israel.   For, in Christ all that is really Israel's, finds its proper centre and its ultimate destination ; where He, the King of Zion is, there is Israel's ascendency, Israel's seed of blessing, Israel's distinctive glory ; and the best and highest thing for Jew and Gentile alike is to share in the dominion of Christ, and with Him to possess the kingdom.

To sum up, then, in regard to this series of words so peculiarly indicative, as a whole, of the nature and tendency of the Gospel of Christ:—The generic idea of renovation, or radical change from a worse to a better state, is here presented to our view under successive stages and developments. We see it beginning in the region of the inner man—in the awakening of a sense of guilt and danger, with earnest strivings after amendment (μετά-νοια); then, through the operation of the grace of God, it discovers itself in a regenerated frame of spirit, the possession of an essentially new spiritual condition (παλιγγενεσία); this, once found, proceeds by continual advances and fresh efforts to higher and higher degrees of spiritual renovation (ἀνακαίνωσις); while, according to the gracious plan and wise disposal of God, the internal links itself to the external, the renovation of soul paves the way for the purification of nature, until, the work of grace being finished, and the number of the elect completed, the bodies also of the saints shall be transformed, and the whole material creation shall become a fit habitation for redeemed and glorified saints (ἀπακατάστασις). What a large and divine-like grasp in this regenerative scheme! How unlike the littleness and superficiality of man! How clearly bespeaking the profound insight and far-reaching wisdom of God! And this, not merely in its ultimate results, but in the method also and order of its procedure! In beginning with the inner man, and laying the chief stress on a regenerated heart, it takes possession of the fountainhead of evil, and rectifies that which most of all requires the operation of a renewing agency. As in the moral sphere, the evil had its commencement, so in the same sphere are the roots planted of all the renovation, that is to develop itself in the history of the kingdom. And the spiritual work once properly accomplished, all that remains to be done shall follow in due time; Satan shall be finally cast out; and on the ruins of his usurped dominion, the glories of the new creation shall shine forth in their eternal lustre.

SECTION NINTH.

ON THE USE OF *Paraskeuê* AND *Pascha* IN ST JOHN'S ACCOUNT
OF OUR LORD'S LAST SUFFERINGS ; AND THE QUESTION
THEREWITH CONNECTED, WHETHER OUR LORD KEPT HIS
LAST PASSOVER ON THE SAME DAY AS THE JEWS.

IT is simply in connection with this question respecting the
time of keeping the last Passover, that the use of the words
παρασκευή and πάσχα, by St John, in ch. xviii. and xix., is involved
in doubt, or assumes an aspect of importance. And, as we are
firmly persuaded that the question itself has mainly arisen from
some of the historical circumstances being too little regarded, we
shall commence our inquiry by taking these in their order, and
endeavouring to present them in their proper light.

1. The first thing requiring to be noted is the determined purpose formed by the leading men in Jerusalem to make away with
Jesus. The clear revelations He had given, especially on the
occasion of this last visit to Jerusalem, of His own character and
kingdom, and the unsparing exposure He had made of their
ignorance, carnality, and deserved condemnation, had brought
matters, as between them and Him, to a crisis. It was now seen
that, if their authority was to stand, His career must be extinguished. But, in their project for accomplishing this, two points
of special moment are to be noted. In the first place, it was to
be by stratagem (ἐν δόλῳ, Matt. xxvi. 4 ; Mark xiv. 1)—this being,
as they naturally conceived, the only safe course for them to adopt.
They durst not venture on an open assault, as Jesus had evidently
acquired great fame, had come up to the feast with a large retinue
of followers, and by His miracles, His discourses, and His dis-
interested life, had made profound impressions upon many hearts.
Against such a person it would have been a hazardous thing for
them to bring a formal charge of impiety or crime ; it were on
every account wiser to compass their design by the hand of an
assassin, or some secret plot, which might admit of their remaining
in the background. Then, this stratagem was not to be quite

immediately put in force ; not till after the feast. This is expressly noticed in two of the Evangelists (Matt. xxvi. 5 ; Mark
xiv. 2) ; and they both assign the same reason for the delay—
"lest there should be an uproar among the people." These
seemed now to an alarming degree won to His side; they had
attended Him in crowds from Galilee ; they had even borne Him
in triumph, and with every demonstration of enthusiastic joy, as
King Messiah, from Mount Olivet into the heart of the city ; and
it was not to be supposed that multitudes, apparently so full of
confidence in their leader, and so ardently devoted to His cause,
would suffer Him to be openly wronged, without exerting themselves to the utmost in His defence. It was, therefore, the obvious
dictate of prudence to let the crowds again disperse, before the
hand of violence was lifted against Jesus.

2. But all of a sudden a new element came into their deliberations, and their policy took another form, when the treachery of
Judas discovered itself, offering for a sum of money to deliver up
Jesus into their hands. The precise moment when Judas made
this offer to them is not stated. It must, however, have been
sometime between the conclusion of those discourses, in which the
Lord had so plainly exposed and denounced the leading Jews,
and the actual execution of the treachery ; for it is manifest that
the traitor had come to terms with them before the paschal feast
had actually begun, and yet not less manifest that it must have
been after they had formed their plan not to proceed against Jesus
till the feast was over. Subsequently to this resolution on their
part, but prior even to the assignation of any particular time or
place for the accomplishment of the purpose, " he sought how he
might conveniently betray Him" (Mark xiv. 11). The purpose
itself doubtless took shape in the mind of Judas, and reached the
point of action, much in the same way that the Jewish rulers
were led to their resolution to kill Him. From the position
matters had now assumed, it had become for both alike a necessity to get rid of Jesus : His presence was felt to be intolerable.
Indeed, Judas, in his state of mind and his procedure toward
Jesus, might be taken for a representative among the twelve of
those Jewish rulers ; he did within the narrower sphere what they
did in the larger one—delivered up the Holy One of God to His
adversaries ; on which account, in the psalms that spake before

concerning the treachery, the individual traitor is identified with
the whole company of faithless men who were to take the part of
violence and deceit (Ps. lxix., cix.; Acts i. 16–20). Judas had
undoubtedly, at the time of his first connection with Christ, been
known as a person of shrewd intellect, as well as respectable de-
meanour, most probably also as a person of active business habits :
—whence the charge naturally fell to him of managing the
pecuniary concerns of the company, of bearing the purse. With
such natural gifts and acquired habits, he had thought he dis-
cerned enough in Jesus of Nazareth to convince him that this
could be no other than the expected Messiah ; but, beyond doubt,
the Messiah of an earthly cause and a worldly kingdom. And
as the hopes of advancement in this direction began to give way ;
as the plan of Jesus more fully developed itself, and successive
revelations of coming events forced on the mind of Judas the
conviction, that not earthly grandeur or political ascendency, but
sacrifice, self-denial, peril, and shame, were to be the immediate
portion of those who espoused the cause of Jesus, then the spell
was broken to his calculating and worldly spirit. He not only
became depressed and sorrowful, like the others, but totally un-
hinged : his only distinct motives for embarking in the enterprise
were withdrawn from him ; he must be done with the concern.
Symptoms of this recoil had been perceived by the penetrating
eye of Jesus about a twelvemonth before the last Passover, which
led Him to utter the strong expression, that of those He had
chosen one was a devil (John vi. 70). It was only now, however,
that the full effect was produced. The repeated intimations which
Jesus had recently made of His coming death, the specific assurance that He was to be rejected by the chief priests and scribes,
crucified and slain ; the palpable breach that took place between
Him and these rulers of the people on the occasion of His public
entrance into Jerusalem, with the discourses subsequently delivered ; still more recently the reproof individually and pointedly
addressed to Judas, in connection with the personal anointing at
Bethany, and the fresh allusion then also made to His impending
death and burial:—All these following in rapid succession, and
leaving, at length, no room to doubt that a catastrophe was at
hand, consummated the process which had been going on in the
mind of Judas, and impelled him to adopt a course of decisive

action—to resolve on being done with a service which no longer possessed his sympathy or his confidence, and make sure of his interest with those that had. Thus prompted and drawn, he secretly threw himself into the camp of the adversaries, and entered into terms with them for the betrayal of Jesus.[1]

3. But this unexpected occurrence, we may well conceive, cast a new light upon the prospects of Christ's adversaries in Jerusalem, and naturally led to a remodelling of their plans. The discovery that one of His bosom friends was deserting Him, as if he had seen through the imposture, and was even proffering his aid to the accomplishment of their aims, could not fail to beget the conviction, that the cause of Jesus was by no means so powerful, nor His place in the popular esteem so firmly seated, as they had imagined. They now began to think that there was not so much need for stratagem and delay, as they at first imagined; nay, that their best chance for accomplishing the desired result, was by a bold and summary procedure. Most heartily, therefore, did they close with the proposal of Judas, and for the stipulated sum of thirty pieces of silver, agree to act in concert with him. This circumstance, if allowed its due consideration, and followed to its legitimate results, will be found sufficient to account for all the peculiarities and apparent inconsistencies in the evangelical narratives. It first of all led the Jewish rulers to resolve on taking action immediately, the moment Judas might find a favourable opportunity for effecting the betrayal. And it led our Lord, who was perfectly cognizant of what was proceeding in the camp of the enemies, to pursue a course at the very commencement of the Passover, which left Judas no alternative: he must either act promptly that very night, or lose the opportunity of acting at all.

4. This procedure, then, on the part of Christ, is the point that next calls for notice. In compliance with His own instructions, the necessary preparations had been made for holding the feast—an upper chamber was engaged, and the materials requi-

---

[1] It is most likely, on account of the influence exercised on the mind of Judas by what took place at Bethany, that the Evangelists Matthew and Mark mention it in immediate connection with the purpose of Judas to betray. In reality, however, it occurred before several of the last discourses were delivered, and six days previous to the last Passover, John xii. 1.

site for the feast provided. Then Jesus met with the disciples
at the appointed time—we can readily suppose at a somewhat
earlier hour than customary, as He well foreknew what a series
of events had to be crowded into the remaining hours of that
night. The period, it should be remembered, for eating the
paschal lamb, was left somewhat indefinite. The lamb itself was
to be killed any time between the two evenings (Ex. xii. 6;
Lev. xxiii. 5); that is, between the ninth and eleventh hour by
the Jewish reckoning, or the third and fifth in the afternoon by
ours (Joseph. Wars, vii. 9, 3). So that, as our Lord had special
reasons for making the hour as early as possible, we may war-
rantably suppose, that the lamb was killed about three o'clock,
and the feast entered upon about five, or shortly after it. But
scarcely had Jesus and His disciples begun the feast—it was, at
least, only in progress, after the solemn service of the washing of
the disciples' feet had been performed (John xiii. 1–22)—when
Jesus, with evident emotion announced, that one of them should
betray Him.[1] The disciples, as might be supposed, were greatly

[1] Notwithstanding the positive assertions of Meyer to the contrary, there
can be no reasonable doubt, that the feast mentioned in this 13th ch. of
John, at which our Lord washed the disciples' feet, was the same as that
described by the other Evangelists under the name of the Passover. The
great majority of commentators are agreed on this—however they differ
on other points. Stier justly states, that the supper or feast here mentioned,
from the manner in which it is introduced, was manifestly no ordinary supper; and the reference to it again, at ch. xxi. 20, as *the* supper, by way of
eminence, at which John leant on his Master's bosom, confirms the view.
A still further confirmation is derived from the evident allusion, in Luke
xxii. 27, to the action of washing the disciples' feet, which took place at it,
and is recorded only by St John; *there*, however, and with reference to it,
our Lord says Himself, "I am among you as one that serveth." The expression of St John, at the beginning of the chapter, πρὸ τῆς ἑορτῆς τοῦ
πάσχα, which Meyer so strongly presses as conclusively showing, that the
circumstances of this supper were prior to the Passover, and that our Lord
did not keep the Passover at all, have no such necessary import. It is
utterly arbitrary to make them point to all the transactions that followed,
and, indeed, against the most natural and proper sense. The Evangelist
simply tells us, that before the Paschal Feast, at which the things concerning His earthly career were to proceed to their consummation, had actually
arrived—before that, but without any indication of how long before, Jesus,
being cognizant of all that was at hand, and of His speedy return to the
Father, having loved His own, and still loving them, was resolved to give

stunned by the announcement—for a moment looked at one another—then anxiously, in succession, put the question, " Lord, is it I ? " Judas could not afford to appear singular at such a time, perhaps also wished to learn how far Jesus might be acquainted with the secret, and so, followed the rest in putting the question. The reply informed him, that his treachery was known ; but it would seem, the information was so conveyed, as to be intelligible only to the traitor himself. Hence, still revolving the matter, and anxious to attain to certainty regarding it, Peter beckoned to John, who lay next to Jesus, to the intent that he might endeavour to obtain more definite information. The inquiry was evidently made by John in a whisper, as simply between himself and Christ. But the mode adopted by our Lord in giving the reply, of presenting a sop to Judas, while it served the purpose of a sign in regard to the treachery in question, served, at the same time, to connect the act of Judas with the delineations of prophecy (John xiii. 18; Ps. xli. 9). Then, turning to Judas, He said emphatically, " That thou doest, do quickly." This brought the matter to an issue. Judas's time was clearly up ; he had forfeited his place among the disciples of Jesus ; and if the bargain with his new masters was to be implemented, it must be instantly gone about. Hence, without a moment's delay, he hurried off to the Jewish rulers to get them to strike at once, as now only was it likely he could do aught in their behalf.

5. Now, let it be imagined, in what mood he must have found his accomplices at such a time, and what was likely to have been the effect produced on them by his appearance. *His* purpose had been precipitated by what took place in the Passover-room ; and this necessarily led them to precipitate theirs. It was a great crisis with them—now or never. Even scrupulous men could not be expected to be very nice in such a moment ; and since

them a palpable and personal proof of it, by washing their feet before the feast properly commenced. So substantially, after multitudes of earlier commentators, Alford, Stier, Luthardt. The precise period of washing, however, is wrongly put in our version, by the words in ver. 2, " and supper being ended ;" it should be, " supper having come "—for it is quite clear from what follows, that it had not ended, nor even in any proper sense begun. There was, at most, before the washing the προεόρτιον or ante-supper, as it was called, from which (ver. 4) Jesus rose and went about the washing ; after which came the supper itself, the Paschal Feast.

they now had what they could never look for again, the oppor-
tune help of one of the companions of Jesus, they must venture
somewhat, though it should oblige them to depart a little from
use and wont—the rather so, as it was probable that the matter
might be brought to quite a speedy termination. Let it be
remembered, that it was but a comparatively limited number of
persons, who were actively engaged in the business—only a few
of the more resolute and daring members of the Sanhedrim.
When Judas presented himself before these, it was in all probability still the earlier part of the evening, considerably before
persons in *their* rank of life would be accustomed to sit down to
the Passover-feast. And as there was no time to lose, as everything, in a manner, depended upon their seizing the favourable
moment, and as they could eat their Passover any time between
night and morning, what was more likely than that they should
agree to postpone their participation of the feast till they had
got through with this urgent business ?   It was possible enough
they might have it despatched before midnight, when still it
would not be too late for them to eat the Passover. Such, it
might seem, would be the natural, and, on every account, the
most advisable course, for them to pursue in the circumstances.
Judas in the first instance, and then the party with whom he
was in concert, had both, sooner than they anticipated, been
thrown into the vortex of active and violent operations, through
the overruling providence of Him, who bounds and restrains
even the wrath of the wicked, so as to render it subservient to
His purposes. And as they *could* postpone their paschal solemnity for a certain period, but could *not* postpone concurrence
with the proposal of Judas to proceed immediately against Jesus,
they hastily concerted their measures, and commenced their
course of action, by sending along with Judas an armed band
to the garden of Gethsemane, for the purpose of arresting the
Son of Man, and dragging him to the tribunal of judgment.

6. So far the traitor had calculated aright. Jesus *was* found
in the well-known garden. He had there already passed through
that solemn and affecting scene of agony, in which, with thrice-
repeated and ever-increasing earnestness, He had prayed to the
Father that the cup might be removed from Him. The season
of watching and prayer was no sooner ended than Judas and his

company presented themselves. It could not, therefore, be late; as it was still near the beginning of April, when the nights are too cold in Palestine to admit of persons remaining at an advanced hour in the open air, without harm; and hence, when it did become late, Peter is spoken of as shivering with cold, and going near to warm himself at the fire that had been kindled (John xviii. 18). We cannot reasonably suppose the time of the meeting in Gethsemane to have been beyond eight, or, at the furthest, nine in the evening, according to our mode of reckoning. What ensued upon the meeting need not at present detain us. Jesus proved Himself to be fully equal to the occasion—with mingled majesty and meekness met the assault of His adversaries, kept them for a time awe-struck and powerless, by word and deed showed how easily, had He willed, He could have smitten them to the ground; but, that the Father's counsel might be fulfilled, freely yielded Himself into their hands. Thereafter He was conducted by them to the house of the high priest; first, indeed, to Annas, the father-in-law of Caiaphas, then to Caiaphas himself, where the chief priests and elders—such of them as could be got together on such hasty notice—had meanwhile assembled to give formal judgment against Him. Here, however, they met with an unexpected difficulty; for, while Judas had put them in possession of the obnoxious party, he had but poorly provided them with grounds of guilt, or evidence to establish it. "They sought for witness against Jesus to put Him to death—and found none" (Mark xiv. 55). So that, after fruitless efforts to make good a charge of felony, and considerable time spent in the endeavour, they were obliged to fall back on the claims of Jesus regarding His person, and extorted from Him a confession of His assuming to be, in a sense altogether peculiar, the Son of the living God. This they held to be blasphemy, and thereby obtained, indeed, the materials of a capital offence; since, by the law of Moses, blasphemy was punishable with death. But a new difficulty sprung up on this very ground, for, as it was necessary to obtain the sanction of the Roman governor to the doom before it could be put in execution—the charge being a strictly religious, not a civil one—how should they manage to get Pilate to accredit it? They must, however, make the trial; Pilate's consent was indispensable; and they must present themselves with the prisoner at

the judgment-hall, in order to press the sentence of judicial condemnation. Thither, accordingly, they went.

7. By this time it was past midnight; it is even said in John
xviii. 28, that, when they got to the judgment-hall or prætorium
of Pilate, it was πρωί; not merely past midnight, but early morn.
This is implied also, in the circumstance that, before leaving the
palace of the high priest, the crowing of the cock, indicating the
approach of dawn, had been heard, awakening the cry of guilt
in Peter's bosom. It might still further be inferred, from the
accounts given by the several Evangelists of the processes of trial
and examination gone through, followed by the scenes of mockery
and dishonour, during which, it is evident, many hours must have
been consumed. And, indeed, the very purpose for which they
went to the prætorium is a proof that it must have been about
the break of day ; since they could not sooner have expected an
audience of the governor on a matter of judicial administration.
Early in the morning, then—it might be a little before, or a little
after sunrise—they led Jesus to the prætorium ; and when there,
they presented Him before Pilate for summary condemnation,
as a person whom they had ascertained to be a rebel against the
government of Cæsar, forbidding men to give tribute, and perverting the nation (Luke xxiii. 1). This took place, apparently,
at the door of the prætorium, and they doubtless hoped that
Pilate would instantly accede to their proposal, and allow them
to take their own way with the prisoner. Such, however, was
not the result ; the same over-ruling Providence, which controlled
their proceedings before, controlled them again ; instead of summarily pronouncing judgment, Pilate took Jesus into the hall for
the purpose of examining more closely into the matter. But
thither, it is said (John xviii. 28), His accusers refused to follow,
"they did not go in to the judgment-hall, lest they should be
defiled, but that they might eat the Passover."

8. Now, it is here that the first, and indeed the main difficulty
presents itself, in reconciling St John's account of the transactions with the accounts of the other Evangelists, and with what
may seem to have been the facts of the case :—a difficulty which
has given rise to a variety of conjectural explanations; in particular, to the supposition, on the part of some, that Jesus kept
the Passover with His disciples a day earlier than the Jews gener-

ally; and, on the part of others, to the supposition that the eating
of the Passover mentioned in the passage just quoted, referred,
not to the eating of the Paschal lamb itself, but to the subsequent
and supplemental provisions of the feast.   Both views carry a
somewhat unnatural and arbitrary appearance; and can neither
of them stand a rigid examination.

9. The latter view, which would take the expression "eating
the Passover" in an inferior sense, of the things to be eaten only
on the second and other days of the feast, has the usage of the
Evangelists wholly against it.   The expression occurs in five other
places—Matt. xxvi. 17; Mark xiv. 12, 14; Luke xxii. 11, 15—
and always in the sense of eating the Passover strictly so called.
It is true, as is still urged by Luthardt, that in Deut. xvi. 2,
offerings of the herd and flock to be presented during the feast
are called the paschal sacrifices, and that the word Passover itself
is used by John frequently of the feast generally (ii. 23, xiii. 1,
xviii. 39).   But these things will never prove, or even render
probable the idea, that the phrase of "eating the Passover" might
be used of any other part of the feast, exclusive of the very thing
from which all the rest took its character and name; and the
plain meaning of the expression, in all the other passages where
it occurs, must be held conclusive against it.   Then, as regards
the other opinion, that our Lord kept the Passover on a day
earlier than the Jews generally, it places the account of John in
direct opposition to that of the other Evangelists.   They clearly
represent the day observed by our Lord as the one looked forward
to with common expectation for the keeping of the Passover.   In
Matt. xxvi. 2, Jesus is represented as saying at the close of His
discourses, "Ye know (as if there could be no doubt upon the
matter) that after two days is the Passover, and the Son of Man
is betrayed to be crucified;" again at ver. 17, "And on the first
day of unleavened bread the disciples came to Jesus, saying unto
Him, where wilt Thou that we prepare for Thee to eat the Passover?"   So also in Mark xiv. 1, it is intimated, as a matter of
public notoriety, "After two days was the feast of the Passover,
and of unleavened bread;" and still again in Luke xxii. 7, "Then
came the day of unleavened bread, when the Passover must be
killed."   With such clear and explicit statements on the subject,
it is not too much to say with Lücke, that "it is impossible to

extract from the text of the Synoptical Gospels even the semblance
of an anticipation of the Passover." And if we hold by the
historical fidelity of their accounts, no ingenious theorisings as
to the probability, or moral fitness of the day preceding that of
the ordinary Passover, being observed, can have any effect in
countervailing the force of the testimony delivered in the above
passages. Of such theorisings none has been pressed with more
frequency or confidence than the requirements of type and antitype—not merely as understood by the Jews, and urged by commentators like De Wette, Lücke, Meyer, Ewald, Bleek; but also
as demanded by the nature of things. So Mr Gresswell, for example, presses the consideration : circumstances of time and place
were indispensable to the constitution of the paschal offering as a
type; it must be slain on the 14th of Nisan, and only in the
place where God had put His name, latterly in the city ot
Jerusalem; otherwise, the ordinance was not kept in its integrity.
And " who then," asks Mr Gresswell, " shall say, that they were
not equally indispensable to the antitype ? Had Christ suffered,
though He had suffered as a victim, on any day but the 14th of
Nisan could He have suffered as the Jewish Passover ? Had
Jesus suffered, though He had suffered anywhere but at Jerusalem,
could He have suffered as the Jewish Passover ?"[1] But why stop
simply there ? Why not insist upon other correspondences of a
like kind ? The Jewish Passover was expressly required to be a
lamb of a year old; and could Christ have suffered as the Jewish
Passover, if more than a year had elapsed since He entered on
His high vocation ? The Jewish Passover, wherever and however killed, must have its blood poured around the altar; and
could Christ have suffered as the Jewish Passover, if a like service was not performed with His life-blood ? If such merely
outward correspondences are pressed, we shall not find the reality
after all ; and *that* not here alone, but in the ordinances generally which had their antitypical fulfilment in the history and
work of Christ. The demand for these proceeds on mistaken
views of the relation between type and antitype; as if the one
stood upon the same level with the other, and were equally dependent upon conditions of place and time.[2] And, besides, what,
in the circumstances supposed, should become of our Lord's own

¹ Harmony, vol. iii., p. 163.   ² See Typology of Scripture, vol. i., p. 57.

Passover? The precise day *did* enter as an important element into the Old Testament ordinance; and was He, who came to fulfil the law, to change at will the Divine appointment? Was it by infringing upon one part of a typical institution, that He was to make good another? To say with some, among others Stier, that it was probably the right day for the Passover our Lord and His disciples kept, and that the Jews erred a day in their calculations, is a mere assertion, and against the manifest bearing of the evangelical statements already adduced. Such lame and halting respect to the ordinances of heaven, could neither be pleasing to God, nor satisfactory to men; and Christ's accomplishment of the things written beforehand concerning Him in type and prophecy, must be placed on another footing, if it is to approve itself to our religious feelings and intelligent convictions. We dismiss, therefore, all pleadings of the kind now referred to; and hold to the plain import of the historical statements in the Evangelists, that our Lord and His disciples knew of no day for observing the Passover, but the one which the law required, and which was common to them with their countrymen.[1]

---

[1] The reasoning in the text is directed only against those who hold the idea of an anticipated Passover being kept by our Lord, without impugning the historical accuracy of the Synoptical Evangelists. But most of the German writers, who think that our Lord either did not keep the Passover at all, or, at least, that He did not keep it on the common day, give up the historical accuracy of the Synoptists. So, for example, Meyer and Ewald (the latter in his *Geschichte des Volkes Israel,* v. p. 409, *sq*), who both, though Meyer most sharply and offensively, hold John's narrative to be irreconcileable with the other accounts; that he, however, gave the correct one, while the others erroneously identify the feast kept by our Lord with the proper Jewish Passover. They followed a mere tradition; and Meyer supposes the tradition to have originated in the Lord's Supper coming to be identified with the Paschal Feast; whence the day of its institution was first viewed as an *ideal* 14 Nisan, and by-and-by was taken for a *real* 14 Nisan. Precious writers of sacred history—to say nothing of their inspiration—who could thus, all three, confound the *ideal* with the *real,* which is here, in plain terms, the *false* with the *true!* Considering the importance which attached to the last festal solemnity of Jesus, we ask, with Luthardt, how *could* such an error in the tradition have sprung up, especially under the eyes of the apostles, and gained an established footing? Or, if such a thing *had* been possible, what must one think of the intelligence and the memory of the Synoptists? The very proposing of such a solution seems like an affront to one's understanding, as well as an assault on one's faith.

10. In truth, the supposition, that our Lord and His disciples anticipated by a day the proper time for observing the Passover, when closely examined, fails to explain the statement, for the solution of which it was more peculiarly adopted : it does not, if it were true, account for the refusal of our Lord's accusers to enter the prætorium. This has been well pointed out by Friedlieb, in a passage quoted by Alford, " The Jews would not enter the prætorium, that they might not be defiled, but that they might eat the Passover. For, the entrance of a Jew into the house of a Gentile made him unclean till the evening. It is surprising, that, according to this declaration of the holy Evangelist, the Jews had still to eat the Passover; whereas Jesus and His disciples had already eaten it on the previous night. And it is no less surprising, that the Jews in the early morning should have been afraid of rendering themselves unclean for the Passover; since the Passover could not be kept till the evening; *i.e.* till the next day (for the day was reckoned from evening to evening); and the uncleanness which they dreaded, did not, by the law, last till the next day." Had these Jews, therefore, been simply concerned about fitness for eating the Passover on the day following that observed by Christ and His disciples, they did not need to have been so sticklish about entering the prætorium; the uncleanness they were anxious to avoid contracting would of itself have expired by the time they behoved to be free from it; at sunset they should again have been pure. So that the supposition, which is historically groundless, is also inadequate for the purpose of a proper explanation.

11. Friedlieb himself, along with not a few critical authorities, in former as well as present times, is disposed to fall in with the other supposition, and to regard the eating of the Passover, in John xviii. 28, as referring to subordinate parts of the feast. After stating that the passage labours under no small exegetical difficulties, which, perhaps, cannot be solved for want of accurate knowledge of the customs of the time, he adds, " Possibly the law concerning Levitical defilements and purifications had in that age been made more stringent, or otherwise modified; possibly they called some other meal, beside the actual Passover, by its name. This last we certainly, with our present knowledge of Hebrew antiquities, must assume." We might, indeed, have

to do so, and take what satisfaction we could from the possible solution thereby presented, if the circumstances of the case absolutely required it. But it is here we demur: we see no necessity for having recourse to the merely possible and conjectural, when the actual (if duly considered) may suffice. It is to be borne in mind, we again repeat—though constantly overlooked by the authors of those hypothetical explanations—that the persons mentioned by the evangelist as afraid to contract uncleanness by entering the prætorium, and thereby losing their right to eat of the Passover, formed no fair representation, in this matter, of the Jews at large. The Evangelist, in the whole of this part of his narrative, is speaking merely of the faction of the chief priest and elders, the comparative handful of men who conducted the business of our Lord's persecution, and never once refers to the general population of the Jews. Once, indeed, and again, he calls them by the name of Jews (ch. xviii. 31, xix. 7, etc.) partly to distinguish them from Pilate, the heathen, and partly also from his custom of using the general name of Jews, where the other Evangelists employ the more specific names of Scribes and Pharisees (v. 16, 18, ch. vi. x., etc.). He still, however, leaves us in no doubt, that the persons really concerned were the mere party of the high priest, the accomplices of Judas. This base faction had, as already stated, been driven by circumstances, over which they had no control, to a course of proceeding different from what they had contemplated. When preparing to partake of the Passover, they suddenly found themselves in a position which obliged them to act with promptitude, while it did not appear to exclude the possibility of their being able, at a more advanced period of the night, to eat the Passover. In the urgency of the moment they allowed the feast to stand over till the business in hand was despatched. But unexpected difficulties met them in the way; in the midst of which the night wore on, and at last the morning dawned, without the desired result being reached. They did not, however, on that account, abandon the purpose of eating the Passover—no doubt conceiving that the greatness of the emergency justified the slight deviation they had to make from the accustomed order. Hypocrites and formalists, in all ages, when bent on the execution of some cherished project, have been notorious for their readiness in

accommodating their notions of duty to the exigencies of the
moment; they can swallow a camel when it suits their purpose,
while at other times they can strain at a gnat. Nor were the
chief actors on the occasion before us ordinary hypocrites and
formalists; the more forward of them at least belonged to the
Sadducean party, the members of which, it is well known, never
scrupled to make religious practice bend to self-interest or political expediency. It is vain, therefore, in a case like the present,
to summon a host of witnesses (as Mr Gresswell does, *Harmony*,
iii. p. 156) to the great regard which the Jews as a people paid
to the Sabbath, and to the consequent improbability of their
pressing forward such judicial proceedings against Christ, on the
supposition of the time being the first day of the Paschal Feast,
which by the law was to be observed as a Sabbath. A single
fact or two, coupled with the known characters of the actors, is
perfectly sufficient to put all such general testimonies to flight.
Looking into Jewish history, we find it related of a period very
shortly after that now under consideration, during the commotions,
which took place under Cestius, that while the Jews were celebrating the Feast of Tabernacles, they heard of the governor's
approach with an army toward Jerusalem; and immediately (to
use the words of Josephus, Wars, ii. 19, 2), " they left the feast,
and betook themselves to their arms; and, taking courage greatly
from their multitude, they went in a sudden and disorderly
manner to the fight, with a great noise, and without any consideration had of the rest of the seventh day, although the
Sabbath was the day to which they had the greatest regard; but
that rage, which made them forget the religious observance,
made them too hard for their enemies in the fight." Here, both
the solemnities of the feast and the hallowed rest of the Sabbath
were unhesitatingly sacrificed to the demands of a civil emergency.
And at a somewhat later stage of affairs, instances are recorded
by Josephus, which show, that the men who then chiefly ruled in
Jerusalem came even to count nothing whatever sacred, in comparison of their own mad policy; that the most hallowed things
were turned, without scruple, to a profane use whenever the
interests of the moment seemed to require it; so that, from what
passed under his observation, the historian is led to express his
conviction that, if the Romans had not come and put an end to

such impieties, some earthquake, or supernatural visitation from heaven, must have been sent to revenge the enormities (Wars, v. 13, 6).

12. Now, it is only ascribing a measure of the same spirit, and in a far inferior degree, to the few leaders of this conspiracy against Jesus, when we suppose them to have been hurried on by the progress of events beyond the proper time for eating the Passover; yet, without abandoning the intention, and the hope of still partaking of it, after the business in hand was brought to a close. They were consequently anxious to avoid contracting a defilement, which would have prevented them from eating the Passover during the currency of the first day of the feast. Were it not better that they should strive so to keep the feast, than omit its observance altogether? Undoubtedly, they would reckon it to be so. For the delay that had occurred beyond the appointed time, they would plead (as with *their* views there was a fair pretext for doing) the constraint of circumstances; they would rest in the conviction, that they had come as near to the legal observance of the institution as it was practicable for them to do. And as to the special objection of the first day of the feast being a Sabbath, and, as such, unfit for the prosecution of such a matter as now engaged their attention, the same considerations, which could reconcile them to the postponement of the feast, would also appear to warrant the active operations they pursued. It was not as if matters were moving in a regular and even current, and they could shape their proceedings in accordance with their own deliberate judgments; the rush of unexpected circumstances had shut them up to a particular course. Nor are there wanting instances in what is presently after recorded of them in Gospel history, in perfect keeping with the view now taken of their procedure. On the day following the crucifixion, which, by the testimony of all the Evangelists, was not only a Sabbath, but a Sabbath of peculiar solemnity, they waited upon Pilate, for the purpose of getting him, on that very day, to set a watch around the sepulchre of Jesus, lest the body should be stolen (Matt. xxvii. 62, 63). And at an earlier period, we learn from John vii. 32, 37, 45, the Pharisees sent out officers to apprehend Jesus on the last day of the Feast of Tabernacles, which by the law was also to be observed as a Sabbath. So that either they did not look

upon such judicial proceedings as work unsuited to a Sabbath, or they thought the urgency of the occasion justified its being done. How much more, then, in the matter now under consideration, when every thing, in a manner, was at stake? It is proper also to add, that while the first day of the Paschal Feast was appointed to be kept as a Sabbath, it was not possible, from the amount of work that had to be done in connection with the feast, that it could have so much the character of a day of rest as an ordinary Sabbath. And, indeed, the law regarding it expressly provides, that such work as was necessary to the preparation of victuals and travelling to their respective abodes, was allowable (Ex. xii. 16; Deut. xvi. 6, 7); ordinary avocations merely were prohibited, in order that the observances proper to the feast might proceed.

The conclusion, therefore, to which on every account we are led is precisely that which the statement in John xviii. 28 itself requires us to adopt. The expression of " eating the Passover" there employed, by invariable usage points to an actual participation on that very day of the proper feast; and the more closely the circumstances of the time, and the character of the actors are considered, the more reason do we find for the belief, that it was the same passover of the 14th of Nisan which our Lord had kept, and which they were still intent on celebrating, though from urgent circumstances, it had to be postponed a little beyond the due season.[1]

13. So much for the more peculiar passage in St John's Gospel on this subject; but there are one or two others that also require explanation. These have respect to the Sabbath, and in

---

[1] It is not necessary to do more than refer to an objection that might be raised against this conclusion, drawn from the procedure of our Lord Himself, going out with His disciples after eating the Passover. This Mr Alford mentions as a reason for thinking of another than the exact day and feast prescribed by the law being kept; since in Exod. xii. 22, it was ordered that none should leave his house till the morning. But it was equally ordered, that all should eat the Passover, attired as travellers, and ready for a journey—though we know, the prescription was not kept in later times, and was understood to be temporary. So and much more must the other have been; for, keeping the Passover, as multitudes necessarily did, in other people's houses, it must often have happened that they were obliged to go out afterwards.

particular what is called the *paraskeuê*. Speaking of the time, when Pilate was going to pronounce judgment against Jesus, it is said in John xix. 14, ἦν δὲ παρασκευὴ τοῦ πάσχα, it was the paraskeue or preparation day of the Passover. This, it has been alleged, points to the proper passover-day as still to come, and fixes it to be the day following the one of which the transactions are recorded. It would certainly do so, if the expression, as used by the Evangelist, meant a preparation-day *before* the keeping of the Passover. But this does not appear to be the case. He uses the word paraskeue twice again in the same chapter, and each time in reference to the Sabbath : ver. 31, "The Jews, therefore, because it was the paraskeue, that the bodies should not remain upon the cross on the Sabbath-day (for that Sabbath was an high day) besought Pilate that their legs might be broken, and that they might be taken away;" and ver. 42, "There laid they Jesus therefore because of the Jews' paraskeue ; for the sepulchre was nigh at hand." Here, plainly, it is with the Sabbath, that the term is specially connected ; and the natural inference is, that in the earlier passage, although it is called the paraskeue of the Passover, yet what is meant is not a paraskeue of the feast itself, but a Sabbath paraskeue during the feast. This is confirmed by what is written in the other gospels. Thus, at Matt. xxvii. 62, with reference to the application made to Pilate for a guard on the day after the crucifixion it is said, "Now on the following day, which is the one after the paraskeue" (ἥτις ἐστὶν μετὰ τὴν παρασκευήν) ; the following day, beyond doubt, was the ordinary Sabbath ; and the name paraskeue had become so common as a designation of the preceding day, that the Sabbath itself, it would seem, was sometimes denominated from it. Not merely, the evening after sunset of the sixth day, as Michælis, Kuinoel, Paulus, and Alford suppose (though even so, the words would apply to what was strictly the Jewish Sabbath); but *the following morn*, as the τῇ ἐπαύριον of the Evangelist properly means. This we may the rather believe to be the meaning, as it is against all probability, that the thought of placing a guard around the sepulchre during the night between the second and the third day, should have occurred so early as the very night of the crucifixion ; it has all the appearance of an after-thought, springing up when reflection had got time to work. In

Mark xv. 42, we have not only the same word applied to designate the time preceding the Sabbath, but an explanation added, " And evening having now come, since it was paraskeue, which is προσάββατον, fore-Sabbath." Luke says, ch. xxiii. 54, " and it was paraskeue day" (καὶ ἡμέρα ἦν παρασ.). The day which preceded the Sabbath, was called by way of emphasis, the *preparation*, on account of the arrangements that had to be made on it in anticipation of the approaching Sabbath, with the view of spending this in perfect freedom from all ordinary labour. So much account was made of such preparatory arrangements, in the later periods of Jewish history, that the name paraskeue came to be a familiar designation for the sixth day of the week, and even to have a certain decree of Sabbatical sacredness attached to it. Josephus gives a decree of Augustus securing, among other liberties to the Jews, exemption from judicial proceedings on Sabbath, and on paraskeue, after the ninth hour (Ant. xvi. 6, 2). Irenæus, in his account of the Valentinian System, represents them as connecting the creation of man with the sixth day, because it was the paraskeue (I. 14, 6).   And in a passage, quoted by Wetstein, at Matt. xxvii. 62, from a Rabbinical authority, the days of the week are given thus: the first, second, third, fourth, fifth paraskeue, Sabbath. Clearly therefore the word in question had come to be familiarly applied to denote the day corresponding to our Friday, to denote that day as a whole, not merely some concluding fragment of it; but we have no evidence of any such appellation being customary in regard to the Passover Feast. Nor, indeed, can we conceive how it should have been thought of. For, as already stated, even on the first day itself of the feast, a certain freedom was allowed for travelling and preparing victuals; and the day preceding it must usually have been one of considerable bustle and activity. We hold it, therefore, as established beyond all reasonable doubt, that the paraskeue is the day preceding the regular Jewish Sabbath ; and that when the Evangelist John speaks of the paschal paraskeue, he is to be understood as meaning simply the Jewish Saturday, the fore-Sabbath of the Passover-solemnity ; in other words, not an ordinary preparation-day, but that heightened by the additional solemnities connected with the Passover—such a paraskeue as was itself a sort of Sabbath.

Hence he makes the further explanatory statement, that the Sabbath following was an high day, or, literally, " Great was the day of that Sabbath." Why should it have been called great ? Not surely—though this is very often alleged—because the first day of the Jewish Passover coincided with the ordinary Sabbath ; for a great deal had to be done on the first day of the feast, which tended rather to disturb Jewish notions of Sabbatical repose :—the killing of many thousand victims (Josephus even speaks of so many as 200,000), the pouring of the blood around the altar, the hurrying to and fro of persons performing these services, and all the labour and bustle connected with the cooking of so many suppers. A day, on which all this went on, could scarcely be regarded among the Jews as emphatically a great Sabbath. They were much more likely to apply such an expression to the Sabbath immediately following the Paschal Supper, when, the activities of the feast being over, the assembled people were ready, in vast numbers, and with excited feelings, to engage in the public services of the sanctuary.

Thus, every expression receives its most natural explanation ; no constraint is put upon any of the words employed either by St John or by the other Evangelists ; while, by giving full play to the historical elements mentioned in the narrative, we have the best grounds for concluding, both that our Lord kept the Passover with His disciples on the 14th of Nisan, on the day prescribed by the law, and observed by the great body of the Jews, and that a faction, but in point of number, only a small faction of these, lost the opportunity of observing it till a later period of the same day. If these positions have been successfully made out, then, in this case, as in so many others connected with the sacred writings, the apparent discrepance in the different statements, as seen from a modern point of view, coupled with the satisfactory explanation, which arises from a careful examination of the circumstances, affords a strong confirmation of the thorough truthfulness and integrity of the writers—greatly more than if their narratives had presented a superficial and obvious agreement.

PART THIRD.

THE USE MADE OF OLD TESTAMENT SCRIPTURE IN THE WRITINGS OF THE NEW TESTAMENT.

THE use here referred to has respect simply to the formal quotations made in the New Testament from the Old, and the purposes to which they are applied. There is a more general use pervading the whole of the New Testament writings, and appearing in the constant appropriation of the truths and principles unfolded in Moses and the prophets, of the hopes and expectations that had been thereby awakened, and the very forms of thought and expression to which, as subjects of former revelations, the minds of God's people had become habituated. In all these respects the New is the continuation and the proper complement of the Old. But beside this general use, which touches more or less on every department of theological inquiry, there is the more formal and specific use, which consists in the citations made by our Lord and His apostles from the inspired writings of the Old Covenant. These are of great number and variety; and are marked by such peculiarities, that it may justly be regarded as one of the chief problems, which modern exegesis has to solve, to give a satisfactory explanation and defence of the mode of quoting and applying Old Testament Scripture in the New. If this cannot be made to appear consistent with the correct interpretation of the Old Testament, and with the principles of plenary inspiration, there is necessarily a most important failure in the great end and object of exegetical studies.

It is proper, however, to state at the outset, that a very considerable number of the passages, which may, in a sense, be reckoned quotations from Old Testament Scripture, are better omitted in investigations like the present. They consist of silent, unacknowledged appropriations of Old Testament words or sentences, quite natural for those, who from their childhood had been instructed in the oracles of God, but so employed as to involve no question of propriety, or difficulty of interpretation. The speakers or writers, in such cases, do not profess to give forth the precise words and meaning of former revelations ; their thoughts and language merely derived from these the form and direction, which by a kind of sacred instinct they took ; and it does not matter for any purpose, for which the inspired oracles were given, whether the portions thus appropriated might or might not be very closely followed, and used'in connections somewhat different from those in which they originally stood. For example, when the Virgin Mary, in her song of praise, says, " He hath filled the hungry with good things," she uses words exactly agreeing in our version with those in Ps. cvi. 9, and in the original differing only in its having the singular for *hungry* and *good*, where the other has the plural : but nothing scarcely can be said to be either gained or lost by bringing the two passages into comparison, nor can we even be certain, that the later passage was actually derived from the other. Or, when the Apostle Peter, in ch. iii. 14, 15, of his first epistle, gives the exhortation, " Be not afraid of their terror, neither be troubled, but sanctify the Lord God in your hearts," there can be no doubt, that he substantially adopts the language of Isaiah, in ch. viii. 12, 13 ; but as he does not profess to quote what had been written by the prophet, so he reproduces the passage with such freedom, as to manifest, that it was the substance of the exhortation, rather than the *ipsissima verba* containing it, which he meant to appropriate. There are multitudes of similar examples, which in an exegetical respect involve no difficulty, and call for no special remark ; and if noticed at all, it should only be as proofs of the extent to which the ideas and language of the Old Testament have given their impress to the New. Taking in all the instances in which the expressions of the Old Testament are thus used by the authors of the New, as well as the more direct and formal quotations, a number exceeding 600 has been made out.[1] No proper

---

[1] See the volume of Mr Gough, " The New Testament Quotations collated with the Scriptures of the Old Testament," Walton and Maberly, 1855 ; a volume which shows pains and industry, but is not distinguished for critical ability ; and is, besides, too cumbrous and expensive to be of general use.

end, however, could be served here by exhibiting such a lengthened array as this; it would tend rather to embarrass than promote the object we have in view.   Our business must be chiefly
with citations of a more formal and explicit kind, fitted, from the
manner in which they are employed, to raise the inquiry, whether
they are fairly given and legitimately applied.

There are properly, however, two points of inquiry—one
bearing respect to the form in which the citations appear; the
other, to the application made of them.   These are two distinct
questions.   Are the passages quoted from the Old Testament in
the New fairly dealt with, simply as quotations?   And are the
purposes for which they are adduced, and the sense put upon
them, in accordance with their original meaning and design?
In answer to the first question, it is found, that the quotations
fall into four different classes; the first, a very large one, in
which they exactly agree with the Hebrew (often also with the
Septuagint); the second, likewise a considerable one, in which
they substantially agree with the Hebrew, the differences being
merely formal or circumstantial, and indicating no diversity of
sense; the third, those, in which the Septuagint is followed,
though it diverges to some extent from the Hebrew; and the
fourth, a class of passages, in which neither the Hebrew nor the
Septuagint is quite exactly adhered to.   The whole of the passages might be ranged under these different classes; but for
purposes of reference and consultation this would give rise to
inconvenience; and we shall, therefore, follow the order of the
citations themselves, as they occur in the New Testament.   In
adopting this course, however, we shall not lose sight of the
several classes, which shall be marked respectively, I. II. III.
IV., and one or other of them appended to each quotation, indicating the class to which it belongs, with a figure besides,
denoting its number in that class.   A summation will be given
at the close of the results obtained, and such explanatory remarks added as may seem to be called for.   This will occupy
the first section.

Another section will be devoted to the second point noticed—
the sense put upon the passages quoted, and the purposes to
which they are applied; in other words, the principles involved
in the application made of them.   In the great majority of cases,

however, the application is so manifestly in accordance with their original meaning and design, that it requires no vindication. All of this description, therefore, will be passed over, and attention directed only to such as involve some apparent license in interpretation.

SECTION FIRST.

QUOTATIONS FROM THE OLD TESTAMENT IN THE NEW, CONSIDERED IN RESPECT TO THE MANNER OF CITATION.

THE capital figures employed after each quotation, it will be borne in mind, refer to the several classes indicated above. I. Those in which the Greek exactly corresponds with the Hebrew. II. Those in which it substantially agrees with the Hebrew, the differences being merely circumstantial, and indicating no diversity of sense. III. Those in which the Septuagint is followed, though it diverges to some extent from the Hebrew. IV. Those in which neither the Hebrew nor the Septuagint is exactly adhered to. The numerals subjoined to these figures give the number of that class, reckoning from the commencement of the Gospels. In all cases the exact translation will be given, whether precisely agreeing with the authorised version or not.

ST MATTHEW'S GOSPEL.

Ch. i. 22, 23. In order that it might be fulfilled, which was spoken by the prophet, saying, Ἰδοὺ ἡ παρθένος ἐν γαστρὶ ἕξει καὶ τέξεται υἱὸν, καὶ καλέσουσιν τὸ ὄνομα αὐτοῦ Ἐμμανουήλ : Isa. vii. 14. Behold the virgin shall be with child and shall bring forth a Son, and they shall call His name Emmanuel. II. 1.

The deviation here from the exact rendering of the original is very slight and unimportant ; it relates only to two expressions, putting "shall be with child" for "shall conceive," הָרָה,

and " they shall call" for " thou shalt call," קָרָאת. In both cases the Septuagint is closer to the original; it has ἐν γαστρὶ λήψεται, and καλέσεις.

Ch. ii. 5, 6. For thus it is written by the prophet, Καὶ σὺ Βηθλεὲμ γῆ Ἰούδα, οὐδαμῶς ἐλαχίστη εἶ ἐν τοῖς ἡγεμόσιν Ἰούδα· ἐκ σοῦ γὰρ ἐξελεύσεται ἡγούμενος, ὅστις ποιμανεῖ τὸν λαόν μου τὸν Ἰσραήλ: Micah v. 2. And thou Bethlehem, Judah-land, art by no means least among the rulers of Judah; for out of thee shall come forth a Governor, who shall rule My people Israel. IV. 1.

Here the differences are very considerable both from the Hebrew and from the Septuagint. (1.) Instead of Ephratah, after Bethlehem, the Evangelist puts γῆ Ἰούδα—an elliptical expression for situated in the land of Judah, and, coupled with Bethlehem, making substantially the same meaning as is sometimes expressed in the Old Testament by the compound term, Bethlehem-Judah (Judg. xvii. 7; Ruth i. 1). It merely distinguishes that Bethlehem from another in a different locality. So far, the addition of the Evangelist serves much the same purpose as the Ephratah of the prophet, which defined Bethlehem as the place that originally bore the name of Ephratah (Gen. xxxv. 19). The Septuagint has οἶκον Ἐφραθά, which gives no proper sense. (2.) Instead of " thou art by no means least among the rulers of Judah," the Heb. has " thou art little to be (too small to be reckoned) among the thousands of Judah"—צָעִיר לִהְיוֹת בְּאַלְפֵי יְהוּדָה. The Septuagint gives this part of the passage with substantial correctness, ὀλιγοστὸς εἶ τοῦ εἶναι ἐν χιλιάσιν Ἰούδα. The words of the Evangelist express a meaning *formally* different, yet *materially* the same. Looking at the substance of the original, it intimates, that Bethlehem, little in one respect, scarcely or not at all able to take its place among the ruling divisions of the land, was yet destined to be great in another—as the appointed birth-place of the future Governor of Israel. This twofold idea is precisely that also which the words of the Evangelist convey—only they contemplate the preceding littleness as in a manner gone, on account of the now realised ultimate greatness: *q. d.* Thou wast, indeed, among the least, but thou art no longer so, for thou hast already attained to what in the Divine purpose was to make thee great. So that this change, as well as the preceding one, proceeds on the principle of explaining while it quotes—modifying the language, so as, without changing the import, to adapt it to the Evangelist's times. (3.) The remaining clause is a quite correct, though somewhat free translation of the original, which hardly admits of a very close rendering—lit. " Out of thee there shall come forth for Me to be Governor in Israel," מִמְּךָ לִי יֵצֵא לִהְיוֹת מוֹשֵׁל בְּיִשְׂרָאֵל, that is, One shall be raised up there by My special providence, who shall possess the government in Israel ; all one in substance with the Evangelist's " out of thee shall come forth a Governor, who shall rule My people Israel."[1]

Ch. ii. 15. In order that it might be fulfilled which was spoken of the Lord by the prophet, saying, Ἐξ Αἰγύπτου ἐκάλεσα τὸν υἱόν μου : Hos. xi. 1. Out of Egypt have I called My Son. I. 1.

The passage of Hosea is here given with the greatest exactness. The Septuagint is more loose, Ἐξ Αἰγ. μετεκάλεσα τὰ τέκνα αὐτοῦ, apparently taking the word for My Son, לִבְנִי, as a plural, sons, or children.

Ch. ii. 18. Then was fulfilled that which was spoken through Jeremiah the prophet, saying, Φωνὴ ἐν Ῥαμᾶ ἠκούσθα, [2]κλαυθμὸς καὶ ὀδυρμὸς πολύς, Ῥαχὴλ κλαίουσα τὰ τέκνα αὐτῆς, καὶ οὐκ ἤθέλησεν παρακληθῆναι, ὅτι οὐκ εἰσίν : Jer. xxxi. 15. In Rama was there heard a voice, lamentation and great mourning, Rachel bewailing her children, and refused to be comforted, because they are not. II. 2.

The departures from the Heb. original are here quite trifling; they consist merely in substituting " great mourning" for " bitter weeping," or weeping of bitternesses, בְּכִי תַמְרוּרִים, a correct, though not the most literal translation ; and omitting the second mention of her children, which is found in the prophet—" refused to be comforted for her children," while the Evangelist simply has, " refused to be comforted," namely, for the loss of her children.   What is not expressed is clearly implied.

Ch. ii. 23. And he came and dwelt in a city called Nazareth,

[1] For some explanation of the circumstances connected with the fulfilment of the prophecy, and especially its relation to the governorship of Syria by Cyrenius, as stated in Luke ii. 2, see Appendix.

[2] The received text has θρῆνος before κλαυθμὸς, but it wants authority.

so that it might be fulfilled which was spoken through the prophets, ὅτι Ναζωραῖος κληθήσεται, He shall be called a Nazarene. IV. 2.

The words here given as a quotation from the prophets are not found in express terms in any one of them; and the mode of quotation, as from the prophets generally, seems to import, that the Evangelist had in view, not a single prediction, but a series of predictions, respecting Messiah, the substance of which might be compressed into the sentence, He shall be called a Nazarene; that is, He shall be a person of low and contemptible appearance, as the inhabitants of Nazareth were in a somewhat peculiar sense esteemed (John i. 46). The reference appears to be to such passages as Isa. iv. 2, xi. 1; Jer. xxiii. 1; Zech. iii. 8, vi. 12, in which the Messiah was spoken of as the offspring of David, that was to grow up as a *nezer*, or tender shoot; in plain terms, rise from a low condition, encompassed for a time with the emblems of poverty and meanness. Nazareth itself was probably derived from *nezer*; so that sound and sense here coincided.

Ch. iii. 3. This is he that was spoken of by Isaiah the prophet, saying, Φωνὴ βοῶντος ἐν τῇ ἐρήμῳ, Ἑτοιμάσατε τὴν ὁδὸν Κυρίου, εὐθείας ποιεῖτε τὰς τρίβους αὐτοῦ: Isa. xl. 3. The voice of one crying in the wilderness, Prepare ye the way of the Lord, make His paths straight. II. 3.

The same passage is also quoted in Mark i. 3; Luke iii. 4, and in precisely the same words. They are directly taken from the Septuagint, except the last expression, τρίβους αὐτοῦ, for which the Septuagint has τρίβους τοῦ Θεοῦ ἡμῶν. Both renderings, however, differ slightly from the expression of the prophet, which is "highway for our God," מְסִלָּה לֵאלֹהֵינוּ. The sense is entirely the same, only less fully and boldly exhibited by the Evangelists.

Ch. iv. 4. It is written, Οὐκ ἐπ᾽ ἄρτῳ μόνῳ ζήσεται ὁ ἄνθρωπος, ἀλλ᾽ ἐν παντὶ ῥήματι ἐκπορευομένῳ διὰ στόματος Θεοῦ: Deut. viii. 3. Not on bread alone shall man live, but by every word that cometh forth through God's mouth. I. 2.

The passage is most fitly assigned to the first class of quotations; for it is a close translation of the original, down to the last word, the name of God. This is Jehovah in the original, which is usually given in the Greek by Κύριος; but here the Septuagint has Θεοῦ, and it is followed by the Evangelist, as it is also throughout, except in the substitution of ἐν παντὶ instead of ἐπὶ παντί. The insertion of ῥήματι in the Septuagint and the Evangelist, without any thing corresponding in the original, is only done to render the sense plain, and cannot justly be regarded as a deviation from the original.

Ch. iv. 6. For it is written, Ὅτι τοῖς ἀγγέλοις αὐτοῦ ἐντελεῖται περὶ σοῦ, καὶ ἐπὶ χειρῶν ἀροῦσίν σε, μή ποτε προσκόψῃς πρὸς λίθον τὸν πόδα σοῦ : Ps. xci. 11, 12. He shall give His angels charge concerning thee, and upon their hands they shall bear thee up, lest thou dash thy foot against a stone. I. 3.

The meaning of the original is quite exactly given, and given in the words of the Septuagint—only a clause is omitted in ver. 11 of the Psalm, " to keep thee in all thy ways." No change is thereby introduced into the passage, which, as far as it goes, is a faithful reproduction of that in the Psalm.

Ch. iv. 7. It is again written, Οὐκ ἐκπειράσεις Κύριον τὸν Θεόν σου : Deut. vi. 16. Thou shalt not tempt the Lord thy God. I. 4.

This must also be regarded as an exact translation ; for it merely adopts the singular for the plural—*thou* for *ye* ; an interchange that is constantly made in the Pentateuch itself, according as Israel was contemplated as a plurality or a unity. The Septuagint here adopts the singular ; so the words of the Evangelist exactly correspond with it.

Ch. iv. 10. For it is written, Κύριον τὸν Θεόν σοῦ προσκυνήσεις, καὶ αὐτῷ μόνῳ λατρεύσεις : Deut. vi. 13. Thou shalt worship the Lord thy God, and Him only shalt thou serve. III. 1.

The same words are given in Luke iv. 8 ; they are those of the Septuagint ; but they differ so slightly from the Hebrew, that the passage might almost with equal propriety be ranked under class I. The only divergence is in putting " thou shalt worship," for " thou shalt fear," תִּירָא. The fear undoubtedly includes worship, as its chief outward expression.

Ch. iv. 14–16. In order that it might be fulfilled, which was spoken by Esaias the prophet, saying, Γῆ Ζαβουλὼν καὶ γῆ Νεφθαλείμ, ὁδὸν θαλάσσης πέραν τοῦ Ἰορδάνου, Γαλιλαία τῶν ἐθνῶν, ὁ λαὸς ὁ καθήμενος ἐν σκοτίᾳ φῶς εἶδεν μέγα, καὶ τοῖς

καθημένοις ἐν χώρᾳ καὶ σκιᾷ θανάτου, φῶς ἀνέτειλεν αὐτοῖς:
Isa. ix. 1, 2. Land of Zabulon, and land of Nephthalim,
way of the sea beyond the Jordan, the people that sat
in darkness saw a great light, and for them that sat in
the region and shadow of death, light sprung up to
them. IV. 3.

It is but a part of Isaiah's prophecy that is here cited; the
Evangelist begins in the middle of a sentence, and does not give
even the whole of what follows. The entire passage may be
thus literally rendered: " As the former time degraded the land
of Zabulon and the land of Nephthalim, so the latter makes
glorious the way of the sea, the farther side (עֵבֶר) of Jordan,
Galilee of the Gentiles. The people (viz. of this Galilee), those
walking in the dark, see a great light, the dwellers in the land
of the shadow of death, light rises upon them." It thus appears,
that there are considerable differences between the Evangelist
and the prophet, but chiefly in the way of abridgment. His
purpose did not require him to produce the whole, and he gives
only a part—very naturally, on this account, beginning with a
nominative, γῆ Ζαβ., while a fuller quotation would have required
the accusative. For the ὁδόν in the next clause, see at p. 28. It
has very much the force of a preposition, and means alongside, or
by the tract of, viz. the sea; the sea-board portions of the tribes of
Zabulon and Naphthali. The only deviation worth naming, in
the portion that is fully quoted, from the precise meaning of the
original, is in substituting " the people that sat," for " the
people, those walking"—הָעָם הַהֹלְכִים; and " in the land and
shadow of death," for " in the land of the shadow of death"—
בְּאֶרֶץ צַלְמָוֶת. The difference in both respects is quite immaterial,
and seems to have been adopted for the sake of greater distinctness. The Septuagint differs so much, both from the original
and from the Evangelist, that it has manifestly exercised no
influence here.

Ch. viii. 17. So that it might be fulfilled which was spoken by
Esaias the prophet, saying, Αὐτὸς τὰς ἀσθενείας ἡμῶν ἔλαβεν
καὶ τὰς νόσους ἐβάστασεν: Isa. liii. 4. Himself took our sicknesses and bore our pains. I. 5.

The Septuagint has here οὗτος τὰς ἁμαρτίας ἡμῶν φέρει, καὶ περὶ
ἡμῶν ὀδυνᾶται, This one bears our sins, and on our account is put

to grief. So that the rendering of the Evangelist strikingly departs from it, and does so by adhering more closely to the original. There can be no doubt that this is the case respecting the first clause, "Himself took (*i.e.*, took upon Him נָשָׂא) our sicknesses," or diseases. But it holds equally of the second clause, which is וּמַכְאֹבֵינוּ סְבָלָם, " and our pains He bore them." The only peculiarity in the Evangelist is, that he employs νόσους in the sense of *pains;* which, however, is a very common meaning of the word, though not elsewhere found in the New Testament.

Ch. ix. 13 (xii. 7). But go and learn what is Ἔλεος θέλω καὶ οὐ θυσίαν : Hos. vi. 6. I desire mercy and not sacrifice. I. 6.

The passage is again quoted on another occasion by our Lord, at ch. xii. 7, and in precisely the same words. They give the literal meaning of the original, and adhere more strictly to the form than the Septuagint, which has Ἔλεος θέλω ἢ θυσίαν. This gives undoubtedly the substantial meaning—I desire, or delight, in mercy rather than sacrifice—but it is obtained by a sort of paraphrase.

Ch. xi. 10. For this is he of whom it is written, Ἰδοὺ ἐγὼ ἀποστέλλω τὸν ἄγγελόν μου πρὸ προσώπου σου, καὶ κατασκευάσει τὴν ὁδόν σου ἔμπροσθέν σου : Mal. iii. 1. Behold I send My messenger before Thy face, and he shall prepare Thy way before Thee. II. 4.

In the original it is simply, " Behold I send My messenger (or angel), and he shall prepare the way before Me." As given by our Lord, there is a change of person not found in the Hebrew—*I* send . . . before *Thy* face, prepare the way before *Thee;* and it is also a little more explicit—not simply send, but send *before Thy face*, and prepare, not the way merely, but expressly *Thy* way. The alterations are, like others of a like kind already noticed, plainly for the sake of explanation. It was in reality the same Divine Being who sent the messenger, and before whom the messenger was to go, preparing the way. But when that Divine Being had become man, and was Himself in the condition of one sent, it was fit that He should somehow indicate the diversity that thus appeared in connection with the unity. And it was quite naturally done by the change of person introduced, by which the sender appeared in some sense different

from the person before whom the messenger went; yet, as
the messenger had just been declared to be greater than all the
prophets (ver. 9), who could *He* be, whose way the messenger
went before to prepare, but the Lord Himself, that sent him?
This was evident to any thoughtful mind; and to show it was
the same, and yet in one sense another, of whom in both parts
the prophet spake, was our Lord's object in slightly altering the
original words. The real meaning was not thereby altered; it
was only adapted to existing circumstances, and to a certain
extent explicated. The Septuagint mistook the meaning of the
second clause of the verse, apparently from not knowing that the
verb פָּנָה in the Piel signifies to *clear* or *prepare*; so, they rendered פִּנָּה דָרֶךְ by ἐπιβλέψεται ὁδόν, he shall survey the way.

Ch. xii. 17–21. In order that it might be fulfilled which was
spoken through Esaias the prophet, saying, Ἰδοὺ, ὁ παῖς
μου, ὃν ᾑρέτισα, ὁ ἀγαπητός μου, ὃν εὐδόκησεν ἡ ψυχή μου· θήσω τὸ
πνεῦμά μου ἐπ' αὐτὸν, καὶ κρίσιν τοῖς ἔθνεσιν ἀπαγγελεῖ. οὐκ ἐρίσει οὐδὲ
κραυγάσει, οὐδὲ ἀκούσει τις ἐν ταῖς πλατείαις τὴν φωνὴν αὐτοῦ· κά-
λαμον συντετριμμένον οὐ κατεάξει, καὶ λίνον τυφόμενον οὐ σβέσει, ἕως
ἂν ἐκβάλῃ εἰς νῖκος τὴν κρίσιν. καὶ τῷ ὀνόματι αὐτοῦ ἔθνη ἐλπίουσιν:
Isa. xlii. 1–4. Behold my servant, whom I have chosen,
My beloved, in whom My soul is well-pleased; I will put
My Spirit upon Him, and He shall announce judgment to
the Gentiles. He shall not strive, nor cry, nor shall any
one hear His voice in the streets. A bruised reed shall
He not break, and smoking flax shall He not quench, till
He have brought forth judgment into victory. And in
His name shall the Gentiles trust. IV. 4.

By much the greater part of this passage might be assigned to
the first class; for it gives a faithful representation of the original
—in this differing favourably from the Septuagint, which presents a very loose and incorrect translation. It merely has,
" whom I have chosen," instead of " whom I uphold" אֶתְמָךְ־בּוֹ;
also, " He shall not strive, nor cry," instead of " He shall not cry
nor lift up," לֹא יִצְעַק וְלֹא יִשָּׂא; the former being only more explicit, and affixing to the lifting up of the prophet the more definite
sense of boisterous and wrangling procedure. But at the close
of ver. 20, we have " till He have brought forth judgment into
victory," while in the original it is, " He shall bring forth judg-

ment into truth"—לְאֶמֶת יוֹצִיא מִשְׁפָּט—or rather, " for truth (in the interest of truth) He shall bring forth judgment;" that is to say, His administration shall be in accordance with the principles of truth; and that is not materially different from the sense of the Evangelist, who represents the Lord's servant going on in His quiet, peaceful exercise of goodness, shunning everything that might lead to violent measures, or insurrectionary movements, till judgment—*i.e.*, righteousness in act and power—shall have been rendered triumphant over all that was opposed to it. It is a free rendering of the words of the original, but one that gives with perfect fidelity their scope and import. And the same also may be said of the last clause, " in His name shall the Gentiles trust," which is the Septuagint rendering for what is literally, " the isles shall wait for His law." In prophecy " the isles " is often put for the Gentiles; and these being said to wait for His law, is as much as, they look to Him as their Lord, they trust in His name.

Ch. xiii. 14, 15. And in them is fulfilled the prophecy of Esaias, which saith, Ἀκοῇ ἀκούσετε καὶ οὐ μὴ συνῆτε· καὶ βλέποντες βλέψετε καὶ οὐ μὴ ἴδητε· ἐπαχύνθη γὰρ ἡ καρδία τοῦ λαοῦ τούτου, καὶ τοῖς ὠσὶν βαρέως ἤκουσαν, καὶ τοὺς ὀφθαλμοὺς αὐτῶν ἐκάμμυσαν, μὴ ποτε ἴδωσιν τοῖς ὀφθαλμοῖς, καὶ τοῖς ὠσὶν ἀκούσωσιν, καὶ τῇ καρδίᾳ συνῶσιν, καὶ ἐπιστρέψωσιν, καὶ ἰάσομαι αὐτούς: Isa. vi. 9, 10. Ye shall verily hear, and shall not understand, and shall verily see, and shall not perceive; for this people's heart has waxed gross, and in their ears they are dull of hearing, and their eyes they have closed, lest at any time they should see with their eyes, and should hear with their ears, and should understand with their heart, and should convert, and I shall heal them. III. 2.

The quotation accords throughout with the Septuagint, differing only in the transposition of a single word, putting αὐτῶν after ὀφθαλμούς instead of after ὠσίν. Nor does it any otherwise differ from the Hebrew, than by using throughout the future instead of the imperative; what *shall* be done, according to the Septuagint and the Evangelist, the prophet represents himself as *commanded* to do. But this was only a stronger form of the future; it ordered the melancholy results spoken of to be accomplished, because these were so clearly foreseen as going to take place, that the Lord might as well instruct His servants to bring them about. Winer, Gr. § 44, 3. So that the Greek version is but the plainer and milder form of the prophetic declaration. In Acts xxvii. 26, 27, it occurs again in the same form; and in John xii. 40, it is given historically as a state of things actually brought about by the Lord, " He hath blinded their eyes," etc.; because what, in such circumstances, was commanded to be done, might equally be represented as in the eye of God already in being. In all the places of New Testament Scripture, in which the original passage is cited, it is applied to the mass of the Jewish people of the apostolic age, as if directly spoken of them. But it is clear from the passage itself, that it was uttered respecting that people generally, and that the prophet spoke for a long time to come.

> Ch. xiii. 35. So that it might be fulfilled which was spoken by the prophet, saying, Ἀνοίξω ἐν παραβολαῖς τὸ στόμα μου, ἐρεύξομαι κεκρυμμένα ἀπὸ καταβολῆς: Ps. lxxviii. 2. I will open my mouth in parables, I will utter things that have been hidden from the foundation [of the world]. II. 5.

In the first member the citation literally agrees with the Septuagint, and only so far differs from the Hebrew, that it puts parables in the plural, instead of in the singular. In the second member, however, the Evangelist very markedly differs from the Septuagint, which has φθέγξομαι προβλήματα ἀπ᾽ ἀρχῆς, I will utter problems—dark sentences, enigmas—from the beginning. This is a pretty close rendering of the original Hebrew, אַבִּיעָה חִידוֹת מִנִּי־קֶדֶם; excepting that " from of old," " from ancient time," would have been a little closer than " from the beginning;" but the meaning is the same. The version of the Evangelist, which expresses the same general sense, was obviously intended to present a simpler meaning, and to give a sort of explanation of the dark sentences spoken of, and of the ancient time. They were defined to be things that had been hid, not properly understood, and that from the beginning of the world. The ἐρεύξομαι of the Evangelist exactly corresponds to the Hebrew, both signifying properly to sputter, or belch out, then to give forth, or utter.

> Ch. xv. 4. For God said, Τίμα τὸν πατέρα καὶ τὴν μητέρα· καὶ,

'Ο κακολογῶν πατέρα ἢ μητέρα θανάτῳ τελευτάτο : Ex. xx.
12, and xxi. 16. Honour father and mother; and, He
that curseth father or mother, let him die the death. I. 7.
This may justly be assigned to the first class; for it gives the
exact meaning of the original, only omitting the personal pronouns, *thy* and *his*, after father and mother, merely on account of
the citations being turned from the form of a direct address into
that of a general charge. The Septuagint no further differs,
than in having the pronouns, σου in the first verse after father
and mother, αὐτοῦ in the second; and in having τελευτήσει instead
of τελευτάτο. In Mark vii. 10, the σου is retained in the first part
of the citation, but not in the second. Otherwise, it agrees with
Matthew.

Ch. xv. 8, 9. Esaias prophesied concerning you, saying, 'Ο
λαὸς οὗτος τοῖς χείλεσίν με τιμᾷ, ἡ δὲ καρδία αὐτῶν πόῤῥω ἀπέχει
ἀπ᾽ ἐμοῦ· μάτην δὲ σέβονταί με, διδάσκοντες διδασκαλίας, ἐντάλματα ἀνθρώπων : Isa. xxix. 13. This people honoureth Me
with the lips, but their heart keeps far from Me; but
in vain do they worship Me, teaching doctrines, commandments of men. III. 3.

The Evangelist here so nearly gives the words of the Septuagint, that the passage may be substantially regarded as an adoption of its words. The only difference is, that the Evangelist
abbreviates the commencement a little, puts the verb after λαός
in the singular, τιμᾷ instead of τιμῶσι, and, at the close, while
using the same words, places them in another order; the Septuagint has, διδάσκοντες ἐντάλματα ἀνθρώπων καὶ διδασκαλίας. It is
in the last part chiefly, that this version differs from an exact
impression of the original. For the sentence, "But in vain do
they worship Me, teaching doctrines, commandments of men,"
the Heb. is וַתְּהִי יִרְאָתָם אֹתִי מִצְוַת אֲנָשִׁים מְלֻמָּדָה, literally, "and their
fear toward Me has become a precept of men, taught" (viz. by
men, as contradistinguished from God). An abrupt and somewhat obscure sentence, of which the Septuagint version is a kind
of paraphrase, giving what is substantially the same meaning in
a fuller and plainer form. They seem to have taken וַתְּהִי for
וְתֹהוּ, and יִרְאָתָם for the second person plural Kal of the verb, thus
obtaining the sense, "in vain do they worship Me." This is not
distinctly stated in the original, but it is implied; for their fear

toward God being characterised as a fruit of man's teaching, necessarily bespoke its vanity.

Ch. xix. 4, 5. Have ye not read, that He who made them
at the beginning, made them male and female, and said,
῞Ενεκα τούτου καταλείψει ἄνθρωπος τὸν πατέρα καὶ τὴν μητέρα,
καὶ κολληθήσεται τῇ γυναικὶ αὐτοῦ, καὶ ἔσονται οἱ δύο εἰς σάρκα
μίαν; Gen. ii. 24. Therefore shall a man leave father
and mother, and shall be joined to his wife, and they two
shall be one flesh. II. 6.

The Septuagint is here all but adopted, and, for any practical
purpose, it is of no moment whether we should say, the Hebrew is
rendered with substantial correctness, or the Septuagint is in the
main followed. The Septuagint differs only in having αὐτοῦ
after πατέρα, which the Evangelist omits, and in putting προσκολ-
ληθήσεται πρὸς τὴν γυναῖκα instead of κολληθήσεται τῇ γυναικὶ—variations of no moment. Nor is the difference much greater from
the Hebrew : this has *his* father, and *his* mother ; and instead of
they *two* shall be one flesh, it has simply *they* shall be one flesh ;
by the *they*, however, plainly meaning the two in the preceding
context. The sense, therefore, is the same.

Ch. xix. 18, 19. Οὐ φονεύσεις, οὐ μοιχεύσεις, etc. Thou shalt
not kill, thou shalt not commit adultery, etc., precisely as
in Ex. xx. 12, *sq.*, and Lev. xix. 18. I. 8.

Ch. xxi. 4, 5. In order that it might be fulfilled which was
spoken through the prophet, saying, Εἴπατε τῇ θυγατρὶ
Σιών, ᾽Ιδοὺ, ὁ βασιλεύς σου ἔρχεταί σοι, πραὺς καὶ ἐπιβεβηκὼς
ἐπὶ ὄνον καὶ ἐπὶ πῶλον υἱὸν ὑποζυγίου : Zech. ix. 9. Say ye to
the daughter of Zion, Behold, thy King cometh to thee,
meek and mounted on an ass, and on a colt the foal of a
beast of burden. II. 7.

There is a peculiarity in the commencement of this citation,
the " Say ye to the daughter of Zion" being found, not in Zech.
ix. 9, from which what follows is taken, but in Isa. lxii. 11 ; so
that there is properly the joining together of two Old Testament
passages. They both relate to the same thing—the one more
generally, the other more particularly. Isaiah says, " Behold
thy Salvation cometh ; behold His reward is with Him, and His
work before Him." Zechariah proclaims, not the salvation
merely, but the Saviour Himself, and His appearance and cha-

racter. It is, no doubt, on this account that the two passages
are thrown together, and considered as one; although, as it is
merely the preamble of Isaiah's that is taken, the prophecy
quoted as now fulfilled is strictly that of Zechariah. As given
by the Evangelist, it does not differ much from the Septuagint,
but it comes somewhat nearer to the original—omitting, however,
one clause, "He is just and having salvation." The last expression in the original, בֶּן־אֲתֹנוֹת, more exactly means, son, or foal of
she-asses; according to a common Hebraism, by which the
young of a creature is denominated the offspring of that kind of
creatures generally; for example, בֶּן־בָּקָר, son of the herd, offspring of cattle. The Evangelist gives the import more generally, foal of a beast of burden—including asses of course, but
not specifically designating them. The Septuagint had also
given the meaning in a general way—ἐπιβεβηκὼς ἐπὶ ὑποζύγιον καὶ
πῶλον νέον; and this, no doubt, was partly the reason of the rendering adopted by the Evangelist.

Ch. xxi. 13. And He said unto them, it is written, Ὁ οἶκός μου
οἶκος προσευχῆς κληθήσεται· ὑμεῖς δὲ αὐτὸν ποιεῖτε σπήλαιον
λῃστῶν: Isa. lvi. 7; Jer. vii. 11. My house shall be
called a house of prayer, but ye make it a den of thieves
(or robbers). I. 9.

It is only the first part of this passage that is properly a citation; and it is a literal version of a part of Isa. lvi. 7. It stands
there, "My house shall be called a house of prayer for all nations." Matthew omits the "for all nations," as Luke also does,
but it is given in Mark xi. 17. The other part of the passage is
the word of Christ Himself, charging the persons before Him
with an entire depravation of the character of the temple and a
frustration of its design; but He does so in language borrowed
from Jer. vii. 11, where the prophet indignantly asks of the
priests and elders of his day, "Is this house, which is called by
My name, become a den of robbers in your eyes?" Our Lord
purposely threw His accusation into this form, to impress on the
men of His generation, that the iniquities of Jeremiah's age had
again returned, and that consequently like judgments also might
be expected. It is an allusion, however, to the prophet's words,
rather than a formal citation of them.

Ch. xxi. 16. Have ye never read, Ὅτι ἐκ στόματος νηπίων καὶ

A A

θηλαζόντων κατηρτίσω αἶνον : Ps. viii. 2.   Out of the mouth of
babes and sucklings Thou hast perfected praise.   III. 4.
A transcript from the Septuagint.   The Hebrew has עֹז יִסַּדְתָּ,
Thou hast founded, or, more generally, prepared strength.   Earlier
commentators gave the sense of *praise* here, and in some other
places to, the noun ; and it is still one of the meanings ascribed to
it by Gesenius.   Such also must have been the view of the Septuagint translators.   In the passages, however, where it is conceived
to bear this meaning, it rather indicates the strength, by which
God gets praise to Himself over His enemies, than the praise
itself.   In the eighth Psalm particularly, the idea of such
strength is appropriate ; for children are plainly brought in there
to show how God, even by such weak and foolish instruments,
can put to shame His powerful adversaries ; the strength of babes
is sufficient for His purpose.   So that we must regard our Lord
here as adopting the current version of the Septuagint, giving
the general sense, though not the precise shade of meaning in
the original.   It merely differs in directing attention, more to
the result aimed at, less to the means of accomplishing it.

> Ch. xxi. 42. Have ye never read, Λίθον ὃν ἀπεδοκίμασαν οἱ οἰκοδομοῦν-
> τες, οὗτος ἐγενήθη εἰς κεφαλὴν γωνίας· παρὰ Κυρίου ἐγένετο αὕτη,
> καὶ ἔστιν θαυμαστὴ ἐν ὀφθαλμοῖς ἡμῶν : Ps. cxviii. 22, 23.   The
> stone which the builders rejected, the same has become
> the head of the corner ; it was the Lord's doing, and it
> is marvellous in our eyes.   I. 10.

The Septuagint is followed verbatim, as it is also in Mark
xii. 10, 11 ; Luke xx. 17 ; and, as far as the quotation goes, in
Acts iv. 11 ; 1 Pet. ii. 7.   But the Septuagint here gives a
close translation of the original.

> Ch. xxii. 24. Moses said, If any one die, etc.   The reference
> is to Deut. xxv. 5 ; but the passage cannot justly be
> regarded as a quotation ; it merely professes to give the
> substance of a provision in the Mosaic law.

> Ch. xxii. 31, 32. Have ye not read that which was spoken
> unto you by God, saying, Ἐγώ εἰμι ὁ Θεὸς Ἀβραὰμ, καὶ ὁ
> Θεὸς Ἰσαὰκ, καὶ ὁ Θεὸς Ἰακώβ : Ex. iii. 6.   I am the God
> of Abraham, and the God of Isaac, and the God of
> Jacob.   I. 11.

At once coincides with the Septuagint, and closely adheres to the Hebrew, but omits what is in both, after I am, " of thy father," as not bearing on the point in hand.

Ch. xxii. 37. Jesus said to him, ᾿Αγαπήσεις Κύριον τὸν Θεόν σου ἐν ὅλῃ τῇ καρδίᾳ σου, καὶ ἐν ὅλῃ τῇ ψυχῇ σου, καὶ ἐν ὅλῃ τῇ διανοίᾳ σου : Deut. vi. 5. Thou shalt love the Lord thy God with (or in) all thy heart, and with all thy soul, and with all thy mind. I. 12.

The passage keeps closer to the Hebrew than to the Septuagint, which uses the preposition ἐξ instead of ἐν. The only apparent deviation from the exact import of the original, is at the close, in rendering בְּכָל־מְאֹדֶךָ with all thy mind, as strength is the more proper meaning of the noun; but it is *mental* strength that is meant; and consequently *mind* is really the same, denoting the full bent and purpose of soul.

Ch. xxii. 39. ᾿Αγαπήσεις τὸν πλησίον σου ὡς σεαυτόν : Lev. xix. 18. Thou shalt love thy neighbour as thyself. I. 13.

An exact translation, found previously in the Septuagint.

Ch. xxii. 43, 44. How then doth David in Spirit call Him Lord, saying, Εἶπεν Κύριος τῷ κυρίῳ μου· Κάθου ἐκ δεξιῶν μου, ἕως ἂν θῶ τοὺς ἐχθρούς σου ὑποκάτω τῶν ποδῶν σου : Ps. cx. 1. The Lord said to my Lord, Sit Thou at My right hand, until I make Thine enemies Thy footstool. I. 14.

Also an exact translation, and differing from the Septuagint only in having ὑποκάτω instead of ὑποπόδιον. The sense is the same in both. The passage is cited in the same terms in Mark xii. 36; Luke xx. 42; Acts ii. 35; Heb. i. 13; but in the three last with ὑποπόδιον.

Ch. xxvi. 31. For it is written, Πατάξω τὸν ποιμένα, καὶ διασκορπισθήσονται τὰ πρόβατα τῆς ποίμνης : Zech. xiii. 7. I will smite the Shepherd, and the sheep of the flock shall be scattered abroad. II. 8.

The rendering here is nearer to the Hebrew than the Septuagint, but it differs in putting the first verb in the first person future instead of in the imperative, as in the Hebrew, and also in adding τῆς ποίμνης, for which there is nothing to correspond, either in the Hebrew or in the Septuagint. This addition is omitted in Mark xiv. 27. The passage, as given in Matthew, is merely the simpler and more explicit form of that in Zechariah; by using the first person future of the verb πατάσσω, the action

is more distinctly referred to God; and by calling the sheep the
sheep of the flock, they are more pointedly described as the
Lord's select people. Both, however, were implied in the original
passage.

Ch. xxvii. 9, 10. Then was fulfilled that which was spoken
by Jeremy the prophet, saying, Καὶ ἔλαβον τὰ τριάκοντα
ἀργύρια, τὴν τιμὴν τοῦ τετιμημένου, ὃν ἐτιμήσαντο ἀπὸ υἱῶν
᾿Ισραὴλ, καὶ ἔδωκαν αὐτὰ εἰς τὸν ἀγρὸν τοῦ κεραμέως, καθὰ
συνέταξέν μοι Κύριος : Zech. xi. 13. And they took the
thirty pieces of silver, the price of Him that was valued,
whom they valued from (i.e. on the part of) the children
of Israel, and gave them for the potter's field, according
as the Lord appointed me. IV. 5.

The most striking peculiarity in connection with this citation,
is the circumstance of its being ascribed to Jeremiah, while in
reality it is found in the writings of Zechariah. This point will
be considered in Section Second, as it bears upon the mode of
application. Viewing the words as those of the prophet Zechariah, there certainly are considerable differences between the
original Hebrew and the Evangelist's version, though they affect
the form only, and not the substance. The Septuagint differs
again so materially from both, that it can have exercised no
influence. The passage in Zechariah runs literally thus, " And
the Lord said to me, Cast it (viz. the price, mentioned immediately before) to the potter, a glorious price which I was prized
at of them (מֵעֲלֵיהֶם, from off them, on their part) ; and I took
the thirty pieces of silver, and cast them into the house of the
Lord for the potter (i.e. that they might be given to the potter)."
Here, the whole assumes the form of a transaction between the
Lord and the prophet, who personates the Divine Shepherd,
thus meanly rated by the people ; in the Evangelist, the people
themselves are represented as doing all—as might, indeed, have
been understood, would be the case, when the prophecy passed
into the reality. The change in this respect, therefore, is entirely
of the same kind with that which was made at ch. xi. 10 and xiii.
14; a change from the first person to the third, to adapt the
words more palpably to the historical fulfilment, and render them
more transparent in meaning. The same object led to the other
alterations. In the original, the passage is very strongly enig-

matical; and so, instead of literally quoting it, the Evangelist presents a sort of paraphrase of the words. But there are in both the same leading ideas,—viz. that the Lord's representative, the Shepherd of Israel, had a price set upon Him—that this price was the miserable sum of thirty pieces of silver—that the transaction was gone into on the part of the people, and consequently by those who had to do with the house of the Lord— that, in token of the baseness of the transaction, the money was to be somehow consigned to the potter—and that the hand of the Lord was to be remarkably seen in the ordering of what took place. The words at the close, " according as the Lord commanded me," answer to the preamble in the prophet, "And the Lord said to me," coupled with the imperative form of what follows. The disposal of the price of blood was described as of the Lord's appointment; and, in like manner, in the history, while Jewish rulers alone are mentioned as doing all, it is plainly implied, that the hand of God directed the course of events into the particular channel they took.

Ch. xxvii. 46. And about the ninth hour Jesus cried with a loud voice, saying, Ἠλί, Ἠλί, λαμὰ σαβαχθανί; τουτέστιν, Θεέ μου, Θεέ μου, ἵνα τί με ἐγκατέλιπες; Ps. xxii. 1. My God, My God, why hast Thou forsaken Me? I. 15.

The Hebrew is exactly given, but given in the words of the Septuagint. Mark only so far differs, that instead of Θεέ he has ὁ Θεός, and instead of ἵνα τί he has εἰς τί. The sense is quite the same.

ST. MARK'S GOSPEL.

Ch. i. 2, 3. As it is written in Esaias the prophet, Ἰδοὺ ἀποστέλλω τὸν ἄγγελόν μου πρὸ προσώπου σου, ὃς κατασκευάσει τὴν ὁδόν σου· Φωνὴ βοῶντος ἐν τῇ ἐρήμῳ, ἑτοιμάσατε τὴν ὁδὸν Κυρίου, εὐθείας ποιεῖτε τὰς τρίβους αὐτοῦ: Mal. iii. 1; Isa xl. 3. Behold I send My Messenger before Thy face, who shall prepare Thy way. The voice of one crying in the wilderness, Prepare ye the way of the Lord, make His paths straight. II. 9.

The Old Testament passages have been already noticed—the latter at Matt. iii. 3, where it appears in precisely the same form;

the former at Matt. xi. 10, from which the words here no further
differ, than in substituting ὅς for καὶ before κατασκευάσει, merely
turning the second member of the verse from an independent
into a relative clause; and by leaving out at the close ἔμπροσθέν
σου. This abbreviates the passage, and so far departs from the
original, but the meaning is not altered. For the principle of
coupling two prophets together, and under the name only of one
introducing quotations from both, see the remarks in Section
Second, No. VIII., near the close.

 Ch. iv. 12. In order that βλέποντες βλέπωσιν καὶ μὴ ἴδωσιν, καὶ
  ἀκούοντες ἀκούωσιν καὶ μὴ συνιῶσιν, μή ποτε ἐπιστρέψωσιν καὶ
  ἀφεθῇ αὐτοῖς : Isa. vi. 9, 10. Seeing they might see, yet
  perceive not, and hearing might hear, yet understand
  not, lest at any time they should convert, and it be forgiven to them. IV. 6.

The Evangelist does not expressly cite these words; and we
only know, from their substantial agreement with the passage referred to in Isaiah, that they are a virtual quotation from the
prophet. From the manner in which the passage is given, however, it is evident that the Evangelist only meant to give the
substance of what was written. And accordingly, the words
actually produced are a sort of compound of the first and second
part of the original passage ; and, intent on the spiritual import
of the prophecy, the closing member, " and it be healed to them,"
is here turned into " and it be forgiven to them." This, doubtless,
was what was really meant; but in so changing the passage here,
and in the other parts, it is plain that the Evangelist thought it
enough to give the substance.

 Ch. vii. 6, 7. See at Matt. xv. 8, 9.
 Ch. vii. 10. See at Matt. xv. 4.
 Ch. x. 7. See at Matt. xix. 5.
 Ch. xi. 17. See at Matt. xxi. 13.
 Ch. xii. 11. See at Matt. xxi. 42.
 Ch. xii 26. See at Matt. xxii. 32.
 Ch. xii. 29, 30. The first commandment of all is, Ἄκουε,
  Ἰσραήλ, Κύριος ὁ Θεὸς ἡμῶν Κύριος εἷς ἐστίν· καὶ ἀγαπήσεις
  Κύριον τὸν Θεόν σου ἐξ ὅλης τῆς καρδίας σου, καὶ ἐξ ὅλης τῆς
  ψυχῆς σου, καὶ ἐξ ὅλης τῆς διανοίας σου, καὶ ἐξ ὅλης τῆς
  ἰσχύος σου : Deut. vi. 4, 5. Hear, O Israel, the Lord our

God is one Lord; and thou shalt love the Lord thy God out of all thy heart, and out of all thy soul, and out of all thy mind, and out of all thy strength. IV. 7.

It is necessary to assign this quotation to the last class; since, while very nearly coinciding with the Septuagint, it still slightly differs, without following the Hebrew. The difference is increased by the clause, ἐξ ὅλης τῆς διανοίας σου, for which there is nothing corresponding either in the Septuagint or in the Hebrew; but it seems doubtful, if the clause should form part of the text. Tischendorf omits it. Besides this, however, there is the substitution of ἰσχύος for the δυνάμεως of the Septuagint. The change renders it fully more close to the Hebrew; and (supposing the clause above noticed being unauthorised) the only departure from the exact translation of the Hebrew is in the preposition ἐξ, instead of ἐν—pointing more distinctly to the *action* of Divine love, as being from within outwards, and not simply to its having its *seat* within.

Ch. xii. 31. See at Matt. xxii. 39.

Ch. xii. 36. See at Matt. xxii. 43, 44.

Ch. xiv. 27. See at Matt. xxvi. 31.

Ch. xv. 28. And the Scripture was fulfilled, which said, Καὶ μετὰ ἀνόμων ἐλογίσθη, and He was numbered with the transgressors. The passage is a literal translation of Isa. liii. 12; but the whole verse is wanting in the best MSS., A B C D X, and it is consequently omitted in the later editions of the text.

Ch. xv. 31. See at Matt. xxvii. 46.

ST LUKE'S GOSPEL.

Ch. i. 17, comp. with Mal. iv. 5, 6; ver. 37, comp. Gen. xviii. 14; ver. 46, comp. with 1 Sam. ii. 2, sq.; ver. 76, comp. with Mal. iii. 1; ver. 78, comp. with Mal. iv. 2;—in these and various other parts of the first chapter of this Gospel, there are references to passages in Old Testament Scripture; but they are concealed references, the meaning of the original Scriptures being adopted, and their language, with more or less exactness, also employed,

but without any formal citation of them.   The object of
the references, indeed, is as much for the purpose of elucidating the Old, as confirming the New ; and hence there
is a considerable freedom in the mode of using the original.
Ch. ii. 24. According to that which is said in the law of the
Lord, ζεῦγος τρυγόνων ἢ δύο νεοσσοὺς περιστερῶν : Lev. xii. 8.
A pair of turtle-doves, or two young pigeons.   I. 16.
The translation is as literal as it could well be ; for the expression in the original, " two sons of a pigeon," is but a Hebraism
for " two young pigeons."   The rendering of the Evangelist very
nearly accords also with the Septuagint.
Ch. iii. 4–6. As it is written in the book of the words of
Esaias the prophet, Φωνὴ βοῶντος ἐν τῇ ἐρήμῳ· ἑτοιμάσατε
τὴν ὁδὸν Κυρίου, εὐθείας ποιεῖτε τὰς τρίβους αὐτοῦ· πᾶσα φάραγξ
πληρωθήσετε, καὶ πᾶν ὄρος καὶ βουνὸς ταπεινωθήσεται, καὶ ἔσται
τὰ σκολιὰ εἰς εὐθείας, καὶ αἱ τραχεῖαι εἰς ὁδοὺς λείας, καὶ
ὄψεται πᾶσα σὰρξ τὸ σωτήσιον τοῦ Θεοῦ : Isa. xl. 3–5.   The
voice of one crying in the wilderness, Prepare ye the way
of the Lord, make His paths straight.   Every valley
shall be filled up, and every mountain and hill shall be
made low ; and things crooked shall be [made] into
straight [paths], and rough ways into those of smooth-
ness ; and all flesh shall see the salvation of God.   III. 5.
The citation so nearly agrees with the Septuagint, that the
Evangelist may justly be held to have followed it.   The first
part of the passage occurred also in Matthew and Mark ; and
here too, as with them, the departure from the Septuagint and
the Hebrew merely consists in substituting αὐτοῦ for τοῦ Θεοῦ
ἡμῶν. This Evangelist alone gives the latter and longer part of the
passage ; and the language, throughout, with only very slight
and superficial differences, is that of the Septuagint.   The Septuagint has πάντα before τὰ σκολιὰ ; it has τραχεῖα instead of
τραχεῖαι, and πεδία instead of ὁδοὺς λείας : no difference in meaning, grammatical diversities chiefly.   The last clause, which
according to the Hebrew is, " And all flesh shall see it together,"
is in the Septuagint and Evangelist, " And all flesh shall see the
salvation of God."   The object to be seen—the salvation of God
—appears to have been introduced for the sake of explanation.
The manifestation of God spoken of was plainly that of God as

the Saviour of His people ; and the Septuagint translator merely expressed what was implied in the preceding context.

Ch. iv. 4.   See at Matt. iv. 4.

Ch. iv. 8.   See at Matt. iv. 8.

Ch. iv. 10, 11.   See at Matt. iv. 6.

Ch. iv. 12.   See at Matt. iv. 7.

Ch. iv. 17–19.   Opening the book, He found the place where it was written, Πνεῦμα Κυρίου ἐπ᾽ ἐμέ· οὗ εἵνεκεν ἔχρισέν με εὐαγγελίσασθαι πτωχοῖς, ἀπέσταλκεν με [ἰάσασθαι τοὺς συντετριμμένους τὴν καρδίαν—of somewhat doubtful authority], κηρῦξαι αἰχμαλώτοις ἄφεσιν, καὶ τυφλοῖς ἀνάβλεψιν, ἀποστεῖλαι τεθραυσμένους ἐν ἀφέσει, κηρῦξαι ἐνιαυτὸν Κυρίου δεκτόν : Isa. lxi. 1, 2.   The Spirit of the Lord is upon Me ; because that He anointed Me to preach good tidings to the poor, sent Me to heal the broken-hearted, to proclaim deliverance to the captives, and recovering of sight to the blind, to set at liberty them that are bruised, to proclaim the acceptable year of the Lord.   IV. 8.

Supposing the clause within brackets to be a part of the text, the Evangelist has followed the Septuagint precisely as far as ἀνάβλεψιν ; but after that he inserts the clause, ἀποστεῖλαι τεθ. ἐν ἀφέσει, not found in the Septuagint, and in the last clause, which *is* in the Septuagint, substitutes κηρῦξαι for καλέσαι.   It is obvious, that the Septuagint has been mainly followed, even though its rendering is not very literal.   Thus, instead of *poor*, as the persons preached to, the Hebrew expresses rather *humble* or *meek*, עֲנָוִים ; and for *healing* the broken-hearted, it has *bind up*. But in such a connection binding up and healing convey much the same meaning, and the poor must plainly be understood, partly at least, in a moral sense.   The clause, " recovering of sight to the blind," corresponds to what in the authorised version of that part of Isaiah, runs " the opening of the prison to them that are bound."   But the original, וְלַאֲסוּרִים פְּקַח־קוֹחַ, literally is, " and to the bound open-opening," or complete release from the evil under which they laboured.   The evil itself is not distinctly expressed; and it is only by a sort of conjecture that *prison* has been inserted.   The verb is almost always used of opening blind eyes (for example, in Isa. xlii. 7, l. 10), which accounts for the rendering of the Septuagint.   The translator merely sought to bring out the meaning more definitely; and even now—after all the helps of modern learning have been called into requisition—this substantially is the sense that approves itself to some as the best. Dr Alexander holds, that " the only natural sense which can be put upon the words, is that of spiritual blindness and illumination." The clause, ἀποστεῖλαι τεθ. ἐν ἀφέσει, appears to have been imported from another part of Isaiah, ch. lviii. 6. But how it should have come to be introduced here, is incapable of any proper explanation.

Ch. vii. 27. See at Matt. xi. 10.

Ch. x. 27. See at Matt. xxii. 37, and Mark xii. 29.

Ch. xix. 46, xx. 17, xx. 42, 43. See at Matt. xxi. 13, xxi. 42, xxii. 43, 44.

Ch. xxii. 37. For I say unto you, that this that is written must yet be accomplished in Me, ὅτι καὶ μετὰ ἀνόμων ἐλογίσθη: Isa. liii. 12. And He was numbered with the transgressors. I. 17.

An exact rendering of the Hebrew, and but slightly differing from the Septuagint, which has ἐν τοῖς ἀνόμοις.

Ch. xxiii. 46. Εἰς χεῖράς σου παρατίθεμαι τὸ πνεῦμά μου: Ps. xxxi. 6. Into Thy hands I commit My spirit. I. 18.

The words exactly accord with the original, and only so far differ from the Septuagint, that the latter has παραθήσομαι, the future, instead of the present. The received text has also the future; but there can be no doubt that the other is the correct form, which is that exhibited in the older MSS.

ST JOHN'S GOSPEL.

Ch. i. 23. See at Matt. iii. 3. There is here the substitution of εὐθύνατε for ἑτοιμάσατε.

Ch. ii. 17. His disciples remembered, that it was written, Ὁ ζῆλος τοῦ οἴκου σου καταφάγεταί με: Ps. lxix. 9. The zeal of thine house consumes me. I. 19.

It only differs from the Septuagint by using the present instead of the past tense of the verb. The Septuagint has κατέφαγε. The original is closely adhered to.

Ch. vi. 31. According as it is written, Ἄρτον ἐκ τοῦ οὐρανοῦ ἔδωκεν αὐτοῖς φαγεῖν: Ps. lxxviii. 24. He gave them bread out of heaven to eat. II. 10.

The more precise rendering of the Hebrew is, " Corn of heaven (דְגַן־שָׁמַיִם) He gave them." The Septuagint corresponds with the Evangelist, excepting that it has simply οὐρανοῦ, without the preposition and the article.

Ch. vi. 45. It is written in the prophets, Καὶ ἔσονται πάντες διδακτοί Θεοῦ: Isa. liv. 13. And they shall be all taught of God. II. 11.

The form of citation is very general : " in the prophets," as if our Lord had various passages in view, the substance of which alone He meant to give. The words, however, so nearly coincide with the passage in Isaiah referred to, that this is justly regarded as the original. The sense only is given ; the more exact rendering is, " All thy children shall be taught of the Lord ;" with which also the Septuagint agrees.

Ch. x. 34. Is it not written in your law, ὅτι ἐγὼ εἶπον, Θεοί ἐστε ; Ps. lxxxii. 6. I said, Ye are gods. I. 20.

In accordance both with the Hebrew and the Septuagint.

Ch. xii. 14, 15. According as it is written, Μὴ φοβοῦ, θύγατηρ Σιών· ἰδοὺ ὁ βασιλεύς σου ἔρχεται καθήμενος ἐπὶ πῶλον ὄνου: Zech. ix. 9. Fear not, daughter of Zion, behold thy King cometh to thee upon an ass's colt. IV. 9.

Comp. at Matt. xxi. 5. The passage is here given in a somewhat abbreviated form, and so as merely to convey the general sense. It hence does not literally accord with the Hebrew, yet differs but slightly from it, as far as the quotation goes : there is " fear not" instead of " rejoice," and " sitting" instead of " riding" —differences of no moment.

Ch. xii. 38. That the saying of the prophet Esaias might be fulfilled, which he spake, Κύριε, τίς ἐπίστευσεν τῇ ἀκοῇ ἡμῶν; καὶ ὁ βραχίων Κυρίου τίνι ἀπεκαλύφθη; Isa. liii. 1. Lord, who hath believed our report? and to whom has the arm of the Lord been revealed? I. 21.

The Septuagint is here followed in the closest manner ; but the Hebrew, at the same time, is literally rendered. Only the passage begins with a Κύριε, which is in the Septuagint, but has nothing corresponding in the Hebrew.

Ch. xii. 40. See at Matt. xiii. 15.

Ch. xiii. 18. In order that the Scripture might be fulfilled,
Ὁ τρώγων μετ᾽ ἐμοῦ τὸν ἄρτον, ἐπῆρεν ἐπ᾽ ἐμὲ τὴν πτέρναν αὐτοῦ:
Ps. xli. 9. He that eateth bread with Me, lifted up his
heel against Me. II. 12.

The words are fully nearer to the Hebrew than the Septuagint, and differ from it so little, that the sense is no way interfered with. The precise import of the Hebrew is, " He that ate
My bread, magnified against Me the heel." To magnify the heel
is a peculiar expression, and undoubtedly means the same as the
simpler phrase, " Lift up the heel;" namely, for the purpose of
kicking, or overthrowing his benefactor.

Ch. xv. 25. In order that the word might be fulfilled, which
is written in their law, ὅτι ἐμίσησάν με δωρεάν: Ps. cix. 3.
They hated Me without a cause. II. 13.

The original is יִלָּחֲמוּנִי חִנָּם, they fought against Me gratui-
tously, or without a cause ; which the Septuagint also expresses
by ἐπολέμησαν. The fighting, of course, implied the hatred, and
was but the expression of it ; so that the sense is substantially the
same. And possibly this mode of rendering was adopted to indicate more distinctly the moral nature of the conflict, and divert
the minds of the disciples from external weapons of violence.

Ch. xix. 24. In order that the Scripture might be fulfilled,
Διεμερίσαντο τὰ ἱμάτιά μου ἑαυτοῖς, καὶ ἐπὶ τὸν ἱματισμόν μου
ἔβαλον κλῆρον: Ps. xxii. 18. They parted My garments
among themselves, and upon My vesture they cast lot. I. 22.

The words are taken verbatim from the Septuagint, which
here exactly render the Hebrew.

Ch. xix. 36. In order that the Scripture might be fulfilled,
Ὀστιοῦν οὐ συντριβήσεται αὐτοῦ: Ex. xii. 46. A bone of Him
shall not be broken. I. 23.

The words again correspond with the Septuagint, and give a
literal rendering of the Hebrew, with the trifling exception of a
change of person and voice in the verb, to agree better with the
application made of the prescription : instead of " Ye shall not
break a bone," " A bone shall not be broken."

Ch. xix. 37. Another Scripture saith, Ὄψονται εἰς ὃν ἐξεκέντησαν:
Zech. xii. 10. They shall look unto Him whom they
pierced. I. 24.

An exact rendering of the original, with simply a change of

person, to adapt it to the occasion, as a word spoken *of* the Messiah, not *by* Him, as in the prophet : hence, look unto *Him*, not, unto *Me*. The Septuagint expresses it quite differently, ἐπιβλέψονται πρὸς μὲ, ἀνθ᾽ ὦν κατωρχήσαντο.

ACTS OF THE APOSTLES.

Ch. i. 20. For it is written in the book of Psalms, Γενηθήτω ἡ ἔπαυλις αὐτοῦ ἔρημος, καὶ μὴ ἔστω ὁ κατοικῶν ἐν αὐτῇ : Ps. lxix. 25. Let his habitation be desolate, and let there be none dwelling in it. II. 14.

The sense is entirely that of the original ; only what is there in the plural is here applied to an individual, and in the last clause, " in their tents" is omitted, and a reference made by the pronoun to the habitation in the preceding clause. The Septuagint does not differ materially.

Ch. i. 20. And τὴν ἐπισκοπὴν αὐτοῦ λάβετο ἕτερος : Ps. cix. 8. Let another take his office. I. 25.

An exact version of the original, and a transcript of the Septuagint, except in having λάβετο for λάβοι.

Ch. ii. 16–21. But this is that which was spoken by the prophet [Joel], Καὶ ἔσται ἐν ταῖς ἐσχάταις ἡμέραις, etc. The whole of this long passage is, with a few exceptions, a transcript of the Septuagint, and, as the Septuagint is here very faithful to the Hebrew, it is at the same time a close version. The ἐν ταῖς ἐσχ. ἡμέραις of the Evangelist is substituted for μετὰ ταῦτα of the Septuagint, and אַחֲרֵי־כֵן of the Hebrew ; there is a change of order in the two clauses of the second division of ver. 17 ; at the close of ver. 18 the Evangelist adds, καὶ προφητεύσουσιν, apparently for the purpose of rendering more explicit the intended result of the Spirit's effusion, resuming what had been in that respect indicated before ; and, lastly, in ver. 19, there is for ἐν οὐρανῷ of the Septuagint, ἐν τῷ οὐρ. ἄνω ; also for καὶ ἐπὶ τῆς γῆς, there is καὶ σημεῖα ἐπὶ τῆς γῆς κάτω. The slight additions are all of an explanatory kind ; they seem to have been designed to render the meaning at certain places somewhat more pointed and

explicit. Though the passage approaches very nearly to
the first class, it should perhaps strictly be ranked with
the second. II. 15.

Ch. ii. 25-28. For David saith respecting Him, Προορώμην τὸν
Κύριον ἐνώπιόν μου διαπαντός, etc. : Ps. xvi. 8, sq. The passage throughout is taken verbatim from the Septuagint.
But the translation gives the original very faithfully—
the only, and that a very slight deviation, being in ver. 8,
second member, where the original expresses, " Because
He is at my right hand, I shall not be moved ;" while
the other has, " Because He is at my right hand, in order
that I may not be moved." In rendering, however, so as
to give the meaning at once of the Hebrew and of the
Greek, the first clause should run, not as in the English
version, " I foresaw the Lord," but " I proposed," or
set, " the Lord ;" and again, at ver. 27, instead of,
" Thou wilt not leave My soul in hell," the exact import is, " Thou wilt not leave (give up, abandon) My
soul to Hades," οὐκ ἐγκαταλείψεις τὴν ψυχήν μου εἰς ᾅδην.
I. 26.

Ch. ii. 34, 35. See at Matt. xxii. 44.

Ch. iii. 22, 23. Moses said, "Ὅτι προφήτην ὑμῖν ἀναστήσει Κύριος
ὁ Θεὸς ὑμῶν ἐκ τῶν ἀδελφῶν ὑμῶν, ὡς ἐμέ· αὐτοῦ ἀκούσεσθε κατὰ
πάντα ὅσα ἂν λαλήσῃ πρὸς ὑμᾶς. "Εσται δὲ, πᾶσα ψυχὴ ἥτις ἂν
μὴ ἀκούσῃ τοῦ προφήτου ἐκείνου, ἐξολεθρευθήσεται ἐκ τοῦ λαοῦ :
Deut. xviii. 15, 18, 19. The Lord your God shall raise
up to you of your brethren a Prophet, like me ; Him
shall ye hear, in all things whatsoever He may speak to
you. And it shall come to pass, that every soul which
will not hear that Prophet, shall be destroyed from
among the people. IV. 10.

This citation differs as remarkably from the Septuagint as
that of ver. 25–28 coincides with it ; there is some resemblance
between them in the first part of the passage, but in the latter
part, not an expression is the same. Ver. 22 is an exact rendering of the Hebrew, as far as " Him shall ye hear," with
which Deut. xviii. 15 terminates. But instead of proceeding
right onwards, or passing over to ver. 19, in what follows the
substance is given of the latter part of ver. 18, together with

ver. 19. " He shall speak unto them," it was said, in ver. 18,
" all that I shall command Him." This substantially is added
after the quotation from ver. 15, " Him shall ye hear, in all
things whatsoever He may speak to you"—the things, namely,
that the Lord should command Him to speak. And then the
general import of ver. 19 is given. According to the original it
is, " And it shall come to pass, that whosoever will not hearken
to My words, which He shall speak in My name, I will require
it of him." St Peter makes it somewhat more specific, putting
" every soul," instead of " whosoever," and " he shall be destroyed from among the people," instead of " I will require it of
him." Not different in reality.

Ch. iii. 25. Saying to Abraham, Καὶ ἐν τῷ σπέρματί σου ἐνευλογηθήσονται πᾶσαι αἱ πατριαὶ τῆς γῆς : Gen. xxii. 18. And
in thy seed shall all the families of the earth be blessed.
II. 16.

It follows the Septuagint, with the exception of πατριαί, which
it substitutes for ἔθνη. The Hebrew has גוֹי, and consequently
agrees with the Septuagint. In the original call, however, as
given at Gen. xii. 3, the term for *families* is used, although the
Septuagint there uses φυλαί.

Ch. iv. 11. See at Matt. xxi. 42.

Ch. iv. 25, 26. Who didst speak through the mouth of thy
servant David, Ἵνα τί ἐφρύαξαν ἔθνη, καὶ λαοὶ ἐμελέτησαν κενά ;
παρέστησαν οἱ βασιλεῖς τῆς γῆς, καὶ οἱ ἄρχοντες συνήχθησαν ἐπὶ
τὸ αὐτὸ κατὰ τοῦ Κυρίου καὶ κατὰ τοῦ Χριστοῦ αὐτοῦ : Ps. ii.
1, 2. Why did heathen rage, and peoples imagine vain
things ? The kings of the earth stood forth (or up), and
the rulers were gathered together, against the Lord and
against His Christ. I. 27.

A literal transcript of the Septuagint, and also a fair version
of the Hebrew.

Ch. vii. 3, 6, 7, 26, 27, 28, 32, 33, 34, 35, 37, 40, 42, 43, 49,
50 :—In all these verses the words of Old Testament
Scripture are referred to, and cited, in the course of Stephen's speech. With only one or two slight verbal exceptions, the Septuagint is followed, in which the plain
sense of the Hebrew for the most part is given. But as
the passages are recited in a merely historical way, and

no specific application made of them, further than what
is implied in their having a place in such a speech, it is
unnecessary to exhibit them here in detail. No principle
of interpretation is involved in the use made of them by
Stephen.

Ch. viii. 32, 33. Here again there is a simple production of
an Old Testament passage, as found in the extant Greek
translation, and perused by the eunuch in his carriage.
The version accords generally, though not exactly, with
the Hebrew.

Ch. xiii. 32, 33. And we declare unto you glad tidings, how
that the promise which was made unto the fathers, God
hath fulfilled the same unto us their children, having
raised up Jesus, as also in the second Psalm it is written,
Υἱός μου εἶ σύ, ἐγὼ σήμερον γεγέννηκά σε : Ps. ii. 7.   Thou art
My Son, to-day have I begotten Thee. I. 28.

The words are precisely those of the Septuagint, which closely
render the Hebrew. As to the form of quotation, some MSS.
have ἐν τῷ πρώτῳ ψαλμῷ, which is preferred by Lachmann and
Tischendorf. If this be the correct reading, the apparent incorrectness is easily accounted for by the known practice of the
Jews, to regard the first psalm as a sort of general introduction
to the whole collection. In that case, what is now reckoned the
second psalm would naturally be viewed as the first.

Ch. xiii. 34. But that He raised Him from the dead, no longer
going to return to corruption, He spake after this manner,
ὅτι δώσω ὑμῖν τὰ ὅσια Δαυεὶδ τὰ πιστά : Isa. lv. 3.   I will
give you the sure mercies of David. I. 29.

The words again are those of the Septuagint, which correspond
with the Hebrew; only δώσω is introduced at the beginning, as
necessary to give a complete sense.

Ch. xiii. 35. See at ch. ii. 27.

Ch. xiii. 40, 41. Beware, therefore, lest that come upon you,
which is spoken of in the prophets, Ἴδετε, οἱ καταφρονηταί,
καὶ θαυμάσατε καὶ ἀφανίσθητε· ὅτι ἔργον ἐργάζομαι ἐγὼ ἐν ταῖς
ἡμέραις ὑμῶν, ἔργον ὃ οὐ μὴ πιστεύσατε ἐάν τις ἐκδιηγῆται ὑμῖν :
Hab. i. 5.   Behold, ye despisers, and wonder and vanish ;
for I will work a work in your days, a work which ye will
in no wise believe, if one should declare it to you. III. 6.

The Septuagint is followed with such slight variations as are scarcely worth noticing. It omits the καὶ ἐπιβλέψατε of the Septuagint, which form its second clause, and also θαυμάσια, which it has after θαυμάσατε. It also inserts a second ἔργον— ἔργον ὁ οὐ μὴ—which is wanting in the Septuagint. The Hebrew expresses substantially the same meaning, but instead of " ye despisers," has " ye among the heathen"—which undoubtedly points to the moral condition of the persons addressed, their heathenish, ungodly state of mind, rather than to their local position ; and it also has nothing precisely corresponding to the ἀφανίσθητε of the Greek. The idea conveyed by this is implied rather than expressed in the original. That the passage is quoted so generally as " from the prophets," is to be explained, partly, from the circumstance to be noticed in the elucidation of Matt. xxi. 5,—that the minor prophets are scarcely ever individually mentioned ; and partly because there is probably a reference to the very similar prophecy of Isa. xxviii. 14, which may be regarded as the foundation of that in Habakkuk.

Ch. xiii. 47. For so hath the Lord commanded us, Τέθεικά σε εἰς φῶς ἐθνῶν, τοῦ εἶναί σε εἰς σωτηρίαν ἕως ἐσχάτου τῆς γῆς : Isa. xlix. 6. I have appointed Thee for a light of the Gentiles, that Thou shouldst be for salvation to the ends of the earth. I. 30.

The Septuagint is again followed, excepting that the Hebrew is more closely rendered at the beginning, by the τέθεικά σε, for which the Septuagint has δέδωκά σε εἰς διαθήκην γένους. The passage before us differs from the Hebrew only in the latter expressing My salvation, instead of simply, salvation.

Ch. xv. 16, 17. As it is written, Μετὰ ταῦτα ἀναστρέψω καὶ ἀνοικοδομήσω τὴν σκηνὴν Δαυεὶδ τὴν πεπτωκυῖαν· καὶ τὰ κατεσκαμμένα αὐτῆς ἀνοικοδομήσω, καὶ ἀνορθώσω αὐτήν· ὅπως ἄν ἐκζητήσωσιν οἱ κατάλοιποι τῶν ἀνθρώπων τὸν Κύριον, καὶ πάντα τὰ ἔθνη ἐφ' οὓς ἐπικέκληται τὸ ὄνομά μου ἐπ' αὐτούς, λέγει Κύριος ποιῶν ταῦτα : Amos ix. 11, 12. After these things I will return, and will build up the tabernacle of David, which has fallen down ; and I will build again the ruins thereof, and I will set it up ; so that the residue of men may seek the Lord, and all the Gentiles upon whom My name is called, saith the Lord who doeth all these things. III. 7.

The citation is made almost verbatim from the Septuagint; but instead of μετὰ ταῦτα ἀναστρέψω, the commencement, the Septuagint has ἐν τῇ ἡμέρᾳ ἐκείνῃ. The latter is what the original expresses; and the explanation of the diversity here in the address of James is, no doubt, to be found in the desire to indicate briefly the period to which the prophecy referred, as implied in the context : it was to be after the times of judgment and humiliation there threatened had run their course. The Septuagint also, at least in most MSS., wants the τὸν Κύριον in the second verse, though this seems requisite to complete the meaning ; and it has after the ἀνορθώσω αὐτήν, what is omitted here, καθὼς αἱ ἡμέραι τοῦ αἰῶνος, as in the days of eternity, or of old. Down to this point, or throughout the first of the two verses quoted, the Septuagint renders the original closely ; but after that it deviates very considerably from the Hebrew, though it still expresses the general sense. The meaning of the original, however, is so plain, that it is difficult to understand how it should have been so rendered. " So that they may possess (or inherit) the remnant of Edom, and of all the heathen"—this is what in the Septuagint is turned into, " So that the residue of men may seek [the Lord], and all the Gentiles." It has been supposed they might have had a text, of which that was the literal rendering ; but this is doubtful, as all the MSS. give the reading of the received text. The reasons for the deviation can be only conjectural. But as it is clear, that Edom was particularised by the prophet, only on account of the enmity which animated the heathen toward Israel having assumed in them its keenest form,— so that " Edom and all the heathen" was as much as " all the heathen, not excepting even Edom,"—consequently, the rendering of the Septuagint, adopted by Luke, " the residue of men and all the heathen," comes, though in a general way, to much the same thing ; it denotes all sorts of heathen, wherever a residue of the old tribes might be found. And that instead of Israel *possessing* them, they should be represented as themselves *making inquiry* after God, the great fact is still indicated, that there was to be an entire change of relationship between the covenant-people and the heathen ; instead of hating and fighting against them, the heathen were to make suit to them, and press forward to obtain a share in their peculiar privileges. But this, in substance, is all one with Israel possessing them, in the sense meant by the prophet; he meant, that Israel was to become, in what was really important, the head of all the nations, and all were to come to them for blessing. So that, while the import is very much generalised in the rendering adopted, the leading ideas of the prophet are still conveyed. And they are quite apposite to the point at issue; for they imply, that there were to be tribes of men seeking after God, yea, over whom His name was called as peculiarly His own, who yet were formally different from the family of Israel.

Ch. xxviii. 26, 27. See at Matt. xiii. 14.

ROMANS.

Ch. i. 17. As it is written, Ὁ δὲ δίκαιος ἐκ πίστεως ζήσεται : Hab. ii. 4. But (or, now) the just shall live of faith. II. 17. According to the original it is, And the just shall live by his faith; or, as it may be rendered, And the righteous through his faith shall he live. The apostle, undoubtedly, gives the virtual import; for, as the suffix in the original, אֱמוּנָתוֹ, undoubtedly refers to the righteous person, the apostle could, without the least injury to the sense, leave out the *his*. The saying is again quoted in Gal. iii. 11, and Heb. x. 38. The Septuagint only differs from the apostle's citation by inserting μου after πίστεως.

Ch. ii. 24 and iii. 4 adopt the words of Isa. lii. 5, and Ps. li. 4, as given by the Septuagint, and correctly expressing the original; but the words are simply appropriated as suitable to the subject of the apostle's remarks, and are not introduced as having any special or prophetical reference to it.

Ch. iii. 10–18 is a series of quotations, in like manner, from Ps. xiv. v. 9, cxl. 3, x. 7 ; Isa. lix. 7, 8 ; Ps. xxxvi. 1,— cited merely as proof texts on the subject of human depravity and corruption, and without any peculiar Christian application. They are all taken from the Septuagint, with occasional slight alterations, which indicate no material difference of meaning, and call for no explanatory remark.

Ch. iv. 3. For what saith the Scripture, Ἐπίστευσεν δὲ Ἀβραὰμ τῷ Θεῷ, καὶ ἐλογίσθη αὐτῷ εἰς δικαιοσύνην : Gen. xv. 6. And Abraham believed God, and it was counted to him for righteousness. I. 31.

The rendering is that of the Septuagint, and it gives the original with sufficient exactness. What in the one is " He counted it," is merely put passively in the other, " it was counted to him."

Ch. iv. 6, 7. According as also David saith, Μακάριοι ὧν ἀφέθησιν αἱ ἀνομίαι, καὶ ὧν ἐπεκαλύφθησαν αἱ ἁμαρτίαι· μακάριος ἀνὴρ ᾧ οὐ μὴ λογίσηται Κύριος ἁμαρτίαν : Ps. xxxii. 1, 2. Blessed are they whose transgressions are forgiven, and whose sins are pardoned : blessed is the man to whom the Lord does not impute sin. I. 32.

The plural is here adopted in the first of the two verses,— " blessed they—sins—transgressions ;" while the original has the singular. But the words are there evidently used in a collective sense ; so that there is no real difference. The apostle follows the Septuagint exactly.

Ch. iv. 17. As it is written, ὅτι πατέρα πολλῶν ἐθνῶν τέθεικά σε : Gen. xvii. 5. A father of many nations have I made thee. I. 33.

From the Septuagint, and a literal rendering of the Hebrew.

Ch. iv. 18. As it is written, Οὕτως ἔσται τὸ σπέρμα σου : Gen. xv. 5. So shall thy seed be. I. 34.

The same as the preceding example.

Ch. viii. 36. As it is written, Ὅτι ἕνεκεν σοῦ θανατούμεθα ὅλην τὴν ἡμέραν, ἐλογίσθημεν ὡς πρόβατα σφαγῆς : Ps. xliv. 23. For Thy sake we are killed all the day long, we are counted as sheep for slaughter. I. 35.

Again quite literal.

Ch. ix. 7, 9, 12, 13, 15, contain passages from Gen. xxi. 12, xviii. 10, xxv. 23 ; Mal. i. 2, 3 ; Ex. xxxiii. 19, which are merely historically referred to, and are cited almost uniformly in the words of the Septuagint.

Ch. ix. 17. For the Scripture saith to Pharaoh, Ὅτι εἰς αὐτὸ τοῦτο ἐξήγειρά σε, ὅπως ἐδείξωμαι ἐν σοὶ τὴν δύναμιν μου, καὶ ὅπως διαγγελῇ τὸ ὄνομά μου ἐν πάσῃ τῇ γῇ : Ex. ix. 16. For this same thing did I raise thee up, that I might show forth in thee My power, and that My name might be declared throughout all the earth. I. 36.

Here the Septuagint is not precisely followed in the first part, and the rendering is more close to the Hebrew. The Septuagint has ἕνεκεν τούτου διετηρήθης, ἵνα.

Ch. ix. 25. As He saith also in Osee, Καλέσω τὸν οὐ λαόν μου, λαόν μου, καὶ τὴν οὐκ ἠγαπημένην, ἠγαπημένην: Hos. ii. 23. I will call the not-My-people, My people; and the-not-beloved, beloved. IV. 11.

Here again the Septuagint is departed from, notwithstanding that it gives a pretty literal version. The exact rendering of the Hebrew is, "I will have pity on the not-pitied (lo-ruhamah), and will say to the not-My-people (lo-ammi), My people art thou." The Septuagint, in the first part, expresses, I will love the not loved, ἀγαπήσω τὴν οὐκ ἠγαπημένην; otherwise, it is quite exact. The apostle gives substantially the same meaning, but he expresses the sense somewhat paraphrastically.

Ch. ix. 26. Καὶ ἔσται ἐν τῷ τόπῳ οὗ ἐρρέθη αὐτοῖς, Οὐ λαός μου ὑμεῖς, ἐκεῖ κληθήσονται υἱοὶ Θεοῦ ζῶντος: Hos. i. 10. And it shall come to pass, that in the place where it was said to them, Ye are not My people, there shall they be called sons of the living God. I. 37.

The Septuagint is here followed, excepting that instead of ἐκεῖ κληθ., it has κλη. καὶ αὐτοί. But the Hebrew is faithfully rendered.

Ch. ix. 27, 28. But Esaias crieth for Israel, Ἐὰν ὁ ἀριθμὸς τῶν υἱῶν Ἰσραὴλ ὡς ἡ ἄμμος τῆς θαλάσσης, τὸ ὑπόλειμμα σωθήσεται· λόγον γὰρ συντελῶν καὶ συντέμνων ἐν δικαιοσύνῃ· ὅτι λόγον συντετμημένον ποιήσει Κύριος ἐπὶ τῆς γῆς: Isa. x. 22, 23. If the number of the children of Israel be as the sand of the sea, the remnant shall return; for He is finishing His word and cutting it short in righteousness; because a word cut short will the Lord accomplish in the earth. IV. 12.

The citation approaches pretty nearly to the Septuagint, yet does not exactly accord with it; nor does it, in the latter part, give more than the general sense of the Hebrew. The first part is a close rendering: If the number of the children of Israel be as the sand of the sea (referring to the promise to Abraham),

the remnant (viz. that mentioned in the verse immediately preceding, " the remnant shall return unto the mighty God"—this,
but only this, not the countless, sand-like multitude) shall return.
Then the reason follows ; which in the original runs, For the
Lord God of hosts is making a consumption, and (or, even) determined, in the midst of all the earth. The sentence is obscure ;
and a paraphrastic rendering is given of it by the apostle. It evidently points to a work of judgment, which the Lord was going
to execute generally in the earth, and from which the covenant-
people were by no means to escape : Even in respect to them,
He was not going always to forbear ; and, while He saved a remnant, He would, at the same time, accomplish a work of judgment upon the many. This also is what is expressed by the
apostle, and more distinctly. The Lord was going, according to
it, to bring His word to an issue—an abrupt and determinate
issue—that would signally display His righteousness ; implying,
of course, from the connection, that Israel was to share in the
severity of its inflictions. So that this does not differ, in sense,
from the consumption determined, which the literal rendering
yields. .

Ch. ix. 29. And as Esaias said before, Εἰ μὴ Κύριος σαβαὼθ
ἐγκατέλιπεν ἡμῖν σπέρμα, ὡς Σόδομα ἂν ἐγενήθημεν, καὶ ὡς
Γόμορρα ἂν ὡμοιώθημεν : Isa. i. 9. If the Lord of hosts had
     not left us a seed, we should have become like Sodom,
     and should have been made like to Gomorrha. III. 8.

The Septuagint is here followed verbatim : it differs from the
Hebrew only in one word, in rendering a seed, σπέρμα, what in the
original is remnant, שָׂרִיד. It means, of course, barely a seed—
a remnant so small, that it should merely suffice for preserving a
seed. So that the difference is only in form.

Ch. ix. 33. As it is written, Ἰδοὺ τίθημι ἐν Σιὼν λίθον προσκόμματος
     καὶ πέτραν σκανδάλου, καὶ ὁ πιστεύων ἐπ᾽ αὐτῷ οὐ καταισχυνθήσεται :
     Isa. xxviii. 16, combined with ch. viii. 14. Behold I lay
     in Sion a stone of stumbling and rock of offence, and he
     that believeth on Him shall not be put to shame. IV. 13.

There are here brought together two related passages of the
prophet Isaiah ; the principal one referred to is ch. xxviii. 16, but
certain epithets, descriptive of the stone in respect to those who
refused to use it aright, are borrowed from an earlier passage, in

ch. viii. 14. There alone is the stone designated " a stone of stumbling and rock of offence." The apostle, combining thus two passages together, uses some freedom, as might be expected, in the manner of quotation. He does not adhere closely either to the Septuagint or to the Hebrew. The Hebrew, indeed, is so nearly followed, that it may be said to be all but literally rendered. The only deviation worth noticing is in the last expression : the Hebrew is לֹא יָחִישׁ, shall not make haste ; while the apostle, after the Septuagint, gives it, " shall not be put to shame." Not different in meaning, however; for the making haste of the prophet undoubtedly points to that hasty flight which they should betake to who made, not this foundation-stone, but *lies,* their refuge : these should very soon be found in a state of trepidation and flight; while the others, resting calmly on God's foundation, should stand fast, as having no occasion for rash and precipitate measures.—The last clause is again cited at ch. x. 11.

Ch. x. 5. For Moses saith, ὅτι ὁ ποιήσας αὐτὰ ἄνθρωπος ζήσεται ἐν αὐτοῖς : Lev. xviii. 5. The man that doeth these things shall live therein. I. 38.

The precise words of the Septuagint, but also corresponding with the Hebrew.

Ch. x. 6–8. But the righteousness of faith speaketh on this wise, Μὴ εἴπῃς ἐν τῇ καρδίᾳ σου, τίς ἀναβήσεται εἰς τὸν οὐρανόν ; τοῦτ᾽ ἔστιν Χριστὸν καταγαγεῖν· ἤ, τίς καταβήσεται εἰς τὴν ἄβυσσον ; τοῦτ᾽ ἔστιν Χριστὸν ἐκ νεκρῶν ἀναγαγεῖν.—Ἐγγύς σου τὸ ῥῆμά ἐστιν, ἐν τῷ στόματί σου καὶ ἐν τῇ καρδίᾳ σου : Deut. xxx. 12, *sq.* Do not say in thy heart, who shall ascend into heaven? That is, to bring Christ down again. Or, who shall descend into the abyss? That is, to bring Christ again from the dead. (But what saith it?) The word is nigh thee, in thy mouth and in thy heart.

This is not a quotation in the strict sense, but merely the free use of certain words in Deuteronomy, which conveyed a meaning adapted to the apostle's purpose, and is intermingled with comments or explanatory remarks of his own. The parts employed are given pretty nearly in the version of the Septuagint.

Ch. x. 11. See at ch. ix. 33.

Ch. x. 15. As it is written, Ὡς ὡραῖοι οἱ πόδες τῶν εὐαγγελιζομένων ἀγαθά : Isa. lii. 7. How beautiful are the feet of those that publish good things. I. 39.

The original is here exactly rendered, only the apostle omits " upon the mountains," as not required for his purpose. The Septuagint differs considerably, and mistakes the meaning of the first part, rendering ὡς ὥρα ἐπὶ τῶν ὀρέων.

Ch. x. 16. For Esaias saith, Κύριε, τίς ἐπίστευσεν τῇ ἀκοῇ ἡμῶν ; Isa. liii. 1. Lord, who hath believed our report ? I. 40.

A transcript of the Septuagint, and a close rendering of the Hebrew.

Ch. x. 18. Εἰς πᾶσαν τὴν γῆν, κ.τ.λ. An exact citation of the words in Ps. xix. 5, as found in the Septuagint, and also correctly representing the Hebrew; but the words are only appropriated, not formally quoted.

Ch. x. 19. First Moses saith, Ἐγώ παραζηλώσω ὑμᾶς ἐπ' οὐκ ἔθνει, ἐπὶ ἔθνει ἀσυνέτῳ παροργιῶ ὑμᾶς : Deut. xxxii. 21. I will move you to jealousy by [what is] no-people ; by a foolish people I will provoke you to anger. I. 41.

A close translation, but taken from the Septuagint.

Ch. x. 20, 21. But Esaias is very bold, and saith, Εὑρέθην [ἐν] τοῖς ἐμὲ μὴ ζητοῦσιν, ἐμφανὴς ἐγενόμην τοῖς ἐμὲ μὴ ἐπερωτῶσιν. But to Israel he saith, Ὅλην τὴν ἡμέραν ἐξεπέτασα τὰς χεῖράς μου πρὸς λαὸν ἀπειθοῦντα καὶ ἀντιλέγοντα : Isa. lxv. 1, 2. I was found of them that sought Me not, I became manifest to them that asked not after Me. All day long I stretched forth My hands unto a disobedient and gainsaying people. III. 9.

The Septuagint is followed in both verses, only the order is somewhat varied ; what forms the first clause here being the second in the Septuagint, and the ὅλην τὴν ἡμέραν in the second verse being thrown farther back. But the import of the Hebrew is not exactly given. According to it the first verse is, " I was sought of those that asked not, I was found of those that sought Me not." And, in the closing part of the second verse, there is but one epithet applied to the people — not " disobedient and gainsaying," but simply " rebellious." There is no real difference of meaning ; but the sense is somewhat more paraphrastically expressed in the Greek.

Ch. xi. 3, 4. Two passages from Elijah's history are here

quoted, but merely in a historical respect, as indicative of the state of things existing at the time. In both the Hebrew is pretty closely adhered to, more so than in the Septuagint.

Ch. xi. 8. As it is written, Ἔδωκεν αὐτοῖς ὁ Θεὸς πνεῦμα κατανύξεως, ὀφθαλμοὺς τοῦ μὴ βλέπειν, καὶ ὦτα τοῦ μὴ ἀκούειν: Isa. xxix. 10, combined with Deut. xxix. 4. God gave to them the spirit of slumber, eyes that they should not see, and ears that they should not hear. IV. 14.

The apostle seems here to have combined two passages, as at ch. ix. 33. The spirit of slumber is spoken of in Isa. xxix. 10 as judicially inflicted on the people ; and an explanation is given of what is meant by this in words derived from Deut. xxix. 4. What might be expected in such a case, was that the general sense should be expressed, rather than a very exact translation; and so in reality it is.

Ch. xi. 9, 10. David saith, Γενηθήτω ἡ τράπεζα αὐτῶν εἰς παγίδα, καὶ εἰς θήραν, καὶ εἰς σκάνδαλον, καὶ εἰς ἀνταπόδομα αὐτοῖς· σκοτισθήτωσαν οἱ ὀφθαλμοὶ αὐτῶν τοῦ μὴ βλέπειν, καὶ τὸν νῶτον αὐτῶν διὰ παντὸς σύγκαμψον: Ps. lxix. 22, 23. Let their table become a snare, and a net, and a stumbling-block, and a recompense to them ; let their eyes be darkened that they may not see, and bow down their back alway. III. 10.

The Septuagint is here followed with some very slight variations ; chiefly the leaving out of ἐνώπιον αὐτῶν before εἰς παγίδα, and inserting εἰς θήραν, which does not exist in the Septuagint. Substantially, however, the apostle follows the Septuagint, though this departs considerably from the Hebrew. The precise meaning of the latter is, " Let their table before them become a snare, and for peace (lit. peaces, salâms, salutations of peace) for a gin (i.e. what seemed to be for peace, let it become for a gin). Let their eyes become dark, so that they shall not see, and their bones continually shake." The rendering of the Septuagint, adopted by the apostle, however it may have been brought about, gives the general sense, though somewhat paraphrastically : the *snare* of the one, and its substitution of a gin for indications of peace, is amplified into " a snare, and a net, and a stumbling-block, and a recompense," that is, into things entirely the reverse, but such as

they had deserved by their own treachery. The other verse varies
less from the original; it merely substitutes, " bow down their
back alway," for " let their bones continually shake :"—only a
different mode of expressing a state of oppressive and enfeebling
bondage.

Ch. xi. 26, 27. As it is written, "Ηξει ἐκ Σιὼν ὁ ῥυόμενος, ἀποστρέ-
ψει ἀσεβείας ἀπὸ 'Ιακώβ· καὶ αὕτη αὐτοῖς ἡ παρ' ἐμοῦ διαθήκη,
ὅταν ἀφέλωμαι τὰς ἁμαρτίας αὐτῶν: Isa. lix. 20, 21. The
Redeemer shall come out of Zion, He shall turn away
ungodliness from Jacob; and this is the covenant from
Me to them, when I have taken away their sins.   IV. 15.

This citation differs less from the Septuagint than from the
Hebrew, but it does not exactly accord with either.   " The Redeemer shall come to Zion," is the first clause in the original, or
" for Zion," לְצִיּוֹן ; the Septuagint has ἕνεκεν Σιὼν ; but the apostle
says " out of Zion."   And in the following clause, what is in the
original, " unto them that turn from transgression in Jacob,"
becomes with the apostle, who here follows the Septuagint, " He
shall turn ungodliness from Jacob."   Peculiar as these changes
are, they proceed upon the same principle as that which we have
so often had occasion to notice in previous examples ; without in
reality altering the meaning, the apostle throws the passage into
a form, which virtually explains while it quotes; as our Lord,
for instance, slightly altered the words of Malachi, to render them
of easier understanding to those who lived when they were passing into fulfilment (See at Matt. xi. 10).   In like manner here,
we have such an alteration put upon the original passage, as
might render the only fulfilment it could henceforth receive
more easy of apprehension.   Christ, it intimates, will again come
to Zion, as He has already done, and come to such as turn from
transgression in Jacob—namely, for the purpose of blessing them
and doing them good.   But having already come and finished
transgression, Christ has put an end to the old state and constitution of things, so that the Zion that then was is now abolished:
Zion, in the proper sense, is above, the residence of the Divine
King; and when He comes to visit His people for the full execution of His covenant, He must come out of Zion, even while, in
a sense, He may be said to come to it.   And, as regards the Jewish
people, now rooted in apostasy, He must also, in connection with

that coming, turn them *from* ungodliness ; for only thus could the ends of the covenant in their behalf be accomplished, and the Lord's coming be attended by the benefits pointed at by the prophets. It is, therefore, the same prophecy still—only, by the verbal alterations he puts on it, the apostle adapts it to the time when he wrote, and renders it more distinctly indicative of the manner in which it was to find what still remained of its accomplishment.

The last clause, " when I have taken away their sins," is a brief and compendious expression for the state of blessing and acceptance, in which the people are contemplated by the prophet, and which with him is more especially connected with the indwelling agency of the Spirit. The Lord's coming finally to redeem and bless, will take place, only when the barrier raised by their guilt and alienation shall have been removed, and their personal state shall correspond with their privileges and prospects.

Ch. xii. 19. For it is written, Ἐμοὶ ἐκδίκησις, ἐγὼ ἀνταναποδώσω, λέγει Κύριος : Deut. xxxii. 35. Vengeance is Mine, I will repay, saith the Lord. II. 18.

The passage is not far from a literal rendering of the Hebrew, which is, " Vengeance is Mine, and recompense." The λέγει Κύριος is introduced for the purpose of indicating more expressly, that it is the Lord Himself who there speaks.

Ch. xii. 20. Contains a reiteration, and in the words of the Septuagint, of the exhortations originally given in Prov. xxv. 21, 22. But they are not formally cited.

Ch. xiii. 9. Contains citations of the commandments of the second table of the law, where there was no room for variation.

Ch. xiv. 11. For it is written, Ζῶ ἐγὼ, λέγει Κύριος, ὅτι ἐμοὶ κάμψει πᾶν γόνυ, καὶ ἐξομολογήσεται πᾶσα γλῶσσα τῷ Θεῷ : Isa. xlv. 23. As I live, saith the Lord, to Me shall every knee bow, and every tongue confess to God. II. 19.

The original passage is abbreviated; but it is so near to the Hebrew, that the deviations make no difference in the sense. Instead of "I live, saith the Lord," the prophet has, " I have sworn by Myself, the word is gone out of My mouth in righteousness, and shall not return"—a fuller declaration, but not different in sense. " Every tongue shall confess" is also sub-

stantially the same with "every tongue shall swear," which is
the expression in the prophet.   For in the Old Testament usage
swearing to, or in the name of the Lord, is simply to own and
confess Him as the one living God.

Ch. xv. 3. As it is written, Οἱ ὀνειδισμοὶ τῶν ὀνειδιζόντων σε ἐπέπεσαν
ἐπ᾽ ἐμέ: Ps. lxix. 9.   The reproaches of them that re-
proached thee fell upon Me.   I. 42.

From the Septuagint, but exactly rendering the Hebrew.

Ch. xv. 9. As it is written, Διὰ τοῦτο ἐξομολογήσομαί σοι ἐν ἔθνεσιν,
καὶ τῷ ὀνόματί σου ψαλῶ: Ps. xviii. 49.   For this cause
will I confess (or, give thanks) to Thee among the Gentiles, and sing praise to Thy name.   I. 43.

Again from the Septuagint, and a literal translation of the
Hebrew.

Ch. xv. 10. Again he saith, Εὐφράνθητε, ἔθνη, μετὰ τοῦ λαοῦ αὐτοῦ:
Deut. xxxii. 43.   Exult, ye Gentiles, with His people.
I. 44.

Here the Septuagint is quite different; it has εὐφ. οὐρανοὶ ἅμα
αὐτῷ.   The apostle follows the Hebrew, only inserting the preposition between Gentiles and people, for the sake of distinctness.
" Exult ye Gentiles, His people," is the precise rendering of the
original; addressing the Gentiles as now among God's people,
having one place and character with them.

Ch. xv. 11. And again he saith, Αἰνεῖτε πάντα τὰ ἔθνη τὸν Κύριον,
καὶ ἐπαινεσάτωσαν αὐτὸν πάντες οἱ λαοί: Ps. cxvii. 1.   Praise
the Lord all ye nations, and laud Him all ye peoples.
I. 45.

From the Septuagint, which literally renders the Hebrew.

Ch. xv. 12. And again Esaias saith, Ἔσται ἡ ῥίζα τοῦ Ἰεσσαί,
καὶ ὁ ἀνιστάμενος ἄρχειν ἐθνῶν, ἐπ᾽ αὐτῷ ἔθνη ἐλπιοῦσιν: Isa.
xi. 10.   There shall be a root of Jesse, and He that
ariseth to govern the Gentiles, in Him shall the Gentiles
trust.   III. 11.

Follows the Septuagint.   The Hebrew is, " In that day there
shall be a root of Jesse, that shall stand as a banner of the Gentiles; to it (or him) shall the Gentiles seek."   The Greek is a
free translation, but gives the sense in a simpler form.   To be a
banner to the Gentiles, is, in plain language, to take the leader-
ship or government of them; and to seek to Him, in such a

connection, must be all one with repairing to Him in confidence and hope.

Ch. xv. 21. As it is written, Ὁῖς οὐκ ἀνηγγέλη περὶ αὐτοῦ, ὄψονται, καὶ οἱ οὐκ ἀκηκόασιν, συνήσουσιν: Isa. lii. 10. To whom He was not announced, they shall see, and they that had not heard, shall understand. III. 12.

Again following the Septuagint, which differs from the original only in some points that merely affect the form. It has " *what was not announced or told them,*" and, at the close, " they shall consider," implying, doubtless, that they should so do it, as to understand.

I. CORINTHIANS.

Ch. i. 19. For it is written, Ἀπολῶ τὴν σοφίαν τῶν σοφῶν, καὶ τὴν σύνεσιν τῶν συνετῶν ἀθετήσω: Isa. xxix. 14. I will destroy the wisdom of the wise, and the understanding of the prudent I will set aside. II. 20.

The citation agrees with the Septuagint, except in the last word, which is κρύψω in the Septuagint, I will hide. The translation, however, though not the most literal that could be made, undoubtedly gives the plain meaning of the original. The chief difference is, that the thing is spoken of in the original merely as done, while here God is directly represented as doing it; this was certainly what the prophet also meant. To make men's understanding to become hidden, and to set it aside, are obviously but different modes of expressing the same thing.

Ch. i. 31. An abbreviated form of the sentiment contained in Jer. ix. 24, and not strictly a quotation.

Ch. ii. 9. As it is written, Ἃ ὀφθαλμὸς οὐκ εἶδεν, καὶ οὖς οὐκ ἤκουσεν, καὶ ἐπὶ καρδίαν ἀνθρώπου οὐκ ἀνέβη, ὅσα ἡτοίμασεν ὁ Θεὸς τοῖς ἀγαπῶσιν αὐτόν: Isa. lxiv. 4. Things which eye saw not, and ear heard not, and upon the heart of man came not up, the things which God has prepared for them that love Him. IV. 16.

This citation agrees neither with the Hebrew nor with the Greek of any particular passage of the Old Testament. It comes nearest, however, to Isa. lxiv. 4, where the exact rendering of the original is, " And from the beginning of the world they heard not, they perceived not by the ear, the eye saw not, O God, beside Thee (or, a God beside Thee), who will do for him that trusteth on Him." It is an obscure passage, and is rather paraphrased than translated by the apostle. The " neither hearing nor perceiving by the ear," is a kind of reiteration for the purpose of strongly asserting, that the matters referred to lay entirely remote from any cognizance of men's faculties; but the apostle, instead of giving this duplicate reference to ear knowledge, carries it into the region of the heart, and uses words substantially taken from the cognate passage of ch. lxv. 17, " it came not up upon the heart." The Septuagint has in the latter place, οὐ μὴ ἐπέλθη αὐτῶν ἐπὶ τὴν καρδίαν, so similar to the phrase here employed by the apostle, that one can scarcely doubt he had it in view. The citation, therefore, proceeds on the principle of bringing distinctly out, by a sort of paraphrastic interpretation, the import of the passage, and, while doing so, availing himself in part of language furnished by another passage in Isaiah's writings.

Ch. iii. 19. For it is written, Ὁ δρασσόμενος τοὺς σοφοὺς ἐν τῇ πανουργίᾳ αὐτῶν : Job v. 13.   He taketh the wise in their own craftiness.   I. 46.

The original is closely rendered, but not in the words of the Septuagint.

Ch. iii. 20. And again, Κύριος γινώσκει τοὺς διαλογισμοὺς τῶν σοφῶν, ὅτι εἰσὶν μάταιοι : Ps. xciv. 11.   The Lord knoweth the thoughts of the wise, that they are vain.   II. 22.

It differs from the Septuagint, and also from the Hebrew, only by putting " the wise," instead of " man." But as *man* is used emphatically by the Psalmist, as much as the most skilful, the most aspiring of men, it comes to the same thing as the apostle's *wise.*

Ch. ix. 9. For in the law of Moses it is written, Οὐ φιμώσεις βοῦν ἀλοῶντα : Deut. xxv. 4.   Thou shalt not muzzle the ox that treadeth.   I. 47.

A literal translation, and in the words of the Septuagint.

Ch. x. 7. As it is written, Ἐκάθισεν ὁ λαὸς φαγεῖν καὶ πιεῖν, καὶ ἀνέστησαν παίζειν : Ex. xxxii. 6.   The people sat down to eat and drink, and rose up to play.   I. 48.

Another literal translation, and in the words of the Septuagint.

Ch. xiv. 21. In the law it is written, Ὅτι ἐν ἑτερογλώσσοις καὶ ἐν χείλεσιν ἑτέρων λαλήσω τῷ λαῷ τούτῳ, καὶ οὐδ' οὕτως εἰσακούσονταί μου, λέγει Κύριος : Isa. xxviii. 11, 12. For in other tongues, and in lips of other persons (strangers), will I speak to this people; and not thus [even] will they listen to Me, saith the Lord. II. 22.

Here the Septuagint is quite forsaken, being palpably incorrect. The meaning of the Hebrew is given, though not by a close translation : what is there " stammering lips and another tongue," is here put in an explicated form by " other tongues and lips of strangers ;" i.e. unaccustomed modes of speech and address. The same thing seems to be meant by both forms of expression.

Ch. xv. 25, 27, 32, 45. The language is adopted of the following passages : Ps. cx. 1, viii. 7 ; Isa. xxii. 13 ; Gen. ii. 7.

Ch. xv. 54. Then shall be fulfilled the word that is written, Κατεπόθη ὁ θάνατος εἰς νῖκος: Isa. xxv. 8. Death is swallowed up into victory. I. 49.

A literal translation ; for לָנֶצַח means to perfection, or to glory, as well as to perpetuity ; but quite different from the Septuagint, which has κατέπιεν ὁ θάνατος ἰσχύσας.

II. CORINTHIANS.

Ch. vi. 2. For He saith, Καιρῷ δεκτῷ ἐπήκουσά σου, καὶ ἐν ἡμέρᾳ σωτηρίας ἐβοήθησά σοι: Isa. xlix. 8. In an acceptable time I heard thee, and in a day of salvation I succoured thee. I. 50.

A close translation, taken verbatim from the Septuagint.

Ch. vi. 16. As God said, ὅτι ἐνοικήσω ἐν αὐτοῖς καὶ ἐμπεριπατήσω, καὶ ἔσομαι αὐτῶν Θεός, καὶ αὐτοὶ ἔσονταί μου λαός : Lev. xxvi. 11, 12. I will dwell among them, and I will walk among them, and I will be their God, and they shall be My people. II. 23.

The meaning entirely accords with the Hebrew ; only, instead of " I will set My tabernacle," it has " I will dwell ;" and it uses

throughout the oblique instead of the direct form of address, as
in the original and the Septuagint.

Ch. vi. 17, 18. Διὸ ἐξέλθετε ἐκ μέσου αὐτῶν καὶ ἀφορίσθητε (saith
the Lord), καὶ ἀκαθάρτου μὴ ἅπτεσθε· κἀγὼ εἰσδέξομαι ὑμᾶς,
καὶ ἔσομαι ὑμῖν εἰς πατέρα, καὶ ὑμεῖς ἔσεσθέ μοι εἰς υἱοὺς καὶ
θυγατέρας—saith the Lord Almighty : Isa. lii. 11, 12 ;
Jer. xxxi. 9, 33.   Wherefore come out from among them,
and be ye separate—saith the Lord—and touch not the
unclean thing ; and I will receive you, and will be a Father
unto you, and you shall be to Me sons and daughters—
saith the Lord Almighty.   IV. 17.

The first of these two verses is a free translation of Isa. lii. 11,
and a portion of verse 12, which contains an address to the Lord's
people, as redeemed, to go forth from their state of bondage and
depression, and to separate themselves from all the defilements,
amid which they were placed ; with the assurance, that if they
did so the Lord Himself would go with them and defend them.
Undoubtedly, the substance of the prophet's declaration is given
by the apostle.   The remaining part of the passage seems to be
a compressed exhibition of the purport of several verses—in particular, the two referred to in Jeremiah.   Jer. iii. 19 might also
be included, and 2 Sam. vii. 14 has sometimes been thought to
be referred to.   In all these passages the same sentiment is undoubtedly expressed, viz., the acknowledgment of a filial relationship on the part of God toward those who should forsake
their sins, and give themselves to His service.   But as to the
formal character of both these verses, it may be questioned whether they should be regarded strictly as a quotation—or, rather,
as an utterance of the Lord's mind by the apostle himself ; though
couched in the style of ancient prophecy, and with reference to
certain passages contained in it.   So that we might say, *substantially*, the Lord spake thus in former times ; *formally*, and
explicitly, He speaks thus now.

Ch. viii. 15. As it is written, Ὁ τὸ πολὺ οὐκ ἐπλεόνασεν, καὶ ὁ τὸ
ὀλίγον οὐκ ἠλαττόνησεν : Ex. xvi. 18.   He that [got] the much
had no surplus, and he that [got] the little had no lack.
I. 51.

A close translation, and very nearly the same as the Septuagint.

Ch. ix. 9. As it is written, Ἐσκόρπισεν, ἔδωκεν τοῖς πένησιν, ἡ δικαιοσύνη αὐτοῦ μένει εἰς τὸν αἰῶνα : Ps. cxii. 9. He dispersed, He gave to the poor, His righteousness endureth for ever. I. 52. The same precisely as in the last example.

GALATIANS.

Ch. iii. 8. The Scripture preached before the Gospel to Abraham : ῞Οτι ἐνευλογηθήσονται ἐν σοὶ πάντα τὰ ἔθνη : Gen. xii. 3. In thee shall all nations be blessed. I. 53.

The original, in Gen. xii. 3, has *families* instead of *nations ;* the Septuagint φυλαὶ; but this is all one with nations; and the word for the latter is frequently used in the repetition of the promise: Gen. xviii. 18, xxii. 18.

Ch. iii. 10. For it is written, ὅτι ἐπικατάρατος πᾶς ὃς οὐκ ἐμμένει ἐν πᾶσιν τοῖς γεγραμμένοις ἐν τῷ βιβλίῳ τοῦ νόμου, τοῦ ποιῆσαι αὐτά: Deut. xxvii. 20. Cursed is every one that continueth not in all things that are written in the book of the law, to do them. II. 24.

The citation differs only in a few unimportant particulars from the Septuagint, and from the Hebrew only in being a little more full and explicit. The latter has, " Whosoever does not confirm," or ratify, " the words of this law to do them." Evidently the kind of ratification meant is that of a steady adherence to them.

Ch. iii. 11, 12. See at Rom. i. 17, x. 5.

Ch. iii. 13. For it is written, ᾿Επικατάρατος πᾶς ὁ κρεμάμενος ἐπὶ ξύλου: Deut. xxi. 23. Cursed is every one that hangeth on a tree. II. 25.

The Hebrew has merely *hanged* in the verse actually quoted, but the preceding verse uses the fuller expression, *hanged on a tree ;* so that there is no real difference between the citation and the original. The apostle, however, abbreviates the other part of the verse; he says simply, " cursed," while the original has " cursed of God."

Ch. iii. 16. He says not to seeds, as of many, but as of one, Καὶ τῷ σπερματί σου: Gen. xxii. 18. And to thy seed (which is Christ).

The passage was already cited at Acts iii. 25. But here it is coupled with a peculiar interpretation, for which see No. XV.

Ch. iv. 27. For it is written, Εὐφράνθητι στεῖρα ἡ οὐ τίκτουσα, ῥῆξον καὶ βόησον ἡ οὐκ ὠδίνουσα, ὅτι πολλὰ τὰ τέκνα τῆς ἐρήμου μᾶλλον ἢ τῆς ἐχούσης τὸν ἄνδρα : Isa. liv. 1. Rejoice thou barren that bearest not; break forth and cry aloud, thou that didst not travail; for more are the children of the desolate than of her that hath an husband. I. 54.

The Septuagint is followed throughout; but it gives the original with fidelity.

Ch. iv. 30. What saith the Scripture? Ἔκβαλε τὴν παιδίσκην καὶ τὸν υἱὸν αὐτῆς· οὐ γὰρ μὴ κληρονομήσει ὁ υἱὸς τῆς παιδίσκης μετὰ τοῦ υἱοῦ τῆς ἐλευθέρας : Gen. xxi. 10. Cast out the bond-woman and her son; for the son of the bond-woman shall not be heir with the son of the free-woman. I. 55.

This is also a literal translation; only, it generalises the closing words, by putting " with the son of the free-woman," instead of with " my son, with Isaac." Naturally; for the words were originally Sarah's; but as the Lord sanctioned the principle announced in them, the apostle fitly quotes them as spoken by the Lord of Sarah's offspring.

EPHESIANS.

Ch. iv. 8. Wherefore He saith, Ἀναβὰς εἰς ὕψος ᾐχμαλώτευσεν αἰχμαλωσίαν, ἔδωκεν δόματα τοῖς ἀνθρώποις : Ps. lxviii. 18. Having ascended up on high, He led captivity captive, He gave gifts to men. II. 26.

The rendering here adopted, which in the latter part only differs from the Septuagint, is a faithful representation of the original, so far as the substantial import is concerned. The only deviation from the literal meaning is in using the oblique, for the direct form of statement, and substituting gave, for received, in respect to the gifts of grace. The two words exhibit but different aspects of the same thing.

Ch. v. 14. Wherefore He saith, Ἔγειραι ὁ καθεύδων καὶ ἀνάστα ἐκ τῶν νεκρῶν, καὶ ἐπιφαύσει σοι ὁ Χριστός : Awake thou that sleepest, and arise from the dead, and Christ shall give thee light.

The passage is introduced with a very general reference to

Divine authority, specifying no particular Scripture where the saying was to be found; and as the words do not occur in any book of the Old Testament, some have even doubted if there is a reference to any passage in it. The mention of Christ at the close plainly shows, that an exact or literal quotation was not meant; but rather a free use of one or more passages read in the light of the Gospel. Such passages exist in Isa. lx. 1, 2, comp. with xxvi. 19.

Ch. v. 31. See at Matt. xix. 4, 5.

I. TIMOTHY.

Ch. v. 18. See at 1 Cor. ix. 9.

II. TIMOTHY.

Ch. ii. 19. And,"Ἔγνω Κύριος τοὺς ὄντας αὐτοῦ: Numb. xvi. 5. The Lord knoweth them that are His. II. 27.

The words of the Septuagint are taken, except that Κύριος is put for Θεός. In the original it is rather, The Lord will make known who are His—not only knows them, but will make His knowledge to appear. This is all the difference; the one indicating simply the fact, the other the visible manifestation, of the Divine knowledge.

HEBREWS.

Ch. i. 5. (on first quotation, see at Acts xiii. 32, 33, and No. XII. of the Second Part). And again, Ἐγὼ ἔσομαι αὐτῷ εἰς πατέρα, καὶ αὐτὸς ἔσται μοι εἰς υἱόν: 2 Sam. vii. 14. I will be to him a Father, and He shall be to Me a Son. I. 56.

In the words of the Septuagint, which correctly render the Hebrew.

Ch. i. 6. And when again He brings His first-begotten into the world, He saith, Καὶ προσκυνησάτωσαν αὐτῷ πάντες ἄγγελοι

Θεοῦ : Ps. xcvii. 7. And let all the angels of God worship Him. III. 13.

Coincides with the Septuagint, except in using the oblique instead of the direct form of speech. The original has *Elohim*
instead of *angels;* and there is the same difference at ch. ii. 7,
where see what is said in explanation.

Ch. i. 7. And as to the angels, He saith, Ὁ ποιῶν τοὺς ἀγγέλους
αὐτοῦ πνεύματα, καὶ τοὺς λειτουργοὺς αὐτοῦ πυρὸς φλόγα : Ps.
civ. 4. Who maketh His angels (messengers) winds, and
flame of fire His ministers. I. 57.

The Hebrew is exactly rendered, and in the words of the
Septuagint, excepting in the last expression, which is there πῦρ
φλέγον.

Ch. i. 8, 9. And to the Son, Ὁ θρόνος σου, ὁ Θεός, εἰς τὸν αἰῶνα
τοῦ αἰῶνος, κ.τ.λ.: Ps. xlv. 6, 7. Thy throne, O God, is
for ever and ever, etc. I. 58.

Throughout from the Septuagint, with no variations worth
naming, and giving a close translation of the Hebrew.

Ch. i. 10–12. And, Σὺ κατ᾽ ἀρχάς, Κύριε, τὴν γῆν ἐθεμελίωσας,
κ.τ.λ.: Ps. cii. 25, 26. Thou, Lord, in the beginning
didst lay the foundation of the earth, etc. I. 59.

Precisely as in the last example.

Ch. i. 13. See at Matt. xxii. 44.

Ch. ii. 6–8. But one testified in a certain place, saying, Τίς
ἔστιν ἄνθρωπος ὅτι μιμνήσκη αὐτοῦ; κ.τ.λ.: Ps. viii. 4–6.
What is man that Thou art mindful of him? etc. III.
14.

The citation is made entirely from the Septuagint, and differs
from the Hebrew only in one clause. What is here ἠλάττωσας
αὐτὸν βραχύ τι παρ᾽ ἀγγέλους, Thou hast made him somewhat
less than the angels, is in the Hebrew תְּחַסְּרֵהוּ מְעַט מֵאֱלֹהִים Thou
hast made him want little of Elohim (God). There is, however, an ambiguity in the Greek; for the βραχύ τι may refer
either to space or to time—lessened him either for a short period,
or by a little degree, though the latter is the more natural. The
Hebrew is more definite, and indicates littleness in respect to
degree or space. The application made of the passage consists
with the one aspect as well as the other; as will be shown in
the remarks at No. XVIII. of Second Section. And in regard to

the Elohim, it is plain, that when man is spoken of as wanting but a little of this, that is, of Deity, the term cannot be taken in its strictest sense; it cannot mean the Supreme Jehovah, in His personal properties and perfections; for the highest of creatures stand at an *infinite* distance from Him. It must be understood, therefore, in the looser sense, of something Divine-like in condition and dignity. It is so used in Ps. lxxxii. 6; Ex. xxii. 9, comp. with John x. 34. In the same sense it must also be understood in Ps. xcvii. 7, cited in ver. 6 of the preceding chapter, where the Elohim are called to do worship to one higher than themselves. Divine-like honour and dignity, therefore, are all that, in such cases, can be fairly understood by the term. And as the angels stand highest in this respect among created intelligences known to men, they are not unnaturally regarded as the beings, that most fully answer to the description. Substantially, therefore, the Greek version here gives the sense of the original; and some of the best commentators still concur in it as the most appropriate rendering that can be given. "The angels," says Delitzsch on the passage, "are called Elohim, as pure spiritual natures that have been produced from God, and are the purest reflections of the Divine essence."

Ch. ii. 12. Saying, Ἀπαγγελῶ τὸ ὄνομά σου τοῖς ἀδελφοῖς μου, ἐν μέσῳ ἐκκλησίας ὑμνήσω σε: Ps. xxii. 22. I will declare Thy name to My brethren, in the midst of the Church (or congregation) will I sing praise to Thee. I. 60.

The Septuagint is followed, except in the first word, for which it has διηγήσομαι; and the Hebrew is strictly adhered to.

Ch. ii. 13. And again, Ἐγὼ ἔσομαι πεποιθὼς ἐπ' αὐτῷ, I will put My trust in Him. And again, Ἰδοὺ ἐγὼ καὶ τὰ παιδία ἅ μοι ἔδωκεν ὁ Θεός, Behold I and the children which God hath given Me: Isa. viii. 17, 18. I. 61.

The Septuagint is literally followed in both parts of the citation; and without any material difference it exhibits the meaning of the original.

Ch. iii. 7-11. As the Holy Ghost saith, Σήμερον, ἐὰν τῆς φωνῆς αὐτοῦ ἀκούσατε, κ.τ.λ.: Ps. xcv. 7. *sq.* To-day, if ye will hear His voice, etc. I. 62.

The words are again those of the Septuagint, but the division made of them is not precisely the same; for here we have "saw

My works for forty years," while in the Septuagint, and also in the original, there is a pause after "saw My works," and the following sentence begins, "Forty years was I grieved." The sense is still the same, and by coupling the forty years with the seeing of God's works additional emphasis is given to the guilt of the people.

Ch. iv. 4. For He spake in a certain place, Καὶ κατέπαυσεν ὁ Θεὸς ἐν τῇ ἡμέρᾳ τῇ ἑβδόμῃ ἀπὸ πάντων τῶν ἔργων αὐτοῦ: Gen. ii. 3. And God rested in the seventh day from all His works. I. 63.

The passage is somewhat abbreviated, but it is exactly rendered, and in the words of the Septuagint.

Ch. v. 6. As He saith in another place: Σὺ ἱερεὺς εἰς τὸν αἰῶνα κατὰ τὴν τάξιν Μελχισεδέκ: Ps. cx. 4. Thou art a Priest for ever after the order of Melchisedek. I. 64.

The Hebrew again rendered in the words of the Septuagint.

Ch. vi. 14. God sware by Himself, saying, Εἰ μὴν εὐλογῶν εὐλογήσω σε, καὶ πληθύνων πληθυνῶ σε: Gen. xxii. 17. Surely blessing I will bless thee, and multiplying I will multiply thee. I. 65.

There is no deviation from the Hebrew and the Septuagint, except in putting σε at the close instead of σπέρμα σου. It makes no difference as to the sense.

Ch. viii. 5. As Moses was divinely instructed, Ὅρα γάρ, φησίν, ποιήσεις πάντα κατὰ τὸν τύπον τὸν δειχθέντα σοι ἐν τῷ ὄρει: Ex. xxv. 40. For see, says He, thou shalt make all according to the pattern that was shown thee in the mount. I. 66.

The words are again to a nearness those of the Septuagint, the only difference being the use of the aorist participle instead of the perfect δεδειγμένον. The original is correctly exhibited.

Ch. viii. 8–12. For finding fault He saith to them, Ἰδοὺ ἡμέραι ἔρχονται, λέγει Κύριος, καὶ συντελέσω ἐπὶ τὸν οἶκον Ἰσραήλ, κ.τ.λ.: Jer. xxxi. 31–34. Behold the days come, saith the Lord, and I will establish with the house of Israel, etc. I. 67.

There is no difference worth naming between this citation and the corresponding passage in the Septuagint; it is substantially a quotation from the Septuagint—only in one or two instances it substitutes a phrase of like import for another—such as συντελέσω ἐπὶ τὸν οἶκον for διαθήσομαι τῷ οἴκῳ, and διαθήκην ἐποίησα for διεθέμην. Throughout also the meaning of the Hebrew is closely rendered; nor does any exception need to be made for the clause at the close of ver. 9, where the writer of the epistle, following the Septuagint, has κἀγὼ ἠμέλησα αὐτῶν, and I regarded them not. In the original it is וְאָנֹכִי בָּעַלְתִּי בָם, which in the English Version, and many others, has the sense put on it, "though I was married to them." The same expression occurs at Jer. iii. 14, and has received the same rendering. But the propriety of that rendering is justly called in question, and the translation of the Septuagint is rather to be maintained. The primary meaning of the verb is to possess, or have dominion over; then to possess a wife, to marry ; but finally, according to Gesenius, to loathe, to reject, in which sense he takes it in the two passages referred to. " The common meaning," he says, "may do in ch. xxxi., if it be rendered, ' Although I was their Lord ;' but it gives a harsh sense ; and what weighs with me more, the signification of loathing is not foreign to the primary power of the verb. For there are also other verbs, in which the sense of subduing, being high over, ruling, is applied to the signification of looking down upon, despising, contemning."

Ch. ix. 20. Saying, Τοῦτο τὸ αἷμα τῆς διαθήκης ἧς ἐνετείλατο πρὸς ὑμᾶς ὁ Θεός: Ex. xxiv. 6. This is the blood of the covenant which God hath enjoined unto you. II. 28.

The sense of the original is substantially given, though differing slightly in form, and also departing somewhat from the Septuagint. The more exact rendering is, " Behold the blood of the covenant, which the Lord hath made with you."

Ch. x. 5–7. Wherefore when He cometh into the world He saith, Θυσίαν καὶ προσφορὰν οὐκ ἠθέλησας, σῶμα δὲ κατηρτίσω μοι, ὁλοκαυτώματα καὶ περὶ ἁμαρτίας οὐκ ηὐδόκησας· τότε εἶπον, Ἰδοὺ ἥκω—ἐν κεφαλίδι βιβλίου γέγραπται περὶ ἐμοῦ—τοῦ ποιῆσαι, ὁ Θεός, τὸ θέλημά σου: Ps. xl. 6–8. Sacrifice and offering I did not desire, but a body hast Thou prepared for Me ; burnt-offerings and offerings for sin Thou hadst no pleasure in. Then I said, Lo I come—in the volume of the book it is written of Me—to do Thy will, O God. III. 15.

This citation follows the Septuagint so closely, that the variations from it are quite inconsiderable. Instead of οὐκ ηὐδόκησας

it has οὐx ἤτησας, which is the more exact rendering of the original;
but the idea is the same ; and it is substantially all one, whether
the offerings in question are represented as not sought, or not
delighted in, on the part of God. The one implies the other.
There is, however, a very peculiar rendering given of a clause in
ver. 5. In the Hebrew it is אָזְנַיִם כָּרִיתָ לִּי, ears hast Thou dug
through (laid thoroughly open) for Me; the meaning is, Thou
hast formed in Me a willing and obedient spirit, so that I preserve
an open and listening ear to all Thy commands. It is difficult to
understand, how this should have come to be put into the form
given it by the Septuagint, " a body hast Thou prepared for Me."
But the sentiment conveyed by it is substantially the same ; for
by the preparing of a body, in such a connection, is evidently
meant, a body formed and qualified for the service of God—
ready in all its powers to yield the obedience required. The
contrast here is, between the sacrifices of slain victims, and the
free-will sacrifice of a living body, or a listening and obedient
spirit.

Ch. x. 16, 17. See at ch. viii. 8–11.

Ch. x. 30. For we know Him that hath said, Ἐμοὶ ἐκδίκησις, ἐγὼ
     ἀνταποδώσω, λέγει Κύριος. And again, κρινεῖ Κύριος τὸν λαὸν
     αὐτοῦ : Deut. xxxii. 35, 36. Vengeance is Mine, I will
     recompense, saith the Lord. The Lord will judge His
     people. II. 29.

The only difference is in the form of the first declaration ; as
put in the original it is, Mine is vengeance and recompense.
Here the latter word is turned into an independent sentence, to
give additional emphasis to the meaning.

Ch. x. 37, 38. There is here a substantial appropriation of
     the language of Hab. ii. 3, 4; but there is no express
     citation, and the original is used with some freedom.

Ch. xi. 21. Καὶ προσεκύνησεν ἐπὶ τὸ ἄκρον τῆς ῥάβδου αὐτοῦ : Gen.
     xlvii. 31. And worshipped upon the top of his staff.
     I. 68.

This is not given as a quotation, but it is actually one, being
the precise words of the Septuagint. According as the words
in the original are pointed, they admit of a different rendering ;
either that just produced, or the one given in the English version, according to the Mas. punctuation, " He bowed himself

(or, worshipped) upon the bed's head." The other is the more probable meaning.

Ch. xii. 5, 6. And ye have forgotten the exhortation, which speaketh unto you as unto children, Υἱέ μου, μὴ ὀλιγώρει παιδείας Κυρίου, μηδὲ ἐκλύου ὑπ᾿ αὐτοῦ ἐλεγχόμενος· ὃν γὰρ ἀγαπᾷ Κύριος παιδεύει, μαστιγοῖ δὲ πάντα υἱὸν ὃν παραδέχεται: Prov. iii. 11, 12. My son, despise not the Lord's chastening, nor faint when thou art rebuked of Him; for whom the Lord loveth He chasteneth, and scourgeth every son whom He receiveth. III. 16.

The Septuagint is followed verbatim, which only in the last clause departs from the Hebrew; but here it does so rather singularly. The Hebrew is וּכְאָב אֶת־בֵּן יִרְצֶה, and (or, as) a father the son he delighteth in. The Septuagint apparently read the first word as if it were יְכָאֵב, and so turned it into a verb, having God for its nominative, and making it mean, " and chastiseth the son whom He receiveth," or delighteth in. As this introduced no change into the sentiment conveyed in the passage, but only omitted the allusion to the earthly father, which, however, the apostle shortly afterwards takes occasion to bring out in words of his own (ver. 9), he simply adopted the rendering of the Septuagint.

Ch. xii. 20, 21. In these two verses the general import merely is given of passages in the Old Testament. Ex. xix. 12, 13, 16; Deut. ix. 19.

Ch. xii. 26. Now hath He promised, saying,῎Ετι ἅπαξ, ἐγὼ σείσω οὐ μόνον τὴν γῆν, ἀλλὰ καὶ τὸν οὐρανόν: Hag. ii. 6. Yet once, I will shake not only the earth, but also the heaven. II. 30.

The citation differs from the Septuagint and from the Hebrew only in form: for the purpose of bringing out more prominently the heaven as included in the shaking, what according to the original is, " the heaven and the earth," is here made, " not only the earth, but the heaven."

Ch. xiii. 5. For He Himself hath said, Οὐ μή σε ἀνῶ, οὐδ᾿ οὐ μή σε ἐγκαταλίπω: Josh. i. 5. I will not leave thee, nor will I forsake thee. I. 69.

Follows the Hebrew closely, but differs in form from the Septuagint. The same sentiment occurs in Deut. xxxi. 8.

Ch. xiii. 6. So that we may boldly say, Κύριος ἐμοὶ βοηθὸς, καὶ
οὐ φοβηθήσομαι· τί ποιήσει μοι ἄνθρωπος ; Ps. cxviii. 6. The
Lord is my helper, and I shall not be afraid ; what shall
man do to me ? I. 70.

The Septuagint is cited, but it gives the original quite correctly; for, " the Lord is my helper," is substantially one with
" the Lord is for me," which is the literal rendering of the Hebrew.

JAMES.

Ch. ii. 8, 23. See at Matt. xxii. 39, and Rom. iv. 3.

Ch. iv. 5. Do ye think that the Scripture saith in vain, πρὸς
φθόνον ἐπιποθεῖ τὸ πνεῦμα ὃ κατῴκισεν ἐν ἡμῖν ; the spirit that
dwelt in us lusts to envy ?

The reference seems to be to the passages which condemn an
envious or covetous spirit, as naturally working in men's hearts
—such as the tenth commandment of the law, Eccl. iv. 4, etc.
But it is only a reference to the general import of such passages,
not an explicit quotation.

Ch. iv. 6. Wherefore He saith, Ὁ Θεὸς ὑπερηφάνοις ἀντιτάσσεται,
ταπεινοῖς δὲ δίδωσιν χάριν : Prov. iii. 34. God resisteth the
proud, but giveth grace to the lowly. III. 17.

The Septuagint has precisely these words in the passage referred to. The Hebrew so far differs, that in the first member
it expresses, " Surely He scorneth the scorners." It is undoubtedly the scorn of a proud and elated spirit that is meant; so
that the meaning is virtually the same. A very similar antithesis also is found in Prov. xxix. 23.

I. PETER.

Ch. i. 16. Because it is written, Ἅγιοι ἔσεσθε, ὅτι ἐγὼ ἅγιος :
Lev. xi. 44. Be ye holy, for I am holy. I. 71.

An abridged quotation, but quite literal.

Ch. i. 24, 25. For, πᾶσα σὰρξ χόρτος, καὶ πᾶσα δόξα αὐτῆς ὡς
ἄνθος χόρτου· ἐξηράνθη ὁ χόρτος, καὶ τὸ ἄνθος ἐξέπεσεν· τὸ δὲ ῥῆμα

Κυρίου μένει εἰς τὸν αἰῶνα : Isa. xl. 6, 7. All flesh is grass, and all the glory of it as the flower of grass; the grass withereth, and the flower fadeth; but the word of the Lord abideth for ever. I. 72.

The Septuagint is followed, which adheres closely to the Hebrew.

Ch. ii. 6. See at Rom. ix. 33. The apostle here merely adds a few epithets from Isa. xxviii. 16, which were omitted by St Paul.

Ch. ii. 7. See at Matt. xxi. 42, and Acts iv. 11.

Ch. ii. 9, 22, 24. In each of these verses there is a silent appropriation of Old Testament passages—Ex. xix. 6; Isa. liii. 9, 5,—in perfect accordance with the Hebrew, and in the words of the Septuagint. But there is no formal citation.

Ch. iii. 10–12. Another silent appropriation of an Old Testament passage—Ps. xxxiv. 12–16—almost entirely in the language of the Septuagint, and quite faithful to the original.

Ch. iii. 14, 15. A similar adoption of the language of Isaiah, in ch. viii. 12, 13.

Ch. iv. 8. A substantial, though not quite literal, appropriation of the words of Prov. x. 12.

II. PETER.

Ch. ii. 22. It has happened unto them according to the true proverb, κύων ἐπιστρέψας ἐπὶ τὸ ἴδιον ἐξέραμα, καὶ ὗς λουσαμένη εἰς κύλισμα βορβόρου : The dog is turned to his own vomit again, and the sow that was washed to her wallowing in the mire.

This is not properly a scriptural quotation, but the application merely of a common proverb to a spiritual case. The first part of it occurs substantially in Prov. xxvi. 11, yet not precisely as presented here.

REVELATION.

Throughout the book of Revelation there is the constant appropriation of the language of Old Testament Scripture ; sometimes
—as at ch. ii. 27, v. 10—sentences are adopted entire ; but of
proper and formal citation there is no example, as, indeed, the
nature of the book did not admit of it.

GENERAL RESULT.

It thus appears, that of the four classes of citations mentioned
at the outset, there are—not reckoning repeated citations of the
same passages in the same or other books—72 belonging to the
first, 30 to the second, 17 to the third, and 17 to the fourth. In
other words, considerably more than the half of the whole, in
which the passages from the old Testament are closely rendered
—very commonly in the words of the Septuagint, but also occasionally by an independent translation.   In 30 more the difference between the original and the citation is merely of a formal
kind, some slight alteration being adopted in the phraseology,
usually for the purpose of adapting it better to its place as a citation, but without making any assignable difference in the meaning of the passage.   Indeed, so narrow often is the boundary
between this class of quotations and the first, that it is of no
moment, practically, whether they should be assigned to the first
class, or should form one by themselves.   The third class presents
17, in which the Septuagint is followed, in preference to the
Hebrew ; but here again the variations are commonly of a formal
kind ; and even when they exhibit a substantial difference, it is
only by a sort of paraphrastic explanation being given of the
original, or by a distinct expression being imparted to a particular
aspect of the truth, such as specifying a result or a cause, which
the original did nothing more than indicate.   In none of the
cases are we presented with a different sense, but simply with a
modified representation of the same sense.   And in the remaining
17, in which neither is the Hebrew nor the Septuagint strictly
followed, there is a common principle pervading them ; that,

namely, of rendering something peculiar or obscure in the original more clearly intelligible to those who were immediately in the eye of the New Testament writer, or to readers generally in Gospel times. In the whole of this class of cases, as well as of the immediately preceding one, the general meaning of the ancient Scripture is still preserved, and nothing in doctrine or precept is built upon the superficial differences existing between the citation and the original.

It is, therefore, a groundless and unwarranted application to make of these occasional departures from the exact import of the original, when they are employed as an argument against the plenary inspiration of Scripture. So, for example, Dr Davidson, in his Hermeneutics (p. 513); he holds, that the freedom with which the New Testament writers cite the Scriptures of the Old Testament, is a conclusive proof against such inspiration. For, he argues, " the terms and phrases of the Old Testament, if literally inspired, were the best that could have been adopted. Why, then, did not the writers of the New Testament give, as nearly as possible, these best terms and phrases? They should have adhered to the *ipsissima verba* of the Holy Spirit (seeing they were the best), as closely as the genius of the Hebrew and Greek languages allowed. But, instead of this, they have widely departed from them." We are afraid this argument, if valid, would go much further than establish a conclusion against what is termed *verbal* inspiration. The question cannot be one merely of words; for if not the main import, yet the precise shade of meaning, is necessarily affected by the deviations; so that, on the principle in question, the New Testament writers are liable to the charge of having chosen an inferior thing to what lay actually before them; they altered, to some extent, the statements of Scripture, and altered them to the worse. But the argument rests upon a fallacy—the fallacy of supposing, that what is the best in certain circumstances, what may have been best when the ancient prophets wrote, must also be the best when apostles and evangelists brought into notice the fulfilment of their words. By that time circumstances were materially changed; and it may have been expedient, it may even have been required by the highest spiritual wisdom, to adopt some slight modification of the original passage, or to give an explanatory rendering of its terms, so as to adapt it the better to the purpose of its application. Even in those cases, in which, for anything we can see, a closer translation would have served equally well the purpose of the writer, it may have been worthy of the inspiring Spirit, and perfectly consistent with the fullest inspiration of the original Scriptures, that the sense should have been given in a free current translation; for the principle was thereby sanctioned of a rational freedom in the handling of Scripture, as opposed to the rigid formalism and superstitious regard to the letter, which prevailed among the Rabbinical Jews. The Church of the New Testament, we are thereby taught, is not bound by the pedantic trammels which Jewish authorities imposed, and which, by spending its solicitude upon the shell, comparatively neglected the kernel. The stress occasionally laid in the New Testament upon particular words in passages of the Old, and even on the number and tenses of words—as at Matt. xxii. 32, 45; Gal. iii. 16; Heb. i. 5, v. 10—sufficiently proves what a value attaches to the very form of the Divine communications, and how necessary it is to connect the element of inspiration with the written record as it stands. It shows that God's words are pure words, and that, if fairly interpreted, they cannot be too closely pressed. But in other cases, when nothing depended upon a rigid adherence to the letter, the practice of the sacred writers, not scrupulously to stickle about this, but to give prominence simply to the substance of the revelation, is fraught also with an important lesson; since it teaches us, that the letter is valuable only for the truth couched in it, and that the one is no further to be prized and contended for, than may be required for the exhibition of the other.

The practice in this respect of the sacred writers is followed every day still, and followed by persons who hold the strictest views of inspiration. They never imagine, while they quote passages from a current translation, though it may not give the meaning to the nicest shade, or themselves slightly modify the form of words to suit the particular application made of them, that they are thereby compromising the plenary inspiration of Scripture. They do not the less hold every jot and tittle of it to be sacred, that they at times find it unnecessary to press what is comparatively *but* a jot or tittle. Indeed, the matter in this aspect of it has been quite properly put by the writer just quoted, and in a manner, that seems to accord ill with what fell from him on verbal inspiration. "It is unreasonable to expect," he says, "that the apostles should scrupulously abide by the precise words of the passages they quote. By a slight deviation from the Greek, they sometimes rendered the sense clearer and more explicit; at other times they paraphrased, rather than translated, the original Hebrew. In every instance we suppose them to have been directed by the superintending Spirit, who infallibly kept them from error, and guided them in selecting the most appropriate terms, where their own judgments would have failed." (P. 470.)

There *is*, however, a point connected with the citations from the Old Testament, which seems somewhat strange, and admits of no proper explanation—although it can scarcely be said to touch upon the doctrine of inspiration, or to involve any question of principle. It is in respect to the apparent capriciousness of the treatment given to the Septuagint translation. Sometimes it is followed with great regularity for a series of passages, and then, it is suddenly abandoned at places where its rendering is not less, or even more exact. Thus at Matt. xxvii. 9, 10, a rendering is preferred markedly differing from the Septuagint, itself too one of the most peculiar, while in several preceding quotations the words of the Septuagint were almost literally adopted. So again, at John xv. 25, the Septuagint is departed from, where it literally renders the original, but in the two following citations it is implicitly followed. There are similar irregularities elsewhere, particularly in the Epistle to the Hebrews, where, usually, the Septuagint is closely followed, while yet at certain passages a somewhat different rendering is preferred (see ch. ix. 20, x. 30, xii. 26). This alternating use and disuse of the Septuagint as a translation of Old Testament Scripture finds no explanation in any existing relations, or spiritual principle, with which we are acquainted.

SECTION SECOND.

QUOTATIONS FROM THE OLD TESTAMENT IN THE NEW, CONSIDERED IN RESPECT TO THE MODE OF APPLICATION.

IT is but a comparatively small number of the passages, which have been already produced and compared with the original Scriptures, that require to be brought up for consideration here. The use made of them in the New Testament is, for the most part, so transparently reasonable and proper, that among thoughtful and sober-minded Christians there can be but one opinion regarding it. We shall, therefore, as formerly intimated, limit our inquiry to the examples which have chiefly created embarrassment, and require explanation.

I.
Matt. i. 22, 23 ; Isa. vii. 14.

It is remarkable, that the application of no testimony of Old Testament Scripture to the transactions of the New, has given rise to more variety of opinion, or is more frequently called up for fresh discussion, than the one, which meets us at the very threshold of the Gospels,—in Matt. i. 22, 23, where we are told, that the things concerning the miraculous conception of Christ took place, that the prophecy in Isa. vii. 14 might be fulfilled, which said, " Behold the virgin shall conceive, and bear a son, and they shall call His name Immanuel." By a large body of interpreters it is held, that in this application there is a certain accommodation of the prophecy to what was not primarily, if at all, contemplated in it; and that the child to be born and called Immanuel was, in the first instance at least, to be a child produced in the ordinary course of nature, and within a very short period from the deliverance of the prophecy. They argue this on the ground, that the birth of the child was to form the sign of Judah's speedy deliverance from the hostile assaults of Syria and Israel ; insomuch that, before he should know to discern the evil and the good, those two lands should be forsaken of their kings (ver. 16). They, therefore, conceive, that by the child-bearing virgin must primarily be meant a then living maid—a maid presently to be married, and to have offspring; that to this offspring a symbolical name should be given, as a pledge of the Divine favour and protection, and that the pledge should be verified within two or three years by the removal of the kings of Syria and Israel. So that the Evangelist Matthew must, either have *accommodated* a prediction to Christian times, which did not originally and properly point to them, or the prediction of itself admitted and justified such an application because of a typical relationship between the nearer and the more remote birth—the one being like the foreshadowing sign of a much greater future. Many subordinate differences exist among the interpreters, who concur in the more fundamental part of this view; they only differ as to the particular *almah,* or virgin, and child that may be meant, and the way in which the ultimate is to be connected with the primary application. But as such shades of difference do not affect the *principle* of the interpretation, or obviate the objections, to which in *any* form it appears to me liable, there is no need for going into details.

I. (1.) To begin with the negative aspect of the matter, or the objections that present themselves to this mode of interpretation, we remark, first of all, that there is obviously in it the want of a proper *nexus* between the two events, such as the application of the Evangelist seems to indicate, and as the nature of the relation itself would require. We take for granted, that there *was* a relation of some kind; for the *mere* accommodationists are not worth arguing against. The Evangelist, then, plainly appears to have found, in the words of the prophet, an explicit and definite announcement of Messiah's wonderful birth and person, as being in Himself a marvellous combination of the Divine and human, and as born into this world the singular offspring of a virgin. However he may have found this in the prophecy, he certainly appears to *have* found it; and can the right to do so be justified on such a relationship between the immediate and the ultimate as the view under consideration, in any of its forms, supposes? One can conceive of a birth among the chosen people so brought about and so circumstanced, as that

it might fitly enough be taken for a prophetical sign or prefigu-
ration of Christ's birth.   The birth of Isaac was pre-eminently
one of that description ; there was a quite special and supernatural element in the one as well as in the other ; and in both
cases alike connected with the higher interests of the Divine
kingdom.   Such, too, in a measure, was the case with Solomon,
the immediate successor of David on the throne of the kingdom.
But in such cases there was a peculiarity connected with the
parentage ; a typical relationship already existed there, forming
the ground of the *prospective* reference of the birth ; and it
became comparatively easy to pass from the immediate to the
future, and to see the one imaged in the other ; especially when
there was a prophetic word uttered over the nearer event, which
naturally carried the thoughts onward to the remoter and greater
things of the kingdom.   But here, on the interpretation in question, there is nothing properly special, either in the parent or the
child ; it might have been (for aught that appears) *any* young
woman in Judea, *any* child born of such a woman, in the ordinary course of nature, whether in the line of Messiah's parentage or not.   One cannot even see why, on the supposition in
question, the single specification should have been made, of the
mother being at the time an unmarried person—granting, what
we by no means admit, that the *almah* of the prophet denotes
only a marriageable maid, though not necessarily a virgin ; for
there seems no proper call for the mother being a maid, if the
child was to come by ordinary generation, and if it was to be the
pledge of Divine protection and deliverance only by the period
of its birth.   In such a case, it seems arbitrary in the prophet
to lay stress on the point of her maidenhood, especially when no
particular maiden was indicated ; and still more arbitrary in the
Evangelist to find in the child of this indefinite mother, with its
immediate adjuncts, a distinct and circumstantial presage of
Messiah's birth.

(2.) Then, the name assigned to this child, for the purpose of
indicating its nature and destiny, taken in connection with the
prophet's own subsequent references to it, seems incompatible
with the idea of its being a common child, produced by ordinary
generation.   That a maiden or virgin, without further specification, should be announced as the prospective mother of a child,

that was to bear, as a fit designation, the name Immanuel (God-with-us), would certainly be peculiar—we may even say, without a parallel—if in that child there was nothing supernatural in respect to its generation or its birth. The very imposing of such a name seems to import, that Divinity was somehow to be peculiarly manifested in the Being produced. Not only so, but in ch. viii. 8, the prophet addresses Him as the rightful proprietor of the land ; for, speaking of the adversary, he says, " The stretching out of his wings shall fill the breadth of Thy land, O Immanuel." And in the very fact of that proprietorship, he descries the sure ground of a final deliverance from all oppression and violence : " Take counsel," he says to the enemies, " and it shall come to nought ; speak the word, and it shall not stand, *because of Immanuel*" (ch. viii. 10). Thus Immanuel is plainly regarded by Isaiah as the God-man, the proper Lord of the heritage, supreme Head of the kingdom. And still again, in another part of the same line of prophecy, in the glorious announcement with which it closes (ch. ix. 6), the prophet evidently points back to the original passage, and invests it with the full meaning of which its words were susceptible :—in the one, " a virgin conceives and bears a son ;" in the other, " unto us a child is born, a son is given ;" " God-with-us" is the name by which the first is to be called, and of this, in like manner, it is said, " His name shall be called Wonderful, Counsellor, the Mighty God, the Everlasting Father, the Prince of Peace." With such marked resemblances, it is impossible almost to doubt the identity of the two ; and looking at the whole of these subsequent references to the prediction of the Immanuel, it is not too much to say, that the prophet himself stretches out the hand to the Evangelist.

(3.) Thirdly, the interpretation we oppose would find only comfort and encouragement in what was announced to the house of David ; and thereby leaves altogether unexplained the element of indignation and threatening with which it is so pointedly introduced. " Is it a small thing for you to weary men, but will ye weary my God also ? *Therefore* the Lord Himself shall give you a sign ; Behold, the virgin shall conceive," etc. Does it seem a natural or satisfactory way to understand this address, to read it as if it meant, Because ye have wearied men by your faithless

and foolish procedure, and are proceeding to do the same with
God, therefore the Lord will Himself give you the most asto-
nishing sign of His gracious nearness and protection. This,
surely, would have been a premise and a conclusion that hung
strangely together; and so some of its propounders have felt;
for they have endeavoured to turn the *therefore* (לָכֵן) into a *nevertheless*, which would, indeed, make an intelligible meaning, but
it is entirely unwarranted by the usage of the word. There
were, no doubt, at the time, pious individuals in the kingdom of
Judah, and of these some probably in the house of David, who
needed a word of encouragement, and for whom also it was provided, in the communication actually given; but such persons
are not formally brought into notice. It is with the false and
backsliding portion, that the prophet directly and ostensibly
deals; hence, whatever of a hopeful nature might be wrapt up in
the message he delivers, we are constrained to look for something
also—something even of a striking and palpable kind—which involved a work of rebuke and judgment. In presenting nothing
of this description, the interpretation under review entirely fails to
account for a prominent feature in the prophetic announcement.

These objections, which are derived mainly from the Old Testament passage itself, seem fatal to the view, under any modification, which would find in the Immanuel an ordinary child,
born at that particular time. In urging them, no reference has
been made to incidental topics—such as the attempt sometimes
made to identify this child with that said, in ch. viii. 1–4, to be
born of the prophet and the prophetess; for this identification is
utterly arbitrary, the latter child having both a different parentage ascribed to it, and a different name; nor can it be consistently understood otherwise than of a transaction in the ideal
region of prophetic vision.[1]

II. It is one thing, however, to make good, or to appear to
make good a negative, and quite another thing to establish satisfactorily a positive, view of a controverted subject. And as the
strength and plausibility of the class of interpretations now considered lie in the apparent necessity of finding a present birth
to render the child a sign (as it is supposed the prophet meant

---

[1] See Prophecy in its Distinctive Nature, etc., p. 505.

it to be considered) of an immediately approaching deliverance, it is necessary to show how, on the supposition of the Messiah being directly contemplated in the prediction of Immanuel, this objection can be met.

(1.) Now, it is at the outset to be borne in mind, that the prophecy has in its very form something enigmatical—*purposely* has it; both from the nature of the subject, which refers to the deep things of God, and from the condition of the people, which was such as to call for what would, in a manner, drive them from their superficial mode of looking at Divine things. Our Lord Himself sometimes, for like reasons, spoke enigmatically; He did so, for example, near the commencement of His ministry, when He said, " Destroy this temple, and in three days I will raise it up"—an announcement which none present at the time understood, and which was not even *intended* to be understood, except by such as would give themselves to prayerful and earnest inquiry. The real import and bearing of Isaiah's prediction, in like manner, lay beyond the depth of those who had no eye to look beneath the surface, and might even baffle the research and inquiry of those who possessed such an eye, till farther revelations and the course of Providence had thrown additional light on it. Undoubtedly, there is no want of similar announcements in Isaiah and the other prophetical books.

(2.) Another thing to be kept in mind is the precise starting-point, or crisis of affairs, out of which the prophecy originated, and which it was designed to meet. The combination formed by the kings of Syria and Israel had for its object, not merely the invasion of Judah and the subjugation of the king, but the entire displacement of the house of David, and the substitution of another dynasty under the son of Tabeal (ver. 6); in other words, the avowed aim of the hostile party was to make void God's covenant with the house of David. This was the audacious design which called forth the first word of God on the occasion, and led Isaiah to give to Ahaz and his people a solemn assurance that the scheme should certainly miscarry (ver. 8, 9). Yet, in the very act of doing this, he distinctly intimated, that for Ahaz and his house there still was danger—danger arising, not so much from any plans or power of their open adversaries, as from their own faithless and ungodly spirit; for the word concluded by saying, " If ye will not believe, surely ye shall not be established." As much as to say, Even the overthrow of your immediate enemies, and the defeating of their hostile policy, cannot secure to you and your family the possession of the throne, and the establishment of the kingdom in your hands— unless you rid yourselves of the evil spirit of unbelief, and learn to rest in the word and power of Jehovah.

(3.) Then, partly with the view of bringing out this fatal de- fect in the character of Ahaz, and partly for the purpose of un- folding God's own design as to the establishment of the kingdom in the house of David, the prophet represents himself as giving Ahaz the option of a sign—a sign of what? A sign, we are constrained by the connection to think, of God's purpose to maintain inviolate the covenant with David, and perpetuate the kingdom therein granted to his seed. Ahaz, however, as if al- ready satisfied, pretended to regard the offer as superfluous, and declined asking a sign—while really his heart was set upon earthly confidences, and from want of faith in the assurances given him, he was calling in the aid of the king of Assyria (2 Chron. xxviii. 16, 20). Hence, the Lord interposes to give a sign ; but of what nature ? Such a sign, we naturally expect in the circumstances, as would show at once His determination to maintain the covenant, and His just displeasure with, or even virtual repudiation of, the existing representatives of the house and throne of David. While men should be made to see that God's covenant must stand fast, they must also see, it would be in a way that should augur no good to persons in such ill accord- ance with its design.[1]

(4.) In this state of matters, when there was given *the* sign of a virgin conceiving and bringing forth a son, whose name should be Immanuel, we are, if not absolutely necessitated, at least most naturally led to think of a son, that should bear directly and con- clusively upon the point at issue ; namely, the establishment and perpetuation of the kingdom in conformity with the covenant of

---

[1] It makes no difference, as to the essential nature and purport of the re- presentation above given, if we suppose the transactions and words to have passed in vision ; for in that case the offer of the sign to Ahaz and his refusal would simply have served as a cover to bring out his actual state of mind ; precisely as in the eighth chapter of Ezekiel with the elders of Judah.

David :—a son who, by his very birth and being, should form the truest sign of the full realisation of all that properly belonged to it. Such a sign, could it be given, would settle, as nothing else could, the pending controversy. And what the connection thus seems to point to, is confirmed by the implied contrast between this Son of the virgin, the destined possessor of David's throne, and what had previously been said of the possessors of the two rival thrones in Syria and Israel (ver. 8), "The head of Syria is Damascus, and the head of Damascus is Rezin (*these* and nothing more—they ascend no higher than a mere earthly city and a frail human being) ; and in sixty-five years Ephraim shall be broken, that it be not a people." That is, both the two have about them the weakness and instability of the world ; they shall presently become striking examples of its fleeting and transitory existence. But now, on the other hand, when the prophet turns to the kingdom of David, the Divine comes prominently into view along with the human ; to establish it, Deity itself is to become incarnate ; and the inference, therefore, is plain—all attempts to overthrow it must be fruitless ; it moves in the element of immortality, and shall abide for ever.

(5.) But the mention of such a good implied for existing parties a corresponding evil ; the sign given bespeaks a fall as well as a rising ; and a contrast was indicated, not merely between the kingdom of David and the kingdoms of Syria and Israel, but also between the child Immanuel and the degenerate house of Ahaz. For in this Divine purpose and provision for a better future, the existing royal house is entirely overleapt ; silently passed by on account of their unfaithfulness and corruption, when the higher interests of the kingdom and its ultimate stability come into consideration. The sign, in which the nature and destiny of the kingdom were to be imaged, bursts upon the view as a prodigy from an unknown quarter ; it is to be a child born, not to the *present* occupant of the throne, nor to any *future* occupant, but to a virgin ; and even she marked out by no distinct specifications of place or time,—foreseen only by the omniscient eye of God. He it is alone, who charges Himself with the accomplishment of the result ; in His own time He will bring forth the *almah* and her Son—as if Ahaz and his successors in the kingdom had no personal interest in the matter !

(6.) This alone is ominous of evil, but what follows is much more so. And in what follows we include, not merely ver. 15 and 16—with which commentators usually and unhappily stop —but all the concluding portion of the chapter. There is no real break or proper termination at the close of ver. 16, as if the prophet intended to shut up his present communication there, and commence afresh with something different. The whole, to the end of the chapter, is but one message, and is required in its totality to make out a full and consistent meaning. From what follows, then, it appears that the Son, on whose birth all hope hung, was to grow up in the midst of a depressed state of things ; such as betokened a terrible and wide-spread previous desolation. The precise time is left altogether indefinite. From anything that is said in the prophecy, it might be comparatively near or remote ; but the position and aspect of affairs, amid which Immanuel was to appear, is distinctly indicated to be one in which the reverse of prosperity and strength should prevail. For no sooner does the child appear, than butter and honey are assigned as His food (ver. 15), and not for Him only, but the people in the land generally are afterwards spoken of as having these for their support (ver. 22) ; and butter and honey are most fitly regarded here as the symbols of a reduced and prostrate condition, being the products of a land, far from barren indeed, but yielding of its resources after little or no cultivation. It tells us, that at the period of Immanuel's birth, and while He should Himself be still in the feebleness of childhood, all around should be in a weak, dilapidated, impoverished condition—in the kingdom of Judah, not less than in the regions of Syria and Israel. These, indeed, should experience the calamity first ; before the child should have out-grown His childhood, they should have " been forsaken of both their kings.". This does not mean, as is very commonly assumed, that the then reigning kings of Syria and Israel should have ceased to fill the throne ; far more than that—the land in both its divisions was to be bereft of *those holding the state and office of king ;* it should have ceased to *have* kingdoms. There was no need, therefore, for the true children of God to be greatly concerned about *them ;* Immanuel, when He came, with the manifestations of Divine power and glory, should not find them even in existence. But, if the earlier and the greater prostration should befall them, the house and kingdom of David should also be marred with symptoms of humiliation and decay. This is more briefly indicated in ver. 15 by the eating of butter and honey—nature's products in pastoral countries—and then more pointedly and fully at ver. 17, where the prophet, turning to the ungodly Ahaz, says, " The Lord shall bring upon *thee,* and upon *thy people,* and upon *thy father's house,* days that have not come, from the day that Ephraim departed from Judah," etc. In a word, the substance of the message was, God's covenant should certainly stand fast, and the sign to be given of its stability should eventually be brought to pass ; but, meanwhile, the kingdom of David, in its existing form, together with the kingdoms of Syria and Israel, should undergo a sad and calamitous reverse ; *they* should altogether go down, while *it* should be diminished and brought low. And the kingdom of David, as the object of faith and hope to the Lord's people, was to spring as from a fresh starting-point in the person of Immanuel, and out of poverty and weakness rise to its proper magnitude and glory.

Such, by a careful consideration of the original passage, appears to be the progress of thought and the richness of meaning embodied in the prophecy here referred to by the Evangelist Matthew. If we are right in the view that has been given of it, the Evangelist was undoubtedly right in the use, to which he applied it ; and not a tendency to catch at some obvious and superficial meaning, but a capacity to apprehend the real import of the prediction, was what determined him in turning it to such an account. Understood in the light, in which it has now been presented, it stands in no need of the embarrassing hypothesis of a double birth, nor of the fanciful supposition of Hengstenberg (Christology, vol. ii.), and also of Ewald (if I rightly understand his view of the passage)—the supposition of the promised child being ideally present in his birth and growth to boyhood before the spiritual eye of the prophet, and constituting, as so present, the sign of a speedy deliverance of Judah from Syria and Israel. Such an impersonation were far too subtle and involved for the purpose in question ; and it would, besides, most incongruously confound together the ideal and the real—making the prophet's internal apprehension of a future event, a sign to the people of a more immediate external reality. The sign, however, as already

stated, was not intended to be directly or properly a pledge of
Judah's deliverance from her impending evils; it was strictly a
sign of God's purpose to ratify His covenant with David, and
build up his throne to all generations; and a sign so conceived
and announced as to speak at once of judgment and of mercy to
the existing representative of David's house.

II.
Matt. ii. 15 ; Hos. xi. 1.

There can be no doubt, that the portion of Hosea here applied
to the circumstance of our Lord's recall from His temporary
sojourn in Egypt, was in its original connection simply a historical statement respecting what God had done for the national
Israel in the commencing period of their history. The whole
passage is, " When Israel was a child, then I loved him, and I
called my son out of Egypt." The question, therefore, is, how
the Evangelist could find in such a passage any proper pre-inti-
mation of the circumstance in our Lord's life to which he has
so specifically applied it ? The application can only be understood and vindicated on the ground of a typical relationship
between the literal Israel and the Messiah ; but on this ground
it admits of a satisfactory explanation. The relationship in question was not obscurely indicated even in Old Testament Scripture ; and particularly in the latter portion of Isaiah's writings,
where there is a constant transition from Israel in the literal
sense to an ideal and prospective Israel—from an Israel called,
indeed, to the enjoyment of high privileges, and the discharge of
important obligations, but still compassed about with imperfection,
backsliding and trouble, to an Israel, in whom the calling was to
find its adequate fulfilment—God's elect, in whom His soul
delighted, and by whom His name was to be glorified, sin and
evil purged away from the condition of His people, and the world
restored to the favour of Heaven. (Compare, for example, on the
one side, ch. xlii. 19–25, xliii. 22–28, xlviii. 18–22, lix. 1–19 ;
and on the other, xlii. 1–8, xlix. 1–13, liii., lix. 20, 21, lxi.)
The same sort of relationship was indicated in another class of
prophecies, between the son of David in the literal sense, and a
son sometime to appear, who should occupy an unspeakably higher
position, and raise the kingdom to a state of purity and bliss it

could never otherwise have reached. (Compare here also, on the one side, 2 Sam. vii. 14; Ps. lxxxix. 30–32, 38–45; 1 Kings xi. 36–39; Amos ix. 11; and on the other, Ps. ii., xlv., lxxii., cx.; Isa. ix. 6, 7, etc.) There was no essential difference between this later covenant with the house of David, and the earlier covenant with Abraham or Israel; they both aimed at the same great end of obtaining salvation and blessing for the world, in connection with the establishment of truth and righteousness:— only, what the one proposed to accomplish through the seed of Israel, the other, more specifically and individually, sought to work out by the administration of a kingdom, in the hands of a son of David. The design of each covenant should be realised, when (as it might be indifferently expressed) the kingdom among the sons of men had become the Lord's, or all the families of the earth were truly blessed in Him. Fundamentally, therefore, the relation of the promised Messiah to David's immediate son was the same with that of Christ to Israel; it was such as, in God's dispensations, subsists between the present and the ultimate, the preparatory and the final—that is, in both there were relatively the same place and calling, but these in the earlier connected with an inferior line of things, partaking more of the human, and the external,—in the later, rising more into the sphere of the spiritual and Divine; consequently, in the one case inter-mingled on every hand with imperfection and failure, in the other, attaining to heavenly excellence and perfection. Such generally is the relation between the Old and the New—between type and antitype; and such it is also here. Christ is at once the anti-typical or the true Israel, and the antitypical or true Son of David; since in Him all the promises made concerning these were to stand fast, and the high calling of God was to find its proper realisation. Hence, the prophetic announcements respect-ing Abraham's seed of blessing, and David's son and heir, are, in their higher bearing and import, ascribed to the Messiah; they have no adequate accomplishment till they find it in Him (Acts ii. 25, 26, xiii. 33; Heb. i. 5).

Now, as before the incarnation the Spirit gave forth a series of prophetical utterances, based on the relationship of Israel to the Messiah, and again a series based on His relationship to David, it was quite natural, that the writers of the New Testa-

ment, under the guidance of the same Spirit, should at times
mark how the things concerning both were discovering themselves in the history of Christ. And in doing so, we might
expect them to take, not merely the prophetical passages, which
on the ground of the typical relationship, in either of its forms,
pointed to the coming future, but also, occasionally at least, to
render prominent the relationship itself, and show how, by remarkable coincidences in God's providence, Jesus was, in a manner, identified with the literal Israel, or with the house of David.
In the nature of things, there could not be more than occasional
coincidences of the kind referred to; for it had been impossible,
or, if possible, it had been on many accounts unsuitable, that
Jesus should have been made to pass through all the recorded
experiences belonging either to Israel at large, or to David's
house. It were enough, if a few noticeable agreements took
place, fitted from their own nature, or from the manner in which
they were brought about, to serve as finger-posts to direct the
eyes of men to Him that was to come, or, like Heaven's seal on
the connection between the beginnings and the end, to certify
them that the old was at length in its higher form coming into
being. Such was the birth of Jesus at Bethlehem, the city of
David,—fulfilling, indeed, a prophecy which had been announced
regarding it (not overlooked by the Evangelist, ch. ii. 5, 6), but
itself, especially when effected by so singular turns of Providence, a sign from above, that the long-expected Son of David
was born into the world. Of the same kind, and pointing to
the other form of the typical relationship, was the removal of the
infant Saviour for a time to an asylum in Egypt, and His recall
thence when the season of danger was over; it was substantially
doing over again what had been done in the infancy of the
national Israel, and thereby helping a weak faith to recognise
in this remarkable babe the new Israel, the child of hope for the
world. Of the same kind, again, was His withdrawal, through
the Spirit, into the wilderness, to be tempted of the devil, and
His sojourn there for forty days—the number, and the place,
and the object, all pointing back to Israel's forty years' temptation in the desert; but by the day for a year (instead of, as in
their case, a year for a day), and by the baffling of the tempter
in every assault, showing how infinitely superior the new was to

the old, and that here, at last, was the Israel in whom God was to be fully glorified.

If these principles in the Divine government are kept in view, no difficulty will be found in the application made by the Evangelist of Hos. xi. 1 to our Lord's return from Egypt. His temporary descent thither, and subsequent recall to the land appointed for the fulfilment of His high vocation, as just noticed, was one of the more striking and palpable coincidences between His outward history and that of Israel, which were ordered and designed by God to point Him out as the true Israel, the antitype of the old; and the passage in Hosea, which records the earlier event, necessarily formed, by reason of the typical connection, a virtual prophecy of the corresponding event in the future. It embodied a typical fact; and so, when viewed in connection with God's ulterior design, it enclosed a presage of the antitypical counterpart. Substantially the requirements of the type might have been met, if some other local asylum had been provided for the youthful Saviour than the literal Egypt— precisely as, afterwards, the circumstantials of His temptation differed in time and place from the prior temptation of Israel. But to render the correspondence here more obvious and convincing, the new was made *formally*, as well as *substantially*, to coincide with the old; so that, for those who were watching and desirous to learn from the footsteps of Providence, there might be the less difficulty in discerning the fulfilment of the typical prediction, when the Lord anew called His Son out of Egypt.

III.
Matt. ii. 18; Jer. xxxi. 15.

The application of Jeremiah's prophecy, about Rachel bewailing her lost children, and refusing to be comforted on account of the apparently hopeless deprivation she had sustained, to the slaughter of the children at Bethlehem, undoubtedly proceeds upon a certain connection between the earlier and the later event. But from the very nature of things, and the terms of the passage cited, the connection could not be regarded as of such a close and organic kind, as that indicated in the last quotation. *There* stress was laid even on the external resemblance between what befell Christ, and what had anciently befallen

Israel; the connection of both with Egypt formed the immediate and ostensible ground of the word, spoken originally of
the one, being extended to the other. *Here*, on the other hand,
there is a palpable diversity as to the external circumstances; for
the scene of action in the one case was Rama, a city in the tribe
of Benjamin, a few miles to the north of Jerusalem, while in the
other it was Bethlehem, a city about the same distance to the
south, in the tribe of Judah; and, consequently, if respect were
had to literal exactness, Leah, the ancestral mother of Judah,
should have been addressed as the chief mourner on the present
occasion, as Rachel had been on the former. In such circumstances of obvious and palpable disagreement, the Evangelist
could not possibly mean, that the passage he quoted from Jeremiah had either been directly uttered of the scene at Bethlehem,
or even that the original mourning at Rama had a typical relation,
in the stricter sense, to that at Bethlehem. And hence he does
not say, as he usually does, that the circumstances took place *in
order that* the word might be fulfilled, but merely that *then was
fulfilled* what had been spoken by Jeremiah. The *kind* of fulfilment indicated must be determined by the points of agreement
in the two related transactions. Even in its original application,
the passage is highly poetical in form, and cannot be interpreted
as a piece of prosaic writing. It was at Rama, as we learn from
Jer. xl. 1, that the last band of captives was assembled by the
captains of Nebuchadnezzar, before they were sent into exile;
and either in anticipation of this sore calamity, or in reference
to it after it had taken place, the prophet represents Rachel, the
ancestral mother of the tribe, where the hapless exiles were
gathered, bewailing the fate of her offspring, and giving way to
an inconsolable grief, as if all were gone. The introduction of
Rachel is, of course, a mere cover, to bring out in vivid colours
the sadness of the occasion, and the apparently hopeless character of the calamity; to human eye, and especially to the passionate fondness of maternal affection, it seemed as if Israel had
utterly perished under the stroke of Nebuchadnezzar. Yet it
was not so in reality; and the prophet presently goes on to
assure the disconsolate mother, that her grief was inordinate,
that her children should return again from the land of the
enemy, and that there was hope in her end.

Now, with all the circumstantial diversities that distinguish the original event at Rama, and the message it called forth, from the slaughter of the infants in Bethlehem, there still is a fundamental agreement in the more peculiar features of both. Herod was the new Nebuchadnezzar, who, by his cruel and crafty policy, sought to do what, after another fashion, the Chaldean conqueror thought *he* had done, viz., extinguished for ever the better hopes and aspirations of Israel. When the one, after having razed the foundations of Jerusalem, bore away from Rama the shattered remnants of her people, he had struck, as he conceived, a fatal blow at their singular pretensions and distinctive glory. And, in like manner, when Herod smote the children at Bethlehem, with the impious design of embracing in the slaughter the new-born " King of the Jews," he would, had his aim been accomplished, have buried in the dust all that was to render Israel pre-eminent among the nations. They might as well, thenceforth, have ceased to exist, gone to a hopeless exile, or a dishonoured grave. So that, looking upon matters with the eye of sense, the ancestral mother might, as of old, have raised anew the wail of sorrow, even such as might appear incapable of any true solace. Yet God, in His paternal faithfulness and oversight, had provided against the worst, and here again had taken the wise in his own craftiness. As regarded the main object in view, the stroke fell powerless to the ground ; the bird escaped from the snare of the fowler. But situated as matters now were—not only with a Herod in the seat of power, but with a Herodian party, who thought that the best thing for the people was to maintain the Herodian interest, it was well to bring this memorable transaction of Gospel times into formal connection with the ancient catastrophe—to show that Herod was virtually now what Nebuchadnezzar was then—and that, so far as concerned the real glory and salvation of Israel, to look for help from the existing representative of the worldly power in Judea, was like going to Babylon for pity and succour. From such a quarter misery and despair, not life and hope, were what might surely be looked for.

IV.
Matt. viii. 17 ; Isa. liii. 4.

The explanation given of the terms, by which the Evangelist

renders the original in this quotation, has shown the faithfulness
of the rendering. It is at once more specific, and more literal,
not only than the Septuagint, but also than the authorised version of the passage in Isaiah, which has, " He hath borne our
griefs, and carried our sorrows." Sicknesses and pains, however,
are the more exact synonyms for the Hebrew terms; and it is
not bearing and carrying, anyhow, that is ascribed to the Messiah respecting them, but more specially taking them on Himself, as a burden bearing them on His person. Such also is the
sense put upon them by the Evangelist. Yet Meyer says, " The
passage is cited according to the original, but not in conformity
with its *import*, since, according to this, the Messiah is represented as an atoning sin-bearer; for the parallel verbs, λαμβάνειν
and βαστάζειν, must here be rendered (against the meaning of the
corresponding Hebrew words) to *take away*, to *remove*, on account
of the historical connection in which the citation is found."
There is, however, no such necessity; and Meyer here, as in
many other cases, merely adopts a superficial historical sense as
the only tenable one, and then pronounces an arbitrary and pre-
sumptuous judgment on the sacred record. It is, first of all, not
sins, but sicknesses, or diseases and pains, that primarily and
directly are the subject of discourse. And, secondly, while the
sense of bearing away or removing these would have suited the
connection, it is not absolutely required by it; nay, the other
and literal rendering gives us, though a less obvious, yet a much
profounder insight into our Lord's connection with the troubles
and distresses of mankind. In respect to these also He had a
vicarious relation to fill—to charge Himself with the burden of
human sorrows, as well as with the guilt from which they spring;
and, in order to remove them, He must bring them into contact
with His own sympathies, and powers, and benevolent working.

Hengstenberg, in his comment on the original passage (Christology, vol. ii.), maintains the rendering above given, and justifies
the use made of it by the Evangelist. He says, " According to
the opinion of several interpreters, by diseases all outward and
inward sufferings are figuratively designated; according to the
opinion of others, *spiritual* diseases, sins. But, from the relation
alone of this verse to the preceding, it appears that here, in the
first instance, diseases and pains, in the ordinary sense, are

spoken of; just as the blind and deaf, in ch. xxxv., are, in the first instance, they who are naturally blind and deaf. Diseases, in the sense of *sins*, do not occur at all in the Old Testament. The circumstance, that in the parallel passage, ver. 11, 12, the bearing of the transgressions and sins is spoken of, proves nothing. The servant of God bears these also in their consequences, in their punishments, among which sickness and pains occupy a prominent place. Of the bearing of outward sufferings, נָשָׂא חֳלִי occurs also in Jer. x. 19. If the words are rightly understood, then at once light falls upon the apostolic quotation, in Matt. viii. 16, 17, which deserves the more careful consideration, as the Evangelist intentionally deviates from the Alexandrine version. In such an application there is not an external meaning given to that, which is to be understood spiritually; but when the Saviour healed the sick, He fulfilled the prophecy in its most proper and obvious sense. . . . He has not only *put away* our sicknesses and pains, but He has, as our substitute, *taken them upon him;* He has healed us by His having Himself become sick in our stead." This, of course, implies, as Hengstenberg goes on to state, Christ's personal appropriation of our sins, of which His sufferings were the consequence. But it implies also, that the troubles and disorders of humanity were themselves, in a sense, laid upon Christ; He had to make these also His own; and showed that He did so by applying His Almightiness to remove them. Even here there was the proof of an infinite condescension, and the indication of a vicarious work.

In 1 Pet. ii. 24, 25, there is undoubtedly a reference to the 53d of Isaiah; and the sin-bearing of Jesus is expressed in the very words used by the Septuagint in rendering the first clause of ver. 4. But there is no ground, on that account, for supposing that Peter meant the words to be understood as expressing his view of the passage. He is merely unfolding, in language, which the thoughts and words of that chapter had rendered current, the great truth, which doubtless formed the centre of the prophet's representation, as well as the main theme of the apostle's teaching.

V.
Matt. xiii. 35 ; Ps. lxxviii. 2.
It is in connection with the change introduced into our Lord's

E E

method of teaching, when He began to speak in parables, that the passage from Ps. lxxviii. 2 is cited.   He did so, the Evangelist states, " that it might be fulfilled which was spoken by the prophet, I will open my mouth in parables, I will utter things that have been hidden from the foundation of the world."   The stress is plainly meant to be laid upon the first part of the passage ; it was that, which now more especially had its verification in the procedure of Christ ; the hidden or enigmatical nature of the things discoursed of was but a consequence, that, in greater or less degree, attached itself to the other.   Now, in considering the fitness of this application of the Psalmist's language, we are first of all met with a source of doubt and uncertainty in regard to the proper meaning of the word rendered *parables*.   This in the original is מָשָׁל, *mashal;* and opinions have been, and still are, divided on its precise import in certain applications—some making it bear mainly upon the form and character of the discourse, others upon its style and diction.   To the former class belongs Hengstenberg, who says in his work on Balaam, on Num. xxiii. 7, " The noun *mashal* originally means likeness, comparison, and properly maintains this sense always.   When it is used of sentences, proverbs, and songs, then it denotes these, not simply as such, but only in so far as the idea of likeness, comparison, prevails in them."   As used by Balaam, he conceives it to have respect more particularly to the poetic elevation in them, which naturally led to a considerable infusion of the figurative modes of conception, in which poetry delights to indulge.   And there are other portions of the prophetic Scriptures—such, for example, as Isa. xiv., and the prophecies of Ezekiel (comp. ch. xv. 49), to which also the word is applied—in respect to which from the play of fancy and the large employment of figure that appears in them, we can readily perceive the appropriateness of a term that is indicative of images and similitudes.   But when the same term is applied to such didactic pieces, as Ps. xxxix. (ver. 4), or to such narrative discourses, as Ps. lxxviii., which are not characterised by any flights of fancy, or by figurative speech, one is at a loss to see, how, if the word *always* retains the sense of comparison or likeness, it should be applied to compositions which seem to have so little about them of the distinctive quality.

It is partly on this account, that the other shade of opinion respecting *mashal* has been adopted, and which would find the idea of similitude or likeness, that forms the root-meaning, in the parallelism of the sentences. Thus Gesenius, while he represents the word as often applied to parabolical and figurative discourses, holds it to be also employed of songs and other compositions, " the particular verses of which consist of two hemistichs of similar argument and form." In this case there might be no figure, or illustrative style of thought employed in developing the subject handled ; nothing, indeed, marked or peculiar beyond the digesting of what was uttered into a series of parallelistic members. This view, however, appears to give undue prominence to the mere structure of the sentences, which is never rendered prominent in Scripture itself, and only takes, in certain cases, the parallelistic form, from the requirements of the kind of instruction, or the species of discourse, with which it is associated.

The fault probably lies in making the import and bearing of the word too determinate either way. The sense put upon it by Lowth, which may be said to include both the shades of opinion now mentioned—giving chief prominence to the characteristics of the discourse, yet not altogether excluding the external form, into which its utterances are cast—is perhaps the correcter mode of representation. He takes it to be a term " expressive of the poetic style. Many interpreters designate it parable ; a word in some respects not unsuitable, but by no means embracing the entire compass of the Hebrew term ; which, taken in its full strength, and according to its current use, will be found to signify a sententious, figurative, and elevated kind of discourse."[1] He means one or other of these, as the occasion may require; and in the kind of discourse he would include also its appropriate style of expression. When applied, therefore, to such a piece of composition as the 78th Psalm, in which by a poetico-historical rehearsal of the transactions of former times, the inspired writer seeks to convey lessons of instruction for the future, it may be regarded as calling attention, not so much to the parallelism of the sentences,—if to that at all, in a quite subordinate manner— but chiefly to the underlying parallelism of circumstances conceived as existing between the Israel of former generations and those yet to come ; and to the profound, sententious form, in which

[1] Prælec. de Heb. Poesi, 4.

the instruction inlaid in the one was exhibited for the benefit of
the other. It was a turning of history into prophecy; for while
ostensibly but rehearsing the past, it aimed at presenting in this
a mirror of the future.

Precisely similar was the object of our Lord's parables; differing only in so far as they employed for the cover of the instruction, not the records of actual history, but the ideal narratives of
parabolical discourse. This, indeed, was a form of speech and
instruction, that still more distinctly and fully realised the idea of
the *mashal*, than the 78th Psalm—containing, as it did, more of
the poetical element, and more palpably basing its instruction on
the similitude of one class of relations to another. And as all
preceding teachers, who in any measure possessed and exercised
the spirit of prophecy, were but so many forerunners and types
of Him, who was to be emphatically *the* teacher and prophet of
His church, so, what by any one of these had been uttered of
His calling and His work, might with fullest propriety be applied
to Christ, as destined to find in Him its truest realisation. Nor
could any thing of that description be more fitly so applied, than
the saying before us, which pointed to a method of instruction,
that in one of its forms was carried by our Lord to the highest
degree of perfection, and which, at once for what it unfolded and
for what it wrapt in temporary concealment, was peculiarly
adapted to the ends of His mission. The exterior form conveyed
to those, who heard, the *image* of the truth ; and purporting to be
but the image, it naturally served both to prompt their desires, and
to direct their inquiries after the reality.

VI.
Matt. xxi. 42 ; Ps. cxviii. 22, 23.

The application, first by our Lord, and afterwards by His
apostles, of the figurative passage in the 118th Psalm, respecting
the rejection of the stone by men, and its elevation by God to
the head stone of the corner, to the things which were to befal
Himself, proceeds upon the same relation of Christ to Israel,
which has been explained under No. II. The psalm speaks in
the first instance of the literal and collective Israel ; but of this
with reference to its election of God, its higher calling and
destiny. The experiences, therefore, to which it relates, while

they had an earlier verification in the history of the covenant-people, necessarily had a higher development, a kind of culminating exemplification in the person and kingdom of Christ. As a prophecy, it is of that class which may most justly be said to have " springing and germinant accomplishment," while "the height and fulness of them" are to be found only in the things which relate to the Messiah. The conflict, which the psalm describes, between the speaker and the ungodly adversaries around Him, was in some form perpetually proceeding. The purpose of God to bless Israel, and to make them the one channel of. blessing to the world, was ever and anon calling forth the ungodly opposition of the world—sometimes within the natural Israel itself, as in the struggles through which David, the chosen servant of God, had to make his way to the throne—but more commonly with Israel as a community, when set on by the jealous rivalry and malice of surrounding nations. More especially did this conflict come to a height under the old relations, when the worldly power, headed by the king of Babylon, scattered the force of the chosen people, and, in boastful opposition to them, claimed to be recognised as the ruling dynasty among men. Israel was then like a stone rejected by the builders, deemed altogether unworthy of a place in their proud scheme of earthly dominion and personal aggrandisement. But when Babylon herself fell from her high position, and Israel not only survived the calamities which crushed their conquerors in the dust, but was sent back with honour, and the clear signs of Heaven's favour, to lay the foundations of a new, and, ultimately, a nobler destiny in their native land, it then strikingly appeared how God's purpose respecting them prevailed over the power and malice of men ; and how the rejected stone was by Him appointed to be the head of the corner. At such a time, even thoughtful persons among the heathen were constrained to say, " The Lord hath done great things for them ;" and the covenant-people themselves naturally sung their song of triumph, and exclaimed, " It is the Lord's doing, and wondrous in our eyes."

In all probability, the event now referred to was the historical occasion on which Psalm 118th was composed and originally sung; a probability that is greatly strengthened, and rendered all but certain by the recorded fact, that at the laying of the

foundation of the second temple, the returned exiles sung in re-
sponsive strains (such as actually belong to this psalm), and
strains that commenced precisely as it does.   For we are told, at
Ezra iii. 11, that they then " sang together by course, in praising
and giving thanks unto the Lord, because He is good, for His
mercy endureth for ever toward Israel."   But the principles of
the Divine government, which then received such a striking
exemplification in the case of Israel, were again to be exhibited,
and in a yet higher form, in the personal history of Messiah.
Many. prophecies had pointed in this direction—all, indeed,
which spake of the Messiah as executing His work, and rising to
the place of pre-eminent power and glory, through a course of
trying experiences and headstrong opposition.   These, one and
all, betokened a contrariety between the views of men and the
purpose of God, in respect to the Author and the plan of salvation ; and never failed to make manifest the ultimate triumph
of Heaven's counsels over the perversity and malice of the world.
But among these prophecies, there were several which connected
the struggle and triumph of Messiah with substantially the same
idea as that employed in Ps. cxviii.   In Isaiah, for example, ch.
viii. 14, speaking of the Lord's more peculiar manifestation of
Himself, which was to take place in the future, it is said, " And
He shall be for a sanctuary ; but for a stone of stumbling and a
rock of offence to both the houses of Israel."   Again, at ch.
xxviii. 16, with a more special and pointed reference to the work
of Christ, " Therefore thus saith the Lord God, Behold I lay in
Zion for a foundation a stone, a tried stone, a precious corner-
stone, a sure foundation ; he that believeth shall not make haste."
In Zechariah also the promised appearance of the Lord's Branch
—the Messiah, as the scion of the house of David—is associated
with the erection of a temple, of another and a nobler kind than
that which was in process of erection by the returned captives,
and in that, of course, Messiah Himself was to occupy the most
prominent place (ch. vi. 12, 13).   So that, when in Ps. cxviii.,
mention is made of the stone rejected by the builders, yet exalted
by the Lord to be the head of the corner, and on that very account He is magnified as the God of salvation, the thoughts of
believers, even in ancient times, might as readily have been led to
think of the future as of the past.   And had not a judicial blind-

ness been on the hearts of the people, when our Lord asked them, "Have ye never read in the Scriptures, The stone which the builders rejected is become the head of the corner ?" they would have seen, that to continue their opposition after all the mighty works that had showed themselves forth in Him, was but to enact anew, and with infinitely less excuse, the part which of old the heathen had acted toward Israel, or which the Sauline party had acted toward David. The same controversy was pending as of old, and the same disastrous results must inevitably befal those who set themselves against the manifested purpose of God.

It thus appears, that while the passage had a primary respect to Israel, it from the first included the Divine purpose, with which Israel was more peculiarly identified—their election of God to be the instrument and channel of blessing to the world, and as such to have the chief place among men. But as this purpose was to find its proper accomplishment in Christ, so to apply the passage personally to Him was in perfect accordance with its original import and design.

VII.
Matt. xxii. 31, 32 ; Ex. iii. 6.

This is one of the few passages in which it has sometimes been alleged our Lord occasionally fell in with the cabalistic mode of handling Scripture, which was current among the Rabbinical Jews. It is only, however, with the more extreme and reckless section of the Rationalists that this allegation is found ; for, however often interpreters of Rationalistic tendencies have failed to bring out the full force of our Lord's reasoning, they have commonly admitted that the argument He draws is based on a solid foundation ; and even Paulus, in the last edition of his Commentary on the Synoptical Gospels, says, "Jesus reasons here in a subtle manner, yet by no means so that there did not really lie in the premises what He deduces from them." It is not undeserving of notice, that, amid all the sayings which have been gathered out of ancient Jewish writings, for the purpose of elucidating New Testament Scripture, none has been found that bears any proper resemblance to the words of Jesus, before us. In a comparatively modern Jewish writer, the words themselves, and the reference of Christ, have been substantially appropriated ; the passage is quoted by Schöttgen, on this part of Matthew's Gospel. It is from R. Menasse Ben Israel de Resur., p. 68 : " When the Lord first appeared to Moses, he is reported to have said, I am the God of your fathers, the God of Abraham, the God of Isaac, the God of Jacob. But God is not the God of the dead, because the dead are not ; but of the living, because the living exist. On that ground, therefore, it is rightly inferred that, in respect to the soul, the patriarchs still live." Rabbinical men could in some measure perceive the force of the argument, when it was formed to their hand, but they wanted depth and discernment of spirit to discover it for themselves. Indeed, the argument is perfectly simple, and must appear so to all, the moment they apprehend what is implied in the relationship which God, *as God*, admitted to subsist between Himself and those patriarchs. He owns Himself *their* God ; their God still, though for hundreds of years their bodies had been mouldering in the cave of Mamre. In His account they were yet alive ; and He, being their God, it necessarily behoved Him to do for them whatever a God is able to perform in their behalf—just as a father is bound to do for his children whatever he really can to promote their welfare. But cannot God—He who at first breathed into those patriarchs the breath of life, again raise them from the dust of death, and clothe them with strength and beauty ? Doubtless He can ; and because He can, He will—nay, He must, since He has Himself assumed the name, and thereby pledged Himself to make good all that it imports. He who would have been ashamed to be called their God, if He had not provided for them a city, would much more have been ashamed so to call Himself, if their bodies, a part of their very natures, were left for ever as a prey to corruption.

VIII.
Matt. xxvii. 9, 10 ; Zech. xi. 13.

There are two points that require explanation, in the use that is made here of the words of ancient prophecy ; one more general, and another more specific. The first has respect to the propriety of understanding the Messiah as the person who was to be so unworthily treated, and rated at the mean price of thirty pieces

of silver—the price of a slave.   This admits of a full justification ;
for, in the preceding context, the subject of discourse plainly is
about the false shepherds, on the one side, and the true Shepherd,
on the other.   Reproving and judging the former, the Lord
Himself, whom the prophet personates, undertakes the office, and
in doing so, feeds the misled and injured flock, and cuts off those
who had impoverished and oppressed them.   But, so far from
meeting with a kind reception and grateful acknowledgment from
those whose cause he undertook, "their soul rebelled against him,"
and he resolved on withdrawing in disgust ; but demanded of them
a reward for his services in their behalf.   This, they are represented as answering, by weighing out the contemptuous sum of
thirty pieces of silver : a transaction which evidently bespoke the
light estimation in which they held him and the work he had performed amongst them.   Hence they are again given up to bad
shepherds, and disorder and trouble rush in as before.

Now, since the Lord Himself is the Good Shepherd spoken of,
and the transaction about the rating, carries a peculiarly personal
aspect, it is scarcely possible to understand it otherwise than as
referring to some manifestation of Godhead more objective and
realistic than any that had taken place in ancient times.   The
people, under the relations of the Old Covenant, might be represented as selling themselves (Isa. lii. 3), but they neither were,
nor could fitly be, spoken of as selling the Lord.   Such a mode
of representation pointed to another and more palpable exhibition
of Godhead than had hitherto appeared ; it pointed to the appearance of the Divine Shepherd, of whom the earlier prophets had
so often and so distinctly spoken (Ps. ii. 9, lxxii. ; Isa. ix. 6, 7 ;
Jer. xxiii. 4, 5 ; Ezek. xxxiv. 23).   And when, in addition to
this, we look to the particulars of the account given by the prophet of the treatment of the shepherd, we may justly say, with
Hengstenberg, "The agreement of prophecy and fulfilment is so
striking, that it would force itself upon us, although it had been
indicated by no declaration of the New Testament.   What could
the last and most fearful expression of ingratitude towards the
Good Shepherd here predicted be, other than the murderous plot
by which the Jews rewarded the pastoral fidelity of Christ, and
for whose accomplishment Judas was bribed ?" (Christology).

The differences that present themselves between the terms of the prophecy and the record of its fulfilment, are such merely as respect the form, not the reality of things. In the prophecy, the shepherd demands the payment of a sum, and that in the shape of a reward for his services ; but this is only for the purpose of bringing out more distinctly the fact that he had appeared to them in the character of one doing them important service, and that, when they came formally to surrender their interest in him, the time and circumstances of the transaction might fairly be taken as an evidence of the value they set upon him. In a word, it would inevitably and justly be regarded as a proof of blackest ingratitude toward him, and senseless disregard of their own highest interests. Not only so, but as Divine Providence ordered it so that the ministers of the temple paid the price, and the price was again taken back and thrown down in the temple ; so in reality all came to be, in a manner, transacted before the Lord ; it was done as under His immediate eyesight. As for the command in the prophecy to cast the price to the potter, it was but a strong form of the future (as in Isa. vi. 9, noticed under, Matt. xiii. 14), and merely denoted the certainty with which the event should come to pass.

But another point here calls for consideration, of a somewhat more special kind ; viz. why should the price have been so explicitly adjudged to the potter ? This seems to imply, that somewhere already mention had been made of a potter, in such a connection, as rendered the destination of this money to the same quarter a natural and proper thing. The prophecy here, therefore, must lean on some earlier portion of Scripture, which it either resumes, or takes for granted as known and understood. Now, it is only in Jeremiah that we find anything of that description. There, but there alone, is mention made of the potter, in a way that is fitted to throw light on the passage under consideration. In ch. xviii. 2, the word of the Lord comes to Jeremiah, saying, "Arise, and go down to the potter's house, and there will I cause thee to hear My words." From the use of the definite article, *the* potter, we are naturally led to think of some one being meant, who had a well-known and recognised place in connection with the temple ; and from the prophet being ordered to *go down* to him, we are not less naturally led to think of his workshop as being situated in a lower place, probably in the valley that lay adjacent to the temple.. This, however, is rendered certain in ch. xix. 2, where, after being commanded to get a potter's earthen bottle, he was instructed to proceed, in company with the priests and elders of the people, " into the valley of the son of Hinnom," and proclaim certain words. This valley had first been the scene of frightful abominations, when idolatry was at its height in Jerusalem ; and afterwards, to mark his abhorrence of these, Josiah had polluted the place, by throwing into it carcases and bones—into that part of it more especially, which was called Tophet, and in which children had been made to pass through the fire to Moloch (2 Kings xxiii. 10 ; comp. Jer. vii. 31). When the prophet, then, had gone down to the potter, he saw a vessel become marred in the potter's hand ; on which the word of the Lord came, intimating that the Lord *could* do the same with the children of Israel, and, on account of their sins, might even be expected to do it. But the second special message was the one recorded in ch. xix., when the prophet was commanded to throw an earthen vessel of the potter into the valley of Hinnom, and accompany the action with these appalling words, " Behold I will bring evil upon this place, the which whosoever heareth, his ears shall tingle. Because they have forsaken Me, and have estranged this place, and have burned incense in it unto other gods, whom neither they nor their fathers have known, and have filled this place with innocent blood ; therefore behold the days come, saith the Lord, that this place shall no more be called Tophet, nor the valley of the son of Hinnom, but the valley of slaughter. And I will make void the counsel of Judah and Jerusalem in this place ; and I will cause them to fall by the sword," etc. " Even so will I break this people and this city, as one breaks the vessels of a potter, which cannot be made whole again, and they shall bury in Tophet, till there be no place to bury."

Now, when in Zechariah it was said, regarding the thirty pieces of silver, without any farther explanation, " cast them to the potter," there can be no doubt, that he refers to these transactions in Jeremiah. And the meaning of the appointment was to this effect, Let these pieces of silver become, like the potter of Jeremiah and his vessels, the symbol of the people's consummate guilt and impending doom. They are the price of

innocent blood—blood that must still more surely draw down
the vengeance of heaven, than that which was of old shed in the
valley of Hinnom ; let them, therefore, be identified with the
potter's field, the place emphatically of pollution and crime, as
a sign and warning to all, that the former desolations are ready
to come back again. Such was the natural import of the prediction ; and it affords by far the most fitting explanation of the
apparent anomaly in the reference of the Evangelist, who, when
quoting a passage of Zechariah, ascribes it to Jeremiah. Many
suppositions have been made to account for this, such as, that
there may have been a lost passage in the writings of Jeremiah
to the same effect—that the portion of Zechariah's writings
quoted from may really have belonged to Jeremiah—that the
Evangelist's memory may have failed him, etc. The real reason, however, is, that the Evangelist had in his eye the insepar-
able connection between the prediction in Zechariah and the
earlier announcements in Jeremiah ; that he regarded the one
only as a later and more specific application of the other ; and
that as he wished the people to consider the denunciations of
guilt and judgment most graphically portrayed in the original
prophecy, so he couples the prophecy with the name of the earlier
rather than of the later prophet. This view, which was first
distinctly propounded by Grotius, who says, Cum autem hoc
dictum Jeremiæ per Sach. repetitum hic recitat Mat., simul
ostendit tacite, eas poenas imminere Judæis, quas iidem prophetæ
olim sui temporis hominibus prædixerant, has been more fully
vindicated and established by Hengstenberg, in his Christology,
on Zechariah. He justly says, " Matthew might, indeed, have
cited both prophets. But such prolixity in citation is entirely
contrary to the custom of the authors of the New Testament ;
which may be explained by a twofold reason. They presuppose
their readers to possess an accurate knowledge of Scripture ;
and then the human instrument was kept far behind the
Divine Author, the Spirit of God and of Christ, who spake in
all the prophets in the same manner. Very frequently, therefore, the human author is not mentioned at all ; they content
themselves with such forms of citation as " the Scripture saith,"
" according as it has been written," " for it is written," " as saith
the Holy Ghost," etc.

The explanation of Hofmann, in his *Weissagung und Erfullung*, differs only in some subordinate points.   He also thinks, that the Evangelist cannot be supposed to have attributed to Jeremiah a passage of Zechariah, as if by mistake; especially as he has taken the chief circumstance, with which the citation is formally connected, not from Zechariah but from Jeremiah— that, namely, which respects the purchase of the potter's field. Hofmann, however, would confine the reference to Jeremiah to the xviii. ch., making no account of ch. xix.; and would regard the link of connection between the passage in Zechariah and that of Jeremiah, as consisting simply in this—that the shepherd in Zechariah treats the temple-court as a clay-pit, and under the conviction, that this was destined soon to become a clay-pit, casts down in that holy place the money that was to be given to the potter as a worker in clay.   On which account a curse is pronounced upon the place by the prophet, as had been done by Jeremiah; and hence the combination of the two passages together by the Evangelist.   The explanation has somewhat of a recondite and artificial appearance; and the other seems simpler.

It should be borne in mind also, that the throwing together in the way now supposed of two passages of Old Testament Scripture, is nothing absolutely singular.   We have already had an example of it at ch. xxi. 4, 5, where a portion of Isa. lxii. 11 is conjoined with Zech. ix. 9, while the Evangelist simply introduces the words as having been spoken by the prophet.   In Rom. ix. 33, also two prophecies of Isaiah are thrown together, and treated as if they formed a continuous utterance.   But the most striking example, next to the one under consideration, is at Mark i. 2, 3, where, according to the correct text, the Evangelist says, " As it is written in Esaias the prophet, Behold I send my messenger before thy face, who shall prepare thy way. The voice of one crying in the wilderness," etc.   Here, the two prophecies of Malachi and Isaiah are coupled together, and cited only in connection with the name of Isaiah; partly, doubtless, because he was both the earlier and the greater prophet, and, partly, because the prophecy in Malachi was but the resumption of that in Isaiah, only cast into a somewhat more personal and specific form.   It is remarkable, too, and lends further confirma-

tion to the view now given, that while there are numerous
references to Malachi and Zechariah in the New Testament,
the prophets themselves are never named. Zechariah is quoted
four times beside the occasion before us—Matt. xxi. 5, xxvi.
31; John xii. 14, xix. 37, and always with a general formula.
Hosea alone of the minor prophets, and he but once, is expressly
mentioned (Rom. ix. 25); for, it seems very doubtful if the
reference in Acts ii. 16 to the prophet Joel should go further
than simply, " But this is that which was spoken by the prophet." The minor prophets were usually regarded as a single
book of prophecies by the Jews, somewhat of the nature of an
appendage to the larger prophetical books. Hosea stood at the
head of the list, and it was natural to name him, but scarcely
less natural to refer to the others in a more general manner; or
even, when the passage taken from any of them coincided in
substance with what had been uttered by one of the greater
prophets, to bring out its connection with the more prominent
name. These things undoubtedly indicate a peculiar mode of
contemplation in respect to the point at issue, and lend confirmation to the explanations given above.

IX.
John xix. 36; Ex. xii. 46.

The prescription regarding the Passover lamb, that a bone of
it should not be broken, is applied by the Evangelist to our Lord,
as a Scripture that required to find its correspondence, or meet
with its verification in His person. The application proceeds, of
course, on the ground of a typical relationship between that sacrificial lamb and Christ, as the author of redemption to His people;
on account of which it is said by the apostle, " For also our
Passover, Christ, was sacrificed" (1 Cor. v. 7); and our Lord
Himself, pointing to the same relationship, said, at the celebration
of the last Passover He held with His disciples, " With desire I
have desired to eat this Passover with you before I suffer; for I
say unto you, I will not any more eat thereof, until it be fulfilled
in the kingdom of God" (Luke xxii. 15, 16). It will at once be
admitted by all, who believe in the fact of this relationship, that
it involved the necessity of Christ's sacrificial death, as the means
whereby the stroke of deserved judgment was to be averted from

their heads. And not only that, but that this new passover-sacrifice was to hold relatively the same place as the old—was to be the formation of a new era for the Church, the redemptive act, that provided for her members' life and blessing. But persons may admit this, without perceiving any necessary connection between the preservation of our Lord's limbs from the violence done to those crucified beside Him, and the order to break no bone of the Paschal Lamb. For, why, it may be asked, this specific formal agreement—while so many others were wanting? The lamb, for example, was to die, by having its blood shed with a knife, which was afterwards to be poured out or sprinkled; the flesh of it also was to be roasted entire, and eaten the very night it was slain. These were prescriptions respecting the mode of treating the lamb, as well as that about the bones, while yet we see no formal agreement with them in the personal history of Christ. Why, then, should there have been such an agreement in regard to this one particular? The precise relation of things may be thus stated:—The ordinance of the Passover had this as a distinctive feature in its institution, that the lamb, which had been the provisional means of deliverance from impending destruction, the source, in a sense, of material life, should also be the food and support of the life so preserved; it must be eaten, and eaten entire, by those for whom it had provided a ransom; and for this end it had to be roasted, without suffering mutilation. Now in this, the ordinance was to find its counterpart in the new dispensation, by the appropriation of Christ for strength and nourishment, on the part of all, who should be saved by His death; they must continue to live upon Him, and can only do so by making His fulness of life and blessing their own. And to give, even outwardly, a sign of this unbroken wholeness of Christ—of the necessity of it, and of the believer's fellowship with it, to salvation—the Lord interfered, by a singular act of providence, to preserve the body of the crucified intact. The type might, indeed, without this external conformity, have been substantially verified; but it was given as a special token or seal from the hand of God, to authenticate the antitype, and to point men's thoughts back to the ordinance, which had been framed so many ages before in anticipation of the reality. The fulfilment here, therefore, belongs to the same class as those referred to in

No. II. ; a fulfilment that manifested an external correspondence, fitted to help an imperfect discernment, or a feeble faith, but one that, at the same time, bespoke a more inward and deeper correspondence lying beneath. It was, so to speak, but the outer shell of the antitypical development, which is noticed by the Evangelist ; yet such, that through it discerning minds might discover the rich kernel of spiritual and abiding truth, of which it was the index.

X.

John xix. 37 ; Zech. xii. 10.

We have here another example of that kind of fulfilment of ancient Scripture, which has been treated of in the last number —in something outward and corporeal a verification of a word, which reached much farther and deeper. Here, however, it is connected, not with a typical transaction of former times, but with an emblematic announcement of ancient prophecy. Describing prospectively the repentance of the people, whose blindness and folly had alienated them from the Lord, and involved them in misery and ruin, the Prophet Zechariah represents them as looking to Him whom they had pierced, and mourning. It was, undoubtedly, a spiritual grief—a grief on account of sin, of which the prophet spake, and in connection with that, a spiritual direction of the eye to their offended Lord; for the whole is described as the consequence of a spirit of grace and supplication being poured out upon their souls. In such a case the *piercing*, which more especially caused the mourning, must also have been of a like profound and spiritual kind; it could be nothing less than the heart-grief experienced by the Shepherd of Israel on account of the wrongs and indignities He had received from His people. But the Evangelist John, who had a peculiar eye for the symbolical, and was ever seeing the spiritual imaged in the visible, descried in the piercing of our Lord's side by the soldier's spear a sign of that other piercing. It was an indignity that formed, indeed, so far as it went, a proper fulfilment of the prophetic word, yet still one that touched the surface only of its dark meaning, and was important, more for what it suggested than for what it actually embodied.—(Comp. John xii. 32, 33).

XI.
Acts i. 20 ; Ps. lxix. 25, cix. 8.

The manner in which St Peter brought these passages from the Psalms to bear on the case of Judas, is such as to leave no doubt that they had in this their most legitimate and proper application. He prefaced the use made of them with the words, " Men and brethren, this Scripture must needs have been fulfilled, which the Holy Ghost, by the mouth of David, spoke before concerning Judas." There was a Divine necessity in the case ; Judas was so definitely in the mind of the inspiring Spirit, that the things written must have their accomplishment in the fate that befell him. And when we reflect, that this was the very first application of a prophetic Scripture by any of the apostles after they had been instructed by Jesus respecting all things that were written of Him " in the law of Moses, in the prophets, and the Psalms" (Luke xxiv. 44), we cannot doubt that it was made on the express warrant and authority of their Master. It is chiefly valuable, on account of the insight it affords into the position and character of Judas. For, as the hostile party portrayed in Ps. lxix. and cix., sometimes as an individual, sometimes as a band of adversaries, stands arrayed in the darkest features, alike of guilt and of condemnation—as in the delineation given we see ingratitude of the blackest dye, malice and wickedness taking entire possession of the soul, and rendering it incapable of yielding to the impressions of love and holiness, capable only of rushing headlong to destruction—so we are taught by the personal application of the words to Judas (what the evangelical history itself teaches), that it was no accidental circumstance, his having found a place among the number of the apostles, and no misapprehension merely, or precipitancy of judgment (as some would have it), which led him to take the part he did, in betraying the Son of Man. Judas, within the bosom of the twelve, did what his countrymen generally did, in respect to the world at large—betrayed the Lord of glory to His enemies. He was, therefore, the unconscious representative and leader of these enemies—the impersonation of those elements of evil, which rendered them what they ultimately became to Christ, and the cause of the Gospel. He was but accidentally separated from

F F

them—fundamentally and in spirit he was one with them. Hence, it was quite legitimate to take what is written in Ps. lxix. 25, of the adversaries as a body, and apply it, as St Peter does, individually to Judas:—what was to find its realisation in the unbelieving portion generally of the Jewish people, was, in a concentrated form, to take effect upon him, who, with peculiar aggravations, acted the treacherous part, which they also pursued. In him, as an individual, their guilt and punishment were alike reflected—as the one first, by his own perversity, so of necessity the other, by Divine ordination. Happy, had they but read in time the sign it was intended to afford of their inevitable doom! In that case, even the melancholy fate of the son of perdition might have proved a beacon, to warn them away from that coming wrath, which laid their habitations desolate like his, and drove them from the office they had been called to fill, as the channels of blessing to mankind.

XII.

Acts xiii. 33 ; Ps. ii. 7.   Acts xiii. 34 ; Isa. lv. 3.

The peculiarity in the use of these passages of Old Testament Scripture lies in their being placed in such immediate connection with the resurrection of Christ. It has been doubted by some, whether in ver. 33 the apostle *is* speaking directly and specially of the resurrection : they would rather regard the raising up (ἀναστήσας) there mentioned as pointing to the natural birth of our Lord, or His official appointment as Messiah. This is argued on the ground, more especially, that the word ἀνασ. does not necessarily imply a raising up *again;* that it occurs, for example, at ch. iii. 22, of the simple existence and manifestation of Jesus as the great prophet like unto Moses ; and that when the raising up has respect to the resurrection of Christ, it is coupled with ἐκ νεκρῶν—as in the very next verse to the one under consideration. These grounds are urged, for example, by Treffry, on *the Eternal Sonship,* p. 299, who therefore thinks, that the apostle " begins to speak of the resurrection only in ver. 34," and that the raising up of Jesus mentioned in ver. 33, was His being brought forth, not from the dead, but from the seed of David, as at ver. 23.

This view might have been held with some appearance of reason, if the apostle in his address had not distinctly introduced the resurrection of Jesus in the immediately preceding context. But this he *has* done; he has even brought it prominently out, as the point, on which all, in a manner, hung for the Messiahship of Jesus, and in support of which the apostolic testimony was more peculiarly given. "God raised Him from the dead," he had said, "and He was seen many days of them which came up with Him from Galilee to Jerusalem, who are His witnesses unto the people. And we declare unto you," he continues, "glad tidings, how that the promise which was made unto the fathers, the same has God fulfilled unto us their children, having raised up Jesus; as it is also written in the first Psalm, Thou art My Son, this day have I begotten Thee." It were, perhaps, wrong to say, that this passage in the Psalm is brought in simply and exclusively with reference to the resurrection of Christ; but the connection seems plainly to indicate, that both in that, and in the raising up of Jesus, it is to the resurrection that allusion is more peculiarly made. All, according to the apostle's view, seemed to point to, and find its consummation in, the risen Saviour; this realised the hopes nourished by ancient prophecy, and proved Jesus to be emphatically the Son of God. It is to be remarked, also, that this was but the first of a series of like testimonies from St Paul; above all the apostles, he delights to connect the promise of God and the Messiahship of Jesus with the resurrection. When standing on his trial before Felix, he put the whole question, as between himself and his accusers, thus, "I believe all things, which are written in the law and in the prophets, and have hope toward God, which they themselves also allow, that there shall be a resurrection of the dead, both of the just and unjust" (Acts xxiv. 14, 15). And again, when pleading before Agrippa, he represented the hope, that God would raise the dead, as at once "the promise made of God unto the fathers, and that for which he was accused of the Jews" (Acts xxvi. 6, 7). "If Christ has not risen," he elsewhere wrote, "your faith is vain, ye are yet in your sins" (1 Cor. xv. 17). It was precisely by His resurrection, that Christ was "declared to be the Son of God with power" (Rom. i. 4); and by virtue also of a fellowship in the power of His resurrection, that sinners are quickened to newness of life, and constituted sons of God: Himself first, by reason of His resurrection, the first-begotten from the dead, and then, the life—the causal life—to many, who were dead in sin (Rom. viii. 29 ; Col. i. 18, iii. 1–4, etc.).

It was probably on account of Christ's having appeared to Paul as the risen Saviour, and wrought thereby such a marvellous change on his condition and prospects, that his thoughts took so strongly this direction.   Not, however, as if there were anything properly singular in such a mode of representation—for the same substantially is found in the discourses of Christ, and the writings of the other apostles ; but in those of Paul it assumed a more remarkable prominence.   It proceeds on the contemplation of Christ's work as the actual restoration of man from the curse of death, which came in by sin.   The promise of such a restoration was the grand hope of the fallen, for which the children of faith were ever waiting and longing.   And Christ, by His resurrection from the dead, and ascension to the heavenly places, actually brings in the hope ; now at length it passes into a living reality; and He, who prevails thus to bring life out of death, and enter in the name of His elect on the heirship of immortality, is found, by the very act, to be, what He was long ago declared, God's peculiar Son—for He could have done it only by having life in Himself, even as the Father hath life in Himself.

Such is the ground of the apostle's application of the word in Ps. ii. 7 to Christ, in connection with His resurrection from the dead.   It does not mean, that He was *constituted* God's Son by the resurrection ; but that the *power* of the resurrection belonged to Him as God's Son, and by the exercise of this power was His Sonship made incontrovertibly manifest.   And it is merely by following out the same line of thought, that the other passage— that from Isaiah—is applied to the *perpetuity* of Christ's risen life.   It was not enough for the apostle's purpose to exhibit a risen Saviour ; he must show this Saviour to be the possessor of an *endless* life ; for, otherwise, the realisation of the world's hopes would not be complete; the covenant could not have been established on a sufficient basis.   Therefore, the promise is called in, which spoke of " the sure mercies of David"—the mercies which had for their guarantee the everlasting faithfulness of Jehovah. Here there is no room for failure, as in the case of merely human gifts or promises ; the covenant once ratified by the appearance and triumph of Jesus, stands fast for ever; living in the presence

of the Father, He can see no corruption, and of His kingdom of .
grace and blessing there can be no end.

XIII.
Rom. i. 17 ; Hab. ii. 4.

The only question that can be raised upon this citation is,
whether the word rendered *faith* is taken by the apostle precisely
in the same sense in which it is used by the prophet. The word
is undoubtedly employed in different senses; sometimes as an
objective matter-of-fact property—stability, the settled condition
of things ; sometimes as a personal property of God, His fidelity
or truthfulness ; and sometimes, again, as a personal property
of men, their truthfulness in word or deed, stedfast adherence to
what is felt to be right and good. Some have hence sought to
identify it, as used by Habakkuk, with the righteous principle
generally ; and Hitzig even says, on the passage, that it might
as well have been said, that the righteous man shall live by his
righteousness. But to this it is justly replied by Delitzsch, that
"in a passage which treats, not of the relation of God to man,
or of man to his fellow-men, but of *man to God*, it may fitly designate the state of him who, in respect to God, is named נֶאֱמָן,
faithful or steady. But he is so named, whose spirit clings to
God with unwavering stedfastness, whose mind is firmly fixed
upon God (Ps. lxxviii. 8 ; 1 Chron. xxix. 18). The property here
marked, accordingly, is that of an unshaken confidence in God,
a firm adhesion to God, or unwavering direction of the soul upon
Him. If, then, the subject of discourse is the gracious promises
of God, the term before us will denote an unshaken resting upon
these, or firm confidence in them ; in short, *faith*, for this settled
acquiescence, this firm confidence, this tenacious cleaving, is the
very soul, the constituting element of a living, life-giving, justifying faith." As used by the prophet, it is of the general principle of faith, as an humble, confiding trust in God's power and
faithfulness—of this, as opposed to the proud, self-reliant spirit
of the Chaldean, that the prophet speaks. He who has such
faith shall live ; for the living God is on his side, and infinite resources of grace and blessing are at his command. But it is so
still, the apostle affirms ; the principle is an all-pervading one ;
and whenever life in the higher sense is attained, it comes only

through faith in the manifested grace of God, realizing and trusting in what this has provided.

XIV.
Rom. xi. 9, 10 ; Ps. lxix. 22, 23.

The verses here quoted and applied to the apostate part of the Jewish people, are from one of the psalms, which the Apostle Peter had applied to Judas (Acts i. 20). This application of it confirms the view taken of the subject at the place referred to. Judas and the Jewish people are identified ; their sin was substantially the same, and such also must be their condemnation. In both cases alike, the falsehood and treachery that had been manifested toward the cause of Heaven, must be repaid into their own bosom.

XV.
Gal. iii. 16 ; Gen. xxii. 18.

The Apostle Peter, very shortly after the ascension of our Lord, had applied the promise to Abraham, about all the families of the earth being blessed in his seed, in such a way as clearly to imply, that the fulfilment was to be found in Christ. All were to be blessed in Abraham's seed ; and God having raised up His Son Jesus hath sent Him (says Peter) to bless *you first*—meaning, to give the seed of Israel precedence in the enjoyment of the benefit, which yet was to be diffused through every tribe and region of the world (Acts iii. 25, 26). By implication at least, this really involves the principle of the Apostle Paul's formal explanation in Gal. iii. 16. For he merely asserts, that the Abrahamic promise of blessing concentrates itself, as to vital efficacy, in Christ, and so is enjoyed by such, but only by such as are in organic union with Him. Not to seeds, therefore, as of many—not to Abraham's offspring indiscriminately—the various families and tribes that looked to him as their common fleshly head ; but to the one seed that combined the spiritual with the carnal bond of affinity to Abraham—the seed of which Christ was to be the public representative, and the one living Head. This seed, throughout all its generations and members, is properly but one, having its standing, its characteristics, its destiny in Christ. So that by Christ, as the one seed, the

apostle does not mean Christ individually, but Christ collectively
—Christ personally, indeed, first, but in Him, and along with
Him, the whole of His spiritual body the Church. This is put
beyond all doubt by ver. 28, 29, where he says of believers,
that they are all one (εἷς) in Christ—one corporate being—and
that being Christ's, they are Abraham's seed (σπέρμα)—a collective unity, as regards the heirship of blessing. The term Christ
is used in a precisely similar manner at 1 Cor. xii. 12, where our
Lord and His people are compared to the body with its many
members, and are simply designated Christ. If the apostle had
meant in either case the simply personal Redeemer, he would
doubtless have said, Christ Jesus. Considered thus, the argument of the apostle is perfectly legitimate, and there is nothing
whatever of the Rabbinical in it. The use of the singular from
the first showed, as Tholuck has justly remarked, " that the
prophecy had a *definite* posterity in view, namely, a *believing*
posterity ; and had *seeds* been employed, it would have indicated,
that all the posterity of Abraham, who sprung from him by
natural descent, were included." This was not meant ; the seed
of blessing was to hold of Abraham in a spiritual respect, still
more essentially than in a carnal ; and the apostle merely affirms,
that it has its spiritual standing, and with that its organic oneness, in Christ. No otherwise could it be a seed of blessing.

XVI.
Heb. i. 6; Ps. xcvii. 7.

The chief peculiarity in this application of an Old Testament
passage to Christ, is in respect to the time or occasion with which
it is more particularly associated. The Lord, it is said, commanded all the angels (or Elohim) of God to worship the Son,
when He introduced Him as the first-begotten into the world.
To what occasion or period does this refer ? There is nothing
in the Psalm itself to enable us to give a very specific answer.
It describes in figurative and striking terms a contemplated
manifestation of God—such as should confound all the adversaries of Zion, and to Zion herself bring peace, security, and
blessing. There can be no doubt, that this was to be accomplished in the highest degree by the incarnation and work of the
Lord Jesus Christ, and no otherwise could it be effectually

accomplished. He alone was to put for ever to shame the
enemies of God's truth, and establish the interests of righteousness—to establish them on such a sure foundation, that the
people of God should be able to rejoice with a joy unspeakable,
and full of glory. The Psalm, therefore, in regard to its main
theme, might be associated generally with the manifestation of
Christ's person and the execution of His mediatorial work ; especially as in the pregnant and ideal style of prophecy particular
stages and precise moments of the Divine kingdom are often less
contemplated than its general character and results. At the
same time, as the Psalmist seems to have more properly in his
eye the final processes of the work of Christ, and speaks of the
whole world having become the theatre of the manifested glory
of God in Him, it is most natural to understand the language
as pointing more immediately to the time of the end, when every
thing shall be brought to its proper consummation. This seems
also to be the view adopted by the inspired writer of this epistle ;
for the πάλιν is most naturally coupled with the verb that follows
—" when He (God) *again* bringeth in the first-begotten into the
world"—as if there had been an earlier and preliminary bringing
in, which was regarded as past, and another were anticipated, to
which the description of the Psalmist more especially applied.
The epithet *first-begotten* also, as a designation of Christ, seems
to point in the same direction ; for, as used elsewhere, it has a
predominant reference to the (either in fact, or in destination)
risen, perfected God-man, in whom all humanity, in so far as it
is an heir of blessing, has its life and head. So that, when in
this respect He is spoken of as being again brought into the
world, we naturally think of His return in glory. Even at His
first advent, however, angels worship and serve Him, on account
of what appeared in Him and was done by Him ; and when the
passage before us is placed in special connection with the event
of the second advent, it is not as if the affairs of the first were
altogether excluded.

XVII.

Heb. i. 10–12 ; Ps. cii. 25–27.

It strikes one at first sight as strange, that a passage, which
proclaims the eternity and immutableness of God, in marked

contrast with the created universe, should have been applied, without a note of explanation, to Christ, as if He were beyond any doubt the subject of the representation.   But it must be remembered, the sacred writer is not here arguing with Jews, who might have been disposed to question the ground on which the application is made.   He is addressing believers, Jewish Christians, who were already persuaded of the truth of Christ's Messiahship, and who, therefore, understood, that in Christ Divine and human met together—that by Him, as the Great Revealer of Godhead, the worlds were originally made, and all the provisions and arrangements connected with the Old Economy brought into existence.   It is in truth as the Divine Head of the covenant with Israel, and in particular with the house of David, that the Lord is addressed throughout the 102d Psalm ; and the thought of the eternal being and unchangeableness of God is brought in, not absolutely and as an independent consideration, but in connection with the hopes of His Church and people. There were troubles, the Psalmist well foresaw, lying in the future—calamities and desolations enough to make the pious soul conscious of gloom and horror at the prospect.   But he re-assured himself, and would have afflicted believers in every age to re-assure themselves, by realising their connection with their eternal and glorious King.   He is infinitely exalted above the mutable and the perishing; He fails not with created things, which He made by the word of His mouth, and which He can again change at His pleasure, or fold up as a decayed garment ; —And we also, who by faith have become heirs of God, and have an imperishable interest in all that is His, are, on this ground, secured against failure, in respect to our hopes of final bliss.   This is the train of thought in the Psalm ; and the passage, therefore, is in the strictest sense applicable to the Divine Redeemer, by whom the worlds were made, and through whom all the operations of Godhead have been, and are executed in our fallen world.

XVIII.
Heb. ii. 6–8 ; Ps. viii. 4–6.

The use here made of a portion of the 8th Psalm has been so well vindicated by Hengstenberg, as to the ground on which it rests, that we shall do little more than quote what he has said on the subject in his introductory remarks on the Psalm. " The Psalm stands in the closest connection with the first chapter of Genesis. What is written there of the dignity with which God invested man over the works of His hands, whom He placed as His representative on earth, and endowed with the lordship of creation, that is here made the subject of contemplation and praise. We simply have that passage in Genesis turned into a prayer for us. But how far man still really possesses that glory, what remains of it, how much of it has been lost,—of this the Psalmist takes no thought. His object was merely to praise the goodness of God, which still remained the same, as God, whose gifts are without repentance, has not arbitrarily withdrawn what He gave; only man, by his folly, has suffered himself to be robbed of it. But even with this single eye upon the goodness of God, which, on His part, continues unabated, it is to be understood, that the entire representation holds good only at the beginning and the end; and but very imperfectly suits the middle, in which we, along with the Psalmist, now stand. When this middle is placed distinctly before the eye, man is represented quite otherwise in the Old Testament than we find him here—as a sheep, a shadow, a falling leaf, a worm, as dust and ashes. And why God is here thanked, see especially Isa. xi. 6–9, where the same reference is made as here to Gen. i., and where a restitution is promised to man, in the times of Messiah, of the relation he originally held to the earth, but which is now in a state of prostration. Accordingly, the matter of the Psalm can find its full verification only in the future; and for the present it applies to none but Christ, in whom human nature again possesses the dignity and glory over creation, which was lost in Adam. By-and-by, when the moral consequences of the fall have been swept away, this also shall come to be the common inheritance of the human family." Contemplated thus, the application of the 8th Psalm to the temporary humiliation and final exaltation of Christ, as the Head of redeemed and glorified humanity, admits of a perfect justification. Only, when viewed *simply* in reference to Christ, the words descriptive of the nearly Elohim-dignity of man necessarily become, at the same time, indicative of a relative, though temporary humiliation. " With the man of

creation the βραχύ τι is an abiding inferiority of degree, connected with his creaturely existence ; but the Son of God, who
has humbled Himself to the condition of man, in order that He
might exalt it to the lofty position which it is destined to occupy,
cannot remain in that low estate ; and so, that which with man
as such was a *paululum* of degree (much as at 2 Sam. xvi. 1),
becomes changed into a *paululum* of time (βραχύ τι as at Isa.
lvii. 17, and commonly with the Attics) ; and while with man
the *paululum* of degree has his glory for a correlate, with Jesus
the *paululum* of time has His glory for a contrast. Thus, the
sense of the βραχύ τι suffers a kind of necessary, but by no
means arbitrary turn, in the application to the Man Christ
Jesus of the words that were originally spoken of man generally."—(Delitzch). There still are commentators, among
others, Stier, who would regard the Psalm as pointing more
directly to Christ, and to the restitution of all things to be
brought in by Him. But this view cannot be deemed so
natural as the other ; and it is not needed to justify or explicate
the argument of the apostle.

XIX.
Heb. ii. 13 ; Isa. viii. 17, 18.

Three passages are here appealed to in proof of the kindredness
of Messiah to those whom He came to redeem. One is from
Ps. xxii., which is strictly Messianic ; the other two from the
eighth chapter of Isaiah. By not a few commentators the propriety of these latter applications is doubted ; at least, they are
judged applicable only in a secondary sense, as the prophet himself is considered to be the speaker ; so that only by way of
accommodation, or typically, can the words be understood of the
Messiah. This, however, may justly be questioned, and *is* questioned, by a large body of interpreters. They hold, that as in
the immediately preceding verse, it is the Messiah who appears
to be the speaker—in the words, " Bind up the testimony, seal
up the law, among My disciples"—so He ought to be understood
as continuing to speak in ver. 17 and 18, declaring His trust in
the Father, and pointing to the spiritual seed the Father had
given Him. The passage is unquestionably an obscure one ;
but even if we should prefer considering the prophet as more

directly the speaker, he must be viewed as speaking in a representative character—personating the being, and maintaining the
cause of the Immanuel. The whole discourse, from ch. vii. 14
to ix. 7, is perpetually turning upon " the God with us," as the
great security and hope for Israel; and, mediately or immediately,
the words in question must be regarded as pointing in that
direction. Either way, the use made of them in the epistle is
perfectly legitimate.

In the remaining passages of Old Testament Scripture quoted,
either in the Epistle to the Hebrews, or in the general epistles,
there is nothing very peculiar, as regards the use that is made of
them by the inspired writers. We may simply state, in regard
to the application made of Ps. xl. in Heb. x. 5–10, to the personal obedience and offering of Christ, that it is not to be understood as excluding an inferior reference to the Psalmist himself.
He knew perfectly, in regard to his own spiritual state and calling, that a willing surrender of himself to God ranked higher
than the mere presentation of animal victims; and substantially
the same idea is expressed elsewhere, in passages that undoubtedly have a direct reference to the Psalmist and his fellow-wor-
shippers in Old Testament times (Ps. l. 7–15, li. 16, 17). It is
not necessary, therefore, to suppose, that in Ps. xl. no respect
was had to that self-dedication to the Divine service, which even
under the ancient dispensation was preferred to all burnt-offerings. But as little should the remarkable words there written
be confined to that; and the defects and shortcomings, of which
the saints of God in those earlier times were painfully conscious,
as mingling with all their personal surrenders to God, could not
but dispose them to look for the proper realisation of what was
written in one higher and greater than themselves. The
spiritual Israel in every age aimed at it; but He alone, in whom
Israel's state and calling were to find their true accomplishment,
could in the full sense appropriate the words, and embody them
in action.

APPENDIX.

THE HISTORICAL CIRCUMSTANCES THAT LED TO CHRIST'S BIRTH
AT BETHLEHEM—CYRENIUS AND THE TAXING (p. 359).

THE application of the prophecy in Micah v. 2 to the birth of
our Lord at Bethlehem, by the Evangelist Matthew, involves in
itself no peculiar difficulty; for the prophecy itself is so specific,
and was so readily understood and applied by the Jews themselves to the great event it contemplated, that the use made of
it in this connection cannot justly be questioned by any fair interpreter of Scripture.   The difficulties which do hang around
the subject have sprung up in connection with the historical
circumstances, which are mentioned by the Evangelist Luke, as
the more immediate causes that led to the birth of Christ at
Bethlehem.   These circumstances relate, in the first instance, to
the decree issued by Augustus, appointing a general census or
enrolment to take place; and, secondly and more especially, to
the incidental notice as to the time when this decree was carried
into effect, that it was while Cyrenius was governor, or had the
presidency of Syria—αὕτη ἡ ἀπογραφὴ πρώτη ἐγένετο ἡγεμονεύοντος τῆς
Συρίας Κυρηνίου.   This latter being the more special difficulty, and
one also on which recently some new light has emerged, we
shall here give it our first and chief attention.

I. Giving to the words of St Luke what seems their natural
and grammatical rendering, " this first enrolment was made (or,
it was first made) when Cyrenius was governor of Syria," they
appear plainly enough to indicate, that at the time the presidency of Syria was in the hands of Cyrenius, and possibly also
(though that is not so clear) that the census now under consi-

deration was an earlier as contrasted with a later one. Dis-
missing, however, for the present, the question, whether reference
is made to a second census, we have to face the position which
seems involved in the historical statement of the Evangelist,
that the particular census, which led to the birth of Jesus at
Bethlehem, took place during the time that Cyrenius was governor of Syria.   And this, it is alleged, was impossible ; for, to
quote the words of Meyer, " at the time of the birth of Jesus Q.
Sentius Saturninus was president of Syria, and P. Sulpicius
Quirinus did not become so till about ten years later ;" *i.e.* ten
years after the *real* period of our Lord's birth, but only six after
the *common era*, which is four years too late.   There can be no
doubt that Cyrenius, or Quirinius (as the name ought rather to
be written, and as we shall retain it in what follows), did receive
the presidency of Syria at the later period mentioned, and
shortly afterwards did conduct a census in Judea.   So that, if
this were the only presidency of Syria held by Quirinius, and
the only census taken contemporaneously with it, the statement
of the Evangelist must be pronounced erroneous.

It certainly would be very strange if such were the case ; for,
apart altogether from the inspiration of St Luke, it would indicate a degree of looseness in historical information, which would
ill comport with his assertion at the outset, of possessing " perfect understanding of all the matters" he was going to write
about ; and it would just as little correspond with the remarkable accuracy exhibited in his other historical notices.   The
most searching results of modern inquiry have not only confirmed the general fidelity of his allusions to political affairs and
current events, but have established his correctness even in
minute details, and in respect to points on which for a time his
testimony lay under a measure of suspicion.   The narrative in
Acts xxvii. of St Paul's voyage and shipwreck, in which every
particular has been subjected to the severest scrutiny, and has
thereby become but the more clearly marked with the attributes
of truth, is itself a convincing evidence of this.   But one or two
examples more may be taken, and these more closely connected
with the point under discussion.   In Acts xviii. 12, Gallio is
called " pro-consul " (Eng. version, deputy) of Achaia ; and
Achaia was, indeed, originally a senatorial province ; but

Tiberius changed it into an imperial one. In that case *pro-prætor* would have been the proper name for the representative of the Roman state. Strabo expressly calls it "a prætorian province;" and not only had great perplexities thence arisen among the learned, but Beza even took the liberty to correct the text, substituting *pro-prætor* for *pro-consul*. But we learn from Suetonius, that the Emperor Claudius restored the province to the Senate; and as this change took place only about five or six years before the time referred to by St Luke, pro-consul had then become the proper designation. Again, in Acts xiii. 7, 8, Sergius Paulus is called the pro-consul of Cyprus, although Cyprus is known to have been ranked as an imperial province, and might still have been reckoned so by the learned, but for a notice in Dio Cassius, which contains the information, that Augustus restored it to the Senate. "And so," says Tholuck, who after Lardner refers to the passage, "as if purposely to vindicate the Evangelist, the old historian adds, 'Thus pro-consuls began to be sent into that island also.'"

Now, it is surely against all probability, that a historian, who has shown in such things the most exact and scrupulous fidelity, and whose reputation for accuracy has been in danger of suffering, not from our possessing too much, but rather from our possessing too little of collateral testimony—it is against all probability, that he should have committed the gross anachronism of connecting Quirinius with Syria, at a period ten years before his presidency actually commenced. It is the less likely in this case, that there should have been such an erroneous antedating of a public event, as there is every reason to suppose that the Evangelist himself was a native of Syria, most probably a citizen of Antioch, and, consequently, must have had every facility for becoming acquainted with the political history of the district.

A conviction of the extreme improbability of any error in this direction, has led many persons—among others in the last century Lardner, and in the present Ewald and Greswell—to adopt an unusual translation of the passage in Luke, so as to make it point to a future, not to an existing, presidency of Quirinius. They would render, "And this enrolment was made *before* that Quir. had the presidency of Syria." Certainly an unnatural, if

even (in the circumstances) an admissible, representation of the
meaning; and one that could only be resorted to, if it were
otherwise impossible to vindicate the truthfulness of the narrative!
But we are saved from this alternative by the recent progress of
research in the historical territory, which has again, and in a
very singular manner, lent its confirmation to the scrupulous
accuracy of the Evangelist. The person who, in this instance
has conducted the investigation is Augustus W. Zumpt, the
author of a very learned work on Roman Antiquities—entitled
*Commentationes Epigraphicæ ad Antiquitates Romanas perti-
nentes.* In the second volume of this work he has a chapter on
Syria as a Roman province from Cæsar Augustus to Titus Vespasian, in which he treats of the successive governors of the province, and the leading features of their respective administration.
It is an entirely literary, or antiquarian investigation; and simply
as connected with the subject of the Syrian presidencies, the passage in Luke ii. 2 comes into consideration. The inquiry is
conducted with great patience and acuteness ; and in so far as
it bears on the point before us—for it frequently branches off in
other directions—we shall present an outline of the argument.

Taking the words of the Evangelist Luke in their apparent
sense, as denoting the contemporaneousness of a presidency of
Quirinius over Syria with the event that led to Christ's birth at
Bethlehem, Zumpt conceives that there is the more reason for
adhering to that sense of the Evangelist, and accrediting the
testimony it delivers respecting Quirinius, that the Fathers in
various connections deliver a like testimony. Thus Eusebius,
Hist. Eccl. i. 5, "Now this was the forty-second year of the
reign of Augustus, and the twenty-eighth from the subjugation
of Egypt, and the decease of Antony and Cleopatra, with which
last event terminated the dynasty of the Ptolemies in Egypt,
when our Lord and Saviour Jesus Christ was born in Bethlehem
of Judea on the occasion of the first census being taken, and
while Quirinius was governor of Syria." The reckoning here
given dates from the time that Augustus was first made consul ;
from which time there were forty-one years complete to the third
before the Christian era, and twenty-eight after the subjugation
of Egypt. At that period, therefore, which to a nearness coincides with the real time of Christ's birth, Eusebius plainly be-

lieved, that Quirinius presided over Syria, and that a census was taken: and so also did Irenæus, Haer. ii. 22, 6 ; Tertullian adv. Jud. c. 9; Clemens Alex. Strom. i. p. 147, etc. In all these passages both the fact of a general census, and the presidency of Quir. over Syria, at the time of Christ's birth, are distinctly asserted. Of what nature the census might be, or whether the time of its being taken might precisely accord with the exact period of Christ's birth, is not now the question. But in regard to the Syrian presidency of Quir. there is an important notice in Tacitus, Annal. iii. 48, which he introduces in connection with the death of Quir., A.D. 21. *Nihil ad veterem et patriciam Sulpiciorum familiam Quir. pertinuit, ortus apud municipium Lanuvium: sed impiger militiæ et acribus ministeriis consulatum sub divo Augusto, mox expugnatis per Ciliciam Homonadensium castellis insignia triumphi adeptus datusque rector C. Cæsari Armeniam obtinenti Tiberium quoque Rhodi agentem coluerat. Quod tunc patefecit (viz. Tiberius) in Senatu laudatis in se officiis et incusato M. Lollio, quem auctorem C. Cæsari pravitatis et discordiarum arguebat.* Hear we learn respecting Quir., first, that he was a man of comparatively obscure origin ; then, that he had approved himself to be expert in military affairs, and services that called for stringent measures, in consequence of which he had attained to the consulship under Augustus, by-and-by also got the triumphal badges for having stormed the fortresses of the Homonadenses,[1] and was afterwards appointed counsellor or guardian to Caius Cæsar on receiving Armenia. He had also paid court to Tiberius, when residing at Rhodes in a sort of exile, and Tiberius reported to the Senate in laudatory terms the services rendered to him by Quir., while he charged M. Lollius with having led C. Cæsar into vicious and quarrelsome courses. Now, as the C. Cæsar here mentioned, one of the grandsons of Augustus, is known to have obtained Armenia in the year B.C. 1, and as Quir. was raised to the consulship in B.C. 12, it is manifest, that the conquest of the Homonadenses must

[1] The triumphal badges or ornaments were the honours granted in place of a triumph, after triumphs ceased to be held except by the Emperors. They consisted in the permission to receive the titles bestowed on those who did obtain triumphs, to wear in public the robes peculiar to them, and to bequeath triumphal statues to their descendants.

G G

have been accomplished in the interval. It remains, therefore, to be inquired who these people were, and in what position Quir. was, when he made himself master of their fortified places.

The Homonadenses are mentioned by Pliny, Hist. Nat. v. 23, 94, as a people in the farthest parts of Cilicia, near the Isauri, with a fortified town, Homona, and forty-four strongholds situated in rugged valleys or ravines. Strabo also occasionally mentions them, and places them in the rough parts of Cilicia, near the Isauri, and the Pisidians, xiv. 1, 4, 24. There can be no doubt, therefore, about their character and position; they were evidently a hardy and troublesome set of mountaineers, occupying a number of forts in the more inaccessible parts of Cilicia, and re- quiring a vigorous and energetic warrior, like Quir., to bring them into subjection. But how should he have come into con- flict with them? Or what might be the province held by him, when he gained such victories over the Homonadenses, and triumphal ornaments on account of them?

Various provinces might be, and have been thought of. (1.) Proconsular Asia; but this will not suit. For the Homona- denses did not live within the bounds of that province; and, besides, proconsular Asia having come before this into a state of entire subjugation, had no legion stationed in it (Tac. Ann. iv. 5); and hence there could have been no such victories won by its governor as to secure for him triumphal honours. (2.) Nor could it be Bithynia and Pontus; for Galatia lay between this province and the region of the Homonadenses. It was also a senatorian province, and had no legionary force; even Pliny, in Trajan's time, had none, though his case was somewhat peculiar, having been sent to put things in order. It was usually as- signed, too, to men of only prætorian rank (Dio, liii. 12); so that, unless we should betake to merely groundless conjectures, the province of Bithynia and Pontus must be excluded from the number of those with whom Quir. might be supposed to have been connected. (3.) Galatia has been pointed to as the probable region; but this also fails in the requisite conditions; for the possessor of it had no legion assigned him, with which he might carry on such warlike operations as would entitle him to trium- phal honours. Nor were the Homonadenses situated in Ga- latia, but on its borders; so that the governor of the province,

even if he had the command of a legion, could have had no call to
make war upon those Cilician mountaineers.   It is also known,
that the province of Galatia was wont to be committed to a man of
prætorian rank (Eutrop. vii. 5 ; Euseb. Chron. p. 168).   (4.)
Cilicia alone remains, which seems to be indicated by Tacitus as
the province—so far, at least, the province of Quir., that the
people, whose forts were scattered through it, lay within his jurisdiction.   But Cilicia by itself was by much too small a province
for a consular man, at the head of a legion ; it must have been
conjoined with some other district.   It is stated by Dio, liii. 12,
that when Augustus surrendered, in the 27th year of his reign, the
thoroughly reduced and quiet provinces to the Senate, he reserved
Cilicia (because of the fierce and warlike tribes that were in it),
and also Cyprus.   Afterwards, however, in B.C. 22, Cyprus was
granted to the Senate (Dio, liv. 4).   It, therefore, could not have
been coupled with Cilicia to make out a sufficient province; and
it seems impossible to think of any other region than Syria.

The conclusion thus arrived at from the examination of the
passage in Tacitus, is confirmed by evidence from other sources.
For example, in the year B.C. 17, Syria and Cilicia appear to
have been associated under one provincial administration; since,
when Cn. Piso then obtained the presidency of Syria, and required
to levy troops against Germanicus, he sent an order to the chiefs
(reguli) of the Cilicians to furnish him with supplies of men
(Tac. Ann. ii. 70, 78).   It is by no means probable, that either
he would have issued such an order, or that they would have
complied with it (especially in a war against Germanicus), unless the governor of Syria had a legal right to their services.
And in the course of the proceedings that followed, during
which Piso himself acted treacherously, he is reported to have
seized the fortress of Celenderis, which Tacitus designates a
town in Cilicia (Ann. ii. 80), and Strabo also places in the highlands of Cilicia (xiv. 4).   But it is also connected with Piso's
province, which was Syria ; for Piso was accused by Tiberius to
the Senate of seeking to possess *the province* (the province,
namely, over which he had been appointed) by force of arms—
armis repetita provincia (Tac. Ann. iii. 12)—and on this very
account the Emperor is said to have been implacable toward
Piso, that he had taken arms against the province—ob bellum

provinciæ inlatum (Ann. iii. 14).   In another passage of Tacitus,
Ann. vi. 41, it is stated that Vitellius, president of Syria, sent
troops, A.D. 36, to subdue the Clitæ, a people of Cilicia, as work
that properly fell under his administration.   It thus appears,
that both about B.C. 25, and A.D. 36, Cilicia was conjoined with
Syria into one province, and placed under the sway of one imperial
representative; and so it remained till the times of Vespasian.

From these data there seems no avoiding the conclusion, that
Quir., at the time he possessed himself of the forts of the Homonadenses throughout Cilicia, was the legate of Augustus and
pro-prætor of Syria.   It only remains to be ascertained, more
narrowly, if such a thing be possible, over what period his presidency was spread, and how far down it reached.   The determination of this point is to be sought in another series of passages,
and chiefly in those which connect Quir. with Caius Cæsar.   As
the date of his elevation to the consulship precluded his connection with Syria at an earlier period than B.C. 12, so his relationship to C. Cæsar fixes its termination to a period not later than
about the commencement of the Christian era.   For it was at
the very close of the year B.C. 2, or the beginning of B.C. 1, that
C. Cæsar obtained the government of Armenia, when it was
threatened with war by Phraates the Parthian king.   Velleius,
ii. 101, states, that he set out for Armenia a short time after his
mother Julia was banished for her incontinence; and this
banishment is known to have taken place before Kal. Oct. of
B.C. 2.   It was sometime after this that Caius set out, and he
took Greece, Egypt, Palestine, on his way.   He even appears
to have spent the winter at Samos, where he was visited by his
stepfather Tiberius, at that time resident in Rhodes (Suet. Tib.
c. 11).   The year immediately B.C. must, therefore, have been
nearly spent before he left Samos; and in the following year,
A.D. 1, he was designated consul, and set forth toward the region
over which he was appointed.   The year after this he brought
Phraates to a conference, in which the Parthians agreed to
abandon Armenia.   But in a subsequent war with Tigranes the
Armenian, he received a wound, of which he died in A.D. 4, the
wound itself having been received in the third year.   So that
Quir., on being appointed *rector* to C. Cæsar, evidently did
not require to quit his Syrian presidency sooner than some time

in the year B.C. 2, and it might even be supposed, on a hasty
consideration, that about two years later might have been soon
enough. But as the determination of this point is one both of
some nicety and of some importance, it is necessary to look a little
more closely into the circumstances of the time.

In the passage formerly quoted from Tacitus, the Emperor
Tiberius was represented as commending Quir. for the part
he had acted toward Caius Cæsar, while standing in the relation of *rector* to him, and, at the same time, severely blaming
M. Lollius.[1] Tacitus does not expressly say, though his language seems to imply, that Lollius held the same relation to
C. Cæsar that Quirinius had done. But Suetonius distinctly
calls him *comitem et rectorem C. Cæsaris* (Tib. c. 12, 13), and
adds, that from the charges made by Lollius against Tiberius,
Tiberius perceived, when he went on a visit to C. Cæsar at
Samos, that the mind of the latter had become alienated from
him. And it also appears from a passage in Velleius, ii. 102,
that when the conference was held with the Parthian king,
Lollius was present, and represented himself as appointed by
Augustus to be a sort of regulator to his youthful grandson—
veluti moderatorem juventæ filii sui. It thus appears, that M.
Lollius had become *rector* to C. Cæsar about the end of B.C. 1
or the beginning of A.D. 1, when the young commander was
passing the winter at Samos, and that he continued to hold the
same position for a year or two afterwards. What time, then,
must be assigned for Quir. being rector? It has been thought
by Norisius (in Cenot. Pisan. ii. 9), that he succeeded Lollius in the office, as it is mentioned by Tacitus in connection
with C. Cæsar's obtaining Armenia. But this is untenable.
For in the Latin idiom he is said to obtain Armenia, who has
acquired the legal right to preside over it, whether he may
actually have taken possession of it or not. And from the position and import of the words in the passage of Tacitus (insignia
triumphi adeptus, datusque rector C. Cæsari—Tiberium quoque
Rhodi agentem coluerat), it seems plain, that Tiberius was at
Rhodes at the time when Quir. had obtained his triumphal

---

[1] The rector was not a guardian in the ordinary sense, but a person of
skill in war and experience in affairs, who could act as confidential adviser and
counsellor to a youthful prince, at the commencement of his public career.

honours and had become rector to C. Cæsar. Hence M. Lollius must have succeeded Quir., and not this the other. It is also certain on another account; for by comparing Tacitus, Ann. iii. 22 and 48, it appears that Quir. had, in A.D. 21, been married about twenty years to Lepida, a lady of high rank at Rome, whom Augustus had destined for Lucius Cæsar, the brother of Caius. But this Lucius died in A.D. 2; and hence Quir. must have gone to Rome, and become married to Lepida about the time that Caius actually entered on his Armenian administration. It is clear, therefore, that Quir. must have been made *rector* to C. Cæsar immediately on the latter crossing the sea on his way to the East, and remained with him for a year or so, and that M. Lollius was sent to take his place toward the beginning of the first year of the Christian era. It seems probable also, that Quir. accompanied C. Cæsar to Egypt, and that both together paid a visit to Tiberius at Rhodes, with which the latter was well pleased; while by the time Tiberius visited Caius at Samos, Lollius had become rector, and had begun to alienate the mind of Caius from his stepfather.

Such, then, are the successive links of the history, as brought out by this investigation: Quir., it is ascertained, was governor or president of Syria, some time subsequent to B.C. 12, when he obtained the consulship, and before A.D. 1 or 2, when he seems to have gone to Rome, and become married to Lepida;—after entering on his Syrian presidency, he carried on a difficult, and, no doubt, somewhat arduous conflict, with the warlike mountaineers of Cilicia, and on account of his successes against them obtained triumphal honours;—about a year before the Christian era he was appointed rector to C. Cæsar, in order to prepare him for the administration of affairs in Armenia, for which both military prowess and a considerable measure of diplomatic skill were requisite;—it was, however, while he was governor of Syria that he held this office of rectorship, for it was *as* governor of that province that he was more peculiarly qualified to give the counsel and aid that were needed to one who was going to fulfil a difficult and dangerous mission in the neighbouring region of Armenia—whence Lollius, and another person, who succeeded him in the one office, also succeeded him in the other—they became both presidents of Syria and rectors of C. Cæsar. But since the common Christian era is four years later than the actual birth of Christ, it follows that Quir. must have been governor of Syria about the time that Christ was born, and for a year or two subsequent to the event. And thus the statement of St Luke, reiterated by several of the Christian fathers, that Quir. was president of Syria at the time when Jesus was born at Bethlehem, is fully vindicated, though the proof is reached only by a minute and lengthened deduction, and it is again the paucity, not the fulness of the collateral sources of information, which has brought into suspicion the accuracy of the sacred historian.[1]

II. The other points connected with the subject need not de-

[1] In the text, we have given only the evidence bearing on Quir.'s presidency about the time of our Lord's birth. But since the investigations of Norisius, referred to in the preceding discussion, it has been held by most writers on the subject (for example, by Greswell, *Harmony, Vol. I., Diss. XIV.*, Meyer, Alford, etc.), that Saturninus was president of Syria at the time of Christ's birth, that in the year of His birth (viz. U.C. 750) Varus became president, and continued, probably, for five years, till he was succeeded by another Saturninus. It is admitted, however, for instance, by Mr Greswell, that coins have come to light, which do not readily correspond with this representation. And the more careful inquiries of Zumpt tend to establish the following as the real succession:—C. Sentius Saturninus became president of Syria in the year 9 B.C. (*i.e.* before the common Christian era), as may be inferred from Jos. Ant. xvi. 9. 1, who also speaks of him as a man of consular rank, and of great authority, xvi. 11. 3, etc. ; then, it appears from coins and other collateral evidence, that Varus obtained the Syrian presidency in B.C. 6, and continued for about two years. The precise time when this Varus was superseded is doubtful; for here, both the notices of Josephus, and other accounts of Syrian affairs, are somewhat meagre and confused. Evidence, however, has been produced of L. Volusius Saturninus having held the government of Syria ; and it is certain that he must have quitted it in the year 6 A.D., because then Quir. was appointed to Syria, with the design of reducing Judea to a Roman province, and annexing it to Syria. But between this 6th year after A.D., and the 6th before it, when Varus entered on his office, there is room, according to the usual practice of Augustus, for at least one legate, and possibly more than one, to fill up the space. And it is here that the legation, first of Quir. and then of Lollius (both of a somewhat special character, and lasting but a short time), come in. So that the succession stands thus:—C. Sentius Saturninus became president B.C. 9 ; P. Quinctilius Varus, B.C. 6; P. Sulpicius Quirinius, B.C. 4 ; M. Lollius, B.C. 1 ; C. Marcius Censorinus (mentioned by Velleius as for a short time after Lollius, who killed himself, rector of C. Cæsar and governor of Syria), A.D. 3 ; L. Volusius Saturninus, A.D. 4 ; P. Sul. Quirinius, A.D. 6, etc.

tain us long. They refer to the nature of the census, for which, it is said, a decree was issued by Cæsar Augustus, and to the compass of territory it embraced—whether the whole Roman world, or simply that portion of it which was bounded by the regions more immediately in the eye of the Evangelist.

In regard to this part of the inquiry—which, as already stated, is not touched upon by Zumpt—it ought to be borne in mind, that here also our information is extremely scanty; and it is very possible, that if ampler materials were within our reach for determining the political relations and movements of the time, all would become perfectly plain. In such a matter, it should be enough, if there is nothing obviously irreconcileable with the evangelical narrative, and certain things that make it reasonably probable. It should also be noted, that while the Evangelist says that the census was taken while Quir. was governor of Syria, he does not affirm it to have been personally conducted by him in Judea. It merely happened to be coeval with his Syrian presidency, and formed a first census, as contradistinguished from a second. St Luke being himself a native of Syria, and very probably writing to a Syrian, quite naturally indicated the name of the governor presiding at the time over the region, and the relation of this census to another, with which the governor was known to be officially connected.

In regard to the ἀπογραφή itself, it is impossible to arrive at any very definite conclusion. The word strictly means an *enrolling*, though very commonly an enrolment with a view to taxing— taking an account of men's persons and goods for the purpose of laying on them an equitable proportion of the public burdens; and hence it might often with propriety be rendered by our word *taxing*. But, undoubtedly, there were cases in which this term would be too specific; in which, at least, the immediate act was not directly associated with any pecuniary rating. Those who, with Lardner, would regard the Evangelist as writing of the whole world in the restricted sense—that is, as embracing merely the districts more immediately in his eye, the provinces subject to the jurisdiction of Herod—think they discover a probable account of the transaction in certain notices of Josephus respecting the latter days of Herod's reign. In the Ant. xvi. 9. 3, 10. 9, it is stated that Herod, toward the close of his life, " lost the

Emperor's favour, and was forced to submit to many disgraces and affronts;" in consequence of which he sent an ambassador to Rome, who succeeded, though not without difficulty, in explaining matters and effecting a reconciliation. Further, in Ant. xvii. 2, 6, the historian, having mentioned the Pharisees as a powerful and subtle party, ready to attempt anything against those who were obnoxious to them, adds, " When, therefore, the whole Jewish nation took an oath to be faithful to Cæsar and the interests of the king, these men, to the number of above 6000, refused to swear." He proceeds to mention, that for this act of contumacy they were fined by Herod, while, on their part, they declared that God had decreed to put an end to the government of Herod and his race. This came to the ears of Herod, and proved the occasion of death to not a few of their number.   Now, it is supposed that the oath of fidelity here spoken of as having been exacted towards Cæsar and the interests of Herod, might be identical with the enrolment or census of St Luke; the rather so, as the time must have been nearly the same in both cases, and the national expectation of another king than Herod, or any that could spring from his family, did then also assume a very definite and specific form.

Whatever truth, however, there may be in all this, as regards Herod and the people of his dominions, it must be owned that it scarcely meets the conditions of the historical statement presented by the Evangelist.   In the account of the Jewish historian the matter seems to lie between Herod and his people, and to be altogether of local interest; while with the Evangelist it is the decree of the Emperor—δόγμα παρὰ Καίσαρος Αὐγούστου—which alone comes into notice ; and the object of this is represented in the most general terms, as ordering an enrolment for the whole world, πᾶσαν τὴν οἰκουμένην. Of course, not absolutely the whole; the words must in any case be understood with some limitation ; for wide as the Roman empire was, there still were, in the age of Augustus, regions of considerable extent and ample resources, respecting which he would never have dreamt of issuing a decree of the kind here specified.   We are constrained to think, at the very utmost, of a universality co-extensive with Cæsar's acknowledged supremacy: but to that, both the words themselves and the connection in which they stand, seem most naturally to point. There is some reason to believe, as Mr Greswell has shown (Harmony, vol. i., p. 536 sq.), that Augustus did take measures

for effecting, not merely partial censuses—of which various are
incidentally noticed by the ancient historians—but also surveys
of a more general kind.   There appears, for example, to have
been made in his reign a general geometrical survey of the empire,
which, though nǒt mentioned by any historian extant, is yet explicitly referred to by several writers, especially by such as treat
of rural affairs.   Thus Frontinus de Coloniis says, Huic addendæ
sunt mensuræ limitum et terminorum ex libris Augusti et
Neronis Cæsarum ; and speaks further of a surveyor Balbus, qui
temporibus Augusti omnium provinciarum et civitatum formas
et mensuras compertas in commentarios contulit, et legem
Agrariam per universitatem provinciarum distinxit ac declaravit.
Various other authorities are cited by Mr Greswell to the same
effect.   And it certainly can be regarded as by no means unlikely,
that along with a general measurement of the empire, Augustus
should have sought to obtain a general census of its inhabitants.
The one could scarcely fail to seem the proper complement of the
other.   And it is also known that Augustus left behind him what
is called *breviarium imperii* (Tac. Ann. i. 11 ; Suet. Aug. c. 102 ;
Dio, lvi. 33), which it took many years to complete, and which
would in all probability be based to some extent on returns regarding the population of the empire.   But the accounts we have
of it are brief, and the history, in particular, of Dio appears to be
defective in respect to this period.

Supposing such a measure to have been prosecuted by Augustus,
there is no need for imagining that the decree ordering the returns
must have been issued for the whole empire at once, and appointed
to be carried out simultaneously throughout all the provinces.
It would be more likely to be carried into effect piecemeal ;
although, when speaking of it in connection with any particular
province, a writer of the period would naturally connect the
special work in his region of the empire with the decree of the
Emperor ordering its general accomplishment.   So the Evangelist
may be conceived to have done.   And it tends still further to
confirm this view of the nature and design of the census here
spoken of, that the very mode of taking it seems to indicate a
specific difference between it and the census afterwards taken by
Quirinius, when Judea was formally annexed to Syria.   Of the
latter it is said, that the express design of it was to take an
account of the people's substance ; and Quir. himself is designated

an appraiser of their means—τιμητὴς τῶν οὐσιῶν (Ant. xviii. 1).
Had the first census been of this description, there could have
been no need for so early a renewal of it.   And, besides, the circumstances noted by the Evangelist in regard to the holy family,
seem to indicate that other things than property were in question ;
since, instead of being enrolled where their dwelling and substance
(if they had any) existed, they repaired to what was reckoned their
own city—theirs, it would appear, only by genealogical descent
and personal claims ; for, if any property had belonged to them
there, they should not have been obliged to lodge in the mere out-
houses of the inn.   Such things seem best to accord with a census
of persons merely, apart from the valuation of their property.

Finally, as to the relation of the census to the Syrian presidency, it should be borne in mind, that the accounts both of the
census itself, and of the Syrian presidents at this time, are extremely brief and indistinct.   As it was about the very time of
our Lord's birth, that Quir. appears to have taken the place of
Varus, one can quite easily conceive, that the enrolling may have
partly fallen under the one administration, and partly under the
other.   It is also quite conceivable, and even probable, that, as the
appointment of Quir. seems to have been made (according to
the notice of Tacitus) for the more immediate purpose of bringing into subjection the Homonadenses in the western and less
accessible parts of the province, Varus, his predecessor, may
have been ordered to remain for some time in the east, till
Quir. was at liberty to enter on the regular administration of
the affairs of the province.   These are quite natural suppositions
in the circumstances ; and they may sufficiently account for the
mention made by Josephus of Varus in Ant. xvii. 9, 3, as being
still president of Syria, shortly after Herod's death.   He may
have been so, in point of fact, as regards the eastern part of the
province, although not strictly the president of Syria at the
time.   But the notices are so partial and incomplete, that it is
impossible to exhibit more than a probable view of the circumstances of the period.   From what *has been* established, there is
valid ground for asserting, that it is not our Evangelist who has
reason to fear the fullest inquiry, and that the more the actual
relations of the time are known, the more patent and conclusive
shall be the proof of his historical accuracy.

INDEX OF SUBJECTS.

INDEX OF TEXTS ILLUSTRATED.

THE END.

MURRAY AND GIBB, PRINTERS, EDINBURGH.

Other Solid Ground Classic Reprints

Homiletics & Pastoral Theology by William G.T. Shedd
W.G.T.Shedd expounds almost every aspect of preaching, analyzing its nature, outlining the main features which should characterize powerful preaching and describing the approach, plan, actual construction and refinements of a sermon.

A History of Preaching by Edwin Charles Dargan
This two volume set, published in 1905, was written as a tribute to Dargan's homiletics professor at Southern Baptist Seminary, John A. Broadus. Dargan later became a colleague and then the successor to Broadus in the chair of Homiletics at SBTS in Louisville, KY.

Lectures on the History of Preaching by J.A. Broadus
John A. Broadus delivered these five lectures in May 1876 at Newton Theological Institute near Boston, and they immediately caused a stir of interest for their publication. It was lectures like these which later moved his student E.C. Dargan to desire to spend his life studying the history of preaching.

The Preacher and His Models by James Stalker
This volume consists of the 9 lectures delivered in 1891 at The Yale Lectures on Preaching. Appended to the volume is a sermon Stalker preached at an Ordination Service in 1879. Alexander Whyte encouraged the publication of that sermon when it was first delivered. As with all of Stalker's works both light and heat fill every page.

The Scottish Pulpit by William M. Taylor
William M. Taylor was one of the few men asked to return and deliver a second series of lectures at the Yale Lectures on Preaching. Those who were able to hear these lectures did not regret the invitation to return. His chapter on John Knox is worth the price of the book.

Call us toll free at **1-877-666-9469**
E-mail us at **sgcb@charter.net**
Visit our web site at **solid-ground-books.com**

Printed in the United States
84703LV00008B/28/A